MANAGEMENT
Text and Cases

Third Edition

R. SATYA RAJU
Former Principal, College of Arts and Commerce
Andhra University, Visakhapatnam

A. PARTHASARATHY
Former Professor
Postgraduate Department of Commerce
MES College, Bangalore

PHI Learning Private Limited
Delhi-110092
2018

₹ 495.00

MANAGEMENT: Text and Cases, Third Edition
R. Satya Raju and A. Parthasarathy

ISBN-978-93-88028-04-2 (Print Book)
ISBN-978-93-88028-05-9 (eBook)

Eleventh Printing (Third Edition) ... ... **August, 2018**

Published by Asoke K. Ghosh, PHI Learning Private Limited, Rimjhim House, 111, Patparganj Industrial Estate, Delhi-110092 and Printed by Raj Press, New Delhi-110012.

Contents

Preface

We have been teaching over three decades to the postgraduate students of Commerce and Management. Nowadays, several books on management are either difficult to understand or their standards are not meeting the demand of the readers.

Our aim is to provide a book to the students of management as well as professionals in the area, which would clearly set forth the principles and practices of management. Therefore, we have strived to explain the basic concepts of management which are required for students and executives. While reading this book, the readers will have a clear knowledge of what management is all about, and how to acquire managerial skills and execute them in the organizations.

This revised edition covers some additional information on Corporate Respect, Corporate Social Responsibilities, Quality Management Systems and Six Sigma. As per the requirement of the students, some of the chapters have been revised and new case studies have been included. This book is different from other textbooks in India as it gives management orientation on several conceptual issues and practices to the students in this field.

For instance, concepts like Total Quality Management, Quality Management Systems, Six Sigma, Management Education, Productivity Management, Managing Business Values, Executive Education, Organizational Behaviour [Change Management, Stress Management, Organization Culture and Effectiveness] and Case Method of Learning are not included in many books on this subject. All these chapters are unique in providing useful and interesting information. The case studies are expected to help learners understand the practical aspects of management. Every chapter in the book provides learning objectives, summary, review questions and further reading for the benefit of students.

Any constructive comments and suggestions for improving the contents of the book will be warmly appreciated.

R. SATYA RAJU
A. PARTHASARATHY

Preface to the First Edition

We have been teaching management for the last several years to the postgraduate students of Commerce and Management. Today, there are several books on management which are either difficult to understand or whose standard is not up to the mark. Our aim is to provide a book to the students of management as well as professionals in the area, which would clearly set forth the principles and concepts of management. Therefore, we have tried to explain the basic issues of management which are required for everyone. While reading this book, the readers will have a clear idea of what management is all about, and how to acquire managerial skills and manage their organizations. The objective of this book is to enable the readers to learn the main concepts and contribute their best in managing their respective organizations for achieving their mission and objectives.

This book is different from other text books in India in giving management orientation to the students of management on several conceptual issues and practices. For instance, Total Quality Management (Chapter 13), ISO 9000 Certification (Chapter 14), Management Education in India (Chapter 15), Productivity Management (Chapter 17), and Case Method of Learning (Chapter 18) are not included in many books on management. All these chapters are unique in providing useful and interesting information. The case studies are expected to help learners understand the practical aspects of management. Every chapter in the book provides learning objectives, summary, review questions and further reading for the benefit of students.

Any constructive comments and suggestions for improving the contents of the book will be warmly appreciated.

R. SATYA RAJU
A. PARTHASARATHY

Acknowledgements

We express our gratitude to all those who helped us in the preparation of this book. We are indebted to our teachers, K.K. Das, K.V. Sivayya, R. Radha Krishna, G. Subrahmanyam, C.S. Venkata Ratnam, V.B.M. Das, J.V.P. Rao, K.R.S. Murthy, K. Satyanarayana, R. Ramam, Nangegowda, Seshadri Iyengar, Srinivas Murthy, Radhakrishna, Akhilesh, M.R. Rao, K. Ramachandran, G. Nageswar Rao and V. Umamaheswara Rao.

We also wish to thank colleagues and friends, R.K. Vijayasarathy, A.N. Sharma, B.A. Rao, D.P. Rao, I.M.K. Rao, M.M. Rao, K.R.M. Rao, G.S. Narayana, G.S. Rao, I.V.R.L.N. Rao, N.K. Babu, M. Sarada Devi, R. Suneetha, Challarao and Narayana Gupta for their cooperation at various stages. The research scholars who have completed their research and those who are pursuing their research at present, are to be highly appreciated for their cooperation.

We sincerely thank our parents, spouses Raniraj and Rajyalakshmi Parthasarathy, and our children for the encouragement and support they have given while we were busy in preparing this book.

Finally, we wish to thank the Chairman and the Managing Director, the management staff and all employees of PHI Learning for their meticulous care in processing the manuscript, both at the editorial and production stages.

R. SATYA RAJU
A. PARTHASARATHY

Abbreviations

AAMO	Asian Association of Management Organizations
AICTE	All India Council of Technical Education
AIM	Asian Institute of Management
AIMA	All India Management Association
AIMS	Association of Indian Management Schools
AMDISA	Association of Management Development Institutions in South Asia
APESMA	Association of Professional Engineers, Scientists and Managers, Australia
APFPM	Asia-Pacific Federation for Personnel Management
AQC	Acceptable Quality Level
ARTDO	Asian Regional Training and Development Organization
ASCI	Administrative Staff College of India
BEPA	Best Ethical Performance Award
BGL	Bharat Gears Limited
BIS	Bureau of Indian Standards
CATWOE	Customer, Actors, Transformation, World Wide Owners and Environment
CCI	Container Corporation of India
CCMS	Canadian Consortium of Management Schools
CME	Centre for Management Education
CPM	Critical Path Method
CWQC	Company-Wide Quality Control
DPA	Departmental Purpose Analysis
DSS	Decision Support System
EASH	European Agency for Safety and Health
EEC	European Economic Community
EWMA	Exponentially Weighted Moving Average
FICCI	Federation of Indian Chambers of Commerce and Industry
FMEA	Failure Mode and Effect Analysis
GATB	General Aptitude Test Battery
GMAT	Graduate Management Aptitude Test

HSL	Hottem Street London
IBM	International Business Machines
IFPMM	International Federation of Purchasing and Materials Management
IFTDO	International Federation of Training and Development Organization
IGNOU	Indira Gandhi National Open University
IIM	Indian Institute of Management
IIMM	Indian Institute of Materials Management
IIP	Improve Internal Process
IIRA	Indian Industrial Relations Association
ILO	International Labour Organization
ISABS	Indian Society for Applied Behavioural Science
ISO-9000	International Organization for Standards-9000
ISTD	Indian Society for Training and Development
JIT	Just-In-Time
MBO	Management by Objectives
META	Management Education Technological Advancement
MIS	Management Information Systems
MITI	The Ministry of International Trade and Industry
MOU	Memorandum of Understanding
NHRD Network	National Human Resource Development Network
NIOSH	National Institute of Occupational Safety and Health
NIPM	National Institute of Personnel Management
NTPC	National Thermal Power Corporation
ONGC	Oil and Natural Gas Corporation
PDCA	Plan Do Check and Act
PERT	Programme Evaluation and Review Technique
PGDM	Postgraduate Diploma in Management
PPA	Potential Problem Analysis
QFD	Quality Function Development
RINL	Rashtriya Ispat Nigam Limited
SBU	Strategic Business Unit
SCLA	Steel Contract Labour Association
SEC	Swagat Engineering Corporation
SPC	Statistical Process Control
SQC	Statistical Quality Control
TCIC	Twin Cities Insurance Company
TISCO	Tata Iron and Steel Company
TNP	Tennessee Plant Toshiba
TPM	Total Plant Maintenance
TQC	Total Quality Control
TQM	Total Quality Management
WFPMA	World Federation of Personnel Management Associations

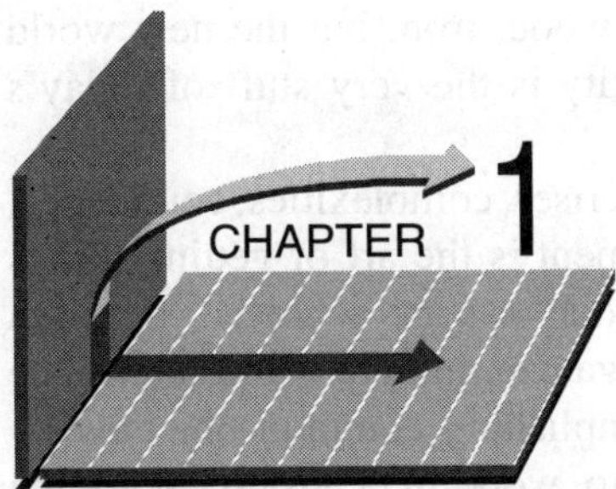

Invitation to Management

CONTENTS

INTRODUCTION

Every organization requires management for its sustained success and survival. When we take a look at the existing organizations all over the world, we find that some are highly successful, some are striving hard for success, and some are unsuccessful. There are certain factors influencing their success. Managers in their organizations perform the functions of planning, organizing, staffing, directing, leading, and controlling for success. We are aware that all organizations in the world are either proprietary concerns, or partnership firms, or cooperative societies, or companies.

Management is a key factor for the success of any organized activity. It is an essential accompaniment of all social organizations. Management is a discipline and culture. It is the life-giving and dynamic organ of any institution it manages. Management refers to the series of functions, and also to the people who discharge it. As Stafford Beer puts it, "the old world was characterized by the need to manage resources like stone, wood, iron; but the new world is characterized by the need to manage complexity as complexity is the very stuff of today's world."

Today, management refers to managing changes, challenges, crises, complexities, confidence, culture, and credibility, to succeed and to accomplish. Management is the art of getting things done through or by people. It is a vital means by which all goals can be achieved, and is a directing and unifying force in all group efforts. It is to plan, organize, integrate and interrelate organizational activities and resources for the purpose of accomplishing common objectives.

Primarily, man is a social being and he always prefers to work in a group. With the growth of science and technology, the birth of large-scale industries, development of trade and commerce, a revolution in transport and communication, the need for organized group efforts has become more important. This group effort has to be properly planned, organized, coordinated and controlled. In a nutshell, it has to be managed effectively.

Management principles are universal in character. Management is essential for all types of organized life. Public/private and joint sector industries, capitalist, communist and mixed economies, government departments, defence organizations, hospitals, hostels, educational institutions and all kinds of business enterprises require management for their survival, growth, expansion and excellence.

DEFINITIONS

There is no universally accepted definition of management. Management experts have defined management differently. The following are some of the definitions of management:

F.W. TAYLOR: Management is the art of knowing what you want to do in the best and cheapest way.

JOHN F. MEE: Management may be defined as the art of securing maximum prosperity with a minimum of effort so as to secure maximum prosperity and happiness for both the employer and the employee and give the public the best possible service.

WHEELER: Management is centred on the administration or managers of the firm who integrate men, material and money into an effective operating unit.

LAWRENCE A. APPLEY: Management is the development of people and not the direction of things... Management is personnel administration.

HAROLD KOONTZ and HEINZ WEIHRICH: Management is the process of designing and maintaining an environment in which individuals work with such performance for optimising efficiency in reaching goals.

OLIVER SHELDON: Management proper is the function in industry, concerned in the execution of policy within the limits set up by the administration and the employment of the organization for the particular objects set before it.

In spite of these various definitions, it has become increasingly difficult to formulate a single and universally acceptable definition of management. However, all these definitions are relevant, meaningful and functional in different contexts. They are nothing but the reflections of different experts and their perspectives. Most of the definitions are limited in their outlook and range. Some of the definitions are oriented towards *decision making*, *leadership* or *human administration*. But these definitions are not comprehensive.

In our opinion, management is managing people and other resources in the organization and outside the organization for achieving the mission and objectives of the organization. It is nothing but managing people with tact; managing people for achieving targets.

The above definition is based on the process approach and is equally significant, as it implies the ongoing and increasing cyclical operations in the form of management. A process also indicates the dynamic nature of management. Management implies managing change also.

CHARACTERISTICS

The following are the characteristics of management:

Management is a distinct process: Management is a unique process. A manager will perform the job of getting things done through planning, organizing, staffing, directing and controlling.

Management is an organized activity: Management, as a process in group activities, essentially requires coordination among individuals and sub-groups. This results in an organized activity, which may be rigid and formal or informal.

Management aims at the accomplishment of predetermined objectives: Management as a group effort aims to achieve predetermined objectives. These objectives become the ultimate goals of any organization. All managerial activities are systematically directed in the accomplishment of such goals.

Management is both a science and an art: It is considered a science because it has developed certain principles, laws, activities and generalizations which are applicable to group activities. Even though *science* is considered a systematic body of knowledge, it cannot be considered as exact as the natural and physical sciences. *Art* refers to the application of knowledge. Management is regarded as an art because it can be applied effectively for solving various organizational problems.

Management is a group activity: Management cannot be done in isolation; it is not an individual activity. All the major achievements in society have been made possible only through group activities. It also helps in integrating human effort through organized group activities.

Management principles are universal in nature: They are applicable in government organizations, business enterprises, military organizations and educational institutions. Henry Fayol suggested this for the first time, and he pointed out certain principles of management which generally apply to every group situation. Even though management principles are universal in nature, they are flexible. They provide working guidelines which can be adapted according to the required situations.

Management integrates human and other resources: The process of management usually results in integrating human and other resources so as to accomplish effective results. Of all resources, human resources are the most precious and difficult to manage. It is essential to manage human resources effectively for the efficient functioning of all the organizations in society. It is for senior managers to ensure that all personal goals of the individual are harnessed and fulfilled in the accomplishment of organizational goals.

Is management a profession? Of late, management is regarded as a profession, as it fulfils the following fundamental characteristics of a profession:

- It has a body of knowledge that is transferable.
- Its basic principles can be identified, mastered and practised.
- It has a scientific approach.
- It involves specific skills, tools and techniques.
- It has to adhere to a code of ethics.

Management is the skill of getting things done through people: Management acts as an effective executive in getting things done through people. It is the process or agency through which management policies are planned and work is supervised.

Management has a distinctive significance: Increased productivity, a favourable organizational climate and positive attitude of the employees are nothing but reflections of good management. In this sense, management has a separate existence from the body of administration at the top. Management has a separate entity in the other sense also. It differs from ownership. The owner may be a manager, but a manager need not be an owner. The effectiveness of a manager, whether he is an owner or not, depends upon how he applies the knowledge and skill required for the job.

Management is essential at different levels of the organization: The "level" suggests the arrangement of managerial positions in an organization in working order. The upper level of management is known as *top management*. The middle level or echelon of management is referred to as *middle management*. The lower level of management is composed of foremen and supervisors. But irrespective of these levels, all managers must perform the basic managerial functions of planning, organizing, directing, and controlling, in different degrees.

Management principles are dynamic in nature: The very concept of management involves a certain degree of dynamism; therefore, the principles laid down under it are also dynamic. The principles of management are not stagnant; they keep changing. They are basically vibrant and respond practically to any major changes in the environment.

Management utilizes a multi-disciplinary approach: Management, as a fast developing subject, has attained significance over the years. Many new techniques and principles have been added to this discipline and now it has become a fully developed subject. Computer engineering, industrial psychology, sociology, anthropology, economics, quantitative techniques and such other subjects have enriched the areas of management discipline. Management thinkers and practitioners have utilized these new developments in other fields to their best advantage. Decision makers have started applying the systems approach and complex quantitative techniques.

Management is a system of authority: Management can also be defined as a system of authority. It has a special ability to visualize things in the right perspective, to recognize, analyze and define the objectives of a problem. It suggests and synthesizes various alternatives for a particular problem, and tests the conclusions to prove its applicability.

MANAGEMENT AND ADMINISTRATION

There are several views on the concept of management and administration. Some of these are as follows:

SHELDON: Administration is the function in industry concerned in determining the corporate action and policy, the coordination of finance, production and distribution, the settlement of the compass of the organization, and the ultimate control of the executive, whereas management is the function in industry concerned in the execution of policy within the limits set by the administration, and the employment of the organization for the particular objects set before it.

WILLIAM SPRIEGEL: Management is essentially an executive function and deals particularly with the active direction of human effort. Administration is determinative in nature, i.e., it sets forth the general purpose of an enterprise, establishes its major policies, formulates the general plan of procedures, inaugurates the board programme and approves the specific major projects that fall within the general programmes.

WILLIAM SCHULZE: Administration is concerned with the formulation of objectives and overall policies of an enterprise and management is executive, i.e., with the execution of policies.

KIMBALL and KIMBALL: The authors of *Principles of Industrial Organization*, however, consider management as a wider concept, embracing all duties and functions that pertain to the initiation of an enterprise and the establishment of all major policies. Administration, in their view, is concerned with the actual work of carrying out those policies.

E.F.F. BRANCH: Administration is that part of management which is concerned with the installation and carrying out of the procedures by which a programme is laid down and the progress of activities is regulated and checked against plans.

To conclude, administration is concerned with the determination of overall corporate objectives, policies and major strategies. It determines mainly the coordination of different major functions in the organization. Administration is more concerned with the determination of a proper organizational climate and also acts as the central controlling authority in the organization.

Management, on the other hand, is more concerned with the execution of plans and policies as laid down by the administration. Administrative functions are mainly legislative and determinative. Management functions are executive. Administration is more or less concerned with the top level management. Management is more related to the middle and lower levels of management. Administration needs more of administrative rather than technical ability. The functioning and importance of administration increases at higher levels and decreases at lower levels.

MANAGEMENT AS A PROCESS

George R. Terry, a well-known author, is of the opinion that management is a distinct process consisting of planning, organizing, directing and controlling, which are performed to determine and accomplish objectives by the use of people and resources. The process of management involves various sub-processes, setting objectives, like planning for the future, division of work, assigning responsibilities, employing people, directing, evaluating the performance of people and work. Planning, organizing, staffing, directing and controlling are the essential responsibilities of all managers in the accomplishment of determined objectives. Management is a process, in the sense that it is concerned with planning, executing and controlling the activities of an enterprise. It is basically concerned with the interrelationship of people at work, mainly with *directing* the performance rather than with the quantum of work done.

MANAGEMENT AS A SCIENCE

Science refers to a systematic body of knowledge acquired through observation, experimentation and intelligent speculation. *Management* deals with the systematic knowledge of acquiring the skill of getting things done through others. It has become a discipline, which is more organized and systematized. Management has evolved general principles relating to planning, organizing, coordination and controlling which have become more scientific. Science has spread to all areas throughout the world, and management is an accepted science as a way of solving problems and taking decisions. In fact, most modern management problems are being solved by the use of computers, which are nothing but scientific brains.

As a science, management is a fast-developing subject. The principles of management are universal in nature and are being applied in every branch of human activity. As it deals with human beings, it is considered a social science also. A manager has to develop new knowledge, new principles and accept thoughts of new schools of management. A scientific attitude is absolutely essential for a manager in problem solving and decision making.

MANAGEMENT AS AN ART

George Terry states that management is an art, which is the "bringing about of a desired result through the application of skill". In fact, *art* mainly refers to the practical application of theoretical knowledge. Management is an art because management principles are evolved and accepted not merely for the sake of knowledge, but to apply them to the actual practical situations in problem solving and decision making.

A manager is not only a scientist but also an artist. At times, he has to depend upon his own experience, intuition and judgement in taking managerial decisions. In fact, as a decision maker, a manager is more of an artist. This art of decision making has to be acquired by continuous effort and practice.

But in the day-to-day experience of a manager, he has to be both a scientist and an artist. For him, both are essential, mutually interdependent and complementary. For any successful manager, even in this computer age, judgement, imagination, intuition and experience are absolutely essential.

MANAGEMENT AS A PROFESSION

Louis A. Allen states that a professional manager is one who specializes in the work of planning, organizing, leading and controlling the efforts of others, and he does so through systematic use of classified knowledge, a common vocabulary and principles, and who subscribes to the standards of practice and code of ethics established by a recognized body.

With the industrial and managerial revolution throughout the world, ownership and management are becoming totally distinct in nature. So, pure management divorced from ownership has become professional in most of the industrialized economies.

The concept of a profession presupposes the following important elements:

- A well-developed body of knowledge
- Professional tools
- Specialization
- Definite standards of entry and practice
- A code of conduct (or an ethical code)
- Prescribed course training
- A professional association

Management is now a developed and highly specialized body of knowledge. The tools of management, like statistics, quantitative techniques, data processing, accounting, business law, and industrial psychology, have become more popular and are providing more practical utility to the science of management. Management as a specialized study has been introduced in many universities and institutes in the field of higher learning. Their training programmes and seminars are becoming popular and functional. Management is becoming a more and more specialized activity. Experts and highly qualified people are needed to manage each functional area of management. Management associations have become popular in promoting the principles and ideals of management.

MANAGERIAL SKILLS

Modern management requires various skills. Technical, human, conceptual and decision making skills are absolutely essential in solving some of the complex problems of modern management. Resource appraisal is also one such technique or skill that can be used effectively as a basis for formulating strategies and taking decisions. Robert L. Katz identified three kinds of skills—technical, human and conceptual. Koontz and Weihrich added the fourth one—design skill.

Technical Skill

Technical skill is the ability to work with resources in a particular area of expertise. A surgeon must know how to do surgery. An accountant must know how to keep accounts. Without technical skill, one is not able to manage work effectively. The first-line supervisor in a manufacturing industry needs greater knowledge about the technical aspects of the job compared to his top boss. In a small manufacturing organization, even the top boss who owns the company needs to have a lot of technical skill.

Human Skill

Human skill is the manager's ability to work effectively as a group member and to build cooperative effort within the team he leads. Every managerial level requires managers to interact with other people, whereas technical skill is primarily concerned with working with things (processes or physical objects). The first-level manager is involved on a regular basis with the personal problems and life events of many non-managers.

Conceptual Skill

Conceptual skill means the ability to see the organization as a whole and recognize how the various functions of the organization depend on one another. It also makes the individual aware how changes in any one part of the organization affect all the others. It extends to visualizing the relationship of the individual business to the industry, the community and the political, social and economic forces of the nation as a whole. Thus, the manager gains an insight into improving the overall welfare of the whole organization.

Design Skill

Design skill involves the ability to solve problems of the organization. Top and middle managements must be able to do more than see a problem.

In every company, there will be different levels of management, as the logical organizational structure demands the existence of such different levels. These levels are:

1. Top-level management
2. Middle-level management
3. Lower-level or operational management.

Skills of top-level management

1. Formulation of vision and mission status.
2. Outsourcing knowledge, people and process development.
3. Top-level management has to deal with environmental forces.
4. It has to plan, organize, control and take policy decisions.
5. It should provide overall leadership.
6. It must effectively apply conceptual and decision-making skills.

Skills of middle-level management

1. Transparency
2. High expertise
3. Fact based decisions
4. Innovations
5. To act as an intermediary between top management and operating management
6. To translate plans into specific action programmes
7. To coordinate inputs, production and outputs
8. To effectively apply human and technical skills.

Skills of lower-level or operational management

1. To translate middle-management plans into short-range operating plans
2. To assign specific jobs to personnel and to watch, evaluate and correct performance
3. To maintain personal and regular rapport with the workers.

CONCEPTS OF MANAGEMENT

There are various concepts of management. Raymond G. Leon, in his book *Manage more, by doing less*, has explained the following concepts for effective management.

Management by Communication

Communication determines the effectiveness of management since a manager spends 90 per cent of his time in communication for getting things done through others. Communication is a continuous, coordinated process of telling, listening and understanding. According to this concept, the success of management depends upon effective communication.

Management by Systems

The concept of management by systems refers to:

- Recognizing problems, analyzing them and defining the objectives
- Collection and analysis of the necessary data
- Finding out various possible alternatives
- Reviewing and evaluating each such alternative
- Testing the conclusions, if possible
- Selecting the best alternative
- Reviewing the results and taking corrective action, if necessary.

Management by systems is more concerned with experimentation and analysis rather than with blind principles or age-old tradition.

Management by Results

The concept of management by results states that the end-results are significant. Development or progress can be evaluated by looking at the end-results. Management should be result-oriented: the success and strength of the management are determined from the results that it can bring in.

Management by Participation

Management by participation means taking workers into confidence. Workers are given opportunity in the decision-making process. It also involves the doctrine of trusteeship. This concept helps in creating a sense of involvement among the workers.

Management by Motivation

Motivation is the dynamic aspect of management, distinct from the mechanical one. According to E.F.L. Brech, "The problem of motivation is the key to management in action and in its executive form, it is among the chief tasks of the general manager."

Management by Exception

Management by exception is a special skill of managing by attending only to exceptionally important matters and taking vital decisions. Routine matters are to be handled by the lower-level officers.

Management by Objectives

Management by objectives (MBO) is a dynamic system which seeks to integrate the company's need to clarify and achieve its profit and growth goals with the manager's need to contribute and develop himself/herself. It is a demanding and rewarding style of managing a business.

The concept of MBO provides a simple but systematic way of creating values and established systems and targets and such other means whereby the efforts of each manager are harnessed to achieve the objectives. All such objectives are the sub-components of a total network, all of which aggregate to the achievement of overall objectives of the unit. According to Peter F. Drucker, "The only principle that can give full scope to individual strength and responsibility, common direction of vision, effort and teamwork is management by objectives." John Humble calls it "a dynamic system which integrates the company's need for more contribution and their [the managers'] personality development."

Reddin, who is an operations expert in MBO, defines it as the "establishment of effectiveness, standards for managerial positions and the periodic conversion of those into measurable time-bound objectives linked vertically and horizontally and with future planning."

Objectives of MBO

- To identify problems and opportunities in business
- To convert identified opportunities into clear goals
- To set up a system to convert these goals into achievements
- To review the organization in the light of the objectives
- To establish the objectives of each job and unit
- To clarify the policies and systems to accomplish the objectives
- To set up a review system.

Steps in MBO

- To establish long-term and short-term organizational goals
- To establish long-term and short-term objectives for each manager, clarifying the key performance standards
- Periodic review of performance
- Encouraging managers to accept responsibility.

Benefits of MBO

- The need for planning will be recognized.
- It provides for objectives and accountability for performance.

- It encourages participative management.
- It helps in job enrichment.
- It provides for a good feedback system.

To conclude, planned objectives are obviously necessary if a company is to operate successfully. But this depends upon the individual performance of managers and their staff. Management by objectives provides a system which identifies the objectives and contribution of individuals with the overall company objectives and performance.

FUNCTIONS OF MANAGEMENT

Henry Fayol has classified managerial functions into planning, organizing, command, coordination and control. Urwick states that there are six management functions. They are:

1. Forecasting
2. Planning
3. Organizing
4. Commanding
5. Coordinating
6. Controlling.

Along with those functions, he also considers research and communication as vital functions of management. Luther Gluick provides a term called POSDCORB to classify the functions of management. POSDCORB refers to the functions of:

1. Planning (P)
2. Organizing (O)
3. Staffing (S)
4. Directing (D)
5. Coordinating (CO)
6. Reporting (R)
7. Budgeting (B).

Newman and Summer classify the functions of management into:

1. Planning
2. Organizing
3. Leading
4. Measuring and controlling.

Koontz and O'Donnell classify the management functions into:

1. Planning
2. Organizing
3. Staffing
4. Directing
5. Controlling.

J.L. Massie classifies management into:

1. Planning
2. Decision making
3. Organizing
4. Staffing
5. Controlling
6. Directing.

From the above classifications, it can be concluded that planning, organizing, staffing, directing/leading, and controlling are the primary functions of management.

Planning

Planning is bridging the gap between the present and the future. It is to foresee things in the right perspective, it is the primary function of any management activity, and begins with the determination of the objectives of the organization, i.e. deciding the future course of action. Planning is all-pervasive. It is essential at all levels of management, and includes objectives, strategies, policies, procedures and programmes. Planning basically involves foreseeing and decision making.

Organizing

Group effort has to be harnessed and organized for the success of any activity. It involves division of activities, assigning duties, delegating authorities and fixing responsibilities. It also includes blending together different resources like men, machinery, material, money and markets. Departmentation, decentralization and delegation are the essential sub-functions of the organization. The organization also determines the authority-responsibility relationship, and provides a mechanism for the management to execute plans.

Staffing

People are responsible for the progress or the problems of any organization. The right person should be employed for the right job. Staffing provides proper personnel who are competent, qualified and with the essential skills to perform the job efficiently. This needs manpower planning and manpower management. Scientific selection and training of personnel, proper remuneration and performance appraisal are the important tasks of the staffing function.

Leading

Leading refers to providing a positive and dynamic leadership. It also implies the creation of a favourable work environment which can provide the maximum opportunities for workers to give expression to their creative powers and skills. The directing function takes up the responsibility of guiding and supervising the activities and operations in an organization. Directing also involves proper motivation of personnel. It refers to managing managers, managing workers and managing the work environment. Direction also refers to the ability to command people.

Controlling

Henry Fayol states that "Control consists of verifying whether everything occurs in conformity with the plan adopted, the instructions issued, and principles established. It has the object of pointing out weaknesses and errors in order to rectify them and prevent recurrence. It operates on everything: things, people, actions." Control refers to the evaluation and correction of the performance. E.F.L. Brech defines control as the process of checking actual performance against the agreed standards or plans with a view to ensuring adequate progress or satisfactory performance. Control involves establishment of standards, appraisal of performance and taking corrective action.

PRINCIPLES OF MANAGEMENT

The 14 Principles of Management enunciated by Henry Fayol are as follows:

1. *Division of work*: People need specialization for effective performance.
2. *Authority*: Managers must be given authority to get things done.
3. *Discipline*: All the employees and the shareholders must respect the rules, regulations and agreements that govern the organization.
4. *Unity of command*: An employee in an organization must receive instructions from only one person.
5. *Unity of direction*: The operations relating to a particular job must be directed by only one manager.
6. *Subordination of individual interest to the common good*: The interest of all the employees should also be linked with organizational objectives.
7. *Remuneration*: The compensation payable to the employees in the organization should be fair and reasonable.
8. *Centralization*: Authority and responsibility must be centralized in any organization, with adequate decentralization policies.
9. *Hierarchy*: The line of authority in an organization should be very clear and the organization chart has to provide all the information.
10. *Order*: Employees must be at the right place and at the right time.
11. *Equity*: Managers must be friendly and fair with their employees.
12. *Stability of staff*: The organization should not have high employee turnover.
13. *Initiative*: Employees should be given freedom to function in the organization with creativity and innovation.
14. *Espritdecorps*: Promoting team spirit helps a lot in achieving organizational goals.

FLAT WORLD

According to the Bible, God created the world in six days and on the seventh day, he rested. Flattening the world took a little longer time. The world has flattened by the convergence of some major political events, innovations, and establishment of new companies. We have to keep it in our mind that we are managing business enterprises in the flat world of the twenty-first century. The ten forces that flattened the world are:

1. New age of creativity
2. New age of connectivity
3. Work-flow software
4. Uploading
5. Outsourcing
6. Off-shoring
7. In-sourcing
8. Informing
9. Supply chaining
10. The steroids—digital, mobile, personal and virtual.

CORPORATE EXCELLENCE

In their book, *In Search of Excellence*, Peters and Waterman identified 43 companies that they considered excellent. In choosing some of the firms, the authors considered measures such as growth of assets and equity, average return on total capital and similar measures. They also asked industry experts about the innovativeness of the companies. The authors identified eight characteristics of excellent enterprises as follows:

1. *A bias for action*: A preference for doing something—anything—rather than sending a question through cycles and cycles of analyses and committee reports.
2. *Staying close to the customer*: Hearing his or her preferences and catering to them.
3. *Autonomy and entrepreneurship*: Breaking the corporation into small companies and encouraging them to think independently and competitively.
4. *Productivity through people*: Creating the awareness in all employees that their best efforts are essential and that they will share in the rewards of the company's success.
5. *Hands-on, value-driven policies*: Insisting that executives keep in touch with the firm's essential business.
6. *Stick to the knitting*: Remaining with the business the company knows best.
7. *Simple form, lean staff*: Few administrative layers, few people at the upper levels.
8. *Simultaneous loose-tight properties*: Fostering a climate in which there is dedication to the central values of the company, combined with tolerance for all employees who accept those values.

A survey by *Fortune* magazine of 31 industrial groups showed the following ranking of the 10 most admired companies in the USA:

1. International Business Machines (IBM)
2. 3M
3. Dow Jones (printing and publishing)
4. Coca-Cola
5. Merck (pharmaceuticals)
6. Boeing
7. Rubbermaid
8. Procter & Gamble
9. Exxon
10. J.P. Morgan (banking).

In addition, companies were rated on eight attributes of reputation. IBM ranked first in the following five categories: quality of management, long-term investment value, financial soundness, the ability to attract, develop and retain talented people, and the use of the assets of the corporation. In the other three categories, these companies ranked first: Dow Jones in quality of products and service, Citicorp in innovativeness, and Eastman Kodak in community and environmental responsibility.

The world's most admired top 20 companies in 2008 were:

1. Apple
2. Costco Wholesale

3. General Electric
4. UPC
5. Toyota Motor
6. IBM (tie)
7. Berkshire Hathaway
8. PepsiCo (tie)
9. Procter & Gamble
10. Cisco Systems
11. FedEx
12. Boeing
13. Johnson & Johnson
14. Wal-Mart Stores
15. Target
16. Honda Motor
17. BMW
18. Coca-Cola
19. Microsoft
20. Caterpillar

Most admired top 20 Indian companies in 2008 were:

1. Infosys Technologies
2. ITC
3. Bharti Airtel
4. Bajaj Auto
5. Maruti Suzuki India
6. HCL Technologies
7. Tata Consultancy Services
8. Ranbaxy Laboratories
9. Reliance Communications
10. State Bank of India
11. Wipro
12. Hindustan Unilever
13. Reliance Industries
14. HDFC Bank
15. ICICI Bank
16. Dabur India
17. Tata Motors
18. Idea Cellular
19. Hero Honda Motors
20. Colgate–Palmolive (India)

The best innovative companies in India in 2008 were:

1. Deccan Airline
2. ITC
3. Jet Airways
4. Dabur India
5. Mahindra & Mahindra
6. LG Electronics
7. Tata Motors
8. Apollo Hospitals
9. Citibank India
10. Arvind Eye Care
11. Maruti Suzuki India
12. SRL Ranbaxy
13. HDFC Bank
14. Narayana Hrudayalaya
15. ICICI Bank
16. Infosys Technologies
17. Philips Electronics
18. Wipro Technologies
19. Samsung Electronics
20. Dr. Reddy's Laboratories

The factors considered for ranking were: number of employees employed, reliability, constant innovation, enjoyability, and the investor's confidence.

CORPORATE RESPECT

The new business environment has created a mindset among the professional managers on issues related to competitiveness, cost reduction, quality consciousness, innovation, value culture, customer delight, corporate excellence, managing for future results, etc. in the global village. Several management schools, management development centres, consultancy organizations and professional organizations have been focusing their attention on creating a culture for corporate respect and excellence through leadership development.

Culture creation is a key role of the CEO because it plays an important part in the success or survival of any organization. Culture is the totality of beliefs, customs, traditions and values of an organization. We all know that, "Rome was not built in a day". Same is the case with culture which requires a lot of interest and investment on the people and processes. CEOs of the most respected companies have been striving hard to build good corporate culture and corporate governance for corporate respect.

Studies on Corporate Respect

The Business World, *Business Today*, etc. have been conducting surveys on the most respected Indian companies and corporate respect from time to time. These studies reveal certain interesting insights. The survey results have also been published in various issues of business magazines. Though there is every care taken, some human errors may also be considered in ranking. Therefore, the results of such surveys need not be taken into consideration for any negative remarks. We congratulate the business magazines and experts for creating a mindset among the Indian CEOs for maintaining corporate respect.

As per the survey of the *Business World* in 2001, the top ten most respected companies in India are Infosys, HUL, Reliance Industries, Wipro, ICICI, L&T, ITC, Dr. Reddy's, Ranbaxy and Nestle-India.

When the first survey was conducted in 1987, Hind Lever was at the top among India's most respected companies, followed by Tata Steel, Telco, ITC, L&T, Bajaj Auto, ... In the second survey (1990), Tata Steel was the topper followed by Telco and Hind-Lever. In the 1992 survey also, Tata Steel maintained the same position followed by L&T and Tata Engineering. There is some change in the ranking of the companies over a period of time. For instance, Hind Lever ranked first in 1987, third in 1990, ninth in 1992, tenth in 1994, first in 1996, second in 1999 and again second in 2001. Some top companies in 1987 were not listed in the survey of 2001.

The Parameters

The parameters considered for rating these corporate enterprises are:

1. Number of times a company was chosen
2. Overall quality
3. Top management leadership
4. Depth/quality of talent
5. Ability to attract/manage/retain talent
6. Believes in transparency
7. Ethical organization
8. Socially responsive organization
9. Environmentally conscious organization
10. Quality of products/services provided
11. Believes in customer satisfaction

12. Record of product/corporate brand management
13. Dynamism in organization
14. Responds quickly to business scene changes
15. Believes in continuous innovation
16. Has global competitiveness
17. Has a record of steady corporate performance
18. Gives good returns to shareholders
19. Ability to create value for stakeholders.

CEO's Response

Some CEO's response of various organizations during different years have been given as per the following:

- "We've striven hard for respectability and to create an ethical organization. There are certain expectations that we haven't fulfilled. But, we've also a very young organization and in areas like track record of management, we may be low because we've yet to show longevity" (Naryana Murthy).
- "We execute innovation and product quality. By focusing on 30 brands, we have been able to concentrate our resources" (M.S. Banga).
- "Reliance is passionate about attaining global leadership" (Mukesh Ambani).
- "At Wipro, we have dared to dream. We have put in place strategies to execute the dreams. We achieved all targets set for 2000. We have now articulated our vision for 2004. Among other targets, we want to be among the top 10 IT services companies globally by 2004" (Azim Premji).
- "We run a meritocracy over here and I can attract talent at will. I get worried when senior people leave. We play hardball with competition which can call it unethical." I can build, and I will, a world class IT Company of the size of India's top 5" (A.M. Naik).
- "We are a conscious corporation in all aspects of our contribution to the society" (Y.C. Deveswar).
- "To be able to change in a dynamic world calls for some management thinking" (Satish Reddy).
- "There is no company in the world that has delivered consistent performance over a span of 12–15 years" (K.V. Kumar).
- "Ranbaxy has not frittered away its focus. It stands for high integrity" (D.S. Brar).
- "In an environment where MNCs are not welcomed, it's important to do better than normal" (Carlo Donati).

Key Factors

The following information provides the key factors for respect in various organizations.

Infosys	• Top management leadership • Commendable • Company on growth path • Competitiveness • Export orientation • Good employee relations
HLL	• New initiatives in marketing • Excellent corporate governance • Continuous performance standards
Reliance Industries	• Capable of marshalling resources • Thinks big • Savvy tax management • Growth-oriented strategies
Wipro	• Good corporate governance • Transparent and professional • Visionary leadership • All round achievements
L&T	• Engineering excellence • Professionally managed company • Consistent profitability • Good employee relations
ITC	• A big company consistently making profits despite adverse regulations • Smart diversifications
ICICI	• Returns to shareholders • Visionary leadership
Dr. Reddy's	• Innovation and growth in high tech pharmaceuticals • Quality research and development
Ranbaxy	• First indian firm started pharma R&D • Developed drugs that have patented abroad • Best pharma firm in India
Nestle India	• Market savvy company • Maintains quality • Professional management • Fair practices • Clean organisation

In India, the best employers have been continuously following several practices such as:

1. High degree of employee satisfaction
2. High degree of commitment and morale
3. A sense of ownership and belongingness
4. Depth, breadth and consistency in application and GHR practices
5. Unique HR practices—many of them were home-grown and based on employee suggestions

6. Sensitivity towards balance between work and personal life
7. Alignment of HR practices with business context
8. Stature of organisations in the business community as evidenced by employer and corporate initiatives.

The new generation management professionals who pursue their studies from various business schools in India and abroad, are expected to play a crucial role in the click and chick economy for creating wealth through value culture. As per the studies, it is a well-known fact that they have more intellectual skills and high score on knowledge. These intellectual and knowledge people have to understand the present scenario and prepare their minds to serve the mighty or mini organizations. Though they are not expected to learn all the management tools and techniques in a short span of their study period, they have to study beyond their curriculum. They need knowledge on both global and national organizations and are expected to prepare their vision and mission statements. They have to undergo training in India and abroad through various programmes for acquiring knowledge on global and local companies. All the skills required for leadership are to be acquired and improved.

According to Stephen R. Covery, the principle-centred leaders have certain traits. They read valuable literature, get training and train others, listen to people and develop new skills and competencies. They always practice four principles:

1. Personal (X – relationship with himself)
2. Interpersonal (X – relationship and interactions with others)
3. Managerial (X – responsibility to get a job done with others)
4. Organisational (X – need to organise people).

Trustworthiness at personal and interpersonal levels is highly essential for managing people. The CEOs of several organizations continuously learn, are service minded, radiate positive energy, believe in people, lead balanced lives, see life as an adventure, are synergistic and exercise for self-renewal. They are also called either **transformational** or **transactional**.

Covey also states the seven habits of highly effective people which are given below:

1. Be proactive
2. Begin with the end in mind
3. Put first things first
4. Think win-win
5. Seek first to understand, then to be understood
6. Synergize
7. Sharpen the saw

He also stated the eighth habit of people is effectiveness to greatness.

These habits are observed in several CEOs. The successful CEOs are proactive and always take initiation and responsibility. They feel the weather is always favourable for them, whether it rains or shines. They are value-driven by producing good quality of work.

'To begin with the end in mind' means to start with a clear understanding of our destination—where we are now and where we have to go. The mission statements for individuals, family and organizations are essential to achieve. The successful CEOs are habitual of doing things priority-wise and follow the win-win policy. They first understand the environment and activities themselves, and then ask others to understand everything. Synergy is an important concept in their minds which they implement in their activities. They always learn new things and follow new methods with a creative outlook. They sharpen their minds and environment with new ideas and thinking.

The future CEOs need not think about their pay and perks if they possess the required qualifications and qualities. The salary structure of CEOs in India is quite attractive and interesting for the new generation professional managers. They will certainly be successful either as professional managers or as administrators, or consultants, or entrepreneurs in the new era as they possess a member of qualities such as honesty, high integrity and values, high emotional quotient, patience, tolerance, creativity, innovations, and respect towards people and society along with a high degree of patriotism. They have to change the pace of people at all levels by facing several challenges. When the managers and new generation professionals come forward to share the responsibility of building culture with care for creating wealth and health in the corporate world, then the mission of our visionary leaders will certainly be fulfilled.

LEVELS OF MANAGERS

Lower-level Managers

These managers are in direct contact with the employees, who usually produce goods or services of an organization. They are referred to as **supervisors** or **foremen** in some organizations.

Middle-level Managers

These managers are those with a number of responsibilities and linking or connecting activities. They direct the activities of the lower-level managers.

Top-level Managers

Top-level managers are a small group of policy makers responsible for the overall strategic management of the organization. It is the responsibility of the top managers to develop the objectives and strategies of the organization.

SUMMARY

1. Management is getting things done through people. Planning, organizing, staffing, leading and controlling are the functions of management.
2. Managing changes and the challenges is essential.
3. Management is a distinct process of organized activity, aimed at predetermined objectives.
4. Management is both—a science and an art: it is universal in nature.
5. Management is a profession.

6. Administrative functions are legislative and determinative, whereas management functions are executive.
7. Technical skills, human skills and conceptual skills are required for managers.
8. Fayol's 14 Principles of Management are very important in management.
9. The ultimate objective of management is achieving excellence.

REVIEW QUESTIONS

1. Define management and discuss its main characteristics.
2. "Management is a trinity of art, science and profession." Discuss.
3. "Management is the art of getting things done through and with people in formally organized groups." Explain.
4. Distinguish between management and administration.
5. Discuss the basic functions of management.
6. Explain the role and importance of management in present society.
7. Explain Fayol's Principles of Management.
8. Explain the required managerial skills.
9. What are the characteristics of excellent companies?

CASE STUDY

Asia Businessman

On the evening of March 3, 2008, more than sixty leading figures from Japan's business community gathered in the Grand Hyatt Tokyo for the presentation of the *Fortune Asia Businessman of the year* award.

In 2008, the recipient was Minoru Mori, president and CEO of Mori Building, the Japanese property development company best known for the Roppongi Hills complex in Tokyo and the soaring World Financial Centre in Shanghai.

Presenting the award, Clay Chandler, Asia editor of *Fortune*, praised Mori for his vision, his commercial acumen, his patience, his willingness to take risks, his ability to build consensus and, more than anything, his fine sense of style. With Asia growing more prosperous, there is a lot of ill-thought-out development taking place, but Mori, said Chandler, "shows us how much is to be gained when development and urban planning is done right."

Mori expounded his building philosophy in a witty acceptance speech, "The taller the building, the smaller the footprint and thus the greater the area created for greenery, tall buildings also reduce urban sprawl and cut commuting times to contribute to a better quality of life." Asked to comment on his future plans, Mori spoke about the potential of 'underground high-rise buildings', and his desire to assist the Japanese government with his twin initiatives of turning Tokyo into a genuine global financial centre, and boosting tourist numbers.

Questions for Discussion

1. What are the main issues in the case?
2. Explain the skills and qualities required for the CEO.

FURTHER READING

Business Today, April, 2008.

Chester, B.I., *The Functions of the Executive*, Harvard University Press, (Mass.), Cambridge, 1938.

Drucker, Peter, F., *The Frontiers of Management*, Heinemann Professional Publishing Co., London, 1986.

Drucker, Peter, F., *The Practice of Management*, Heinemann, London, 1955.

Fortune, **157**, No. 5, p. 40, 2008.

Friedman, Thomas, *The World is Flat*, Penguin Books, New York, 2006.

Koontz, Harold and O'Donnell, C., *Principles of Management*, McGraw-Hill, New York, 1972.

Koontz, Harold and Weihrich, Heinz, *Essentials of Management*, McGraw-Hill, New York, 1990.

Steiner, G.A., *Business and Society*, Random House, New York, 1971.

Stoner, James A.F., Freeman, R. Edward and Gilbert, Daniel R. Jr., *Management*, 6th ed., Prentice-Hall of India, New Delhi, 1995.

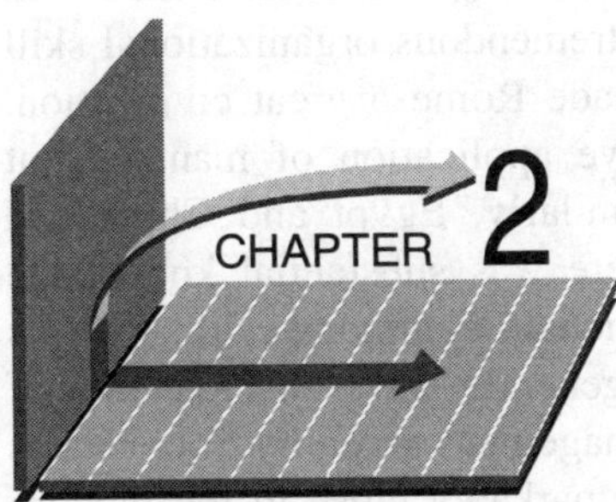

Evolution of Management Thought

CONTENTS

INTRODUCTION

Management was unknown anywhere about two and a half centuries ago, and now it is well known everywhere in every activity, and every enterprise—from small family business to multinational corporation. It is considered to be an important activity and part of life of every human being.

MANAGEMENT THOUGHT

Management, both as a theory and practice, has a long history. Through the ages, the idea of management was there in some form or the other. However, its method has been varying from time to time, depending upon the state of social and technological factors. Since the dawn of civilization, there was an organized effort in the accomplishment of desired objectives.

In the ancient times, there were groups of priests who directed and controlled people by virtue of their authority as the representatives of God. In Rome, the organization was supreme. The city of Rome was expanded into an empire with tremendous organizational skill and order. The scalar and delegation of authority principles made Rome a great civilization. The Roman Catholic Church was another example of effective application of management and organizational technique to fulfil religious objectives. Similarly, Egypt and China had introduced concepts of managing people. In early Greece, there was substantial knowledge of the principles of management. The very existence of the Athenian commonwealth, with its councils, popular courts, administrative officials and board of generals, gave an indication of their appreciation of managerial functions. The definition of management given by Socrates, as a *skill* separate from technical knowledge and experience, is remarkably close to the modern understanding of the concept.

The study of administration of the cities of Mohenjodaro and Harappa of the ancient Aryans in 2000 BC, Buddha's order and the Sangha in 530 BC, provides sufficient evidence in India about the use of the principles of management. However, major management techniques were not available till the second half of the nineteenth century, as the structure of industry was not highly developed.

The Industrial Revolution of the eighteenth century was a great landmark in the economic history of mankind. With the advent of the Industrial Revolution, organizational structure underwent a great change. Mass production, international marketing and technological specialization resulted in the creation of new economic relationships among people and nations. It created a new order and a system of modern management.

In America, it was Alexander Hamilton (1757–1804) who brought out the famous "Report on Manufacturers", which emphasized the constructive, purposeful and systematic role of management. In *management*, he found the engine of economic and social development, and in *organization* the carrier of economic advancement. Henry Clay (1777–1852) published *American System,* which is popularly known as the first blueprint for systematic economic development. But it was Robert Owen (1771–1858), an industrialist in Scotland, who actually became the first manager. He tried to tackle the problems of productivity and motivation, of the relationship of the worker to work, of the worker to the enterprise, and of the worker to the management.

In Germany, George Siemens (1839–1901), who developed the Deutsche Bank into a leading financial institution of continental Europe, designed an effective top management model for the first time and tackled the basic problems of communications and information in a large organization.

In Japan, Eiichi Shibusawa (1840–1931) in the seventies and eighties first raised basic questions regarding the relationship between business and national objectives, business needs and individual ethics.

It was Frederick W. Taylor (1856–1915) who made a major attempt to study work in the actual work situation. It has become fashionable today to look down on Taylor and to decry his outmoded psychology, but he was the first man in the history of mankind who did not take work for granted, but looked at it and studied it.

Almost during the same period, in France, Henry Fayol (1841–1925) for the first time thought of an organizational structure. Walter Rathenall (1867–1922) of Germany raised the most relevant questions on the social responsibilities of business for the first time. Hugo Muensterberg (1863–1916) first tried to apply the social and behavioural sciences like psychology to modern organization and management. After the First World War, Herbert Hoove (1874–1964) became very popular by applying the principles of management to the first massive foreign-aid operation in history.

Thomas J. Masaryk (1850–1937) conceived the idea of using management as an instrument to restore the economies of Europe after their destruction by war. In the early twenties, Pierre S. du Pont (1870–1954) and Alfred P. Sloan Jr (1875–1966) in America, first developed organizational principles for the new kind of "big business". Julius Rosenwald (1862–1932) and Robert E. Wood (1879–1969) built the first business based on the marketing approach.

After Taylor, the discipline of management was further developed by Frank (1868–1924) and Lillian Gibreth (1878–1972), Henry Gantt (1861–1961). Mary Parker Follet (1868–1933) and Chester Barnard (1886–1961) first studied the process of decision making in organizations and the relationships between formal and informal organizations. Cyril Burt (1883–1972) in England and the Australian Elton Mayo (1880–1949) working at Harvard, respectively, developed industrial psychology and human relations and applied it to enterprise and management.

James McKinsey (1889–1937) and Lynolall F. Urkinesey started management consultancy on a large scale. But it was Peter Drucker who brought a new breeze to different areas of modern management. He introduced tremendous changes in the organization and management of large-scale institutions and he regarded management as the life-giving dynamic organ of the institution. He has exerted a major influence on the management practice of the present century. Drucker has studied and explored the management problems and systems in Great Britain, Western Europe, USA, Japan and Latin America. He identified the areas of organized ignorance in the field of management, and introduced the concept of *Management culture* to overcome it. Drucker states clearly that "Management is a discipline and management is a practice."

Besides these developments, during the pre-Taylor period, there were other scholars who made some significant contributions in the field of management. Charles Babbage of the UK (1792–1871) suggested the use of proper data in the management of an organization. He felt that modern science and mathematics could be applied to the operation of factories and invented a calculating machine called "The Differential Engine". James Watt Jr and M.R. Boulton, the sons of the inventors of the steam engine, used marketing research and forecasting techniques, planned machine layout, production planning, standardization of components, record keeping, provision of welfare of personnel, and schemes for developing executives in their engineering factory at Birmingham.

MANAGEMENT APPROACHES

The evolution of management thought can be classified into two different stages:

1. Traditional approaches
2. Modern approaches.

Traditional Approaches (Early approaches)

The traditional approaches are based on the following four important factors:

1. *Scientific management model:* This school based its experiments on: science, not rule of thumb; harmony, not discord; cooperation, not individualism; maximum output, not restricted output; the development of each man to his greatest efficiency and prosperity.

Taylor made significant contributions in improving the methods of production and efficiency. Standardization, increased wages, research and cooperation were given due importance. Gantt, Gilbreth and Emerson also made remarkable contributions to enrich the ideas of F.W. Taylor.

2. *Administrative management model:* Henri Fayol provided this theory, which prescribes concepts like the scalar principle, unity of command, the exception principle, span of control, and departmentation. Mooney and Railey, Simon and Urwick also contributed a lot to develop the ideas of Fayol. The administrative management theory includes:

(a) 14 Principles of Management as stated by Fayol
(b) Line and staff structure
(c) Management functions like planning and organizing.

This model is also termed *ideal bureaucracy.* But it is power-centred at the institutional level without providing many opportunities for the development of individuals.

3. *Human relations model:* As every organization exists in society, it has to satisfy the people living in that society. When people are protected and provided good working conditions, we can observe high productivity in the organizations. Even the employees have to consider the interest of their employer along with their interest. Participative style of leadership helps a lot in this model.

4. *Bureaucratic model:* Business is a social system. It has to provide employee satisfaction. The employee requires financial and non-financial rewards. Employee relations are very essential in management. In the present sense of the term, *bureaucracy* means the negative consequences of a large organization like red-tapism, inordinate delays, unnecessary procedures, etc. But Max Weber, a German sociologist, provided this theory and stated that bureaucracy is the most efficient form of a complex organization. He provided a model which included:

- Hierarchy of authority
- Division of labour
- A system of rules
- Impersonality of interpersonal relationships
- A system of work procedures
- Placement of employees based upon technical competence
- Legal authority and power.

But bureaucracy has its own glaring defects like rigidity, impersonality, higher cost of control, self-perpetuation, etc. It does not provide opportunity for job enrichment or management development.

Modern Approaches

The following are the modern approaches of management:

1. *Behavioural approach:* It is an improvized or extended form of the classical theory. The neo-classical theory emphasized the people who work behind the machine. The behavioural science approach to management is the base of this neo-classical theory. Psychology, human sentiments and social values are important in this theory. The classical theory concentrated on Theory X, while this theory emphasized Theory Y. The behavioural science approach shifted the importance from the bureaucratic to the participative management style. Elton Mayo, Maslow, McGregor and Whitehead are some of the experts who have made significant contributions in enriching this theory. This theory prefers democratic style of leadership.

2. *Quantitative approach:* Coordination of different teams of scientists from several fields is one of the main characteristics of this school of management thought. This school utilizes all the scientific techniques and tools for providing a quantitative basis of managerial decisions. It believes that management is a logical process which can be expressed in terms of mathematical symbols and relationships. The main contributors to this school are Taylor, Gilbreth, Gantt, Joel Dean, Newmann, Ackoff and Hicks.

The application of quantitative methods to military and logistical decision problems during and after World War II resulted in the development of operations research. Operations research includes linear programming, queueing, theory of probability (which helped more in product design and development), inventory control, and quality control of raw materials and finished goods.

Quantitative techniques have become popular because of their wide application in several countries. *Linear programming* helps in input-output analysis and product mix. *Queueing theory* helps in inventory control, traffic control, telephone trunking systems and radio communications. *Sampling theory* helps in profit planning, inventory control and manpower requirement study. *Information theory* helps in data processing, systems design and organization analysis. Nowadays, computers are being used in solving management problems.

Mathematical techniques have helped management in developing systematic thinking and improved its accuracy. But these quantitative techniques can only be considered as tools in decision making, rather than a "be all and end all" of management. There are various problem areas in management which cannot be solved by mere mathematical application or quantitative techniques.

3. *Systems approach:* The systems approach analyzes the entire activities of an organization in terms of system inputs, processing, and outputs to develop operational efficiency. This approach was developed with the success of operations research after 1950.

The Greek term *system* basically refers to blending or bringing together. The systems approach may be regarded as "a way of thinking about the job of managing which provides a framework for visualizing internal and external environmental factors as an integrated whole".

Managers are encouraged to take into consideration real-life situations and practical problems in their decision making. That is why the systems approach has been considered as more realistic than the other approaches to the study of management problems. Various physical, biological and social scientists have contributed to develop this school of thought.

Kenneth and Boulding extended the application of this approach to management areas, Katz and Kahn to the social systems, Ludwing von Bertalanffy to other sciences, Forester to industrial systems, Stafford Beer, Hertz, Morse and others to operations research, and Norbert Wiener to the feedback theory.

4. *Contingency approach:* The contingency or situational approach emphasizes the relevance of management actions to the specific characteristics of the situations of such actions. Management must adapt itself to the environment. A manager has to identify the significant variables in the situation. In areas like organization, design and leadership, this approach has been widely applied. The major contributors to this school of thought in management are Joan Wood, Fiedlar and Lawrence. Table 2.1 lists the eminent management thinkers and their contributions.

Table 2.1 Management thinkers and their contributions

Name	*Chief publications*	*Major contributions*
Henry Fayol (1841–1925)	1. *Administration Industrielle et Generale* (1916)	Stressed that the theory of administration was equally applicable to all forms of organized human cooperation
Harrington Emerson (1853–1931)	1. *Efficiency as Basis for Operation and Wages* (1900)	Studied the Sante Fe Rail-road and promoted "scientific management" in general usage
	2. *The Twelve Principles of Efficiency* (1912)	
	3. *The Scientific Selection of Employees* (1913)	
Frederick W. Taylor (1856–1915)	1. *A Piece-Rate System* (1895)	Father of scientific management. Developed high-speed cutting tools. Introduced time study to industry
	2. *Shop Management* (1903)	
	3. *On the Art of Cutting Metals* (1906)	
	4. *The Principles of Scientific Management* (1911)	
Karl Pearson (1857–1936)	1. *On the Correlation of Fertility with Social Value* (1913)	Developed basic statistical tables and statistical techniques, including the chi-square test and the standard deviation concept
	2. *Tables for Statisticians* (1933)	
Henry L. Gantt (1861–1919)	1. *Work, Wages and Profits* (1910)	Emphasized relation of management and labour. Stressed conditions that have favourable psychological effects on the worker. Developed charting techniques for scheduling
	2. *Industrial Leadership* (1916)	
	3. *Organizing for Work* (1919)	
Max Weber (1864–1920)	1. *The Theory of Social and Economic Organization* (translated by Henderson and Parsons in 1947)	The foremost pioneer in the development of the theory of bureaucracy
	2. *From Max Weber: Essays in Sociology* (translated by Gerth and Mills in 1946)	

Name	*Chief publications*	*Major contributions*
Frank Gilbreth (1868–1924)	1. *Concrete Systems* (1908) 2. *Motion Study* (1911)	Searched for "the one best way". Introduced motion study to industry
Mary Parker Follett (1868–1924)	1. *Dynamic Administration* (edited by Metcalf and Urwich, 1941)	Led in practical observations about the value of human relations to the basic principles of organization
G. Elton Mayo (1880–1949)	1. *The Human Problems of an Industrial Civilization* (1933) 2. *The Social Problems of an Industrial Civilization* (1933)	Stressed the importance of human and social factors in industrial relationships. Questioned the overemphasis on technical skills at the expense of adaptive social skills. Led a team of researchers in extensive studies at the Hawthorne plant of Western Electric Company
Chester I. Barnard (1886–1961)	1. *The Functions of the Executive* (1938) 2. *Organization and Management* (1948)	Leader in stressing sociological aspects of management. Concentrated on the concept of authority, the importance of communication, and informal organizations in management
Kurt Lewin (1890–1947)	1. *Resolving Social Conflicts Field Theory in Social Science* (1951)	Developed the theory of group dynamics
Ronald A. Fischer (1890–1962)	1. *Statistical Methods for Research Workers* (1925) 2. *The Design of Experiments* (1935)	Pioneer in the use of statistical methods in research. Made valuable contributions to the design of experiments
Walter A. (1891–1972)	1. *The Economic Quality Control of Manufactured Products* (1930)	Applied theory of probability and statistical inference to economic problems at Bell Laboratories. Developed statistical control charts
F.J. Roethlisberger (1898–1974)	1. *Management and the Worker* (with W.J. Dickson, 1939) 2. *Management and Morale* (1941) 3. *A New Look for Management* (1948)	Made a comprehensive report on the Hawthorne experiment. Led in experimental research on human factors in management
Peter Drucker (1909–)	1. *The Practice of Management* (1954) 2. *Innovation and Entrepreneurship* (1985) (And several other books on management)	Developed the concept of management by objectives. As a consultant and writer, popularized new developments in management
G.B. Dantzig (1914–)	1. *Maximization of a Linear Function of Variables Subject to Linear Inequalities* (1947)	Developed the basis for practical applications of linear programming
Claude Shannon (1918–)	1 *The Mathematical Theory of Communication* (1948)	Laid the theoretical foundation for information theory

Name	Chief publications	Major contributions
Herbert A. Simon (1916–)	1. *Administrative Behavior* (1947)	Winner of Nobel Prize in Developed Economics Theory building from behavioural and quantitative bases for modern management
	2. *Models of Man* (1957)	
	3. *Organization* (1958)	

Source: Joseph L. Massie, *Essentials of Management*, PHI, New Delhi, 1987.

Management Theory Jungle

With the growth and development of the above theories and approaches to management over a period of time, perspectives have also changed. Harold Koontz called it the "management theory jungle" in 1961. Koontz analyzed that there were six different schools of management in 1961. But, after several years, Harold Koontz, O'Donnell and Weihrich found almost 11 approaches to management. They are:

1. Empirical or case approach
2. Interpersonal behaviour approach
3. Group behaviour approach
4. Cooperative social systems approach
5. Socio-technical systems approach
6. Decision theory approach
7. Systems approach
8. Mathematical or "management science" approach
9. Contingency or situational approach
10. Managerial roles approach
11. Operational theory.

After this observation, several attempts were made to synthesize the various schools of thought. As a result, Koontz and Weihrich suggested the adoption of the "operational approach" to management analysis. George R. Terry advocated the modified management process approach to take the best from what was available in the management thought. The approaches to management are presented briefly in Table 2.2.

Table 2.2 Approaches to management

Characteristics/contributions	Limitations
Empirical or case approach	
Studies experience through cases identifies successes and failures	Situations are all different. No attempt to identify principles. Limited value for developing management theory
Interpersonal behaviour approach	
Focus on interpersonal behaviour, human relations, leadership, and motivation, based on individual psychology	Ignores planning, organizing, and controlling. Psychological training is not enough to become an effective manager

Characteristics/contributions	*Limitations*
Group behaviour approach	
Emphasis on behaviour of people in groups. Based on sociology and social psychology. Primarily study of group behaviour patterns. The study of large groups is often called "organization behaviour"	Often not integrated with management concepts, principles, theory, and techniques. Need for closer integration with organization structure, design, staffing, planning and controlling
Cooperative social systems approach	
Concerned with both interpersonal and group behavioural aspects leading to a system of cooperation. Expanded concept includes any cooperative group with a clear purpose	Too broad a field for the study of management. At the same time, it over-looks many managerial concepts, principles and techniques
Socio-technical systems approach	
Technical system has great effect on social system (personal attitudes, group behaviour). Focus on production, office operations and other areas with close relationship between the technical system and people	Emphasis only on blue-collar and lower-level office work. Ignores much of other managerial knowledge
Decision theory approach	
Focus on the making of decisions, persons or groups making decisions, and the decision-making process. Some making as a springboard to study all enterprise activities. The boundaries of study are no longer clearly defined	There is more to managing than making decisions. The focus is at the same time too narrow and too wide
Systems approach	
Systems concepts have broad applicability. Systems have boundaries, but they also interact with the external environment, i.e. organizations are open systems. Recognizes importance of study of interrelatedness of planning, organizing, and controlling in an organization as well as many subsystems	Analyses of the interrelatedness of systems and subsystems as well as the interactions of organizations with their external environment. Can hardly be considered a new approach to management
Mathematical or "management science" approach	
Managing is seen as mathematical processes, concepts, symbols, and models. Looks at management as a purely logical process, expressed in mathematical symbols and relationships	Preoccupation with mathematical models. Many aspects in managing cannot be modelled. Mathematics is a useful tool, but hardly a school or an approach to management
Contingency or situational approach	
Managerial practice depends on circumstances (i.e. a contingency or a situation). Contingency theory recognizes the influence of given solutions on organizational behaviour patterns	Managers have long realized that there is no one best way to do things. Difficulty in determining all relevant contingency factors and showing their relationships can be very complex

Characteristics/contributions	*Limitations*
Managerial roles approach	
Original study consisted of observations of five chief executives. On the basis of this study, 10 managerial roles were identified and grouped into (a) interpersonal, (b) informational, and (c) decision roles	Original sample was very small. Some activities are not managerial. Activities are evidence of planning, organizing, staffing, leading and controlling. But some important managerial activities were left out (e.g. appraising managers)
McKinsey's 7-S framework	
The seven S's are (a) strategy, (b) structure, (c) systems, (d) style, (e) staff, (f) shared values, and (g) skills	Although this experienced consulting firm now uses a framework similar to the one found useful by Koontz et al. since 1955 and confirms its practicality, the terms used are not precise and topics are not discussed in depth
Operational approach	
Draws together concepts, principles, techniques, knowledge from other fields, and managerial approaches. The attempt is to develop science and theory with practical application. Distinguishes between managerial and non-managerial knowledge. Develops classification system built around the managerial functions of planning, organizing, staffing, leading and controlling	Does not, as some authors do, identify "representing" or "coordination" as a separate function. Coordination, for example, is the essence of managership and is the purpose of managing

CONTRIBUTIONS OF MANAGEMENT THINKERS

Several management thinkers have contributed a lot to the growth of management. Some of them are: Taylor, Emerson, Gilbreth, Follett Gantt, Mayo, Mooney, Railey Sheldon, Barnard and Fayol.

F.W. TAYLOR: Frederick Winslow Taylor is widely known as the father of the scientific management movement. He was the first to identify and emphasize the need to have a scientific approach to the task of managing an enterprise. In his popular book, *The Principles of Management,* he states three main reasons for writing the book:

1. To point out, through a series of simple illustrations, the great loss which the whole country is suffering through inefficiency in almost all types of daily acts.
2. To try to convince the trader that the remedy for his inefficiency lies in scientific management.
3. To prove that the best management is a true science resting upon clearly-defined rules, laws and principles, and these principles of scientific management are applicable to all kinds of human activities from one simple, individual act to the work of a great corporation.

Taylor first published his theory on management in a paper entitled, "A piece rate system", presented to the American Society of Mechanical Engineers in 1895. Further, he developed it and published *Shop Management* in 1903 and *Principles of Scientific Management* in 1911.

According to Taylor, the principal object of management should be to secure the maximum prosperity for each employer, coupled with the maximum prosperity of each employee. Taylor has laid down four major principles of management:

1. Development of a true science of work
2. Scientific selection and progressive development of the workmen
3. Bringing together of the science of work and scientifically selected and trained men
4. Constant and intimate cooperation of management and men.

Taylor basically recommended making management a science resting on "well recognized, clearly defined and fixed principles". He emphasized five basic concepts on which management theory and practice could be based:

1. Research
2. Standards
3. Planning
4. Control
5. Cooperation.

Taylor also suggested:

1. Replacing the rule of thumb with scientific determination of each element of a man's work
2. Scientific selection and training of workers
3. Mental revolution
4. More equal division of responsibility between managers and workers.

Standardization, time and motion studies, functional foremanship, production planning and control, and the piece rate system of payment were some of the main ideas enunciated by Taylor. Though "Taylorism" was severely criticized by many, his contribution to the field of scientific management remains significant. As Oliver Sheldon, a British management expert, remarked, "So, finally the torch was handed over from one generation to another till, amidst the immense structure of American industry, it was passed on to the hands of F.W. Taylor."

HARRINGTON EMERSON: Emerson was an engineer in the USA, who proclaimed that the railroads could save a million dollars a day by introducing scientific management methods. He published his famous work, *Twelve Principles of Efficiency,* in which he states them as:

1. Clearly defined goals
2. Common sense
3. Competent counsel
4. Discipline
5. Fair deal
6. Reliable, immediate, accurate and permanent records
7. Despatching
8. Standards and schedules
9. Standardized conditions
10. Standardized operations
11. Written standard practice instructions
12. Reward for efficiency.

Emerson was a reputed efficiency engineer who popularized concepts like standard cost, standard time, preventable waste, etc. He also suggested the concept of *line and staff organization* instead of *functional foremanship*.

F.B. GILBRETH: Gilbreth developed motion study as a primary tool for managers. He maintained that there was one best way to perform a given job. Gilbreth proved the truth of his idea by simplifying the motions used in the bricklaying industry. He reduced the number of motions from 18 to five, and increased the hourly number of bricks laid from 170 to 350, thus increasing productivity by 100 per cent. He applied, for the first time, a motion picture camera to record and analyze performance. He classified human motions into 18 elements. Those are: search, find, select, grasp, transport load, position, assemble, use, hold, disassemble, inspect, preposition, release load, transport empty, rest, unavoidable delay, avoidable delay and plan.

MARY PARKER FOLLETT: She was educated at Cambridge and Harvard universities with academic accomplishments in philosophy, history and political science. Her publications on *The new state and creative experience* and *Dynamic administration* have become popular. She made significant contributions regarding the human relationships within industrial groups. She advocated the use of reason and explanation, rather than power, in managing the affairs of an organization.

HENRY L. GANTT: Henry Lawrence Gantt worked with Taylor and made significant contributions to the study of scientific management. His famous Gantt Chart has become very popular, and it was the forerunner of modern techniques like PERT and CPM. He concentrated mainly on developing graphic methods of presenting plans. Another contribution made by Gantt was the task and bonus system of remunerating workers for performance.

GEORGE ELTON MAYO: Born and educated in Australia, Mayo led some of the remarkable experiments at Harvard with the Hawthorne Plant of Western Electric Company. These experiments proved that workers respond to their work situation as a whole, and that their attitudes and social relations constitute an important part of the total situation. He emphasized that emotional and non-logical attitudes and sentiments were more important in economic relationships than in logical, economic ones.

MOONEY and RAILEY: Mooney wrote a book, *Principles of Organization*, and co-authored *Onward Industry* with Allan C. Railey. Mooney stated that the principles of organization employed by all great leaders throughout history were the same. He primarily dealt with three principles of organization. They are:

1. Principle of coordination
2. Scalar principle
3. Functional principle.

OLIVER SHELDON: Oliver Sheldon L was a British industrial consultant. He wrote *Philosophy of Management*. He primarily dealt with the determination of policy and coordination of functions, execution of policy and the process of consigning the work of individuals or groups with the faculties necessary for its execution.

CHESTER BARNARD: The book, *The Functions of the Executives,* was a major contribution. According to Barnard, the executive functions are:

1. Maintaining organization communication
2. Securing the essential services of individuals
3. Formulating purposes and objectives.

Barnard made it clear that organizations are systems of cooperative effort and coordinated activities.

HENRY FAYOL: As a French administrator, Fayol developed a theory of general management for universal application. In 1916, he published his well-known work in French, entitled, *Industrial and General Administration*. While Taylor worked primarily at the operative level from the bottom of the industrial hierarchy upwards, Fayol concentrated on the managing director and worked downwards in the hierarchy. Fayol classified all industrial activities into six groups. They are:

1. Technical activities concerning production
2. Commercial activities concerning buying, selling and exchange
3. Financial activities like procurement of capital, optimum utilization of capital
4. Security activities concerning protection of property
5. Accounting activities concerning final accounts, costing and statistics
6. Managerial activities concerning planning, organizing, commanding, coordinating, and controlling.

According to Fayol, an efficient manager must possess the following:

1. Physical qualities
2. Mental qualities
3. Moral qualities
4. A sound general education
5. Special knowledge
6. Experience.

To conclude, in the words of Urwick, "the work of Taylor and Fayol was, of course, essentially complementary. They both realized that the problem of personnel and its management at all levels is the 'key' to industrial success. Both applied scientific methods to this problem. Taylor worked primarily on the operative levels from the bottom of the industrial hierarchy upwards, while Fayol concentrated on the managing director and worked downwards, which was merely a reflection of their very different careers."

MANAGERIAL ROLES

The following are the managerial roles identified by Mintzberg.

Interpersonal Roles

1. Figurehead role (performing ceremonial and social duties as the organization's representative)
2. Leader's role
3. Liaison role (particularly with outsiders).

Informational Roles

1. Recipient role (receiving information about the operation of an enterprise)
2. Disseminator role (passing information to subordinates)
3. Spokesperson role (transmitting information to those outside the organization).

Decision Roles

1. Entrepreneurial role
2. Disturbance-handler role
3. Resource-allocator role
4. Negotiator role (dealing with various persons and groups of persons).

Several management experts feel that the following are issues of concern for the managerial role:

1. Managers work with and through other people.
2. Managers are responsible and accountable.
3. Managers formulate goals and set priorities.
4. Managers must think analytically and conceptually.
5. Managers are mediators.
6. Managers are not politicians.
7. Managers are diplomats.
8. Managers are inspirers.
9. Managers take decisions.
10. The foremost goal of managers is to make their organization effective.
11. Profit maximization and stockholders' interests are not the central goals of managers.
12. Attending to customers is very important.
13. Integrity is a highly rated factor by managers at all levels.
14. Pressure to conform to organizational standards is essential.
15. Spouses are important in helping their mates grapple with ethical dilemmas.
16. Most managers seek the advice of others in handling ethical dilemmas.

Management plays an important role in any activity. It helps in the success of an activity or organization. It organizes the factors of production for effective utilization. Whether small or large, family-owned or factory-type, an organization should implement the principles of management for the success and survival of the enterprise. Management at local, state and national levels of the government helps in improving efficiency. Transnational corporations and also other organizations all over the world, including non-government organizations, hospitals, hotels and clubs, need management for utilizing resources to the maximum possible extent.

SUMMARY

1. Management has a long history—as old as mankind.
2. Taylor, Emerson, Gilbreth, Parker, Gantt, Mayo, Fayol, etc. have contributed a lot to the field of management.
3. Management theories are both classical or traditional and neo-classical or modern.
4. The role of managers is very important in the success of an organization.

REVIEW QUESTIONS

1. Explain the evolution of management thought.
2. What is meant by scientific management? Discuss the various elements of scientific management.
3. Outline Taylor's scientific management and examine its relevance to management in present-day business.
4. Explain Fayol's contribution to management?
5. "Scientific management involves in its essence a complete revolution on the part of workers and an equally complete revolution on the part of those on the management side." Explain.
6. "The work of Taylor and Fayol was essentially complementary." How far do you agree with this statement?
7. Discuss the contributions of Elton Mayo, Chester Bernard and Mary Parker Follet to the development of management thought.
8. Write a note on the different schools of management thought.
9. Explain the role of managers and management.

CASE STUDIES

1. Rasish Computers

Raman came with a good proposal and discussed it with his friends Siva and Shyam. Under the changing social, economical and political environments, the three entrepreneurs with professional expertise would like to start an organization in Bangalore to manufacture computer spare parts. All the entrepreneurs have an engineering background and are financially sound. They were fresh graduates and their knowledge of the practical aspects of management is inadequate. They would like to be world leaders in a period of 10–15 years in manufacturing computer spare parts.

Questions for Discussion

1. What should these entrepreneurs know about management?
2. How can they become world leaders?

2. Rehin Sons

"Our vision is to globalize our business with cost leadership. We would like to expand our business by establishing footwear shopping malls by 2010. Two of our family members, my son and nephew, were asked to join our business after completing their studies in management education", stated Sen Kwong, the managing partner of the business enterprise, Rehin Sons. He also said, "Our father, Jao Tang Chang, was an entrepreneur who used to run a small enterprise in China in the beginning and later continued in India. He migrated from a village in China to Kolkata (India) along with some of his friends to achieve his mission."

In the beginning, their father Jao Tang started a firm with four partners, which was highly successful. Later, they had some disputes. They dissolved the firm and then, Jao Tang started a new venture, Rehin Sons with a meagre capital of ₹10,000 in 1958. He carried out the business successfully until his demise in 1987. Sen said, "From our family, myself and younger brother (On Kwong) joined our father in managing the business and continued the journey for 50 years. We had been celebrating the golden jubilee of our business." When the case writer had a discussion with the entrepreneurs [Sen Kwong and On Kwong], they were happy to share their business experiences. On Kwong, the younger brother, said, "We have been serving the people at their feet for the last fifty years and celebrated golden jubilee of the success of our business. We are happy with the success of our business."

Though the enterprise was established in Visakhapatnam City of coastal India, the entrepreneurs had close contacts with their friends and family members in China. They showed the case writer the photographs of their visit in 2007 to Beijing, Shangai and other places in China. As the case writer had also visited China to attend an international seminar in Beijing in October 2008, they had a detailed discussion on important places of China, including the Great Wall of China, Lama temple, and the traditions and customs of the people of China. The entrepreneurs were happy to share their views and experiences.

About Chinese and Economy of China

We describe here the Chinese networking system, the changing economy of China, their value culture, and the traits of overseas Chinese. The Peoples Republic of China is one of the fast growing economies of the world. The nation had maximum prosperity and wealth during the last three decades. It was due to the people and their discipline, sacrifice and social networking. The economy was liberalized in 1978 and reforms were introduced. The Chinese migrated to different countries and settled well. Chinese had followed the policy of one child family. It helped in raising the standard of living and reducing the fertility rate drastically. The fertility rate slumped to 1.8 children per women in 2008 from 5.8 children about three decades ago, as per the official records.

Li Bin, Director of the National Population and Family Planning Commission, had stated that the Chinese planning campaign, which began about three decades ago, had benefited a lot. Chinese followed the policy strictly in urban areas. The population stood at 1.32 billion by 2007. As a result, the per capita GDP of China had also reached US$2400 in 2007.

The financial crisis in USA had created a greater impact on all nations. Some American companies slashed salaries from 30 per cent to 50 per cent. Some others had drastically reduced

Diwali and Christmas gifts to their employees. China's products were expected to be sold less in quantity. India and other countries buy Chinese goods because of low cost and cost competitiveness. One of the journals published an article entitled, "Made in China and sold in India." As the Chinese goods had cost competitiveness, they had become more popular all over the world. The case writer wishes to have the slogan as "Made in India and sold all over the Globe."

The people who migrated to South East Asia in the last one or two waves were considered to be overseas Chinese. Several people arrived in their new homelands in the later years of the nineteenth century or in the twentieth century. The overseas Chinese had a greater role in national and international trade. An expert on Chinese economy, Xiaotong Fei, had identified five distinctive general characteristics of Chinese networks. Those were: Chinese networks are continuous; Chinese networks have hierarchical and dyadic ties; Chinese networks emphasize uprightness; Chinese networks view morality; and Chinese networks have flexible boundaries.

The Chinese networks had five bases: clan, language, location, guild and trust. The membership in one does not guarantee membership in another. The Chinese philosophical system had historically stressed high ethical standards. Buddhism had more focus on their ethical duties and behaviour. Their relationship from the superior person to the inferior person occurs from: sovereign to minister; father to son; husband to wife; older brother to younger brother; and friendship.

The competitive advantage of the overseas Chinese was based on three factors: speed, knowledge and *guanxi*, which means building networks, and trust. Chinese were considered to be more creative and innovative. The eight management techniques for stimulating creativity among the people were: encouraging people; be not judgemental; helping people; stimulating curiosity; creating necessity; allowing time away from the fray; catalyze group problem solving and require fun.

The top ten emerging markets in the world in 2006 were in trillion US$ China (8.1), South Korea (2.5), Brazil (2.2), India (1.8), Russia (1.5), South Africa (1.0), Mexico (1.0), Malaysia (0.6), Turkey (0.6) and Thailand (0.5). As China had attracted all countries the world, the entrepreneurs would like to globalize the business in having their operations in China and Korea first. Sen Kwong had plans to go global by 2015.

Family Background and Wealth Creation

Jao had five sons and two daughters. Three sons had taken up their career as employees in different companies and daughters, after getting married, were doing business. One of the sons of Jao, Sen Kwong (55) had taken up the business with true spirit after his father's demise. The active members of the family were: himself and his younger brother On Kwong (49). Both of them had been managing the business successfully. As a result, the business celebrated 50 years of its existence. During 2008, some discounts and customer benefit schemes were also offered. They had given ₹50 discount on the purchase of shoes/*chappals*. The entrepreneurs had family network in China and used to go now and then, but had become Indian citizens. They stated that their girl children would also join them in the business.

The case writer asked them the reasons for choosing their career as entrepreneurs. They replied that they entered the business because of their family business and also to derive certain advantages, such as: invulnerability; limited responsibility; to gain experience to develop networking skills; and self-learning. They further stated that the great things of being entrepreneurs were: they can make rules of their own; their baby; no more politics; time flexibility; working as per the convenience; working with their own friends; work life balance; living their own dreams; monetary flexibility; showing a sense of pride and satisfaction.

The members of the family had strong beliefs and customs, and everyone was respected in the family. Family decisions and business decisions were taken collectively by the two brothers, Sen Kwong and On Kwong. Their spouses also would involve in decision making. The successors of the business would be their sons in their family. The had 'all by all' or any other combination type of ownership structure of business and had continuous journey for about 50 years from 1958 to 2008 without any conflicts.

The two brothers had worked hard and increased their wealth every year. Their family wealth was estimated to be ₹20 crores. About 30 per cent of it was locked up in the business. They had certain plants for next generation entrepreneurs, with clear goals and mission. The entrepreneurs had one son each and the elder brother had another two daughters. The daughters of Sen also were highly educated. One daughter got married and later joined their family business in Canada. Thus, they had high human assets and business assets. Their main business was started at Suryabagh, a busy centre in Visakhapatnam during 1958 and later, two branches were established in 1997 at Gajuwaka and RTC complex areas, which were their own business premises, at busy centres of Visakhapatnam city.

Visakhapatnam is located on the coastal belt of India and is one of the fastest growing cities in the world, with a population of about two millions. It has a natural harbour and port along with an integrated steel plant (Vizag steel), Hindustan Shipyard, Hindustan Petroleum, NTPCL, Hindustan Zinc, Bharat Heavy Plate and Vessels and several other large, medium and small enterprises. Some information technology companies were also established in addition to some service and trade enterprises. The city is also called 'the city of destiny.' It is a calm and pleasant place, with global culture and high traditions. Some multinational companies test-marketed their products in Visakhapatnam because of its cosmopolitan culture. Therefore, several entrepreneurs were highly successful in their ventures.

Business Growth

The business had a substantial growth during its five decades of journey. It was started with a meager amount of ₹10,000 in 1958. By 2008, it was expected to be over ₹20.00 crores. The important feature in the business was that they had never borrowed money from banks or financial institutions. They had invested their surplus amount in the business for expansion. Their turnover and profitability positions were quite encouraging and growing very fast.

The turnover and profits of the firm had a significant increase from 1980 to 2008. The turnover increased from ₹10 lakh in 1980 to ₹150 lakh in 2008. The profit of the organisation was also raised from ₹1.0 lakh of ₹30.0 lakh during the corresponding years.

The business had given fame and fortune to the family. Sen and his brother, On Kwong, sent their sons to United States for higher studies in management. The growth rate of business was very high during the last ten years and was expected to increase in future. They had certain projections for future business. There were only two workers in the beginning. Later, the number was increased gradually. About 30 persons (20 permanent and 10 temporary) were working with the firm in 2008. Except five workers, all of them had joined about five years ago. The employees expressed their happiness to have worked with the organisation for a long time.

All over the world, successful entrepreneurs have certain traits. They are: persistence; confidence; vision; action; dedication; faith; integrity; adaptability; courage; and communication. The important traits of the two entrepreneurs were: hard work and discipline. Sen stated that their grandfather and father were more creative and aggressive. They had a manufacturing unit of their own for about twenty years, and manufactured new model shoes at low cost as per the customer requirement.

The two brothers, Sen and On, had some other traits also. Sen was friendly with all and had a positive attitude. Both of them had knowledge of the business. On Kwong was a Rotarian. Both of them had an urge to serve the society and continue their journey for a long time without any break. In near future, they would like to globalize the business by establishing malls at various places in India, China, Canada, South Korea and the USA.

Competitiveness and Business Operations

There was high competition from branded shops. Several new ventures were established for footwear. The important competitors were: Bata, Elite, and Popular. About 200 shops were main competitors. Their market share was expected to be reasonable and it was about 20 per cent in 2008. Modern retail malls such as Big Bazaar, Pantaloon, Reliance Footcare, More for you, Mega Mall, Forum, etc. would also include footwear in their business with international brands. They had high confidence in managing business under severe competition because they had knowledge of the business from their childhood. Their unique selling proposition (USP) was serving at customer's feet at low cost.

They had been buying different models of *chappals* from ABCD cities. Those were Agra, Bombay, Calcutta and Delhi. On Kwong stated that "Agra was the shoe capital of Asia" for a long time. Later, China had got the title, "Shoe capital of Asia and globe." They used to manufacture shoes earlier. Because of modernization and modern mills, they stopped manufacturing shoes and *chappals* and got finished products from different manufacturers. Their sales were mainly at Visakhapatnam. Sometimes, the suppliers dictated business terms. All the purchases were from leading manufactures in India and obtained the products as per the customer's choice. They were not spending much on advertisements. They had mostly cash transactions and trade credit for two to three months and sold goods on cash and credit cards. They also supplied to schools and offices in addition to individual buyers from different areas.

The business had some problems. One of the problems was obtaining raw material. The suppliers had certain restrictions in the trade. As a result of increasing oil prices, there were fluctuations in the business. Hike in oil prices had an impact on synthetic raw material. Religious factor had an impact on leather. As a result, there was a problem of raw material for the manufacturers who were supplying goods to them. Employee turnover and labour cost were also high. Rents were increasing substantially, as well as the power bills. Another important problem was customer behaviour. On Kwong expressed that, the customers had loyalty earlier, but at present the percentage of loyal customers was very low. The customers had low emotional balance. The level of tolerance was low. The customer requirement was super market style shop. In future, customers would certainly require separate malls for footwear.

Due to increase in traffic at Visakhapatnam city, the customers faced parking problem at the shops located at main road junctions. Sometimes, customers complained about parking. Though they had a desire to establish a mall, they did not have enough capital for it. Their business was expanded with their surplus amounts in the business every year, they were not interested to take loans from banks and financial institutions up to 2008. There was no guarantee that their children would certainly join them after completing their studies abroad. Sometimes, they were reluctant to do footwear business. Sen was telling that their intention was to start mega malls to serve all types of customers.

The Future of Business

Sen Kwong and On Kwong had several ideas to expand the business in future. As they did not have any other family member to join them, they were awaiting the arrival of their sons from the states after completing their studies. Meanwhile, the two brothers had decided to start another three branches at different places in Visakhapatnam city. They were also interested to sell goods through online. They would like to open a website shortly for further expansion. They would like to globalize their operations by 2015.

Questions for Discussion

1. What are the main issues of the case?
2. Discuss competitive advantage of China and Chinese Businessmen.
3. What are your suggestions for expansion of the firm Rehin Sons?

FURTHER READING

Business World, January 2008.

Drucker, Peter, F., *Management—Tasks, Responsibilities, Practice*, Allied Publishers, Bombay, 1980.

Koontz, Harold and O. Donnell, C., *Principles of Management*, McGraw-Hill, New York, 1972.

Koontz, Harold and Weihrich, Heinz, *Essentials of Management*, McGraw-Hill, New York, 1990.

Stoner, James, A.F., Freeman, Edward, R. and Gilbert, Daniel, R. Jr., *Management*, 6th ed., Prentice-Hall of India, New Delhi, 1995.

Planning

CONTENTS

- The Concept
- Definitions
- Types of Plans
- Importance of Planning
- Essential Features
- Principles of Planning
- Steps in Planning
- Planning and Forecasting
- Steps in Forecasting
- Forecasting Techniques
- Planning Premises
- Planning and Control

THE CONCEPT

Planning is basically a decision-making process, setting apart different courses of action which an organization and its individual members are to take over a period of time. It also refers to policy formulation and the establishment of goals. The development of alternative courses of action and the selection of the best possible alternative is vital for good planning. Planning is deciding in advance what to do, when and how to do it. Perception and foresight are vital for a good planner. A wise planner can capitalize on his/her opportunities in the competitive world by looking into the future, well ahead of others. However, planning is not only looking into the future but also preparing for it. In fact, it is the blueprint for the future action. It bridges the gap between the present and the future. Planning, therefore, includes setting objectives, laying down policies, procedures and rules, preparing strategies and programmes, budgeting, forecasting and decision making. The top management requires mission, vision and values in preparing strategic planning in the organization.

DEFINITIONS

KOONTZ and O'DONNELL: Planning involves selecting enterprise objectives, departmental goals, and programmes, and determining the ways of reaching them. Planning, thus, provides a rational approach to pre-selected objectives.

PHILIP KOTLER: Planning is deciding in the present what to do in future. It is the process whereby companies reconcile their resources with their objectives and opportunities.

McFARLAND: Planning in business is selecting the best course of action for achieving the predetermined objectives of a business, after making a careful evaluation of present conditions and future trends regarding the external forces and internal resources.

In the light of the foregoing definitions, it is clear that planning involves:

- Determination of objectives and goals of the organization, and laying down specific targets
- Appraisal of current conditions and resources and analyzing factors involved in the realization of the resources
- Collection of relevant data and an intelligent, imaginative understanding of their interrelationships
- Prediction of future developments and their impact on the organization
- Evolving alternative courses of action on the basis of data collected and keeping future trends in view
- Weighing the merits and demerits of each course and deciding on the best course of action, involving the minimum of time, money and other resources
- Working out details of the selected course of action, breaking it down into different items of work, charting a chronological sequence for each, etc.

HUSSEY: Corporate planning includes the setting of objectives, organizing the work, people and systems to enable those objectives to be attained, motivating through the planning process and through the plans, measuring performance and so controlling the progress of the plan and developing people through better decision making, clearer objectives, more involvement and awareness of progress.

Strategic planning is the process of deciding the objectives of the organization, changes in these objectives, on the resources used to attain these objectives and on the policies that are to govern the acquisition, use and disposition of these resources.

Examples of strategic planning in an organization may be: planning growth rate in sales, diversification of business into new lines, type of products to be offered, and so on. This way, strategic planning encompasses all the functional areas of business and is effected within the existing and long-term framework of economic, political, technological, and social factors. Strategic planning also involves the analysis of various environmental factors, particularly with respect to how an organization relates to its environment.

GEORGE R. TERRY: Planning is the selecting and relating of facts and the making and using of assumptions regarding the future in the visualization and formulation of proposed activities believed necessary to achieve desired results.

PETER F. DRUCKER: Planning is the continuous process of making present entrepreneurial decisions systematically and with the best possible knowledge of their futurity, organizing systematically the efforts needed to carry out these decisions and measuring the results of these decisions against the expectations through organized, systematic feedback.

FARMER and RICHMAN: Planning determines organizational objectives and the policies, programmes, schedules, procedures, and methods for achieving them. Planning is essentially decision making since it involves choosing among alternatives and it also encompasses innovation. Thus, planning is the process of making decisions on any phase of organized activity.

To conclude, planning is the basic function concerned with the establishment of objectives to be accomplished in the future.

TYPES OF PLANS

Planning may be of different types. We can classify some of the important types of plans as below, discussed according to the nature of its planning:

1. *Financial or non-financial plans:* Most plans cannot be translated into action if there is no finance. In fact, planning loses all its significance if sufficient financial resources are not mobilized. Plans that require financial resources are considered *financial plans*. Plans relating to the physical resources of an organization may be called *non-financial plans*.

2. *Formal and informal plans:* Mere thinking by managers or contemplation refers to informal plans. When an informal plan is finalized and prepared for implementation, it is considered to be a formal plan.

3. *Specific and routine plans:* Any plan made with a particular object is known as a *specific plan*. Day-to-day normal activities require some type of regular plan, known as a *routine plan*.

4. *Strategic and functional plans:* Strategic planning is the overall planning of the enterprise's objectives determined by the top management. A plan made in a functional area like production, purchase, marketing is referred to as a *functional plan*.

5. *Long-range and short-range plan:* The definition of short- and long-term (or range) planning depends upon the organizational structure, nature of business, the kind of industry, etc. Generally, a *short-term plan* refers to a period covering six to twelve months. A *long-range plan* usually involves a time interval of between three and five years. But the modern concept is to plan for a decade or two.

6. *Administrative and operational plans:* An *administrative plan* provides the base for operative plans. Administrative planning is done by the top- and middle-level management, and operational planning by the lower-level management.

Long-range Planning

Modern organizations, particularly in the corporate sector, have started making long-range plans. These plans are made not only to earn maximum returns on investment, but also to explore new areas of activity which can utilize their human skills, and financial and technical resources to the fullest possible extent. A good plan is one that is flexible. It is designed to put the company in a comfortable position to take maximum advantage of future changes. With this end in view, targets should be fixed for utilizing and developing corporate skills and resources. The company should plan for flexibility by concentrating on such potential areas of innovation and development by setting both quantitative and qualitative objectives.

Another Classification of Plans

A plan can encompass a future course of action. Plans are also classified as follows:

1. *Mission:* The basic purpose of the existence of the business is called the *mission*. For instance, the purpose of a college or university is teaching and research. The purpose of a firm is production and distribution of goods and services.

2. *Objectives:* Objectives are the goals or the end results towards which all management activities are directed. *Objective* is a term commonly used to indicate the end point of a management programme. Objectives should be specific and set for different periods. They are the basic purpose of the enterprise. Well-defined goals or clear objectives are essential for the smooth progress and growth of any organization.

According to Peter F. Drucker, objectives are essential in all the key areas where performance and results directly contribute to the growth and survival of the business. Objectives may be either major or minor, short-term or long-term, economic or social. Major objectives are the main purpose of the concern, and minor objectives are subordinate to the major objectives. The *economic objectives* may be to make more profit, sales, etc. The *social objectives* may be to serve the customers, employees, etc.

Objectives function as reference points for all the efforts of the employees and the management. They also serve as standards for control. All the activities of the concern must be related to the objectives. Objectives are to be given for each person and to each responsibility centre.

Effective management is one that has management by objectives. It is popularly known as MBO. Originally, MBO was proposed by Peter Drucker and later, it was popularized. It is a concept of managing for minimizing external controls and maximizing internal motivation through joint goal-setting by the superior and his subordinates and self-control on the part of all managers. MBO can be introduced through the following steps:

- Formulate long-range goals and strategic plans
- Develop specific overall organizational objectives
- Establish departmental objectives
- Set individual job objectives
- Formulate action plans
- Implement and take corrective action
- Review progress towards objectives
- Appraise overall performance, reinforce behaviour and strengthen motivation.

Peter F. Drucker says that the objectives help to organize and explain the whole range of business phenomena in a small number of general statements; to test those statements in actual experience; to predict behaviour; to appraise the soundness of decisions to enable practising businessmen to analyze their own experience, and as a result, improve their performance.

3. *Strategies:* The term *strategy* originally came from Greece around 400 BC, and it refers to the technique of directing a military force in the light of the enemy force's action. In the management sense also, it has the same competitive implications. It is also regarded as interpretative planning. In the present-day context of a dynamic environment, developing effective corporate strategies is vital for the survival, success and growth of an organization. Strategy is related to the environment and its impact on the organization. It is dynamic in nature, an action to meet the specific demands of the situation. There are *overall strategies, derivative strategies, minor strategies, composite strategies, contingency strategies* and *master strategies.*

4. *Policies:* Policies are guidelines to action. They are the basic statements serving as guides to the thinking and action of subordinates in repetitive situations. They provide broad guidelines. Alford and Beatty have defined a policy as "the mode of thought and the principles underlying the activities of an organization or an institution." It is a regular decision which is applicable to repetitive situations. For instance, a firm has a policy of promoting from within to higher jobs in the organization. The significant and basic policies are administered at the top. The policies at the middle and lower levels should be consistent with the top management policies. Policies are the first major step in converting the objectives into workable propositions. They are the main instruments for delegating authority by a superior manager to his subordinates. Every subordinate can act freely and confidently as long as he operates within the scope of a policy.

Every policy statement must be definite, clear and easily understandable. Policies made by the management should be reasonable, stable, and flexible, based on proper and correct information and sound judgement, and, to accomplish their purpose, be communicated. As far as possible, policies should be in writing.

The different types of policies are as follows:

(a) *Originated policies:* These are the policies formulated by the top management with the intention of guiding the actions of their subordinates. Originated policies help in delegating authority throughout the organization.

(b) *Appealed policies:* If an appeal is made by a supervisor or a manager to his superior regarding a particular decision, the superior may provide a guideline as a precedent, which can serve as a guide for action by the subordinate for all future decisions. Such a policy resulting from an appeal is called an *appealed policy.*

(c) *Imposed policies:* Any policy taken by the influence of some external forces like the government, trade unions, trade associations, etc. is called an *imposed policy.*

(d) *Top management policies:* They are the policies of top management, usually with a long-term perspective. Product line selection, sales forecasting, size of the firm, machine selection, budgeting, etc. are such policies.

(e) *Middle-management policies:* Policies regarding sales, production, research, finance, accounting, training of junior executives, etc. are considered *middle-management policies.*

(f) *Product policies:* 'Make or buy' policies and 'diversification or simplification' policies are *product policies.* They are the policies regarding the designing, developing, or marketing of a product.

(g) *Pricing policies:* Policies regarding the price of a product are considered *pricing policies.* Charging higher price, lower price, differential price, credit facilities, cash terms, etc. are covered under these policies.

(h) *Promotion policies:* Policies to promote may be for utilizing the managerial resources for the best use of the organization, to provide for a fair opportunity to all for advancement and promotion. In the context of marketing, promotion policy refers to a policy of promoting the product line. Promotional activities like advertisement, salesmanship, etc. are considered under this policy.

(i) *Distribution policies:* For the purpose of physical distribution of the goods, selection of channels of distribution, establishing warehouse, certain policies are to be taken. They are called distribution policies.

(j) *Production policies:* They include the decisions regarding automation policy, make or buy policy, inventory level policies, etc.

(k) *Finance policies:* These are policies which consider the method of raising funds and the ratio between the various types of financial resources. They include the rate of return, credit policy, dividend policy, working and fixed capital requirements, etc.

When all the policies of a concern are published in the form of a book or diary, it is called the *policy manual*. It is a written and definite statement of policy, readily available as a reference or guide for all the managers. It makes the policies clear and understandable, avoids misinterpretation, and helps the new workers to acquaint themselves with the policies of the organization.

5. *Procedures:* Procedures provide the manner in which a particular work has to be done. They also provide a sequence of steps to be followed in the execution of a plan. These chronological series of steps constitute a procedure. If a programme indicates *what* is to be done, a procedure indicates *how* it should be done. Procedures are basically guides to *action,* and not guides to *thinking*. Policies can be executed through procedures. A procedure guides in detail how work should be performed, thereby providing a definite way.

A procedure has to be consistent with the objectives and within the broad areas of a policy. It should provide a chronological sequence of performing an activity, and help in maintaining uniformity of performance by setting a standard route. It leads to simplification and elimination of unnecessary steps, as it is more specific, and provides a good standard for superiors to appraise their subordinates.

6. *Rules:* A rule is a guide to action. It is in the nature of a decision made by the management regarding what is to be done and what is not to be done in a given situation. A rule is more rigid. It may or may not be a part of a procedure. Rules will not have any scope for discretion, as they are specific and definite. The breach of rules usually carries a penalty. "No credit facilities beyond 30 days" and "Smoking is strictly prohibited" are examples of rules.

7. *Programmes:* Programmes are sets of goals, policies, procedures, rules and other components required to carry out a course of action.

8. *Budgets:* A budget is a basic plan or statement defining the anticipated cost of attaining an objective. It is an appraisal of the expenses expected against the income anticipated for a particular future period of time. A budget is considered both a planning and a controlling device.

It may be expressed in terms of time, materials, money, machine-hours, man-hours, etc. But usually, money budgets are the common ones. Budgets are very popular as planning devices. The goal of every department is expressed in exact and specific terms, so that the plans of all the departments can be readily coordinated.

9. *Standards:* A standard is a measure of the level of achievement desired. For all future evaluation, it becomes a model. A standard helps in comparing accomplishments with the desired results. If there are major deviations from the plan, standards will help in ascertaining whether there are any deviations from the original plan. If there are any such deviations, they can be corrected.

IMPORTANCE OF PLANNING

Planning helps in focussing attention on future objectives and unity of efforts. Different activities are united towards a single objective by proper planning. It helps in avoiding duplication, overlapping and cross-communication, and provides a continuous stream of objectives which indicates the direction of future growth by utilizing all the available resources.

Planning provides a basic decision-making structure. A comprehensive and long-term corporate plan helps all the managers in different functional areas to prepare their own departmental plans and necessary strategies. A complete, clear, comprehensive master plan will provide a basic decision-making structure for every departmental manager, and there will be unity of purpose.

Planning helps in finding out possible threats and potential opportunities by providing an insight into the future. It helps an organization to identify the potential areas of opportunities and possible threats. It also provides a yardstick to measure performance by helping in fixing up a performance standard through which the performance of a company can be measured. A good plan will help in fixing the targets to be achieved.

Planning helps an organization to adapt to the environment. Environmental forces are so important that an organization has to adapt itself to such changes to achieve success. Planning helps an organization to adjust and adapt to such environmental factors.

ESSENTIAL FEATURES

The following are the essential features of planning:

1. *Planning is objective-oriented:* Every plan has to concentrate on accomplishing certain objectives, and must contribute positively to the accomplishment of these objectives. Planning without a specific goal in mind is meaningless. It becomes a futile exercise.

2. *Planning is an intellectual process:* According to Koontz and O'Donnell, planning is an intellectual process. A good plan reflects directly on the intellectual ability of the staff concerned. It involves thinking to take decisions, and evolve ideas.

3. *Planning is all-pervasive:* Planning pervades the entire organization in all its wings and at every level of management. Top management has to concentrate on policy making and strategic planning. Middle management has to look after the executive planning. Lower management has to concentrate on operational planning.

4. *Primacy of planning:* Planning precedes all other management functions; it is the first function of management. Without it, no work can commence. All other functions like organizing, staffing, directing and control can be performed only after planning.

5. *Planning is a continuous process:* It is a continuous activity and cannot be stopped at any stage in an organization. One plan leads to another, which will be followed by a series of other plans. Today's plan will become tomorrow's action.

6. *Planning is flexible in nature:* The process of planning must be flexible and it has to adjust itself to changing circumstances; it cannot confine itself to one particular cause. As environmental conditions may undergo a change, the process of planning may also have to undergo a change.

7. *Planning is directed towards efficiency:* The concept of efficiency is implicit in planning. The success of any plan depends upon its efficiency, accuracy, precision and exactness. The efficiency of the plan in turn directly depends upon, and is proportional to, the accuracy and precision of forecasting.

8. *Planning is a master coordinator:* Planning provides for a cohesive decision-making framework, which may ultimately help in identifying potential opportunities and threats. It brings together different factors, and coordinates the what, who, how, where, when and why of the managerial infrastructure.

Urwick states the following essential features of a good plan:

- A good plan must be based on well-established objectives. In fact, the management by objectives concept has been widely accepted by all management people.
- A good plan must be simple and understandable.
- It should be flexible to adjust to changing circumstances.
- It should be balanced and provide equal emphasis to all important sectors of business.
- It should provide for a proper analysis and classification of actions.
- It should be reasonable.
- It should be possible for implementation.

Advantages

The following are the advantages of planning:

1. It acts as a significant integrating force. Planning interrelates and integrates all the available resources and activities of an organization to accomplish the common objectives. It provides a coordinated effort by reducing risks and uncertainties.
2. It helps in the process of decision making. Managers can take quick decisions with proper planning.
3. It helps the organization to implement future programmes. Once the programme is chalked out, it becomes easy for managers to implement such future programmes, so that all the activities of the organization can be conducted in a systematic manner to achieve the common goals of the concern.
4. It keeps the organization up-to-date and highly competitive. With the development of modern technology and changes in the customers' needs, the managers of today are

expected to develop the competitive strength of the organization. Planning can suggest the new methodology, techniques, etc. to keep the company competitive.

5. It helps in providing the economies of large-scale operation by avoiding wastage of important resources.
6. It leads to budgeting, which may lead to budgetary control.
7. It provides for a sense of involvement and team spirit.
8. It helps in the smooth performance of all other functions like organizing, coordinating, controlling, etc.
9. It helps in achieving the objectives through proper control.
10. It makes the management most efficient and develops individual managers.

Disadvantages

The following are the disadvantages of planning:

1. Planning is very expensive and time-consuming.
2. Planning makes the organizational structure more rigid.
3. Planning delays the process of decision making.
4. Planning cannot ensure the certainty of future performance.
5. Planning and its precision is determined only on the basis of assumptions. If the assumptions are not accurate, planning may not be a success.
6. Planning may give only approximate results, not definite and assured results.

In spite of these limitations, it is always better to have planning to achieve the desired results.

PRINCIPLES OF PLANNING

Of late, some of the scholars in the field of management science like Koontz, O'Donnell, Weihrich, Lele and Mahajan have made significant contributions in the form of providing some principles for the planning function. They are as follows:

1. *Principle of the contribution to objectives:* Every plan and its components should help in the achievement of organizational objectives.

2. *Principle of the primacy of planning:* Planning is considered as the first and the foremost function to be performed in the process of management. It is followed by other managerial functions like organizing, staffing, directing and controlling.

3. *Principle of the pervasiveness of planning:* Planning is all-pervasive and it percolates to all the levels of management from top to bottom.

4. *Principle of the flexibility of planning:* Every plan should be made in such a way that it adjusts and adapts itself to changed circumstances. There must be a high degree of flexibility in every good plan.

5. *Principle of periodicity:* Long-term plans, medium-term plans and short-term plans are to be integrated and interrelated in such a way as to achieve the organizational objectives effectively and economically.

6. ***Principle of planning premises:*** To develop consistent and coordinated plans, it is essential that planning be based upon carefully considered assumptions and predictions, known as *planning premises.*

7. ***Principle of efficiency of operations:*** Every plan should be designed with its components, such as objectives, strategies, policies, procedures, schedules, budgets, etc., to accomplish efficient realization of the plans.

8. ***Principle of limiting factors:*** There are various limiting factors, such as money, manpower, machinery, materials and management, which are to be taken into consideration while drafting a plan or taking a policy decision or devising a strategy.

9. ***Principle of revision:*** Every plan has to be executed, and in the process of execution, managers should check periodically the events and decisions, and if there is any necessity to redraw and readjust their plan to achieve the organizational objectives. They should make provision for such changes.

STEPS IN PLANNING

There are various steps involved in planning as shown in Figure 3.1. These are as follows:

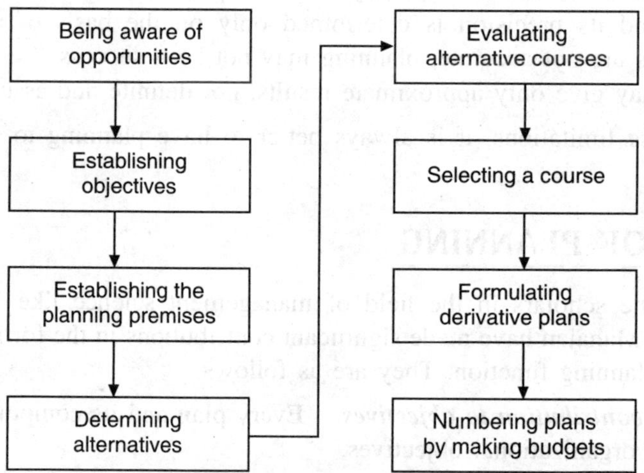

Figure 3.1 Various steps involved in planning.

1. ***Being aware of opportunities:*** Managers have to understand external environment relating to market, competition, customers' requirements, wants, strengths and weaknesses. Later, they have to set realistic goals.

2. ***Establishing objectives:*** Every manager should clearly establish the objectives to be achieved by the enterprise. Every person belonging to the organization should be familiar with these. Major objectives must be clearly stated in realistic or specific terms. They will serve as a guide to action. Objectives must be specific, informative and functional.

3. ***Establishing the planning premises:*** Every plan has to be based on certain carefully considered assumptions and predictions, which are known as *planning premises*. A business organization has to provide for various environmental factors. Planning premises supply important facts and information relating to the future, and because of that, they are very significant to the success of planning.

4. *Determining alternative courses of action:* The next step is to search for and examine alternative courses of action.

5. *Evaluation of alternative courses of action:* Every alternative course of action has to be evaluated, and the relative importance of each one of them should be ascertained. Every alternative will have some strong and weak points, which are to be understood in the right perspective.

6. *Selecting the course of action:* After analyzing and evaluating the available alternatives, the manager has to select the best course of action. In fact, it is the real point of decision making.

7. *Formulating derivative plans:* Every major plan has to be supported and developed by the preparation of other derivative plans. Within the framework of the basic plan, derivative plans are developed in each area of the business. The breakdown of the primary plan into departmental and sectional plans will strengthen the plan base of the organization.

8. *Numbering plans by making budgets:* After setting plans, managers have to numerize each plan and then convert them into budgets. Total budgets of an organization reveal the total income and expenditure of the firm.

PLANNING AND FORECASTING

Planning involves looking into the future, which is known as *forecasting*. This is basically a systematic attempt to analyze the future on the basis of certain known facts so as to help the management in its planning decisions. In fact, it is the calculation of probable or possible events in the future. It refers to the predetermination of events. Fayol has pointed out that a plan is the synthesis of various forecasts. It helps the managers by providing them a fund of information on a lot of vital background situations.

Lyndall Urwick observed that forecasting is involved, to some extent, in every conceivable business decision. A person who starts a business is making an assessment of a future demand for its products. The person who determines a production programme for the next six or 12 months usually bases it on some calculation of future demand. McFarland states that "Forecasting refers to predictions or estimates of the changes, if any, in characteristic economic phenomena which may affect one's business plans." To conclude, forecasting means estimation of future events based on the past and present, enabling a premise to be made on which plans can be developed, and enabling the right objectives to be chosen.

STEPS IN FORECASTING

The process of forecasting involves the following steps:

1. *Analyzing and understanding the problems:* The manager has to identify the actual problem about which the forecast is to be made. It may be regarding the technological conditions, environmental factors, selection of persons, location of site, or mobilizing finance.

By doing this, the manager can concentrate and fix the scope of forecasting only on relevant and specific information.

2. *Preparation and development of a foundation:* In the light of experience and information, the present set-up and rate of development, the management can prepare and develop a good foundation for the future.

3. *Selection and analysis of data:* The management has to select suitable data to analyze them in the light of past fluctuations. There are various statistical tools which can be used to analyze data.

4. *Estimation of future events:* There are trend studies which indicate the possible future events. Keeping some provision for margin of error, these trend analyses can be relied upon. Experience, discretion and judgement also help in estimating future events.

5. *Comparison of actual results with estimated results:* It is always better and safer to compare the actual results with the estimated results. If there is any major difference between the actuals and the estimates, the reasons should be investigated.

6. *To further develop the process of forecasting:* With the knowledge gained from experience, the forecasting process has to be constantly improved and refined.

FORECASTING TECHNIQUES

There are various techniques of forecasting. Every technique has certain special advantages and contents. The time, date, and records are to be considered for using the right technique. The degree of accuracy required and the cost benefit of the forecasting should also be considered before selecting any particular technique. These techniques may be either *quantitative* or *qualitative*. Various quantitative techniques are time series or trend analysis, regression analysis, econometric models, and extrapolation. Qualitative techniques may be the Delphi method, market research method, panel consensus method, morphological research method, visionary forecasts, historical analogy method, relevance tree method, etc. If the data are not readily available, these techniques can be used.

1. *Time series analysis:* It helps in identifying and explaining any regular or systematic variation in the series of some seasonal data or cyclical trends which appear every two or three years. Such patterns or pattern changes can be determined by analyzing the past trends over a period of time. The rate of change may be either an increasing or decreasing one. But this method is useful and possible only when the data for several years are available. At the same time, if there are drastic changes like abnormal increase in sales or a sudden market collapse, such changes cannot be predicted by this technique. In such circumstances, statistical methods like the moving average method, trend projections, or exponential smoothing can be used.

2. *Moving average technique:* This is a technique where each point of moving average time series is the arithmetic or weighted average of a number of consecutive points in the series. *Trend projection* refers to fitting a trend line to a mathematical equation and projecting it for the future through an equation. *Exponential smoothing* refers to a type of moving average wherein more recent data points are given more weight. All these methods are helpful in production control, inventory control, etc.

3. ***Regression analysis:*** If two variables are functionally related, an understanding of one such variable will help in estimating the other. Such relationships between two variables are analyzed through regression analysis, e.g. sales for the last year and the amount spent on advertisement are two such variables.

4. ***Econometric model:*** This refers to a mathematical model for observing the relationship of a number of variables to the company's sales. They are almost like a set of simultaneous equations. Electronic data processing may be used if there is a large number of equations to construct econometric models. This model helps in understanding the various aspects of interrelated problems in quantitative terms.

5. ***Delphi method:*** This is a simple method of selecting a panel of experts to which questionnaires are given to obtain accurate and complete information. The speciality of this method is that the information obtained from one questionnaire is used to prepare and weigh another questionnaire, so that ultimately all the experts will have comprehensive information through such a series of questionnaires.

6. ***Market research method:*** Personal interviews, sending questionnaires, etc. are the methods to conduct market research. When a new product has to be released and sales forecasts have to be made, this method is more useful.

7. ***Panel consensus:*** It is the collective ideas and estimates provided by a group of experts who are familiar with the problem.

8. ***Visionary forecast:*** The intuition, insight, judgement, vision of a person, who is known for this in a particular field may help in forecasting.

9. ***Historical analogy:*** Based on the past records and history of the product, forecasting may be made for new products also.

10. ***Morphological research method:*** It concerns itself with the development and the practical application of basic methods which will allow us to discover and analyze the structural or morphological interrelations among objects, phenomena and concepts, and explore the results obtained for the construction of a sound model. In this method, with the help of various permutations and combinations, all possible technological alternatives can be derived for a given problem.

11. ***Relevance tree method:*** In this method, the basic objectives and their feasibility are determined first, and then efforts are made to accomplish these things through various technological innovations. This method helps in developing various possible alternatives and the best method of accomplishing the task.

Advantages

Forecasting helps:

- in managerial planning by providing key information,
- managers to think for the future and to look ahead,
- in the best utilization of resources through proper direction,
- in accomplishing the objectives practically and positively,
- in minimizing adverse effects and maximizing opportunities,

- the management to follow a definite course of action,
- to improve the efficiency of the management process, by developing the mental faculties of the managers, and
- in coordination and effective control.

Disadvantages

Forecasting is:

- subject to a degree of error, and precision cannot be attained in it,
- sometimes based on guess work which is not fully scientific, and
- based on certain assumptions, so there may be some possibility of error.

PLANNING PREMISES

According to Koontz and Weihrich, planning premises are anticipated environment in which plans are expected to operate. They include assumptions or forecasts of the future and known conditions that will affect the operation of plans.

Management has to take policy decisions based on certain assumptions about future happenings. Such assumptions are known as *planning premises*. Planning premises constitute the very basis of planning. Such assumptions and predictions are absolutely essential to make plans more realistic and workable. Managers usually assume that certain entities will behave in a particular manner. Such assumptions are based on institutional as well as systematic prediction. Planning premises provide a framework within which planning decisions are taken.

Planning premises may be either *external* or *internal*. Managers have to carefully consider all such factors which have a practical bearing on the plan to be made. Systematic forecasting provides sound premises, and past happenings provide a useful guide for having sound planning premises.

Types of Premises

Premises may be classified as follows:

1. *Internal premises and external premises:* *Internal premises* are those that can be obtained from internal factors, like sales forecasts, the programmes and policies of the company, competent personnel, and skilled labour. *External premises* are derived from the external environment, like political, economic, social and technological forces, population trends, income level, employment level, government policies, and national income.

2. *Tangible and intangible premises:* *Tangible premises* are those which can be expressed in quantitative terms. Money, time, units of production, etc. can be expressed in terms of money. *Intangible premises* are those which cannot be measured in quantitative terms. These factors are the goodwill of a business, public relations, employee morale and motivation.

3. *Controllable, semi-controllable and uncontrollable premises:* Factors which can be controlled, such as materials, money and machines are *controllable premises*. These are the factors on which the management has maximum control over its future commitments. *Semi-controllable premises* are those assumptions over which the management can exercise only partial control. Labour relations, marketing strategy, etc. are such areas where partial control can be exercised. *Uncontrollable premises* are those over which the management has absolutely no control. For instance, war, natural calamities, new discoveries and inventions, etc.

4. *Constant and variable premises:* *Constant premises* are those which will act in the same manner, irrespective of the course of action taken. These premises are definite, known and clear, for example, men, money and machines. *Variable premises* are those which differ in relation to the course of action taken, such as union-management relations.

PLANNING AND CONTROL

No management can function effectively without the twin concepts of planning and control. The success of a business is proportionate to the astuteness of its planning and the skill with which it is controlled. The planning process must be conducted in direct relation to the needs of control. Control is that which is present in the business as a force which guides it to a predetermined objective by means of predetermined policies and decisions. It can be done effectively by using cost accounting, budgets, internal audit, control data, etc.

SUMMARY

1. Planning is deciding in advance what to do, when and how to do it.
2. Planning is a goal-oriented process.
3. There are different types of plans: financial and non-financial; formal and informal; long-range and short-range.
4. Planning helps in effective decision making.
5. A good plan has certain essential features.
6. The principles and steps of planning must be followed.
7. The components of planning are objectives, strategies, standards, budgets, policies, etc.
8. Forecasting is a systematic attempt to analyze the future on the basis of certain known facts.
9. Organizations have to follow some policies and strategies.
10. Planning premises are essential to make good plans.

REVIEW QUESTIONS

1. What is planning? State the nature and benefits of planning.
2. Explain the essential features of a good plan.
3. What are the principles of planning? What are the steps in planning?
4. Discuss the process and techniques of forecasting.
5. Explain the procedure and premises of planning.

CASE STUDIES

1. Info Systems Associates

Info Systems Associates (ISA) was set up by three promoters. The company would serve as an excellent service provider from Visakhapatnam to the several organizations all over the world. ISA would like to offer its IT services with a mission to "provide global services at competitive prices". Some of the global services offered by the company were: telemarketing, telebanking, customer service management for international banks, software firms, telecom providers, creditcard companies, market research and surveys, etc. As the competitive services are to be offered as per the customer needs, the company can do the business globally and function effectively by making profits.

MANAGEMENT TEAM

Three promoters Venu, Madhav and Chand were interested to start a private limited company in Visakhapatnam. They all had high professional background with rich experience in the business. Mr. Venu had B.Tech (IT) and MBA qualification. He would like to be the CEO of a new venture. He worked in a government company for 15 years and left the company. Later, he started a consultancy firm which was highly successful. Now, he would like to take up a new venture in information technology sector.

The second promoter Mr. Madhav, who is the only son of Mr. Venu's close friend, Mr. Raghav, had business knowledge with M.Tech qualification. He was a gold medallist in his B.Tech and M.Tech courses. He hailed from a business community associated with family business from his childhood. He had his own business in trade and services activities and he is managing successfully.

The third one is Mr. Chand, who did Chartered Accountancy after M.Com. He is an expert in maintaining accounts and preparing financial statements. He has been a consultant for about 20 organizations in Andhra Pradesh through his firm Chand and Co.

THE BUSINESS

Three friends Venu, Madhav and Chand established a venture under Software Technologies Park of India (STPI) in Visakhapatnam Special Economic Zone (VSEZ). They obtained the necessary permission from the Department of Telecommunications, Ministry of Communication, Government of India, to start the venture from Visakhapatnam. There was a vast potential for the market in the USA and UK. They would like to deliver maximum benefit and cost-effective IT services to the customers abroad. They prepared the mission statement of the business as "to satisfy the customer with quality and cost focus service". They attract customers from various places and succeed in retaining them with their service quality. Fortunately, India has a pool of highly qualified English speaking professionals who are highly required for this venture. The firm will offer telemarketing and other services.

As the telemarketing services had become prominent in the world, some services to be offered by the ISA were telemarketing, telebanking, direct response television, customer service management for international banks, software firms, telecom providers, creditcard companies, market research and surveys, fraud detection, prevention calls, welcome, thank you calls, etc.

India's software industry is successful and it is a sunrise sector at present. The Government of India identified ITES/BPO as a key contributor to economic growth, and for encouraging the enterprises, attractive environment is provided by the Government to start the ventures in IT industry. Moreover, the National Association of Software and Service Companies (NASSCOM) acts as an adviser, consultant and coordinating body for the industry. The market growth is high in the industry, and the scope for several ventures to tap the vast potential market is high.

Several colleges have been providing skilled graduates in IT area. As a result, many professional students are available in Visakhapatnam. The number of existing companies at that time were also very few and except one, all were small in size. The management team had a lot of expertise, knowledge, wisdom and financial soundness. The city is calm and quiet with friendly people. Rents and other living expenses are comparatively low. The climate is also conducive for IT and ITES services. The market is so vast abroad for IT enabled services. The existing ventures of this area are growing and highly successful.

The market is growing and have vast potential. Customers require cost-effective and fast services. ISA was different in providing various services at competitive prices and also different in terms and conditions.

THE PRODUCTS

Info Systems commenced the activities with the following services/products. The promoters would like to start it as a Business Process Outsourcing (BPO) and later, it can be focused on Knowledge Process Outsourcing (KPO).

Important services/products of the industry are: telemarketing products, telebanking, direct response television, airline ticketing and reservation, market research and surveys, third party verification, fraud detection/prevention calls, welcome/thank you calls, continuity sales caller, all kinds of message delivery, and customer care and support services.

PROFITABILITY

As they invested the minimum capital of ₹3 crores with low interest rates, the business would get a profit of ₹30 lakhs in 2009, ₹60 lakhs in 2010, and ₹90 lakhs in 2011. Even after third year, the company would make profits because of the expertise of the entrepreneurs. The software sales are expected to be ₹350 lakhs in 2008, ₹750 lakhs in 2009, and ₹1400 lakhs in 2010.

The estimated expenditure for salaries and maintenance charges are ₹320 lakhs in the first year, ₹690 lakhs in the second year, and ₹1310 lakhs in the third year. These are comparatively low expenses and expected to generate surpluses during the first three years and later.

MARKET ANALYSIS

The USA is the main market for software services accounting for over one-third of the total ITES–BPO exports from India and Western Europe. Even in Asian, African and Australian countries, there is a vast scope. IT sector registered US$3.9 billion in 2003–2004 with a growth rate of 45.3 per cent, estimated to get revenues of US$5.7 billion by the end of the financial year 2004–2005.

Hardware segment also grew from US$3.6 billion in the financial year 2003–2004 to US$4.8 billion in 2004–2005 with a growth of 34 per cent and is expected to reach US$6 billion in the financial year 2004–2005. There is a tremendous growth rate of 87.5 per cent of Indian software exports in the world market in 2008. It is expected to increase in future. Software exports of India were only US$4 million in 1980 and increased to US$27.7 million in 1985, US$668 million in 1995, and US$7,300 million in 2001. It is expected to grow further from 2010 to 2020.

There is a vast scope for the KPO sector also. According to a report, KPO industry is expected to reach US$17 billion by 2010, of which US$12 billion would be outsourced to India. Some other report estimates that India will capture more than 70 per cent of the KPO sector by 2010. Other countries such as Russia, China, the Czech Republic, Ireland and Israel are also expected to join the KPO industry along with India. BPO undertakes data processing, basic data entry, setting up a bank account, department outsourcing, and provides technical support and email support to its customers. KPO is not restricted to information technology. It deals with other challenging sectors, namely business research, clinical research, intellectual property research, etc. KPO exports are expected to be about US$12 billion by 2010. KPO has a bright future. In KPO, the focus is on knowledge expertise with MBA or CA qualification. KPO employees tend to have greater direct contact with international clients. Broadly, KPO is a branch of BPO and it is beyond BPO.

Regarding human resources, India has competitive advantage over other countries. There are several prestigious technical universities and institutes of world class. India produces over 75,000 IT graduates and over 20 lakhs English speaking graduates annually.

The Philippines churns out 380,000 graduates annually, but only 15,000 of them have core technology knowledge. The country has cultural affinities with the US is well versed in US accounting and customer service standards, and has low employee turnover. Russia can claim the third largest number of engineers and scientists, but very few of them can speak English. China's technical schools churn out 50,000 graduates annually, many of whom migrate to the West. Those who stay do not speak English generally. Canada has a good educational system, with a qualified labour force of more than 16 million. In Ireland, relatively small, 14,000 graduates will come out annually, only 5000 of them with technical background. Mexico provides US companies with millions of Spanish speaking people to staff call centres.

It is evident that there will be a huge market potential for software exports in future. The important target segments are: banking, financial services, government organizations, manufacturing companies, retail industry, trading concerns, transport undertakings, travel and tourism sectors, real estate activity, other service sector activities.

The important entry barrier is the language. As the language required is English, this is a real barrier in several countries. Another barrier is culture. Difficulty in accessing customers and convincing people are some of the other barriers. Attracting and retaining talented people is also one of the important constraints in the business.

STRATEGY AND IMPLEMENTATION

ISA started the venture initially with a strategic partner in New York—American Systems Associates (ASA). Mr. David had a proprietory concern for software and was well established for the last 10 years. Mr. David and Mr. Venu happened to meet once in New York when Mr. Venu had been to an international conference on venture capital management. Both of them had an agreement to offer software services in the USA. David provided his services through ASA for ISA products/services and in turn, he will get two per cent of the gross sales. They had also an MoU for strategic partnership in offering services for five years. Later, they would like to have a renewal with new terms and conditions. Initially, Mr. David gets 2 per cent on gross sales. All the expenses except the salary of one office attendant would be met by him at the New York office because David & Co. has been well established.

The business venture operations will be from Visakhapatnam City, which is one of the fast growing cities of India with a total population of about 15 lakhs. The city has a vast potential for business and the software activity is in the introductory stage. It has tremendous opportunities and potential for business. The Governments of India and also Andhra Pradesh have announced some incentives for the software promoters. Special Economic Zones were initiated by the Government at various places including Visakhapatnam (VSEZ). The strategy is to offer cost-effective services globally.

The management team has designed the organizational chart with the managing director, executive director (ED), and four managers under the ED for operations, business development, quality assurance and human resources. Under these managers, supervisors, team leaders, call centre experts, and trainees are functioning.

The technology adopted is available in India. But it is expensive and needs to have about 100 systems. The expected amount spent for the business to install machinery and systems is about ₹50 lakhs. The management raised funds to meet various other expenses.

The human resources required for the business for the last 10 years was assessed. Initially, they had recruited about 60 employees and gradually increased it to 950 within 6 years, and 2500 by the tenth year of business, with 1900 skilled and 600 semi-skilled people.

Mr. Venu needs to have a discussion with the development commissioner, VSEZ, for allotment of a flat at Software Technology Park of India (STPI). The development commissioner provided one flat with 6000 square feet for the operations of the business. They obtained permission to start the venture from the Department of Telecommunications, Ministry of Communications, Government of India and registered the business with the Software Technologies Park of India (STPI) and Visakhapatnam Special Economic Zone (VSEZ). The number of people employed in 2008 were 40 skilled and 10 unskilled. They are prepared to recruit 230 by 2012 and 2500 by 2018.

RISK EVALUATION

In BPO and KPO industry, the important problem or risk is head hunting. The potential entrants in the business may offer attractive compensation and facilities to the skilled people and take them to their ventures. Information security is another constraint in the industry. The policy of the government is also one important factor in understanding the risk in the business.

PROJECTED FINANCIAL POSITION

The total capital requirement of the company was about ₹3 crores. A part of the amount is to be borrowed from banks; the promoters contributed ₹2 crores. They also planned the usage of funds. Office furniture and decoration is expected to cost ₹50 lakhs. The required technology and systems cost was ₹150 lakhs, and the balance was for working capital. They had about ₹2 crores own capital and ₹1 crore borrowed capital.

They expected ₹0.60 crore profits in 2009, ₹1 crore in 2012, and about ₹10 crores by 2018.

Questions for Discussion

1. What are the qualities of the management team?
2. Discuss SWOT analysis of the organization.
3. What are the strategies to be followed by the management in future?

2. Naveen Fisheries Ltd.

The managing director of Naveen Fisheries Ltd. (NFL) received a message from one of the members of the crew that their mechanized boats had sunk at sea off Paradeep Port Trust due to unfavourable weather. The other directors of NFL ascertained the detailed information regarding the incident. All the promoters were fresh graduates.

Naveen, Praveen, Nagin, Ravi and Chandra were the promoters of the organization (NFL at Visakhapatnam), with a capital contribution of ₹25 lakhs each. Three of them had an engineering background. The other two were commerce graduates. They had thought of designing the vessels themselves so that the cost of each mechanized boat would be reduced from ₹30 lakhs (if they bought them) to ₹22 lakhs. They designed three boats and these were sent out with a newly-appointed crew. Two vessels were sent to Paradeep and the third to Kakinada. Unfortunately, the weather was unfavourable. All the vessels sank. The crew also did not have experience. Two workers were injured and the rest arrived safely. There was significant damage to the vessels and the residue was considered scrap. The cost of scrap of the vessels was nominal. As their working capital was scarce, and they were unable to invest more capital, they were in a dilemma whether to continue the business or not.

Questions for Discussion

1. What were the reasons for the sinking of the vessels?
2. How could they reorganize the business?

3. Westward Exports Ltd.

In mid-1984, Mr. Mahmood, the general manager of Westward Exports Ltd., Karachi, Pakistan was striving to implement a management information system. He was facing resistance from Mr. Saleem, his most senior supervisor. Mr. Mahmood wondered what he could do to overcome this resistance.

Westward Exports was an exporter of ladies' cotton garments. It was a private company established in 1971, a family-run business, all four directors being brothers. Over the past 14 years, the exports of the company had grown from ₹0.71 million in 1972–1973 to ₹59.76 million in 1984. Almost 90 per cent of the exports went to the USA. It owned no manufacturing facility of any kind. It purchased cotton cloth from six different textile mills and had the cloth dyed and printed. This fabric was then passed on to 138 stitching subcontractors. The company had been expanding the product line over the years, and by 1983, it was exporting about one million garments in over 100 basic designs. The 100 designs were presented in a range of fabric types, shades, designs and sizes. When seen in the context that the company got all these things done through subcontractors, the managerial control of the operations became quite challenging. The directors, who had always been actively involved in each and every aspect of the business and made all the decisions themselves, felt the heat of the changing situation. They appreciated the problem, and decided to hire some professional assistance to bring more control to their operations.

Mr. Mahmood was hired in late 1983 to be the new general manager. He was an agricultural graduate who had about 15 years of marketing and sales experience with a multinational organization. He had also attended more than a dozen management development courses. The directors were confident that he could introduce some new control measures to help ensure the continued success of the company. Mr Mahmood quickly determined that if Westward Exports was to remain in business, it must immediately eliminate the haphazardness in its operations. No proper costing, no scheduling, no progress sheets or order status reports, no follow-up charts, or for that matter no control procedure worth the name existed. "It was all so nebulous," he concluded. He worked late hours to comprehend fully the nature and scope of the company's business and its coordination and working relationships with the contractors. Almost immediately, he started to design a proper system to help cure the lack of control and information available.

Out of about 200-odd employees in the company, the key operating manager was Mr. Saleem. Saleem joined the company in 1973 as a production officer, nearly the lowest rung in the company's hierarchy. He distinguished himself because of his hard work and was promoted to be a supervisor. By 1982, Saleem, under direct supervision of the directors, was looking after every activity in manufacturing. Right from raw material procurement to packing and shipping of finished garments, he was coordinating all the activities. Because of the varied nature of his duties and his dedication to work, he was able to learn all the ins and outs of the business. Saleem was also considered to be a man with a photographic memory. He virtually ran the whole business from the information stored in his head. "I have an abhorrence for paperwork," said Saleem. "My work load is so great that I am always engrossed in my job. Even my dreams are job-related," he added, "but due recognition has always been accorded to me by my directors." Saleem initially cooperated with Mahmood. However, when Mahmood started to implement some of the new systems and procedures, Saleem refused to go along with them. Saleem even questioned the very need for such a drastic change. "Ask me about anything—any detail of a fabric, any garment, any export order—for that matter anything that has happened in this company since I joined, and I will tell you instantly. Why are you bothering the people here with such clerical burdens? These luxuries are alright for big companies, but not for us. We cannot spare people for such unproductive things." Mahmood understood that

Saleem was close to the director and was the seniormost supervisor. Therefore, his opposition could not be taken lightly. Mahmood also felt that the other might say that he had neither the general management experience, nor any particular experience in the garment industry.

Nevertheless, Mahmood was confident that the company *did* need the change, and as soon as possible. He was troubled, however, with the resistance of Mr. Saleem. Unless he could somehow overcome Saleem's reluctance to accommodate his new systems, he would not be able to do the job.

Questions for Discussion

1. Do you agree with Mr. Saleem that "such luxuries are for big companies, but not for us"? Why or why not?
2. What mistake did Mr. Mahmood make?
3. How should Mr. Mahmood handle the current situation?

FURTHER READING

Business India, December 2007.

Business World, January 2008.

Drucker, Peter, F., *Management—Tasks, Responsibilities, Practice*, Allied Publishers, Bombay, 1980.

Koontz, Harold and Weihrich, Heinz, *Essentials of Management*, McGraw-Hill, New York, 1990.

Laurie, J.M., Management and Organizational Behaviour, *Financial Times*, Pitman Publishing, London, 1999.

Stoner, James, A.F. Freeman, Edward, R., and Gilbert, Daniel, R. Jr., *Management*, Prentice-Hall of India, New Delhi, 1995.

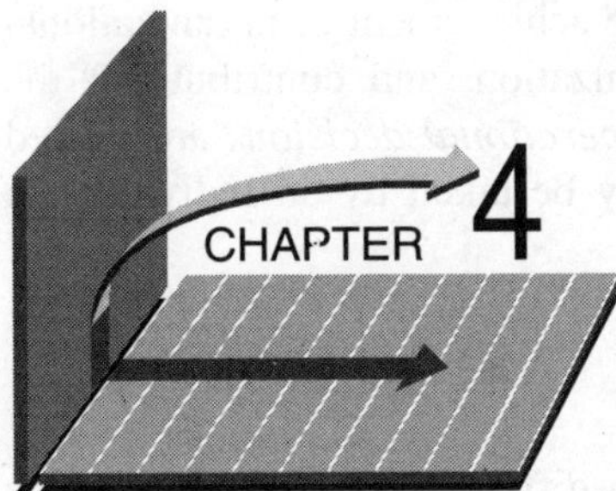

Decision Making

CONTENTS

INTRODUCTION

In any organization, decision making plays an important role for its effectiveness and also excellence. Modern organizations are very particular about the decision making process. Unfortunately, there are several constraints in taking decisions in several public enterprises in India. As a result, they face several problems. It is always better to take the right decision at the right time. Managers have to understand the environment and future for taking right decisions to achieve their goals.

THE CONCEPT

The concept of decision making is defined as "the selection from among alternatives of a course of action; it is at the core of planning". "Decision making is the selection based on some criteria from two or more possible alternatives". We consider that choosing the best course of action from various alternatives for implementation is decision making. It is an essential part of modern management, and also the regular activity of managers.

Decisions are of two types: strategic and tactical. A *strategic decision* is a major choice of actions concerning allocation of resources and contribution to the achievement of organizational objectives. Such decisions have a major impact on the organization, and contribute to the achievement of organizational objectives. Whereas *tactical* or *operational decisions* are related to the day-to-day operations of the organization. Decisions may be taken by an individual in the organization or by a group of persons.

TYPES OF DECISIONS

There are different types of decisions taken by the managers in different organizations. Some of them are as follows:

1. *Personal and organizational decisions:* Personal decisions are to be taken by the managers on their own. Others need not be consulted. For a manager, there is a lot of freedom and independence to take the decision. Organizational decisions are those decisions which the managers take under certain conditions relating to organizations. They take decisions independently or sometimes delegate to other colleagues. The decisions are based on the organizational environment.

2. *Basic and routine decisions:* Basic decisions are also called strategic or important decisions of the organizations. Some of them are: location of the factory, design of the organizational structure, producing products or process of productions, choosing marketing operations—domestic or international or both, etc. Routine decisions are taken by the managers rather regularly. Some of the routine decisions in the organization are: appointment of an employee in the organization, sending the raw material to production process or marketing the product at the same places, etc. These decisions may not have a major impact on the organization.

3. *Programmed and non-programmed decisions:* Programmed decisions are routine in nature. These decisions can be taken by following the standard practices using the available information in the organization. Non-programmed decisions are not routine. Managers can take such decisions based on some judgement. For this, they require some skill and talent for taking right decisions.

4. *Individual and group decisions:* Managers take certain decisions individually without interference of others. These decisions usually are routine decisions without any significant impact. Managers are expected to take certain decisions at critical circumstances. In several organizations, a group of people takes decisions. If any important change is to be introduced, a group of managers and associates discuss the pros and cons and resolve to take decisions. The board of directors, a group of managers from different functional areas, take strategic decisions of their organizations.

5. *Major and minor decisions:* Major decisions are strategic in nature. Important aspects like construction of various blocks, production of the products, expansion of the business are some of the major decisions of an organization. Whereas decisions relating to low cost involvement, less important, and routine in nature are minor decisions.

6. *Departmental and interdepartmental decisions:* Departmental decisions are taken by the chief or head of the department concerned. Usually, the chief takes decisions based on the past experience or opinion of other people in the department. Interdepartmental decisions are taken by two chiefs of two departments or all chiefs of all departments of an organization. Sometimes, senior managers of different departments or general managers take decisions relating to that particular aspect.

DECISION MAKING PROCESS

The following are the various phases in the decision-making process (see Figure 4.1). First, one must understand organizational mission and objectives. Managers have to take decisions to achieve the objectives of the organization.

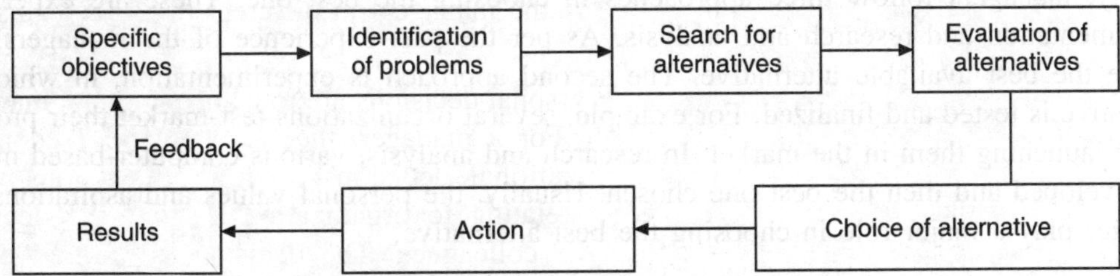

Figure 4.1 Decision making process.

Objectives/Goals

Decisions have to be taken to achieve a particular objective/goal of the organization. The manager has to understand first the specific objective of taking the decisions before diagnosing a problem.

Problem Diagnosis and Analysis

In any particular situation, in order to take a decision, the problem has to be diagnosed first. Just like a doctor diagnosing a disease before prescribing a drug, a manager has to diagnose the real problem in the situation. For example, if there is a high rate of absenteeism in the organization, the management has to analyze the rate of absenteeism from different perspectives. Whether it is uniform throughout the year or in a particular period, of all cadres or only at the lower level, various reasons for such absenteeism, etc. The problem has to be analyzed thoroughly. Thus, the analysis of the problem is very important. If the problem is diagnosed, the half of it is solved.

Search for Alternatives

After diagnosis, the management has to search for alternative solutions. For example, for reducing absenteeism, the management has to announce some incentives/disincentives; take serious action; convince employees to attend work regularly, etc. The manager has to consider the concept of limiting factors also. It means that the corporate culture, financial position, etc.

have to be considered. He has to use several sources for identifying various alternatives: his past experience, corporate practices and innovative ideas.

Evaluating Alternatives

The management has to evaluate the impact and implementation of all the alternatives. The tangible and intangible factors in implementing the decision must be studied. Sometimes, the qualitative and quantitative aspects also have to be considered in evaluating a decision.

Choosing the Best Alternative

From the available alternatives, the best alternative has to be selected for implementation. Usually, managers follow three approaches in choosing the best one. These are experience, experimentation and research and analysis. As per the past experience of the managers, they choose the best available alternative. The second approach is experimentation, in which the alternative is tested and finalized. For example, several organizations test-market their products before launching them in the market. In research and analysis, various computer-based models are developed and then the best one chosen. Usually, the personal values and aspirations of a manager play a major role in choosing the best alternative.

Action

After choosing the best alternative, it is to be implemented by managers. It requires organizational support and cooperation at all levels. The effectiveness of the decision depends upon the active cooperation of the staff.

Result

When the best alternative is implemented, its impact has to be examined. Managers have to take follow-up action in the light of the feedback received from the results. The results are to be verified with the objectives of the organization. If there is any wrong decision, the reasons have to be analyzed and the necessary changes incorporated in taking decisions in future. This review helps a lot in taking the right decisions. .

MODELS

The following are the important decision making models:

1. Economic man model
2. Administrative man model
3. Social man model

Economic Man Model

The economic man model was developed by the classical economists. They believed that man is completely rational in taking decisions: he takes decisions based on the best alternative available. The following are the steps suggested for this decision making model:

- Discover the symptoms of the problem or difficulty.
- Determine the goal to be achieved or define the problem to be solved.
- Develop a criterion against which alternative solutions can be evaluated.
- Identify all alternative courses of action.
- Consider the consequences of each alternative as well as the likelihood of occurrence of each.
- Choose the best alternative by comparing the consequences of each alternative with the decision making criteria.
- Act or implement the decision.

Administrative Man Model

The administrative man model was developed by Herbert Simmon. In it, man uses rationality in his decisions because of the limited information and processing skills. The steps in this model are as follows:

- Set the goal to be pursued or define the problem to be solved.
- Establish an appropriate level of aspiration or criterion level (that is, when do you know that a solution is sufficiently positive to be acceptable even if it is not perfect?).
- Employ heuristics to narrow the problem space to a single promising alternative.
- If no feasible alternative is identified, (a) lower the aspiration level, and (b) begin the search for a new alternative solution.
- After identifying a desirable alternative, evaluate it to determine its acceptability; if the identified alternative is acceptable, implement the solution.
- Following implementation, evaluate the ease with which the goal was (or was not) attained, and raise or lower the level of aspiration accordingly on future decisions of this type.

Social Man Model

The social man model was developed by the classical psychologists. They say that man, being a social animal having a bundle of feelings and emotions guided by his unconscious desires, is also subject to social pressures and influences. Usually, such a person cannot take rational decisions.

CONDITIONS UNDER CERTAINTY AND UNCERTAINTY

Decisions are taken by managers in any organization under two conditions or states of nature. These two are briefly explained in the following sections.

Decision Making under Certainty

Decision making under certainty is easy for any manager. As the conditions and environment are known, decisions can be taken without any problem. Organizations can be managed successfully under this situation. For instance, producing a new product under certain known situation is very easy. Decisions can be taken quickly and correctly.

Decision Making under Uncertainty

When the environmental conditions are uncertain, decision making is somewhat difficult. Then, managers have to follow some techniques for decision making. Those are:

Risk analysis: Usually, managers think more when they are taking decisions under uncertainty. Some are based on probabilities or interaction of important variables. For instance, if the company launches a new product, the variables to be considered are: the cost of production, the cost of introducing the product, the capital investment required, the market, the fixation of price, etc.

Decision tree analysis: Another method of decision making is using the decision tree analysis to analyze the decision under uncertainty. This is considered to be one of the best methods. It is explained in the form of a tree. Therefore, it is called the *decision tree analysis*.

Let us examine how the decision tree analysis of decision making is done by managers in organization. For instance, if a new product is to be introduced in the business, then the manager has to take a decision whether to install a new permanent machinery for manufacturing the product at low cost or to have temporary low cost machinery arrangement with low investment to produce the new product at high cost. Figure 4.2 shows decision tree analysis under two different circumstances.

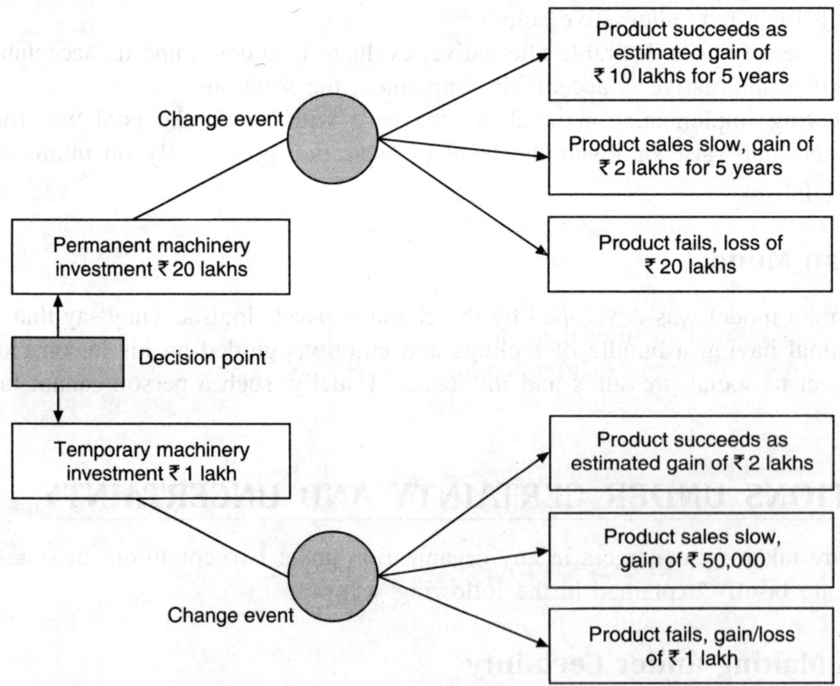

Figure 4.2 Decision tree analysis probabilities.

The decision tree approach helps to understand the future profitability or loss position of the organizations very clearly. Managers analyze the alternatives and take decisions under uncertainty very carefully. They prepare for the consequences in the future. Based on the decision tree analysis, managers get the expected outcome in several companies. Sometimes, managers, judgements as per their experiences play a major role in the decision making process under uncertain conditions. They may not follow the decision tree analysis.

Preference theory (utility theory): In this theory, the manager's risk taking attitude is very crucial. Some managers take greater risks (gamblers), and some take smaller risks (risk averters). The preference for taking risk is based on the attitude of the manager. For instance, when a decision is to be taken by managers sometimes under 80 per cent certainty and 20 per cent uncertainty. Some avoid taking the decision. They think that the organization may suffer loss or some damage. But some managers take decisions because of their attitude for taking risk. They have the confidence in expecting the desired results even the decision is taken under uncertainty.

In the above circumstances—risk analysis, decision tree analysis and preference theory analysis—managers take decision under uncertainty. They have their own experiences in their respective organizations. Mixed feelings were narrated by some managers. In the globalized environment, managers need more skills and knowledge to take right decisions at the right time even under uncertainty.

MANAGEMENT INFORMATION SYSTEMS

A Management Information System (MIS) refers to the system by which the required information is collected, processed and presented to the management to take better decisions. Managers take decisions to get better results in the organization. In MIS, data is the input which is processed to provide output in the form of information reports, summaries, etc. The output helps the manager in the decision-making process. To be effective, MIS must have the following characteristics:

Timeliness: The required information is to be provided at the right time. The information received will be useful only when it is received in time to take a decision.

Accuracy: The accuracy of the information is very important in taking decisions. The manager himself can contribute more when he receives relevant information to take decisions.

Relevance: The information has to be relevant to take the right decisions. The top management needs to have information about changes in the environment which can affect the very survival of his company. Some decisions that the top management makes are oriented towards the future. The management at the middle level is mostly concerned with acquiring and controlling the necessary resources, and is concerned with decision making. Thus, when data are put together in a meaningful form, they constitute *information*. Further, the same data can be used for generating multiple reports for use by different individuals and departments.

DECISION SUPPORT SYSTEMS

According to O.I. Larichev, there is something fuzzy or insufficiently explicit in different decisions of a Decision Support System (DSS). These are universal expert systems that are generally dealt with by specialists in artificial intelligence. Some people say that these are improved computer-based decision-making systems.

Fast development of computers and the emergence of microprocessors and flexible sophisticated programming languages offer considerable opportunities for their application in decision-making problems. But the ways in which the opportunities are used, the extent to which they can actually be helpful in decision making, considerably depends on the arrangement of man-machine interaction.

Decision support systems are guides for thoughts to be presented. Appropriate knowledge representation in an organization can be best understood when it is seen as an element of DSS. According to a well-known definition, DSSs computer-based support for management and for decision makers dealing with semi-structured problems.

The support provided by DSS developed in an organization is the most primitive support providing access to facts or information retrieval. The second level of support involves the addition of filters and pattern recognition ability to this data retrieval. The third level adds more generous computational facilities to the first two, and permits the manager to ask for simple computations, comparisons and projections. The final level of support provides useful models to the manager. Thus, it can be said that development in DSS means growth of structures in the use of knowledge. Decision support systems use computers to facilitate the decision making process of semi-structured tasks. The design of an effective DSS requires a thorough knowledge of how managers take decisions. DSS gives managers an important tool for decision making under their own control.

Evaluation of a Decision and Group Decision Making

The impact of a decision on the organizational climate is very important. The cost of production may be reduced, the quality of the product may be increased, the customer satisfaction may be improved, employee relations may be improved in several decisions. Sometimes, managers need creativity and innovation in taking the right decisions at the right time. Group decision making is also in practice in some organizations. It has advantages and disadvantages.

Advantages

1. Groups can accumulate more knowledge and facts.
2. Groups have a broader perspective and consider more alternative solutions.
3. Individuals who participate in decisions are more satisfied with the decision and are more likely to support it.
4. Group decision processes serve an important communication function as well as a useful political function.

Disadvantages

1. Groups often work more slowly than individuals.
2. Group decision making involves considerable compromise which may lead to less-than-optimal decisions.
3. Groups are often dominated by one individual or a small clique, thereby negating many of the virtues of group procedures.
4. Over-reliance on group decision making can inhibit the management's ability to act quickly and decisively when necessary.

CONSTRAINTS / DIFFICULTIES/LIMITATIONS IN DECISION MAKING

Decision making is very easy for the conditions under certainty. Unfortunately, managers have to take several decisions under uncertainty and some other constraints. The important constraints are:

- Unfavourable environment
- Ineffective communication
- Incorrect place/timing
- Employee's non-cooperation

Managers of a large ice factory take decision to expand its operations. The weather is not favourable, with unexpected rain and continuous transport problem. Then, the business expansion is difficult. Sometimes, ineffective communication from top or bottom creates confusion among managers for taking decisions. Timing or place is other important constraint. Employees of the organization may not cooperate with the management in taking timely and right decisions.

Whatever may be the conditions, the modern managers have to take decisions based on their experience or judgement to manage the organization with competitiveness.

SUMMARY

1. Decision making is the selection from among alternatives of a course of action; it is at the core of planning, and an essential part of modern management.
2. The effectiveness of the organization depends upon the decision-making process in the organization.
3. Decisions are mainly of two types: strategic and tactical. There are different types of decisions.
4. In the decision making process, various steps have to be followed.
5. There are different models of decision making. These are the economic man model, administrative man model and social man model.
6. Decisions are taken under conditions of certainty and uncertainty.
7. Management Information Systems and Decision Support Systems are playing important roles in decision making.
8. Evaluation of a decision is very important after implementation.
9. There are some constraints in decision making.

REVIEW QUESTIONS

1. Explain the concept and the types of decision making.
2. Discuss the process of decision making.

3. Discuss the models of decision making.
4. What is MIS? How is it useful in the decision-making process?
5. Discuss group decision making.
6. Explain decision making under uncertainty.
7. What is a decision tree? Explain decision tree analysis.
8. What are the constraints in decision making?

CASE STUDY

Nakamura Lacquer Company

The Nakamura Lacquer Company of Kyoto, Japan was one of the many hundreds of small handicraft shops making lacquerware for the daily table use of the Japanese people when the American GIs of the occupation army began to buy lacquerware as souvenirs. Young Mr Nakamura, who had just taken over the old family business in 1948, saw therein an opportunity, but soon found that traditional handicraft methods were both too slow and too expensive to supply this new demand. He developed ways of introducing simple methods of machine-coating, machine-polishing, and machine-inspection into what had been purely a handicraft, carried out with the simplest tools. And while the American GI and his souvenir-hunting disappeared with the American occupation in 1952, Nakamura built a substantial business, employing several thousands men, and produced 500,000 sets of lacquer tableware each year for the Japanese mass consumer market. The Nakamura "Chrysanthemum" brand had become Japan's best known and bestselling brand of good quality, for the middle class, and dependable. Outside Japan, however, Nakamura did practically no business, except for selling occasionally to American tourists through his established Japanese outlets such as the big department stores.

This was the situation when, early in 1960—with US interest in things Japanese beginning to grow—Mr Nakamura received in rapid sequence two visitors from the United States, both very highly recommended and equipped with the very highest and best credentials.

"Mr Nakamura," the first one said, "I am Phil Rose of the National China Company, Vice President Marketing. As you probably know, we are the largest manufacturers of good quality dinnerware in the United States with our 'Rose & Crown' brand, which accounts for almost 30 per cent of the total sales. We think that we can successfully introduce lacquer dinnerware to a small but discriminating public in the US. We have investigated the Japanese industry and found that you are by far the best and most modern producer. We are willing to give you a firm order for three years for annual purchases of 400,000 sets of your lacquer dinnerware at 5 per cent more (delivered in Japan), than your Japanese jobbers pay you, provided the merchandise is made for us with our trademark 'Rose & Crown', and provided that you undertake not to sell anyone else in the US lacquerware either with your brand or with any other brand during that period."

Mr. Nakamura had scarcely recovered from this shock when the next visitor appeared. "I am Walter Semmelbach," he said, "Semmelbach, Semmelbach and Whittacher, Chicago's largest supplier of hotel and restaurant supplies in the States, and buyers of dinnerware and similar goods for a number of department stores. We think we can successfully introduce good quality Japanese lacquer dinnerware to our market. In fact, all our customers are willing to try it out. We think there is a market for at least 600,000 sets a year. Within five years it should be a couple of millions. We have investigated your industry and feel you are the only man in Japan who can exploit this opportunity. Now we know your government does not allow you to invest any money abroad; we don't ask you for a penny. We are willing to pay the full costs of introduction. We are willing to budget $ 1,500,000 for the next two years for introduction and promotion. You don't owe us that money. All we ask of you is that (a) we get the exclusive representation for your 'Chrysanthemum' brand for five years at standard commission rates, and (b) that the first 20 per cent on all the sales we make during that time—which we figure is roughly your profit margin—be used to pay off the money we actually spend for promotion and introduction as certified by a firm of independent accountants we want you to name."

Questions for Discussion

1. Discuss the rationale behind the two offers.
2. If you were in the position of Mr. Nakamura, what would be your decision?

FURTHER READING

Barnard, C.I., *The Functions of the Executive*, Harvard University Press, Cambridge, 1937.

Business Today, March, 2008.

Koontz, Harold, and Weihrich, Heinz, *Essentials of Management*, McGraw-Hill, New York, 1990.

Thomas, L. Friedman, *The World is Flat*, Penguin Books, London, 2005.

Toffler, A., Future Shock, *The Adaptive Corporation*, Toronto, 1988.

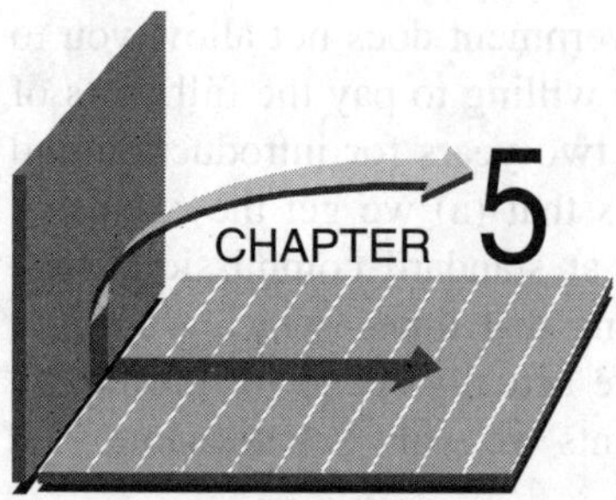

Organizing

CONTENTS

INTRODUCTION

Organization is the task of mobilizing resources. It is a structure involving a large number of people engaging themselves in a multiplicity of tasks, a systematic and rational relationship with authority and responsibility between individuals and groups. Organization involves dividing the entire work into manageable units, departmentation, decentralization, delegation and span of control.

DEFINITIONS

There are several definitions on the concept of organizing. Some of them are as follows:

LOUIS A. ALLEN: Organization is a mechanism or structure that enables living things to work effectively together. The evolution of all forms of life and of human society demonstrates the need for organization.

OLIVER SHELDON: Organization is the process of combining the work which individuals or groups have to perform with facilities necessary for its execution that the duties so performed provide the best channels for efficient, systematic, positive and coordinated application of available effort.

BARNARD: Organization is a system of consciously coordinated activities or forces of two or more persons.

MOONEY and RAILEY: Organization is the form of every human association for the attainment of a common purpose.

JOSEPH L. MASSIE: Organization is the structure and process by which a cooperative group of human beings allocates its tasks among its members, identifies relationships and integrates its activities towards common objectives.

KOONTZ and O'DONNELL: Organization is the establishment of authority and relationships with provision for coordination between them, both vertically and horizontally in the enterprise structure.

ALVIN BROWN: The part which each member of an enterprise is expected to perform and the relations between such members, to the end that their consistent endeavour shall be most effective for the purpose of the enterprise.

A study of the above definitions makes it clear that organization involves: identification and grouping of work, defining responsibility, delegation of authority, establishment of structural relationships, and coordination of interrelated activities. Organization is concerned with (a) the attainment of objectives by grouping the activities, (b) dividing these activities into different departments, divisions, sections and between individuals, (c) providing authority, delegation, coordination and communication, (d) providing physical facilities like buildings, equipment, etc. for the smooth and successful performance of the tasks, and (e) establishing clear structural relationships among individuals and groups.

PRINCIPLES OF ORGANIZATION

1. *Unity of objectives:* The entire organization and every part of it should function effectively to accomplish the basic objectives of the enterprise.

2. *Efficiency:* All the accomplishments of the organization should be at the lowest possible cost. There should not be any waste of human resources.

3. *Span of control or span of management:* Urwick states that a manager can directly supervise a limited number of people. No superior at a higher level should have more than *six* immediate subordinates.

4. *Division of work:* Specialization and division of work should result in separate departments "established to reflect the most efficient breakdown of enterprise activities". Each area of specialization must be interrelated.

5. *Functional definition:* The duties and responsibilities must be properly defined. There should not be duplication or overlapping of activities.

6. *Coordination:* The efforts of everyone in the organization must be coordinated to achieve common goals. Coordination is the orderly arrangement of collective efforts to accomplish a common organizational goal.

7. *Scalar principle (Chain of command):* The line of authority flows from the topmost to the lowest managerial level, and this continuous chain of command should not be broken.

8. *Unity of direction:* There must be only one plan for a group of activities directed towards the same goal. "One person one plan" is the best way of achieving unity of direction.

9. *Unity of command:* Each subordinate should have one superior only. Dual command is always dangerous and confusing.

10. *Delegation:* Delegation should be made upto the lowest competent level. Delegation of authority increases efficiency and smooth operation.

11. *Responsibility:* The superior is responsible for the activities of his subordinates, and the subordinates are responsible to their superiors for their performance. Authority should be consistent with responsibility.

12. *Balance:* There should be a reasonable balance between centralization and decentralization, different sizes of various departments, limited span and longer lines of management.

13. *Communication:* A good organization must have an effective channel of communication for smooth flow of information.

14. *Personal ability:* Ultimately, an organization means people. Proper selection, placement and training of people will go a long way in developing a favourable organizational climate.

15. *Flexibility:* The organization should adopt built-in devices for any change, expansion, etc. with least disturbance. The organizational structure should not be rigid. It should be able to adapt itself to all future changes.

16. *Continuity:* There must be a provision for continuity of management and enterprise. Management development programmes should be encouraged.

17. *Exception principle:* All routine, normal and programmed matters should be handled at the lower level itself. Only exceptionally vital decisions of unusual nature should be handled by superiors, as they have limited time.

FORMAL AND INFORMAL ORGANIZATIONS

An organization may be *formal* or *informal*. In most organizations, formal groups will function as it is essential to execute specific tasks of the formal organization concerned. Chester Barnard states that an organization will be a formal one when the activities of two or more persons are consciously cordial to a given objective. It refers to the structure of positions with clearly defined functions and relationships as determined by the top management. A formal organization is mainly guided by its rules, systems and procedures. In a formal organization, authority, responsibility, and relationships must be clear, fixed and definite. A formal organization is generally based on delegation of authority and it is a legally constituted one. In fact, a formal organization is created and propagated through organization charts, rule books, manuals, procedures, models, etc. Chester Barnard states that a formal organization comes into existence when persons are (a) willing to communicate with one another, and (b) willing to act and share a common purpose. William Brown states that "I personally believe that the more formalization that exists, the more clearly we will know the bounds of discretion which we are authorized to use and will be held responsible for; and prescribed policies make clear to people the area in which they have freedom to act."

A formal organization, according to Keith Davis, "is a pinnacle of man's achievement in a disorganized society. It is man's orderly, conscious, intelligent creation for human benefit. A formal organization is a system of well-defined authority positions and responsibility centres."

Informal organization refers to the activities of people, in particular to their actions in terms of needs, emotions and attitudes. Hawthorne's experiments have sufficiently proved that people have a tendency to form small social groups with their own status systems, behavioural patterns, beliefs and objectives. They emerge from continued social integration and modify or develop the formal organizational structure. This informal gathering or informal organization is not devised or designed by the management. The same location and objective, common timings, common interests and background are the factors which may create such informal organizations. An informal organization is not a planned one. It is created spontaneously. Authority is generally based on personal acceptance. All the inadequacies of a formal organization can be covered in an informal organization. A formal organization requires an office to function, but an informal organization functions through people. A formal organization is rigid, definite and has a written constitution, but an informal organization is flexible and has no such fixed, rigid, written constitution. A formal organization is created by the top management; an informal organization comes up on its own.

Informal organization can be beneficial to management. Keith Davis states that work groups are important as they provide various benefits. Some of them are as follows:

- Informal work groups blend with the formal organization to make a workable system for getting work done.
- Informal work groups lighten the work load for the formal manager and fill in some of the gaps in the manager's abilities.
- Informal work groups provide satisfaction and stability to the organization.
- They provide a very effective channel of communication within the organization.
- Managers will be more careful and effective with the informal work groups.

Management can neither establish nor abolish an informal organization. But any sensible management will try to live with an informal organization and can effectively develop its influence on such an organization for its advantage. It should see that an informal organization remains secondary to the formal organization.

Grapevine: Generally, where an informal organization is strong and effective, it can develop an additional channel of communication, in the form of rumour or hearsay, known as a *grapevine*. Communication moves with a great speed and reaches all levels at the earliest in a grapevine. Such information may be true or false. A grapevine is an informal system of communication for sending confidential or important information through person-to-person talk or gossip. As a grapevine moves with a great speed and without control, there can be distortion also. A good management has to accept the existence of a grapevine and can harness it for the accomplishment of organizational objectives.

STEPS IN ORGANIZATION

Once the necessary plans and objectives are formulated, the organizational process can be started. Every type of activity has to be grouped into workable units of similar activities. All the work has to be classified, employees identified and an arrangement made for the assignment of work to the employees. Terry states that organization is the establishment of effective behavioural relationships among selected workplaces so that their groups can work together efficiently.

The logical steps in the process of organization are as follows:

- Determine and formulate objectives, strategies, plans and policies.
- Determine the activities involved to accomplish the objectives.
- Grouping of similar activities into tasks, sections and departments.
- Define responsibility and accountability for every person.
- Delegate the required authority to perform the task.
- Integration of activities through authority relationships and communication networks.
- Provide adequate physical facilities to perform the tasks effectively.

IMPORTANCE

Organization is the backbone of the management; it helps the enterprise in its progress and prosperity. Today, organization has become more important than ever before because of the many advantages it offers to the modern-day complex society.

1. *Encourages specialization:* Specialization is the direct result of organization, which helps in increasing the productivity and efficiency.

2. *Eliminates the problem of duplicating and overlapping:* Proper and clear division and delegation of authority and responsibility avoid duplication and overlapping.

3. *Brings order and cohesiveness:* Determining a clear line of authority will bring in order in the concern. Everything in its place and a place for everything can be introduced by organizing the concern.

4. *Improves administration:* Administrative policies and day-to-day operation of the enterprise will become effective and functional with proper organization.

5. *Stimulates creative thinking:* A good organization provides maximum opportunity for creative people to develop their ideas for the benefit of the concern. It also provides the ways and means of doing things in a better way.

6. *Facilitates effective communication:* With the clear definition of authority, an organization can develop the most efficient channels of communication.

7. ***Helps in providing a balanced emphasis on various activities:*** Organization, by clearly defining the importance of activities through division, departmentation, etc. gives more priority to urgent and important problems. Routine problems can be decided at the lower or middle level. Managing change, managing crisis, managing credibility become easy through proper organization.

8. ***Helps to build up and expand the enterprise:*** An organized enterprise can build up a team of executives and workers who can develop much faster. Organized team effort helps in expanding the firm. Today, every organization is expanding smoothly into unimaginably large-sized units because of organized effort.

9. ***Helps in the smooth delegation of authority:*** When executives delegate authority downwards, that can get the things done smoothly. It also helps in fixing responsibility for tasks. A good organization clearly defines the authority, responsibility and relationship.

DELEGATION OF AUTHORITY

Delegation and decentralization are very important tasks in modern management. "Delegate and get the things done" is the essence of modern management. "Delegate and things will be done" is also another principle of management. According to Louis A. Allen, "Delegation is the dynamics of management." It is the process a manager follows in dividing the work assigned to him and entrusting work to his subordinates, so that they perform it as he would do it himself. Delegation refers to the entrustment of responsibility and authority to another and the creation of accountability for performance. It also refers to conferring authority to another, usually a subordinate.

Need for Delegation

Delegation is essential in modern management practice to accomplish effective results. It has become important for the following reasons:

1. ***Limitations of one man's ability and time:*** However capable an individual might be, he has limited energy and time. So, he has to delegate to get things done by dividing the work load and assigning it to different workers at different levels. Thus, an executive can multiply himself into numerous workers by delegation.

2. ***Specialized and technological needs:*** Modern organizations need the services of different specialists and technicians. One man cannot be specialized in different fields of activities. So delegation becomes essential.

3. ***Tendency to diversify and decentralize organization:*** A modern large-scale business has a tendency to diversify and decentralize its activities. All such divisions and branches should be managed effectively, even though they are away from the head office. Delegation of authority to the branch managers can make these diversified and decentralized branches function effectively.

4. ***Employee motivation:*** More and more interest and enthusiasm can be introduced through delegation to the workers, so that they can feel that they are also participating in the decision making.

5. *Managerial development:* Delegation, by providing sufficient opportunity for the workers to take decisions and to accept more and more responsibility, can create new generation managers. Initiative, involvement and constant participation will provide continuity of management. So, delegation can be considered as a means of management development.

6. *Management by exception:* Modern managers manage by exception. Delegation will relieve the botheration of managers in attending to routine decisions, which others can attend to efficiently. So, delegation will let managers concentrate on exceptional vital aspects of management.

Delegation is assigning work to others and give them authority to do it. The features of delegation are:

- It is authorization to the person.
- The subordinate receives authority.
- The authority delegated can be withdrawn.
- It is general or specific.

Authority

According to Henry Fayol, authority is the right to give orders and the power to exact obedience. Koontz and O'Donnell define authority as "the power to command others, to act or not to act in a manner deemed by the possessor of the authority to further enterprise or departmental purpose." Authority may be official or personal. *Official authority* refers to authority of a superior which he possesses because of his official position and placement in the organizational structure. Subordinates should accept the official authority of the superior because of the propriety and legality of the rules involved. *Personal authority*, on the other hand, is the authority which a person enjoys because of his popularity, good public relations, excellent charismatic personality, etc.

Authority may be either expressed or implied. It may be a power to command or order. It may be either to purchase machinery, employ people, borrow money, etc. Authority cannot be unlimited also. The amount of authority should be proportional to that of the duties performed or responsibilities held.

Responsibility

According to Theo Haimann, "Responsibility is the obligation of a subordinate to perform the duty as required by his superior." McFarland states that "responsibility refers to such duties and activities which are assigned to a position or to an executive. When an executive delegates his authority to his subordinate, he cannot delegate responsibility." A manager is responsible for the performance of his duties, even though he may delegate his authority to a subordinate for the performance of the same task. Responsibility cannot be transferred.

Responsibility is exacted upwards and authority flows downwards. Responsibility may be in the form of continuing obligation or special assignment. Responsibility cannot exist without sufficient authority.

Accountability

Accountability is the logical conclusion of any authority. McFarland states: "Accountability refers to the fact that each person who is given authority must recognize that the executive above him will judge the quality of his performance." It is a logical derivative of authority. Accountability is the obligation on the part of the subordinate to carry out the responsibility by exercising authority. Every subordinate is accountable to his superior for the tasks assigned to him. Delegation requires creation of accountability, conferring authority and assigning a particular duty, or task fixation.

Authority and responsibility can be delegated to subordinates. Accountability cannot be delegated fully by any manager. For instance X, Y and Z are three levels of managers at different level.

X is the general manager, Y is senior manager, and Z is manager. When Y, the senior manager, delegates authority and responsibility to Z, the manager, Y is accountable to X, the general manager. X's accountability cannot be delegated. Y remains accountable to X, the general manager, for the work done. Thus, accountability of a person cannot be delegated fully.

Advantages

Delegation develops coordination: Delegation, by establishing structural relationships in the organization, helps in securing coordination and team spirit.

Reduction in the burden of the executives: Delegation relieves the executives from minor and time-consuming burdens and allows them to concentrate on major responsibilities and important tasks.

Development of subordinates: Delegation, by allowing subordinates to exercise authority and make decisions, helps in increasing their efficiency and developing their abilities.

Provides continuity: Developing subordinates regularly helps the organization in maintaining a regular decision-making cadre, so that no managerial problem is created in the organization.

Facilitates expansion: Delegation always encourages expansion and diversification of the business. The art of delegation can lead to industrial expansion and success.

Provides motivation: Delegation helps in giving expression to the innate talents of subordinates. It encourages subordinates to look forward to promotions and good opportunities in the future. It improves the employee's morale.

Disadvantages

There are some practical difficulties or problems in the process of delegation. It may be because of the superior's ego or the attitude of the subordinate. Some of the obstacles for successful delegation are as follows:

From the point of the superior:

Superior's unwillingness to delegate authority: If a superior is an autocrat or a person who thinks that delegation will reduce his importance in the organization, he may not delegate authority.

Superior's attitude: The superior may feel that he can do the job much better himself and as such, may not like delegation.

Lack of confidence in subordinates: A superior may be reluctant to part with authority if he feels that the subordinate is not capable of accepting the responsibility.

Psychological barriers: A superior may be precise and perfect in his job by his very nature. He may not like to take chances and so he may perform the job himself.

Absence of control: If there are no developed control techniques, a manager will not be able to know the impending problems. So, a manager may like to delegate without knowing the consequences.

From the point of the subordinate:

Inability to take independent decisions: If a subordinate feels that it is easier to ask the boss rather than to decide himself about how to deal with a problem, he may not like to take up independent responsibility and naturally, he cannot be delegated any major and independent authority.

Fear of criticism: A subordinate may not like to get delegation for fear of criticism for mistakes. He may be very cautious and may try to play safe. He may not like to take risks and face embarrassing situations for fear of criticism.

Lack of necessary information and resources: If a subordinate thinks that acceptance of a new assignment requires a lot of information and resources without which he may not be equipped, he may hesitate to accept the new assignment.

Lack of self-confidence: If a subordinate has no confidence in facing a particular problem, he may not accept delegation.

Lack of incentives: If the brilliant performance of a worker is not recognized or appreciated by the superior, it may discourage the subordinate from accepting further delegation.

The following are the guidelines to make delegation effective:

1. Define the objectives in clear terms.
2. Select proper persons for delegation and train them.
3. Motivate subordinates through various incentives.
4. Establish a favourable work climate free from fear and frustration.
5. Determine the tasks to be delegated.
6. Delegate sufficient authority to perform the job.
7. Provide all possible assistance.
8. Establish proper control and conduct regular reviews.
9. Adhere to the principles of delegation.
10. Evaluate the final results.

DEPARTMENTATION

Organization involves the division and grouping of work. Every task has to be identified so as to form individual jobs, jobs into sections, sections into departments. This departmentation is the process of analyzing and dividing related activities into units and sub-units so that it becomes manageable in the form of departments.

Koontz and O'Donnell define a department as a distinct area, division, or branch of an enterprise over which a manager has authority for the performance of specified activities. So, departmentation is the simple process of dividing or grouping activities into units for purposes of administration. Taylor states that the work of every person in the organization should be confined to the performance of a single, leading function. The logical conclusion of this statement is that every function has to be performed by a single specified group which can be called a *department*.

The main purpose of departmentation is to divide the entire organization into smaller, flexible administrative units to manage the business successfully. Each small unit is headed by a manager to discharge the functions of that particular department.

Advantages

1. *Specialization:* Departmentation automatically provides the benefit of division of labour and specialization. It increases the efficiency and performance level of the organization. All the specialized skills and individual talents can be fully utilized by creating specialization through departmentation.

2. *Determining responsibility:* Departmental heads should be free to take decisions for the smooth and effective performance of their units. At the same time, responsibility will also have to be fixed for their performance.

3. *Coordination:* The departmentation process ensures coordination among different units.

4. *Skills and talents can be developed:* Individual skills and talents can be developed to the fullest possible level in the departmental system of work distribution.

Basis of Departmentation

The activities of an organization can be grouped into departments on any of the following bases:

1. *Function:* Departments can be created on the basis of functions like production, sales, personnel, finance, etc. This is the most popular basis of departmentation.

2. *Product or service:* Large companies with different product lines can set up separate departments for each product or service that it produces or provides. Specialized product knowledge and fixing of specific responsibilities are the merits of this division. This is also called *divisionalization*.

3. *Customers:* Departmentation may be done on the basis of the customers of the concern. A marketing company may have separate departments to cater to the wholesalers, retailers, mail-order customers, etc.

4. *Location:* This is also called *territorial division* or *departmentation*. A company may have separate departments to serve the southern region, northern region, etc. It has the advantage of the intimate knowledge of local conditions.

5. *Time:* When a working unit called a *department* works in different shifts, for each shift the working unit or department may be separate.

6. *Process:* Different departments can be created on the basis of functional processes, e.g. bleaching department, drying department, printing department, etc.

7. *Combination:* One or more bases can be adopted to constitute a department according to the necessity of the organization.

The following factors are to be considered in forming departments in an organization:

1. *Cost factor:* The cost of creating a new department should be considered. It should be economical.

2. *Functional specialization:* A new department should be based on this important factor of functional specialization. For every separate function like marketing, personnel or purchase, a separate department has to be created to secure the economies and benefits of functional specialization.

3. *Control centre:* One should see whether creation of a department can serve as an effective control centre for that particular group of activities.

4. *Integration of different activities:* Various connected activities can be brought together into one department. Sometimes even different activities which are not closely related can be brought together.

5. *Personnel factors:* While creating a department, one has to see whether there is a proper personnel manager to manage the department effectively.

CENTRALIZATION AND DECENTRALIZATION

Centralization

According to Louis Allen, "Centralization is the systematic and consistent reservation of authority at central points within the organization". Most decisions are taken by those who are at the higher levels of the organization. Every manager has to reserve a certain authority for effective planning, organization, command, motivation and control. If authority is not delegated, it means it is centralized.

Benefits of centralization

1. Top management can take vital decisions affecting the entire organization.
2. Having a uniform policy and coordination of all activities are possible.
3. Higher-level people in the organization can take more effective and intelligent decisions.
4. Centralization offers a more flexible base for the organizational structure.
5. Crisis and emergency situations can be effectively managed.
6. The benefits of higher specialization can be secured.
7. Duplication of effort can be avoided.
8. Control and communication become easier.

Limitations of centralization

1. Decisions are not taken by the people who face situations and problems in their area.
2. Lower- and middle-level management will not have interest and initiative in the job.
3. Top management unnecessarily has to waste a lot of time and energy on unimportant and routine matters.
4. It hampers effective communication.

Decentralization

Henry Fayol states that "Everything that goes to increase the importance of the subordinate's role is decentralization, everything which goes to reduce it is centralization." Louis Allen states that "Decentralization is the systematic and consistent delegation of authority to the levels where the work is performed." Keith Davis states that wide distribution of authority and responsibility must be made to the smallest-sized units that is practical throughout an organization. It is an advanced form of delegation to operating units. McFarland defines decentralization as "the degree to which an organization places authority and responsibility for decisions as far down in the organization as efficient management permits". So, decentralization refers to creating a number of relatively autonomous units under a central organization and delegating appropriate powers to them; it is a policy of the top management towards employee development programmes. In a decentralized organization, the decision-making power will be widespread. It is a systematic effort to delegate authority to the lowest levels.

The factors which determine the degree of decentralization of authority are:

- Cost involved in the decision
- Desire for uniform policy
- Size and character of the organization
- History and culture of the enterprise
- Management philosophy
- Desire for independence
- Availability of managers
- Control techniques
- Decentralized performance
- Business dynamics: the pace of change
- Environmental influences.

Benefits of decentralization

- Relieves top management of the burden of decision making and forces upper-level managers to participate effectively.
- Encourages decision making and assumption of authority and responsibility.
- Gives managers more freedom and independence in decision making.
- Promotes establishment and use of broad controls which may increase motivation.
- Makes comparison of performance of different organizational units possible.
- Facilitates setting up of profit centres.

- Facilitates product diversification.
- Promotes development of general managers.
- Aids in adaptation to a fast-changing environment.

Limitations of decentralization

- Makes it more difficult to have a uniform policy.
- Increases complexity of coordination of decentralized organizational units.
- May result in loss of some control by upper-level managers.
- May be limited by inadequate control techniques.
- May be constrained by inadequate planning and control systems.
- Can be limited by the availability of qualified managers.
- Involves considerable expense for training managers.
- May be limited by external forces (national labour unions, governmental controls, tax policies).
- May not be favoured by economies of scale of some operations.

SPAN OF MANAGEMENT

Span of management refers to the problem of "how many subordinates can be effectively managed by a manager". General Hamilton, who was the first person to introduce the concept of 'Span of Control' in his famous book, *The Soul and Body of the Army*, states that "The average human brain finds its effective scope in handling from three to six other brains. The nearer we approach the supreme head of the whole organization, the more we ought to work towards groups of six". Lyndall Urwick, the famous British consultant, in 1938 found that "No superior can supervise directly the work of more than five or at the most six subordinates whose work interlocks." If the number of subordinates is larger, then the superior may find it very difficult to supervise and coordinate their activities effectively.

Factors Determining the Span of Management

A superior cannot manage a large number of persons, but if the number of subordinates is too small, it is uneconomical. So, he has to determine the optimum span of management. It depends upon various factors. They are as follows:

1. ***Qualities and abilities of the executives:*** A better qualified, versatile and experienced superior can supervise a large number of employees effectively, can understand their problems quickly, can get along with them, can command loyalty and respect from them without much problem.

2. ***Nature and significance of the tasks:*** If the work is repetitive, the span of management would be larger as the work becomes more mechanical, requiring less attention and supervision. If it is a specialized task, e.g. major project work involving complex decision making and coordination, the number of subordinates should be less. If the jobs are similar, the span of management would be wider, and if the jobs are dissimilar, the span would be narrower.

3. ***Capacity and quality of subordinates:*** If the subordinates are dynamic, competent, well-trained and experienced, the manager can manage a large number of such subordinates. If there is perfect understanding and team spirit among the employees, he can manage more workers. If the manager has no confidence in the ability of his subordinates, the span will be narrower.

4. ***Levels of management:*** At higher levels of management, a lesser number of people can be managed; the lower the level of management, more workers can be managed.

5. ***Clarity, precision and perfection of plans and responsibility:*** If plans and programmes are fixed and clear and the responsibility is definite, the task of supervision becomes easier and the span of management can be wider. If the management has introduced two-way communication channels which are effective, then also the span can be wider.

6. ***Degree of decentralization:*** If there is decentralization, an executive can effectively supervise more people; with centralized authority, an executive can have only a narrow span of management.

LINE AND STAFF

For achieving the goals of an organization, line managers take up the responsibility and the staff support and cooperate with the line in discharging their functions. The staff function is to advise or support or assist line managers. When line and staff functions are not clear in an organization, then the staff may perform line functions and vice versa. Actually, line and staff positions are different in their authority and power. In modern organizations, these two functions must be very clear for performing the roles of employees and executives.

Line managers have the power and authority for taking decisions and also performing their duties, whereas staff cannot exercise power. In practice, both are very important in performing the activities of an organization.

Conflict between Line and Staff

A line and staff relationship is established to work together to achieve the objectives of the organization. But, frequently, there is friction and even conflict in the organization. Rivalry may be common. The reasons are briefly given as under.

The line viewpoint

- Line managers feel that the staff do not have any responsibility but only enjoy authority.
- Line managers feel that the staff encroach their authority.
- Line managers' authority is diluted as a result of encroachment by the staff.
- The staff fail to give sound advice.
- The staff get the credit when the goals are achieved but are not responsible for the failures.

The staff viewpoint

- The staff always feel that the line authority command them for support services.

- Line managers usually resist new ideas given by the staff.
- The staff also feel that they do not get enough authority from the line managers.

Reducing Conflicts between Line and Staff

In any organization both line and staff are important. It is common for them to have conflicts, but one has to minimize them. The following suggestions may be useful in minimizing conflict:

- The line and staff should understand their proper positions and functions in the organization.
- The line should be educated and encouraged to use the staff effectively.
- The staff should realize that resistance to change is partly natural, so they should work for overcoming resistance to change.
- The staff should realize that they command respect and reputation in the organization due to their skill and expert knowledge in a particular field: they should constantly strive to acquire and increase its proficiency.
- The staff should render complete advice on the problems concerned: they should present realistic recommendations and solutions based on full consideration of all the pertinent facts.

COMMITTEES

The Board of Directors constitutes an important committee at the highest level. It is a policy-making, decision-taking body of an organisation.

Advantages

1. Benefits of specialized and collective knowledge of two or more persons.
2. Creative and more intelligent solutions can be secured for complex problems.
3. It helps in democratizing the internal administration of the organization.
4. It acts as a motivating factor for intelligent officers by providing participation.
5. It is useful in coordinating plans and in their execution.
6. It serves as an effective instrument of communication.
7. It provides united action and mutual understanding.
8. Representation for different group interests can be accommodated.
9. It is a method of executive development.

Disadvantages

1. It is a time-consuming process.
2. There is a tendency to compromise on every issue.
3. Aggressive groups may dominate and control the entire committee.
4. No individual accepts any personal responsibility because of the principle of collective responsibility.

5. Most of the time, a committee remains undecided, or diluted solutions are given.
6. To manage and maintain a committee is very costly.

To ensure effective committee operation, the following guidelines are suggested:

- Define the scope, purpose and authority of the committee clearly.
- Select committee members carefully and limit their number.
- Select an effective chairman with competence and experience.
- Prescribe proper procedures.
- Provide appropriate and adequate assistance.
- Evaluate its performance periodically.

Easy flow of communication: A new department should be created to improve the flow of communication. Both formal and informal communication channels should be utilized to make the department effective.

Scope for incorporating future changes: The departments established should provide for any possible future changes. They must be flexible.

STRATEGIC BUSINESS UNIT

Recently, companies have started using an organizational device generally referred to as a *strategic business unit* (SBU). These are distinct little businesses set up as units in a larger company to ensure that a certain product or product line is promoted and handled as an independent business unit. This organizational unit was introduced to ensure that each product or product line of the company gets the same attention it would if it were developed, produced, and marketed by an independent company. The device has also been used in some cases by companies for a major product line. Several companies have different SBUs.

To be called an SBU, it has to meet specific criteria. An SBU, for example, must have its own mission, distinct from other SBUs; have definable groups of competitors, prepare its own integrative plans fairly distinct from other SBUs; manage its resources in key areas; and have a proper size, neither too large, nor too small. In practice, it might be difficult to define SBUs that meet all these criteria.

SUMMARY

1. Organization is a task of mobilizing the necessary resources.
2. There are certain principles of organization.
3. Organizations are of two types: formal and informal.
4. Delegation of authority is essential to manage effectively.
5. Departmentation is a part of total organization.
6. Line and staff functions are required in an organization.
7. Centralization and decentralization are also required in the organization.
8. An appropriate span of management is to be followed for effective functioning.

REVIEW QUESTIONS

1. Define organization. What are the principles of organization?
2. Describe formal and informal organizations.
3. Explain delegation of authority.
4. Discuss centralization and decentralization.
5. Explain "span of management".
6. Explain line and staff functions in an organization.

CASE STUDIES

1. Major Tools Ltd.

Robert, one of the field sales managers of Major Tools Ltd., had been promoted to his first headquarters assignment as an assistant product manager for a group of products with which he was relatively unfamiliar. Shortly after he had taken over this new assignment, one of the company's vice-presidents, Smith, called for a meeting of product managers and other staff to plan marketing strategies. Robert's superior (the product manager) was unable to attend, so the director of marketing, Reynolds, invited Robert to the meeting to help and orient him to his new job.

Because of the large gathering, Reynolds was rather brief in introducing Robert to Smith. After the meeting began, Smith—a crusty veteran with a reputation for bluntness—began asking a series of probing questions, which most of the product managers were unable to answer in detail. Suddenly, he turned to Robert and questioned him quite closely about his group of products. Somewhat confused, Robert confessed that he really did not know the answers.

It was immediately apparent to Reynolds that Smith had forgotten or had failed to understand that Robert was new to the job and was attending the meeting more for his own orientation than to contribute to it. He was about to offer a discreet explanation when Smith, visibly annoyed with what he took to be Robert's lack of preparation, snapped, "Gentlemen, you have just seen an example of sloppy staff work, and there is no excuse for it."

Reynolds had to make a quick decision. He could interrupt Smith and point out that he had judged Robert unfairly, but that might embarrass both his superior and his subordinate. Alternatively, he could wait until after the meeting and offer an explanation in private. As Smith quickly became engrossed in another conversation, Reynolds followed the second approach. Glancing at Robert, Reynolds noted that his expression was one of mixed anger and dismay. After catching his eye, Reynolds winked at Robert as a discreet reassurance that he understood and that the damage could be repaired. After an hour, Smith, evidently dissatisfied with what he termed the "inadequate planning" of the marketing department in general, abruptly declared the meeting over. As he did so, he turned to Reynolds and asked him to remain behind for a moment. To Reynolds' surprise, Smith immediately raised the question of Robert himself. In fact, it turned out to have been his main reason for asking Reynolds to remain behind. "Look," he said, "I want you to tell me frankly, do you think I was too rough with that kid?" Relieved, Reynolds said, "Yes, you were. I was going to speak to you about it."

Smith explained to Reynolds that Robert was new to his job had not registered in his mind adequately when they had been introduced, and that it was only some time after his own outburst that the nagging thought began to occur to him that what he had done was inappropriate and unfair. "How well do you know him?" he asked. "Do you think I hurt him?"

For a moment Reynolds took the measure of his superior. Then he replied evenly, "I do not know him very well yet, but, yes, I think you hurt him."

"Damn, that is unforgivable," said Smith. He then telephoned his secretary to call Robert and ask him to report to his office immediately. A few moments later, Robert returned, looking perplexed and uneasy. As he entered, Smith came out from behind his desk and met him in the middle of the office. Standing face to face with Robert, who was 20 years and four organization levels his junior, he said, "Look, I have done something stupid and I want to apologize. I had no right to treat you like that. I should have remembered that you were new to your job, but I did not. I am sorry."

Robert was somewhat flustered. He muttered his thanks for the apology. "As long as you are here, young man," Smith continued, "I want to make a few things clear to you in the presence of your boss's boss. Your job is to make sure that people like myself do not make stupid decisions. Obviously, we think you are qualified for your job or we would not have brought you in here. But it takes time to learn any job. Three months from now I will expect you to know the answers to any questions about products." "Until then," he said, "thrusting out his hand for the younger man to shake, "you have my complete confidence. And thank you for letting me correct a mistake."

Questions for Discussion

1. What do you think was the effect on Robert and the other managers of Smith's outburst at the meeting?
2. Was Smith right to apologize to Robert or should he have left well enough alone?
3. What do you think the apology meant to Robert?
4. What would it be like to have Smith as a superior? As a subordinate?
5. How does Smith define Robert's responsibilities as an assistant product manager? How does he define his own role as a top manager?
6. What is the most important aspect of the relations between management levels in this company?

2. Electric Manufacturing Corporation

Roy, the president and founder of Electric Manufacturing Corporation (EMCORP), is wondering how he can follow the advice of his doctor, who had told him to take it easy after last year's coronary attack. EMCORP manufactures a full line of fractional horsepower electric motors sold to both original equipment manufacturers and distributors throughout the country. At present, the company employs approximately 1,000 people.

Roy, an engineer, has maintained tight control over all major functions throughout the years, and though each of the heads of the engineering, manufacturing, sales, finance and personnel departments has the title of Vice President, they come to Roy for approval before making any change in procedure. Usually, each of these executives sees Roy several times a day. The personnel director once suggested a weekly meeting, but Roy voted the idea as too time-consuming. Now, worried about his health as well as the problems of the company, Roy is beginning to feel the need for some relief from the constant pressure.

The manufacturing department shows a picture of rising costs, consistent failure to meet delivery schedules, and an increasing number of quality complaints. John, Vice President Manufacturing, admits to poor performance, but says that the cost figures from accounting are pure history and of no use since they do not reach manufacturing until the fifteenth of the month following the month in which the work is completed. He states that his failure to meet delivery schedules is due almost entirely to the fact that the sales department makes unrealistic promises, and does not bother to check manufacturing schedules. John attributes most of the quality problems to the incessant flow of engineering changes that come without warning and with no time to work out the production problems present in all new products. Roy admits to himself that he had asked Smyth, Vice President Engineering, to put all the approved changes into production immediately.

The Vice President and general manager of sales, Rita, recognizes that she has no knowledge of the manufacturing schedules and realizes that she, too, is being criticized by Roy for many broken promises in regard to delivery dates. However, Rita's chief complaint at the present time is the result of having sold a large order of Standard Motors to a distributor having a supply of replacement parts in stock, and then discovering that engineering had changed specifications: a change that made all replacement parts in the field obsolete. Another irritant for Rita is the tightening of credit requirements instituted by the finance department without prior consultation with the sales department. Again, Roy admits to himself that it is the same engineering change which caused so much trouble in manufacturing that is causing trouble for the sales department and making obsolete the existing stock of replacement parts. He also realizes that at his request, due to an unusually short cash position, the finance department tightened up on credit requirement.

Questions for Discussion

1. Define the major problem of EMCORP's management.
2. Will the formation of a committee be of any value in this situation? If a committee is needed, assign a title to the committee and indicate who should be the members of the committee?
3. Is there a need for an outside member on the committee?
4. Will an ad hoc committee be of any value?
5. In the event that Roy decides to retire, will the presence of a committee make it easier or more difficult for Roy's successor? Discuss.

3. Rama Corporation

John Tan, the service manager, had Ram Lim as a supervisor in the equipment service section to oversee the work of the servicemen. The supervisor was a nice person, but a bit soft in dealing with people. After working for four years, Ram Lim left the company for a new job elsewhere. A new supervisor was recruited from outside.

Roy Lee, a senior technician who had 10 years of service with the company, was disappointed because he was not considered for the supervisor's post. Robert had maintained a good record all along, and in fact, came up through the ranks from trainee to senior technician.

The new supervisor, Mehra, was generally a more aggressive person. Shortly after taking over the job, he started asking his subordinates to record the actual hours spent on various activities and idle time, if any. (Prior to this, the hours spent on each job were based on some kind of estimate.) The technicians were not happy with this, but unwillingly complied with the demand.

The relationship between the supervisor and his workers deteriorated when Mehra started to change certain routine matters which were supposed to improve the flow of work and reduce overtime.

A few months later, two servicemen resigned. Then the senior technician also tendered his resignation and complained to the service manager accusing Mehra of trying to create more work for them unnecessarily. However, these complaints were found to be not fully justifiable, but to a great extent were the result of misunderstandings between Mehra and his men.

The service manager did not want to lose the senior technician, and managed to persuade him to stay on and reconcile with the supervisor. Shortly after, the supervisor left the company.

Questions for Discussion

1. Do you consider the actions taken by the new supervisor not tactful enough? What would have been the tactful approach?
2. There is a general tendency for employees to resist changes in routine, particularly when such changes may encounter initial teething problems and affect the morale of the employees. In view of this, what should be the right approach in implementing changes?
3. If you were the service manager, would you let the senior technician or supervisor go? What are your reasons? Is there any other way of handling this situation?

FURTHER READING

Allen, Louis, A., *Management and Organisation*, McGraw-Hill, New York, 1980.

Business India, April 2008.

Indian Management, June 2008.

Prasad, L.M., *Principles and Practice of Management*, Sultan Chand & Sons, New Delhi, 1990.

Stoner, James, A.F. and Wankel, Charles, *Management*, Prentice Hall Inc., Englewood Cliffs, New Jersey, 1987.

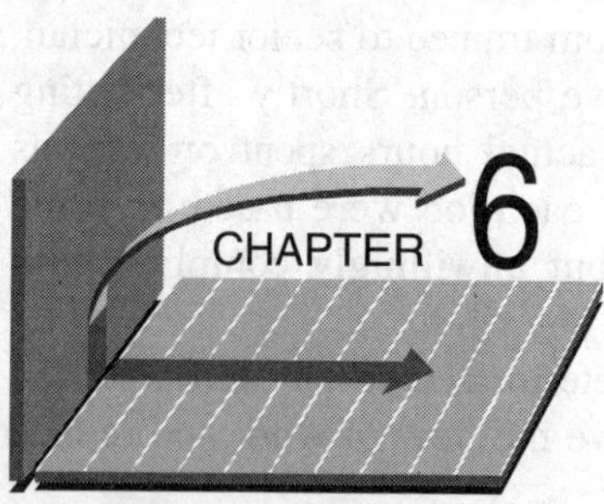

Staffing

CONTENTS

INTRODUCTION

Management is the art of getting things done through people. The process of recruitment, selection, development, training, identifying, assessing, placing, evaluating and developing people can be called *staffing*. Haimann states that "staffing relates to the recruitment, selection, development, training, compensation of subordinate managers".

Staffing has become one of the very important functions of management, along with planning, organizing, directing and controlling. Staffing is more concerned with the human elements, which are dynamic in nature. But this job can introduce a lot of complexity and challenge also. Staffing has become very significant as it involves a lot of investment in the recruitment, selection, training and placement of workers. So, to make the whole exercise meaningful, the best available people are to be secured, and their skills and abilities developed for the benefit of the organization. Staffing involves human resource planning, i.e. estimating the size and nature of the personnel required, the recruitment and selection of the best training them effectively, inducting them, rewarding them, and having regular and effective communication with them. It calls for comprehensive manpower planning.

MANPOWER/HUMAN RESOURCE PLANNING

Adwin B. Geisler states that "manpower planning is the process by which a firm ensures that it has the right number of people and right kind of people, at the right time, doing things for which they are economically most useful". So, manpower planning involves the determining of the manpower requirements for a period, which includes the acquisition, employment, and development of human resources. It helps in the selection and development of personnel, and also in effective control over labour costs by avoiding shortages and surpluses of manpower. Manpower planning as a process includes job analysis, skills, inventory and personnel forecasting. Now, it is considered to be human resource planning.

JOB ANALYSIS

Job analysis is the process of collecting the relevant job information and determining the component elements of a job by observation and study. It is the process of determining the pertinent information related to a specific job, and the record of such a process. Job analysis is the fundamental method through which proper manpower management can be done. It is the careful study of the activities of an employee on a job to determine different operations which may help in job description and job specification. Job analysis helps in the preparation of specifications for recruitment, placement, selection, training and guidance of employees. It can secure information about jobs through interviews, observation, activity sampling, questionnaires, etc. Job analysis as a report can help in time and motion study also.

Steps in the Process of Job Analysis

The following are the steps in the process of job analysis:

- Identification of the component tasks of a job
- Examining the causes, effects and the timings of task performance
- Identifying the main duties of the job
- Identifying the areas of responsibilities regarding the assignment of work, money, equipment, etc.
- Considering the personal demands of a worker.

Methods of Securing Job Information

There are several methods of securing information for job analysis. These are as follows:

1. ***Interviews:*** To conduct interviews of workers and supervisors is the most common method of collecting such information. Personal conversation with the worker can provide vital information. It can be further checked with similar jobs. But while conducting such interviews, care should be exercised on the study of the job or position of a person, rather than the study of the person himself.

2. *Observation:* There are certain situations where direct observation is possible while workers are in action. Experts may study the jobs at the performance centres, where manual content in the job is significantly high. But after observation, it has to be followed up by interviews and discussions to make the job analysis accurate and meaningful.

3. *Activity sampling:* It is almost performing the job actually for getting first-hand knowledge of the job. But it takes a lot of time to select a sample job, and it is also a costly method.

4. *Questionnaires:* Different questions relating to the jobs can be listed and these can be sent out to the job holders to get their answers. Questionnaires should be so designed as to get the responses in time. They are very economical and time saving. In some cases, it is better to follow it up by personal discussions with selected job holders.

Job Description

When the record of the job analysis is prepared with its result in a condensed form, it is called a *job description.* It is a written statement of the main duties and responsibilities of a particular job. Job description includes the job title, job number, function of the job and the responsibilities involved, the machinery used, equipment and tools used, how and why they are used, working hours involved, working conditions, method of remuneration, job relationships, job sequence, and qualifications required. It provides task contents and occupational requirements.

A job description should emphasize the functional responsibilities. It should be clear, simple and informative. It should be descriptive, complete and comprehensive. But job description has a serious limitation. It describes the job only but not *how* it should be done. It is essential to obtain the approval of the employee and the supervisor to finalize the job description so that it becomes acceptable.

Job Specification

If job description is a detailed and complete one, job specification basically emphasizes the personal requirements and inclinations necessary for the successful performance of a job. The mental or educational, technical or physical qualities required to do a job can be obtained from the job specifications for selecting the best persons for the best performance. A job specification is also called a *man specification.*

Advantages

1. It provides vital information for selecting the right man for the right job.
2. It helps in developing a foolproof training curriculum.
3. It helps in establishing physical requirements for workers from the standpoint of safety.
4. It helps in conducting salary surveys.

Job Evaluation

Job evaluation is a process by which the factors in each job are identified. Such factors are identified and measured so that the determination of the remuneration to be paid for the job becomes easy.

RECRUITMENT AND SELECTION

After ascertaining the manpower requirements through job analysis, the next process will be recruitment and selection. Recruitment is the process of identifying the sources for potential candidates and to motivate them to apply for jobs. Proper steps should be taken to have the right type of people in the right number and at the right time. It should be ensured that the people selected will remain in the organization. The right number of workers required for a concern depends upon the scale of operation, the degree of automation, computerization and the work methods. There should be a sound plan for the recruitment of labour. Recruitment should be based on certain principles.

Principle of procedure: A proper procedure should be established to conduct interviews and tests to find out the details of the candidates.

Principle of administrative convenience: The method of recruitment should be reasonable and without unnecessary complexities or undue delays. The interview should not be too long or too short.

Principle of fairness: The method of recruitment should be fair and reasonable.

Sources of Recruitment

Recruitment has to be done to get the right type of manpower needed. There are various techniques or sources to recruit people (Figure 6.1). But each such technique has to be evaluated properly by maintaining records of the success or failure of various techniques, regarding the different types of employees recruited. There are mainly two sources of recruitment which are effective: *internal sources* and *external sources*. Internal sources refer to the recruitment within the organization such as transfers and promotion. External sources are recruitment from outside.

Internal sources: Recruitment can be made by transfer or by promotion. Promotion means elevating the position of an employee towards higher responsibilities enjoying increased authority and prestige. So, higher positions can be filled up by promotion. But transfer involves the shifting of a worker from one job to another without involving any change in the responsibilities, rank and pay. Lay-off means temporary retrenching of the employee from the employment on the initiative of the employer. In such circumstances, the employee may be recalled after the commencement of work.

External sources: Resignation of employees, expansion of the company, creation of new departments, death, retirement or dismissal of employees can create more job opportunities. In such cases, recruitment has to be made from external sources. Casual applications received may be taken from the applications received file and they can be considered. If the present employees recommend the names of their relatives and friends, they can be employed so that the goodwill of the present employees can be retained and reliable candidates can also be recruited on the responsibility of the present workers. Sometimes, for technical or unskilled vacancies, a notice board can be displayed either at the gate or the central place of the concern; usually, a large number of job seekers come to the factory gates everyday. If there is any necessity to fill up casual vacancies or for unskilled workers, they can be employed at the gate. The services of contractors can also be used to obtain labourers. Management consultancy firms can help in recruiting managerial personnel.

Educational institutions like colleges, universities, university employment bureaus, institutes of technology, management can be used for recruiting graduates to be trained for positions of responsibility. Public employment exchanges can provide the required manpower for organizations. They are very helpful in providing employment opportunities for the physically challenged, ex-servicemen, Scheduled Castes and Scheduled Tribes, university graduates and professional and executive personnel. They can also provide employment market information and employment surveys. Newspapers or journals also help in recruiting staff. An advertiser can select the most appropriate and effective media and newspapers for advertisement. Labour unions can also play an important role in providing personnel. Private employment agencies can render good service in employing people. There is another medium called *scouting* by which professional athletes and semi-professional and amateur athletes at educational institutions are recruited.

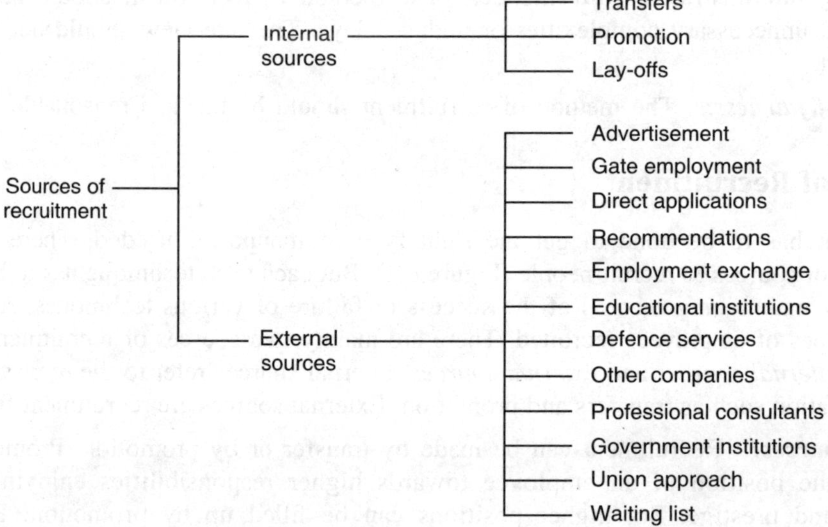

Figure 6.1 Sources of recruitment.

Advantages of internal sources

- Continuity of service and stability.
- Employees have a feeling of security.
- Fosters loyalty, integrity and honesty among the employees.
- Familiarity with the organizational set-up; induction is not necessary.
- Encourages low grade workers to work forward to higher posts.

Advantages of external sources

- New perspectives and fresh viewpoints can be introduced.
- New experience, skill and technology can be introduced.
- There can be a change in the outlook and habits.

Selection

The selection process starts after securing applications from different sources of recruitment. Selection plays a vital role in reducing costly labour turnover. Careful screening of all applications is essential. Selection is a process of selecting the right persons with necessary skills, abilities and personality to fit in their respective jobs in the organization. To select a highly competent, qualified and effective team, one has to take care and be objective. The selection procedure has a history. J.L. Lundy states that some of the darkest days in the history of personnel selection and administration occurred when phrenologists, physiognomists, palmists, graphologists and astrologers were selling their services throughout the business world. They claimed to be specialists in personality evaluation. Phrenologists studied the bumps on one's chin, nose and ears and the colour of one's eyes and hair. Palmists by studying the hand, and graphologists by studying the handwriting, were 'analyzing' personality. But these pseudo-scientific techniques proved futile in selecting the right people for the right job. Modern techniques can help in avoiding the selection of inappropriate personnel. They help in discovering the most talented, promising and suitable candidates. It automatically means that the least qualified and less suitable persons are eliminated in the process. The number of rejected or eliminated will be usually higher than the number selected. Yorder states that recruitment is a positive process, whereas selection is negative.

Steps in the selection procedure

The selection procedure is the process through which eligible candidates are selected. It involves the following steps:

1. Conduct job analysis and job description.
2. Keep the man specification ready.
3. Find out the sources of recruitment.
4. Scrutinize the applications received.
5. Conduct preliminary interviews.
6. Send application blanks.
7. Conduct different employment tests.
8. Conduct personal interviews.
9. Check the references.
10. Conduct medical examinations.
11. Final selection.
12. Placement and induction.

The employer has to conduct the job analysis and prepare a job description. With this background, a man specification should be prepared and proper sources of recruitment must be considered. Efforts must be made to get applications from these sources. They should be screened in such a way that unsuitable applicants are automatically eliminated, and they are informed accordingly to avoid the problem of further processing.

Preliminary interviews: Such an interview will act as the first hurdle for the applicant. They are short interviews to know the nature of the job required from the applicant, and also to ascertain whether he is suitable for the existing job. It does not probe deeper into the details of skill, abilities, and experience. It only covers the application. It can be used economically to prevent further processing of an unnecessary case.

Application blanks: Blank application forms are sent to the candidates who are successful in the preliminary interview, for getting further information. An application blank should be brief, definite and comprehensive. It should avoid superfluous questions. An application blank helps the concern to get the details about the candidate regarding his ability to spell, to write, to provide facts. It can also serve as a guide for interviews, and a record where waiting lists are kept.

Selection or employment tests: Various standard tests are available to find out those possessing the required intelligence, abilities, aptitudes, interests and personality. *Intelligence tests* are conducted to identify the mental capabilities. *Ability tests* are available to measure the efficiency or proficiency in specific areas. *Vocation tests* are designed to show a candidate's suitable vocation. *Personality tests* are conducted to measure various traits of a candidate. Similarly, there are various tests like performance tests, psychological tests like interest tests, dexterity tests, achievement tests, and attitude tests. Such tests should only *supplement* other selection techniques. The tests should be conducted under standardized conditions to minimize external influences on the results. These tests themselves should be subjected to periodic testing to ascertain whether they can still serve their purpose or not. The strength of a test depends upon its ability to discriminate between individuals. A good test will be consistent, reliable and objective.

There are other important types of employment tests which are widely used by many modern organizations. The General Aptitude Test Battery, popularly known as GATB, was first introduced by the US Department of Labour. This test can determine the competence of candidates in their numerical skill, ability to perceive things in the right perspective, general intelligence level, and finger dexterity. Another such popular test is the Career Maturity, inventory test, which determines the level of competence in the candidate. It identifies the judgement, sequence, operational ability, job responsibility, and decision-making abilities of the candidate. Another such test is the in-basket test. It is an achievement test which determines the productivity, action, interaction, analyzing ability, planning skill, priorities, peer group interaction, informality of nature, and ability to manage work schedules.

The above tests can provide very useful information to employers. In advanced countries, experienced psychologists conduct clinical interviews to find out the emotional stability and balance of the candidate. Human resource utilization and development, to a major extent, depends upon such special tests.

The following are the advantages of tests:

1. Tests help in increasing accuracy in selection.
2. They enable employers to make most objective and purposeful selection.

3. They can prove economical in the long run.
4. They can tap talent located at even distant and remote areas.
5. They can be made acceptable to applicants.
6. They help in reducing the employee turnover.

The following are the disadvantages of tests:

1. Tests are not infallible.
2. They can only help in minimizing errors and cannot eliminate them completely.
3. Candidates may not score in the test proportionate to their abilities.
4. Verbal or written questions may create interpretation problems.
5. If they are used by unqualified personnel, they can be defective.

Conducting personal interviews: For every type of job, the interview has become an important tool. In fact, in most organizations, the interview is the *only* tool adopted to select personnel. It helps in assessing the total personality of the prospective employee. An interview enables assessment of the motivation, attitude and overall personality of the candidate and is vital for all types of skilled and technical jobs, being the best selection device of major importance as a valuable means of evaluating such factors like pleasing disposition and appearance of the candidate. Interviews may be structured, semi-structured, or unstructured. A *structured interview* formulates definite questions to use for all applicants in general, with the same list of questions. In a *semi-structured interview*, some questions are predetermined and others asked during the interview. An *unstructured interview* usually will have no such predetermined or readymade checklist. It may create a rapport between the interviewer and the interviewee. A panel of recruiting officers from the personnel, works, and general divisions can be formed to judge the ability and suitability of candidates. Interviews may be in the following forms:

1. Formal
2. Informal
3. Depth
4. Stress
5. Group
6. Panel

The *stress interview* technique attempts to deliberately confuse the candidate, put him on the defensive and keep him under emotional pressure. Questions may be silly, blunt, or ambiguous. But this technique has to be used with great care. The persons conducting an interview cannot make a comprehensive analysis of the ability and attitude of a candidate in one interview. The personal likes and dislikes of the interviewer should not influence the interview. It is better to explore the possibility of *multiple interviews* so that a comparative evaluation can be made.

Checking references: The viewpoints and opinions of others regarding the applicant can be obtained through references. Applicants are usually required to provide two or three references. References can provide useful information about the character, history and reputation of the candidate. References can be made to the previous employers, the college authorities or the references mentioned in the application. If it is essential, the present employer of the candidate can also be contacted on the phone; a personal visit can provide still better information.

Supervisors' approval: If the supervisor or the immediate boss is not involved in the interview, then he should be given an opportunity to carefully verify the physical and mental capacities of the candidates. This has to be done in the light of the job specification.

Medical or physical examination: Workmen's compensation regulations have made the process of physical examination a very important one. Physical fitness should be one of the primary considerations in selection. If the physical defects of an employee are not discovered, then the employer will be liable for all the health hazards to the employee. Physical fitness can be ascertained through a detailed medical examination.

Final selection: After the completion of all the above exercises, the final selection of the candidate can be made by sending a job offer to the selected candidate.

Placement and induction: Selected people should be put on the job. In fact, it is the final step in the selection process. An employee should be introduced to the organizational culture and environment. He should be made familiar with the policies, objectives, rules and regulations of the company. Induction training refers to the introduction of a new employee to the work group, supervisor and organization.

TRAINING

Training and development activities are highly required in any organization to prepare the employees to work in the organization as per the requirement. As these are playing a significant role in the organizational success, several companies have established separate training and development centres to provide training and development activities.

The employees will become useful assets when proper training and development activities are provided. Here, we discuss the issues relating to training and development, types of training, significance of training, and identification of training needs.

Objectives of Training and Development

The following are the objectives of training and development activities of an organization:

Induction: Training is used for inducting new employees into the organizations. This induction training is given for introducing the employees to the policies, procedures, people, peers in the organization so that they can adjust quickly and associate themselves with the organization.

Updating: Training is used for periodical updating of skills of the employees. It is mandatory because of changing policies and launching of new products. The refresher courses conducted by banks for employees helped them a lot to get accustomed to the work.

Preparing for future: Training is used as a toll to prepare people for handling higher responsibilities in the future. It is also conducted to build loyalty among the employees. Infosys invests a huge amount on training employee selected by it. In fact, it has set up a global training centre at Mysore for training of its employees in various cadres on a continuous basis.

Competency development: The identification of training needs and competency development are increasingly recognized as important parameters. Some companies have adopted core competencies programmes. Five areas were identified by one bank: marketing, credit, cash management services, treasuring and HRM. The selected candidates are given extensive training in training colleges and also in workplaces.

Simulation and game play: For technical subjects and complicated projects, organizations locate simulated work conditions to train the employees. In aviation industry, pilots are trained in a simulated environment. In armed forces, recruitment and selection is made through game plays which help to improve the candidate's decision-making skills.

Definitions

The terms 'training' and 'development' are used synonymously. But there is some distinction between these two concepts. Training is for non-executive personnel, while development is for the executive personnel. Training is given on technical and mechanical operations of the company, while development is on theoretical and conceptual skills. Training is for short term, but development is for long term. Both are highly required to educate employees. They understand organizational mission, vision and values. Every organization allocates some amount for training and development purposes.

Flippo defines training as "the act of increasing the skills of an employee for doing a particular job". Training is a process of learning the sequence of programmed behaviour. Thus, behaviour being programmed is relevant to a specific phenomenon that is "a job".

Training denotes "a systematic procedure for transferring technical know-how to the employees to increase their knowledge and skills for doing a particular job. It focuses on skill development which is necessary to perform a particular job."

Development has several definitions. It is all those activities and programmes which, when recognized and controlled, have substantial influence in changing the capacity of the individual to perform his assignment better and in doing so are likely to increase his potential for future assignments.

Any activity designed to improve the performance of existing managers and to provide for a planned growth of managers to meet future organizational requirements is management development.

The term 'development' is holistic and aims at the overall personality development. The content of a development programme includes conceptual or theoretical inputs, strategic thinking or focusing on behavioural aspects like leadership skills and managing teams.

Distinction

Training is imparted to operatives whereas development is mainly used for executives or managers. The impact of a training programme ends with learning the skill, while that of a developmental programme is a continuous and ongoing process. Management development is based on the assumption that there always exists a gap between the individual's performance and his potential for the performance.

Development requires clean setting of goals and conducive environment. One author has differentiated the two terms in the following words: training courses are typically designed for a short term, stated set purpose such as operations of some pieces of machinery or IT tools, while development involves a broader education for long-term purposes.

Based on the foregoing discussion, the distinction between training and development can be given as follows:

Learning dimension	*Training*	*Development*
• Who	• Non-managerial personnel	• Managerial personnel
• What	• Technical and mechanical	• Conceptual idea
• Why	• For specific job	• For a variety of jobs
• When	• Short term	• Long term

Significance

Training is an important component of HRD in managing people. The reason is that employees have to understand their jobs and their roles. The morale of the employees increases when they are given proper training. Sometimes, behaviour of employees can be changed through training. The objectives of training and development are as follows:

- To get skills of employees
- To update skills and knowledge
- To prepare for higher responsibilities
- To develop job related attitude
- To mould employees to adapt to organizational changes.

The significance of training is understood on the basis of the skills required for getting output/result. Training increases efficiency. In the ever-changing technology, training is required to maintain the minimum level of output. For example, working on automatic machine requires skills different from those required to handle manually operated machines. Raw employees cannot handle such machines.

Help high morale: Employees learn something new and thus, their ego is satisfied. It helps in improving employee morale.

Better quality of human relations: Growing complexity of organizations has led to various human problems. Many of the problems can be overcome by suitable human relation training. Many techniques have been developed through which people can be trained and developed to tackle problems of social and psychological nature.

Reduced supervision: Employees require less supervision. When they are trained, they require more autonomy and freedom. Such autonomy can be given if the employees are well trained. With reduced supervision, managers can increase the span of management.

Increased organizational flexibility: Trained people can maintain organizational viability and flexibility. Viability relates to survival of the organization during problems, and flexibility relates to sustain its effectiveness despite the loss of its key personnel, and making short-term adjustment. With the existing personnel, adjustment is possible if the organization has trained personnel.

Identification of Training Needs

Training depends on the correct identification of the needs. The elements that follow need identification are:

- Developing training objectives for the programme
- Contents of the programme
- Selecting appropriate training methodologies
- Drawing out a schedule
- Designing tshe system for evaluation of training
- Conducting the training programme
- Measuring results of training.

As training is for improving the performance of a person in his current job, it is necessary to collect and store the following data for identification of training needs:

- Job descriptions of individuals as perceived by them and their superior against individual profile.
- Job performance review. The level of performance of the employees will be measured.
- Potential of individuals to grow within the organization, keeping in view the growth rate of the organization and its future objectives.
- Managerial ability and traits of the individual which can contribute towards the performance of the job.

The training manager of an organization will perform the function with the assistance of the line manager. The training manager is primarily responsible for the design and conduct of suitable training programmes for the employees in the organization as per the organizational objectives.

Training needs are identified on the basis of organizational analysis, job analysis and people analysis. Training methods and course content are to be planned on the basis of training basis. Training needs are those aspects which are necessary to perform the job in an organization.

Training needs are based on the job and organizational requirements and employees' skills.

Organizational analysis: It involves analyzing organizational strengths and weaknesses in different areas such as accidents, frequent breakage of machinery, labour turnover, market share and other marketing areas, quality and quantity of output, production schedule, raw materials and other production areas, personnel, and finance.

Departmental analysis: Departmental strengths and weaknesses are based on continuously acquiring skills, knowledge in operating computer, accuracy and values of accounting personnel, etc.

Job analysis: It includes the study of jobs, design of jobs due to changes, job enlargement, job environment, etc.

Employees analysis: It means analyzing individual strengths and weaknesses in the areas of job, knowledge, skill, etc.

The following criteria are used to assess the training needs:

- Organizational requirements/weaknesses
- Departmental requirements/weaknesses
- Job specifications and employee specifications
- Identifying specific problems
- Anticipating future problems
- Management requests

- Observations
- Interviews
- Group discussions
- Questionnaire surveys
- Checklists
- Performance appraisal

The following is the list for identifying training and development requirements:

- Review training documents for adequacy
- Observe training and trainees in the learning environment of a classroom, a shop, or a laboratory
- Interview trainers and trainees
- Poor organization and training deficits
- Inadequate supervision
- Poor communication
- Unclear policies, poor job design
- Equipment material problems, work methods
- Compare job description and applicant specifications with personnel records
- Analyze performance ratings
- Analyze all the records of an enterprise to identify the possible deficiency
- Identify and analyze operating problems
- Use interviews, questionnaires, group discussions, tools and work samples to determine training problems
- Analyze enterprise plans, policies and forecast to determine their potential impact on staffing needs
- Identify and analyze future systems, equipment, technique and procedures to determine their impact on staffing needs and requirements
- Finally, development objectives and guidelines following the procedures laid down for the purpose

Methods of Training

1. On-the-job methods:
   (a) Training methods:
      (i) Apprenticeship
      (ii) Job instruction training.
   (b) Development methods:
      (i) Coaching/understudy
      (ii) Job rotations
      (iii) Special committee assignments
      (iv) Internship.

2. Off-the-job methods:
   (a) Training methods:
      (i) Class room instruction
      (ii) Lectures
      (iii) Seminars/conference
      (iv) Programmed instruction
      (v) Audio-visual.
   (b) Development methods:
      (i) Simulation
      (ii) Case study
      (iii) Role play
      (iv) Management games
      (v) In-basket and behavioural modelling.

Success of Training

The success of any training programme depends upon the following factors:

- Top management's support and participation
- Support of immediate supervisors and peers
- Reward for trainees
- Mandatory attendance
- Long-term evaluation of results
- Rewards for employees.

Role of Training and Development Manager

The following are the roles of training and development manager:

- Need analysis and diagnosis
- Determining appropriate training approach
- Programme design and development
- Developing material resources
- Managing external resources
- Individual development planning and counselling
- Job performance related training
- Conducting classroom training
- Organization and group development
- Training research
- Managing working relationships with managers and clients
- Managing training and development function
- Professional self-development.

EXECUTIVE DEVELOPMENT

Executive or management development is an educational process utilizing a systematic and organized procedure by which managerial personnel learn conceptual and theoretical knowledge. Management development includes all those activities and progammes, both recognized and controlled, which have substantial influence in changing the capacity of the individual to perform his/her present assignment better in future. Management development is a planned, systematic and continuous process of learning and growth, designed to induce behavioural change in individuals by cultivating their mental abilities and inherent qualities through knowledge acquision, understanding new knowledge, insights and skills as they are needed for the effective performance of the organisation.

Techniques

The techniques of development are classified into two major categories:

On-the-job methods

The main aim of all on-the-job methods is to increase the ability of executives to work while performing their duties with exposure to the real work situation.

***On-the-job coaching*:** In this method, the immediate superior guides the subordinate in various ways to do the job efficiently. The superior only guides and does not reach, although he extends his assistance whenever needed. Periodic feedback and evaluation are also part of the coaching activity. The merits of this method lie in the fact that it provides real and practical job experience to the executive.

The advantage of on-the-job coaching is increased motivation for the trainee and minimization the problems of transferring learning from theory to practice. It is primarily a device for ensuring that individuals grow within the boundaries set by their jobs and their organizational units.

Understudy: The trainee is prepared to perform the work or fill in the position of another. He is a trainee who, in the future, will assume the duties and responsibilities of the position currently held by his immediate superior when the latter separates from the job because of transfer, promotion, resignation, retirement, etc. The understudy technique is similar to on-the-job coaching with the difference that the department manager may pick up one individual from his unit to come for his understudy. He will then guide him to learn his job and grapple with the problems that confront the manager daily.

The major advantage of this method is that it ensures the ready supply of competent people whenever the vacancy arises due to promotion, transfer, retirement or resignation of the present occupant of the position. This method has built-in motivation because it is considered a step towards promotion of the trainee.

Job rotation: The executive is given all the normal duties and responsibilities which go along with the job to which he is transferred. This method broadens the outlook of the executive.

Job rotation serves to bring the feeling of superiority of one department over the others. When a number of executives have served in each other's department, they can also understand the reasons why a certain function must be done in a particular way. Thus, interdepartmental cooperation will be enhanced. Job rotation injects new ideas into the different departments of the organization.

Boards of executives: In this method, permanent advisory committees of managers are constituted. These committees study various problems and make recommendations to the top management. The advisory committees operate in a staff capacity. Therefore, the recommendations made by these can be rejected by the top management if their suitability is questionable. This method has the advantages of being relatively inexpensive, developing team work, and group decision making among managers.

Committee assignment: A committee is a group of persons appointed to investigate and make recommendations regarding some matter relating to the organization. The committees study the problem or issue in accordance with the terms of reference. For example, a committee may be set up to analyze the feasibility of introducing a new product. This committee may have persons from finance department, engineering department, research and development department, etc. The committee will study the question of feasibility of a new product from all the angles and make recommendations.

A committee is an excellent means of training. The trainee is placed on a committee which is constituted to make recommendations on a particular problem. Through discussions and deliberations in committee meetings, the trainee becomes acquainted with different viewpoints and acquires a wide background.

Off-the-job methods

The following are off-the-job methods which are highly useful:

Role playing: Role playing may be described as a technique of creating a live situation, usually one involving conflict between people, and then having persons in a group play the part or roles of specific personalities. In industry, it is used primarily as a technique for modifying attitudes and interpersonal skills. Role playing brings about the following merits:

- When one is asked to put one's self in someone else's place and play the role of that person, it generally increases awareness of the other's problems.
- The process helps the participants to appreciate that behaviour is often a consequence not only of their personalities but also of the situation, and helps them to identify and recognize some of their own faults.
- The trainee can broaden his experience by trying different approaches, while in a real situation he has only one chance. By evaluating the different ways of handling the same situation, the executive is able to see the strengths and weaknesses of the approaches.
- Role playing is more than an experience because it permits observation, discussion and emphasis that are not customarily a part of experience.

Sensitivity training/laboratory training: Sensitivity or T-group training is an important technique of "laboratory training". The main objective of sensitivity training is the development of awareness and sensitivity to one's own behavioural pattern through interaction with others. The sensitivity training programme is absolutely unstructured. The main goals are: increased openness with others, increased understanding of any change in the attitude; group learning, increased awareness and concern about others, improvement in skills for listening to others, increased interpersonal competence, developing trust and accepted support.

The following are the benefits of sensitivity training to the organization:

- Emergence of innovative ideas
- Increased commitment of trainees
- Increased vertical and horizontal cooperation
- Increased productivity at all levels
- Reduction in intergroup conflicts
- Increased adaptability to the organizational change.

Syndicate training: The purpose of the syndicate technique is to "expose a participant to a milieu in which he is persuaded into reflecting upon his experiences as an executive, updating his knowledge, improving his executive skills and developing a great insight into human behaviour." This method is used for the development of the executives whose age ranges between 35–45 and who have 10–15 years experience in some area of management to be fit for taking up higher responsibilities. The participants are the directors of the programme before actually joining it.

Conference training: A conference is a group meeting conducted on some important issues. As a member, a person can learn from others by comparing his opinions with those of others. The trainee learns to respect the viewpoints of others and to realize that there is more than one workable approach to a problem. As a conference leader, a person can develop his skill to motivate people through his direction of discussions. The trainee learns the effects of closely controlling and dominating the discussion as compared to adopting a more permissive type of direction.

Simulation training: The basic idea behind simulation is to construct a situation which closely represents the actual one. It provides an opportunity to conduct trial or test runs under the conditions that are as close to reality as feasible. Based on empirical data, a model is constructed and then subjected to the same influences and forces that occur in actual practice. These techniques are business games, in-basket exercises and case studies.

1. *Business games:* A business game has been described as a dynamic training exercise utilizing a model of business situation. It is essentially a group exercise in sequential decision making under simulated organizational conditions.
2. *In-basket training:* This technique emphasizes the necessity for skills in decision making. The trainee is presented with a situation where he must take over for a manager who is absent. He is provided with an in-basket full of materials with which he must deal. These materials may be phone calls, meetings to set up, complaints to handle, orders to make and other demands which supposedly duplicate the tasks he would face, if he were holding such a position. This may require a list of priorities.
3. *Case study:* A case study is used for training thorough description of some events that actually occurred in an organization. Usually, it involves some problem that has to be solved. The trainees read the case and present alternative solutions. These suggestions may then be discussed where the individual is able to obtain information about how others felt about the case.

Evaluation

Training programme can be evaluated on the basis of various factors like production factor, general observations, human resource factor, performance tests, cost, value, and relationship.

General observations should not be overlooked as a means of training evaluation. The immediate supervisor is often a good judge of the skill level of his subordinates. For on-the-job training programmes, the supervisor is, in effect, the judge of his own efforts. If the supervisor is treated as a part of the professional management of the organization and is properly selected and trained, this self-analysis and appraisal can be quite accurate and objective. The efficient supervisor decides accurately the level of skill and knowledge acquired by the trainee during the training programme. He also decides how effectively the trainees apply the acquired skill and knowledge to the present and future jobs.

Training programme can also be evaluated on the basis of employee satisfaction, which, in turn, can be viewed on the basis of:

- Decrease in employee turnover
- Decrease in absenteeism and accidents
- Betterment of employee morale
- Reduction in time to earn piece rate
- Decrease in number of discharge/dismissal
- Improvement in working environment and discipline

SUMMARY

1. Staffing is one of the important functions of management.
2. Staffing requires manpower planning, job analysis, job description, job specification and job evaluation. The required staff have to be employed, based on the job.
3. A recruitment and selection process is required to take the right person for the right job.
4. The sources of recruitment are both external and internal.
5. Personal interviews are required in the selection process.
6. Induction and placement are followed by the selection process.
7. The selected staff are provided training related to their jobs.
8. Training methods are both on-the-job and off-the-job.
9. Management development is being given importance in Indian industries.

REVIEW QUESTIONS

1. Why does staffing become an important managerial function in an organization?

2. Briefly explain the selection procedure followed by an industrial organization with which you are familiar.

3. Briefly explain the steps of the staffing process.
4. What are the various sources of recruitment?
5. Discuss the different types of employment tests.
6. What do you mean by job analysis, job description and job specification?
7. What are the different types of training? Explain.
8. Discuss management development in the Indian environment.

CASE STUDIES

1. Hindustan Chemicals Ltd.*

The Hindustan Chemicals Ltd. (HCL) is a public sector firm engaged in petrochemical business. It employs about 1,600 workers, most of whom are well-qualified, fairly young (average age 32) and have typically an urban background. HCL has retained one reputed consulting and training organization each to impart training in supervisory skills for their junior managers, human resource management programme with emphasis on organization analysis and behaviour modification skills for middle managers, and advanced management programmes for senior managers. HCL wanted to train all managerial employees over a period of 12 to 15 months in batches of 20 per month at junior and middle levels, and 20 senior managers once in every two months.

IAM, a renowned management institute, was assigned the responsibility to impart training to middle managers.

A couple of months after the start of the training intervention, the top management learnt of a growing tendency on the part of some of the employees on night shift to sleep while on duty. Since it was a tightly manned petrochemical complex, any negligence or dereliction of duty in certain critical areas could be potentially hazardous and extremely risky. Therefore, the director (Personnel) and a couple of members of the top management team visited the plant one night, without any prior information to the plant people about their visit. They caught red-handed four persons sleeping on duty, recorded evidence, and proceeded with taking steps to initiate disciplinary action the following day. When the charge sheets were being prepared, trade union leaders descended on the scene, persuaded the top management to be lenient, as an exception in this case, to the persons concerned. The union leaders also assured that they would advise their members not to sleep while on duty. In the interest of maintaining good industrial relations, the top management did not pursue the cases.

This gesture on the part of the top management was perceived as a sign of their weakness by the officers' association and its members. They protested to top management whether they (the latter) would be equally considerate in cases involving them (the managers). The workers felt that so long as there is no problem in the plant, management would be considerate enough. With the result, the incidence of sleeping on night duty began to grow. Top management became alarmed. The personnel department was asked to advise all line managers, particularly shift

* The case was prepared by C.S. Venkataratnam and B.K. Srivastava.

incharges, to keep a vigil on those who have a tendency to sleep, and report cases of persons who are found guilty of sleeping on duty. The circular did not have any impact on the middle and junior managers. Instead, they derisively laughed and ignored the circulars. They also felt that "the top management's perception of industrial relations dynamics at the plant is very different from that of junior and middle level managers."

Seeing no improvement in the situation, the top management asked IAM to include a module on Handling Indiscipline with role play sessions on 'How to Conduct Domestic Enquiry'. The programme coordinator readily agreed to the suggestion because he felt that in doing so, he was making it tailor-made to the needs of the organization.

When the module was first offered to the fifth batch of middle managers, the participants wondered why this subject was additionally introduced. They wanted to know why it did not form an integral part of the programme from the colleagues who attended the programme from the beginning itself, and whether the need for including the topic was felt by their colleagues who attended the programme in the previous batches or by the top management. When they learnt that it was at the latter's instance, they stoutly protested in chorus and said, "We know the importance of discipline. In fact, with growing violence our physical security is often threatened due to sabotage, violence and vandalism by a handful of unruly elements. Discipline, therefore, is not merely an organization need, but also a personal need for us, whereas for the top management, it is a bargainable aspect of shop-floor industrial relations. What we need is not training but proof that top management means what it says. We demand that the top management supports and sustains the actions we initiate in maintaining discipline. We will be able to have confidence in top management if it shows us the way by first initiating actions on the cases they themselves have booked."

Such restiveness affected the receptivity in what was on the agenda in the training schedule for that afternoon. But the trainees became intensely involved the following day when they were doing the organization analysis in small groups. Most participants wondered what happened to the suggestion their predecessors made while presenting the findings of their group discussions on organization analysis before some members of the top management team on the last day of every programme held thus far. One participant asked: "our colleagues gave their feedback to the top management. We understand the latter agreed on most points. But we see no evidence of follow-up of any kind." A second one argued with the programme coordinator, "Why are you asking us to give vent to our feelings? Do you realize that our top management is merely using you and the other faculty as a buffer?". A third one queried of personality and situation, "Now tell us whether top management is merely wanting to change our personality but does not want to change the situation. We do not know whether discussion on aspects concerning their personality should remain a taboo since projection will not help us."

Question for Discussion

1. Discuss the key issues in this case. Identify the lessons for developing training strategies. What remedial steps would you suggest in this case?

2. Aero Space Inc

Srinu was the manager of the systems development department of Aero Space Inc. During his 15 years with the company, he trained many managers and encouraged their development, only to see many of them leave the firm after they got their advanced degrees. The company had a liberal policy of educational reimbursement (75 per cent of tuition costs and books), and many engineers (about 50 per cent of them had a member's degree in a technical field) took advantage of the educational opportunities. Ms Sridhar, an electrical engineer, came to see her boss Srinu, who congratulated her on getting a master's degree in business administration, which she received through the assistance of the firm's educational programme.

Ms Sridhar, to the surprise of Srinu, said that she was leaving the company to go to a competitor because she did not see any opportunities for advancement in the firm.

Srinu was furious because this had happened several times before. He wanted to see the vice president of operations immediately and complain about the educational reimbursement policy and the lack of a systematic approach to staffing.

Questions for Discussion

1. What might be the reasons that employees left after receiving their degrees through education reimbursement?
2. If you were the vice president, what would you do?
3. How can such labour turnover be prevented?

3. OPTEL

The general manager of OPTEL, a medium-scale industry, received a complaint against a worker in the production department who was not only careless in his work, but often disobeyed the supervisor and challenged his authority. He was habitually late on duty, and did not like anyone questioning his behaviour. The union leaders criticized his behaviour when he was absent, and defended him in his presence. He had spent 15 years in the industry, and his past records showed that he was graded among the few good workers. This change in his behaviour and conduct was noticed particularly after the change of leadership in the union as well as the change of his immediate supervisor.

Question for Discussion

1. Analyze this case. What action would you suggest to the general manager?

FURTHER READING

Flippo, E.B., *Personnel Management*, McGraw-Hill, New York, 1984.

Laurie, J.M., Management and Organizational Behaviour, *Financial Times*, Pitman Publishing, London, 1999.

Venkataratnam, C.S. and Srivastava, B.K., *Personnel/Human Resource Management*, Tata McGraw-Hill, New Delhi, 1994.

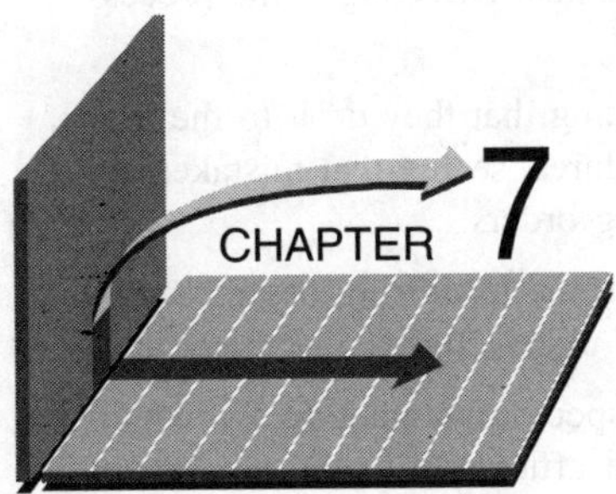

Leading

CONTENTS

INTRODUCTION

In modern management, leading plays an important role in managing business. Earlier, the concept of leading was explained by many management experts as "directing". Now, they feel that *directing* and *leading* are synonymous terms, but leading is more appropriate in modern business. *Leading* is the managerial function of initiating organized activity to fulfil organizational objectives. *Direction* is the regular task of making decisions and converting them into specific and general orders and instructions. *Directing* also refers to providing continuous guidance to people. It is a process by which the activities and achievements of all workers are guided towards the accomplishment of common goals. In simple words, directing means, telling people what to do and to see that they do it to the best of their ability.

DEFINITIONS

HAIMANN: Leading consists of the process and techniques utilized in issuing instructions and making certain that operations are carried on as originally planned. Directing is the process around which all performance revolves.

EARNEST DALE: Leading is telling people what to do and seeing that they do it to the best of their ability. It includes making assignments, explaining procedures, seeing that mistakes are corrected, providing on-the-job instruction, and, of course, issuing orders.

URWICK and BRECH: Leading is the guidance, the inspiration, the leadership of those men and women that constitute the real core of the responsibilities of management.

KOONTZ and O'DONNELL: Leading is the interpersonal aspect of managing by which subordinates are led to understand and contribute effectively and efficiently to the attainment of enterprise objectives.

MARSHALL E. DIMOCK: The leading function is the heart of administration which involves determining the course, giving orders and instructions, providing the dynamic leadership.

From the above definitions, it is clear that leading includes issuing instructions, providing guidance, exercising supervision, organizing leadership and inspiring subordinates.

Nature of Leading

Leading is a process of actuation. It provides an electrifying effect to the organization, makes people action-oriented and bridges gaps within the organization. Distribution of work, delegation of authority and supervision of work should be done meticulously. The top management should create departments and direct the departmental managers to function as per the broad policies and objectives of the concern. The middle-level managers should direct the operative-level managers, who in turn should direct the workers and supervise them, so that direction flows from top to bottom so as to perform the necessary jobs efficiently and effectively.

ELEMENTS OF LEADING

Joseph Massie states that directing concerns the total manner in which managers can influence the action of subordinates. The entire organization is activated with leading.

The aim of leading is to:

- issue clear, complete, comprehensive orders, within the capabilities of subordinates to accomplish,
- provide continuous training to subordinates by instructing them to carry out the particular assignment in the existing situation,
- inspire the subordinates so as to secure their best cooperation,
- supervise the work performance of subordinates,
- maintain order and discipline within the organization, and
- communicate with the worker so as to make the process meaningful.

CHARACTERISTICS OF LEADING

The leading function of management possesses the following characteristics:

It is one of the major functions of management: Planning, organization and employment of persons may not be meaningful unless the employed people are directed properly.

It is a continuing activity: Instructing the employees, their supervision and execution of plans will be a continuous activity. There is a need to lead the subordinates and motivate them regularly.

Leading functions from top to bottom: The top management will direct the middle-level management, and it has to regularly direct the operative management. So, leading is performed by managers at all levels.

It includes not only issuing orders but also regular supervision: Managers and supervisors should not only issue orders, they should also supervise the activities of subordinates regularly.

Leading deals with the human factor: Managers should direct individuals with different ambitions, aspirations and attitudes. Every individual will have a lot of energy, which he can conserve, waste or use for productive purposes. The manager's task is to see that such energy is utilized for the benefit of the organization and the individual concerned.

Leading and other managerial activities: Direction can induce efficiency and effectiveness both for the individual and for the organization.

Naturally, leading has a direct impact on various managerial activities, which are as follows:

Authority and responsibility: A manager who directs should know his limits of power and authority, the relationship of authority and responsibility, span of control, reaction to authority from the peer group, subordinate and superior groups, and degree of accountability.

Decision making: The direction function requires a special skill in tending to certain problems, participative ability at different levels of the organization, and ability to take risks and convert them into opportunities.

Communication: Direction can be effective with different communication skills, by keeping communication channels open for flow of accurate and useful information, by formal and informal methods of communication, and good feedback.

Leadership: Direction will be result-oriented if the person who directs has the qualities of an effective leader. The knowledge of democratic, free-rein and autocratic approaches to management of an organization helps.

Perception, learning and creativity: Direction can be a continuous process of learning and instructing from individual groups within an organization, to develop potentialities, refine existing skills, create a good climate for personal growth and creative expression, and for improved perception.

Innovation and change: Change is a constant factor and leading can be improved by adjusting to technological, managerial, and organizational changes, inviting innovation through increased motivation and improving the morale.

Supervision: It means to supervise or oversee subordinates and their performance level and ascertain that it is in accordance with the original plan/policies.

IMPORTANCE

Leading is a significant function in modern management. Wherever the human factor exists, it has to be properly directed. Every man appointed by the organization should be told about the work that he should perform. The directors are the representatives of the shareholders, who are expected to direct the tasks and take the organization in the right direction. Every job of a manager, like issue of orders, memos, notices, instructions, giving out programmes, policies, procedures, plans, involves directing. Complex human factors have to be directed properly to achieve organizational goals.

Instructions or orders: Issuing instructions is one of the major tasks of a manager. Every manager is expected to know the art of issuing instructions. An *instruction* is the impetus by which an organization is activated. Every instruction is functional in nature, as it initiates, modifies or stops an activity. It is also popularly known as an *order*, *command*, or *directive*. As Koontz and O'Donnell state, as a directional technique, an instruction is understood to be a charge by a superior requiring a subordinate to act, or refrain from acting, in a given circumstance.

A good order or instruction must have the following characteristics:

- The order should be reasonable.
- It should be attainable and capable of immediate compliance by subordinates.
- It should be crystal-clear and unambiguous.
- It should be one with the objective of the organization.
- The order should be time-bound, i.e. specifying the time within which it has to be carried out.
- The order should be complete and comprehensive.
- The tone of the order should be appropriate.
- Every order issued must be followed up properly.
- The order should be in writing.

Written orders and oral instructions: The order may be oral or written. But it is always better and safer to issue instructions in writing because of certain advantages, which are as follows:

- It makes the purpose of the order very clear.
- There will be continuity and clarity of thought before the issue of order.
- A written order can be understood easily, quickly and properly.
- It avoids the possibility of misunderstanding.
- Subordinates can study the instructions in detail and can execute them correctly.
- An order, if written, can be communicated simultaneously to many people.
- It can be precise, accurate and to the point.
- It improves accountability.
- It serves as documentary evidence for future reference.

But there are certain disadvantages also of a written order. They are as follows:

- It is time-consuming and expensive.
- It is very rigid.
- It is difficult to revise a written order.
- The subordinate cannot be creative, as he has to act as per the written order.

To conclude in the words of Haimann, "Oral orders are almost invariably used when the action required is relatively simple in character or routine. Also, in times of emergency, oral orders are almost always used. In order to strike a happy medium between the advantages and disadvantages of a written instruction, it is often expedient to put only the important points of the instructions in writing and to give additional information orally."

SUPERVISION

Supervision is an important element in the process of directing/leading. It is also known as *supervising management*. Supervision involves actual translation of plans into action. It means overseeing or observing the work of subordinates with authority. They should provide day-to-day guidance and instructions to the operative workers. They are also known as first-line managers, or as foremen, overseers, section heads, etc. The bottom line management has got a basic responsibility of supervising the workers in their day-to-day performance. It should be in direct touch with the actual workers.

Functions of Supervisors

Supervisors are basically line executives. Hence, they are expected to give orders, issue instructions, inform the methods, identify the procedures, explain the objectives and policies of the organization. Supervisors should keep the workers in good spirits: motivation is one of their important functions. They are responsible for the accomplishment of group tasks. Supervisors have to maintain the workers, machinery and equipment in efficient condition and secure efficient performance from them. They are delegated authority by departmental managers which they can exercise in getting work done through people. Supervisors are responsible and accountable for performance to the delegator, and the continuous chain of delegation will ultimately end up with them. They should help the workers by providing all the necessary assistance in executing their tasks. Every supervisor should have complete technical skill to guide the workers in their operations. He should also have human relations skill, so that he can secure, and develop team spirit and performance standards.

Role of Supervisors

Supervisors are placed in a strategic position in the organizational structure. They enjoy maximum authority over their workers and are considered a vital link between the management and the workers. Supervisors have to maintain order and discipline in their work groups and motivate the workers and get things done through them as per the schedule. For all practical purposes, *they* are the management for the workers. Supervisors should perform all the activities of the management. The top management and the middle-level management function through long-term planning. But the supervisors are more concerned with the short-term planning and organization. Even though the supervisors are the people performing the actual direction, still, in many organizations, they are not given a prominent position. Supervisors in such concerns are not provided with required powers and authority, with sufficient opportunities to participate in the decision making process, and are overshadowed and undermined by the staff specialists like the personnel manager, industrial engineer, cost accountant, and inspector. In most organizations, this unhappy state of affairs exists because of the fact that the supervisors are not properly trained. The quality and status of the supervisors will be substantially improved if they are properly trained and their position is recognized by the management.

Qualities of a Good Supervisor

- He must be technically competent to perform the tasks by himself.
- He must have all the qualities of a good leader.
- He should be objective and prompt in taking decisions.
- He must be a model for all the workers in efficiency, honesty and sincerity.
- He must not be short-tempered, but be patient.
- He must have a humane approach to all the problems of the workers.

Requisites of Effective Supervision

1. ***Technical knowledge of the work:*** Without knowing the methodology and technicalities of the work, the supervisor cannot function effectively. Complete and correct knowledge of the layout, location, machinery, equipment, materials, tools, and operational process is absolutely essential for effective supervision.

2. ***Managerial knowledge:*** Effective supervision requires constant attention to short-term planning, organization, directing and control.

3. ***Knowledge of rules and regulations:*** The knowledge of the policies, principles, plan, programmes, rules, regulations and procedures of the entire organization in general, and his work group in particular, is of significance to improve the effectiveness of a supervisor. It is desirable for a supervisor to possess a working knowledge of labour laws, e.g. the Workmen's Compensation Act.

4. ***Leadership qualities:*** A supervisor has to lead a group of workers. Essentially, he has to be a good leader. He must guide them by proper leading and promote harmony among them. The top management must recognize the status and position of supervisors and delegate sufficient authority and power to them.

5. ***Communication skill:*** A supervisor has to issue instructions and orders continuously to his subordinates. So, he must have perfect clarity in communication: he must have the ability to tell, listen and understand the workers properly.

6. ***Human relations skill:*** A supervisor is expected to treat his subordinates as human beings first. He is mainly concerned with instructing, guiding and inspiring people to perform their jobs effectively and efficiently; he has to motivate them and keep them in good spirits; he must recognize the workers' abilities; and keep them informed about all the developments. Wherever necessary, he has to understand their individual problems and try to provide favourable solutions for such problems. He has to build up a team spirit and unity among workers.

In the words of G.R. Terry, "Material factors, basic information, and technical knowledge are necessary, but the daily challenge to most supervisors lies not in these areas, but in stimulating group members to perform the maximum quantity and quality of work and making it possible for them to achieve contentment and satisfaction for these work efforts."

PRINCIPLES OF LEADING

Effective leading can be accomplished by the following principles:

1. *Principle of unity of objectives:* A supervisor has to integrate the personal objectives of individuals with the objectives of the organization.

2. *Principle of unity of command:* Every supervisor must have subordinates who will get commands only from *him,* and report to him *only*. Dual command is always misleading. Every worker should get the instructions only from one supervisor.

3. *Principle of direct supervision:* It is always better to have direct supervision: it will make the instruction clear and complete, and not keep the workers in doubt. Direct supervision will improve employee morale.

4. *Principle of effective communication:* Effective leading is possible only when there is an effective communication system. Channels of communication should be kept open so that the workers can also give expression to *their* ideas and feelings. Effective communication will help in avoiding misunderstanding and misinterpretation.

5. *Principle of good leadership:* The success of leading depends upon the effectiveness of the leadership. If the manager provides good leadership, subordinates will be happy to work with him. The leader should be an able guide and should counsel the workers and understand their problems.

6. *Principle of motivation:* Direction, to be effective, must inspire subordinates to do the job with interest and vigour. To make the workers perform tasks voluntarily and with the maximum interest, they must be motivated properly.

LEADERSHIP

Leading will become meaningful and effective only if there is a good leadership. *Leadership* refers to the quality of an individual who is the most influential in the group to bind the group together and to motivate the members of the group towards achievement. Leadership is absolutely essential to inspire people and inculcate team spirit.

Definitions

McFARLAND: Leadership is a process of interpersonal influence by which the executive or manager influences the activities of others in choosing and attaining given ends.

GEORGE R. TERRY: Leadership is a relationship in which one person, the leader, influences others to work together willingly on related tasks to attain that which the leader desires.

KOONTZ and O'DONNELL: Leadership is the ability of a manager to induce subordinates to work with confidence and zeal.

ROBERT TANNENBAUM, WESCHLER and MASSARICK: Leadership is a process of interpersonal relationships through which a manager attempts to influence the behaviour of others towards the attainment of predetermined objectives.

S.A. SHERLEKAR: Leadership is the influence relationship in which the leader influences others in a given situation to work together on related tasks to attain that which the leader desires. It is the ability to influence the behaviour of others in a particular direction.

DUBIN: Leadership is the exercise of authority and making of decisions.

HEMPHILL: Leadership is the initiation of acts which result in a consistent pattern of group interaction directed towards the solution of a mutual problem.

E.B. REUTER: Leadership is an ability to persuade or direct men without use of the prestige or power of formal office or external circumstance.

B.M. BASS: Leadership is the assumption of the tasks of initiating, organizing, clarifying, questioning, motivating and formulating conclusions.

According to Robert Tannenbaum, leadership is the interpersonal influence exercised in a situation and directed through a communication process towards the attainment of specified goals. It is the process of influencing the activities of an individual or a group for goal achievement in a particular situation.

Leadership has the following characteristics:

Leadership means certain personal qualities of the leader: By exercising leadership, a leader attempts to influence the behaviour of individuals to fulfil certain specified objectives. Thus, it is a process of influencing the behaviour of others in a particular way.

Leadership is a continuous process of influencing behaviour: It does not end anywhere; a leader provides guidance to his followers, whenever necessary or asked for.

Leadership is related to a situation: The style of leadership is determined by the set of circumstances prevailing. Thus, there is no one style of leadership which can be applied in all situations.

From the definitions, it is clear that leadership is convincing or influencing the followers for the accomplishment of a common goal by building confidence, and team spirit. It includes all such convincing activities resulting in securing voluntary and successful cooperation of all the persons in an organization.

Importance

Leadership is a very important element of effective management. It can influence the behaviour of individuals and motivate them; it has to identify the potential strength in every individual and convert that into reality by giving opportunity both for the individual and for the organization to prosper. A leader has to create a sense of confidence in the minds of the employees and provide motive power to group efforts. It develops a coordinated network within the organization, and directs people psychologically towards the accomplishment of group goals.

Peter F. Drucker states that in business institutions, there can be only leadership groups and not individual leaders. Managers of these institutions can collectively be the leadership groups. But individually, a manager is just another fellow employee.

Drucker also states that even the most powerful and popular heads of companies and corporations are totally unknown to the public. In a large organization, the employees themselves may not recognize the head. The authority and position of a manager is purely because of his institution. According to Drucker, it is inappropriate to speak of managers as leaders. They can only be considered "members of the leadership".

LEADERSHIP THEORIES

Leadership is one of the most fascinating and ancient subjects. Even Plato's writings have discussed leadership. Leadership qualities are different and there are different behavioural theories of leadership depicting these varied qualities of leadership. These include the trait theory and the situational theory.

Trait Theory

The trait theory can also be considered as the "great-man approach to leadership", which emphasizes "charismatic leadership". This is one of the most popular and ancient theories. This theory states that certain physical, intellectual and personality traits distinguish leaders from non-leaders. In fact, Henry Fayol classified these traits into physical, mental, moral, educational and technical, with experience, intelligence, insight, objectivity, a balanced personality, judgement, knowledge, self-confidence and cooperation. This theory says that persons with these traits will become successful leaders. The study of the lives of some of the most successful and popular leaders provides ample evidence for this belief. Even though earlier studies indicated these results, subsequent research has sufficiently proved that these traits *cannot* always ensure successful leadership. But they will place the person in a position of high esteem. Ordway Tead and Chester Barnard have done a lot of research in this field and suggested physical and nervous energy, a sense of purpose and leading, enthusiasm, friendliness and affection, integrity, technical skill, decisiveness, intelligence, teaching skill and faith, as important qualities of a good leader.

However, this theory has been criticized because of certain important defects. They are as follows:

- Studies about this theory have not produced clear results.
- These traits are not common and uniform.
- The comparative importance of various qualities has not been properly understood and reported.
- It does not recognize the influence of situational factors.
- It fails to mention the traits which are necessary to maintain leadership.

Situational Theory

The situational theory states that there are certain situations in particular groups which can mould the leadership skills in a person. The work situation and its influence is a major factor in leadership. A leader, according to this concept, understands the needs of the situation and then acts accordingly.

The situational theory does not recognize the *inborn* qualities of leadership. This theory states that there is no one "best style" of leadership universally applicable to all situations. A particular situation may create a new leader out of a person who was just a follower. The primary aspect of this theory is that leadership is the interaction between the leader and the group. But this theory states that the leadership style adopted for one particular situation may not be relevant in another situation. The situational theory rejects the "one best style" of leadership applicable to all situations. According to the leadership contingency model developed by psychologist Fred E. Fiedler, a manager's effectiveness depends upon three major factors:

- The leader-follower relationship
- The group-task structure
- The authority position of the leader.

These factors will determine whether a given situation is favourable or unfavourable to a leader. A "favourable situation" refers to a situation which enables the leader to exert his influence over the group. If the leader-follower relationship is extremely good, it is the most favourable situation and the leader enjoys the greatest relative position and power with a well-defined task structure. Another situational theory is House's path-goal model based on paths, needs and goals. This theory states that the leader will clear the path to work goals and provides rewards for the progress. Another theory of situation is Hersey and varies according to the maturity level of the followers and the demands of the situation.

Follower Theory

F.H. Sanford states that followers will make leadership possible and effective, and they will depend on leaders to satisfy their social and personal needs.

Composite Approach

Of late, there is a loud thinking that leadership is the result of the following:

- The traits
- Followers and their problems
- Situation
- Group interaction.

This provides a comprehensive view of leadership.

LEADERSHIP STYLES

There are different styles of leadership. At the beginning of the century, the leader was almost a dictator, with strong and ruthless behaviour. "Might is right" was the philosophy of such leaders. They were like aggressive and successful warriors, with their self-centred and ultra-individualistic attitudes. These industrial leaders were known as "robber barons". Any appeal for generosity and kindness only resulted in a cold response. "Survival of the Fittest", "Business is Business" and "Mind your Business" were their strategies.

Gradually, these business leaders realized that they could get things done even without being harsh. Kindness and understanding started getting place of consideration. The new leaders, called *Patternalistic*, functioned with parental affection towards the workers. But they expected loyalty, demanded respect and provided the employees with facilities which *they thought* were good for them. This change made them the most successful leaders in their ventures and they were able to compete and win against autocratic industrialists.

A lot of study has been done to understand the types or styles of leadership in different countries. Kurt Lewin suggested that leadership may be in three different styles:

- Autocracy
- Democracy
- Laissez-faire.

Rensis Likert developed the following four systems of management at the University of Michigan along with his research associates:

1. Exploitive authoritative
2. Benevolent authoritative
3. Consultative
4. Participative group.

System 1 leaders are highly autocratic and they do not trust subordinates. They manage people through punishments and creating fear. Sometimes they give some rewards also.

System 2 leaders always patronize confidence and trust in subordinates.

System 3 leaders have some confidence and trust in their subordinates. They consult the subordinates for getting their ideas and opinions for taking decisions to some extent.

System 4 leaders have trust and confidence in their subordinates. They receive the ideas of subordinates and give importance to their views while taking decisions.

Likert also observed that System 4 was highly successful and accepted by several leaders and liked by many employees. Therefore, several companies are following participatory style of management, which proved to be successful.

Autocratic Leadership

Autocratic leadership generally creates an immediate impression of a strict, inconsiderate leader with arbitrary rule. An autocratic leader keeps all the authority and decision-making power with himself and assumes full responsibility for situations. He expects implicit obedience from subordinates and never allows them to influence his decisions. Threats of punishment are used frequently. These types of leaders can succeed in emergency or crisis situations. But it can only be a temporary success and can be effective only with untrained, illiterate and unorganized labour. But in the long run, it can only bring down the morale of the employees and it may be strongly resisted also.

Management development programmes are not encouraged by such leaders. Edwin B. Flippo in his, *Management: A Behavioural Approach*, states that autocratic leader may be of three kinds. They are:

1. Hard-boiled autocrats
2. Benevolent autocrats
3. Manipulative autocrats.

A *hard-boiled autocrat* uses strong and negative influences and passes orders to subordinates which may result in employees becoming resentful and quarrelsome. A *benevolent autocrat* uses good techniques of positive leadership. He uses appreciation and praise to secure personal loyalty and to make workers accept his decisions. A *manipulative autocrat* is a decision maker by himself, but creates an impression among subordinates that they too are participating in the decision making. Autocratic leadership can create obstacles for coordination and group cohesion, and the unity of objective may be destroyed.

Democratic or Participative Leadership

Democratic leadership is also called *consultative leadership*. A leader functions through joint action; he takes decisions through discussion. A democratic manager would be willing to decentralize authority; he believes in persuasion rather than punishment. A leader of this style will encourage ideas and suggestions of subordinates. He will inspire them and encourage their intelligence, skill and creative talents. This style of leadership is more effective in developing a favourable and efficient work climate.

Democratic leadership will create self-confidence in workers and help the leader to win the confidence, loyalty and cooperation of all the subordinates. If the subordinates are educated and organized, this leadership functions more effectively. Democratic leadership paves the way for better labour relations, high employee morale, collective decision making, development of skill and abilities, reduction of employee complaints and more job satisfaction for workers.

Laissez-faire or Free-rein Leadership

Laissez-faire is a kind of leadership which gives full authority to the group to make its own decisions. A free-rein manager will entrust decision making to his subordinates with the least intervention. The subordinates are expected to plan, organize and execute; the group enjoys complete freedom and the leader can help the group when needed. This permissive style of leadership can function effectively if the subordinates are highly competent and duty-conscious. It provides an opportunity for every individual worker to give expression to his creative talents, self-discipline and self-control.

The research of Lewin and White clearly demonstrates that the democratic condition is superior to the autocratic condition. Laissez-faire or free-rein leadership was the poorest from every angle. A democratic leader was the most popular. Reduced conflict and increased cooperation were the result of such leadership: subordinates assumed responsibilities and independence. In democratic leadership, work continued when the leader left the room, but in autocratically-led groups, members quit work when the leader stepped out. A greater "We" feeling prevailed in the democratically-led groups, and an outsider could not divide them. In autocratically-led groups, there was a tendency for cliques to form, and an outsider could cause the group members to turn against one another.

Managerial Grid

Robert R. Blake and Jane S. Mouton have done in-depth studies of leader behaviour and its impact on groups. Various leadership styles with reference to such behaviour are presented by Blake and Mouton, in what is popularly known as a *managerial grid*. They have considered two important factors, viz. "concern for production" and "concern for people". "Concern for production", according to Blake and Mouton, "could be seen in the quality of policy decisions; the number of creative ideas that, applied to research, turn into useful products, procedures or processes; the number of accounts processed; the quality and toughness of staff services; work load and efficiency measurements; and the volume of sales or units of physical output". "Concern for people" is concern for a degree of personal commitment to completing the job one is responsible for; accountability based on trust rather than obedience; self-esteem or the personal worth of an individual; establishing and maintaining good working conditions; and maintaining an equitable salary structure and fringe benefits. In their managerial grid concept, Blake and Mouton accept the fact that there will be conflict between the concerns for production and people. They have described five different types of leadership based on concern for production (tasks) and concern for people (relationship). They are as follows:

1. Impoverished
2. Country club
3. Task
4. Middle-of-the-road
5. Team.

Impoverished leadership [1, 1] will have less concern for both production and people. Country club leaders [1, 9] have great concern for people, but lack of production orientation. Task masters [9, 1] are production-oriented leaders and have less concern for people. Middle-of-the-road [5, 5] leaders show common concern both for production and people. Team leaders [9, 9] will maintain a high degree of concern both for production and people. By such an analysis, Blake and Mouton have provided a "method of analysing leaders without labelling them as either autocratic or democratic". Figure 7.1 reveals these grid dimensions clearly.

LEADERSHIP QUALITIES

To make an effective leader, many of the following qualities are essential. These qualities will enlighten and enrich the skill of a person to lead effectively. Varied qualities have been suggested by different experts to enable good leadership.

George Terry

- Energy
- Emotional stability

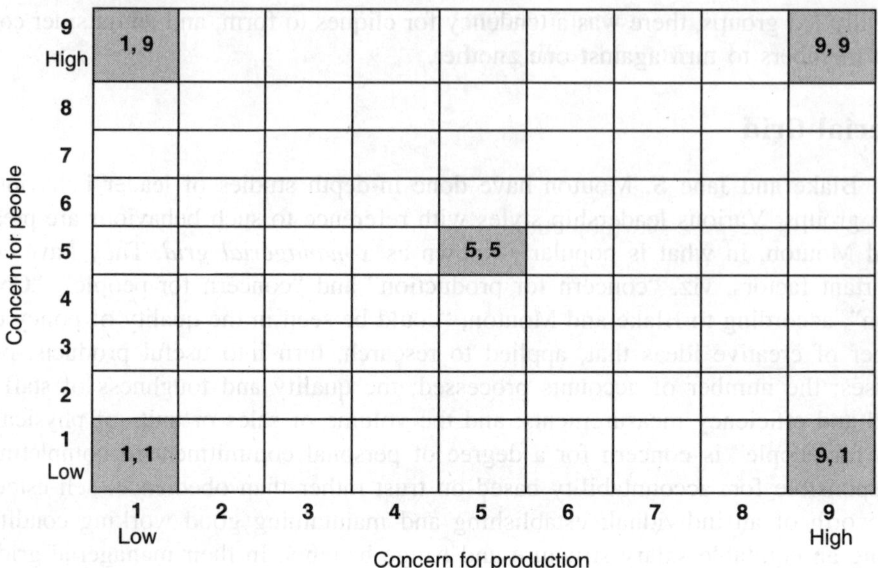

Figure 7.1 Managerial grid.

- Human relations skill
- Empathy
- Objectivity
- Personal motivation
- Communication skill
- Teaching ability
- Social skill
- Technical competence.

Field Marshal Viscount Montgomery

- Courage
- Will power
- Judgement
- Flexibility
- Knowledge
- Integrity.

N.R.F. Maier

- Ability to present and communicate

- Ability to clarify the area of freedom
- Respect for the rights and feelings of others.

Ordway Tead

- Physical and nervous energy
- A sense of purpose and objection
- Enthusiasm
- Friendliness and affection
- Integrity
- Technical mastery
- Decisiveness
- Intelligence
- Teaching skill
- Faith.

Chester Barnard

- Commanding subordinates' admiration by an outstanding physique
- Skill
- Technology
- Perception
- Knowledge
- Memory
- Imagination and developing individual superiority by determination, persistence, endurance and courage.

Mary Smith

- Intelligence
- Good decision-making power
- Insight
- Imagination
- Responsibility
- Sense of humour
- Balanced personality
- Sense of justice.

Ralph-Stogdill

- Capacity (which includes intelligence, alertness, verbal facility, originality and judgement)
- Achievement (which includes scholarship, knowledge, and athletic accomplishments)

- Responsibility (which includes dependability, initiative, persistence, aggressiveness, self-confidence, and the desire to excel)
- Participation (which includes activity, stability, cooperation, adaptability, and humour)
- Status (including socio-economic position and popularity)
- Situation (including mental level, status and skill).

Parkinson and Rustomji

- Knowledge of subordinates
- Good training
- Ability to understand and handle grievances
- Ability to get along
- Ability to distinguish and to manage by example
- Effective communication
- Motivation ability
- Ability to anticipate crisis
- Cost consciousness
- Sincerity.

Cecil E. Goode

- The leader is somewhat more intelligent than his followers.
- The leader is a well-rounded individual from the standpoint of interests and aptitudes; he tends towards interests, aptitudes, and knowledge with respect to a wide variety of fields.
- The leader is mentally and emotionally mature; he has come of age mentally and emotionally, as well as physically.
- The leader has a powerful inner drive or motivation which impels him to strive for accomplishment.
- The leader is fully aware of the importance of cooperative effort in getting things done, and therefore understands and practices the so-called social skills very effectively.
- The leader relies on his administrative skills to a much greater extent than he does on any of the technical skills which may be associated directly with his work.

MANAGER AND LEADER

The distinctions between a *manager* and a *leader* are as follows.

Manager	*Leader*
(a) Does things right	(a) Does the right things
(b) Efficient in climbing success ladder	(b) Chooses the right wall for leaning the ladder

Manager	*Leader*
(c) Works well in peacetime	(c) Works well in crises also
(d) Plans and budgets	(d) Sets direction
(e) Performs organizing and staffing functions	(e) Performs aligning function
(f) Utilizes material resources	(f) Utilizes human resources
(g) Uses authority	(g) Uses power
(h) Manages people	(h) Inspires people

PRACTICES OF LEADERSHIP

The following are the practices of exemplary leadership according to some experiences. Leadership is mostly related to behaviour. It focusses on modeling the way; inspiring a shared vision; challenging the process; enabling others to act on mission, and encouraging the people.

SUMMARY

1. Leading plays an important role in managing a business.
2. Leading has direct concern with various managerial activities.
3. Supervisors play a strategic role in an organization.
4. The supervisor must have all the qualities of a good leader.
5. The theories of leadership show the qualities of a leader.
6. There are different styles of leadership.
7. Various leadership styles based on human relationships were advocated by Blake and Mouton.
8. Several management gurus have listed the qualities of good leaders.
9. Leaders always inspire people.

REVIEW QUESTIONS

1. Explain briefly the features and principles of leading.
2. Define an "order". Bring out the essentials of a good order.
3. What is meant by supervision? What are the requisites of effective supervision?
4. Explain the various functions of a supervisor.
5. Define "leading". Bring out its characteristics.
6. Explain briefly the concept of a managerial grid.
7. What are the qualities of a successful leader?
8. "Good leadership is an integral part of effective direction". Elucidate.
9. Distinguish between a manager and a leader.

CASE STUDY

Twin Cities Insurance Company

Rajesh is 22 years old and will be receiving his masters degree in human resources management from the University of Hyderabad at the end of this semester. He had spent the past two summers working for Twin Cities Insurance Company (TCIC), filling in on a number of different jobs while employees took their vacations. He has received and accepted an offer to join TCIC on a permanent basis upon postgraduation, as a supervisor in the policy renewal department.

Twin Cities is a large insurance company. In the headquarters office alone, where Rajesh will work, they have 5,000 employees. The company believes strongly in the personal development of its employees. This translates into a philosophy, emanating from the top executive offices, of trust and respect for all TCIC employees. The job Rajesh will be assuming requires him to direct the activities of 22 clerks. Their jobs require little training and are quite routine in nature. A clerk's responsibility is to ensure that renewal notices are sent on current policies, tabulate any changes in premium from a standardized table, and advise the sales division if a policy is to be cancelled as a result of non-response to renewal notices.

Rajesh's group is composed entirely of women, ranging from 19 to 62 years of age, with a median age of 23. For the most part, they are matriculates with little prior working experience. The salary range for policy renewal clerks is ₹920 to ₹1,070 per month. Rajesh will be replacing a long-time TCIC employee, Manohar. Manohar is retiring after 37 years with TCIC, the last 14 spent as policy renewal supervisor. Since Rajesh had spent a few weeks in Manohar's group last summer, he was familiar with Manohar's style and also knew most of the group members. He anticipated no problems from any of his soon-to-be employees, except possibly for Subhash. Subhash was well into his fifties, had been a policy renewal clerk for over a dozen years, and as the "grand old man", carried a lot of weight with group members. Rajesh concluded that without Subhash's support, his job could prove very difficult.

Rajesh is determined to get his career off on the right foot. As a result, he had been doing a lot of thinking about the qualities of an effective leader.

Questions for Discussion

1. What are the critical factors that will influence Rajesh's success as a leader? Would these factors be the same if success were defined as group productivity?
2. Do you think that Rajesh can choose a leadership style? If so, describe the style you think would be most effective for him. If not, why?
3. What suggestions might you make to Rajesh to help him win over or control Subhash?

FURTHER READING

Fielder, F.E., *A Theory of Leadership Effectiveness*, McGraw-Hill, New York, 1967.

Maslow, Abraham, *Motivation and Personality*, Harper & Row, New York, 1954.

Stoner, James A. et al., *Management,* Pearson/Prentice Hall, New Delhi, 2005.

Communication

CONTENTS

INTRODUCTION

Communication is essential to minimize conflict, confusion and chaos. It eliminates friction, frustration and helps in motivating people. Communication is a vital link, a process of linking executives to workmen and workers to superiors. It is a dynamic interactive process of connecting people to people. As Raymond V. Lesikar states in his *Business communication,*

70 per cent of our active hours are spent in communicating verbally, listening, speaking, reading and writing—in that order.

The term *communication* is derived from the original Latin word *communis*, which means "common". It involves the act of imparting a common idea or understanding to another person and covers any behaviour that affects an exchange of meaning. Communication basically refers to the meaningful transmission of ideas to others, either orally or in writing. It can also take the form of symbols, codes, electronic impulses or even silence. Communication has become a very significant subject today not only for management experts, but also for technicians, engineers, psychologists, sociologists and organizational theorists.

IMPORTANCE

Communication is very important for the smooth functioning and survival of any organization. Chester Barnard states that "the very first function of a manager is to develop and maintain a system of communication as it is the foundation of cooperative group activity". The success of all management functions depends on successful communication. It shapes and moulds the strength and character of the organization. It links people and purposes together in an organization.

Communication is very important because planning requires perfect *understanding*. Communication is the art of telling, listening and understanding. It is significant because information regarding alterations must be communicated to help executives in the decision-making process. After decision making, decisions have to be communicated for their execution. It is also essential to know whether plans are being achieved. In the light of this, it is obvious that without proper communication, even the basic functions like planning, organizing, directing and controlling cannot be performed. A regular and effective system of communication will help workers to understand the needs and objectives of the organization. It will help in integrating group efforts. Executives are expected to communicate not only within the organization, but also with outsiders like customers, shareholders, government officers and union leaders.

Communication helps in promoting the efficiency and success of managers. George R. Terry states that "Communication serves as the lubricant fostering the smooth operation of the management process." The very concept of management is to get things done through others, which means communication is the *only* means of getting things done through others. It helps workers to develop faith in their work, and results in satisfactory performance. Communication increases group understanding and team work. A manager can convey his ideas, feelings and decisions, workers can convey their responses, feelings, decisions, attitudes, problems and complaints to the managers through the medium of communication. Secrecy and silence are always dangerous in any group endeavour as they create suspicion and jealousy. It may also create a lot of misunderstanding. Understanding through regular communication will avoid such possibilities. Effective communication will help in developing mutual trust and confidence between superiors and subordinates and provide more job satisfaction to workers.

In the pre-Industrial Revolution era and in its early stages, communication was confined only to the issue of instructions or orders. But, gradually, the research activities of behavioural scientists and human relations experts emphasized the growing need for effective communication in a wider perspective. The growing strength of trade unions and their desire to share information with the management is another factor responsible for the growth of communication. Modern business organizations are expected to fulfil their social obligations towards customers, shareholders, the government, etc. These organizations are expected to inform such concerned segments regularly about their efforts. Modern organizations are so complex and huge that they essentially require sound and stable systems of communication.

DEFINITIONS

CYRIL L. HUDSON: Communication in its simplest form is conveying of information from one person to another.

LOUIS A. ALLEN: Communication is the sum of all the things one person does when he wants to create understanding in the mind of another. It is a bridge of meaning. It involves a systematic and continuous process of telling, listening and understanding.

THEO HAIMANN: Communication is the process of passing information and understanding from one person to another.... It is the process of imparting ideas and making oneself understood by others.

CHARLES E. REDFIELD: Communication is the broad field of human understanding and interchange of facts and opinions and not the technologies of telephone, telegraph, radio and the like.

KOONTZ and O'DONNELL: Communication is an exchange of facts, ideas, opinions or emotions by two or more people.

KEITH DAVIS: Communication is the process of passing information and understanding from one person to another. It is essentially a bridge of meaning between people. By using this bridge of meaning, a person can safely cross the river of misunderstanding that separates all people.

NEWMAN and SUMMER: Communication is an exchange of facts, ideas, opinions or emotions by two or more persons.

Careful scrutiny of the above definitions will reveal that communication essentially involves at least two people: only one person cannot communicate. Communication is both information and understanding. It includes all possible means by which matter is conveyed from person to person. Communication is directed towards a response.

COMMUNICATION PROCESS

Communication is a process. This process is applicable to all forms of communication and includes the following elements:

- Source
- Encoder
- Message
- Channel
- Receiver
- Decoder
- Understanding
- Feedback

Source → Encoder → Message → Channel → Receiver → Decoder → Understanding → Feedback →

Source: Any person who conveys a thought, idea or information can be considered a *source*. He is also called a *sender*. He will initiate an idea to be transmitted.

Encoder: All such ideas, feelings, mental perceptions translated into a code is *encoding*. The sender puts the meaning of his idea in some organized form or series of symbols.

Message: It is the actual subject matter of communication. It may be in the form of spoken words, printed letters, facial expressions or even gestures of the body.

Channel: After encoding the message, the sender has to select a medium or channel for sending the information. The *channel* is the link connecting the sender and the receiver.

Receiver: The person receiving the message is called the *receiver*. The process of communication will be incomplete without a receiver.

Decoding: A receiver, after receiving a message, has to decode it so that it can be understood.

Understanding: After decoding the message, the receiver has to understand it in the *same sense* in which it was sent.

***Feedback*:** If the receiver understands the message and is willing to act or react or respond, he will send feedback information to the sender. It helps the sender to know whether or not his message has been understood in the right perspective.

PRINCIPLES OF COMMUNICATION

Important principles of communication are:

- Clarity
- Completeness
- Consciousness
- Courtesy
- Correctness.

PROBLEMS OF COMMUNICATION

Communication problems are mainly of four types:

1. *The perception problem:* *Perception* is the ability to perceive things in the same sense. People have a tendency to perceive things only in a set pattern, depending upon their experience. People may receive only things liked by them and omit those which conflict with their experience. Variation in perception is a problem. Perception may differ because of difference in the individual's ability to hear, see, feel, smell, etc. The perception of women will be different from that of men. The perception of the educated will be different from that of the uneducated. Communication can be made more effective if proper awareness is created about this problem of perception.

2. *The semantic problem:* *Semantic* means the systematic study of the meaning of words. The meaning of a word can itself create a communication problem: a person may say one thing and the receiver may hear it differently, even though the word is the same. If the word used is a complex, infrequently used or abstract one, then this problem may crop up. If a word has got two meanings, then also there is a possibility of misunderstanding.

3. *The technological problem:* There may be a problem in the accurate transmission of certain symbols. Such problems are technological in nature. Cybernetics is a comparatively new discipline which provides precise meanings for some terms to overcome this problem. Technological problems may also be present in the process of transmission, e.g. "snow" in the television and "disturbance" in the radio. This may result in a loss of information because of noise.

4. *The effectiveness problem:* This is a problem pertaining to effectiveness of communication. If the communication is straight or direct, it is more effective. If the distance or the levels are more, or the size of the organization increases, the communication problem also increases. If the message is transmitted across efficiently and if it is accepted effectively, then communication will be more effective.

FUNDAMENTALS OF COMMUNICATION

Peter F. Drucker states that there are four fundamentals of communication:

1. *Communication is perception:* According to this concept, communication is created not by the sender but by the receiver. In a forest if a tree crashes down and if there is no one around to hear, there will not be any sound. There are sound *waves* only. It becomes a sound only when a person *perceives* it, as sound is created by *perception*. Drucker states that communication is effective when people perceive things in the correct perspective. When something is said, different people can understand it differently, depending upon their intimacy, hostility, mood, etc. The executive has to create a favourable environment so as to generate proper perception.

2. *Communication is expectation:* Everyone's psychology is to hear or see only what he *expects* to hear or see. If there are unexpected events, either they are not heard, or not seen. It is a subconscious attempt to ignore such unexpected things. Even though a lot of information is transmitted, workers will have the tendency of selecting and receiving only such information which they expect. It is better for a manager to understand such expectations of employees so that he can make the communication better and effective.

3. *Communication makes demands:* Every communication tries to act on others. Words are not meant for mere information: they carry emotional charges also. Words which have a pleasant impact will be received and retained, words with an unpleasant or threatening impact will be suppressed, as communication demands the receiver either to *do* something or to *believe* something. The manager should know the nature of such demands, and should make them pleasantly and convincingly so as to make them acceptable to his subordinates.

4. *Communication and information are different:* Indeed, they are largely opposite, yet interdependent. Where communication is perception, information is logic. Information is formal and impersonal. If the information is free from emotions, values, expectations and perceptions, it will become more authentic, valid and reliable. In fact, it becomes increasingly informative. So, an executive has to send the message in the language in which the receiver can understand it with authenticity.

COMMUNICATION BASED ON DIRECTION

There are mainly four different structures or types of communication based on the direction. These are as follows:

1. ***Upward communication:*** It is the communication fed to managers by subordinates to enable management to know the effectiveness of execution of orders. Such feedback to the higher authorities may be in the form of complaints, suggestions, activity reports, opinions, grievances, etc. Management can itself try to get such communication to know the feelings and response of the subordinates. If communication goes upwards voluntarily, much of it may not be heard. Managers may not lend their ears to juniors. Sometimes, information reaching the top may be distorted. So, the final success of this type of communication depends upon the attitude and receptivity of the management. If managers can develop an open door policy and receive information with open minds, they can get the real picture of the situation. Distortion is the main problem in upward communication. If there are yes-men around the managers, then all vital information gets distorted. So, managers at strategic points should develop an internal check or cross-check to ascertain the accuracy of the information.

Upward communication encourages participative management. It can create a feeling of belongingness; help to evaluate the communication; and make the subordinates happy as the managers can show a concern for the suggestions, opinions and ideas of each individual. Upward communication should be real and not fictitious. If an executive announces an open door policy and invites people, he should be sincere. If he constantly checks his watch, his appointment diary, calendar, or wall clock, the very purpose will be defeated.

2. ***Downward communication:*** The process of delegation of authority can itself take the form of downward communication. When a communication is sent down the line in the organizational hierarchy, it is known as downward communication. Management can give orders, issue directives, and instructions, so that the subordinates can initiate actions. Downward communication will provide information about the system, objectives, plans, procedures and practices. This method of communication is helpful in having effective control also. But downward communication is considered a traditional concept of organizational behaviour. In downward communication, most managers believe that the more information, the better. Such executives believe that more information will improve performance, quality of work, satisfaction and the morale of the workers. But it is not the quantity of communication, it is the quality of information which is more important. In fact, quality of communication is the key to success. Downward communication has two functions: it should communicate and motivate simultaneously, and should make the people feel that they are well-informed.

3. ***Horizontal communication:*** Richard L. Simpson observed that communication among foremen was mainly horizontal in view of the mechanized nature of their work. Horizontal communication is transmission of information among people at the same level. In many cases, horizontal communication will be of an informal nature. This type of communication helps to achieve coordination and team work.

4. ***Diagonal communication:*** It is a type of communication which exists at different levels of an organization. It crosses different departmental boundaries at different levels to increase organizational efficiency.

COMMUNICATION NETWORK

A communication network reflects the interconnecting links or interaction among the members of an organization. It provides channels of information to the organizational structure. There are five popular types of networks: Wheel, Circle, Free flow, Chain and Y-type networks.

1. ***Wheel type network:*** It is a network where all communication of subordinates must necessarily pass through the person at the centre. For example, if there are five people in a structure, four people can communicate only with the fifth person at the centre. It does not provide any scope for interactions among the subordinates. Communication will be quick, effective and intimate in this network. But as subordinates are expected to communicate only with the manager, it encourages autocratic leadership and reduces employee morale.

2. ***Circular network:*** It is a type of network where each person can communicate with his two neighbours only. It provides a three-level structure, giving importance to all the executives. It is more democratic in nature; increases employee morale; and is effective, particularly for complex problems. But it is slower, and correct information cannot be fully transformed.

3. ***Free flow or all-channel network:*** In this network, all the subordinates in the structure are free to communicate with others. There is free flow of communication in all directions. This provides the maximum opportunity for free expression to everyone.

4. ***Chain network:*** A chain network includes five different levels in which communication can take place. It is a vertical type of network.

5. ***Y network:*** This is a type of network with a Y shape. It has a four-level structure. It is a harmonious blend of both the wheel and chain networks. At the higher level, it takes a wheel shape, and at the lower level, a chain network.

OTHER TYPES OF COMMUNICATION

1. ***Formal communication:*** It is a type of communication in which all official orders, instructions and messages are routed through hierarchical channels. The authority and responsibility relationships will also be formal in this communication. The principles of unity of command and control can be followed smoothly in formal communication. Most formal communication will be in writing. But formal communication is not flexible.

2. ***Informal communication:*** Besides general formal communication, there will be many informal communication channels in an organization. They are not officially recognized or routed through established channels. Most such communication can be developed through the informal interaction of groups in an organization. Informal communication does not function in a predetermined authority and responsibility relationship.

3. *Grapevine:* It is an important type of informal communication. Grapevines arise from the social and personal interests of people, rather than the formal requirements of an organization. The term grapevine probably came into being because it was thought to be a long-winding means of communication from one point to another, like a real grapevine, i.e. one that bears grapes. A grapevine provides expression to the natural motivation of people to communicate. It is a much faster and more direct form of communication. Even though a grapevine is more common among workers, it is equally active among managers. It is a matter of fact that wherever there are people, there are grapevines. It is a person-to-person method of relaying secret reports that cannot be obtained through regular channels.

Keith Davis, who conducted a study on grapevine, revealed that the wife of a plant supervisor had a baby at 11 pm and a plant survey the next day at 2 pm revealed that 46 per cent of the managerial personnel knew of it through the grapevine. A grapevine functions wherever formal communication cannot function. In certain cases, it supplements formal communication. A grapevine is fast and dynamic if the news is very significant. The people who keep this grapevine active are called *liaison individuals*. Most of them will usually partly act in a predictable manner, which helps the management in influencing the grapevine. A grapevine exists largely through word of mouth and observation. As the grapevine has no reliable source to which people can refer to confirm facts, it can carry rumour or distorted information. But a good management can make use of a grapevine to spread certain urgent messages. Management has to allow grapevine communication as it is one of the primary sources of upward communication. In management groups, a grapevine is more spontaneous and flexible. Management should understand the source, channels and impact of the grapevine in the organization and should try to develop it into positive, rather than negative communication. Even though a grapevine is not formal communication, it represents normal management communication.

4. *Rumour:* Rumour is the negative by-product of a grapevine. In fact, the concept of a grapevine has been misunderstood by many because of rumour. It is the untrue or incorrect part of a grapevine. Sometimes rumours can come to be true, but it is unusual. Rumours get distorted when they pass from person to person.

5. *Propaganda:* Communication can also be propaganda. Propaganda is different from open discussion or objective conversation. It comes into action during war or periods of crisis. Either the union may make propaganda or the management can. If propaganda is intense, it can be very powerful. According to Peter F. Drucker, the danger of total propaganda is not that the propaganda will be believed, but that every communication becomes suspect. In the final analysis, no communication will be received with trust. The end results of total propaganda are not fanatics, but cynics.

COMMUNICATION METHODS

There are three important methods of communication. They are as follows:

1. *Verbal communication:* It is a face-to-face type of communication involving conversation. Conversation is a natural human activity, and a more effective method of communication. It provides clarity, accuracy, certainty and nearness for communication. Verbal communication can also be made through mechanical devices like telephones, intercoms, dictating machines, etc. In organizations, verbal communication is popular both for downward and upward communication. Instructions, lectures, orders and counselling are done through verbal communication. It helps in getting quick responses and good feedback. It develops a friendly environment, cooperation and team spirit. In emergency situations, it is the best method of communication. But the problem is distance or misunderstanding. It creates legal difficulties also as there will not be any documentary evidence.

2. *Written communication:* It is the most important medium of communication. Orders, instructions, circulars, manuals, handbooks, etc. are provided only through written communication. It can be transmitted simultaneously to numerous persons. Workers can also give their suggestions and grievances in writing. Written communication serves as a permanent reference; it is official and more effective; it should be drafted clearly, correctly, completely and convincingly to make it effective.

3. *Gesticulation:* It is a method supplementary to verbal communication. A handshake, a pat on the back, can be effective gesticulation, communicating appreciation or praise.

THE ART OF LISTENING

Communication is a continuous process of telling, listening and understanding. But most people who can talk and convince are not good at listening. Research conducted by Harry Goldstein in this regard states that the USA has overlooked a very important element in its educational system, that of refining the ability to listen. He also states that it is perfectly possible to listen to a speech, without losing comprehension, at three times the normal speaking rate. Richard Hubbell, another expert, declared without equivocation that 98 per cent of all that a man learns is by his ears. After the publication of this research, several business houses, industries and government departments in the United States instituted listening training programmes for selected management personnel. A good listener will always be hunting for real and practical and profitable information, and can store that away at the back of the mind. Listeners should bother more about the *substance* than the *form* of communication.

ESSENTIALS OF GOOD COMMUNICATION

1. *Have clarity of thought:* The idea to be communicated should be clear and complete without any conflict or confusion. Employee communication in particular should be specific, meaningful and clear, without any abstract ideas and vagueness. The language spoken should be common and understandable.

2. *Communication should be functional:* A superior who states that he will trust the workers and then proceeds to make unnecessary or too many checks on the workers will fail in communication. He must say what he means, and he must mean what he says. A manager who insists on the punctuality of workers can make the communication functional only when *he* is punctual. This is essential because it is human psychology to discount a message when the attitudes and actions behind it contradict it.

3. ***Develop participation:*** Communication cannot be a one-way traffic. Both the communication channels should be kept open. Workers are not mere listeners; they also will have something to say. Managers should encourage participative communication so as to have an objective and perfect understanding of situations.

4. ***Plan the transmission:*** A communicator has to plan carefully about what to communicate. One has to plan about the media and channels to make the communication most effective. A harmonious blend of both formal and informal channels will make the communication more effective.

5. ***Develop listening systems:*** Listening plays a vital role in the perfect understanding of a communication. It is an art which can be developed by continuous practice. There is a tendency on the part of managers not to listen to workers with real interest, which should be avoided. Good listening is good understanding.

6. ***Maintain cordial superior-subordinate relationship:*** Effective communication is possible only when the employer-employee relationship is cordial. There must be mutual trust, faith and perfect understanding on both sides. Coordination on the part of managers and cooperation on the part of workers will help in making the communication more effective.

7. ***Regulate the flow of information:*** Communication flow should be optimum without any shortage or overloading. Communication should not create a gap because of shortages, or be a burden because of overloading. Top management need not go through all the incoming messages. Only exceptionally important messages can be handed over to the top management and the remaining routine matters can be decided at the lower level itself.

8. ***Use feedback effectively:*** Feedback will give a suitable response to the sender of the communication. Immediate and prompt feedback will make the communication very clear.

BARRIERS TO COMMUNICATION

There are various barriers to good and effective communication. But the main barrier is the fact that many organizations really do not provide or encourage two-way communication. There are other barriers causing breakdowns, distortion or rumours. If these barriers are removed, a considerable degree of effectiveness and accuracy can be achieved in communication. The following are the important barriers to communication:

1. ***Barriers in organizational structure:*** A rigid and ultra-formal organizational structure creates problems of communication. Ulrich and Booz have stated that good communication exists where anyone in the organization is free to contact whoever can help him with his problems. Long lines of communication, great distance of subordinates from superiors, lack of proper and regular instructions, and overloading of work at certain levels of authority may also create barriers of communication.

2. ***Semantic barriers:*** Semantics is the science of *meaning*. The receiver of the message should perceive and understand the message in the same sense in which the sender has communicated it. As words will have different meanings, they may be understood in different senses by different people.

3. ***Difference in status or rank:*** Difference in rank and status is always a source of misunderstanding. The placing of persons in superior and subordinate relationships may inhibit a free flow of information, ideas, suggestions and questions. What the superior sees in his position as *responsibility*, the subordinate sees as *power.* Sometimes, mild criticism or a small piece of advice given by a superior to help a subordinate may be taken as a strong reprimand. The greater is the rank difference, the greater will be the distortion. Factors which increase the rank barriers are unavailability at short notice, special executive chambers, elaborate offices, etc. The superior with his status may feel that he cannot fully admit to his subordinates those problems, conditions or results which may reflect adversely on his ability and judgement.

4. ***Badly expressed messages:*** Messages which are vague, abstract, lack coherence, have poor sentence formation, are repetitive, etc. may affect the quality of the communication.

5. ***Faulty translation:*** Language is an important barrier. Every type of information has to be translated into understandable pieces of information.

6. ***Loss by transmission and retention:*** In oral communication, 30 per cent of the information is lost in each transmission. Even in written communication, there may be poor retention.

7. ***Distrust of the communicator:*** If a superior has no trust and confidence in his employees, he will tend to listen to them in a prejudiced or biased manner. Ultimately, this may result in inaccurate responses and ineffective communication.

8. ***Faulty listening:*** Telling will be meaningless unless someone is listening to it. Listening requires thinking, processing and understanding the message. One must have patience, interest and active participation in listening.

9. ***Emotional approach:*** When a communication is packed with emotion, there will not be any objectivity in it.

10. ***Resistance to change:*** When new ideas are introduced, they may not be welcomed by employees as they may prefer to maintain status quo. Change in timing or methodology may not be received immediately and accepted well.

11. ***Overloading of communication:*** Overloading of communication channels may create a traffic jam in the channels resulting in noise and irrelevant messages, as happens often in telephones.

One can overcome all such barriers by planning the communication system properly, and by recognizing the human elements involved in it. Messages must be direct and simple; the language should be understandable; provision for a good feedback system has to be made; listening should be proper and effective; and there must be coherence, clarity and consistency in communication.

Methods of Overcoming Communication Barriers

- Each and every employee in an organization should take responsibility for sending message.
- For communicating a particular message, the management has to follow the upward, downward or horizontal systems.

- The management has to inform all employees about the need for communication.
- The message should be sent in a simple and clear language.
- A good information system should be established.
- If necessary, communication should be sent informally.
- Employees must send correct information.

Effective Communication

For effective communication, the American Management Association has identified the following points:

- A clear message
- Advantage of communication
- Understanding the physical and human environments
- Consultation with other experts in preparing the information
- Discussion on important aspects of communication
- The values of the receiver
- Importance of the communication
- Follow-up action
- Completing the job as per the communication
- Possessing good listening skills.

SPECIAL COMMUNICATION

There are various special types of communication which are not basically verbal communication. The following are important elements of such communication:

1. ***The face:*** The face is the index of the mind; one can read it and understand the whole personality. The face is considered the primary source of information of the real feelings like happiness, surprise, fear, anxiety, anger, etc. It helps in providing good feedback. It can also be used to hide many feelings.

2. ***The eyes:*** The eyes are considered the "Portals to the Soul". They help in initiating communication. To start any communication with others, we first try to catch their eye. If a person is not interested in talking to someone, he will avoid eye contact.

3. ***The body:*** The entire body, its posture and, gestures can provide non-verbal communication and be interpreted easily. A dancer can "speak" completely for hours together through her body only.

4. ***The posture:*** The very fact that managers usually assume a more relaxed position than their subordinates communicates the status of relationships. When a subordinate enters the chamber of an officer, he usually remains standing until a seat is offered by the officer.

5. ***Touch:*** Nodding the head indicates welcome, liking, acceptance and greeting. It is a positive communication which is widely accepted. People who give a firm, meaningful handshake are

perceived better by other men than those who give a weak handshake. A pat on the back may indicate encouragement, sympathy, understanding and liking or support.

6. ***The appearance:*** The neatness, physical appearance, and dress of a person often influence others. The first impressions are usually based on how the person looks.

PATTERNS OF COMMUNICATION

Communication, in most cases, gets blocked because people have fear and pain within them. In such cases, communication becomes self-deceptive, as the person loses his sense of identity and integrity. John Powell and Sharu S. Rangnekar state that as a person grows, he can improve communication which will pass through five different stages, as follows.

1. ***Cliché conversation:*** In this, there is no real communication. Persons will be isolated, with pretension and unnecessary mannerisms and sophistication. Paul Simon sings:

And in the naked night I see ten thousand people, be more; people talking—without speaking, people hearing—without listening, people writing songs that voices never shared, no one dared—Disturb the sound of silence.

It is at this stage that silence becomes communication.

2. ***External communication:*** In this, a person will be supremely happy to speak to others only about mundane affairs or routine matters as narrated by others. In the process, he will never offer any personal comments, and no one will be able to identify the personality of the communicator.

3. ***Self-communication:*** In this, the basic ideas and thinking of a person finds expression. In this communication, the communicator is cautious, and if the other shows signs of hostility, the message is immediately withdrawn, and silence, change in the subject, or more pleasing topics are then discussed.

4. ***Real feeling communication:*** Real feelings will differentiate one man from another. Ideas and thoughts may be similar, but the feelings may be different. The feelings and sentiments may not be appreciated by others, and people put up gentlemanly appearances and try to develop superficial relationships.

5. ***Peak communication:*** Understanding, perfection, precision, and honesty have expression in this. Communication will be at its peak and relationships will be normal, real and sincere. Immature communication will change into effective and mature communication.

Sharu R. Rangnekar has classified the different games and roles people play to avoid real communication. This classification is very interesting. These models are as follows:

- *All heart.* He is highly sentimental and excessively tender, as a compensation for his sadistic tendencies, he shows special concern.
- *The body beautiful.* Physical vanity as a compensation for the growing sense of inferiority of a person.
- *The braggart.* Has a desire to feel very important as a compensation for being ignored; knows fully well that he is not at all important.
- *The clown.* Believes that he can get recognition and attention only by acting foolishly.

- *The competitor.* Converts every situation into a challenging win-or-lose situation.
- *The conformist.* He will never take risk of non-acceptance by others, and always expect positive decisions and acceptance.
- *The crank.* He cannot tolerate any disgust or frustration.
- *The cynic.* A demoralized non-realist who will be an expert in commenting on others, without much concern for facts.
- *The dominator.* Basically inadequate and cannot control others; will always maintain an extraordinary desire to dominate and control others.
- *The dreamer.* Always thinks of a world of fantasy and getting honour, status and recognition in such a fantasy world; can never get such things in real life situations, so escapes to such a fantasy world.
- *The addict.* Becomes an addict to something, even communication, to forget his personal problems.
- *The flirt.* Tries to get recognition when emotions are trivial and superficial.
- *The fragile.* Is explosive and hypersensitive; attaches little value to himself.
- *The gossip.* Cannot fully exploit his own skill and ability; may prefer to elevate self-esteem by undermining the esteem of others.
- *The hedonist.* Exposes his pleasure and pleasure needs before all others to control his own emotional immaturity.
- *The inferior.* Submits himself to everything due to guilt feelings.
- *The indecisive.* Has lingering fears on taking any positive decision; thinks that if his decision proves wrong, he will lose respect and recognition.
- *The inflammable.* The man who will react violently to almost everything due to subconscious hostility.
- *The intellectual.* Who will be uncomfortable with his feelings; as a result, always stays at a superficial level.
- *The messiah.* Pretends or poses as a saviour of the human race as a reaction to the fear of insignificance.
- *The pouter.* Exposes his sad look widely and refuses to discuss it with others, knowing fully well that his grievance is irrational.

These are all the roles played by people to cover their own limitations. If they get out of such roles, they will be free and objective in their communication. Only then will the communication be real.

To conclude, for an effective communication, one must always try to hear what others are *not* saying and what they will never be able to express. William James has stated that "whenever two people meet, there are really six people present. There is each man as he sees himself, each man as the other person sees him, and each man as he really is".

The gateways (measures) to effective communication are as follows:

- Effective listening
- Interpersonal trust
- Proper feedback

- Understanding non-verbal cues (body posture. eye contact, etc)
- Non-directive counselling (expressing ideas, feelings, attitudes).

GUIDELINES FOR EFFECTIVE LISTENING

1. ***Stop talking:*** You cannot listen if you are talking. Polonius (Hamlet): "Give every man thine ear, but few thy voice."

2. ***Put the talker at ease:*** Help a person feel free to talk. This is often called a *permissive environment*.

3. ***Show a talker that you want to listen:*** Do not read your mail while someone talks. Listen to *understand,* rather than to *oppose*.

4. ***Remove distractions:*** Do not doodle, tap, or shuffle papers. It will be quieter if you shut the door.

5. ***Empathize with talkers:*** Try to help yourself see another person's point of view.

6. ***Be patient:*** Allow plenty of time; do not interrupt a talker; do not start for the door or walk away.

7. ***Hold your temper:*** An angry person gets the wrong meanings of words.

8. ***Go easy on argument and criticism:*** This puts people on the defensive, and they may 'clam up' or get angry. Do not argue: even if you win, you lose.

9. ***Ask questions:*** This encourages a talker and shows that you are listening. It helps to develop points further.

REPORT WRITING

A report is an important management tool used in decision making. In small enterprises, report writing may not be highly required. But in large organizations, it is highly essential to understand various functions and activities to take decisions.

The reports may be oral or written. Impressions of people or observations will be communicated in oral communication. It has limitation of lack of evidence and document. Written report is permanence record of the organization. These reports may be periodic or routine reports or social reports.

Characteristics of a Good Report

The following are the characteristics of a good report:

- Precise and brief
- Accuracy of facts
- Grammatical accuracy
- Relevance
- Reader orientation

- Objectivity
- Simple language
- Clarity
- Brevity.

NEW TRENDS IN COMMUNICATION

Yesterday, communication was through sounds, gestures and pictures. Today, communication is a mix of conventional skills and new age of technology. Tomorrow, communication is set to be increasingly electronic and dehumanized.

The new concepts in communication are the following:

- E-mails
- E-commerce
- E-business
- Networking systems
- Data warehousing
- Teleconferencing
- Video conferencing
- Short messages system.

SUMMARY

1. Communication is essential for effective management.
2. Communication is a process.
3. The problems of communication have to be considered carefully.
4. There are different types of communication.
5. Communication should be free from barriers.
6. There are 9 guides for effective listening.

REVIEW QUESTIONS

1. Discuss the role and importance of communication in modern business.
2. Explain the elements of the communication process.
3. What are the types of communication? Discuss grapevine communication.
4. What are the various barriers to communication? How can one overcome these barriers?
5. Explain the problems of communication.
6. Explain the various methods of communication.
7. What are the 9 guides for effective listening?

CASE STUDIES

1. Late or Not Late*

Kailash reported for work at 10.40 am. Madan, Kailash's boss, expressed his displeasure to Kailash for being late without permission and yet signing in the register quietly even without offering a word of apology. Madan felt that probably this was not the first time he was behaving like this. He, therefore, called Kailash. The following conversation took place between them.

Madan: Kailash, what is wrong with you?

Kailash: Why? Nothing.

Madan: I want to know why you signed in the register quietly when you were late.

Kailash: I am not late. What do you mean when you say, "I have signed quietly?"

Madan: What time is it now?

Kailash: 10.40 am.

Madan: What time does the office open?

Kailash: 9 am.

Madan: Then?

Kailash: Then, What?

Madan: You are late by 100 minutes.

Kailash: No, I am not late. Yesterday, Ghai Saab (Madan's boss) gave me an envelope and asked me to deliver it in person before going to the office. I started off at home much earlier than I normally do, and this is the reward I get!

Madan: Is that so? I do not know about it. OK, forget it. You are not late.

(Kailash leaves the place. After a while, Madan gets a nagging doubt. Is he (Kailash) telling me the truth? Or, is he pulling a fast one on me? So, he picks up the receiver and speaks to Ghai. Ghai was busy at that time and fails to recollect having sent Kailash on some work. Instead, he retorts, "Why would I send your man?" Madan is furious. That fellow, Kailash, not only came late but also bluffed blatantly. So, he called Kailash again and gave him a mouthful.)

Madan: You not only came late but also bluffed me so blatantly. How dare you do that? I can have you charge-sheeted.

Kailash: What is it you are talking?

Madan: I am referring to the incident in the morning. You came late.

Kailash: I thought you also agreed with me, earlier, that I was not late.

Madan: Yes, I did because I foolishly believed your words. Now, I realize I should not have.

Kailash: You guys feels that you are the only virtuous people and we are all cheats. Come, let us go and speak to Ghai and sort out the matter.

Madan: That is not necessary. I have already checked with him.

Kailash: Since you don't believe me, I cannot believe you either.

Madan: How dare you say that to me?

---

* The case study was prepared by C.S. Venkataraman and B.K. Srivastava.

Kailash: Why should I be afraid of speaking the truth? Let us go to Ghai Saab. He is not like you. Let me prove to you that I am honest and truthful.

(Both go to Ghai's cabin. As they open the door, Ghai looks at them, figures out why they came and even before they could walk nearer and explain the purpose of their visit, he beams and says loudly.)

Ghai: Oh boy! I know why you people are after me. I did send Kailash on some work. And, Madan, I am sorry neither did I inform you yesterday nor could I recollect it today when you rang up. You see, these days I am so much preoccupied with the deal we are trying to clinch.

(Kailash stares menacingly towards Madan. Madan tries to be cool in the presence of his boss.)

Madan: Kailash, I am sorry about it, but you knew the confusion arose because I did not know anything about it. Okay, let's forget. You are not late.

Questions for Discussion

1. What are the main issues in the above case?
2. How do you tackle this type of situation?

2. Delhi Televisions

Ramesh works in the assembly department of a company, called Delhi Televisions, that manufactures televisions. The operation requires that men work in teams. Ramesh has been employed by the company for six years. During the first two years, he showed aptitude for the job, but his attendance record was so irregular that he was warned twice that he would be dismissed unless he got to work regularly. For the past four years, he had a good attendance record and he is a competent, experienced employee. Although Ramesh gets along well with his fellow employees, he has always been very quiet and reserved, and company records do not contain any explanation of his early absences. Three days ago (Monday), Ramesh did not show up for work, nor did he phone that he was sick—which company rules require a man to do so when he is ill. On Tuesday, the same thing happened and the personnel manager got no answer when he tried to call Ramesh's home. Again, on Wednesday, no Ramesh. This morning Ramesh appeared on time, but looking a bit dishevelled and glum. The superintendent of the assembly department asked the supervisor under whom Ramesh works, to send him to his office.

The interview with Ramesh went as follows:

Superintendent(S): Ramesh(R):

S: Hello, Ramesh, it is good to see you. Sit down a minute.

R: (Taking a chair beside the desk) Thanks.

S: Ramesh, we have missed you for the last few days.

R: (Half to himself) Yes, been out all week, until this morning.

S: That's right, but I am sorry to say, you know how one man out upsets your crew. We did not have a substitute most of the time.

R: (Pause) Yeah, afraid I caused some trouble.

S: And not calling in, Ramesh, that made matters worse because we did not know what to plan on. You have been here long enough to know how important it is to keep full crews in assembly.

R: (Again, half to himself) Should have called in, that's right.

S: Tell me, when you realize how important it is, how could you just disappear for three days? We could not even get an answer at your home.

R: I just could not make it, and missed calling in. Sorry, I caused so much trouble.

S: Ramesh, I have looked over your record. The last four years have been fine. We need good men like you. A few years back the absences were pretty serious, and I am sure we are not going to slide back to that trouble again. Yet, the recent record looks real good. (Pause.) What do you think, Ramesh, can you keep that record as clean as it has been the last couple of years?

R: I would sure like to. I have been trying . . . (pause).

S: We need good men like you. You know the work, and you pitch in when we have to get work out in a rush. But we have to be able to depend on the men we keep in your spot. If you think this won't happen again, we are mighty glad to have you back.

R: Well, I need my job, and I will do the best I can.

S: OK. That's all the assurance we need.

Questions for Discussion

1. Analyze the communication breakdowns between the superintendent and Ramesh.
2. If you were the superintendent, how would you approach the problem?

3. MNC Corporation

At MNC Corporation, a foreman of inspection noticed a mistake in the assembly of transmitter cases. The foreman, a shy man when speaking to his immediate superiors, mentioned this matter to the senior supervisor in a weak, ineffectual manner. The senior supervisor nodded his head and continued to work on a report that he was writing. Later, a production slowdown occurred, and it was discovered that this flaw in the transmitter was the cause. The chief of production engineering, upset because this error had passed inspection unnoticed, reproved the senior supervisor in a brusque manner.

The senior supervisor called in the foreman of inspection and asked why this error had not been brought to his attention. The foreman said, "I told you the other day they were missing some of the punch-outs in those transmitter cases." The senior supervisor said, "Yes, but you did not pound the desk when you told me!"

Questions for Discussion

1. Why did the communication problem arise?
2. What do you suggest to prevent the communication problem?

4. Ram Dhin*

The National Globe Company of Calcutta put in an advertisement in the situations vacant column of *The Statesman* for a typist, and applications came in from all over the country. After screening the applications, Ram Dhin, 25 years old and a graduate of Bihar University, received an appointment letter from the company. Ram Dhin joined the company on 1 June, 1980. He was asked to report to the section officer incharge of the typing section. Ram Dhin was on probation for a period of six months.

During the first month, it was observed that Ram Dhin did his work on time and intelligently. According to one filing clerk, he grasped his work so quickly and easily that it made some of his colleagues green with envy. Usually, after having finished his own assignments, he helped other people in the section.

After about six months when the probation period was over, the section officer noticed that Ram Dhin started leaving his room quite often. Having observed Ram Dhin for about a week in his new habit, the section officer, Mr Saxena, called him in to his room.

Saxena: Ram Dhin, I see you leaving your seat too often these days.

Ram Dhin: When I finish my work, I go to the canteen to take my tea.

Saxena: It is against office discipline to go to the canteen during the working hours. You can go to the canteen during the lunch interval.

Ram Dhin: You should be satisfied as long as I do my work. If my visit to the canteen interferes with my work, then I will stop going out.

Saxena followed up his conversation by keeping Ram Dhin under close observation. The section officer started giving Dhin more work than was due to him. One morning there was unpleasantness between Dhin and Saxena. Saxena had asked him to carry out an additional assignment.

Ram Dhin: Ever since I started going to the canteen for tea, you have been wanting my blood. If I default in my assignment, you have every right to pull me up. Why for relaxing after every two hours? You are now giving me an assignment which is in addition to my normal work. Is it fair?

Saxena: You are exceeding your limits, Dhin. In this office you have to accept what I say. You have to carry out my say. You have to carry out my instructions. You will have to do this assignment also or be prepared to suffer the consequences....

Ram Dhin: You are threatening me now! I know your motive. The motive is not to get work done. It is to teach me a lesson.

Saxena: I warn you, your behaviour is undesirable....

Ram Dhin: I know what you are driving at. I might as well tell you it is not easy to dismiss me. Even if you succeed in dismissing me, there is no dearth of jobs for a good typist.

Having said this, Ram Dhin walked out. Saxena reported this to the manager incharge of the section. The manager called him and administered a strict warning.

---

* The case study was prepared by proferser Neela Megham, Delhi University.

Manager: Saxena has told me everything. You have to observe office discipline regardless of your efficiency. And also avoid using strong language when talking to superiors.

Ram Dhin: Yes sir....

Manager: Try to mend your ways. That is all I want to tell you.

Questions for Discussion

1. Explain the main problem in the case.
2. How do you tackle this type of situation as a manager?

FURTHER READING

Drucker, Peter F., *The Frontiers of Management*, Heinemann, London, 1987.

Laurie, J.M., Management and Organizational Behaviour, *Financial Times*, Pitman Publishing, London, 1999.

Rangnekar, S., *In the World of Corporate Managers*, Vikas Publishing House, New Delhi, 1996.

Sayles, L.R., *Managerial Behaviour*, McGraw-Hill, New York, 1997.

Stoner, James A.F., *Management*, Pearson Prentice Hall, New Delhi, 2005.

Wofford, J.C., et al., *Organisational Communication*, McGraw-Hill, Kogakusha, Tokyo, 1977.

Motivation

CONTENTS

INTRODUCTION

A worker is basically a human being. He is a person first and then only a worker. Every manager has to understand that a worker cannot be considered a mechanical system. A worker has to be inspired and actuated to accomplish the objectives of an organization. An order issued may not work, but an order *accepted* will be executed. To accept an order and to execute it with interest and vigour requires an element of actuating or motivating.

As management is the art of getting things done by the workers, this art of getting work done will depend mainly on whether a person has been motivated properly or not. Motivation creates a sense of responsibility and special interest in the work. It increases the desire to work; it is enthusiasm to work.

To motivate means to provide a motive; to impel people to action; and to create incentives to work. Motivation inspires people to work efficiently and effectively. Technically speaking, motivation is an energizer of human behaviour: it is a special urge to move in a particular direction. Motives are also the expression of the needs of a person. With motivation, a person can be made to work willingly with zeal and enthusiasm.

A manager has a job not with the products, but with *people*. He can handle them only when he can understand their motives and motivate them to take the desired actions. So, the skill of motivation is vital for successful management in an organization. A manager has to bring the ability of the workers to expression.

DEFINITIONS

MICHAEL J. JULIUS: Motivation is the act of stimulating someone or oneself to get the desired course of action.

KOONTZ and O'DONNELL: Motivation is a general term applying to the entire class of drives, desires, needs, wishes, and similar forces.

DUBIN: Motivation refers to the complex of forces starting and keeping a person at work in an organization. To put it generally, motivation starts and maintains an activity along a prescribed line. Motivation is something that moves the person to action and continues him in the course of action already initiated.

MARCH and SIMON: Motivation is the process or the reaction which takes place in the memory of individuals. It refers to the combination of forces or motives maintaining human activity.

IMPORTANCE OF MOTIVATION

Motivation results in creating a favourable work environment within an organization. It adds the *will to work* along with the ability to work for a worker. Motivation will act as an activator and energizer by directing the behaviour of persons towards the accomplishment of goals. Understanding of motives and motivation theories provides a great deal of insight into the reasons why different individuals exhibit different behavioural patterns. It also helps in understanding why the same person exhibits different reactions to the same stimulus at different times.

Motivation helps in securing voluntary cooperation from workers. It creates the will to work, and confidence in the workforce. Motivation helps to satisfy the needs of workers; naturally there will be a sense of belongingness and total involvement on the part of the workers in the achievement of organizational goals. The knowledge and skill of the workers can be used to the best advantage of the organization and there will be increased efficiency. All this will result in increased productivity and quality of work. Motivated people are the most satisfied people. They will function with a sense of responsibility and commitment to the organization. Naturally, it results in a low rate of labour turnover and absenteeism. A properly motivated team will not have unnecessary friction with the management and with its fellow workers. This will help in maintaining very good industrial relations.

Motivation is the drive to satisfy a want or goal, and satisfaction is experienced when the outcome has been achieved. A person might have high job satisfaction, but a low level of motivation for the job, or the reverse.

THEORIES OF MOTIVATION

Workers should be persuaded, inspired and motivated for contributing their best efforts in achieving the objectives of the organization. To motivate people effectively, managers should prepare certain plans. There are various plans, strategies or theories of motivation. There are different theories of motivation based on content and process.

Some important content theories of motivation are:

- Maslow's theory of hierarchy of needs
- Alderfer's modified need hierarchy
- Herzberg's two factory theory
- McClelland's achievement motivation theory.

Some process theories of motivation are:

- Expectancy based models (Vroom)
- Equity theory (Adams)
- Goal theory (Locke)
- Attribution theory (Heider, Kelley).

Some of these theories are briefly explained here.

Be strong theory or fear and punishment theory: The philosophy of might is right characterized the thinking of aggressive and authoritarian managers. Managers developed a strategy of forcing people to work by threatening to punish or dismiss them, or to cut their rewards if they did not work well. This theory is based on the military principle, "Neither make reply nor question why, but do or die", and the assumption is that people would work efficiently and with interest if they were driven by fear and punishment. There was tight control and rigid supervision over workers. This strategy was successful in the early days of the Industrial Revolution. But in the present circumstances, this theory is not practicable. It is resisted and condemned by workers as it is authoritarian.

Efforts and rewards theory: This strategy or approach tried to establish a direct relationship between efforts and rewards. F.W. Taylor conceived this idea in his piece-rate system of wages. Management thought that people could perform and contribute better to the extent they were rewarded. To practise this theory, managers should establish the standards of performance, monitor the behaviour of employees and decide about the rewards and penalties based on the degree of performance.

Monastic theory: This is almost like the efforts and rewards theory. Here, the management assumes that people work for money only. This theory seeks a single cause of behaviour. It assumes that all the activities of men are directed only towards earning money. More effort will provide more wages, which will further encourage the workers to more effort. This is also known as the *effort-reward-effort theory*. But this theory is criticized on the basis that rewards can serve as motivators upto a particular point only, and not beyond that.

Carrot and stick theory: This theory suggests a judicious combination of both rewards and penalties for motivation. This theory is based on the strategy of putting a carrot in front of a donkey and hitting it with a stick from behind so that it has to run. The carrot refers to incentives like money and other inducements, and the stick refers to penalties, fear of dismissal, demotion, etc.

Be good or paternalistic theory: After experiencing the 'Be strong' theory and its limitations, some managers implemented a new strategy. They were kind, generous and had the interests of the employees at heart. They functioned much as parents towards their children. But they expected loyalty, demanded respect and provided their employees what they thought was good for them. They were fair but firm. Employees in many cases responded to this strategy favourably. As a result, the paternalistic theory was successful in its approach and effectively competed with the "Be strong" and "fear and punishment" theories. High wages, job security, good facilities for education, health, recreation and good work environments were provided to gain loyalty and increase efficiency and productivity. But this theory was disliked by some people on the ground that they had to depend on the employers for everything, as children on their parents.

McGregor's theory: Douglas Murray McGregor classified the basic assumptions on human behaviour into two parts and called these sets of propositions Theory X and Theory Y.

McGregor's theory X: This theory was indirectly conceived and applied by F.W. Taylor. But it was McGregor who stated Theory X in very clear terms. In his own words, Theory X states that:

> Management is responsible for organizing the elements of productive enterprise—money, materials, equipment, people in the interest of economic ends.
>
> With respect to people, this is a process of directing their efforts, motivating them, controlling their actions, modifying their behaviour to fit the needs of the organization.
>
> Without the active intervention by management, people would be passive—even resistant—to organizational needs. They must therefore be persuaded, rewarded, punished, controlled. Their activities must be directed. This is management's task. We often sum it up by saying that management consists of getting things done through people.

- The average man is by nature lazy and he works as little as possible.
- He lacks ambition and dislikes responsibility.
- He is inherently self-centred, indifferent to organizational needs.
- He is by nature resistant to change and he is not very bright.

So, Theory X assumes that authority should be clear and flow directly from the superiors to subordinates without any reservation. It implies that management should be hard and strong. Close supervision and tight control over individual behaviour has to be introduced as work by nature is distasteful and people will try to shirk work and responsibility. But if the management believes in this theory, it will result in a lot of problems.

McGregor's theory Y: In view of the above misleading assumptions and practical difficulties, McGregor declares, "We require a different theory of the task of managing people based on more adequate assumptions about human nature and human motivation. I am going to be so bold as to suggest the broad dimensions of such a theory. Call it Theory Y if you will." His observations on Theory Y are as follows:

- Management is responsible for organizing the elements of productive enterprise—money, materials, equipment, people—in the interest of economic ends.
- People are not by nature passive or resistant to organizational needs. They have become so as a result of experience in organizations.
- Motivation, the potential for development, the capacity for assuming responsibility, the readiness to direct behaviour toward organizational goals, are all present in people.

Management does not put them there. It is the responsibility of management to make it possible for people to recognize and develop these human characteristics for themselves.

- The essential task of management is to arrange organizational conditions and methods of operation so that people can achieve their own goals best by directing their own efforts towards organizational objectives.

Theory Y is basically a process of creating opportunities, releasing potential, removing obstacles, encouraging growth and providing guidance. It also provides for two-way communication, participative management, decentralization and delegation of authority, emphasis on self-control, self-responsibility and self-discipline, emphasis on satisfaction of higher-level needs and maximum scope for management development programmes. Theory Y also assumes that work is as natural as play, provided the conditions are favourable.

Ouchi's theory Z: William Ouchi proposed Theory Z as an alternative theory of organizational behaviour. Theory Z organizational culture comprises three major characteristics: *trust*, *subtlety*, and *intimacy*.

Theory Z outlines a complete transformation of the motivational principles underlying high-performance organizations and implies a revolutionary change in management practices. The main characteristics of the theory are as follows:

- Long-term employment
- Emphasis on training
- Seniority-based rewards
- The Ringi system of collective decision making
- Emphasis on self-discipline
- Holistic concern for employees and their families.

Maslow's theory: Human needs can be classified into: (a) basic physiological needs or primary needs and (b) social and psychological needs or secondary needs. Abraham Maslow states that individuals have these needs and they are motivated to satisfy these unsatisfied needs. If they are satisfied, they do not motivate individual behaviour. Needs are arranged according to a hierarchy of importance from the basic physiological to the complex self-actualization needs. The need at any level of the hierarchy will emerge only when the lower-level needs are fully satisfied.

Maslow states that individual needs are arranged in a hierarchy from the lower-level physiological needs to the higher needs for self-actualization.

Basic physiological needs are the primary needs of an individual. The survival of an individual depends upon the satisfaction of these needs, namely, food, clothing, shelter, sex, air, water and other necessaries of life. The organization helps an individual to satisfy their basic needs by providing reasonably good salaries, benefits and working conditions. Once these needs are satisfied, the individual will get an idea about the higher level needs.

Safety and security needs are considered immediately after satisfying the psychological needs of individuals. These needs can be satisfied from job security, income, provision for old age, insurance, and safer working conditions.

Social needs are also called belonging needs. When basic needs and safety needs are satisfied, social needs become important. Social affiliation will make the job interesting. These needs are: love and affection, friendship, and so on.

Esteem needs or ego needs or status needs develop a concern for getting recognition, status, importance and respect from others. These needs are independence, achievement, competence, skill, knowledge, initiative and success. A very good organizational climate and more opportunity for development, responsibility, praise and promotion can play a vital role in satisfying esteem needs.

After the satisfaction of the esteem needs, the highest level of need, self-actualization, will become an important need. It involves realizing one's potentialities, capabilities for continued self-development and self-fulfilment. It is a personal achievement. Such challenges and achievements provide more satisfaction to a person.

The above hierarchy of needs stated by Maslow proves the fact that the second and subsequent needs do not dominate until the first and the previous needs are reasonably satisfied. Wants are continuous in nature and there cannot be an end to satisfaction. The speciality of Maslow's theory is that the needs arise in a *certain order* of preference.

Even though Maslow's theory of hierarchy of needs (Figure 9.1) has become popular, it is still subjected to a lot of criticism. The experience in continental European countries and Japan has shown that this theory does not apply effectively to their executives. Most of the American workers do not very much bother about their physiological and safety needs. Workers in Belgium and Spain feel that their esteem needs are better satisfied than their security and social needs. Money can be a good motivator only for physiological and social needs, but not for satisfying higher-level needs. Some people may remain contented with the satisfaction of physiological needs only, without developing any further needs.

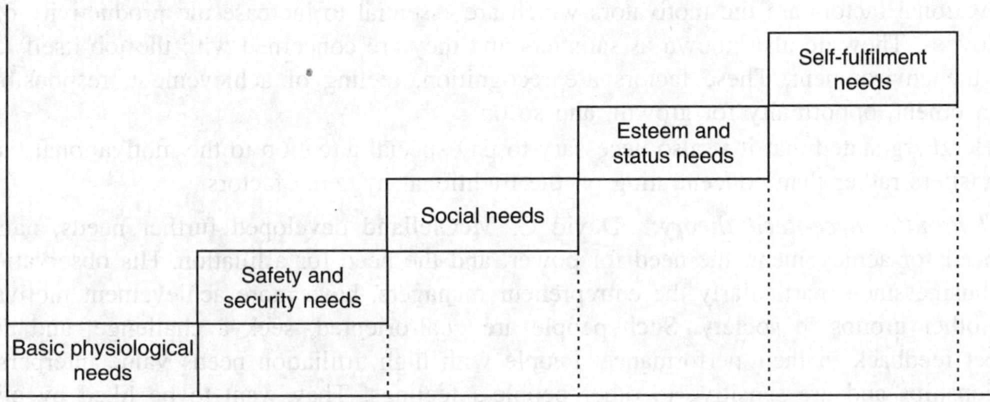

Figure 9.1 Maslow's theory of hierarchy of needs.

Herzberg's hygiene motivation theory: Frederick Herzberg and his associates conducted research based on the interview of 200 engineers and accountants working in 11 different firms in the Pittsburg area. Herzberg developed a theory with two factors. They are *hygiene factors* and *motivational factors*. The dissatisfiers are known as *hygiene factors* because they support the mental health of the workers. Another set of job conditions operates primarily to build strong motivation and high job satisfaction. They are called *motivational factors*. The need structure is shown in Figure 9.2.

Hygiene factors, as stated by Herzberg, are related to the work environment and are external to the job. They include wages, fringe benefits, status, job security, working conditions,

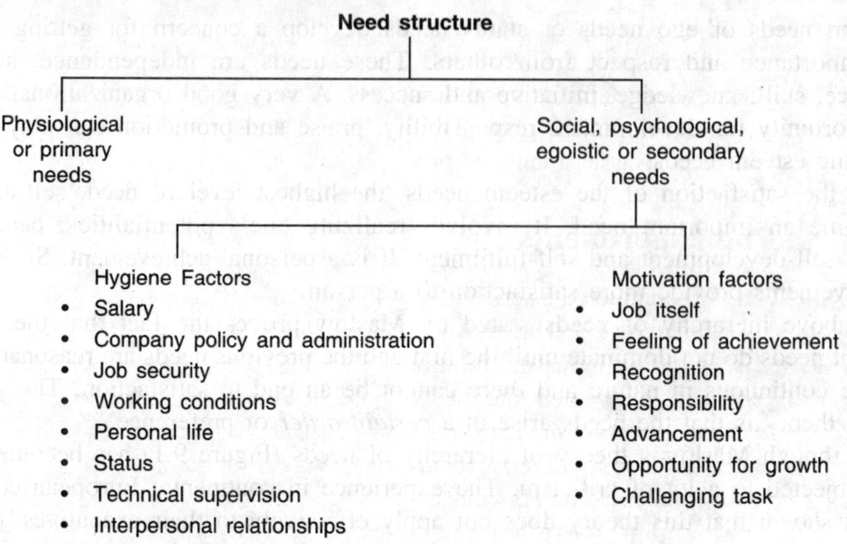

Figure 9.2 Herzberg's hygiene motivation theory.

company policy, administration, and interpersonal relations. The presence of these factors at a satisfactory level prevents job dissatisfaction, but they do not provide motivation to the workers. Even though they are not motivators, they will prevent the individual from becoming dissatisfied. Motivational factors are the motivators which are essential to increase the productivity of the employees. They are also known as satisfiers and they are concerned with the job itself rather than the environment. These factors are recognition, feeling of achievement, responsibility, advancement, opportunity for growth, and so on.

Herzberg stated that it is also necessary to pay special attention to the motivational factors of satisfiers rather than concentrating on the traditional hygienic factors.

McClelland's three-need theory: David C. McClelland developed further needs, namely, the need for achievement, the need for power, and the need for affiliation. His observation is that businessmen, particularly the entrepreneur managers, have more achievement motivation than other groups in society. Such people are goal-oriented, seek a challenge, and desire perfect feedback in their performance. People with high affiliation needs value interpersonal relationships and are sensitive to other people's feelings. They want to be liked by others. They seek company by joining clubs and associations. On the other hand, people with a strong power need seek to dominate, influence and control others. Such power may be positive or negative. McClelland concludes that the need for achievement is one of the key factors of economic growth.

Vroom's expectancy theory: Vroom, while attacking Herzberg's two-factor theory, offered an expectancy approach to the understanding of motivation. His theory explains three concepts of valence, instrumentality, and expectancy. *Valence* represents the value or significance of an outcome for a person, e.g. increased salaries, promotion. *Instrumentality* refers to the person's perception of the relationship between a first-level outcome. It is the extent to which a person will feel that performance is instrumental in getting him increased salaries or promotion.

Expectancy refers to the extent to which such efforts will lead to the first-level outcome. Vroom's theory explains how the goals of individuals influence their efforts and that the behaviour individuals select depends upon their assessment of the probability that the behaviour will take with success towards the goal. To conclude, Vroom emphasized the significance of individual perceptions and assessments of organizational behaviour.

The Hawthorne Experiments

Elton Mayo of Harvard conducted a series of experiments at the Hawthorne plant of the Western Electric Company, Chicago. The Hawthorne experiments clearly showed that the attitudes of workmen are basic factors in industrial relations as they influence both individual performance and group effort. They also revealed that the business organization is a *social system,* apart from being a *technical economic system*. It established that the worker was not only motivated by economic incentives, but also by diverse social and psychological factors. Increased satisfaction led to increased effectiveness. The Hawthorne experiments emphasized that emotions and non-logical attitudes and sentiments are more important in economic relationships than the logical economic factors.

Michigan University Social Research Institute Experiments

The Institute for Social Research at the University of Michigan conducted certain studies about the motivational characteristics most frequently demonstrated by the more successful managers. Rensis Likert observed that the attitude and behaviour of such managers as being supportive, friendly and helpful. The successful manager displays confidence in the integrity, ability and motivation of subordinates. Such a manager will have high expectations regarding the performance level of his subordinates. He will train and promote his subordinates to higher responsibilities. Rensis Likert concludes by stating that every human being earnestly seeks a secure, friendly and supportive relationship. The successful motivator will understand the significance of such human needs, and create a favourable environment for their fulfilment.

Incentives

Incentives can motivate people. They may be financial or non-financial. For people working at the lower level, money can be an effective motivator. As one goes up higher in the hierarchy, the importance of money decreases and non-financial incentives become more powerful. A good pay with good fringe benefits can be a very good financial incentive. Non-financial incentives may be recognition, promotion, participation, achievement, etc. Such incentives motivate workers effectively. They satisfy the needs of the subordinates and boost the morale of the workers. They increase productivity and create a favourable image for the institution.

Morale

Morale is an important element of motivation, and refers to the zeal for action, the overall tone or climate prevailing among workers. If they are happy, cordial and confident, it is a reflection of high morale. If they are poor, restless, irritated and dissatisfied, it reflects their low morale. High morale speaks of effective motivation, and low morale of lack of such motivation. Morale is an attitude of satisfaction, of a feeling of happiness, of a warm feeling, of conditions of zeal, hope and confidence. In general, it is an attitude of an employee towards his firm. Improved or high morale increases output, reduces labour turnover, waste and industrial unrest, absenteeism, grievances and accidents.

SUMMARY

1. Motivation is an act of stimulating employees by providing incentives and encouragement.
2. There are traditional and modern theories of motivation.
3. McGregor classified the basic assumptions on human behaviour into two theories called Theory X and Theory Y.
4. Maslow's and Herzberg's theories are popular in motivating people.
5. McClelland and Vroom also contributed a lot on this subject.

REVIEW QUESTIONS

1. Define motivation. Bring out the importance of motivation.
2. What are the traditional theories of motivation?
3. Discuss Theory X and Theory Y.
4. Explain Maslow's hierarchy of needs theory.
5. Discuss Herzberg's theory of motivation.
6. Explain Theory Z of management.
7. Explain the Hawthorne and Michigan experiments.

CASE STUDY

Literary Agencies Ltd.

Sneha has been a literary agent with one of the largest literary agencies in New Delhi for four years. Her job entails matching up authors and their manuscripts with book publishers. She has about two dozen established authors whom she represents in negotiations with publishing houses. Sneha also regularly reviews manuscripts of new or less established authors who want her firm to represent them.

"I live and breathe this job. I am up at 5.30 a.m. in the morning and in the office by 7 a.m. I either skip lunch or use lunch as an excuse to meet publishing editors, one of my established authors, or to talk with a prospective client. I am never out of the office before 7.30 p.m., and it is usually closer to 9 p.m. when I get home. I spend an hour or two lying in bed, reading book manuscripts. I only wish I could find another five hours a day so I could squeeze in more things. God, I love my work."

You might be correct in calling Sneha a workaholic. She approaches her work almost compulsively. In college, she played on her school's soccer team. But Sneha's job is now her whole life. She said she had not been on a date in five months, although she had several dozen offers. She had no social life, except that which rotated around her work. Sneha even admitted that she had not had time to dust or run the vacuum cleaner over the rugs in her apartment in six weeks.

"But don't get the wrong impression when I say my apartment is a mess," interjected Sneha. "I don't care. Every morning I pop out of bed and just thank the Lord for having a job that makes so happy. When I run into people who complain about their work, I just shake my head. How lucky I am! I'd rather be negotiating with an editor, making manuscript suggestions, discussing strategy with one of my authors, or reading some unknown author's first book than be clearing the house, jogging around Central Park, or for that matter, making love with Rajesh. I mean it when I say I have got a great job."

Sneha's enthusiasm appears to have had a very positive impact on her job performance. Her boss says she is the best young agent in the office. "She gives a hundred per cent. But of course, she's smart too. Sneha has a bright future in this industry."

Questions for Discussion

1. If you were to learn that Sneha made only ₹30,000 a year in her job, would you be surprised? Explain.
2. Since Sneha makes only ₹30,000, one can safely conclude that money is not her main source of motivation. What types of individual, organizational and job-related factors might account for her high level of motivation?
3. Build a model showing the relationship among the factors that help explain Sneha's high level of performance and motivation.
4. Can you see any possible negative aspects of managing someone like Sneha?

FURTHER READING

Herzberg, F. et al., *The Motivation to Work*, John Wiley & Sons, New York, 1959.

Laurie, J.M., Management and Organizational Behaviour, *Financial Times*, Pitman Publishing, London, 1999.

Maslow, Abraham, H., *Motivation and Personality*, Harper & Row, New York, 1954.

McClelland, David C., *The Achievement Motive*, Appleton-Century-Crofts, New York, 1953.

Stoner, James A.F., *Management*, Pearson Prentice Hall, New Delhi, 2005.

Vroom, V.H., *Work and Motivation*, John Wiley & Sons, New York, 1954.

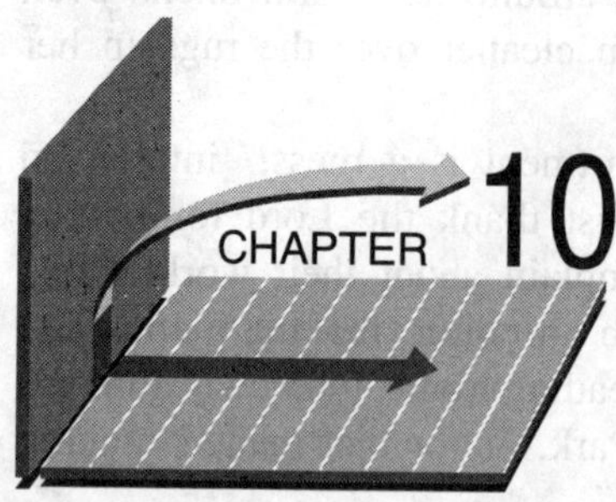

Controlling

CONTENTS

INTRODUCTION

Controlling is a fundamental managerial function or process which measures current performance and guides it towards some predetermined objectives. The essence of control lies in checking progress against plans, setting up individual and organizational performance standards, and seeing that they are achieved as per the plan. Henry Fayol states that in an undertaking, control consists of verifying whether everything occurs in conformity with the plan adopted, the instructions issued and the principles established. Its objective is to point out weaknesses and errors in order to rectify them and prevent their recurrence. It operates on everything: things, people and actions.

The process of control also involves assessment of present or recent operations to identify desirable changes when performance is found to be unsatisfactory. The essence of control is *action,* which adjusts operations to predetermined standards, and its basis is information in the hands of managers. There are various possibilities like confusion, mistakes, delay, loss of effort and friction which may result in deviation from the original plans and programmes. So, mere planning may not be adequate. Control highlights all such deviations as soon as they appear between the performance and the standards prescribed.

DEFINITIONS

KOONTZ and O'DONNELL: Control is measurement and correction of the performance of activities of subordinates in order to make sure that enterprise objectives and plans devised to attain them are being accomplished.

ERNEST DALE: Control is a system which not only provides a historical record of what has happened to the business as a whole, but also pinpoints the reasons why it has happened and provides the data that enable the chief executive or the departmental head to take corrective steps if he is on the wrong track.

GEORGE R. TERRY: Control is determining what is being accomplished, that is, evaluating the performance, and if necessary, applying corrective measures so that the performance takes place according to plans.

The above definitions suggest that control is to find out the variations between the plan and the performance, and to suggest corrective measures to be undertaken.

IMPORTANCE

Control encourages top management for more and more delegation and decentralization. It spots the areas of weaknesses and the range of deviations from the original plans. It stimulates action which will gear up all the departments. McFarland says that "Control is vital to the strength and morale of company employees"—workers will never like a situation to go out of control. Control will help in taking correct and clear-cut decisions. It can make planning effective and meaningful.

LIMITATIONS

1. It is very difficult to establish standards for intangible activities.
2. Control cannot be effectively exercised over external factors which are basically uncontrollable.
3. Intensive control measures may be resisted by employees.
4. Control may not function effectively with untrained and unqualified subordinates.
5. Control may be resisted on the ground that it interferes with freedom of individual thinking and action.

CHARACTERISTICS

1. *Control and planning are inseparable:* No business can exist without these twin concepts in some form or the other. Control cannot exist without planning and, therefore, the planning has to be designed to fit the specification of control. A *standard* is a type of plan which guides in evaluating performance.

2. *Control is a continuous process:* Control is a process of constant revision and analysis of standards, and understanding of the variation between the plans and the performance.

3. *Control is forward looking:* One cannot exercise any control over the past. One can only review the past events. Control is possible only of future performance.

4. *Control is all-pervasive:* Even though the scope of control varies, control as such functions at all levels of responsibility to execute plans.

5. *Control has a positive approach:* Control can never be negative, and it is not an obstacle or a bottleneck; it is a managerial necessity and will help the management in getting positive and successful results.

ELEMENTS OF CONTROL

There are six elements in control systems. An executive exercising control has to understand each element in the context of its necessity. These elements are:

1. Authority
2. Knowledge
3. Guidance
4. Direction
5. Constraint
6. Restraint.

All these elements are absolutely essential to exercise an effective control.

CONTROL PROCESS

K. Boulding states that the barest essential of any organization is a control mechanism. Control is the key factor. If the control mechanism fails, plans and programmes will also fail. A control mechanism or control process has five basic elements. They are as follows:

- Establishment of standards of performance
- Measurement of actual performance
- Comparison of actual performance with the original standards
- Taking corrective action
- Feedback

Establishment of standards of performance: A standard is a criterion against which future results can be measured. Such standards may be *tangible* or *intangible*. A standard should be tangible, for better evaluation. It should be clear and meaningful. Performance standards are expressed in terms of cost, quality, quantity and time. Standards like employee morale, discipline, public relations, image of the concern, etc. cannot be easily quantified, as they are intangible. Quantitative standards can be determined by statistical methods such as sampling.

Measurement of actual performance: The very purpose of control is to check or measure the actual performance. If the standards prescribed are tangible, it is easy to measure the performance in similar units. If the standards are intangible, it is difficult to measure the performance. Work, operations and turnout should be observed, measured, and facts collected. Statistical data, reports, opinions, accounting information, etc. will help in measuring the actual performance.

Comparison of actual performance with the original standards: After measuring the actual performance, it has to be compared with the original standards. The comparison may disclose either agreements or deviations from the standards established. But the manager has to be very clear about the concept of *deviation*: minor or negligible deviations may be ignored, but major and significant deviations should be correctly understood. For this, the manager must have his own range of tolerance, which he can fix with his knowledge and experience.

Taking corrective action: As soon as deviations are reported, the manager concerned should take steps to correct the action. This is essential because measurement of performance should not become just a ritual or post mortem of past events. If the deviation is significant, then the original standard itself has to be rechecked. Corrective action should be taken immediately, without any loss of time. Corrective action may be improving the methodology, techniques, organizational structure, proper selection, training and remuneration of workers, or even effective communication and successful motivation. Corrective action may be either to cure or to prevent such deviations. Wherever possible, automatic, self-regulating mechanisms should be introduced to bring back performance in line with the original plan.

Feedback: Feedback is an important element in the control process. It ties together all the elements of the control mechanism. The controller will receive feedback information regarding actual performance in comparison with the original standards. If the feedback is positive and reveals accomplishment, the manager must encourage and appreciate the subordinates. If the feedback brings negative results, the manager has to take corrective action and alter the operations accordingly. Feedback will help in getting information well in time about the work performance, and it also motivates people.

ESSENTIALS OF A GOOD CONTROL SYSTEM

The following are broad considerations which are essential to have an effective control system:

1. ***Suitability:*** The nature and need of the activity will help in determining a good system of control. Controls in a production department will be different from those used in marketing departments. Control for the production manager will be different from control for a supervisor.

2. ***Prompt reporting:*** If there are any deviations from the plans and standards, they must be reported promptly and immediately.

3. ***Forward-looking:*** A good control system should avoid the possibility of getting similar deviations in future. All potential deviations should be corrected.

4. *Focus on strategic points:* A good system of control not only points out the deviations or exceptions but also pinpoints where they are vital or strategic.

5. *Flexible:* A good control system should remain workable even when the plans are changed or standards are altered.

6. *Objective:* To have effective control, there should be objective, precise and suitable standards. They should be definite, and determinable.

7. *Economical:* The cost of installation and operation of a control system should be justified by its benefits.

8. *Understandable:* A control system should be clear and easily understandable to the people who will use it, so that control becomes easy, smooth and meaningful.

9. *Remedial action:* A good control system not only detects deviation, but also suggests practical corrective action. Koontz and O'Donnell state that an adequate system of control should disclose where failures are occurring, who is responsible for them, and what should be done about them.

10. *Human factor:* A good control system should be worker-centred rather than work-centred. Accountability for major deviations and assistance for improvement should be organized.

To conclude: planning is the basis of control, action is essence, delegation is the key, and information is the guide.

FUNCTIONS OF A CONTROLLER

The Controller's Institute of America has prescribed the following functions for an effective controller:

- To establish, coordinate and administer an integral part of management, or an adequate plan for the control of operations
- To compare the actual performance with the original standards
- To consult all other departments and management segments regarding the attainment of objectives
- To administer policies and procedures
- To coordinate and supervise the preparation of reports to government agencies
- To ensure fiscal protection to the assets and properties of business through adequate internal control and insurance
- To continuously appraise economic and social forces.

TYPES OF CONTROL

Basically, controls can be classified into:

- Pre-controls or forward-looking control
- Feed forward or steering controls
- Yes-no controls
- Post-action controls.

Pre-controls or forward-looking control: Such controls are established before an activity finally takes place, e.g. standard cost control techniques can be adopted to control the cost of a product before starting its commercial production.

Feed forward or steering controls: This type of control is exercised with the background of accurate information and forecasting, before the completion of an operation, so that corrective operation can be taken in the process itself, ensuring complete accomplishment of the objectives.

Yes-no controls: With this control, work is stopped at various stages and at certain preferred events for complete inspection. Such screening can detect if there is any deviation. Only after giving a go-ahead signal, work can be commenced again. Quality controls of various engineering products and automobiles are done like this.

Post-action controls: This type of control is exercised after the completion of the activity for reviewing the results. Budgetary control is an example of post-action control.

TECHNIQUES OF CONTROL

There are various techniques of control. But the most important among them can be classified as:

- Budgetary controls
- Non-budgetary controls
- Network analysis and modern techniques

Budgetary Control

Budgetary control refers to use of a budget as a control technique. A *budget* is an estimate of future need arranged in an orderly basis, covering some or all of the activities of an enterprise for a definite period of time. It is a time-bound financial plan. Budgetary control involves the use of both budgets and budgetary reports for a period to coordinate, evaluate and control the day-to-day operations as per the predetermined objectives.

A budgetary control should be objective-oriented, as it is a planning factor as well as a controlling factor. A budget committee can prepare the details of the budget, taking into confidence all the officers concerned. Employees' views can also be obtained in preparing budgets. Budgets should be flexible, but stable. A budget should be in specific numerical terms, and it should be clear. Budgetary control also involves continuous comparison of actual results.

Benefits

1. Budgetary control brings in efficiency and economy in the working of a business enterprise.
2. It helps in the determination of periodical objectives.
3. It introduces precision, discipline, and direction to the routine activities of the enterprise.
4. It coordinates and integrates the operations of different departments of the enterprise.
5. It provides standards against which the actual performance can be measured.
6. It motivates subordinates.

7. It helps in democratic or participative management.
8. It helps in looking forward to a planned future.

Limitations

1. Spending the entire amount in the budget may be a problem. And if it is not spent, the budget may be reduced in the subsequent years. So, it encourages artificial spending.
2. Budgets create a rigid financial structure and managers have very little choice or discretion over funds.
3. Budgets may be used to judge the results of a manager, rather than the actual results. To keep up with the budget itself, it can be a matter of pride.
4. They sometimes become expensive, meaningless and cumbersome.
5. Budgets may be used to conceal inefficiency.
6. There may be a danger of over-budgeting.

How to make budgetary control effective? Koontz, O'Donnell and Weihrich have suggested certain methods to overcome the limitations of budgetary control and to make it more effective. Budgetary control must be tailored to each job; the managers who are going to administer the jobs should be made responsible for the budget and its preparation; top management should support budget preparation and administration; and there must be a reasonable degree of freedom and discretion for executives in the budget administration.

Non-budgetary Control

Apart from budgetary control, various non-budgetary control devices can be used by managers. They are as follows:

- Statistical data and charts
- Internal audit
- Special reports
- Confidential reports
- Breakeven analysis
- Information control
- Personal observation.

Statistical data and charts: They are the most common form of non-budgetary control. Statistical information of the past and data intended for the future can be used for control. The latest trend is to present such complete statistical information in the form of attractive charts. Charts are self-explanatory, attractive and meaningful.

Internal audit: Management can use the technique of internal audit for checking and controlling the operations. Internal auditors can appraise the performance of the management in relation to its policies and procedures.

Special reports: Executives can give special reports for certain special projects of non-repetitive situations. Such reports can also be given on the progress and performance of individuals and departments. Feedback will help in taking immediate corrective action if necessary.

Confidential reports: In certain organizations, there is a practice of getting confidential reports from the superiors on the working abilities and other information about a subordinate. This can also act as a control device, but it can also be misused.

Breakeven analysis: It is an analysis in chart form depicting the cost-volume-profit relationship. The breakeven point is that where the total cost is equal to the total revenue. This chart shows variable costs like labour, material costs and fixed costs incurred. This chart helps in forecasting, budgeting cash requirement, planning financial needs, make- or buy-decisions, etc.

Information control: With the increased complexities in operations, it has become necessary to have a more sophisticated system of collection, processing, storing and applying the information. This system can be called *information control*. Information technology, management information systems and computer applications have changed the whole concept of information systems. Information control has become one of the most vital and essential tools for effective control today.

Personal observation: Control through personal observation will provide immediate and authentic information regarding the performance and its matching with the standards. But the prejudice or incompetence of the superior may affect the quality of information. It cannot provide quantitative values for performance levels. It is difficult to express the quality of performance observed in numerical terms.

Network Analysis and Modern Techniques

Network analysis is a technique used in different functional areas of management for planning and controlling. It can be used to plan and control the starting or construction of a new factory. It consists of a job or event and its arrangement in a logical network with time estimates. Critical Path Method (CPM) and Programme Evaluation and Review Technique (PERT) and such other techniques of network will help in the starting of a new factory, new product, etc. It focuses attention on the critical elements of the project, and is both a plan and a forward-looking type of control. It helps in reducing work and cost, and in increasing efficiency and profit. The most common among them are control over:

- Policies
- Procedures
- Organizations
- Personnel
- Products
- Product lines
- Production
- Stock or inventory
- Quality
- Wages and salaries
- Sales
- Prices
- External relations
- Overall performance.

The well-known network techniques used by various organizations are:

1. Programme Evaluation and Review Technique (PERT)
2. Critical Path Method (CPM). Some modern techniques are *responsibly centres* such as cost centres, revenue centres, profit centres, and investment centres. All these are briefly explained in the following sections:

Programme Evaluation and Review Technique [PERT]

In project management, PERT is a highly useful technique. Booz used this concept in USA during 1957 for controlling Polaris Missiles Programme. Later, it spread to several places. In this technique, the entire project is broken into a number of clear identifiable activities and are arranged logically. The estimated time for each activity is prepared first. The three sets of time used in this techniques are *optimistic* (shortest) time, *pessimistic* (longest) time and *normal* (most likely) time.

- *Optimistic time estimate:* This is the estimate of the shortest possible time in which an activity can be completed under ideal conditions.
- *Pessimistic time estimate:* This is the maximum possible time it would take to accomplish a job.
- *Most likely time estimate:* This is the time estimate which lies between the optimistic and pessimistic time estimates. It reflects a situation where 'things are normal'.

PERT network is event based. An event indicates a noteworthy or significant point in the project. It is the start or completion of a job and does not consume time or resources. Examples of what an event is and what it is not are:

- Foundation digging started—a PERT event.
- Foundation is being dug—not a PERT event.
- Assemble parts A and B—not a PERT event.
- Electrical design completed—a PERT event.

The following questions are to be asked for preparing a PERT network:

- What event or events must be completed before the particular event can start?
- What event or events follow this?
- What activities can be accomplished simultaneously?

Event or events that immediately come before another event without any intervening events are called *predecessor events* to that event.

Event or events that immediately follow another event without any intervening events are called *successor events* to that event.

Let the problem be of opening a new office and let a few specific events be considered. We shall number these events as:

Event 1	Location of the site started
Event 2	Location of the site completed
Event 3	Building for office selected
Event 4	Cleaning of office building started
Event 5	Interior decorator starts work
Event 6	Interior decorator finishes work

Event 7 Opening of a new office advertised or announced
Event 8 List of invitees for the opening day prepared
Event 9 Invitations sent
Event 10 Office formally opened.

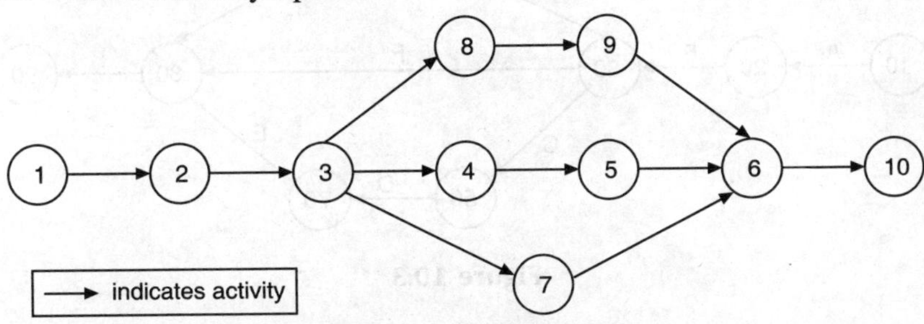

Figure 10.1 The PERT diagram explains the events and activities of opening a new office for starting a commercial airline.

Critical Path Method (CPM)

PERT puts emphasis on events and CPM on activities. Examples of events and activities are as follows:

- Foundation digging started—a PERT event
- Foundation is being dug—an activity
- Site located—an event
- Locate site—an activity
- Assemble parts A & B—an activity

A CPM network is built on the basis of jobs or activities instead of events.
The following are the examples of CPM network:

Activity A Locate the site or street where several buildings are available on net
Activity B Select a building where the office can be accommodated
Activity C Engage cleaners
Activity D Clean the office area
Activity E Decorate the interior
Activity F Advertise or announce the opening of the new office
Activity G Prepare a list of invitees for the opening day
Activity H Send the invitations
Activity I Formally open the office

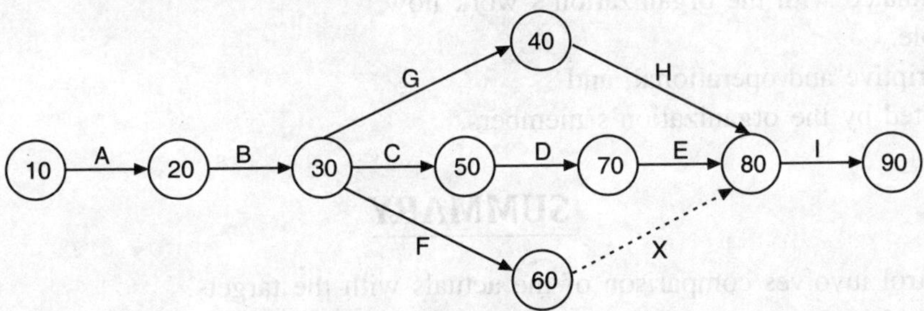

Figure 10.2

The dummy activity can be avoided by reframing the CPM network as follows:

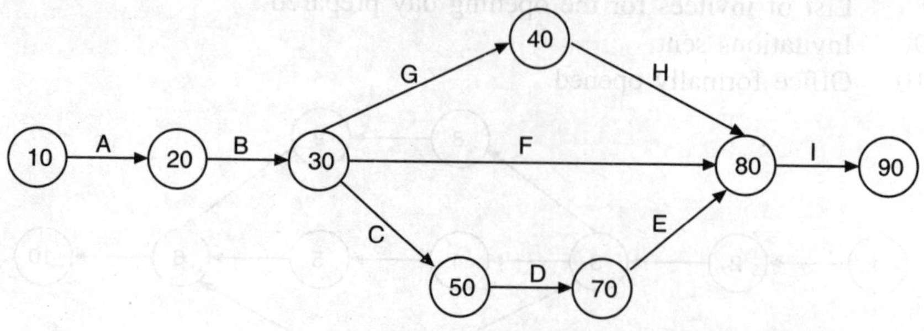

Figure 10.3

Based on the above analysis of PERT and CPM, the activities of an organization can be planned and controlled.

Modern techniques

Responsibility centres help a lot in controlling the activities of an organization. Every organization consists of some departments. Every department is considered to be a cost centre. The manager concerned of the department has the responsibility to control the activities to reduce the cost. Some departments are considered to be revenue centres. The managers of these centres are responsible for generating revenue from different activities. The managers of profit centres are responsible for generating people, whereas the managers of investment centres are responsible for getting return on investment.

CHARACTERISTICS OF AN EFFECTIVE CONTROL SYSTEM

The following are the characteristics of control systems. These should be

- accurate,
- timely,
- objective and comprehensible,
- focused on strategic control points,
- economically realistic,
- organizationally realistic,
- coordinated with the organization's work flow,
- flexible,
- prescriptive and operational, and
- accepted by the organization's members.

SUMMARY

1. Control involves comparison of the actuals with the targets.
2. Control is the measure of the performance of people or processes.

3. Control is forward-looking.
4. A good control system requires certain essentials.
5. Different techniques of control help a lot in achieving the goals of an organization.

REVIEW QUESTIONS

1. "Planning is a futile exercise without controlling." Comment.
2. "Planning is the basis of control, action is its essence, delegation is its key and information is its guide." Comment on the statement.
3. Define control. Explain the importance of control in a modern business enterprise.
4. Discuss the characteristics of the controlling function.
5. What is meant by a control process? Discuss its basic elements.
6. Discuss the requirements of an effective control system.
7. "Budgetary control still continues to be an effective technique of managerial control." Discuss this statement.
8. Discuss various non-budgetary control techniques that may be used in business enterprises.
9. Explain PERT and CPM.
10. Discuss the modern techniques of control.

CASE STUDY

Mehta Bank Ltd.

Venkataraman was an officer in a leading nationalized bank with 25 years of service to his credit. During his long period of service, he worked in different capacities and sections. His attitude and behaviour made him a trusted official in the organization. Having been posted in a big branch based in a large city, he was not keen on getting further promotions.

On one occasion, when he was working as an incharge of the draft issue section, he issued bundles of drawing books from the main stock of the security forms of the branch and kept the same in his custody in an almirah provided to him. One fine morning, he removed three drawing books out of the stock of books valued below ₹10,000 which he had in his own custody and kept them in his house. He then started issuing drafts in various names from his house out of the aforesaid stolen drawing books by allotting correct branch serial numbers obtained from the branch register under his control. The drafts were deposited in different banks/branches of the same bank in different accounts opened in the names of the payees of the drafts. These accounts were introduced by the bank employees, and some of them were in different representations only, like Mr. Venkataraman Aiyar, Mr. Venkataraman Iyengar, etc. The drafts thus deposited were presented in clearing and were passed in the normal course without any doubt or suspicion. In the evening, he would visit the drawee offices concerned and collect such paid drafts.

Having found this technique successful, he tried his hand at yet another. This time he started issuing drafts in fictitious names or in the names of his close relatives drawn on outstations without any vouchers or deposits. After a few days, he would cancel the same drafts by allowing the credits to the respective accounts in his own branch by debiting the head office accounts. He continued to do this for about three months, causing a loss of over ₹700,000 to the bank.

The fraud came to light thanks to the presence of mind exercised by one of the officers at another local office. He found that on the previous day also, he had paid a similar draft with the leaf number previous to the draft presented now. In his view, it was not possible for such a big office to avoid consumption of draft leaves in this fashion. Consequently, the matter was taken up with the issuing branch. Unfortunately for Venkataraman, someone else was working as the incharge of the draft issue section on that day. On checking up the records, it transpired that no such draft was issued. This led to prompt investigations and detection of the whole fraud committed by Venkataraman.

Questions for Discussion

1. How do you view the present fraud case: a human failure or a system failure?
2. What are the main issues in the case, and how can our present system of control prevent such fraud?
3. How would you manage the situation on detection?

FURTHER READING

Anthony, R.N., Dearden, J. and Bedford, N.M., *Management Control Systems*, Richard D. Irwin, Home Wood (Illinois), 1984.

Baig, E.C., America's Most Admired Corporations, *Fortune*, Jan. 19, 1987.

Koontz, Harold, and Weihrich, Heinz, *Essentials of Management*, McGraw Hill, New York, 1990.

Srinath, L.S., *PERT and CPM: Principles and Applications,* Affiliated East-West Press, New Delhi, 2000.

Stoner, James A.F. et. al, *Management*, Pearson/Prentice Hall, New Delhi, 2005.

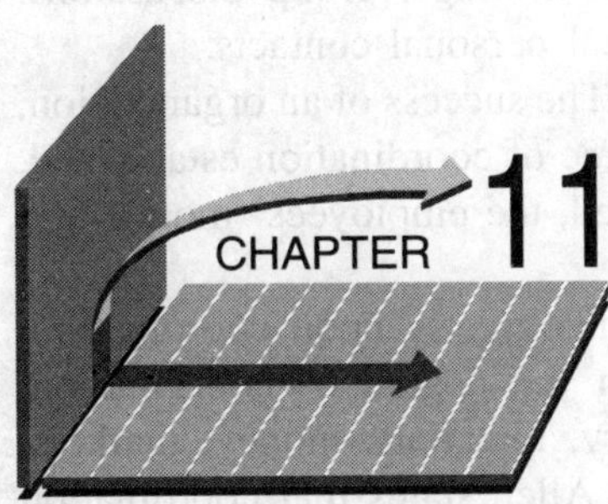

Coordination

CONTENTS

INTRODUCTION

A modern business organization is based on principles like division, departmentation, delegation, and decentralization. Different departments, divisions, branches and sections function to achieve the common objectives of the organization. In all these places, different persons work in different capacities. Under this complex structure and multidimensional system of an organization, there is a vital need for maximum cooperation with minimum conflict, confusion and contradiction. Coordination is an important process of blending together all such functions. It is also considered the essence of management, as every managerial task is in practice an exercise in coordination.

Coordination is the task of arranging group efforts in an orderly manner. It aims at achieving unity of objectives, is all-pervasive in nature, and is essential at all levels of management, and in all departments. The harmonious blending of all organizational activities to achieve unity of action is coordination. Henry Fayol considered coordination as one of the important functions of management. It is the main principle involving all other principles of management, and can be accomplished through departmentation, committees, regular meetings, group discussions, conferences, proper and meaningful communication, and informal personal contacts.

In every organization, the factor of coordination is important. The success of an organization, in general, and management, in particular, depends upon the degree of coordination established. In large organizations, it is critical. Once coordination is achieved, the employees' morale and communication improve automatically.

The success of an army, a play, or a music concert, depends greatly upon coordination. The success of a football or cricket team also depends upon the degree of coordination. Likewise, it is essential in industry also, where men, machinery, materials, money, markets, and methodology are to be managed by maintaining a balance. Allen states that coordination can be accomplished automatically if sound systems of policies, objectives, procedures and organizations are established. Koontz and O'Donnell consider it the essence of management.

DEFINITIONS

JAMES D. MOONEY: Coordination is the orderly arrangement of a group's effort to provide unity of action in the pursuit of a common purpose.

McFARLAND: Coordination is the process whereby an executive develops in an orderly pattern an integrated, orderly, and synchronized pattern of group effort among his subordinates and tries to attain unity of effort in the pursuit of any common goal.

From the above definitions, it is clear that coordination is a continuous activity of managers in the orderly arrangement of group efforts towards unity of action to achieve organizational objectives. It involves the orderly synchronization of group efforts, and avoids organizational bottlenecks or confusion and conflict.

Henry Fayol and some other writers considered coordination as a separate management function. But modern writers regard it as the essence of the management process.

CHARACTERISTICS

Coordination is a continuing activity: Managers in every organization must perform this activity of coordination in the beginning, in the process and at the end regularly for all types of organizational activities. As it is a continuous process, it accomplishes unity of objective.

Coordination is a dynamic process: Coordination has to be done at all levels. It provides a positive and dynamic element to the entire organization and smoothens the process of administration.

Coordination is an orderly synchronization of group efforts: Coordination involves all such efforts which are involved in the harmonious blending of the different parts of an organization. Such an orderly arrangement should result in minimizing of conflict, confusion and friction and maximizing collective effectiveness. Coordination helps in proper timing, balancing and integrating the different activities of an organization.

Coordination is the task of management: As an executive leader, a manager has to perform this task of coordination, which he cannot escape.

Coordination is based on unity of objective: The very purpose of coordination is to accomplish the objectives of the organization. So, all the efforts of different groups should be directed towards the accomplishment of the common objectives.

Coordination should provide for unity of action: All the actions of the individuals are to be blended and directed towards a productive action. Every member should work together with a sense of team spirit.

COORDINATION AND COOPERATION

Coordination is the voluntary effort of individuals to work together and to help each other. It is a managerial effort of harnessing the human resources. The term *coordination* is more comprehensive than the term *cooperation*. Coordination includes the task of the manager to issue proper orders to the right people at the right time so that there is unity of objectives. Cooperation is equally essential to develop team spirit and perfect understanding among the employees.

PRINCIPLES OF COORDINATION

Mary Parker Follett, one of the experts of modern management, has suggested various principles of coordination to make it effective and functional.

Principle of early start: This principle states that it is very easy and convenient to achieve coordination in the early stages of planning and policy making; once this stage is over, and the execution of the tasks starts, it becomes difficult to secure coordination.

Principle of continuity: Coordination should be an ever-flowing and continuous process. Starting from planning up to control, coordination is essential in the entire process of management. It cannot be a temporary or ad hoc factor: it has to go on forever, it is a continuing process. Every manager should coordinate in all his managerial activities as it is a continuous factor.

Principle of direct contact: It is always better for a manager to have direct contact with the people to have effective coordination. It also provides proper feedback and understanding. The problems and potential can be understood better and undue delay can be avoided.

Principle of reciprocal relationship: All the objectives and efforts of different sectors in an organization should be properly blended. Manpower, materials, machinery, money, market, and methodology are interrelated. There should be proper coordination among such factors.

METHODS OF EFFECTIVE COORDINATION

The following are the various methods to secure effective coordination:

Well-defined authority and responsibility relationship: An organization with clear-cut and well-defined authority and responsibility can ensure effective coordination. Authority usually flows from top to bottom through various departments and levels. This will minimize misunderstanding and conflict, and improve coordination.

Proper organizational structure: The organizational structure should be functional. It should neither be oversized nor undersized. If the organization is lop-sided or unwieldy, it will affect smooth operation and coordination becomes difficult. So, modern enterprises are emphasizing on optimum or proper organization, and old organizations are reorganizing themselves for securing better coordination.

Effective communication: An intelligent manager will try to secure the maximum coordination through effective and positive communication. The channels selected for communications should be reliable and regular, and communication should help in accomplishing the objectives. Personal conversation and direct contact are always better for effective coordination.

Cooperation: Cooperation is the voluntary willingness on the part of workers. This method can help to improve the effectiveness of coordination. Cooperation can create harmony and perfect understanding which will smoothen the process of coordination.

Well-defined objectives: Management by objectives (MBO) is of great use in accomplishing perfect coordination. All the workers should try to understand the overall objectives of the organization and provide the maximum contribution through their efforts to achieve such objectives. This unity of action and unity of objectives will make the job of coordination easy.

Dynamic leadership and effective supervision: Effective leadership is able to achieve coordination from the planning level itself. Continuous and effective supervision helps achieve coordination at the execution stage.

TYPES OF COORDINATION

Coordination can be classified into external and internal coordination. Internal coordination can be further classified into vertical, horizontal and diagonal coordination.

External coordination: It is that coordination which is secured by an organization from different external agencies like shareholders, customers, dealers, competitors and the government. Coordination with the environment is absolutely essential for the survival and growth of the organization.

Internal coordination: It is that coordination which is effected between different departments and persons within the organization. Internal coordination can be vertical, horizontal or diagonal coordination.

Vertical coordination: In an organization, there are different levels. It is necessary to have coordination between these different levels of the organization. The marketing manager and the sales supervisor should have coordination for the effective performance of the marketing department.

Horizontal coordination: It is the coordination between departments or positions or persons at the same level of an organization. Coordination between the production department and purchase department, or material department and research department, can be considered horizontal coordination. Superior officers should exercise skill in bringing about such coordination. It can be achieved by regular meetings and cooperation.

Diagonal coordination: In large organizations where there will not be much proximity in the working arrangements, there is a greater necessity for coordination. Such coordination is better known as diagonal coordination.

Along with the above types of coordination, it is essential to have coordination between different zonal offices, branches and regional offices. Decentralization and delegation with unity of objectives can bring about such coordination.

TECHNIQUES OF COORDINATION

Coordination by hierarchy: In an organizational structure, every manager will have authority and he can delegate it to his subordinates. This is a chain of command and all the subordinates are responsible to their executives. This technique was popularized by the traditional management school, particularly by Max Weber and Herbert A. Simon. They stated that the superior, because of his position of authority in the hierarchy over the subordinates, can bring about coordination easily.

Coordination by ideas: This concept has been developed by Luther Gluick. He stated that coordination can be better achieved by motivation and persuasion rather than by command. He also stated that coordination can be achieved by effective leadership and through planning boards and committees.

Coordination by committees: A committee is a group of experts to whom some matter is committed to consideration, advice or decision. Such collective decisions can provide better coordination as they are taken after a careful study of the problem. But committee members must be selected carefully, and the number of members should be few. The committee should be well-informed, functional and a decision-making or recommendatory body. Nowadays, in almost all organizations, for all major decisions or tasks, committees are appointed. But in many cases, committees can postpone decisions, delay unnecessarily, or shift the responsibility.

Coordination by communication: Better and effective communication can bring about greater understanding within the organization. Direct contact and positive communication will minimize the chances of misunderstanding. An effective manager can make use of all the available channels of communication to ensure proper coordination.

Voluntary coordination: When people working in the same department or in another department develop a desire to have mutual talks and mutual trust, it may provide a good system of coordination. If the objectives, departmentation, communication systems, and the superior's concern for coordination are favourable and effective, naturally it will ensure effective voluntary coordination.

Rules, procedures and policies: Standard rules, procedures and policies are to be laid down for effective coordination of various activities. As per the rules and procedures, every department of an organization can be measured and controlled.

Incentives: Providing incentives to employees such as profit sharing and group incentive help a lot in coordination of various activities.

Liaison department: Liaison departments are established in a large organization so that coordination of various activities is easy.

DIFFICULTIES IN COORDINATION

Coordination is very difficult in large organizations. The following are the difficulties for coordination in a large organization:

Time orientation: Employees of different departments give different timings to complete the task. The time for completion of work of a production department may not match with the requirement of the marketing department. There may be differences towards goal achievement. Different employees express their views differently for goal achievement. Coordinating all the views of people is very difficult.

Interpersonal orientation: Interpersonal differences are common in an organization, and managing those differences is very difficult.

Formality of structure: Different departments of an organization have different standards. Evaluation and coordination will become difficult because of different objectives and standards.

Though there are certain difficulties, the manager concerned has to coordinate effectively for achieving the goals of an organization.

MANAGING COORDINATION

Coordination is possible when we pay heed to the following aspects:

- Proper planning and progressive outlook
- Departmentation, delegation and decentralization
- Direct contacts and personal communication with individuals
- Forming committees which are compact, functional and meaningful
- Having regular staff meetings
- Encouraging participation and group discussion
- Developing workable internal strategies and programmes

To conclude, planning itself will not ensure successful results. A powerful and well-planned cricket team may not succeed unless there is a coordinated effort among the captain, batsmen, bowlers and fielders. Collective effort of individuals will be much more effective and powerful than the efforts of each individual applied separately. Coordination will increase productivity, efficiency, performance, standards and regularity. It involves harmony and understanding. Unity of objectives will strengthen the coordination process.

SUMMARY

1. Coordination is the task of arranging group efforts in a systematic manner.
2. The success of an organization depends upon coordination.
3. Coordination is a continuous process in an organization.
4. Coordination is based on the principle of cooperation.
5. There are certain methods of effective coordination.
6. Coordination helps in building understanding and harmony in an organization.

REVIEW QUESTIONS

1. Define coordination. Bring out its characteristic features.
2. Explain the importance of coordination. How does it differ from cooperation?
3. What are the techniques of achieving effective coordination?
4. Explain briefly different types of coordination that exist in an organization.
5. What are the difficulties in coordination?

CASE STUDY

Shahid Fabrics

Mr Lateef, Chairman of Shahid Fabrics, a Hyderabad-based garments and piece goods firm which exported all its products to the USA, faced a decision in August 1985. The US Government had imposed quota restrictions which reduced the exports of his firm by 40 per cent. He had to find a new market for his products.

Shahid Fabrics was one of Pakistan's major exporters of garments and piece goods. Its share was 25 per cent of the exports of these goods of the whole country. It was established in 1954 as a producer of cotton cloth and later, in 1966, it extended production to include garments and piece goods. It had eight local production units and the total number of employees was 8,000. All its garments and piece goods were exported, and branded according to customer specification. All the goods were exported to the USA, and the sales of the firm amounted to US$ 100 million. In 1984, the US Government imposed quota restrictions. By August 1985, Shahid Fabrics exports had been reduced by 40 per cent.

Mr Lateef believed that finding new markets was the only way to survive. The possible alternatives, according to him, were the EEC countries, the USSR, the Middle East and the other Asian countries. The EEC was a very good potential market, but Europeans were very tough buyers. It would be necessary to segregate the EEC from other buyers because of their existing specifications with regard to style, colour and packing. The USSR too was a potential market as far as demand was concerned, but the country did not have enough money in foreign exchange.

The Middle East had money, but their requirements were small due to their smaller population. Second, these countries preferred not to buy Pakistani goods directly from Pakistan.

They would rather like to buy the same Pakistani goods, branded differently from other Western countries, say France.

Asia was a big market, but the Asian countries, including Turkey, were Shahid Fabrics' competition in the international market. Mr. Lateef was deeply concerned with the loss of 40 per cent of his export goods. He was eager to determine which new market offered the highest potential. He wondered what specific information he could use to help in his decision.

Questions for Discussion

1. What information should Mr Lateef develop to evaluate foreign markets?
2. Where should he look for this information?
3. Develop a framework to help Mr Lateef identify his best potential foreign markets.

FURTHER READING

Chester, Barnard, *The Functions of an Executive*, Harvard University Press, Cambridge (Mass.), 1938.

Drucker, Peter, F., *The Frontiers of Management*, Heinemann, London, 1987.

Stoner, James A.F. et al., *Management*, Pearson/Prentice-Hall of India, New Delhi, 2005.

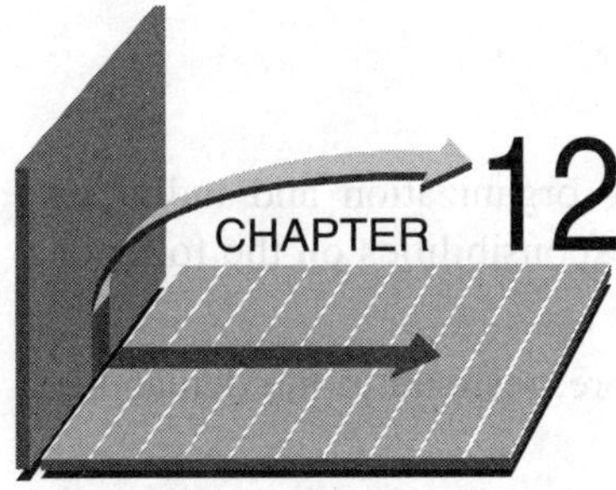

Management and Society

CONTENTS

INTRODUCTION

Social development is the main aim of any form of organization all over the world. Therefore, business has certain responsibilities towards society. Managements are expected to follow the values of the society they work in. In India, everyone is competing for products and profits. But many organizations are not fulfilling their social responsibilities.

Social responsibilities are basic obligations of business organizations. These are described in terms of obligations of business towards the various interest groups as follows:

- Consumers/customers
- Employees
- Owners
- The community
- Fellow business entrepreneurs
- The state

Social responsibilities must be fulfilled by each and every organization and individual. According to George Steiner, a business should assume social responsibilities on the following bases:

1. Corporations are creatures of society and should, therefore, respond to the demands of society.
2. The long-term self-interests of business are best served when business assumes social responsibilities.
3. It is the moral and right thing to do.

CRITERIA FOR SOCIAL RESPONSIBILITIES

Stoner suggests criteria for determining the social responsibilities of business.

- Every business must realize what its social responsibility is, and in deciding what to do, the value and interest of top management's perception of public expectations are the guiding factors.
- Business must be considered to be basically an economic institution with a strong profit motive. Business' search for profitable opportunities may reduce or eliminate many hard social problems.
- Business should take the long-term view and perform socially responsible actions that might temporarily lessen net profit, but are in the profit interests of the company in the long run.
- The greater is the social power of a business, the larger will be its social responsibilities.
- The larger the size of an individual business, the greater its social responsibilities.
- Social responsibilities vary with the type of company.
- Social responsibility should not involve high investment so that it jeopardizes the firm's stability to attract shareholder's investment.
- Business should be obliged to internalize more of its investment costs.

According to Andrew Carnegie, the founder of the conglomerate US Steel Corporation, social responsibility is based on two principles—principle of charity and principle of stewardship. Business owners are like parents, and employees and customers are like children. The charity principle says that more fortunate people of the society have to assist less fortunate people directly or indirectly. The stewardship principle explains that the wealthy business persons are stewards or caretakers of their property, as in trust, for the rest of the society and use it for any legitimate purpose.

SACHAR COMMITTEE RECOMMENDATIONS

The Sachar Committee in its report enumerated the following social responsibilities of a company:

1. It should base its decision not on what is best for its shareholders but on what is best for the community at large.
2. Acceptance of the concept of social responsibility must be reflected in the information and disclosure that the company makes available for the benefit of its various interest groups. Openness in corporate affairs is the first principle in securing responsible behaviour.
3. Companies should be responsive to national problems such as unemployment, rural development, over-population, etc.
4. Companies should prepare a social report at the end of each year indicating and qualifying in as precise and clear terms as possible the various activities relating to the social responsibilities which have been carried out by the company in the previous year.

Some other reasons for increase in consciousness of social responsibility are as follows:

Sense of service: It has modified the greed for profit. Economic order has come to recognize social order as its very foundation. It is now increasingly recognized that what is not for the public good is not for the good of business.

Purchasing power of the public: Industry has come to understand that one of its functions is to manufacture and distribute quality products/services as per the purchasing power of the public. It has led to the business policy of higher wages and lower prices.

Rise of a new relationship between the public and business:

Table 12.1 Model of corporate social responsibility

Type of responsibility	*Societal expectation*	*Examples*
Philanthropic responsibilities	Desired of business by society	• Corporate contributions • Programmes supporting community/education • Community involvement, improvement, volunteerism
Ethical responsibilities	Expected of business by society	• Avoid questionable practices • Respond to 'spirit' of laws • Assume law is a floor on behaviour; operate above minimum required by law • Assert ethical leadership
Legal responsibilities regulations	Required of business by society	• Obey all laws, adhere to environmental laws • Consumer laws affecting all employees • Obey Foreign Corrupt Practices Act, fulfil all contractual obligations
Economic responsibilities	Required of business by society	• Be profitable • Maximize sales revenue • Minimize costs [administrative, production, marketing, distribution] • Make wise strategic decisions • Be attentive to dividend policy

RESPONSIBILITIES TOWARDS CONSUMERS

Consumers, employees, investors, fellow businessmen, community and state represent different interest groups that should be satisfied by management of business enterprises. Since goods are produced, they are to be sold, and consumers need to be satisfied. In fact, in a market-based economy, the consumer is often considered to be "the king". Firms that produce goods which consumers will buy are successful. The consumer not only determines the income of business firms but also affects their success and survival. The goodwill of consumers is, thus, a critical factor for the success of business.

The basic business responsibilities towards consumers may be summed up in terms of five *R*'s—the right quality, right quantity, right time, right place and right price.

To be more specific, business responsibilities towards consumers include the following:

- To produce goods that meet the needs of consumers of different classes, tastes and with different purchasing power.
- To establish fair prices of products consistent with quality, efficiency and reasonable profits to the firm.
- To provide prompt, adequate, courteous, and friendly service to customers.
- To ensure fairly wide distribution of products among all sections of consumers.
- To improve their standard of living in society by producing goods and services which they need.

RESPONSIBILITIES TOWARDS EMPLOYEES

Employees also represent an important interest group to which a business enterprise has certain social obligations. A perfunctory or apathetic approach to employee relations is a thing of the past and must not be considered adequate under the present value system of society. The traditional approach to employee relations needs to be replaced by a more humane and scientific approach towards them. In particular, social responsibilities of business towards employees include:

- Fair remuneration
- Job security and safety
- Proper working conditions and employee welfare
- Trade union rights
- Employee promotion and code of conduct
- Employee participation in management.

RESPONSIBILITIES TOWARDS INVESTORS

- To ensure safety of investment over a period of time
- To provide the highest long-term rate of return on investment
- To provide steady capital appreciation on investment
- To ensure industrial democracy and provide for effective representation of different categories of investors on the board of directors of the company.

RESPONSIBILITIES TOWARDS INTER-BUSINESS RELATIONSHIPS

Every business deals with a number of other business units. For the success of its own business, a company should, therefore, develop healthy and cooperative inter-business relationships. Fair trade practices regarding prices, quality, delivery, payment and service can be an expression of proper discharge of social responsibility in relation to dealers and suppliers.

RESPONSIBILITIES TOWARDS THE COMMUNITY

It is an important responsibility of business to inform the community about the company's policies and programmes, and, above all, how the enterprise contributes to the development of the locality and welfare of the community.

The important aspects of social responsibilities of business towards community include the following:

- Help the local civic administration to provide better public services by providing financial and technical help to municipalities and district boards.
- Promote community help by aiding the Red Cross, hospital boards and medical research institutes.
- Aid schools, colleges and other educational institutions to provide better education to the members of the community—business units should also sponsor research projects.
- Promote cultural enrichment of the community by encouraging greater appreciation of art, music and drama.
- Encourage sports and provide recreational facilities.
- Organize community forums and discussion groups and thus promote better understanding of national and local affairs.
- Minimize the problem of pollution and help community efforts in this direction.
- Abandon ostentatious living and display of wealth, and develop socially desirable standards of living for themselves.

RESPONSIBILITIES TOWARDS THE STATE

In every country, the government is taking keen interest in trade, production, distribution, control and regulation of business. This combination of trade and political power in the government has added to the already existing social responsibilities of business towards the state.

Social Attitudes, Beliefs and Values

According to Koontz and O'Donnell, a number of social beliefs have evolved for social development in the USA. Some important social beliefs are as follows:

- There are opportunities for people who are willing and able to work to take advantage of them.
- Faith in business and respect for business leaders and owners.

- Belief in competition and competitiveness in all aspects of life.
- Respect for the individual, regardless of race, religion, or creed.
- Respect for authority arising from ownership of property, expert knowledge, and elected political position.
- Belief in, and respect for, education.
- Faith in logical processes, science and technology.
- Belief in the importance of change and experimentation to find better ways of doing things.

Suggestions for maintaining social values are:

- Providing clear guidelines for ethical behaviour.
- Teaching ethical guidelines and their importance.
- Setting up controls that check on illegal or unethical deeds.
- Conducting frequent and unpredictable audits.
- Publishing trespassers in a meaningful way.
- Emphasizing regularly that loyalty to the company does not excuse improper behaviour or actions.

THE 10 COMMANDMENTS OF CORPORATE SOCIAL RESPONSIBILITY

1. Take corrective action before it is required.
2. Work with affected constituents to resolve mutual problems.
3. Work to establish industry-wide standards and self-regulation.
4. Admit your mistakes publicly.
5. Get involved in appropriate social programmes.
6. Help correct environmental problems.
7. Monitor the changing social environment.
8. Establish and enforce a corporate code of conduct.
9. Take needed public stands on social issues.
10. Strive to make profits on an ongoing basis.

ETHICS OF MANAGERS

Managers' ethics include a wide range of organizational decisions and actions. A recent study of the values and ethics of managers by Barry Posner and Warren Schmidt found that:

- the foremost goal of managers is to make their organizations effective.
- profit maximization and stockholders' interests were not the central goals of the manager's studies.
- attending to customers was seen as important.
- integrity was the characteristic most highly rated by managers at all levels.

- pressure to conform to organizational standards was seen as high.
- spouses are important in helping their mates grapple with ethical dilemmas.
- most managers seek the advice of others in handling ethical dilemmas.

Robert J. Mockler has identified factors that affect decisions on ethical problems. Some simplify the problems, others complicate them.

SOCIAL AUDIT

The measurement, evaluation and reporting of the performance of an organization in the area of social responsibility is called *social audit*. It is also defined as "A commitment to systematic assessment of and reporting of some meaningful definable domain of a company's activities that have social impact" (Bauer and Fenn).

"Social audit, much like financial audit, is an identification and examination of the activities of the firm in order to assess, evaluate, measure and report their impact on the immediate social environment" (Ahmed Belkaoui).

Social audit helps to determine the areas where the firm could be vulnerable to public criticism. Organizations can inform the public regarding their activities for society. The true picture of corporate accountability can be given to the society. Social audit may be measured in the areas of employment, production, consumer effort, consumer funds absorbed, payrolls, dividends and interest, environmental protection, etc.

The Committee for Economic Development of the United States of America conducted a study on the current business practices of corporate business on social audits. Out of the 284 companies that responded, the main points were:

- 76 per cent of the companies had made an inventory of social audit (three-fourths of the companies performed this function),
- 70 per cent performed this function voluntarily, and
- 30 per cent made their social audit reports available to the general public.

A Ford Foundation support study found that 57 per cent of institutional investors took social considerations into account in the selection of investments. The US Chamber of Commerce also urged business firms to develop social audit procedures.

In the wake of the 1967 summer riots in Detroit, the Michigan Bell Telephone Company announced that it would "adopt" the city's Northern High School and place its own instructors and equipment in the school to supplement, and, in the company's words, to "enrich" the regular teaching programme. Soon after, Chrysler Corporation announced that it would also adopt a Detroit public school.

The Government of Florida (Claude Kirk Jr) subcontracted some of the state's regular police work to a private company which already does similar work for the federal government. The city of New York's mayor (John Lindsay) called in McKinsey & Company to analyze his administration's air pollution problems, and the Traffic Commission invited Sperry Rand, and later IBM, to help to solve the city's growing traffic headache. The Government of California has borrowed business executives whose salaries continue to be paid by their respective companies as consultants in seeking ways to trim the costs of the state government.

In India, this concept was first implemented by TISCO. Gradually, Zuari Agro Chemicals Ltd., Indian Petro Chemicals Corporation Ltd., the Cement Corporation of India, ITC, and several other public and private sector enterprises implemented certain measures of corporate social audit. In TISCO, the social and moral responsibilities of the company were observed in five spheres. They are: (a) customers, (b) employees, (c) shareholders, (d) society and (e) the local community. The organization has contributed towards pollution control, employer-employee relations, consumers, shareholders and community development. The mission of Nagarjuna Group of Industries chief executive was "service to society through industry". Tata's crest is also "Humata" (good thoughts), "Hukhta" (good words), and "Hvarshta" (good deeds).

In the public sector, the Cement Corporation of India has been publishing "Social Accounts" in its annual reports since 1980. The Indian Petro Chemicals Corporation Ltd. has also been following social audit. Several other companies in steel, petroleum, engineering, textiles, etc. also are on the move towards this concept.

The following practices are followed in some of the above enterprises:

- Net income contribution
- Human resource contribution
- Employment to deserving people
- Environmental contribution (pollution)
- Product/service contribution (quality, durability, safety)
- Customer satisfaction
- Service to the society/nation.

Whatever may be the activity of the enterprise, social audit is needed in an organization for satisfying the customer and achieving excellence. Enterprises have to make it a compulsory process at the time of preparing their final accounts. The customer's/community's delight is to be considered as the main purpose of its existence and survival, instead of concentrating only on business expansion or customers. The Total Quality Management concept needs to be introduced in organizations. Each company has to set aside a certain percentage of its profits for in-house R&D on several aspects of management. Implementation of the social audit function should be taken care of by HR professionals along with the people concerned. As stated by Whitehead's Alfred North, "A great society is a society in which its people of business think greatly of their functions."

CSR ACTIVITIES

The CSR activities in the following organizations have been presented:

1. Visakhapatnam Steel Plant (VSP)
2. Hindustan Petroleum Company Limited (HPCL)
3. National Thermal Power Corporation Limited (NTPCL)
4. Steel Authority of India Limited (SAIL)

CSR at Visakhapatnam Steel Plant

In the contemporary corporate business world, Corporate Social Responsibility (CSR) has received a lot of attention in the context of sustainability challenge and the role of corporate entities in addressing the "Triple Bottom Line" *viz.* Economic, Environmental and Social issues in a sustainable way that aims to improve the quality of life for everyone.

CSR is a company's commitment to operate in an economically, socially and environmentally sustainable manner, while recognizing the interests of its stakeholders. This commitment is beyond statutory requirements. In other words, CSR is a concept whereby organizations serve the interests of society by taking responsibility for the impact of their activities on customers, employees, shareholders, communities and the environment in all aspects of their operations (Figure 12.1).

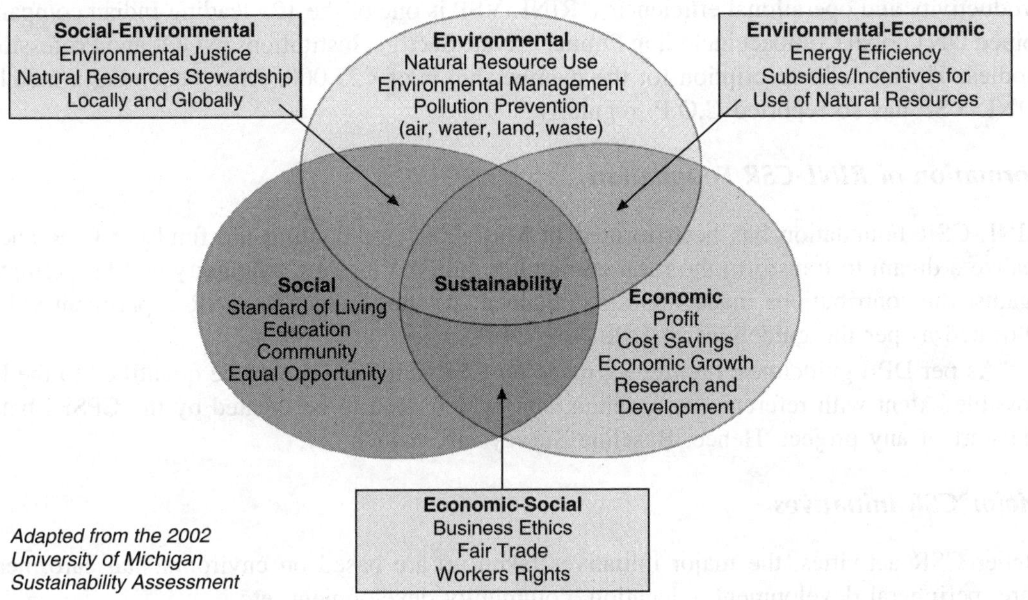

Figure 12.1 The three spheres of sustainability.

Formation of CSR Department

To monitor all the CSR activities of RINL-VSP and to take up the peripheral developmental activities in RH colonies and surrounding villages, a separate CSR department was formed in March, 2007 to have focused attention.

Formation of CSR policy: A policy covering the boundaries of the scope of activities, the initiatives, guidelines on sponsorships and contributions, budgetary allocation, implementation mechanism and delegation of powers for the operation of activities has been framed and approved by VSP Board of RINL in November, 2006.

Scope of the policy: The main focus is to emphasize on—(i) Environmental Care, (ii) Education, (iii) Health Care, (iv) People Care, (v) Peripheral Development, (vi) Cultural Efflorescence, (vii) Activities as a responsible Corporate Citizen, and (viii) To extend help during natural calamities like floods, fire, epidemic, etc.

Membership of Global Compact

The United Nations Global Compact is a strategic policy initiative for business that is committed to aligning their operations and strategies with four issue areas covering ten universally accepted principles on Human rights, Labour practices, Environment and Anti-corruption. Encompassing the above concepts, RINL-VSP joined hands with the UN Global Compact Organization by becoming a member on 6 April, 2006 for demonstrating leadership by producing practical solutions to contemporary problems related to globalization, sustainable development and corporate responsibility in a multi-stakeholder context, managing risks by taking a proactive stance on critical issues, sharing good practices and learning, accessing UN's broad knowledge in development issues and improving corporate/broad management, employee morale and productivity and operational efficiencies. RINL-VSP is one of the 125 leading Indian companies joined UN Global Compact including Public, Private Sectors, Institutions, NGOs and Professional Bodies. The annual subscription for the membership is of ₹25,000. After becoming a member, RINL-VSP has so reported C.O.P. regularly.

Formation of RINL-CSR Foundation

RINL-CSR Foundation has been formed in May, 2007 for holding the funds of CSR and to realize a dream to transform the rural community into a Vibrant Community and IT exemption against the contributions made was also obtained. Annual budget for CSR department will be allocated as per the guidelines of DPE.

As per DPE guidelines, the impact made by CSR activities should be quantified to the best possible extent with reference to baseline data, which need to be created by the CPSEs before the start of any project. Hence, Baseline Surveys are mandatory.

Major CSR Initiatives

Under CSR activities, the major initiatives taken up are based on environmental care, health care, peripheral development, education, community development, etc.

Environmental care

- Environment-friendly project 'Jaladhara' was implemented to provide safe drinking water to 19 tribal villages of Agency area of Vizag District. This project provides filtered, perennial drinking water by gravitation method from a rain-fed source which is at heights, without using electrical power/energy. About 5500 people in 19 villages were benefited. The project was implemented through M/s D. Sarada Trust.
- This program 'Green Visakha' was launched with a view to reduce pollution in the area of Greater Visakha Municipal Corporation (GVMC). The program has been planned with a target of planting 500,000 trees within a period of 5 years (commencing from year 2011) in the GVMC area.
- Solar street lighting and home lighting system was provided to all the homes, libraries and offices in SOS Children village, Bheemunipatnam, Visakhapatnam District. This village for orphan children with 14 houses, schools, libraries and offices were provided with solar powered home lighting system and street lighting, saving the huge electricity bill and power cuts. This benefited about 200 people.

Health care

RINL has taken up a number of activities in this field. Some of the initiatives taken up by RINL-VSP in this direction are:

- RINL made reciprocities arrangement with Sankar Foundation for conducting free eye camps and cataract surgeries under financial aid and for setting up 8 operation theatres in their hospital near Simhachalam. Eye camps were organized since the year 2007 through M/s Sankar Foundation in rehabilitation colonies, peripheral villages of VSP and rural areas of Vizag, Vizianagaram and Srikakulam districts. About 22,000 people were tested and 5000 cataract surgeries were carried out.
- A state of art mobile cancer detection van 'Sanjeevan' equipped with latest cancer detection facilities which enable early detection of cancer for permanent recovery was given to Lions Cancer Hospital. The van is fully funded by RINL with ₹116 lakhs. Lions Cancer Hospital has organized cancer detection camps in rural areas of 5 Districts *viz.* Visakhapatnam, Vizianagaram, Srikakulam, East Godavari and West Godavari. Cancer detection camps were organized and suspected cases have been taken to Lions Cancer Hospital for further investigation and treatment.
- The company contributed to organize cultural programs in Gangavaram, Pedagantyada, Vadlapudi and Aganampudi RH colonies. Programs covering folk act—Burra katha, classical dance, patriotic and devotional songs, were performed in the local communities where the talent of the people is also showcased.
- Supplying treated drinking water to rehabilitation colonies during thirsty summer days.

Peripheral development

RINL has given major thrust to Peripheral Development and has implemented several innovative schemes like:

- Construction of Community Welfare Centres (19 nos.) in rehabilitation colonies and peripheral villages for organizing social events, functions, etc. These can be served as shelters during natural calamities.
- Laying cement concrete roads of length 5.2 km in Vadlapudi rehabilitation colony and peripheral villages.
- Construction of Function Hall for SC/ST community at Pedagantyada RH colony.

Education

In its attempt to ensure that all children have the opportunity to meet basic learning needs, RINL has taken up the following activities:

- **Visakha Vimala Vidyalaya Schools:** Free education to about 1500 children of BPL families at Ukkunagaram and Gantyada in house campus.
- **Arunodaya Special School for Differently Abled Children:** RINL has constructed school building at a cost of ₹200 lakhs, providing free education to 70 children and facilities like physiotherapy, speech therapy, yoga therapy, music therapy, vocational training, etc. located in campus at Ukkunagaram.

- **Additional accommodation at hostels for SC/ST girls/boys:** Additional accommodation was provided at 3 hostels for SC/ST girls/boys in Visakhapatnam city benefiting about 360 students.
- **Additional classrooms:** Constructed additional classrooms in 30 schools in rehabilitation colonies and peripheral villages and provided play equipment to 71 schools.
- **Furniture:** Provided desk-cum-benches to 38 schools benefiting around 4935 students.

People care

People care is an integral part of CSR activities in the company. Activities organized in this direction include:

- **Empowerment programs to women and unemployed youth:** Vocational training programs organized through Jan Shiksha Sansthan (JSS) in rehabilitation colonies and Paderu (tribal area). About 6000 people were trained in courses like Light Motor Vehicle Driving, MS Office, Two-wheeler mechanism, soft-toys making, Ariya work, Beautician, Dress-making, Electrician and income generation programs like manufacturing/producing phenyl, detergent powder etc., at Araku (Agency area of Vizag Dist.).
- The company has supported sportspersons, sponsorship of various sporting events at District and National level including Special Olympics for Physically-challenged children/persons.

As a responsible corporate citizen

RINL as a responsible corporate citizen supported following activities:

- Provided Offset Printing Press for prisoners at Central Prison (Vizag) to create opportunities for a meaningful life.
- Constructed a Police Station building at Kanithi Junction.
- Constructed Road-over-Bridge at Balacheruvu Road.

Help during natural calamities

- Help was extended during floods in Bihar, Andhra Pradesh.
- Help extended for reconstruction of houses devastated during earthquake in Sikkim.
- Contributed steel for reconstruction of houses at Bheemunipatnam (gutted in fire accident).

CSR in Mines Areas

The company has its captive mines for limestone, dolomite, manganese and sand. Activities were taken up in mine areas of Jaggayyapet, Madaram and Garbham. The mining activities are served by employees residing in township area of the mines. CSR activities in the mines cover community and society living in and around that area.

- Vocational training was given to 725 women at Jaggayyapet and Garbham villages in courses like dress-making, ariya works, hand embroidery, fabric painting, etc., for their sustainable living.

- School furniture, library books, computer and other sports material were provided to the schools in mines area at Jaggayyapet and Garbham.
- Power supply was given to water supply scheme at Madaram village.
- Laying of roads and installing bore wells.

CSR at Outstation Branches and Rural India

- Distribution of school kits to 60 students and adoption of 20 girl students of schools at Bengaluru and Jaipur.
- In rural areas of Uttar Pradesh, the company has taken up CSR activities which include:
  - Construction of 8 additional class rooms in existing schools.
  - Providing 350 solar street lights.
  - Providing 261 hand pumps for water supply.
  - Laying of link road in Barabanki district.
  - Providing 1500 solar lanterns to girl students studying in schools of Gonda district.
  - Providing placement-based skill development training to 250 eligible candidates in Gonda district.
- Activities of Branch Office at Kanpur include:
  - Distribution of school bags, educational kit and other items to 400 poor school children in Government/aided schools.
  - Adoption of 50 girl students of below poverty line families, in Government/Aided schools, up to Class XII.
  - Distribution of tricycles to 50 poor and physically-challenged persons.
  - Distribution of desktop computers to 25 brilliant students of Government/Aided schools.

CSR through Visteel Mahila Samiti (VMS)

The ladies arm of RINL is executing several community development and societal support as a part of CSR initiatives on behalf of RINL. Some of the activities by VMS are:

- Providing desk-cum-benches, fans and sports items for students in peripheral villages—Nangineripadu and BC colony of Parawada.
- Distribution of plates and glasses to 370 students in schools in Gangavaram and Pedagantyada rehabilitation colonies towards midday meals.
- Distributing uniforms to students of government schools in Pedagantyada rehabilitation colony.
- Organizing a medical camp at Dayal Nagar near Pedagantyada Rehabilitation colony.
- Immediate response to the occasion, extended relief and succour to the 16 fire accident victim families at Devada, a village in the plant vicinity.
- In health care area, the company has organized general medical camps, de-addiction camps, child immunization, AIDS awareness campaigns, eye check-up camps and medical help during natural calamities and disasters in association with Satya Sai Seva Samithi, doctors from Visakha Steel General Hospital in rehabilitation colonies and peripheral villages of VSP.

- Distribution of artificial limbs and tricycles to 609 poor and needy tribal people in Vizag, Vizianagaram, Srikakulam and West Godavari districts of Andhra Pradesh through M/s Gurudeva Charitable Trust.
- Mother blood bank building was constructed with an outlay of ₹280 lakhs having all necessary equipment for Indian Red Cross Society, Visakhapatnam, and state of art facilities for storage of blood, training needs of technicians, rehabilitation program centres, IRC and YRC training programs. It serves poor and needy from North coastal districts of AP and neighbouring states.
- 3134 Mosquito Nets were distributed in 20 Tribal Welfare Ashram Schools in 9 tribal mandals of Visakhapatnam district, where people are being affected with malaria menace, under the aegis of Integrated Tribal Development Authority (ITDA).
- Dormitory block for AIDS affected children at St. Joseph Hospital, Prathipadu, is under progress.

CSR Initiatives at Hindustan Petroleum Company Limited (HPCL)

HPCL took its first step in CSR during 1985–1986 with a modest budget of ₹18 lakhs for welfare activities to benefit SC/STs and other weaker sections of the society under special component plan. Budget for the CSR projects subsequently rose every year and large portions of under-privileged masses were gradually included in the schemes. As a policy, HPCL allocates certain percentage of the net profit for each financial year to the special component plan and CSR activities. The expenditure for 2005–2006 is for SCP Projects and ₹8 crores for other CSR Projects. An 'HPCL foundation' is now operating to finance the CSR projects and also monitor the implementation of various schemes.

Corporate Level Initiatives

1. ***Swavalamban:*** Providing free vocational training to low income group households.
2. ***Navjyot:*** To increase the health index of slum children.
3. ***Unnati:*** Providing computer training to school children at Visakhapatnam and Vijayawada.
4. ***Nanhi kali:*** To support the girl child for getting quality school education in Mehboobnagar district and Paderu region of Andhra Pradesh.
5. ***Suraksha:*** To prevent HIV/AIDS through training/lecturing truck drivers at highway retail outlets.
6. ***Global warming:*** Providing knowledge to school children at Delhi and Goa through an operating partner CSR&L (Centre for Social Responsibility and Leadership). Apart from the above CSR activities specially undertaken by HPCL for specific groups, the other social development activities include associating with health care, education, environmental protection, agricultural development, rural reconstruction, water supply development, etc. It can be said that HPCL has touched lives qualitatively, acting as a corporate social ambassador by taking up the above activities.

CSR Activities at HPCL Visakhapatnam Refinery

1. Activities on employee welfare

(a) HPCL upholds the freedom of association to all their employees by recognizing the workers' unions.

(b) HPCL has established standard policies and practices to deal with collective bargaining by employees on issues of common interest.

(c) HPCL has signed long-term settlements for salaries, wages and perks of employees.

(d) HPCL also signed agreements with employees' associations that ensure career progression.

(e) Regular meetings are held at HPCL with the representatives of recognized unions for rationalization of manpower, monthly targets, material and inventory maintenance, review of storage facilities, housekeeping, quality, improvements, shift schedules and information sharing.

(f) Senior Managers of HPCL regularly interact with employees to share the details of prevailing business environment, organization performance, growth strategies and future business plans.

(g) HPCL does not support any forced or compulsory labour in any form and adheres to all labour laws in this regard.

(h) HPCL does not engage any person below the age of 18 year as direct employee or even as a contract labour as per the Recruitment policy.

(i) HPCL provides equal opportunity to the citizens of India in employment and avoids discrimination on any ground such as caste, colour, gender and religion.

(j) HPCL strictly follows Government rules with regard to reservation for Scheduled Castes, Scheduled Tribes, Other Backward Classes and physically handicapped persons.

(k) HPCL employed maximum women employees in administrative offices, their percentage as compared to total employees being 7%.

2. Activities to enrich quality of life of the community

(a) HPCL is committed to project human lives both at the workplace and the resident in the vicinity of the company by deploying state of the art technology.

(b) Regular maintenance of equipment is taken up for safety and security of the employees and the inhabitants living in surrounding areas.

(c) HPCL imparted extensive training to regular employees on 'Safety Management' and 'Hazardous Process Management'.

(d) HPCL has an approved policy for handling grievances of employees, shareholders and customers.

(e) HPCL designed the standing orders followed by non-management employees and the conduct, discipline and appeal rules for management employees in compliance with Human Rights.

3. Activities to protect environment

(a) HPCL refineries have developed systems and procedures for attaining compliance with international standards and reduced SO_2 emissions from 36 TPD in 1984 to less than 12 TPD.

(b) HPCL Visakhapatnam refinery has implemented the Environment Management System and has been certified by M/s SGS India Pvt. Ltd. for ISO 14001-2009.

(c) HPCL has reduced dependence on road transport for taking petroleum products to different storage terminals by laying product pipelines. This has reduced the use of trucks for transportation of petroleum products and contributed in reduction of auto-emissions.

(d) HPCL is using environment-friendly technologies such as Diesel Hydro Desulphurization for reducing the sulphur content in Diesel used by automobiles.

(e) HPCL has initiated a novel concept of pay-and-use community cooking with log called *rasoighar* for below poverty line communities who are exposed to harmful smoke due to the use of fire-wood for cooking. This will help them to overcome health problems such as cataract due to smoke. The loss of wages due to collection effort for the fire-wood is also minimized. The negative effects of cutting trees for fire-wood leading to the loss of green cover are also minimized.

4. Computer literacy project

Company has been imparted basic computer training to 3000 students studying in 8th, 9th and 10th standards in 9 schools of Visakhapatnam through NIIT. These students come from poor families and their parents could not afford to buy computer or send their children for paid computer training.

5. Activities under special component plan

In 2007–2008 following activities involving the expense of ₹5.75 crores have been undertaken as a part of CSR:

(a) **Primary education:** Provided uniforms, notebooks, library books, school furniture, stationery items, study material, lab equipment, etc.

(b) **Scholarships:** Scholarships were given to SC/ST and BC students from various colleges and universities for graduation and PG studies.

(c) **Drinking water facility:** Provided bore wells, tube-wells, pumps, water storage tanks in tribal villages.

(d) **Health care:** Conducted medical camps, eye check-up camps and distributed free medicines and spectacles. Provided medical equipment to hospitals and constructed a building for Blood Bank.

(e) **Vocational training:** Provided computer training for women, provided raw materials to artisans to make handicraft items and training was given to rural women.

(f) **Rehabilitation of persons with disabilities:** Provided study material, artificial limbs, speech trainer, group hearing aids, braille computers for blinds, tricycles, PCO kiosks, etc.

(g) **Community hall:** For villages and provided reading room as rural library.

Unique Features of CSR Activities

1. The activities under the Special Component Plan are designed to benefit the less privileged strata of the society directly.
2. The plans are also helpful to provide basic education, vocational training and also higher education to help the beneficiary to develop the skills for taking up a successful career.
3. The income generating schemes for women in tribal settlements and rural areas such as tailor training, toy making, handicrafts, items, etc. are such that the beneficiaries will be able to earn sustainable income for the families.
4. Rehabilitation of persons with disabilities by providing tools that enable the beneficiary to overcome his deficiency and work like a normal person. This will enhance his confidence level and give him the courage to lead a normal life.
5. The health care facilities such as medical camps providing free medicines, hospital equipment and ambulance services are the essential services a corporate should provide as a part of CSR activity.

National Thermal Power Corporation Ltd. (NTPCL)

Drivers of CSR

NTPC has been a socially committed organization since inception. It's mission statement includes "to be a responsible corporate citizen with thrust on environment protection, rehabilitation and ash utilization." In pursuance of the vision and mission, NTPC had a specific corporate objective towards sustainable power development as follows:

- To contribute towards sustainable power development by functioning as a responsible corporate citizen and discharge social responsibilities in the areas of environment protection and rehabilitation.
- The corporation will strive to utilize the ash produced at its stations to the maximum extent possible.
- For achieving its mission and objective, NTPC formulated specific policies, as delineated in subsequent paragraphs of this note. The policies were formulated to address the issue of corporate social responsibility in a comprehensive and systematic manner.

Commitment for CSR

NTPC's sole endeavour is to institutionalize social responsibility at various levels; to add value to the community and society on a sustainable basis through dedicated policies, institutional setup and engagement process; to promote inclusive growth and improve quality of life of people in surrounding areas.

Engagement of community in acceptance of specific CSR initiatives inculcates a sense of ownership among the people and plays a vital role in smooth and successful implementation of schemes. According to Mr. Arup Roy Choudhury (CMD), NTPC states that "we value the partnerships we build with the communities around our units. For us, Corporate Social Responsibility is Corporate Social Relationship."

Pillars of CSR

The pillars include Policies, Structure, Budget and Process the initiation of CSR activity as follows:

- *Initial Community Development (ICD):* Policy mandating CD from project inception.
- *Resettlement & Rehabilitation (R&R):* Policy envisaging CD during project development.
- *CSR-Community Development (CSR-CD):* Policy issued in July 2004 (revised in August 2010 in line with DPE guidelines) for CD activities during operational phase.
- *Committee of the Board for CSR:* To guide, approve and review CSR activity.
- *3-Tier Structure:* At Corporate, Region and Unit with defined responsibilities.
- *NTPC Foundation:* For national level initiatives with focus on persons with special abilities.
- *Budget Allocation:* Overall allocation by Board of Directors and Allocation against specific activities by Committee of Board for CSR.
- *Planning:* Bottom up Approach, Need Assessment Survey, Stakeholder consultation (VDAC, Admin, RPDAC, People's representatives).
- *Implementation:* In project mode with defined deliverables and timelines and through specialized agencies and EVOICE.
- *Monitoring and Evaluation:* Regular monitoring at Units, Regions, Corporate with monthly and quarterly reporting and Internal Audit and Impact Evaluation by external agencies.
- *Documentation and Communication:* Reporting to Committee of Board and Annual Reports, Internet, Intranet, Annual Brochure, etc.

Policies in NTPC on Social Responsibilities

NTPC adopted a visionary approach to address the issue of corporate social responsibility since its inception. NTPC management takes every care to promote and fulfil the recreational and health requirements of the youth and the innate urges of different social groups to meaningfully project their cultural traditions and social values. A sense of pride and respect for the cultural ethos and social moorings of the employees is developed by the management as a conscious effort towards national integration. Besides, the management views the indulgence of its employees in the sports and cultural activities as a source of satisfying their latent needs for creativity, accomplishment, development and recognition. Therefore, the management has endeavoured to provide facilities in all its projects/stations for the welfare of employees and for the pursuit and practice of various games, sports and fine arts namely, dance, drama, music, painting, sculpture, etc. The Corporate Human Resources Department also formulated the policies on "Facilities to be given to land oustees" whose land is expropriated for setting up the power project; policy on educational facilities for the children of employees as early as 1980. Further, institutional mechanism like participative forums for employees and environment groups were established as early as 1980 itself. Specific guidelines were formulated on engagement of contractors, workers and staff. The brief of the policies formulated is given below:

Education and Empowerment

NTPC has been providing quality primary and secondary schooling facilities to the children of its staff and that of neighbouring community in its township located in India. For this purpose, NTPC provides funds to schools for equipments, etc. and to also meet recurring expenditure deficits on need basis in all NTPC opened 45 schools in its township located in India in which approximately 43405 students are studying. The schools are categorised in the following manner:

State schools run on state syllabus and as per State Government norms; Central Schools, which run as per Kendriya Vidyalaya Sangathan (KVS) norms; and Private schools run by various managements such as Delhi Public School, DAV Society, Chinmaya Mission, etc.

Education key initiatives

- Supporting 500 schools, 26 ITIs, 3 Polytechnics and 3 Engineering Colleges around NTPC locations benefiting about 50,000 students every year.
- Construction/repair of classrooms, toilets, boundary walls, kitchen sheds in schools
- Scholarships, awards, solar lanterns, school bags, uniforms, books, and stationeries, etc.
- Benefited close to 3 lakh students so far.

Skill development initiatives

- Skill upgradation programs for women (tailoring, beautician course, embroidery, etc.) Distribution of sewing machines to promote self-employment.
- Programs for village youth like welding, electrician, motor winding, motor driving, IT related training, etc.
- Benefited close to 24,000 in the last three years.

Workers education scheme

The scheme, operated in collaboration with the Central Board of Workers' Education (CBWE), covers all employees in the workman category irrespective of their educational qualification. The policy provides for books and stationery free of cost, daily time off for attending classes, award of certificates on successful completion of the course and cash awards to outstanding participants.

Adult Education Scheme

The scheme is introduced with a view to meet NTPC's social obligations towards propagation of adult education consistent with the aims and objectives of National Adult Education Program. The scheme aims at providing functional adult literacy with a view to endow the illiterate with skills for self-directed learning to reliance and active involvement in their environment. Specifically, it aims to impart functional literacy supportive of self-development program—to improve the level of awareness and communication skills including literacy and functional upgradation.

The scheme is meant for the civilians at large, living in and around NTPC's project areas and is specifically directed towards the adult workers in the employment of NTPC (including their spouses) and its contractor/sub-contractors. The preferred age group of the persons is 15–35 years. The honorarium of ₹800 and ₹400 is being paid to adult education teachers/instructors.

Children's education scheme

The company reimburses the expenditure incurred by the regular employees towards tuition fees and/or hostel charges for their children. NTPC also has a policy of scholarship for the children of regular employees who join professional courses.

Neighbouring communities

For the benefits of the land oustees and the villagers of the neighbouring affected villages, NTPC under the policy on R&R establishes/augments the infrastructure facilities for education like primary school, furniture and equipment in the school. The children of land oustees are also provided with free books and stationery as per need. The land oustees are also sponsored for professional courses for enhancing their employability.

NTPC also has a policy of scholarship for the scheduled Caste/Scheduled Tribe children who join professional courses. The scholarship is provided for 3 years during the course of study.

Health and infrastructure

The organization provides comprehensive medical care to employees and their families inclusive of primitive, curative and preventive health care. It also provides adequate health care to the community around project sites. Having 17 well-equipped project hospitals at its project sites with 700 hospital beds and 58 empanelled hospitals located centrally and at regions, it achieves the above objectives. A fully dedicated team of 250 doctors and around 1000 paramedical staff, NTPC takes scarce quality medical care to the doorsteps of employees in the project in locations where even Govt. Primary Health Care is sadly inadequate. While 7 of the 17 hospitals provide primary and emergency health care, the other 10 major hospitals also provide secondary health care. The empanelled hospitals provide tertiary health care services. With the above efforts, the mean employee age has increased.

Regular employees

All regular employees, trainees and apprentices and their family members are fully covered under the medical policy of NTPC. Full-fledged company hospitals have been established in the project's township. In addition to provision of allopathic system, NTPC promotes the alternative systems like homeopathic and ayurvedic system of medicine.

NTPC also has a policy of annual comprehensive health check-up for the employees above the age of 45 years and health check-up once in two years for the employees in the age group of 40–45. The employees working in hazardous areas in the project undergo regular comprehensive health check-up.

Social security for retired employees

NTPC has a contributory scheme for provision of medical facilities on superannuation for the employees and their spouses.

Land oustees

NTPC has a specific scheme for medical facilities to the land oustees and their families wherein 80 per cent rebate is given for the consultation charges and for indoor treatment in NTPC hospitals. NTPC also facilitates health insurance scheme for land oustees through the insurance companies and contributes partly to annual insurance premium to be paid by the land oustees.

Community development

NTPC provides basic infrastructure for the primary health centres/dispensaries in the affected villages. In addition, NTPC has been extending medical facilities in its project hospitals to the needy and poor people free of cost. Regular health check-ups of students are organized in the neighbouring villages. Spreading the social concern to the surrounding areas, the National Program enforced by the Family Planning camps, Blood donation camps, immunization schedules, Eye camps, Heart disease prevention camps, cancer detection camps, school medical check-ups, etc. are organized for non-entitled people at the project hospitals at places where the Government Primary Health Care is not adequate.

Safe drinking water system

More than 27 villages were benefited with Safe Drinking Water System at Simhadri plant.

- Geological and Hydrological investigation undertaken for source selection.
- Received enthusiastic response from stakeholders through financial (₹9.7 lakhs by village panchayats) and non-financial contribution to execute these schemes.
- Regular monitoring by NTPC, RWS and District Collector.
- Post-completion and commissioning, schemes handed over to respective village panchayats.
- Committee formed by communities for O&M and ensuring scheme's self-sustainability.

Support for physically challenged people and others

NTPC has been organizing free medical camps periodically in many of its projects for the benefit of disabled persons. Special equipment for the aid of disabled persons has also been distributed at the projects. Accommodation is provided by projects to any agency/voluntary organization for the aid of disabled persons, besides providing any other assistance. It provided hearing aids, calipers, tricycles, and wheel chairs, etc. to the identified 172 persons by conducting a camp in association with NIOH, Kolkata.

- 7 Information and Communication Technology (ICT) Centres benefiting more than 1,600 PCPs.
- Disability Rehabilitation Centre (DRC) at 5 NTPC stations providing rehabilitation/restorative surgery to about 24,000 cases, in collaboration with National Institute of Orthopedically Handicap (NIOH).

Rural sports

NTPC also lays stress on rural sports and its projects conduct rural meets on annual basis. It also encourages the local schools in the vicinity to conduct games/tournaments and provides them facilities in terms of sports equipments, grounds, etc. Inter-School Sports Meet within the projects are also held on a regular basis to identify young talent among the children of our employees as well as neighbourhood.

National calamities

NTPC from time to time has donated towards various Relief Funds at the time of natural calamities, such as to the Prime Minister's National Relief Fund, Prime Minister's National Defenses Fund, Chief Ministers Relief Fund of Maharashtra, Gujarat, Rajasthan, Orissa, Madhya Pradesh, West Bengal, etc. In addition to this, NTPC has sent teams of doctors, engineers to the affected areas for restoration works.

NTPC undertook a massive relief and restoration work for the benefit of persons affected by the earthquake that occurred in Bhuj in Gujarat on 26 January, 2001. NTPC undertook to run community kitchens in the affected areas besides providing relief material to the affected persons. Doctors from NTPC worked day and night to provide medical assistance. Engineers undertook to carry out massive repair jobs necessary for restoring electrical distribution systems.

Social security for old age/retirement

NTPC provides the following benefits:

- Employees provident fund.
- Gratuity.
- Employees voluntary benevolent fund.
- Self-contributory superannuation benefit (Pension Scheme).

Safety

- Safety policy has been drawn up and communicated to all the employees at projects/ stations.
- Guidelines have been formulated for constituting committees to conduct inquiries in cases of accidents and dangerous occurrences, to prevent their recurrence in future.
- A detailed procedure for reporting of accidents and dangerous occurrences has been prepared. Safety rules for construction and erection, electrical and mechanical have been prepared to ensure safety of the employees working in Construction, Operation and Maintenance Plants.
- All NTPC projects/stations have Disaster Management Plans to ensure the safety of people and protection of the environment in case of any disaster. Mock drills are organized at regular intervals to educate people and keep the system in readiness.
- Personal protective equipment is provided to all the employees at projects, who are working in hazardous areas. Fire Detection and Protection System have been provided at all vulnerable areas. Effective functioning of the system is ensured through periodical inspection and monitoring.
- Comprehensive Safety Clauses have been incorporated in the General Conditions of the Contract for Construction and Erection and Operation and Maintenance Works to ensure safety of the contractors' employees.

- NTPC organises Safety Audit of all its projects/stations every year by the Safety officers of the other projects. The Safety Audit is done by external professional agencies like National Safety Council, Loss Prevention Association of India, Tata Risk Management Services of India, etc. to identify the hazardous conditions and take appropriate action.
- NTPC projects/stations have received many National/International Safety Awards. During the year 2000, eleven NTPC projects/stations received Safety Awards from British Safety Council. In May 2000, NCPP-Dadri station has also received Shreshtha Surakasha Puraskar from National Safety Council of India for outstanding achievement in Safety Performance and Management.

Resettlement and Rehabilitation (R&R)

During the execution of first generation projects, though there had been no specific guidelines either from the State or Centre on rehabilitation and resettlement, NTPC on its own had implemented limited measures. Progressively, efforts are being made to improve upon the programme implemented earlier.

The following facilities were being considered for the land oustees or nominees of land oustees under the basic guidelines followed by NTPC since 1980:

(i) Employment (subject to vacancies and suitability of land outsees)
(ii) Shop allotment
(iii) Petty contract works

A comprehensive R&R policy was formulated in 1991 and subsequently revised in May, 1993 for implementation at the existing and upcoming projects. R&R is treated as a responsibility and commitment and not as a charity or welfare measure.

The policy has been framed with a clear objective that NTPC will take measures so that PAPs are enumerated on the basis of loss of livelihood and not loss of land alone, and on individual basis instead of family basis. The policy, therefore, is applicable to agricultural labourers, tribals, landless labourers cultivating government land and tenant tillers as well. There are total twelve categories of PAPs. Depending on the category of PAPs, the rehabilitation options include:

- "Land for land"
- Self-employment such as dairy, poultry, handicraft, etc.
- Shops
- Award of petty contracts
- Jobs

The resettlement includes:

- Developed alternate free house plot in resettlement colony with necessary infrastructure facilities.
- Transport arrangement for belongings and reusable material.

For establishing the baseline data for each PAP and to enable the preparation of suitable Rehabilitation Action Plan (RAP), a detailed Socio-Economic Survey (SES) is conducted through reputed institutions. For old projects, a Retrofit Socio-Economic Study (RSES) is carried out through reputed institutions and a Remedial Action Plan (ReAP) is prepared. In addition, the infrastructure facilities are created/augmented based on the findings of survey. The RAP/ReAP is finalized in a consultative manner with PAPs. The RAP/ReAP includes plan for resettling PAPs in resettlement colonies, providing them infrastructure facilities and also ways and means of rehabilitation to be provided to these PAPs as per NTPC R&R policy.

Community development

NTPC has been providing basic infrastructure facilities and amenities in the resettlement colonies and the affected villages to provide a reasonable standard of community life. These include village roads, drainage, drinking water facilities, community halls, augmentation of primary health centres, primary schools, street lights, etc.

Environment

NTPC, while spearheading the process of accelerated development of the power sector in the country, is equally conscious of the environmental degradation and continues to take various pro-active measures for protection of the environment and ecology around its projects. Environmental Auditing and extensive Pollution Monitoring is carried out at all stations leading to better compliance of the environmental norms and has helped in timely renewal of the Air and Water Consents of stations.

NTPC was first among the power utilities in India to start Environment Impact Assessment (EIA) studies to identify and evolve suitable mitigatory measures at the project appraisal stage itself. These measures are in-built in the designs during project engineering stage and are incorporated in the construction stage. Once the plants come into operation, regular monitoring of various environmental parameters and periodic Environmental Audits and Reviews are conducted, and suitable remedial actions are taken to ensure compliance with statutory requirements. Close interaction is maintained with various regulatory bodies and financial institutions in order to keep abreast with latest developments in the field of environment. Efficient operation, maintenance and sound environment management features in all its operating stations.

Environment policy and management system

NTPC is the first public utility in the country to bring out a comprehensive document in November, 1995 entitled 'NTPC Environment Policy and Environment Management System'. The Environment Policy envisages the following principles:

(a) To adopt a pro-active approach in Environmental Protection.

(b) To operate and maintain various pollution control devices and equipments at optimum efficiency.

(c) To adopt latest technologies as far as feasible, and to achieve continual environmental improvement through retrofit, recirculation/reuse, integrated treatment schemes, etc.

(d) To conserve resources by efficient utilisation and to minimize waste to the extent feasible.

(e) To devise environmentally sound policies for maximizing ash utilisation.

(f) To inculcate the culture of environmental care among all employees and further enhance the 'green image' of NTPC.

Accreditation of ISO-14001 certification

As a Corporate Policy, NTPC has taken various pro-active measures for strengthening its environmental management functions and for protection of the environment. Fifteen of its power stations have been accredited with ISO-14001 certification. Actions also have been initiated for achieving ISO-14001 for other stations.

Rewards for environmental performance

In recognition to the initiation and implementation of various environmental measures, the NTPC had received several awards such as:

NTPC-Kahalgaon has received award on "Excellence in Environment Management 1999"; Talcher-Kaniha has received "Pollution Control Excellence Award, 1999" and "Excellent Pollution Control Award" for Kayamkulam from respective State Pollution Control Boards. In addition, Talcher-Kaniha and Ramagundam have received "Environment Performance Awards" and "Feroze Gandhi Unchahar and Dadri Thermal Power Stations have received awards on "Ash Utilisation and Its Safe Disposal" from the Council of Power Utilities and Central Board of Irrigation and Power. NTPC also received "Jawahar Lal Nehru Memorial Award, 1999" for Best Environment and Ecological Implementation from International Greenland Society; "Indo-German Green Tech Environment Excellence Award, 1999–2000 for Corporate Centre", Dadri and Kawas Station and the "Golden Peacock Environment Management Award, 2001" from the World Environment Foundation; "Excellent Environmental and Ecological Implementation Award, 2000–2001" from International Greenland Society, Hyderabad. NTPC Kahalgaon received "Industrial Pollution Control Award, 2000–2001" from Bihar State Pollution Control Board, Patna.

Afforestation

Green belts and massive plantations continue to be done at its projects and till date around 14.9 million trees have been planted at its different projects. Further, in accordance with the decision taken by Ministry of Power, Government of India, necessary action is under way for creation of Special Purpose Vehicle (SPV) for Afforestation.

Afforestation is yet another area which needs careful consideration. Massive afforestation is required in and around power plants to act as a sink to the pollutants. Coal burnt in a 1000 MW power plant is around 4 million tons per annum resulting in around 5 million tons of carbon dioxide emissions annually. In order to sequester this carbon dioxide, around 400 km^2 of forests having plants with 8–10 years of age would be required. In addition, serious attempts may have to be made to reclaim the abandoned ash ponds. Scientific research has shown that wasteland can be successfully converted into green forests if proper care is taken to select the species of plants. Thus, abandoned ash ponds can be reclaimed as already done at Ramagundam.

In NTPC, in view of the above, around 14.9 million trees have already been planted in and around its power stations. Further, a concept of "Special Purpose Vehicle" (SPV) for afforestation has been recently thought of with the objective of creating forest bank to act as sink for greenhouse gas emissions, to increase the national forest cover, as also for speedy forest clearance for power projects. Power plants acquire a sizeable chunk of land for setting up power plants and extending transmission lines. In most of the power plants, acquisition of forest land is also involved which needs forest clearance from State Authorities and MoEF. The existing system of Compensatory Afforestation is a long-drawn process and delays the implementation of power projects resulting in a cost and time overrun of the project. The role of Special Purpose Vehicle (SPV) is envisaged to identify suitable land for afforestation through MoEF and State Forest Department and maintain a buffer of such forest cover. This forest bank is to be treated as 'Compensatory Afforestation' and to be scored off against diversion of forest land for setting up of power plants. This arrangement, if implemented, is expected to increase the national forest cover, convert degraded and denuded forest land into rich forests and also speed up clearance of forest land for Power Plants from Central and State Authorities.

Steel Authority of India Limited (SAIL): CSR Initiatives

SAIL is India's largest and among the leading steel producers in the world. The company owns and operates eight manufacturing plants—five integrated steel plants at Bhilai, Durgapur, Rourkela, Bokaro and Burnpur producing carbon steels, and three plants at Durgapur, Salem and Bhadravati making alloy steel, stainless and special steel.

The company is committed to linking business opportunity and corporate responsibility in ways that fulfil one of SAIL's core purpose—to make a meaningful difference in people's lives. Some of the major initiatives include the following:

Education

The company supports around 138 schools in the peripheral areas of SAIL's plants/units in the country. More than 80,000 children receive education in these centres, a majority of which is located within 1–2 km of the target population making education easily accessible. Also, Special Schools for underprivileged children who have never been to school earlier, have been setup at the five integrated steel plants providing free education, "Akshay Patra" midday meals scheme, free transport, free text-books, stationary items, etc.

Health Care

SAIL has been successfully operating 39 Hospitals, 40 Primary Health Centres and 11 Reproductive and Child Health Centres. These estimates have resulted in access to improved health infrastructure and related benefits for about 2.2 million people. The four general hospitals of SAIL at Bhilai, Durgapur, Bokaro and Rourkela are the nerve centres of the company's health care initiatives. Each equipped with over 700 beds, these are considered to be the apex referral institutes in respective states. The company has organized 49 Health Camps in 6 states (Bihar, Jharkhand, Chhattisgarh, Odisha, West Bengal and Tamil Nadu) providing free health check-ups, pathological laboratory treatment, common medicines, immunization, etc. to over 2.5 lakh of the needy population. Also, the national programme on HIV/AIDS Prevention and Control Programme is being implemented by SAIL in its capacity of an inter-sectoral collaborator of the National AIDS Control Organization under Ministry of Health and Family Welfare, Govt. of India since 1999–2000. SAIL has covered around 6 lakh non-employees and 1 lakh employees in the AIDS awareness programmes since 1999–2000. In 2003, the International Labour Organization documented SAIL's HIV/AIDS programme as a case study for workplace intervention.

Water and Sanitation

Each SAIL plant has ensured that villages within a radius of 20 km of its township have access to potable water. This has been done by installing 1831 water sources including bore wells, hand pumps, overhead tanks, ponds, etc. The company constructs on an average 157 water infrastructure every year for people living in far-flung area.

Roads

SAIL has been involved in the construction and repair of 33 km of *pucca* roads per year, thereby providing nearly 2 lakh people across 435 villages, access to modern infrastructure facilities every year.

Ancillary Development

SAIL has been developing ancillary industries from as early as 1978. Approximately, 1861 units are recognized by the company as ancillary units. On an average, the company has been adding 42 units annually, thus creating employment for more than 700 people each year. The company has reserved a number of items exclusively for procurement from these ancillary units. The company has been supporting these industries by providing land, supply of potable water and other infrastructure facilities.

Creating Sustainable Incomes

SAIL is constantly working to identify various areas where training and help to the communities can be imparted so as to make them self-sustaining units. The programmes promote rural savings and credit, natural resource management, village infrastructure development, increased agricultural productivity through better resource management and intensive cropping.

Sports

Promotion of sports has been an integral part of the corporate philosophy of SAIL right from its inception. The company has setup 4 sports academies *viz.* a hockey academy at Rourkela, an athletics academy for boys at Bhilai, an athletics academy for girls at Durgapur and a football academy at Bokaro. Continuous emphasis on sports activities has helped develop players who have gone on to compete at state and national level tournaments. As an organization, SAIL also undertakes sponsorship of various major sporting events.

SAIL Model Villages

At present SAIL has adopted 79 villages across the country for undertaking comprehensive development as SAIL Model Villages. In these villages, initiatives are being taken with respect to Medical and Healthcare Services, Education, Sanitation, Roads, Employment Generation, etc.

GLOBAL COMPACT AND SOCIAL RESPONSIBILITIES

UN's Global Compact

The UN initiated the Global Compact. It is a framework for businesses that are committed to aligning their operations and strategies with ten universally accepted principles in the areas of human rights, labour, the environment and anti-corruption. As the world's largest, global corporate citizenship initiative, the Global Compact is the first and foremost concerned with exhibiting and building the social legitimacy of business and markets. Responsible business practices can in many ways build trust and social capital, contributing to broad-based development and sustainable markets.

The Global Compact is purely voluntary initiative with two objectives:

- Mainstream the ten principles in business activities around the world.
- Catalyze actions in support of broader UN goals, such as the Millennium Development Goals (MDGs)

To achieve these objectives, the Global Compact offers facilitation and engagement through several mechanisms: *policy dialogues*, *learning*, *country/regional networks*, and *partnership projects*. The Global Compact is not a regulatory instrument—it does not 'police', enforce or measure the behaviour or actions of companies. Rather, the Global Compact relies on public accountability, transparency and the enlightened self-interest of companies, labour and civil society to initiate and share substantive action in pursuing the principles upon which the Global Compact is based. The Compact has become the world's largest voluntary corporate citizenship initiative with more than 3,800 company participants from more than 100 countries, over 60 networks in developed and emerging economies, and a spectrum of learning, dialogue and partnership modalities. Companies have an unprecedented opportunity to further their business and corporate responsibility objectives, while also contributing to the momentum and strength of the Global Compact.

The Global Compact is a network. At its core are the Global Compact Office and six UN agencies:

- Office of the High Commissioner for Human Rights
- United Nations Environment Programme
- International Labour Organization
- United Nations Development Programme
- United Nations Industrial Development Organization
- United Nations Office on Drugs and Crime.

The Global Compact involves all the relevant social actors: governments, who defined the principles on which the initiative is based; companies, whose actions it seeks to influence; labour, in whose hands the concrete process of global production takes place; civil society organizations, representing the wider community of stakeholders; and the United Nations, the world's only truly global political forum, as an authoritative convener and facilitator.

There are numerous benefits to participating in the Global Compact. These include:

- Demonstrating leadership by advancing responsible corporate citizenship.
- Producing practical solutions to contemporary problems related to globalization, sustainable development and corporate responsibility in a multi-stakeholder context.
- Managing risks by taking a proactive stance on critical issues.
- Leveraging the UN's global reach and convening power with governments, business, civil society and other stakeholders.

- Sharing good practices and learning.
- Accessing the UN's broad knowledge in development issues.
- Improving corporate/brand management, employee morale and productivity, and operational efficiencies.

Ten Principles

The Global Compact's ten principles in the areas of human rights, labour, the environment and anti-corruption enjoy universal consensus and are derived from:

- The Universal Declaration of Human Rights
- The International Labour Organization's Declaration on Fundamental Principles and Rights at Work
- The Rio Declaration on Environment and Development
- The United Nations Convention Against Corruption.

The Global Compact asks companies to embrace, support and enact, within their sphere of influence, a set of core values in the areas of human rights, labour standards, the environment, and anti-corruption.

Human rights

- **Principle 1:** Businesses should support and respect the protection of internationally proclaimed human rights; and
- **Principle 2:** make sure that they are not complicit in human rights abuses.

Labour standards

- **Principle 3:** Businesses should uphold the freedom of association and the effective recognition of the right to collective bargaining;
- **Principle 4:** the elimination of all forms of forced and compulsory labour;
- **Principle 5:** the effective abolition of child labour; and
- **Principle 6:** the elimination of discrimination in respect of employment and occupation.

Environment

- **Principle 7:** Businesses should support a precautionary approach to environmental challenges;
- **Principle 8:** undertake initiatives to promote greater environmental responsibility; and
- **Principle 9:** encourage the development and diffusion of environmentally friendly technologies.

Anti-corruption

- **Principle 10:** Businesses should work against all forms of corruption, including extortion and bribery.

Global Compact Society—India

The Global Compact Society (GCS) was formed by some of the organizations from India who are participating in the United Nation's Global Compact Programme. It was registered on 24th November 2003, with the Registrar of Societies, NCT, Delhi, as a non-profit body. Significantly, GCS in India is one of the leading networks of the United Nations Global Compact (UNGC) having legal status. The main objective of the Society is to provide a forum to various Indian companies/organizations to exchange experiences, network, and work together on activities related to corporate social responsibility (CSR). This is expected to promote sustainable growth, besides encouraging good corporate citizenship.

The Society acts as an apex level nodal agency representing various Indian corporate bodies, institutions/NGOs/SMEs, who are committed to the UN's Global Compact principles. The Global Compact Society is planning to undertake a number of activities in related fields to create awareness about UN's Global Compact ten principles on human rights, labour standard, environment and anti-corruption by internalization of these principles, and to facilitate organizations to undertake projects/activities in furtherance of these principles, as part of corporate social responsibility.

Some of the projects planned by GCS include:

- Organizing national convention.
- Interacting with various Indian and UN agencies
- To develop database of members and their activities relating to Global Compact
- To operate a website for information dissemination
- To organize meetings/workshops, etc. for interchange of experience, skill development.
- To facilitate taking up of projects aimed at corporate social responsibility by member companies individually and jointly.

The following are the aims and objectives of GCS—India:

- To create awareness on Global Compact programme
- To promote activities related to labour welfare
- To promote activities aimed at environmental protection and upgradation
- To act in furtherance of the principles relating to protection of human rights and improvement of quality of life, including social and rural development, heritage development of underprivileged sections such as scheduled castes/tribes, backward areas, etc.
- To undertake activities/projects aimed at promoting the cause of human rights, labour standard and environment
- To undertake research, and organize workshops, seminars and conferences for sharing of experiences of respective organizations
- To develop networking with international and national organizations, institutes, etc. for exchange of information, experiences, study and research work
- To develop a database and information system relating to these activities
- To publish journals, magazines, newsletters or information papers or other documents for the members as well as the society for creating awareness about the related areas

- To do all that is necessary, incidental or ancillary to the above purposes, including the right to acquire, receive and hold property of any kind, to enter into contract for, or in connection with, the purposes of the society, to raise monies and funds in such manner as may be deemed fit for and on behalf of the society, and to employ staff.

List of Members in Global Compact Society (India) by 2007

Corporate members

- Aditya Birla Management Corporation Limited
- Balmer Lawrie & Company Limited
- Bharat Heavy Electricals Limited (BHEL)
- Bombay Dyeing & Manufacturing Company Limited
- Central Warehousing Corporation (CWC)
- Chennai Petroleum Corporation Limited
- Gujarat State Fertilizers & Chemicals Limited (GSFC)
- Hindustan Lever Limited (HLL)
- Hindustan Petroleum Corporation Limited (HPCL)
- Hindustan Zinc Limited (HZL)
- Hospital Services Consultancy Corporation Limited (HSCC)
- Housing & Urban Development Corporation (HUDCO)
- Indian Airlines Limited (IAL)
- Indian Farmers & Fertilizers Corporation Limited (IFFCO)
- Indian Oil Corporation Limited (IOCL)
- Infosys Technologies Limited
- Intimate Clothing Private Limited
- Intimate Fashions (India) Private Limited
- Linea Fashions (India) Private Limited
- Mahindra & Mahindra Limited
- National Building Construction Corporation (NBCC)
- National Hydro Power Corporation (NHPC)
- National Mineral Development Corporation (NMDC)
- NTPC Limited
- Oil India Limited (OIL)
- Oil & Natural Gas Corporation (ONGC)
- Paharpur Business Centre & Software Technology
- Power Finance Corporation Limited (PFCL)
- Power Grid Corporation Limited (PGCIL)
- Satluj Jal Vidyut Nigam Limited (SJVNL)
- Tata Motors
- Water & Power Consultancy Services Limited (WAPCOS).

Institutional Members

- All India Management Association (AIMA)
- Artificial Limbs Manufacturing Corporation (ALIMCO)
- Consultancy Development Centre (CDC)
- Construction Industry Development Council (CIDC)
- Federation of Indian Chambers of Commerce & Industry (FICCI)
- Indian Society for Training & Development (ISTD)
- National Power Training Institute (NPTI)
- National Research Development Corporation (NRDC)
- Ryan Foundation for National Socio-Economic Development.

NGO Members

- Global Gandhian Trusteeship & Corp. Responsibility Foundation
- Partners In Change.

The members of the Global Compact Society have been spending a lot of amount towards corporate social responsibilities. Some of them are following creative and innovative practices. For instance: Tata steel has adopted several villages and provided excellent community service under corporate responsibilities. Not only Tata's but also Birla's and several others were taking care of the society. In Visakhapatnam, RINL and NTPCL have been taking several measures for the society. Satyam introduced EMRI service under healthcare. Several companies provided health, wealth, education, water and other services to develop the society.

Ratan Tata, the Chairman of Tata Group, feels the corporate citizenship enhances the competitiveness and global participation. According to him, "A Tata company shall be committed to be a good corporate citizen not only in compliance with all relevant laws and regulations but also by actively assisting in the improvement of the quality of life of the people in the communities in which it operates with the objective of making them self-reliant. Such social responsibility would comprise, to initiate and support community initiatives in the field of community health and family welfare, water management, vocational training, education and literacy, and to encourage application of modern scientific and managerial techniques and expertise. This will be reviewed periodically in consonance with national and regional priorities. The company would also not treat these activities as optional ones but would strive to incorporate them as integral part of its business plan. *The company would also encourage volunteering amongst its employees and help them to work in the committees*. Tata companies are encouraged to develop social accounting systems and to carry out social audit of their operations."

SUMMARY

1. Social responsibilities are the basic obligations of business organizations in society.
2. The interested groups towards social responsibilities are consumers, employees, owners, the community, fellow business entrepreneurs and the state.

3. Business has to follow certain criteria in discharging social responsibilities.
4. The Sachar Committee recommendations are also to be considered in fulfilling this task.
5. Ethics are essential for all managers. Managers without ethics are like a human body without blood vessels.
6. Social audit is an important activity of modern management.
7. The Global Compact Society is taking interest in providing environment for social responsibilities.

REVIEW QUESTIONS

1. What do you mean by social responsibilities of business?
2. Discuss social responsibilities of business towards the interested groups.
3. Explain the criteria for determining social responsibilities.
4. What are the ethics of managers?
5. Discuss the concept of social audit and its implementation in various organizations.
6. What are the activities of members of global compact society?

CASE STUDIES

1. Billionaire's New Avatar

"I would like to retire from my company to do service to the society full time and serve the global poor and needy through our foundation until my last breath", said a billionaire of the world.

William Henry Gates III, popularly known as Bill Gates, had pressed *ctrl + alt + delete* in his career with Microsoft Corporation on July 1, 2008. He founded the software company in 1975. After serving the company as President and CEO for over 33 years, he thought to reboot himself in the avatar of a full-time philanthropist to serve the society much better and with utmost satisfaction.

The world had become a global village by the dawn of the twenty-first century. The number of billionaires had increased in different parts of the globe. The globally known CEOs had a desire to be the richest in the world. Some of the second and third generation CEOs had exceeded in wealth maximization than those of the first generation. For instance, the second generation CEO of Reliance Industries Ltd., Mukesh Ambani, had become the richest person according to a study done recently.

Born on October 28, 1955, Bill Gates had his education at Lakeside School and Harvard University. He founded Microsoft with Paul Allen in 1975. He signed a landmark agreement with IBM for Dos in 1980. In 1995, Windows 95 with integrated internet explorer and MSN were launched and gained almost monopoly. After two and a half decades of innovative business operations, Bill Gates set up Bill and Melinda Gates Foundation. In 2001, Gates introduced

X box gaming console. Gates, the richest man in the world, is well known for his dynamism, creativity, and visionary leadership. Several people in the world tried to follow him.

Several CEOs of India, including Nandan Nilekani, co-founder and co-chairman of Infosys Technologies, had interaction with Gates on several occasions. After hearing Gates' decision to do full-time societal responsibilities, Nilekani said, "The world is fortunate that a man of his genius is putting his enormous wealth and brand value behind social causes and that, too, in the prime of his life at 52 years." Once his client and later his competitor, Steve Jobs of Apple Computers, and an occasional bridge partner Warren Buffett also stated that it was a better place because Gates realized that his goal was not to be the richest guy in the cemetery; his mission was to become a dedicated global social worker by serving the needy and poor of the globe.

Questions for Discussion

1. How do you feel about the billionaire's decision?
2. Explain how it is possible to fulfil his mission?
3. What is the lesson that you learn from the world's richest man?

2. Union Carbide

Shortly after midnight on 3 December, 1984, outside Bhopal (India), a cloud of deadly methyl-isocyanate gas leaked from a pesticide plant owned by the Indian subsidiary of Union Carbide. The choking gas covered the town, quickly killing hundreds—including many children (who were less resistant to the gas than adults), and forcing Bhopal's 670,000 inhabitants to flee in panic. By the end of the week, more than 2,000 had died from inhaling the gas, and 150,000 more had to be hospitalized for respiratory and eye damage, making Bhopal's night of death the worst industrial disaster in history. Images of stunned families burying or burning their dead and blaming Union Carbide for their agony were telecast worldwide.

There were immediate repercussions for Union Carbide and for the chemical industry as well. The Indian Government accused the plant management of failing to take adequate safety precautions and indicated that it held the parent company responsible. Lawsuits brought by American lawyers on behalf of the victims asked for billions of dollars in compensatory and punitive damages and threatened to send the company into bankruptcy. Union Carbide's stock price plummeted, it halted production of methyl-isocyanate at the one West Virginia plant that produced the chemical in the United States.

Officials in the United States and India called for increased regulation and inspection of chemical processing plants. Many US localities considered passing "right to know" laws that would require chemical companies to provide detailed information about hazardous materials to the employees who make them, and to residents living near the plants. Several companies countered with voluntary right to know programmes to head off public sentiment for government regulation. In the wake of protests against Union Carbide in other parts of the world, some multinational corporations claimed that the Bhopal disaster had chilled the international climate for US business.

Union Carbide, which had earned an above-average record on industrial safety over the decade preceding the disaster, appeared paralyzed by the magnitude of Bhopal's suffering.

Corporate Chairman Warren Anderson rushed to India to inspect the site and was briefly arrested by the Indian authorities. Union Carbide's 100,000 employees observed a moment of silence for the dead and injured, many donated money for disaster relief. Top management spent sleepless nights grappling with the company's crushing problems and its uncertain future. Morale at the company was low; production at many plants dropped temporarily. However, while expressing profound sympathy for the Bhopal victims and promising to make fair restitution, Union Carbide maintained its essential innocence. "There is no criminal responsibility here," said Anderson.

Questions for Discussion

1. What are the key issues in this case?
2. If you were a manager of Union Carbide, what effect would the news of the disaster have on you? What would you tell your subordinates?
3. What responsibilities does Union Carbide have to the victims of the Bhopal disaster?
4. What do you think the long-term effects of the disaster will be on the company?

FURTHER READING

Business World, 2008.

Drucker, Peter, F., *The Frontiers of Management*, Heinemann, London, 1987.

Koontz, H. and Weihrich, Heinz, *Essentials of Management*, McGraw-Hill, New York, 1990.

Satyanarayana, P., *Corporate Social Responsibilities: A Study of Selected Organizations*, unpublished PhD Thesis, Andhra University, Visakhapatnam, 2015.

Stoner, James A.F., *Management*, Pearson/Prentice Hall, New Delhi, 2005.

Total Quality Management

CONTENTS

INTRODUCTION

Total Quality Management (TQM) evolved and developed from the concepts of quality control and quality assurance. It focuses on the customer and quality. Quality management is also called quality assurance, quality function, deployment, total quality control and zero defect. The Japanese have applied total quality control since World War II in the name of Company Wide Quality Control (Ishihawi 1985).

THE CONCEPT

During the early 1950s, the concept of Total Quality Control (TQC) was coined by Armand V. Fiegenbaum, who defined TQC in 1954 as an effective system for integrating the quality development, quality maintenance and quality improvement efforts of the various functions of business to enable production and service at the most economic levels to meet full customer satisfaction. The Japanese called it Company Wide Quality Control (CWQC).

One of the most comprehensive definitions of Quality, which looks at it in its various determinates, is by Johnson (1987): "Quality is the capability of a product or service to 'knowingly' satisfy those preconceived composite wants of the User(s) that are intelligibly related to characteristics of performance or appearance and do not cause major overt or covert reactions or actions by other people."

TQM is a company-wide activity, and has to reach every employee within the organization as suggested in the following definition (Oakland, 1989). "Total Quality Management (TQM) is an approach to improving the effectiveness of flexibility of business as a whole. It is essentially a way of organizing and involving the whole organization, every department, every activity, every single person at every level."

It is the combination of socio-technical processes towards doing the right things (externally), everything right (internally), the first time, and all the time, with economic viability considered at each stage of each process.

It is difficult to segregate Total Quality Management (TQM), Total Plant Maintenance (TPM) and Just-In-Time (JIT) Systems. We cannot succeed with TQM when there is excessive floor inventory or frequent breakdown of machines. Likewise, JIT-based production systems cannot be introduced unless they are fully supported by strong TQM and TPM. All the three systems need people's involvement for achieving perpetual improvement. A modified system designed and implemented on the lines indicated in the model has achieved some of the objectives of TQM and JIT, with operators' involvement for seeking perpetual improvement.

Management has to make clear to employees, suppliers, customers, and the world exactly where it stands on quality. It is not enough to lay out stirring words like "excellence" or "TQM" or "customer satisfaction" or "delighting the customer". They mean different things to different people, and do not constitute direction. The policy on quality has to be a statement that cannot be misunderstood. It has to cover conformance to requirements, time and money. It is like saying, "We will deliver defect-free products and services to our customers and co-workers, on time, at agreed costs."

Quality means conformance to requirements. The requirements are all the commitments involved in giving the customer what was agreed upon. Some of them are administrative, some are procedural, some involve product specifications. They are the answers to all the questions involved in running the company. People must learn their jobs and the requirements that are involved, and then learn how to do them exactly. Quality must be achieved by *prevention* rather than *detection*. Think "vaccine" instead of "medicine". The conventional standard for quality is "acceptable quality levels" or "that's close enough". The result of this is that things are not done properly. Imagine, if we had a national standard wherein we were expected to come to a full stop at only 98 per cent of the stop signs!

CHECKPOINTS

Total Quality Management involves major quality checkpoints. These checkpoints are as follows:

Selection and management of upstream systems (i.e. suppliers, vendors, customers—internal or external): This includes the development and maintenance of standards and specifications, whose requirements are open communication channels with the organizational systems from which the organization receives inputs.

Incoming quality assurance: The assurance that you are getting what you wanted, needed, expected or, requested, on time and within specifications.

In-process quality management and assurance: Assuring that key transformation processes (value-adding processes) are effective, efficient and "building" quality into the goods and/or services.

Outgoing quality assurance: The assurance that your organizational system is producing the desired goods and/or services on time and within specifications.

The proactive assurance: The organizational system is meeting or exceeding the customers' needs, specifications, requirements, wants, desires, and expectations.

If an organizational system successfully manages these checkpoints, it will manage quality totally.

FUNDAMENTAL CONCEPTS AND PRINCIPLES

1. TQM is customer-oriented.
2. TQM involves a long-term commitment to the continuous improvement of all processes.
3. TQM success depends upon top management commitment, leadership and continuous involvement.
4. Products and services are the result of processes, and all processes are subject to inherent variation.
5. Much of the knowledge needed to improve a process resides in the workforce and with the customer(s); however, only management can make many of the necessary changes happen.
6. Responsibility for the establishment and improvement of processes lies with the management.
7. Managers are responsible for the quality of supplier products and services received.
8. TQM is a strategy for continuously improving performance at every level and in all areas of responsibility.
9. TQM aims at achieving one broad, unending objective: continuous improvement of products and services.
10. Successful TQM implementation depends on establishing a nurturing, encouraging environment, a disciplined, organizational goal-setting methodology and a formal, structured process-improvement methodology.

The performance of an organizational system is comprised of seven inextricably interwoven criteria:

1. Effectiveness
2. Efficiency
3. Quality

4. Productivity
5. Quality of workers' lives
6. Innovation
7. Profitability (for a profit centre), and budgetability (for a cost centre).

COMPONENTS OF TQM

The following are the important components of TQM:

- Quality policy and its communication
- Team work and participation
- Problem-solving tools and techniques
- Standardization
- Design and implementation of a quality system
- Quality costs/measurements
- Process control
- Customer/supplier integration
- Education and training
- Quality audit and review.

A survey by the National Productivity Council indicates that the common forms of participation are quality circles (42.2 per cent), quality improvement teams or task forces (33.7 per cent), and others such as product committee, quality committee, value engineering (24.1 per cent).

THE TQM MODEL

The TQM model provides a distinctly different way of looking at management style. It develops a participative culture where all employees are involved in a team relating to their work and decisions concerning their work. Team work is organized through quality circles and quality improvement teams.

The second dimension of the model is that it provides the use of quality tools and techniques for problem solving. This system is based on statistical process control techniques and tools aimed at satisfying customer expectations by continuously working across the organization to improve internal and external processes. Over 3,000 companies and about 40 government departments in the USA are practising some form of TQM. In India also, several companies have been following different methods of quality improvement.

The third dimension is management commitment. The quality system integrates the efforts of TQM by providing information on quality, costs and others.

TQM AWARDS

In Japan and the USA, there are prestigious awards instituted for TQM implementation in organizations. Every year, April is celebrated as "quality month" all over the world.

Japan: The highest award in Japan is the Deming Prize. The organizations which have won this award are Toyoto, Matsushita, Canon, etc.

USA: The highest award in the US is the "Baldridge Award". The last winner of this award was Federal Express.

Edward Deming's Principles

- Create constancy of purpose for improvement of products and services.
- Adopt the new philosophy.
- Cease dependence on mass inspection.
- End the practice of awarding business on the price tag alone.
- Improve constantly and forever the system of production and service.
- Institute training.
- Institute leadership.
- Drive out fear.
- Break down barriers between staff areas.
- Eliminate slogans, exhortations and targets for the workforce.
- Eliminate numerical quotas.
- Remove barriers to pride of workmanship.
- Institute a vigorous programme of education and retraining.
- Take action to accomplish the transformation.

APPLICATION OF TQM

The TQM philosophy can be adopted everywhere in an organization. Some of the problem-solving methods are discussed below:

PDCA cycle: All systematic problem-solving and quality improvement processes follow from the basic Deming cycle. It is commonly known as the PDCA cycle. PDCA stands for Plan, Do, Check and Act.

Plan: First make the objective, problem area or improvement and set up the measure to achieve the same.

Do: Put the plan into practice.

Check: Observe the results to see whether or not the desired objective has been achieved.

Act: If there is progress, standardize the plan, otherwise review it.

Continuous rotation of the PDCA cycle progressively brings about improvement in processes. As effective processes are standardized, problems do not surface again. This brings about improvement in quality.

The following short stories, as reported by various people, illustrate the Japanese success with quality control.

The Motorola TV assembly plant in Franklin, Illinois, had an extremely poor record of both productivity and quality. Their records showed that they had 150 defects per 100 completed sets.

All this changed when Matsushita bought this assembly plant. Within three years, Matsushita was able to increase productivity by 30 per cent and reduced defects to well below 4 per 100 sets. This is indeed an outstanding achievement, but still not up to Japanese plants (Wheel Wright, 1981).

When Sanyo bought the ailing Warwick TV plant in Forest City, Arkansas, sales had declined to such an extent that 80 per cent of the plant capacity had been shut down. At that time, Sears owned 25 per cent of the stock and had been buying most of Warwick's production under its own label. However, since quality was so poor, Sears turned to the Japanese manufacturers. Soon, within two months of Sanyo's takeover, quality improved from a defect rate of about 30 per cent to less than 5 per cent. Line productivity also substantially improved (Tsurimi, 1981).

David Garvin (1983) studied room air-conditioner manufacturers in the United States and Japan, and came to the following conclusions. Failure rates of air-conditioners made by the worst producers, which were all American firms, were between 500 and 1,000 *times* greater than those made by the best producers, had 70 times as many defects on the assembly line as the average Japanese manufacture, and made 17 times as many service calls during the first year following the sale. Moreover, the defect percentages of the air-conditioners produced by the worst Japanese manufacturers were less than half of those produced by the best American manufacturers. Companies with the best quality records also had the highest labour productivity. The extra cost of making higher quality Japanese goods was about half the cost of fixing defective products by American manufacturers.

Small-lot production, just-in-time inventory and production control, just-in-time purchasing, extensive preventive maintenance programmes, automated equipment and robots, together with worker involvement and responsibility, all favour a high quality product in Japanese firms. These are some of the ingredients that constitute TQM.

Samtel Color Ltd. (SCL), by virtue of its collaboration with Mitsubishi Electric Co. of Japan, has incorporated some of the Japanese managerial tools in its operational systems. Of significance are computerized unit product flow, operator's responsibility for inspection and quality, employee's involvement at all levels to achieve excellence in internal working, continuous training and development of its operatives and managers, and innovating on products and processes on a continuing basis. SCL has achieved high levels of customer satisfaction, increase in output and reduction in rejects.

In SCL, the philosophy of TQM has three dimensions: Excellence, Universality and Perpetuity. *Excellence* is concerned with delivering error-free (zero defect) and on-time products and services which are produced or designed to meet or *exceed* customers' expectations. *Perpetuity* is achieved through steady, small, progressive steps on the part of all employees to achieve continuous improvement using systematic methods.

The following quote illustrates how Toshiba was able to introduce Total Quality Management in its Tennessee Plant of Toshiba America, Inc. (Traeger, 1983).

> To establish our QC systems at TNP, we transplanted to TNP as much as possible the SQC systems being used in our TV and Microwave Oven plants in Japan. In starting up our TN plant, the most significant problem was with the quality from our US vendors. We found it fundamentally necessary to change the normal U.S. customer-vendor commercial relationship to be successful, i.e.: (1) Vendors' willingness to join in joint evaluation and frank discussions of

quality problems. (2) Develop effective standards and methods of measurement clearly agreed to by both parties (appearance of subjective quality standards were most difficult). (3) Develop credibility with vendors in that, what we declared out-of-specifications was, in fact, out-of-specifications. (4) Willingness to share information regarding counter measures to eliminate problems in the future. The results of implementing these changes have not only been dramatic as a per cent defect received at our plant, but the attitude of our vendors has also been dramatic. They all now agree that the pain and anguish they, and we, went through has more than paid off, for their in-house yields have dramatically increased as well as their reputation for superior quality products, resulting in improved profit and loss for them ..."

ONE HUNDRED METHODS FOR TQM

1. *Acceptable Quality Level (AQL):* To provide a structure of sampling plans, risks and inspection strategies to ensure that the customer receives the quality that the supplier has contracted to deliver.
2. *Affinity diagram:* To organize large amounts of data in groups according to some form of natural affinity.
3. *Arrow diagram:* To show the time required for solving a problem, and which items can be done in parallel.
4. *Bar charts:* To display discrete data collected by check sheets, so that patterns can be discovered.
5. *Basic statistics:* The mean, median, mode, range and standard deviation are ways of summarizing and describing large volumes of data. The first three are measures of location, the last two are measures of spread.
6. *Benchmarking:* To identify and fill gaps in performance by putting in place the best practice, thereby establishing superior performance.
7. *Box and whisker plots:* To provide a simple way of drawing the basic shape of the distribution of a set of data.
8. *Brainstorming:* To generate as many ideas as possible without assessing their value.
9. *Brainwriting:* To generate as many ideas as possible.
10. *Breaking set:* To overcome blocks in thinking by generating new ideas. It is particularly useful in prompting a group to be more receptive to new suggestions.
11. *Buzz groups:* A way of getting the immediate reaction of a group to a new idea or problem.
12. *Cause and effect analysis:* To examine effects or problems to find out the possible causes and to point out possible areas where data can be collected.
13. *C chart:* To identify when the number of defects in a sample of constant size is changing over time.
14. *Check sheets:* To collect data when the number of times a defect or value occurs is important.
15. *Concentration diagrams:* To collect data when the location of a defect or problem is important.
16. *Consensus reaching:* To give a team a methodical way of examining alternatives to reach a collective conclusion which all team members can accept.

17. *Contingency planning:* To avoid "firefighting" and waste resources by planning for contingencies in the completion of a project.
18. *Cost-benefit analysis:* To estimate the real cost and benefits of a project under consideration.
19. *Criteria testing:* To evaluate and compare alternative solutions to a problem by rating them against a list of criteria.
20. *Critical Path Method (CPM):* A project planning technique which separates the work to be done into discrete elements, allowing the key elements that affect the overall project to be identified.
21. *Customers' contingency table:* To understand the needs of both internal and external customers for the fulfilment of customer satisfaction
22. *Cusum chart:* To identify when the mean value is changing over time.
23. *Deming wheel (PDCA):* A management concept to satisfy the quality requirements of the customer by using the cycle: Plan, Do, Check and Act.
24. *Departmental cost of quality:* To provide a financial measure of the quality performance of an organization.
25. *Departmental purpose analysis (DPA):* To review the internal customer-supplier relationship.
26. *Domainal mapping:* To assist in the identification of internal customers and their needs.
27. *Dot plots:* A simple graphic device which presents observations as dots on a horizontal scale.
28. *Error proofing (Pokayoke):* To design an operation in such a way that specific errors are prevented from causing major problems to the customer.
29. *Evolutionary Operation (EVOP):* A sequential experimental procedure for collecting information during on-line production to improve a process without disturbing output.
30. *Failure Mode and Effect Analysis (FMEA):* To assist in the foolproofing of a design or a process.
31. *Fault tree analysis:* To perform a quantitative as well as qualitative analysis of a complex system.
32. *Flowcharts:* To generate a picture of how work gets done by linking together all the steps taken in process.
33. *Force analysis:* To identify external and internal forces at work when developing a contingency plan.
34. *Force field analysis:* Allows you to identify those forces that both help and hinder you in closing the gap between where you are now, and where you want to be.
35. *Gannt charts:* For planning the steps necessary to implement quality improvement.
36. *Geometric moving average:* To identify trends in small changes in the process mean. The geometric moving average is sometimes called the Exponentially Weighted Moving Average (EWMA).
37. *Histograms:* To display continuous data collected by check sheets so that any patterns can be discovered.

38. *Hoshin kanri (quality policy deployment):* To delight the customer through the manufacturing and servicing process by implementing the quality, goals of the organization.
39. *Idea writing:* To bring all participants into group work.
40. *Imagineering:* To assist a company to identify areas of opportunity by concentrating on the ideal outcome, then working back from it.
41. *Improve Internal Process (IIP) plan:* To provide the structure to develop work plan details for a task using various factors, such as measurables, responsible resources, times and previous task owners.
42. *IS/IS not matrix:* To identify patterns in observed characteristics by a structured form of stratification.
43. *ISO 9000:* To demonstrate to yourself, your customers and an independent assessment body that you have an effective quality management system in place.
44. *Just-In-Time (JIT):* To deliver the raw materials or components to the production line to arrive just in time when they are needed.
45. *Kaizen:* A Japanese term meaning "change for the better"; the concept implies a continuous improvement in all company functions at all levels.
46. *Lateral thinking:* A way of transferring from one frame of reference to another, enabling you to break down barriers which inhibit creative thought.
47. *List reduction:* To reduce a list of ideas to one of manageable size.
48. *Matrix data analysis:* To provide a picture of numerical data from a matrix diagram in an efficient way.
49. *Matrix diagram:* To provide information about the relationship and importance of task and methods elements of the subject.
50. *Mind mapping:* A way of generating and recording ideas individually rather than in a group. Mind mapping makes use of word associations, encouraging you to follow your own thought patterns, wherever, they lead. It also provides a written record of the ideas generated.
51. *Minute analysis:* To estimate the survival period of a particular product unit under certain conditions, using a simulated experimental environment.
52. *Morphological forced connections:* To generate new ideas or ways of approaching problems. It combines lists of attributes and forces new connections between them, so triggering new options.
53. *Moving average:* To identify trends in data when short-term variation or cyclical patterns are confusing the long-term picture.
54. *Multi-vari charts:* To show the dispersion in a process over the short and long term, using a graphic control chart.
55. *Multi-voting:* To select the most popular or important items from a list.
56. *Mystery shopping:* A technique involving looking at your business from the outside, and measuring the efficiency of your own key processes from the customer's viewpoint.
57. *Nominal group technique:* A way of generating ideas from a group, and identifying the level of support within the group for those ideas.

58. *NP chart:* To identify when the number of defective items in the sample of constant size is changing over time.
59. *Objective ranking:* Helps to place your current activity in perspective, and enables you to understand the purpose of your efforts.
60. *Opportunity analysis:* Offers the opportunity to quickly evaluate a long list of options against desired goals and available resources.
61. *Paired comparisons:* To help a group to quantify the preferences of its members.
62. *Parameter design:* To determine which factors are important in the manufacturing process, and to find the optimum set of working conditions.
63. *Pareto analysis:* To separate the most important causes of a problem from the many trivial ones. Also, to identify the most important problems for a team to work on.
64. *Paynter charts:* To display information over time in a way that allows changes in patterns of failure to be discovered. Paynter charts will show when one failure mode takes over from another in terms of importance, or when the overall failure rate is changing over time.
65. *P-chart:* To identify when the percentage of defective items in a sample of variable size is changing over time.
66. *Pie charts:* A way of representing data pictorially, pie charts are an effective means of showing the relative size of the individual parts to the total.
67. *Potential Problem Analysis (PPA):* To examine plans to identify what can go wrong with them, so that preventive action can be taken.
68. *Problem prevention plan:* To anticipate what can go wrong, and plan to prevent problems.
69. *Process analysis:* Enables a group to look for opportunities to improve processes. It can also be used to identify standards and measures for critical parts of processes.
70. *Process capability:* To demonstrate whether a process is capable of meeting a specification, and to calculate an index to show this capability.
71. *Process cost of quality:* To provide a financial measure of the quality performance of an organization.
72. *Process decision programme chart:* To focus on possible sequences to help lead to a desirable result and contingency planning.
73. *Programme Evaluation and Review Technique (PERT):* To establish a planning technique for complex and multi-level projects.
74. *Quality circles:* A special type of small group activity which forms a vehicle for the development of individuals.
75. *Quality Function Deployment (QFD):* A technique or discipline for optimizing the process of developing and producing new products on the basis of customer need.
76. *Relation diagram:* To illustrate the relationship between problems and ideas in complex situations. Also, to identify meaningful categories from a mass of ideas when relationships are difficult to determine.
77. *Reliability:* To find the cause of failures and try to eliminate them, and to reduce the effects or consequences of failure.

78. *Rich pictures:* To allow a group to capture all ideas developed, without judgement or analysis, in a pictorial form that allows the strength of the ideas to be recorded.
79. *Robust design (off-line quality control):* To achieve the proper functioning of a component even when affected by interfering factors, whether external, internal or a manufacturing variation.
80. *Sampling:* A method by which a small number of items (the sample) is drawn from a larger number of items (the population), in order to draw a conclusion about the population based upon information from the sample.
81. *Scatter diagrams:* To allow the relationship between cause and effect to be established.
82. *Snowballing:* Sometimes called "pyramiding", snowballing is a technique for gathering information or ideas.
83. *Solution effect analysis:* To examine solutions to problems to find out whether there are any detrimental consequences, and to plan the implementation of solutions.
84. *Spider web diagrams:* To show performance against a target when several criteria are being set.
85. *Statistical Process Control (SPC):* To identify when processes are changing over time.
86. *Stem and lead diagram:* To present raw data and to show their distribution visually.
87. *Stratification:* To assist in the definition of a problem by identifying where it does or does not occur.
88. *Suggestion schemes:* To generate ideas for improvement.
89. *System design:* To apply special scientific and engineering knowledge to produce a basic functional prototype model, having surveyed the relevant technology, manufacturing environment and customer need.
90. *Taguchi methods:* A technique for the optimization of products or processes, Taguchi involves a two-stage experimental design that gives the benefits of robustness and efficiency with the minimum number of experiments.
91. *Tally charts:* To collect data when the value of a defect or problem is important.
92. *Teamwork:* To organize activity which requires a number of people to collaborate and work together for a common goal.
93. *Tolerance design:* To find out by experiment where the variability in a process (product) occurs and where adjustments can be made.
94. *Total productive maintenance:* To help a process which aims at making the most effective and efficient use of existing production structures.
95. *Tree diagrams:* To identify the tasks and methods needed to solve a problem and reach a goal.
96. *U chart:* To identify when the number of defects in a sample of variable size changes over time.
97. *Why-How charting:* When thinking in both abstract and concrete terms, and needing to move between the two, why-how charting enables a goal to be translated into action.
98. *X Moving Range (X-MR) chart:* To identify when a value is changing over time.
99. *X-R chart:* To identify when the means value of a range in a sample of constant size is changing over time.

100. *Zero defect:* To allow teams to experience the success involved in meeting ever more demanding targets, without demotivating them by not achieving absolute success at once.

TQM CULTURE

Total Quality Management evolved and developed from the concepts of quality control and assurance. It focuses on the customer and quality. In the 1950s, the concept was coined by Armand V. Fiegenbaum. It is customer oriented and involves long-term commitment. TQM depends upon top management commitment. In order to satisfy the customer, several companies have been following various quality management practices. In India, B-schools are also competing among themselves to improve quality to satisfy the customer.

European Foundation for Quality Management Model

Fourteen large European MNCs formed the European Foundation for Quality Management (EFQM) to promote TQM principles in Europe. EFQM model for business excellence is based on the following nine factors: leadership (10 per cent); people management (9 per cent); policy and strategy (8 per cent); resources (9 per cent); processes (14 per cent); people satisfaction (9 per cent); customer satisfaction (20 per cent); impact on society (6 per cent); business results (15 per cent).

Malcolm Baldrige Quality National Award (MBQNA) considers the parameters of leadership (90 pts), information and analysis (75 pts), HRM and management (150 pts), education and business process management (150 pts), school performance results (230 pts), and student focus and student stakeholder satisfaction (230 pts).

Components of the Strategic Plan (Vision 2005)

The following are the components of strategic plan, Vision 2005:

- Policy thrust
- Annual plans
- Mission approach
- Project mode
- Team building
- Marketing concept
- Environment building
- Resource generation
- Monitoring and evaluation
- Quality of work Life.

'Perform or perish', 'grow or perish' is the new mantra of some management schools in the globalized era. In the present context, several B-schools have been performing well to meet the global standards. In India, IIMs and IITs are considered to be world class. Indian

School of Business (ISB) is another institution for high quality learning. In addition, about 100 management institutes have been growing fast and performing well. In India, over 1150 institutes and universities have been offering management education full time for two years. Some institutions have been offering part time management programmes (evening) and distance mode programmes for three years. [Thus, Indian B-schools have been offering full time (One year or two years), part time (2 or 3 years) and distance mode (3 years) management education during the last five decades.] In recent period, ISB was established by leading CEOs of India with the objective of offering world class management education in India. It has proved to be a really world class and one of the best B-schools in the world. The school offers one year residential management programme equivalent to MBA, with the collaboration of internationally reputed B-schools. The programme is highly successful, and the students have been getting global placements by several top MNCs and large companies in India.

Initiatives for Quality Management

The Government of India has been taking several measures for quality improvement. Some committees were constituted to suggest measures for quality improvement. The Report of the Education Commission (1964–65), National Policy on Education (1986), the Programme of Action (1995), Vision 2005 are some of the initiatives. The University Grants Commission (UGC), the All India Council for Technical Education (AICTE) at the national level, and State Councils for Higher Education at the state level have been taking several measures for quality. The UGC's National Assessment and Accreditation Council (NAAC) and AICTE's National Board of Accreditation (NBA) have prepared some guidelines for quality.

In addition to the AICTE and the UGC, several other bodies like the Bar Council of India (BCI), the Medical Council of India (MCI), the Indian Nursing Council (INC), the Pharmacy Council of India (PCI), the Dentists Council of India (DCI), the Central Council for Indian Medicine (CCIM), the Veternary Council of India (VCI), the Distance Education Council of IGNOU (DEC – IGNOU), the Rehabilitation Council of India (RCI), have also been established for various activities. The programmes like Special Assistance Programme (SAP), College Science Improvement (COSIP), College Humanities and Social Sciences Improvement Programme (COH SSIP), and some other schemes were initiated by the UGC for quality improvement.

Criteria for Assessment

As per National Assessment and Accreditation Council (NAAC), the following are the criteria for the assessment of an institution:

- Curricular aspects
- Teaching, learning, evaluation
- Research, consultancy and extension
- Infrastructure and learning resources
- Student support and progression

- Organization and management
- Healthy practices.

The criteria for assessment and the points for various institutions are given in a tabular form.

Criteria	*Unit of assessment*		
	Universities (a)	*Affiliated constituent colleges (b)*	*Autonomous colleges (c)*
1. Curricular aspects	15	10	15
2. Teaching, learning, evaluation	25	40	30
3. Research, consultancy and extension	15	05	10
4. Infrastructure and learning resources	15	15	15
5. Student support and progression	10	10	10
6. Organization and management	10	10	10
7. Healthy practices	10	10	10
Total	**100**	**100**	**100**

NAAC is the founder member of the International Network of Quality Assurance Agencies in Higher Education (INQAAHE). Over 120 national agencies of INQAAHE have been engaged in assessment, accreditation and academic audit. At the international level also, some institutions have been getting certification for global recognition and standards.

Competitiveness among B-schools

A world class B-school in India advertises as, "Learn for One Year and Leader for Life". Another B-school states, "Learning for Leadership".

One of the reputed B-schools in India with international focus stresses its strengths as follows: India's first corporate-sponsored B-school with 25 years of excellence in management education and ranked in the top ten B-schools in India; 100 per cent placement in reputed organizations; 36 internationally acclaimed faculty; international collaborations with leading B-schools; state-of-the-art infrastructure; wi-fi campus; multimedia classrooms, lush green and environment friendly campus.

The features of this B-school are: full-time two-year residential programme; 100 per cent since inception; winner of Global Social Entrepreneurship Competition (GSEC) by University of Washington, winner of Microsoft Imagine Cup 2005 at Yokohoma, Japan; winner of Managerial Excellence Award 2005 by Madras Management Association; active collaboration with a public sector giant; a computer centre with a 2-mbps dedicated line and internet facility, accessible round the clock with connectivity to all hostel rooms; air-conditioned library and 1100 online journals; and up-to-date curriculum in tune with the latest industry requirements.

Another B-school says: "we are ranked consistantly among the top-B schools in India; 100 per cent placement record since inception in top organizations; continuous mentoring by industry professionals; student exchange programmes with leading foreign business schools/ universities; strong academic industry interface; and state-of-the-art campus."

"Ours is an ISO 9001: 2000 certified institute. Our B-school nurtures talent with the best in management education. It provides a disciplinary background and extensive work experience that helps in learning the nuances of management principles and the dynamics of global business environment."

"In our B-school, latest courseware and competent teachers facilitate constant upgrading and transform students into leaders who inspire others to aspire. An ISO–9001 certified institute and A rated premier B-school imparting professional education for the last 15 years; separate hostel facility for boys and girls; lush green environment; air-conditioned classrooms and conference hall; well-equipped computer labs and library; library and computer facility at hostels, and mess and canteen facilities."

The Best B-schools

Some organizations in India, such as COSMODE, All India Management Association (AIMA), *Business World*, and *Outlook*, have been conducting surveys on the best B-schools. The latest studies are shown below:

Top 10 Indian B-schools in 2005 (COSMODE study—given in alphabetical order, not by rank):

- Fore School of Management, New Delhi
- Indian Institute of Foreign Trade, New Delhi
- Indian Institute of Management, Ahmedabad
- Indian Institute of Management, Bangalore
- Indian Institute of Management, Calcutta
- Management Development Institute, Gurgaon
- National Institute of Industrial Engineering, Mumbai
- S.P. Jain Institute of Management and Research, Mumbai
- Xavier Institute of Management, Bhubaneswar
- Xavier Labour Relations Institute, Jamshedpur.

Top 10 B-schools in 2005 (All India Management Association Study):

- Xavier Labour Relations Institute, Jamshedpur
- Xavier Institute of Management, Bhubaneswar
- University Business School, Chandigarh
- National Institute of Industrial Engineering, Mumbai
- Institute of Management Technology, Gurgoan
- Institute of Rural Management, Anand
- Institute of Management Technology, Ghaziabad
- Indian Institute of Foreign Trade, New Delhi
- Department of Management Studies, IIT, Delhi
- S.P. Jain Institute of Management and Research, Mumbai.

Parameters considered (Cosmode–*Business World* Survey):

1. Infrastructure (100 points):
   - Physical infrastructure (35)
   - Library (30)
   - Computer and teaching aids (25)
   - Qualitative evaluation (10).
2. Faculty (250):
   - Faculty strength (110)
   - PhDs produced (10)
   - Faculty publications (75)
   - Other programmes (30)
   - Qualitative evaluation (25).
3. Placement (300):
   - Domestic and international (45)
   - Average domestic salary (100)
   - Return on investments (20)
   - Industry interface (15)
   - Alumni (15)
   - Validation and qualitative evaluation (105).
4. Networking (100):
   - Programmes and research (25)
   - Students and research (15)
   - Faculty exchange (15)
   - Member of professional body awards and electives (35)
   - Qualitative evaluation (10).

Parameters considered (AIMA survey):

- Intellectual capital (100)
- Admissions and placements (100)
- Industry interface (100)
- Governance (100)
- Infrastructure (100).

The overall score of top 10 B-schools was 95. Intellectual capital, admissions and placements, infrastructure, industry interface varied from 85 to 95. Governance was observed from 75 to 95.

Other parameters in top 10 B-schools:

- Student to faculty ratio : 4.6
- Student to computer ratio : 1.1
- Auditorium capacity : 7.9

- Number of PhDs : 31
- Percentage of PhDs : 66
- Number of titles published : 20
- No. of papers published : 129
- No. of consultancy projects : 74
- No. of MDPs organized in 2 years : 119
- Salary in last payment : ₹6,27,637

These values varied from the category of B-schools as can be seen from the data given in a tabular form below:

Categorywise B-school Averages

S. No.	*Parameter*	*B-school category*			
		Top ten	*A*	*B*	*C*
1.	Student to faculty ratio	4.6	5	7	11
2.	Student to computer ratio	1.1	1	2	3
3.	Auditorium capacity	719	503	366	499
4.	No. of PhDs	31	12	5	2
5.	No. of papers published	129	32	8	2
6.	No. of consultancy projects	74	22	5	1
7.	No. of MDPs organized in 2 years	119	41	15	1
8.	Salary in last placement (₹ in lakhs)	6.27	3.88	1.86	1.32

New Trends

The new trend is that the one-year MBA course is slowly gaining momentum. IIM Ahmedabad, IIM Calcutta and IIFT New Delhi have already introduced one-year MBA programmes. IIM-A and IIM-C offer the programme full time for one year, and IIFT offers the programme during weekends. IIMs have designed the course for executives with experience who can take a break from their jobs for one year.

Another new feature is that management education at IITs is also going to become highly competitive and expected to reach the top position in the near future.

During January 3–8, 2005, an Indian institution had organized a programme on Advanced Management in Pune with top Harvard's Professors (Krishna G. Palepu, Nitin Nohria Das Narayandas), and the fee for each participant was ₹2.5 lakhs. Several such programmes are organized by various agencies and institutions by collecting huge amounts for short duration programmes. Even ISB in India charges ₹1.5 lakhs to ₹2.5 lakhs for a short MDP with 3 to 5 days duration.

Some B-schools have collaborations with top B-schools abroad and are offering qualitative management education in recent years. The best faculty available abroad has also been sharing their expertise with the Indian B-schools. As a result, the quality of management education has been improving. Even the management of several institutions and the Government of India have also been keen on the quality concept and implementation.

For quality assessment, B-schools have been rated based on the following factors:

Mission, Goals and Organization

1. Mission	:	20
2. Management	:	60
3. Resource utilization (physical and financial)	:	100
4. Academic performance (faculty and staff)	:	150
5. Students	:	100
6. Teaching–learning processes	:	200
7. Supplementary processes	:	50
8. Industry–institute interaction	:	100
9. Research	:	120
10. Innovation	:	50
11. Contribution to community	:	50

Conclusion

Japanese management emphasizes on quality of the product/service. For an international competitive edge, commitment to TQM philosophy is to be developed. The following points should be taken care of for competitive advantage of a firm or nation.

- Change in the organizational structures—multiple layers to be rejected, and moving towards horizontal management
- Developing customer-led, not product-led strategies
- Loving our people
- Initiating a cultural change
- Improving the quality of workers' lives
- Developing partnerships—learning to work with customers and suppliers
- Providing leadership
- Spending as much as one can on training.

SUMMARY

1. TQM was introduced by Armand Fiegenbaum in 1954.
2. It is an approach to improving the effectiveness of flexibility of business as a whole.
3. It is customer-oriented, and a continuous improvement of all processes.
4. Success depends upon top management commitment, leadership and involvement.
5. The model of TQM consists of management commitment, teamwork and quality tools and techniques.

6. Some prestigious awards are instituted for TQM implementation in Japan and the USA.
7. TQM is a culture change.
8. TQM helps in the competitive advantage of a firm or nation.
9. There are several methods for quality management.

REVIEW QUESTIONS

1. Explain the concept of Total Quality Management and its importance in Indian organizations.
2. What are the fundamental concepts and principles of TQM?
3. Discuss the model of TQM.
4. Explain the application of TQM in selected organizations.
5. What are the different methods for TQM?

CASE STUDIES

1. Westward Exports Ltd.

Mr. Abdul Ahmed, Production Manager, Westward Exports Ltd., Karachi, faced a decision in 1984. The rejection rate of their exports of readymade garments was 20 per cent of total production. He also felt that their productivity was not as high as it might have been.

Westward Exports Ltd. was a large Pakistani company exporting ladies fashion garments made of pure cotton. Their main product items were blouses, skirts, dresses, shirts, pants, etc. Their main overseas markets were the USA, Europe, and Japan, and production was ₹100 million. They had about 2,000 workers engaged in production through their various subcontractors.

Production was carried out by 138 subcontractors. They did not utilize assembly line production: each individual worker carried out all the jobs required on each garment. The machinery and equipment used by the subcontractors was about 15 to 20 years old. These domestically manufactured machines had a low output, and were not suited to high technology applications. Mr. Abdul knew that male workers performed 60 per cent of the total production and the rest was done by females. He also knew that while male workers were always willing to work overtime, their absentee rate was greater than that of women. Abdul felt that productivity could be higher, and he wondered how he should approach this issue.

The company purchased raw material (grey cloth) from several sources and had it dyed by different concerns, which sometimes caused variation in the colours. The company subcontracted the stitching of the garments to local suppliers. Both dyeing and inferior stitching caused the rejection rate to rise to 20 per cent of their total production. Mr. Abdul was worried about this high rate of rejection, and wondered what sequence of steps he should take to help reduce this high rejection rate.

Questions for Discussion

1. What alternatives are available to Mr. Abdul?
2. Other than purchasing higher technology machinery, in what ways might Mr. Abdul increase the effectiveness and efficiency of the dyeing and stitching operations?

2. Baba Bearings Company

The quality circle Sigma was started in the heat treatment section of Baba Bearings Company with seven members.

The members prepared the following list of various factors affecting the productivity of the heat treatment section.

1. Distortion of bearing races in sealed quench furnaces.
2. Loss of productivity and energy in sealed quench furnaces.
3. Excess consumption of LPG.
4. Rejection of cages due to scaling during annealing.
5. Shrinkage in tapered roller bearings outer rings.
6. Broadly, bearings are manufactured in the following three stages: (a) Turning, (b) Heat treatment, and (c) Grinding.

The circle members, in their brainstorming sessions, gave priorities to the study aspects with the help of Pareto analysis. Distortion of bearing races in sealed quench furnaces was a major factor affecting the productivity. Hence, the circle decided to take this up for study. Turned rings in the soft condition are hardened and tempered. After heat treatment, it was noted that about 39 per cent of the rings were beyond the specified limits of distortion (ovality). These rings were subjected to straining for rectification.

Straining is a laborious process involving extra manpower and time. It affected schedules and deliveries to customers. The cause and effect diagram was employed for analysis, and the following causes identified:

- design of heating elements
- mesh baskets distortion

The members collected data regarding the heating elements. Rings are loaded into the furnace keeping them in a mesh basket in layers. The rings are heated by corrtherm heating elements; the heat is made to circulate uniformly throughout the furnace by a circulating fan. After the hardening process, it was observed that in general, the rings arranged at the sides of the basket adjacent to the heating elements showed greater ovality (50 per cent) than those at the centre (17 per cent).

The members felt that the rings at the sides were directly exposed to the radiant heat of the elements, and this resulted in a temperature gradient within the cross-section of the rings, causing more distortion. The temperature adjacent to the heating elements was higher by 26 degree Celsius than at the centre of the furnace.

Questions for Discussion

1. What are the measures to be taken to avoid direct effect of heat?
2. Design a quality improvement process for the bearings company.

3. Pepsi-Cola

The U.S. Company Pepsi Co Inc. owns 19 per cent of the company via its overseas beverage unit, Pepsi-Cola International. Philippines is the twelfth-largest market for soft drinks in the world and it accounts for approximately 2 per cent of Pepsi's overseas sales.

Pepsi's sales had been running a distant second to Coca-Cola with a market share of 20 per cent compared to Coke's 78 per cent. In an attempt to take sales from Coke, the Pepsi bottler launched a "Number Fever" promotion campaign in February 1992. Numbers were printed on the underside of Pepsi bottle caps and winning numbers were announced each day. Prizes were awarded to people who brought in caps containing winning numbers. The campaign was trumpeted in ads in newspapers, on the radio, and on TV, proclaiming "Today, you could be a millionaire."

Prizes ranged from 100 pesos to 1 million pesos (approximately $40,000 U.S.). The promotion was a huge success with Pepsi's market share climbing to nearly 40 per cent. Buoyed with the campaign's success, the company extended the campaign for five more weeks for total of twelve weeks. As the campaign wore on, more than 51,000 winners came forward. Most won 100 pesos; however, seventeen people won the 1 million-peso prize. The big winners were incorporated into Pepsi's advertising campaign.

Victoria Angelo, an unemployed mother of five, lives with her family in a tin-roofed shack in a squalid Manila slum. Her husband, Juanito, earned about $4 a day carrying people in his three-wheeled pedicab. As a result of the campaign, they began drinking Pepsi with every meal and snack. Each morning they prayed that they would get a cap with a winning number. Every evening they gathered with their neighbours around a small television set to see if their prayers had been heard.

On May 25, 1992, the number 349 flashed on the screen as the winner. Victoria Angelo searched through her caps, spreading them out on a table and suddenly screamed, "We are a millionaire (sic)." She turned excitedly to her family: "I tell my children you can finish school and go to college. I tell my husband he can buy a [passenger jeep]. I tell myself we can buy a real house. Can you imagine? It is a dream come true!"

Unfortunately, the number 349 appeared on between 500,000 and 800,000 bottle caps. Pepsi quickly realized the mistake when thousands of people began demanding payment. Knowledge that billions of dollars could be at stake, the company refused to pay. Riots broke out and Pepsi delivery trucks were stoned, torched or overturned. Molotov cocktails and homemade bombs were thrown at Pepsi plants and offices. In one incident, a fragmentation grenade was tossed at a parked Pepsi truck. It bounced off the truck and killed a five-year old girl and a school teacher, wounding six other people. Pepsi executives received many death threats.

The violence frightened company officials who quickly decided to offer 500 ($18.50 U.S.) pesos to each winner. More than 480,000 winners have come forward. The original promotion was budgeted at $ 2 million for prizes. Pepsi has paid over $ 10 million in prizes. The cost would have been more than $ 18 billion if the 1 million pesos per winner had been paid as promised.

The violence resulted in more than thirty burned delivery trucks. Approximately 6000 people have filed civil suits for damages. At least 5000 criminal suits charging fraud have been started. All of this is a result of what Pepsi Philippines' officials call a computer error.

Questions for Discussion

1. Explain the main issues of the case?
2. How do you establish sustainable growth of the company?

FURTHER READING

Bank, John, *The Essence of Total Quality Management*, Prentice-Hall of India, New Delhi, 1995.

Juran, J.M., *Leadership for Quality: An Executive Handbook*, New York, The Free Press, 1989.

Kanji, G.K. and Asher, M., *100 Methods for Total Quality Management*, Response Books, New Delhi, 1996.

Oakland, J.S., *Total Quality Management*, Butter Worth-Heinemann, Oxford, 1989.

Stoner, James A.F., *Management*, Pearson/Prentice Hall, New Delhi, 2005.

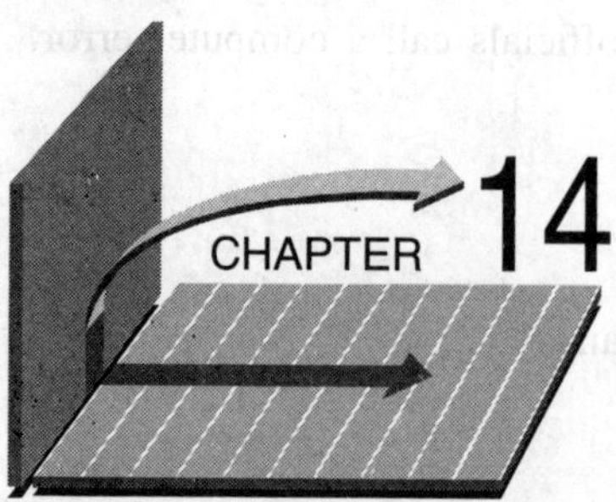

Quality Management Systems

CONTENTS

INTRODUCTION

As natural selection works solely by and for the good of each being, all corporeal and mental endowments will tend to progress towards perfection.

—Charles Darwin, 1809–1882

In the early 20th century, manufacturers began to include quality processes in quality practices. After the United States (USA) entered World War II, quality became a critical component of the war effort—bullets manufactured in one state, for example, had to work consistently in rifles made in another. The armed forces initially inspected virtually every unit of product; then to simplify and speed up this process without compromising safety, the military began using sampling techniques for inspection, aided by the publication of military specification standards and training courses in Walter Shewhart's statistical process control techniques.

The birth of total quality in the United States came as a direct response to the quality revolution in Japan following World War II as major Japanese manufacturers converted from producing military goods for internal use to producing civilian goods for trade. The Japanese welcomed the input of Americans Joseph M. Juran and W. Edwards Deming and rather than concentrating just on inspection, focused on improving all organizational processes through the people who used them.

By the 1970s, U.S. industrial sectors such as automobiles and electronics had been broadsided by Japan's high-quality competition. The U.S. response, emphasizing not only statistics but approaches that embraced the entire organization, became known as *Total Quality Management* (*TQM*).

By the last decade of the 20th century, TQM was considered a fad by many business leaders. But while the use of the term 'TQM' has somewhat faded, particularly in the United States, its practices still continue.

In few years since the turn of the century, the quality movement seems to have matured beyond Total Quality. New quality systems have evolved from the foundations of Deming, Juran and the early Japanese practitioners of quality, and quality has moved beyond manufacturing—into service, health care, education and government sectors.

At first, Japan had a widely held reputation for inferior quality exports and their goods were rejected by international markets. This led Japanese organizations to explore new ways of thinking about quality.

The Japanese welcomed input from foreign companies and lecturers, including two American quality experts:

- W. Edwards Deming, who had become frustrated with American managers when most programs for statistical quality control were terminated once the war and government contracts came to an end.
- Joseph M. Juran, who predicted the quality of Japanese goods would overtake the quality of goods produced in the United States by the mid-1970s because of Japan's revolutionary rate of quality improvement.

Japan's strategies represented the new "total quality" approach. Rather than relying purely on product inspection, Japanese manufacturers focused on improving all organizational processes through the people who used them. As a result, Japan was able to produce higher-quality exports at lower prices, benefiting consumers throughout the world.

American managers were generally unaware of this trend, assuming any competition from the Japanese would ultimately come in the form of price, not quality. In the meantime, Japanese manufacturers began increasing their share in American markets, causing widespread economic effects in the United States—manufacturers began losing market share; organizations began shipping jobs overseas; and the economy suffered unfavourable trade balances. Overall, the impact on American business jolted the United States into action.

At first, U.S. manufacturers held onto their assumption that Japanese success was price-related and thus responded to Japanese competition with strategies aimed at reducing domestic production costs and restricting imports. This, of course, did nothing to improve American competitiveness in quality.

As years passed, price competition declined while quality competition continued to increase. By the end of 1970s, the American quality crisis reached major proportions, attracting attention from national legislators, administrators and the media. A 1980 NBC-TV News special report, "*If Japan Can... Why Can't We*?" highlighted how Japan had captured the world's auto and electronic markets. Finally, U.S. organizations began to listen.

The Chief Executive Officers of major U.S. corporations stepped forward to provide personal leadership in the quality movement. Several other quality initiatives followed. The ISO 9000 series of quality-management standards, for example, were published in 1987. The Baldrige National Quality Program and Malcolm Baldrige National Quality Award were established by the U.S. Congress in the same year. American companies were at first slow to adopt the standards but eventually came on board.

Quality expert Nancy Tague says, "Enough organizations have used it with success that, to paraphrase Mark Twain, the reports of its death have been greatly exaggerated."

Quality is perceived differently by different people. Yet, everyone understands what is meant by "quality." In a manufactured product, the customer as a user recognizes the quality of fit, finish, appearance, function and performance. The quality of service may be rated based on the degree of satisfaction by the customer receiving the service. The relevant dictionary meaning of quality is "the degree of excellence." However, this definition is relative in nature. The ultimate test in this evaluation process lies with the consumer. The customer's needs must be translated into measurable characteristics in a product or service. Once the specifications are developed, ways to measure and monitor the characteristics need to be found. This provides the basis for continuous improvement in the product or service. The ultimate aim is to ensure that the customer will be satisfied to pay for the product or service. This should result in a reasonable profit for the producer or the service provider. The relationship with a customer is a lasting one. Therefore, reliability of a product plays an important role in developing this relationship.

Some of the crucial events in the dairy of International Quality domain, which show how the Quality domain has matured over a century are described below:

- 22 January 1901: Sir John Wolfe-Barry (the man who designed London's Tower Bridge) instigated the Council of the Institution of Civil Engineers to form a committee to consider standardizing iron and steel sections.
- 1911: Frederick W. Taylor published, *The Principles of Scientific Management*.
- 1924: Walter A. Shewhart, a statistician at Bell Laboratories developed the control charts, and principles of statistical process control.
- 1925: Sir Ronald Fisher published the book, *Statistical Methods for Research Workers*, and introduced the concept of ANOVA.
- 1937: Joseph Juran introduced the Pareto principle as a means of narrowing on the vital few.
- 1940: The acceptance sampling plan was developed by Harold F. Dodge and Harry G. Roming.
- 1943: Kaoru Ishikawa developed the cause and effect diagram (also known as fishbone diagram).

- 1946: The Japanese Union of Scientists and Engineering (JUSE) was established.
- 1946: The International Organization for Standardization was founded in Geneva, Switzerland.
- 16 February 1946: The American Society for Quality Control (ASQC) was formed.
- 1947: Dr. Edwards Deming was sent to Japan to help Japanese rejuvenate their industries.
- 1950: Genrich Altshuller developed the theory of inventive problem solving (TRIZ).
- 1951: Deming Prize instituted.
- 1951: Juran published the first edition of *Quality Control Handbook.*
- 1954: Juran's reputation in quality management led the Union of Japanese Scientists and Engineers to invite him to Japan.
- 1960: The first "Quality Control Circles" were formed in Japan and simple statistical methods were used for quality improvement.
- 1960: The concept of Kaizen developed.
- 1961–1964: The concept of Poka Yoke developed by Shingeo Shingo.
- 1966: Dr. Yoji Akao, introduced Quality Function Deployment (QFD) Methodology.
- 1968: Kaoru Ishikawa published the *Guide to Quality Control.*
- 1969: Dr. Shingo Shigeo as a part of JIT, pioneered the concept of Single Minute Exchange of Dies.
- 1969: Ishikawa emphasized the use of Seven Quality Tools.
- 1969: ASQC co-sponsors the first International Congress in Quality Control, hosted by the Union of Japanese Scientists and Engineers in Tokyo.
- 1970: Dr. Taguchi promoted the concept of Quality Loss Function.
- 1977: International Association for Quality Circles founded.
- 1979: BS 5750 was issued. This was later replaced with ISO 9001:1987.
- 1979: Philip Crosby published his book *Quality is Free.*
- 24 June 1980: NBC aired the television documentary "If Japan Can, Why Can't We?"
- 1980: Professor Noriaki Kano developed the Kano model which classifies customer preferences into five categories: Attractive, One-Dimensional, Must-Be, Indifferent, Reverse.
- 1982: In *Out of the Crisis*, originally published in 1982, Deming offers a theory of management based on his famous 14 Points for Management.
- 1986: Six Sigma formulated by Bill Smith in Motorola.
- 1986: Masaaki Imai established the Kaizen Institute to help Western companies introduce Kaizen concepts, systems and tools.
- 15 March 1987: ISO issued the first version of the ISO 9000 series.
- 1987: Malcolm Baldrige National Quality Award was established.
- 1988: Motorola becomes the first company to win Malcolm Baldridge National Quality Award.
- 15 September 1988: Presidents of 14 European companies came together to create the European Foundation for Quality Management.
- 1994: QS 9000 quality standard developed by a joint effort of the 'Big Three' automakers, General Motors, Chrysler and Ford.

- 1994: ISO issued the second version of the ISO 9000 series.
- 1995: General Electric (GE) launched the Six Sigma initiative.
- 1997: ASQC drops 'Control' from its name, becomes ASQ.
- 1999: ISO/TS 16949 1st Edition was released.
- 2000: ISO issued the third version of the ISO 9000 series.
- 2008: ISO issued the fourth version of the ISO 9000 series.

Some of the bitter events in the world which could have been avoided if there are proper quality control practices and implemented are as described below for reference:

- 15 April 1912: The Titanic sank on its maiden voyage. Over 1,500 people lost their lives when the ship ran into an iceberg and sunk in frigid waters.
- 2 December 1984: Bhopal Gas Tragedy—A leak of methyl isocyanate gas and other chemicals from the plant resulted in the exposure of hundreds of thousands of people to toxic environment.
- 28 January 1986: The Space Shuttle Challenger was destroyed 73 seconds after take-off due to a faulty O-ring.
- 26 April 1986: Chernobyl Disaster—The accident was officially attributed to power plant operators who violated plant procedures and were ignorant of the safety requirements needed.
- 6 July 1988: Alpha Piper Disaster—An explosion and resulting fire destroyed it, killing 167 men.
- May 2000: Ford Motor recalled 6.5 million 15-inch Firestone tires fitted to the Ford Explorer SUV. This soon culminated in the resignation of Ford's CEO at the time, Jacques Nasser.
- 2001: Space Shuttle Columbia failed during re-entry into the Earth's atmosphere, resulting in the death of all seven crew members.
- 2006: Sony Notebook Battery Recall—Computer manufacturers recalled batteries after a number of instances where the batteries, made by Sony, overheated or caught fire.
- 2009–2010: Toyota recalled millions of vehicles because of sticking accelerator pedal.
- 20 April 2010: BP Oil Spill—It is the largest accidental marine oil spill in the history of petroleum industry.

EVOLUTION OF QUALITY MANAGEMENT

Over the past few decades, there have been several leaders who have been instrumental in developing the concept of quality as understood today. It is very apt to note some of the vital contributions of these Quality Gurus (Proficient) in this report:

Joseph M. Juran is one of these key figures in the Quality world. Using eastern philosophies learnt in Japan, he advocated the idea that quality is related to 'fitness for use'. Juran believed that this definition of quality fell into two key areas. Higher quality products had a greater number of features which fit with the requirements of the consumer and also had fewer defects. His book *Managerial Breakthrough* published in the 1960s was the first to offer a step-by-step sequence for improvement, while the *Juran Trilogy*, published in the 1980s, produced three definitive quality management processes—quality planning, quality improvement and quality control.

W. Edwards Deming, another 'Founding Father of Quality', also took what he learnt in Japan and brought it to the West. His 14 points were presented in his work *Out of the Crisis*, published in 1982 and had been learnt in Japan following the Second World War. His approach led to the creation of the theory of total quality management and linked the concept of quality with efficient management. Deming said managers were required to have a system of profound knowledge, comprised of appreciation of a system, theory of knowledge, the psychology of change and knowledge about variation.

1. Create and publish to all employees a statement of the aims and purposes of the company or other organization. The management must demonstrate constantly their commitment to this statement.
2. Learn the new philosophy of top management and everybody.
3. Understand the purpose of inspection for improvement of process and reduction of cost.
4. End the practice of awarding business on the basis of price tag alone.
5. Improve constantly and for ever the system of production and service.
6. Institute training.
7. Teach and institute leadership.
8. Drive out fear. Create trust. Create a climate for innovation.
9. Optimize towards the aims and purposes of the company, the efforts of teams, groups, staff areas.
10. Eliminate exhortations for the workforce.
11. (a) Eliminate numerical quotas for production. Instead learn and institute methods or improvement.
    (b) Eliminate management by objective. Instead, learn the capabilities of process and how to improve them.
12. Remove barriers that rob people of pride of workmanship.
13. Encourage education and self-improvement for everyone.
14. Take action to accomplish the transformation.

Philip Crosby is the man behind four absolutes of quality management and furthered the idea that quality was about conforming to a series of requirements, rather than reaching a poorly defined benchmark of goodness. His absolutes centered around the concept that quality should be prevented rather than detected and corrected, the standard for performance should be zero deficits and quality should be measured by the price of non-conformity. Crosby laid out 14 steps for quality improvement, ensuring that the principle is embedded throughout the organization and throughout all business processes.

1. Management commitment
2. Quality improvement team
3. Quality measurement
4. Cost-of-quality innovation
5. Quality awareness

6. Corrective action
7. Ad-hoc committee for the zero defects program
8. Supervisor training
9. Zero-defects day
10. Goal-setting
11. Error-cause removal
12. Recognition
13. Quality councils
14. Do it over again

Indeed, one of Crosby's most commonly quoted phrases is "If quality isn't ingrained in the organization, it will never happen."

Armand Vallin Feigenbaum is an American quality control expert and businessman. He devised the concept of Total Quality Control, later known as Total Quality Management (TQM). Feigenbaum received a Bachelor's degree from Union College, his Master's degree from the MIT Sloan School of Management and PhD in Economics from MIT. He was the Director of Manufacturing Operations at General Electric (1958–1968), and is now the President and CEO of General Systems Company of Pittsfield, Massachusetts—an engineering firm that designs and installs operational systems. Feigenbaum wrote several books and served as President of the American Society for Quality (1961–1963).

His contributions to the quality body of knowledge include:

- "Total quality control is an effective system for integrating the quality development, quality maintenance and quality improvement efforts of various groups in an organization so as to enable production and service at the most economical levels which allow full customer satisfaction."
- "The concept of a 'hidden' plant—the idea that so much extra work is performed in correcting mistakes that there is effectively a hidden plant within any factory."
- "Accountability for quality: Because quality is everybody's job, it may become nobody's job—the idea that quality must be actively managed and have visibility at the highest levels of management."
- 'The concept of quality costs.'

Dr. Kaoru Ishikawa is one of the world's foremost authorities on quality control. He has helped thousands of companies, including IBM, Bridgestone and Komatsu, to turn out higher quality products at much lower costs. His book, *What is Total Quality Control? The Japanese Way* was the best-seller in business books. He has provided leadership in shaping the Japanese quality movement. Dr. Ishikawa said, *Through total quality control with the participation of all employees, including the President, any company can create better products (or service) at a lower cost, increase sales, improve profit and make the company into a better organization.*

Some of the renowned contributions of Ishikawa to the Quality industry are as below:

- The 6 quality control characteristics as mentioned in *What is Total Quality Control? The Japanese Way* are:

  1. Company-wide quality control; participation by all members of the organization in quality control

2. Education and training in quality control
3. Quality control circle activities
4. Quality control audits (for effectiveness)
5. Utilization of statistical methods
6. Nationwide quality control promotion (including training) activities

- True quality characteristics: the customer's view of product performance
- Substitute quality characteristics: the producer's view of product performance
- Proposed the basis of QFD
- Developed seven tools of quality control in *Guide to Quality Control*:
  1. Cause-effect (Ishikawa) diagram
  2. Stratification
  3. Check sheet
  4. Histogram
  5. Scatter diagram
  6. Pareto chart (vital few, trivial many)
  7. Graphs and statistical control charts
- Ishikawa's concept of TQC
  1. Quality first—not short-term profits first
  2. Consumer orientation—not producer orientation (think from the standpoint of other party)
  3. The next process is the customer—breaking down the barrier of sectionalism
  4. Using facts and data to make presentations—utilization of statistical methods
  5. Respect for humanity as a management philosophy, full participatory management
  6. Cross-functional management (by divisions and functions).

Genichi Taguchi, was yet another prominent personality and contributor to the world of Quality. Born on the first day of 1924, Genichi Taguchi studied textile engineering at Kiryu Technical College. After Second World War, he worked for the Japanese Ministry of Public Health and Welfare and conducted the nation's first study on health and nutrition. He also applied his quality improvement knowledge at Morinaga Pharmaceutical and even worked for a candy maker, Morinaga Sieka, to reduce the melting properties of caramel at room temperature.

After the Second World War, Japanese manufacturers were struggling to survive with very limited resources. If it were not for the advancements of Taguchi, the country might not have stayed afloat, let alone flourish, as it has. Taguchi revolutionized the manufacturing process in Japan through cost savings. He understood, like many other engineers, that all manufacturing processes are affected by outside influences, called *noise*. However, Taguchi realized methods of identifying those noise sources which have the greatest effects on product variability. His ideas have been adopted by successful manufacturers around the globe because of their results in creating superior production processes at much lower costs.

Here are some of the major contributions that Taguchi has made to the quality improvement world:

- ***The loss function:*** Taguchi devised an equation to quantify the decline of a customer's perceived value of a product as its quality declines. Essentially, it tells managers how much revenue they are losing because of variability in their production process. It is a powerful tool for projecting the benefits of a quality improvement program. Taguchi was the first person to equate quality with cost.
- ***Orthogonal arrays and linear graphs:*** When evaluating a production process, analysis will undoubtedly identify outside factors or noise which cause deviations from the mean. Isolating these factors to determine their individual effects can be a very costly and time-consuming process. Taguchi devised a way to use orthogonal arrays to isolate these noise factors from all others in a cost effective manner.
- ***Robustness:*** Some noise factors can be identified, isolated and even eliminated but others cannot. For instance, it is too difficult to predict and prepare for any possible weather condition. Taguchi, therefore, referred to the ability of a process or product to work as intended, regardless of uncontrollable outside influences as robustness. He was pivotal in many companies' development of products and processes which perform uniformly, regardless of uncontrollable forces; an obviously beneficial service.

Walter Shewhart is considered as the "Grandfather of Total Quality Management". The original notions of Total Quality Management and continuous improvement trace back to the former Bell Telephone employee named Walter Shewhart. One of W. Edwards Deming's teachers, he preached the importance of adapting management processes to create profitable situations for both businesses and consumers, promoting the utilization of his own creation—the *SPC control chart.*

Dr. Shewhart believed that lack of information greatly hampered the efforts of control and management processes in a production environment. In order to aid a manager in making scientific, efficient and economical decisions, he developed *Statistical Process Control* methods. Many of the modern ideas regarding quality owe their inspiration to Dr. Shewhart.

He also developed the *Shewhart Cycle Learning and Improvement Cycle*, combining both creative management thinking with statistical analysis. This cycle contains four continuous steps: Plan, Do, Study and Act. These steps (commonly referred to as the *PDSA cycle*), Shewhart believed, ultimately lead to total quality improvement. The cycle draws its structure from the notion that constant evaluation of management practices as well as the willingness of management to adopt and disregard unsupported ideas, are keys to the evolution of a successful enterprise.

Having studied the wealth of Quality concepts and body of knowledge provided by all the Quality proponents, it is quite evident that Quality plays a major role in the success of organizations. It is true that the business landscape might have changed to a larger extent since Crosby, Juran and Deming advanced their principles of quality, but undoubtedly they are still much relevant even today.

Many business leaders define quality as being important, according to Chartered Quality Institute (CQI), but only 50 per cent said quality was placed at the heart of their organization and only 23 per cent claimed to be offering a "very consistent" level of quality. Even fewer (16 per cent) claimed their quality is market leading, but this is precisely what companies need to set themselves apart as the economy struggles and consumer spending continues to fall.

In an open, free market economy, with few barriers to market entry, there is little alternative but to compete on quality to win customers from high quality-driven EU competitors and emerging economies with lower production costs. The work in creating a definition and framework for achieving quality has already been done. Organizations must now take steps to apply this to their organization and ultimately, reap the rewards.

For example, there is huge difference between 'quality' management and 'quality management'. Both terms rely on an understanding of the meaning of both 'quality' and 'management', which will vary depending on the context in which they are used. Similarly, quality thinking could be 'quality' thinking or 'quality thinking', i.e. thinking about 'quality' or a 'better and more effective way of thinking'.

Many researchers have attempted to define the magical word "quality" from the past few decades and some of those well suited definitions are documented below which were publicized in the industry:

Quality is:

- 'a measure of excellence'
- 'the characteristics of a product or service that bear on its ability to satisfy stated or implied needs'
- 'better than you would, or could, have ever expected'
- 'what the customer perceives it to be'
- 'doing the right thing right, every time'
- 'the degree to which an item or process meets or exceeds the customers' requirements and expectations'
- 'how closely a product or service meets its design specification'
- 'surpassing customer needs and expectations throughout the life of the product'
- 'a product or service free of deficiencies'
- 'reducing the variation around the target'
- 'a state of mind'
- 'the extent to which products, services, processes and relationships are free from defects, constraints, and items which do not add value for customers'
- 'never having to say you are sorry'
- 'an ever-evolving perception by the customer of the value provided by a product. It is not a static perception that never changes but a fluid process that changes as a product matures (innovation) and other alternatives (competition) are made available as a basis of comparison'
- 'peace of mind'
- 'never an accident'
- 'the inherent features possessed by a product or service'
- 'when what comes back is the client, not the product'
- 'no surprises!'
- 'not achieved by doing different things. It is achieved by doing things differently'.

While there is no right and wrong answer to the definition of Quality, the above opinions include quite a mix of options—from the 'product characteristics' view on one hand, through meeting design specification and reducing variation, achieving (at least) customer satisfaction and other outcomes and to hint about how quality can be achieved. If all of these factors have to be managed, it is clear that we are talking about process quality management rather than just product quality management. And the emphasis has moved from 'just' meeting requirements to 'achieving excellence'. Moreover, terms such as 'sustainability', 'social responsibility' and 'integration' are now as prevalent (if not more so) than 'quality' in its traditional sense. The quality of goods or of a service (or at least a customer's perception of it) can be significantly influenced by the customer's expectations from the product, which in turn can be found on a number of assumptions. Both these factors can be influenced (and manipulated) significantly by the supplier as well as by a number of other factors. This subject is explained in much more detail in Peter Bowbrick's book, *The Economics of Quality, Grades and Brands*. Myron Tribus, former Director of the Centre for Advanced Engineering Study at MIT, puts it another way: "There is no such thing as an immaculate perception. What is seen depends upon what was thought before it was really looked at." Many assumptions made by customers are based on redundant knowledge or on ignorance, yet they have a major impact on how quality is perceived. On the other hand, a supplier can do much to manage expectations and anticipate assumptions, so that the same product is viewed differently under different circumstances. There is a growing realization that quality is multi-dimensional—things do not get done as a result of random acts and events but rather as a sequence of interrelated actions which depend on resources being available and which are affected by a variety of influences. There is also a time element in all of this—company culture, experience and knowledge, reputation and expectations can all take years to develop.

Quality Management Standards

During the Second World War, a number of bombs exploded in factories during assembly. As a result, factories were required to document their procedures and to provide records to show that they were followed. They were then inspected to prove conformity to defined procedures.

In the 1970s some major organizations such as the Ministry of Defense (MoD) and Ford developed their own 'quality management' standards and required their suppliers to define how they operated and provide evidence that they 'conformed' to the defined procedures, with an implied quality of product as an outcome.

In 1979, BS 5750 was developed as a national standard on what constituted a quality system. In the 1980s, the International Organization for Standardization was persuaded by the British government to adopt BS 5750 as an international standard, and it became ISO 9000 standard.

ISO 9000:1987 had the same structure as BS 5750, with three 'models' for quality management systems—ISO 9001:1987 Model for quality assurance in design, development, production, installation and servicing. ISO 9002:1987 Model for quality assurance in production, installation and servicing. ISO 9003:1987 Model for quality assurance in final inspection and test.

Other relevant standards during this period included the 'DEF STAN 05/20 series (MoD)'. DEF STAN 05/21 covered the design, production and service of hardware functions and was broadly equivalent to the 1969 NATO quality management specifications (AQAP). The US did not impose AQAP specifications for their defense contractors but introduced MIL-Q-9858 in its place.

The emphasis of ISO 9000:1987 remained on inspection to ensure conformance with procedures. ISO 9000:1994 emphasized quality assurance by means of preventive actions instead of 'just' checking the final product, but it still required evidence of compliance with documented procedures. So, companies still created volumes of procedure manuals which at times made it more difficult to change and improve.

ISO 9001:2000 was a more significant update, combining 9001, 9002 and 9003 into one standard. It also introduced the concept of 'process management'. ISO 9001:2008 has been released as an upgrade of 9001:2000 without major changes as such and is the current standard today.

Along the way, a variety of sector-specific standards and guidelines (such as TickIT for software development) were produced since it was felt that the generic standards did not translate easily or that a specific industry sector had special requirements. The car industry is another sector which has developed its own standards, despite the fact that the international standards were designed for all sizes of organization and for service companies as well as manufacturing. In truth, the manufacturing origins of ISO 9001 have remained one of the key factors for many managers who have to interpret the standard and relate it to their ways of working.

For the same reason, it has also been a stumbling block in the adoption of the process approach which the year 2000 edition itself promotes. And there remain two other major issues, namely the belief that 'quality' is separate from 'business management' and that producing a 'management system definition' is in some way a substitute for a system by which to manage the business.

New Approaches to Quality Management

Other initiatives and approaches to quality management which have appeared in recent times include TQM (total quality management). According to ISO, TQM is 'a management approach for an organization, centered on quality, based on the participation of all its members and aiming at long-term success through customer satisfaction and benefits to all members of the organization and to society'. It dates back to the 1950s, but was particularly widespread in the 1970s and 1980s.

The Business Excellence Model of the EFQM (European Foundation for Quality Management), established in 1988 in Europe, and the Malcolm Baldrige National Quality Award, established in 1987 in the US, both give organizations a guideline to achieve and measure their success.

Six Sigma is a methodology developed by Motorola to improve its business processes by minimizing defects. Lean manufacturing (lean production) is the optimal way of producing goods through the removal of waste and implementing flow, as opposed to batch and queue.

In reality, the latter two methodologies are aimed at 'process effectiveness' and 'process efficiency', respectively. The first two 'models' focus on key areas.

It is interesting to note that in almost every case, the key elements relate to:

- The objectives which the organization is trying to achieve

- The resources required to ensure that processes can function
- The factors that can influence how (well) the processes operate
- The processes themselves
- The outcomes of the processes.

The fact that all these elements are included in each model serves to emphasize the complete 'system' which enables an organization to operate. The key to process management, and to 'systems thinking', is to appreciate all the factors and component parts which need to exist and to work together—or at least to be managed.

Managing Process

It can be assumed that 'the process approach' promoted in ISO 9001:2008 was an innovation in 'quality' thinking, but it was fundamental to Deming's work in last century. As Dr. Henry Neave (Professor of leadership and management in the Business School of Nottingham Trent University until 2004) pointed out in an article that introduced Dr. Walter Shewhart's work on variation and control charts, which effectively launched Deming's work in the 1920s:

"A fundamental property of all but the most trivial of processes is that there will be some undesirable variation in outputs and the foundation of Deming's guidance on process improvement is the understanding of that variation, so that it can be reduced. Each time a work is performed by the same person there will be some variation. Things are never exactly the same. While variety in products and services can enrich life, variation prevents the customers from enjoying the full benefit. Variation is associated with 'bad quality'. Good quality implies reliability, trustworthiness and no unpleasant surprises. Essentially, a feature of bad quality is too much variation, while a feature of good quality is little variation."

Deming used the example of the Western Electric Company which developed telephone and related equipment and invested to increase its understanding and ability. Initially, this was successful but gradually ran out of steam. Deming later explained: "The harder they tried to achieve consistency and uniformity, the worse were the effects. When any kind of error, mistake, or accident occurred, they went to work on it to tried to correct it. There was only one little trouble—their worthy efforts did not work. Things got worse—they were failing to understand the difference between common causes and special causes, and that mixing them up makes things worse."

In essence, Shewhart's breakthrough was to recognize these two very different types of variation and their very different types of implications as regards improvement efforts, 'control', capability, and so on. What Deming later called *common-cause variation* is the routine variation to be expected because of what the process is, and the circumstances in which it exists and operates. Special-cause variation is anything noticeable beyond that routine variation.

Very different actions are called for, depending on whether something is routine or exceptional. We can distinguish between the two types of variation in practice by using the tool that Shewhart created for the purpose—*the control chart*. It follows that, while we continue to obtain such outputs, it is illogical and impractical to claim that anything specific 'caused' any one particular result, for any such result is the kind of result we know can be produced by the whole system of common causes (Deming simply called it the 'system').

Process monitoring is just fire-fighting and this is not good enough. If process monitoring is all that being perceived using the control chart, it means the main purpose is missed for which Shewhart created it, i.e. process improvement. Process monitoring merely aims to reach and maintain a state of statistical control. But that's only the beginning. The next issue is to understand if the process capable. This means that, when it is in control, is it capable of providing outputs that meet the customers' stated requirements?

Introduction of Third-Party Certification Schemes

During the 1970s, suppliers to the North Sea Oil and Gas Industry found themselves being increasingly audited by every oil major they supplied, with a view to ensure that the goods and services they were buying were of a suitable quality. This, in turn, meant that the oil companies themselves found that they were carrying out more and more audits of their suppliers. In the early 1980s, they got together to divide up their supplier base and work with them to 'encourage' them to obtain third party certification to ISO 9001.

Their objective was to avoid multiple assessments of the same firms by getting a third party to provide independent evidence that the supplier had an established 'quality system' which met an agreed standard (ISO 9001). The thinking was that this would enable them to rely on the supplier to deliver a consistent product—and thus obviate the need to carry out an increasing number of audits themselves.

There remains a major doubt about the success of this policy—second party audits are still carried out (even on suppliers certificated to ISO 9001), and there has been a major concern for some years that the quality of product (goods or services) provided by such suppliers is no better than those without a certificate. So, the time and effort expended does not appear to have been justified, either for the 'customers' or for the suppliers who implemented the required systems.

An Increasing Rate of Change

As with most aspects of modern life, the rate of change in management thinking in general, and in quality matters in particular, has increased exponentially in the last 30–40 years. 'Quality' thinking, in the past, has focused on the reduction of variation and the production of a standard product which meets specifications. Nowadays, however, there is a requirement to find different and better ways of producing better and different products, so the encouragement and support of innovation has become a differentiator for many businesses. Services are delivered by processes which are not predetermined since the customer demands cannot always be anticipated, and the quality of the service is determined by how well the supplier (i.e., their staff) and the delivery process itself is able to react and respond. Reduced variation is not always the measure of customer satisfaction.

The current status of the 'quality' profession, in many ways reflects the evolution of concepts and application of 'quality' thinking over the past 50 years. And yet, the debate suggests that some members are questioning some fundamental aspects of the very reasons for its existence.

Some of the relevant questions being asked are:

- What is Quality?

- How is Quality measured?
- What is the role of the 'Quality Manager' and is there a future for the individual?

The confusion in some people's minds (both within and outside the quality profession) is not helped by the fact, that the 'independent' custodian of international standards in the UK not only provides certification services against these standards, but also promotes and sells consultancy advice and training to organizations which are seeking to develop and define management systems to address these standards. Although other certification bodies maintain a strict independence from product suppliers, the whole certification 'industry' has become so competitive that the value of an ISO 9001 certificate has been seriously questioned by some observers for a considerable number of years.

The perception of the buying public as an entity and of customers involved in an individual transaction, is affected not only by their particular experience on a specific occasion, but also by their overall perception of a supplier's ability to address a wider range of stakeholder requirements at the present time as well as to meet future demands.

The Advent of Systems Thinking

'Systems thinking' is a way of thinking. It is an approach for developing models which can aid understanding of events, the patterns of behaviour resulting in the events and the underlying structure and relationships responsible for behaviour.

In *Computing Business* magazine (August/September 2006), Professor Jim Norton talks of the necessity to align people, process and business needs. He said: "In too many organizations, the business processes and the people who operate them are not fully aligned with the mission and values of the organization. Over time, some processes have failed to adjust to the development of the business and now destroy rather than create value. A major concern for both executive and non-executive directors is to ensure that the key processes in a business are documented clearly, and that those who work with them understand their importance to collective success. Such processes often cross organizational boundaries and are vital to the sharing of knowledge."

The objectives for such processes should always be derived from the organization's mission, performance must be reviewed against these objectives and there needs to be a way to determine whether these objective remain relevant. Systems thinking is 'thinking in terms of systems' rather than in terms of individual components of a system—and the same principles applicable to process management can be applied. Systems thinking can (and should) be used when deciding on the best way to achieve an objective, to respond to an event or to solve a problem. It uses the same logic as root cause analysis and its absence explains the 'law of unintended consequences'. It applies to decision making at all levels. It is also multi-dimensional, in that a process or processes are followed to achieve an objective, but there will also be policies which shape how the organization operates and which, therefore, will affect a number of those processes. It is appropriate to appreciate the interaction of components over time rather than a linear cause-and-effect relationship.

An organization's effectiveness and efficiency is influenced not only by one's own efforts but also by the external environment and events outside one's control. Identifying operational risks and anticipating how the operations may impact on others, are all part of systems thinking.

The same logic applies at all levels, from making a statement during a conversation up to declaring war at the other extreme. Systems thinking is an essential requirement for management success, from the initial assessment of the current situation through planning an organization's business strategy to designing, managing and improving the processes and products delivered. So many factors now affect an organization's operations, future success and even its continuing existence that the concept of 'quality' and how it is applied must expand and change to reflect the reality of business life today.

OVERVIEW OF QUALITY MODELS AND CERTIFICATIONS

Standards and System Certifications in the World

If there were no standards, we could soon notice. Standards make an enormous contribution to most aspects of our lives—although very often, that contribution is invisible.

It is when there is an absence of standards that their importance is truly noticed. For example, as purchasers or users of products, we soon notice when they turn out to be of poor quality, or do not fit, or are incompatible with equipment we already have, or are unreliable or dangerous. When products meet our expectations, we tend to "take this for granted". We do not notice that we breathe oxygen every moment we live. But we feel its importance the moment it is absent. Similarly, we are usually unaware of the role played by standards in raising levels of quality, safety, reliability, efficiency and interchangeability as well as in providing such benefits at an economical cost.

Standards establish an international consensus on terminology, make technology transfer easier and can represent an important stage in the advancement of new technologies. Without the standardized dimensions of freight containers, international trade would be slower and more expensive. Without the standardization of telephone and banking (Credit, Debit) cards in terms of length, width, thickness, etc., life would be highly complicated. Standardized symbols provide danger warnings and information across linguistic frontiers. Consensus on grades of various materials give a common reference for suppliers and clients in business dealings. Agreement on a sufficient number of variations of a product to meet most current applications allows economies of scale with cost benefits for both producers and consumers. An example is the standardization of paper sizes. (A4, A3, A2 and so on). Standardization of performance or safety requirements of diverse equipment makes sure that users' needs are met while allowing individual manufacturers the freedom to design their own solution on how to meet those needs. *Standardized protocols* allow computers from different vendors to 'talk' to each other. Standardized documents speed up the transit of goods, or identify sensitive or dangerous cargoes that may be handled by people speaking different languages. Standardization of connections and interfaces of all types ensures the compatibility of equipment of diverse origins and the interoperability of different technologies.

Agreement on test methods allows meaningful comparisons of products, or plays an important part in controlling pollution—whether by noise, vibration or emissions. Safety standards for machinery protect people at work, at play, at sea, at the dentist's, etc.

There are numerous standards which are existent till date in the industry. There are more than sixteen thousand standards published by International Organization for Standardization

(ISO standards) itself. Some of the widely used standards in the industry are highlighted as below:

- ISO 9001
- ISO 27001
- ISO 14001
- OHSAS 18001
- ISO 22000
- ISO 17025
- ISO 31000
- SA 8000
- SSAE 16
- CMMI (DEV)
- CMMI (SVC)
- ITIL

The details of various widely used models, their structure, model requirements and benefits are discussed below:

International Organization for Standardization (ISO)

ISO (International Organization for Standardization) is the world's largest developer of standards. Although ISO's principal activity is the development of technical standards, ISO standards also have important economic and social repercussions. ISO standards make a positive difference, not just to engineers and manufacturers for whom they solve basic problems in production and distribution, but to society as a whole.

The International Standards which ISO develops are very useful. They are useful to industrial and business organizations of all types, to governments and other regulatory bodies, to trade officials, to conformity assessment professionals, to suppliers and customers of products and services in both public and private sectors, and ultimately, to people in general in their roles as consumers and end users.

ISO standards contribute to making the development, manufacturing and supply of products and services more efficient, safer and cleaner. They make trade between countries easier and fairer; provide governments with a technical base for health, safety and environmental legislation and aid in transferring technology to developing countries. ISO standards also serve to safeguard consumers and users in general, of products and services, as well as to make their lives simpler.

When things go well, for example, when systems, machinery and devices work well and safely, then it is because they conform to certain standards. And IOS is the organization responsible for such thousands of standards which benefit society worldwide as one standard.

Between 1947 and the present day, ISO published more than 15,000 International Standards. ISO's work program ranges from standards for traditional activities, such as agriculture and construction, through mechanical engineering and medical devices, to the newest information technology developments, such as the digital coding of audio-visual signals for multimedia applications.

Without the international agreement contained in ISO standards on quantities and units (kgs, lbs, tons, quintals and so on), shopping and trade would be haphazard, science would be unscientific and technological development would be handicapped.

More than half a million organizations in more than 149 countries are implementing ISO 9000 which provides a framework for quality management throughout the processes of producing and delivering products and services for the customer.

ISO is a network of national standards institutes of 163 countries, on the basis of one member per country, with a Central Secretariat in Geneva, Switzerland, that coordinates the system.

ISO is a non-governmental organization—its members are not, as is the case in the United Nations system, delegations of national governments. Nevertheless, ISO occupies a special position between the public and private sectors.

Because "International Organization for Standardization" would have different abbreviations in different languages ("IOS" in English, "OIN" in French for Organization Internationale de Normalization), it was decided at the outset to use a word derived from Greek, *ISOS*, meaning "equal". Therefore, whatever the country, whatever the language, the short form of the organization's name will always be ISO.

History of ISO

International standardization began in the electrotechnical field—the International Electrotechnical Commission (IEC) was established in 1906. Pioneering work in other fields was carried out by the International Federation of National Standardizing Associations (ISA), which was set up in 1926. The emphasis within ISA was laid heavily on mechanical engineering. ISA's activities came to an end in 1942.

In 1946, delegates from 25 countries met in London and decided to create a new international organization, with the objective "to facilitate the international coordination and unification of industrial standards". The new organization, ISO, officially began operations on 23 February, 1947.

What 'International Standardization' Means

When the large majority of products or services in a particular business or industry sector conform to International Standards, a state of industry-wide standardization can be said to exist. This is achieved through consensus agreements between national delegations representing all the economic stakeholders concerned—suppliers, users, government regulators and other interest groups such as consumers. They agree on specifications and criteria to be applied consistently in the classification of materials, manufacture and supply of products, testing and analysis, in terminology and in the provision of services. In this way, International Standards provide a reference framework or a common technological language between suppliers and their customers which facilitates trade and the transfer of technology.

How ISO Standards Benefit Society

For businesses, the widespread adoption of International Standards means that suppliers can base the development of their products and services on specifications that have wide acceptance in their sectors. This, in turn, means that businesses using International Standards are becoming increasingly free to compete with many more markets around the world.

For customers, the worldwide compatibility of technology which is achieved when products and services are based on International Standards, brings them a wide choice of offers and they also benefit from the effects of competition among suppliers.

For governments, International Standards provide the technological and scientific bases underpinning health, safety and environmental legislation.

For trade officials, negotiating the emergence of regional and global markets, International Standards create "a level playing field" for all competitors on those markets.

For developing countries, International Standards that represent an international consensus on the state of the art constitute an important source of technological know-how. By defining the characteristics that products and services will be expected to meet on export markets, International Standards give developing countries a basis for making the right decisions when investing their scarce resources and thus avoid squandering them.

For consumers, conformity of products and services to International Standards provides assurance about their quality, safety and reliability.

For everyone, International Standards can contribute to the quality of life in general by ensuring that the transport, machinery and tools used are safe.

ISO and World Trade

ISO, together with IEC (International Electrotechnical Commission) and ITU (International Telecommunication Union), has built a strategic partnership with the WTO (World Trade Organization) with the common goal of promoting a free and fair global trading system. The political agreements that reached within the framework of WTO require underpinning by technical agreements. ISO, IEC and ITU, as the three principal organizations in international standardization, have the complementary scopes, the framework, the expertise and the experience to provide this technical support for the growth of global market.

The WTO's Agreement on Technical Barriers to Trade (TBT) includes the Code of Good Practice for the Preparation, Adoption and Application of Standards. The TBT Agreement recognizes the important contribution that International Standards and conformity assessment systems can make to improve efficiency of production and in facilitating international trade. Therefore, where International Standards exist or their completion is imminent, the Code states that standardizing bodies should use them as a basis for standards they develop. The Code requires that standardizing bodies that have accepted its terms, notify this fact to the ISO/IEC Information Centre located at the ISO Central Secretariat. Standardizing bodies having accepted the Code must publish their work programmes and also notify the existence of their work programmes to the ISO/IEC Information Centre. On behalf of the WTO, ISO periodically publishes a directory of standardizing bodies that have accepted the WTO TBT Standards Code.

ISO 9001

ISO 9001: 2008 is the world's foremost quality management standard, used by hundreds of thousands of organizations in over 170 countries around the globe. It sets out the essential requirements for a practical and effective Quality Management System (QMS) which is, in essence, a system for minimizing risk and maximizing opportunity. ISO 9001:2008 was published in November 2008, updating the earlier ISO 9001: 2000.

It is part of a series of quality management system standards, sometimes referred to as ISO 9000. These comprise:

- ISO 9000: *Fundamentals and Vocabulary*, which introduces the basic principles underlying management systems and explains the terminology
- ISO 9001: *Requirements*, which specifies the criteria for certification
- ISO 9004: *Guidelines* for performance improvement goes beyond ISO 9001 by identifying how ISO 9001 can be used as a springboard for improving the efficiency and effectiveness of a quality management system.

This suite of standards is designed to help organizations analyze and improve each element in their operations, from the selection of suppliers to sales and distribution. Among the multiple benefits of ISO 9001, the Standard helps organizations to improve customer satisfaction levels, internal efficiency and employee involvement.

ISO 9001 sets out eight key principles of quality management:

1. Customer focus
2. Leadership
3. Involvement of people
4. Process approach
5. System approach to management
6. Continual improvement
7. Factual approach to decision making

ISO 9001 is used by a diverse array of organizations, from giant multinational corporations to local community groups. The Standard is the first port of call for almost all organizations—large or small, public or private, that have decided to strengthen, streamline or review their management procedures. It can be used to focus on improving performance in a particular department, plant or site. However, it is generally most effective when implemented throughout an organization at every level.

ISO 9001: 2008 Quality Management System (QMS)

ISO 9001: 2008 Quality Management System certification enables you to demonstrate your commitment to quality and customer satisfaction, as well as continuously improve your company's operations. The internationally recognized quality management system standard is the preferred solution for organizations worldwide. In November 2008, the International Organization for Standardization (ISO) introduced a revised Quality Management Standard based on the same process model as the 2000 revision, with an emphasis on measuring customer satisfaction. The goal is for all organizations to seek continuous performance improvement. All requirements for quality management of the product or service are covered in ISO 9001: 2008 which includes a quality planning requirement along with policies, objectives and quantifiable targets.

ISO 9001: 2008 Clauses (Requirements)

ISO 9001:2008 has the following clauses as the requirements to be implemented and demonstrated by an organization to be certified for ISO 9001.

- Clause 1 Scope
- Clause 2 Normative Reference
- Clause 3 Terms and Definitions
- Clause 4 Quality Management System
  - 4.1 QMS General Requirements
  - 4.1 QMS General Requirements—Continued
  - 4.2.1 Documentation Requirements
  - 4.2.2 Quality Manual
  - 4.2.3 Control of Documents
  - 4.2.3 Control of Documents—Continued
  - 4.2.4 Control of Records
- Clause 5: Management Responsibility
  - 5.1 Management Commitment
  - 5.2 Customer Focus
  - 5.3 Quality Policy
  - 5.4.1 Quality Objectives
  - 5.4.2 Quality Management System Planning
  - 5.5.1 Responsibility and Authority
  - 5.5.2 Management Representative
  - 5.5.3 Internal Communication
  - 5.6 Management Review
- Clause 6 Resource Management
  - 6.1 Provision of Resources
  - 6.2 Human Resources
  - 6.3–6.4 Infrastructure and Work Environment
- Clause 7: Product Realization
  - 7.1 Planning of Product Realization
  - 7.2 Customer-Related Processes
  - 7.2 Customer-Related Processes—Continued
  - 7.3.1 Design and Development Planning
  - 7.3.2 Design and Development Inputs
  - 7.3.3 Design and Development Outputs
  - 7.3.4–7.3.7 Verification, Validation and Changes
  - 7.4 Purchasing Process
  - 7.4.2–7.4.3 Purchasing Information and Verification of Purchased Product
  - 7.5.1 Control of Production and Service Provision
  - 7.5.2 Production Process Validation

  - 7.5.3 Identification and Traceability
  - 7.5.4–7.5.5 Customer Property and Preservation of Product
  - 7.6 Control of Monitoring and Measuring Equipment
- Clause 8 Measurement, Analysis and Improvement
  - 8.1 Measurement, Analysis and Improvement—General
  - 8.2.1 Customer Satisfaction
  - 8.2.2 Internal Audit
  - 8.2.3 Monitoring and Measurement of Processes
  - 8.2.4 Monitoring and Measurement of Product
  - 8.3 Control of Nonconforming Product
  - 8.4 Analysis of Data
  - 8.5.1 Continual Improvement
  - 8.5.2 Corrective Action
  - 8.5.3 Preventive Action.

What ISO 9001 Does

- Establishes and streamlines processes through complete documentation
- Improves and establishes training processes
- Defines roles and responsibilities
- Greatly increases operational efficiency
- Increases ability to troubleshoot
- Develops and builds relationships that help to retain existing customers
- Provides advantages over competitors that are not certified ISO 9001:2008
- Builds opportunities for global commerce with international recognition
- Improves customer relations
- Improves relationships with suppliers due to clear, concise production standards
- Provides basis for consistent and fact-based decision making
- Carefully planned improvements, based on documentation and analysis
- Provides for regular audits/reviews of performance.

Benefits of ISO 9001

Some of the benefits of ISO 9001:2008 which were achieved by organizations through this certification are mentioned as below:

- Increases productivity
- Maximizes quality
- Increases revenue
- Improves employee morale and satisfaction
- Saves time and money
- Enhances ability to attract new customers that have adopted requirements for certification
- Improves accountability of management

- Increases employees' understanding of their roles in success of their work and the company
- Creates greater motivation and dedication.

Steps to achieve ISO 9001 Certification

1. Gap Analysis/status appraisal
2. Awareness training to all employees
3. Documentation design and finalization
4. Implementation
5. Conduct of internal audit
6. Management review meeting
7. Review of implementation
8. Stage 1—certification audit
9. Stage 2—certification audit
10. Recommendation for ISO 9001 certification
11. Receiving certificate.

ISO 27001 Information Security Management System (ISMS)

The rising value of information to organizations combined with recent high profile information security breaches, are highlighting the mounting up requirement for organizations to protect their information. In order to ensure the continuity of operations and the safety of data and systems, the security of information systems and critical business information must be constantly and actively managed. Unprotected systems are vulnerable to many threats, including computer-assisted fraud, sabotage and viruses. These threats can be internal or external, accidental or malicious. Breaches in information security can allow vital information to be accessed, stolen, corrupted or lost. It is crucial that every company institutes appropriate controls and procedures in place to avoid such incidents.

The internationally recognized information security management system ISO 27001 (better known as ISO/IEC 27001) is suitable for any organization, large or small, in any sector or part of the world where managing sensitive company information and keeping it secure from outsiders is important. The standard is particularly suitable where the protection of information is critical, such as in the finance, health, public and IT sectors.

ISO 27001 or more precisely ISO/IEC 27001: 2005 Information technology, Security techniques, Specification for an Information Security Management System is an internationally recognized standard that governs the design, implementation, monitoring, maintenance, improvements and certification in the area of Information Security Management Systems (ISMS). ISO 27001 is the formal standard against which organizations may seek independent certification of their ISMS.

The IT department is the main focus of ISO 27001 implementation, but the standard involves areas in the entire company as well. The main driver, sponsor and promoter of the change must be the company's management, while its IT is mainly responsible for its execution. In addition to management and IT, the departments that must be involved include HR, training and education, building security, building maintenance, legal department as well as suppliers, outsourcing, and the employees. ISO/IEC 27001 is also highly effective for organizations that manage information on behalf of others, such as IT outsourcing companies. This standard requires and organization to assure customers that their information is being protected.

ISO 27001: 2005 Information Security Management Systems (ISMS) involves three core principles—confidentiality, integrity and availability, which, in turn, cover eleven areas:

1. Security policy
2. Organization of information security
3. Asset management
4. Human resources security
5. Physical and environmental security
6. Communications
7. Operations management
8. Access control
9. Information systems acquisition, development and maintenance
10. Information security
11. Incident management
12. Business continuity management
13. Compliance.

Basic Requirements

- Analyze risks related to information security
- Define specific and optimal security goals (the standard requires a company to specify its own security goals which an auditor verifies)
- Defined and documented methods which all activities should follow
- Document all risks, goals, and methods
- Implement measures to mitigate and manage risks
- Assign accountability for risk management
- Measure information security
- Embed continuous improvement approach.

What is ISO 27001 Certification

- Demonstrates the integrity of your data and systems and your commitment to information security
- Transforms the organization's culture—both internally and externally
- Allows enforcing information security and reducing the possible risk of fraud, information loss and disclosure
- Demonstrates the independent assurance of internal controls
- Meets corporate governance and business continuity requirements
- Independently demonstrates that applicable laws and regulations are observed
- Provides a competitive edge

- Meets contractual requirements
- Demonstrates to customers that the security of their information is paramount
- Verifies that organizational risks are properly identified, assessed and managed, while formalising information security processes, procedures and documentation.

Benefits of ISO 27001

- Enhances the credibility of an organization
- Opens up new business opportunities with security conscious customers
- Improves employee ethics
- Strengthens the climate of confidentiality throughout the workplace
- Provides a competitive advantage over companies that are not certified against ISO/IEC 27001:2005
- Reduces the risks associated with unsecured data, and
- Formalizes corporate information system structure (infrastructure, buildings, cabling, environment, alarms, fire and flood prevention, access control, etc.)
- Effectively organizes all existing and necessary company IT security processes
- Protects vital business assets with regular backups
- Provides design of ongoing system optimization
- Potentially reduces insurance premiums with proven compliance
- Reduces the potential for lawsuits.

ISO 27001: 2005 Requirements

ISO 27001: 2005 has 11 Domains, 39 Control Objectives and 130+ Controls. Following is a list of the Domains and Control Objectives which have to be implemented and demonstrated by an organization to be certified for ISO 27001. The domains of ISO 27001 ISMS are mentioned below:

1. Security policy
2. Organization of information security
3. Asset management
4. Human resources security
5. Physical and environmental security
6. Communications and operations management
7. Access control
8. Information systems acquisition, development and maintenance
9. Information security incident management
10. Business continuity management
11. Compliance.

ISO 14001 Environment Management System (EMS)

ISO 14001 is an internationally accepted standard that outlines how to put an effective environmental management system in place. It is designed to help businesses remain commercially successful without overlooking environmental responsibilities. It can also help an organization to grow while reducing the environmental impact of this growth. An ISO 14001 system provides the framework to meet the increasingly high customer expectations of corporate responsibility as well as legal or regulatory requirements. An EMS is a system for evaluating environmental risks so that it can be managed in a consistent way. The EMS is systematic and comprehensive; it encompasses all things that affect the environment, at all levels and everyone has a role and responsibilities to this. Following a worldwide standard such as ISO 14001 provides the organizations a consistent, recognized way to merge environmental considerations into the strategic planning process.

Clauses of ISO 14001:2005

- 4.2 Policy
- 4.3 Planning
  - 4.3.1 Environmental Aspects
  - 4.3.2 Legal and Other Requirements
  - 4.3.3 Objectives and Targets
  - 4.3.4 Environmental Management Programs
- 4.4 Implementation and Operation
  - 4.4.1 Structure and Responsibility
  - 4.4.2 Training Awareness and Competence
  - 4.4.3 Communications
  - 4.4.4 EMS Documentation
  - 4.4.5 Document Control
  - 4.4.6 Operation Control
  - 4.4.7 Emergency Planning and Response
- 4.5 Checking and Corrective Action
  - 4.5.1 Monitoring and Measurement
  - 4.5.2 Nonconformance, Corrective, and Preventive Action
  - 4.5.3 Records control
  - 4.5.4 EMS Audit
- 4.6 Management Review

Requirements of ISO 14001:2005

The requirements of ISO 14001 include:

- Development of an environmental policy
- Identification of environmental aspects and evaluation of associated environmental impact
- Establishment of relevant legal and regulatory requirements
- Development and maintenance of environmental objectives and targets
- Implementation of a documented system, including elements of training, operational controls and dealing with emergencies

- Monitoring and measurement of operational activities
- Environmental internal auditing
- Management reviews of the system to ensure its continuing effectiveness and suitability.

Benefits of ISO 14001

- Better environmental management reduces waste and energy use
- Improves efficiency to cut the cost of running a business
- Demonstrate compliance to expand business opportunities
- Meet legal obligations to win greater stakeholder and customer trust
- Prepare for the changing business landscape confidently.

OHSAS 18001 (Occupation Health and Safety Assessment)

OHSAS 18001:2007 is the International Occupational Health and Safety Management Standard. OHSAS 18001 is an internationally recognized standard and is the benchmark for Health and Safety Management Systems certification. It promotes a safe and healthy working environment by providing a framework that allows an organization to consistently identify and control its health and safety risks, reduce the potential for accidents, aid legislative compliance and improve overall performance. The standard has been updated to OHSAS 18001:2007 to parallel ISO 14001 and ISO 9001 for more consistency and to enable easier integration of environment, quality and health and safety management systems into one.

The OHSAS 18001 standard is internationally accepted as a method of assessing and auditing occupational health and safety management systems. Developed by leading trade and international standards bodies, it provides a framework for organizations to instigate proper and effective management of health and safety in the workplace. By having a clearly defined management system in place to identify and control health and safety risks, organizations are able to minimize risks to their workforce and visitors or external contractors on their premises. The standard enables organizations to put in place processes for continually reviewing and improving occupational health and safety.

Key areas that will be assessed by OHSAS certification are:

- Management systems in place
- Planning and risk assessment
- Staff training and awareness
- Communication of safety management systems
- Response to emergency situations
- Monitoring and continual improvement

OHSAS 18001 is suitable for all types of organizations wanting to become more efficient in managing and reducing accidents in the workplace. By setting up systems that are assessed by a third party certification body, organizations will prove to their staff, suppliers and customers that they take health and safety seriously. OHSAS 18001 accreditation provides a framework to help organizations meet their legal obligations to Health and Safety in the workplace.

Benefits of OHSAS 18001:2007

1. Potential reduction in the number of accidents
2. Potential reduction in downtime and associated costs
3. Demonstration of legal and regulatory compliance
4. Demonstration to stakeholders of the commitment to health and safety
5. Demonstration of an innovative and forward thinking approach
6. Increased access to new customers and business partners
7. Better management of health and safety risks, now and in the future
8. Potential reduction public liability insurance costs.

Clauses of OHSAS 18001:2007

- Clause 4.1 General requirements
- Clause 4.2 OH&S policy
- Clause 4.3 Planning
  - Clause 4.3.1 Planning for Hazard identification, risk assessment and determining controls
  - Clause 4.3.2 Legal and other requirements
  - Clause 4.3.3 Objectives
  - Clause 4.3.4 Management program(s)
- Clause 4.4 Implementation and Operation
  - Clause 4.4.1 Resources, roles, responsibility, accountability and authority
  - Clause 4.4.2 Competence, training and awareness
  - Clause 4.4.3 Communication, participation and consultation
  - Clause 4.4.4 Documentation
  - Clause 4.4.5 Control of documents
  - Clause 4.4.6 Operational control
  - Clause 4.4.7 Emergency preparedness and response
- Clause 4.5 Checking and Corrective action
  - Clause 4.5.1 Performance measurement and monitoring
  - Clause 4.5.2 Evaluation of compliance
  - Clause 4.5.3 Incident investigation, nonconformity, corrective action and preventive action
  - Clause 4.5.4 Control of records
  - Clause 4.5.5 Internal audit
- Clause 4.6 Management review

ISO 22000 Food Safety Management Systems (FSMS)

The ISO 22000 family of standards relate to food safety management systems and are designed to help organizations of any size and at any stage in the food chain to ensure they meet the needs of customers and other stakeholders. The standards are published by ISO, the International Organization for Standardization and are available through National standards bodies.

ISO 22000 deals with the fundamentals of food safety management systems. ISO 22000:2005 deals with the requirements that organizations, wishing to meet the standard, have to meet. It has been designed to be compatible with other management system standards such as ISO 9001 and can be implemented within an integrated management system. Independent confirmation that organizations meet the requirements of ISO 22000:2005 may be obtained from third party certification bodies.

ISO 22000:2005 specifies the basic requirements for a Food Safety Management System (FSMS) that an organization must fulfil to demonstrate its ability to consistently produce food products which are safe for the end consumer. The standard can be used for certification/ registration and contractual purposes by organizations seeking recognition of their food safety management system. ISO 22000:2005 delivers safe product and covers all organizations in the food chain—both direct and indirect food chain.

ISO 22000 has been developed to aid harmonization of approaches to managing food safety, not just for one part of the food chain, but for all organizations in the food chain and for those organizations supplying to the food chain, materials and services that could impact on the safety of food. The standard combines the key elements to enable management of food safety along the food chain including—integrating the principles of HACCP and application sequence developed by Codex Aliment Arius Commission; system management; control of food safety hazards through pre-requisite programmes and HACCP plans; interactive communication with suppliers, customers, regulators and consumers and, continual improvement and updating of the management system.

The standard has been developed as a food safety management system applicable to all organizations in the food chain, to suppliers of services and products to the food chain, and has been designed to enhance communication on food safety issues within the food chain to help raise standards of food safety within the food industry and thus harmonize approaches to manage food safety globally. Examples of organizations who can adopt ISO 22000:2005 include:

Direct food chain

- Farmers
- Growers
- Feed producers
- Food manufacturers and processors
- Food ingredient producers
- Food storage, distribution and transport organizations
- Caterers
- Retailers
- Food service operators such as restaurants and fast food outlets.

Indirect food chain

- Producers of chemicals to be used in the food industry

- Producers of equipment used in the food industry
- Producers of cleaning and sanitising equipment
- Producers of packaging materials
- Service providers.

Clauses of ISO 22000:2005

- 4.0 Food Safety Systems Requirements
  - 4.1 Establish a food safety management system (FSMS)
  - 4.2 Document a food safety management system (FSMS)
- 5.0 Food Safety Management Requirements
  - 5.1 Demonstrate a commitment to food safety
  - 5.2 Establish a food safety policy
  - 5.3 Plan a food safety management system (FSMS)
  - 5.4 Clarify a FSMS responsibilities and authorities
  - 5.5 Appoint a food safety team leader
  - 5.6 Establish communications
  - 5.7 Develop emergency response procedures
  - 5.8 Carry out FSMS management review
- 6.0 Food Safety Resource Requirements
  - 6.1 Provide adequate FSMS resources
  - 6.2 Provide adequate human resources
  - 6.3 Provide adequate infrastructure
  - 6.4 Provide adequate work environment
- 7.0 Food Safety Realization Requirements
  - 7.1 Manage realization of safe products
  - 7.2 Establish prerequisite programs (PRPs)
  - 7.3 Get ready to do a hazard analysis
  - 7.4 Perform organization's hazard analysis
  - 7.5 Establish operational prerequisite programs (OPRPs)
  - 7.6 Establish HACCP plan
  - 7.7 Update preliminary documents and programs
  - 7.8 Plan and perform verification activities
  - 7.9 Establish a product traceability system
  - 7.10 Control nonconforming products
- 8.0 Food Safety Confirmation Requirements
  - 8.1 Confirm and improve food safety methods
  - 8.2 Validate food safety control measures
  - 8.3 Control monitoring and measuring methods
  - 8.4 Verify food safety management system (FSMS)
  - 8.5 Improve food safety management system (FSMS)

ISO 17025

ISO/IEC 17025 is the global recognized standard that was developed specifically for testing and calibration laboratories which intended seeking accreditation. It is also the basis for accreditation from an accreditation body. The current release was published in 2005. It covers testing and calibration, performed using standard methods, non-standard methods and laboratory-developed methods.

There are two main clauses in ISO/IEC 17025—Management Requirements and Technical Requirements. *Management requirements* are related to the operation and effectiveness of the quality management system within the laboratory and this clause has similar requirements to ISO 9001. *Technical requirements* includes factors which determines the correctness and reliability of the tests and calibrations performed in laboratory, namely competence of staff; environment control; testing methodology; equipment and measurement traceability; reporting of test and calibration results.

Laboratories that can demonstrate compliance with ISO/IEC 17025 at assessment have demonstrated that they operate using sound management practices and are technically competent to perform specific tests, calibrations and/or measurements as well as at the same time are able to generate technically valid results for which they hold accreditation. To maintain this recognition, laboratories are re-evaluated periodically by the accreditation body to ensure their continued compliance with requirements and to check that their standard of operation is being maintained. The laboratory may also be required to participate in relevant proficiency testing programs between reassessments, as a further demonstration of technical competence.

Accredited laboratories usually issue test or calibration reports bearing the accreditation body's symbol or endorsement, as an indication of their accreditation.

Clients are encouraged to check with the laboratory as to what specific tests or measurements they are accredited for, and for what ranges or uncertainties. This information is usually specified in the laboratory's scope of accreditation, issued by the accreditation body. The description in the scope of accreditation also has advantages for the customers of laboratories in enabling them to find the appropriate laboratory for testing and calibration service. Laboratory accreditation bodies publish the scopes of accreditation for their accredited laboratories in either hard copy directories or on the internet.

ISO/IEC 17025 is the main standard used by testing and calibration laboratories. Originally known as ISO/IEC Guide 25, ISO/IEC 17025 was initially issued by the International Organization for Standardization in 1999. There are many commonalities with the ISO 9000 standard, but ISO/IEC 17025 adds in the concept of competence to the equation and it applies directly to those organizations that produce testing and calibration results. A second release of the standard was made in 2005 after it was agreed that it needed to be more closely aligned with the 2000 version of ISO 9001 in terms of its quality system which includes greater emphasis on the responsibilities of senior management and explicit requirements for continual improvement of the management system itself, particularly communication with the customer.

In the current global scenario, an essential prerequisite of trade is that any product or service which is accepted formally in one economy, must also be free to circulate in other economies without having to undergo extensive retesting. WTO recognizes that non-acceptance of test or calibration results and measurement data is a 'technical barrier to trade'. Thus, accreditation is considered as the first essential step for facilitating mutual acceptance of test or calibration results and measurement data. In seeking of recognition, laboratories need to demonstrate full compliance with both sections of ISO/IEC 17025, namely Management and Technical requirements and successfully go through the third party assessment, i.e. by accreditation body.

Many countries around the world have one or more organizations responsible for the accreditation of their nation's laboratories. Most of these accreditation bodies have now adopted ISO/IEC 17025 as the basis for accrediting their country's testing and calibration laboratories. This has helped countries employ a uniform approach to determining laboratory competence. It has also encouraged laboratories to adopt internationally accepted testing and measurement practices, where possible. In order for accreditation bodies (at various parts of the world) to recognize each other's accreditations, the International Laboratory Accreditation Cooperation (ILAC) worked to establish methods of evaluating accreditation bodies against another ISO standard (ISO/IEC Guide 58—which became ISO/IEC 17011). Around the world, geo-political regions such as the European Community, Asia-Pacific, America and others, established regional cooperation to manage the work needed for such mutual recognition. These regional bodies (all working within the ILAC umbrella) include European Accreditation Cooperation (EA), Asia Pacific Laboratory Accreditation Cooperation (APLAC), Southern Africa Accreditation Cooperation (SADCA) and the Inter-American Accreditation Cooperation (IAAC).

Though, the Management Requirements of ISO/IEC 17025 has similarity with ISO 9001—it cannot be interpreted to be the same as certification against the ISO 9000 series standards. Confidence in accreditation can only be obtained by a transparent system of control over the accredited laboratories and an assurance given by the accreditation body that the accredited laboratory constantly fulfils the accreditation criteria. Thus, demonstration of compliance with Management and Technical Requirements will allow the laboratories to operate a quality management system for their testing and calibration activities that also meets the principles of ISO 9001 and at the same time has people with skills and knowledge, the environment with facilities and equipment, quality control, and the procedures that are required to produce valid results.

This International Standard is applicable to all organizations performing tests and/or calibrations. These include, for example first-, second- and third-party laboratories, and laboratories where testing and/or calibration forms part of inspection and product certification. The standard is also applicable to all laboratories regardless of the number of personnel or the extent of the scope of testing and/or calibration activities.

In addition to the use of this international standard by laboratories in developing their management system for quality, administrative and technical operations, laboratory customers, regulatory authorities and accreditation bodies may also use it in confirming or recognizing the competence of laboratories. However, this International Standard is not intended to be used as the basis for certification of laboratories.

Benefits of ISO 17025

- Increase of confidence in testing/calibration data and of personnel performing work
- Better control of laboratory operations and feedback to laboratories as to whether they have sound Quality Assurance System and are technically competent
- Potential increase in business due to enhanced customer confidence and satisfaction

- Customers can search and identify the laboratories accredited by The Accreditation Member Body for their specific requirements from their website or Directory of Accredited Laboratories
- Users of accredited laboratories will enjoy greater access for their products, in both domestic and international markets, when tested by accredited laboratories
- Savings in terms of time and money due to reduction or elimination of the need for re-testing of products
- Improved national and global reputation and/or image of the laboratory
- Continually improving data quality and laboratory effectiveness.

Clauses of ISO 17025

- 4.0 Management Requirements
  - 4.1 Organization
  - 4.2 Management System
  - 4.3 Document Control
  - 4.4 Review of requests, tenders and contracts
  - 4.5 Sub-contracting of tests and calibrations
  - 4.6 Purchasing services and supplies
  - 4.7 Service to the customer
  - 4.8 Complaints
  - 4.9 Control of nonconforming testing and/or calibration work
  - 4.10 Improvement
  - 4.11 Corrective action
  - 4.12 Preventive action
  - 4.13 Control of records
  - 4.14 Internal audits
  - 4.15 Management reviews
- 5.0 Management Requirements
  - 5.1 General
  - 5.2 Personnel
  - 5.3 Accommodation and environmental conditions
  - 5.4 Test and calibration methods and method validation
  - 5.5 Equipment
  - 5.6 Measurement traceability
  - 5.7 Sampling
  - 5.8 Handling of test and calibration items
  - 5.9 Assuring the quality of test and calibration results
  - 5.10 Reporting the results

ISO 20000—Information Technology Service Management (ITSM)

ISO 20000 is the first international standard for Information Technology Service Management and is fully compatible and supportive of the ITIL (IT Infrastructure Library) framework. ISO/IEC 20000-1:2011 specifies four key service management processes broken into 13 IT processes (see reference diagram below), as follows:

1. Service Delivery Processes: includes Service Level Management, Availability Management, and Capacity Management
2. Relationship Processes: involves interfaces between the service provider and customers and suppliers
3. Resolution Processes: focuses on incidents being resolved or prevented
4. Control Processes: involves managing changes, assets, and configurations.

ISO/IEC 20000-1 requires all processes to be implemented without exception. The standard specifies a number of closely related service management processes that help organizations in the following ways:

- Identify that relationships exist between these processes, and that these relationships will be dependent on their application within an organization
- Provides guideline objectives and controls to enable an organization deliver managed services
- Provides control, greater efficiency, and opportunities for improvement
- Turns technology-focused departments into service-focused departments
- Ensures that IT services are aligned with, and satisfy business needs
- Improves system reliability and availability
- Provides a basis for service level agreements
- Provides the ability to measure IT service quality.

ISO/IEC 20000-1:2011 is a Service Management System (SMS) standard. It specifies requirements for the service provider to plan, establish, implement, operate, monitor, review, maintain and improve an SMS. The requirements include the design, transition, delivery and improvement of services to fulfil agreed service requirements. ISO/IEC 20000-1:2011 can be used by:

- An organization seeking services from service providers and requiring assurance that their service requirements will be fulfilled
- An organization that requires a consistent approach by all its service providers, including those in a supply chain
- A service provider that intends to demonstrate its capability for the design, transition, delivery and improvement of services that fulfil service requirements
- A service provider to monitor, measure and review its service management processes and services
- A service provider to improve the design, transition, delivery and improvement of services through the effective implementation and operation of the SMS
- An assessor or auditor as the criteria for a conformity assessment of a service provider's SMS to the requirements in ISO/IEC 20000-1:2011.

ISO/IEC 20000-1:2011 promotes the adoption of an integrated process approach to effectively deliver managed services in order to meet business and customer requirements. For an organization to function effectively, it has to identify and manage numerous linked activities. Co-ordinated integration and implementation of the service management processes provides ongoing control, greater efficiency and opportunities for continual improvement.

The ISO/IEC 20000 series draws a distinction between the best practices of processes, which are independent of organizational form or size and organizational names and structures. The ISO/IEC 20000 series applies to both large and small service providers, and the requirements for the practice of service management processes are independent of the service provider's organizational form. These service management processes deliver the best possible service to meet a customer's business needs within agreed resource levels, i.e. service that is professional, cost-effective and with risks that are understood and managed.

ISO/IEC 20000 is currently being adopted worldwide. Organizations have realised that an organizational certification is a proof that best practices are in place and that a continual improvement program and internal audits/assessments support the implementation. This is also verified by the certification body performing annual surveillance audits. The advent of ITIL implementations has secured ISO 20000 position as the premier ITSM (IT Service Management) certification for organizations. Prior to ISO 20000, organizations were at the mercy of ITIL practitioners to implement ITIL services that could not be certified. ISO 20000 now provides organizations with a proven ability to audit implementation and accredit (certify) their implementation based on an agreed scope. It also helped organizations understand and conduct risk assessments which improved organization's performance and understanding.

Clause of ISO 20000-1:2011

- Clause 4.0 Service Management System General Requirements
  - Clause 4.1 Management Responsibility
  - Clause 4.2 Governance of processes operated by other parties
  - Clause 4.3 Documentation management
  - Clause 4.4 Resource management
  - Clause 4.5 Establish and improve the SMS
- Clause 5.0 Design and Transition of New Changed Services
  - Clause 5.1 General
  - Clause 5.2 Plan new or changed services
  - Clause 5.3 Design and development of new or changed services
  - Clause 5.4 Transition of new or changed services
- Clause 6.0 Service Delivery Processes
  - Clause 6.1 Service level management
  - Clause 6.2 Service reporting
  - Clause 6.3 Service continuity and availability management
  - Clause 6.4 Budgeting and accounting services
  - Clause 6.5 Capacity management
  - Clause 6.6 Information security management
- Clause 7.0 Relationship Processes
  - Clause 7.1 Business relationship management
  - Clause: 7.2 Supplier management

- Clause 8.0 Resolution Processes
  - Clause 8.1 Incident and service request management
  - Clause 8.2 Problem management
- Clause 9.0 Control Processes
  - Clause 9.1 Configuration management
  - Clause 9.2 Change management
  - Clause 9.3 Release and deployment management

Benefits of ISO 20000-1:2011

- Provides a way to align information technology services with business strategies
- Creation of a formal framework of service management and service improvement
- Provides KPI measurement criteria
- Creates competitive advantage via the promotion of consistent and cost-effective services
- Changes an IT-driven culture into a business-driven culture
- Provides management a clear view of interdependencies across IT and the ISO 20000 processes
- Promotes risk assessment and risk management
- Enhanced reputation and perception for using best practices
- IT becomes proactive rather than reactive
- Improved understanding and relationships between IT and the business/customers
- Creation of a stable framework for both resource training and service management automation.

ISO 31000—Enterprise Risk Management System (ERMS)

Risks affecting organizations can have consequences in terms of economic performance and professional reputation, as well as environmental safety and societal outcomes. Therefore, managing risk effectively helps organizations to perform well in an environment full of uncertainty.

ISO 31000 is a generic risk management standard. It can be used by any organization no matter what size it is or what it does. It can be used by both public and private organizations and by groups, associations as well as enterprises of all kinds. It is not specific to any sector or industry and can be applied to any type of risk. ISO 31000 can be applied to the achievement of any and all types of objectives at all levels and areas within an organization. It can be used at strategic or organizational level to help make decisions and can be applied to all types of activities. It can be used to help manage processes, operations, projects, programs, products, services and assets.

ISO 31000:2009 provides general guidelines for the design, implementation and maintenance of risk management processes throughout an organization. This approach to formalize risk management practices will facilitate broader adoption by companies who require an enterprise risk management standard that accommodates multiple 'silo-centric' management systems.

The scope of this approach to risk management is to enable all strategic, management and operational tasks of an organization throughout projects, functions and processes to be aligned to a common set of risk management objectives.

Accordingly, ISO 31000:2009 is intended for a broad stakeholder group including:

- Executive level stakeholders
- Appointment holders in the enterprise risk management group
- Risk analysts and management officers
- Line managers and project managers
- Compliance and internal auditors
- Independent practitioners.

ISO 31000:2009 gives a list in order of preference on how to deal with risk:

- Avoiding the risk by deciding not to start or continue with the activity that gives rise to the risk
- Accepting or increasing the risk in order to pursue an opportunity
- Removing the risk source
- Changing the likelihood
- Changing the consequences
- Sharing the risk with another party or parties (including contracts and risk financing)
- Retaining the risk by informed decision.

Requirements of ISO 30001:2009

- 3. Risk Management Principles
  - 3(a) risk management should create and protect value
  - 3(b) risk management should be a part of all processes
  - 3(c) risk management should be a part of decision making
  - 3(d) risk management should be used to handle uncertainty
  - 3(e) risk management should be systematic and timely
  - 3(f) risk management should be based on the best data
  - 3(g) risk management should be tailored to the environment
  - 3(h) risk management should consider human factors
  - 3(i) risk management should be transparent and inclusive
  - 3(j) risk management should be responsive and iterative
  - 3(k) risk management should support continual improvement
- 4. Risk Management Framework
  - 4.1 Establish a risk management framework
  - 4.2 Make a commitment to risk management
  - 4.3 Design a risk management framework
    - 4.3.1 Understand the organization's context
    - 4.3.2 Formulate a risk management policy
    - 4.3.3 Make people accountable for managing risk

        - 4.3.4 Build risk management into the organization
        - 4.3.5 Allocate resources for risk management
        - 4.3.6 Establish internal communication mechanisms
        - 4.3.7 Develop an external communication plan
    - 4.4 Implement an approach to risk management
        - 4.4.1 Implement a risk management framework
        - 4.4.2 Implement a risk management process
    - 4.5 Monitor the risk management framework
    - 4.6 Improve the risk management framework
- 5. Risk Management Process
    - 5.1 Apply a risk management process
    - 5.2 Communicate and consult with stakeholders
    - 5.3 Establish a unique risk management context
        - 5.3.1 Establish risk management parameters
        - 5.3.2 Establish organization's external context
        - 5.3.3 Establish organization's internal context
        - 5.3.4 Establish the context of risk management process
    - 5.4 Carry out the organization's risk assessment process
        - 5.4.1 Identify, analyze, and evaluate risks
        - 5.4.2 Identify the organization's risks
        - 5.4.3 Analyze the organization's risks
        - 5.4.4 Evaluate your organization's risks
    - 5.5 Formulate and implement risk treatment plans
        - 5.5.1 Explore the organization's risk treatment options
        - 5.5.2 Select the organization's risk treatment options
        - 5.5.3 Prepare risk treatment implementation plans
    - 5.6 Monitor and review the risk management process
    - 5.7 Maintain a record of risk management activities

SA8000 Social Accountability Management System (SAMS)

Social Accountability 8000 (SA8000) has been developed by Social Accountability International (SAI), known until recently as the Council on Economic Priorities Accreditation Agency. SAI is a non-profit affiliate of the Council on Economic Priorities (CEP). SA8000 is promoted as a voluntary, universal standard for companies interested in auditing and certifying labour practices in their facilities and those of their suppliers and vendors. It is designed for independent third party certification. SA8000 is based on the principles of international human rights norms as described in International Labour Organization conventions, the United Nations Convention on the Rights of the Child and the Universal Declaration of Human Rights. It measures the performance of companies in eight key areas—child labour, forced labour, health and safety, free association and collective bargaining, discrimination, disciplinary practices, working hours and compensation. SA8000 also provides for a social accountability management system to demonstrate ongoing conformance with the standard.

Complying with the requirements for social accountability of this standard will enable a company to:

(a) Develop, maintain, and enforce policies and procedures in order to manage those issues which it can control or influence

(b) Credibly demonstrate to interested parties that existing company policies, procedures, and practices conform to the requirements of this standard.

Benefits of SA8000

The intent of SA8000 is to provide a standard based on international human rights norms and national labour laws that will protect and empower all personnel within a company's scope of control and influence, who manufacture products or provide services for that company, including personnel employed by the company itself, as well as by its suppliers/sub-contractors, sub-suppliers, and home workers.

SA8000 is verifiable through an evidence-based process. Its requirements apply universally, regardless of a company's size, geographic location, or industry sector.

SA8000 Requirements

Child Labour

No use or support of child labour; policies and written procedures for remediation of children found to be working in situation; provide adequate financial and other support to enable such children to attend school; and employment of young workers conditional.

Forced and Compulsory Labour

No use or support of forced or compulsory labour; no required 'deposits'—financial or otherwise; no with-holding salary, benefits, property or documents to force personnel to continue work; personnel right to leave premises after workday; personnel free to terminate their employment; and no use nor support for human trafficking.

Health and Safety

Provide a safe and healthy workplace; prevent potential occupational accidents; appoint senior manager to ensure OSH; instruction on OSH for all personnel; system to detect, avoid, respond to risks; record all accidents; provide personal protection equipment and medical attention in the event of work-related injury; remove, reduce risks to new and expectant mothers; hygiene—toilet, potable water, sanitary, food storage; decent dormitories—clean, safe, meet basic needs; and worker's right to remove from imminent danger.

Freedom of Association and Right to Collective Bargaining

Respect the right to form and join trade unions and bargain collectively. All personnel are free to—organize trade unions of their choice; and bargain collectively with their employer. A company shall—respect right to organise unions and bargain collectively; not interfere in workers' organizations or collective bargaining; inform personnel of these rights and freedom from retaliation; where law restricts rights, allow workers to freely elect representatives; ensure no discrimination against personnel engaged in worker organizations; and ensure representatives access to workers at the workplace.

Discrimination

No discrimination based on race, national or social origin, caste, birth, religion, disability, gender, sexual orientation, union membership, political opinions and age. No discrimination in hiring, remuneration, access to training, promotion, termination, and retirement. No interference with exercise of personnel tenets or practices; prohibition of threatening, abusive, exploitative, coercive behaviour at workplace or company facilities; no pregnancy or virginity tests under any circumstances.

Disciplinary Practices

Treat all personnel with dignity and respect; zero tolerance of corporal punishment, mental or physical abuse of personnel; no harsh or inhumane treatment.

Working Hours

Compliance with laws and industry standards; normal work week, not including overtime, shall not exceed 48 hours; 1 day off following every 6 consecutive work days, with some exceptions; overtime is voluntary, not regular, not more than 12 hours per week; required overtime only if negotiated in CBA.

Remuneration

Respect right of personnel to living wage; all workers paid at least legal minimum wage; wages sufficient to meet basic needs and provide discretionary income; deductions not for disciplinary purposes, with some exceptions; wages and benefits clearly communicated to workers; paid in convenient manner—cash or cheque form; overtime paid at premium rate; prohibited use of labour-only contracting, short-term contracts, false apprenticeship schemes to avoid legal obligations to personnel.

ITIL (Information Technology Information Library)

As the most widely adopted framework for IT service management in the world, it is hard to believe that ITIL is more than 20 years old. Its practical, no-nonsense approach to the identification, planning, delivery and support of IT services to businesses has revolutionised IT service management, and thousands of practitioners now implement ITIL practice in their working environments. The latest editions of ITIL from the Cabinet Office were published in July 2011, and these five publications (*ITIL Service Strategy*, *ITIL Service Design*, *ITIL Service Transition*, *ITIL Service Operation* and *ITIL Continual Service Improvement*) form the core guidance of best management practice. In the early 1980s, the evolution of computing technology moved from mainframe-centric infrastructure and centralised IT organizations to distributed computing and geographically dispersed resources. While the ability to distribute technology afforded organizations more flexibility, the side-effect was inconsistent application of processes for technology delivery and support. The UK government recognised that utilizing consistent practices for all aspects of an IT service life cycle could assist in driving organizational effectiveness and efficiency, as well as achieving predictable service levels. It was this recognition that gave rise to ITIL, which has become a successful mechanism to drive consistency, efficiency and excellence into the business of managing IT services.

Since ITIL is an approach to IT 'service' management, the concept of a service must be discussed. A service is something that provides value to customers. Services that customers can directly utilise or consume are known as *business services*. An example of a business service that has common applicability across many industries would be *Payroll*. Payroll is an IT service that is used to consolidate information, calculate compensation and generate pay cheques on a regular basis, and which relies on other business services such as 'time tracking' or 'benefits administration' to provide the extra information necessary for its calculations. In order for Payroll to run, it is supported by a number of technology or 'infrastructure' services. An infrastructure service does its work in the background, so that the business does not directly interact with it, but nevertheless, this service is necessary as part of the overall value chain to the business service. 'Server administration', 'database administration' and 'storage administration' are all examples of infrastructure services required for the successful delivery of the Payroll business service.

IT organizations have traditionally focused on managing the infrastructure services and technology silos. ITIL suggests a more holistic approach to managing services from end to end. Managing the entire business service along with its underlying components in a cohesive manner ensures that every aspect of modified services must be considered, as well as mechanisms for measuring the service levels, the technology, and the efficiency and effectiveness of processes.

Through the *service transition* phase of the life cycle, the design is built, tested and moved into production to enable the business customer achieve the desired value. This phase addresses managing changes—controlling the assets and configuration items (the underlying components such as hardware, software, etc.) associated with the new and changed systems; service validation; and testing and transition planning to ensure that users, support personnel and the production environment have been prepared for the release to production.

Once transitioned, *service operation* then delivers the service on an ongoing basis, overseeing the daily overall health of the service. This includes managing disruptions to service through rapid restoration after incidents; determining the root cause of problems and detecting trends associated with recurring issues; handling daily routine end-user requests; and managing service access.

Enveloping the service life cycle is *continual service improvement (CSI)*. CSI offers a mechanism for the IT organization to measure and improve the service levels, the technology, and the efficiency and effectiveness of processes used in the overall management of services.

Benefits of ITIL

The main benefits of ITIL include:

1. **Alignment with business needs:** ITIL becomes an asset to the business when an IT organization can proactively recommend solutions as a response to one or more business needs. The IT steering group recommended in *ITIL Service Strategy* and

the implementation of service portfolio management gives the service provider an opportunity to understand the business' current and future needs and develop service offerings that can address them.

2. **Negotiated achievable service levels:** Business and the IT service provider become true partners when they can agree upon realistic service levels that deliver the necessary value at an acceptable cost.
3. **Predictable, consistent processes:** Customer expectations can be set and are easier to meet through the use of predictable processes that are consistently applied. In addition, good-practice processes provide a solid foundation on which to lay the groundwork necessary to meet regulatory compliance requirements.
4. **Efficiency in service delivery:** Well-defined processes with clearly documented accountability for each activity as recommended through the use of a RACI matrix can significantly increase efficiency. In conjunction with the evaluation of efficiency metrics which indicate the time required to perform each activity, service delivery tasks can be optimised.
5. **Measurable, improvable services and processes:** The adage that 'you cannot manage what you cannot measure' rings true here. Consistent, repeatable processes can be measured and therefore, can be better tuned for accurate delivery and overall effectiveness. For example, a critical success factor for incident management is to reduce the time to restore service. When predictable, consistent processes are used, key performance indicators such as mean time to restore service can be captured to determine whether this KPI is trending in a positive or negative direction. Additionally, under ITIL guidelines, services are designed to be measurable. With proper metrics and monitoring in place, IT organizations can monitor service level agreements (SLAs) and make improvements as necessary.
6. **Terms:** A common language Terms are defined in a common glossary.

CMMI—Capability Maturity Model Integration

A Capability Maturity Model® (CMM®), including CMMI, is a simplified representation of the world. CMMs contain the essential elements of effective processes. These elements are based on the concepts developed by Crosby, Deming, Juran, and Humphrey.

In the 1930s, Walter Shewhart began work in process improvement with his principles of statistical quality control (Shewhart, 1931). These principles were refined by W. Edwards Deming (Deming, 1986), Phillip Crosby (Crosby, 1979), and Joseph Juran (Juran, 1988). Watts Humphrey, Ron Radice, and others extended these principles and began applying them to software in their work at IBM (International Business Machines) and the SEI (Humphrey, 1989). Humphrey's book, *Managing the Software Process*, provides a description of the basic principles and concepts on which many of the Capability Maturity Models® are based.

The SEI has taken the process management premise, "the quality of a system or product is highly influenced by the quality of the process used to develop and maintain it," and defined CMMs that embody this premise. The belief in this premise is seen worldwide in quality movements, as evidenced by the International Organization for Standardization/International Electrotechnical Commission (ISO/IEC) body of standards.

CMMs focus on improving processes in an organization. They contain the essential elements of effective processes for one or more disciplines and describe an evolutionary improvement path from ad hoc, immature processes to disciplined, mature processes with improved quality and effectiveness.

Like other CMMs, CMMI models provide guidance to use when developing processes. CMMI models are not processes or process descriptions. The actual processes used in an organization depend on many factors including application domains and organization structure and size. In particular, the process areas of a CMMI model typically do not map one to one with the processes used in an organization.

SEI created the first CMM designed for software organizations and published it in a book, *The Capability Maturity Model: Guidelines for Improving the Software Process* (SEI, 1995).

Today, CMMI is an application of the principles introduced almost a century ago to this never-ending cycle of process improvement. The value of this process improvement approach has been confirmed over time. Organizations have experienced increased productivity and quality, improved cycle time, and more accurate and predictable schedules and budgets (Gibson 2006).

Now more than ever, companies want to deliver products and services better, faster and cheaper. At the same time, in the high-technology environment of the twenty-first century, nearly all organizations have found themselves building increasingly complex products and services. Today, it is unusual for a single organization to develop all the components that compose a complex product or service. More commonly, some components are built in-house and some are acquired; then all the components are integrated into the final product or service. Organizations must be able to manage and control this complex development and maintenance process.

The problems these organizations address today involve enterprise-wide solutions that require an integrated approach. Effective management of organizational assets is critical to business success. In essence, these organizations are product and service developers that need a way to manage their development activities as a part of achieving their business objectives.

In the current marketplace, maturity models, standards, methodologies and guidelines exist that can help an organization improve the way it conducts business. However, most available improvement approaches focus on a specific part of the business and do not take a systemic approach to the problems that most organizations are facing. By focusing on improving one area of a business, these models have unfortunately perpetuated the stovepipes and barriers that exist in organizations.

CMMI® for Development (CMMI-DEV) provides an opportunity to avoid or eliminate these stovepipes and barriers. CMMI for Development consists of best practices that address development activities applied to products and services. It focuses on practices that cover the product's life cycle from conception to delivery and maintenance. The emphasis is on the work necessary to build and maintain the total product.

The CMM Integration® project was formed to sort out the problem of using multiple CMMs. The combination of selected models into a single improvement framework was intended for use by organizations in their pursuit of enterprise-wide process improvement.

Developing a set of integrated models involved more than simply combining existing model materials. Using processes that promote consensus, the CMMI Product Team built a framework that accommodates multiple constellations.

The first model to be developed was the CMMI for Development model (then simply called "CMMI"). Figure 14.1 illustrates the models that led to CMMI Version 1.3.

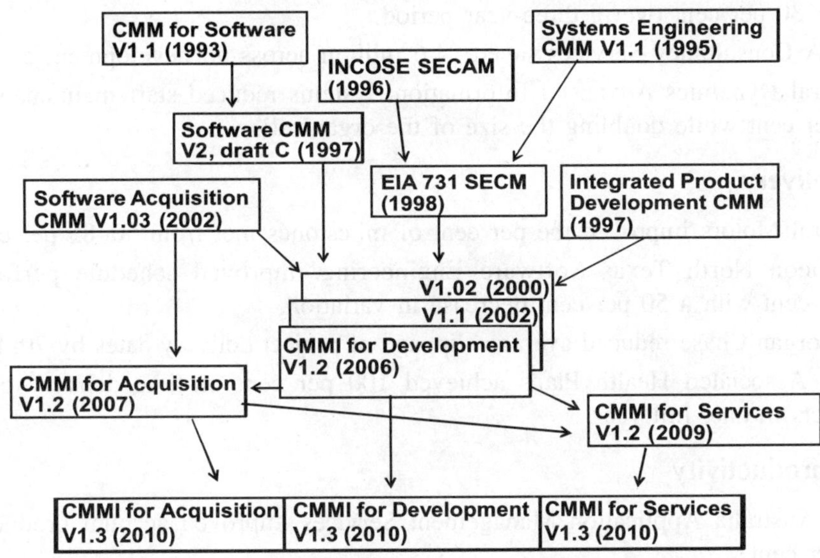

Figure 14.1 History of CMMs.

The CMMI Framework provides the structure needed to produce CMMI models, training, and appraisal components. To allow the use of multiple models within the CMMI Framework, model components are classified as either common to all CMMI models or applicable to a specific model. The common material is called *CMMI Model Foundation* or *CMF*.

The components of the CMF are a part of every model generated from the CMMI Framework. These components are combined with material applicable to an area of interest (e.g., acquisition, development, services) to produce a model.

A *constellation* is defined as a collection of CMMI components that are used to construct models, training materials, and appraisal related documents for an area of interest (e.g., acquisition, development, services). The Development constellation's model is called *CMMI for Development* or *CMMI-DEV*.

Maturity Levels of CMMI

Benefits of CMMI

CMMI provides guidance for efficient and effective improvement across multiple process disciplines in an organization.

It benefits the organization by providing a common, integrated vision of improvement. The ultimate benefit is improved performance which means decreased costs, on-time delivery, enhanced productivity, better quality and improved customer satisfaction.

Another benefit is return on investment. Such a program more than pays for the monetary investment required. These are all reasons why CMMI is the choice for process improvement in multiple industries. Below are some examples of the benefits to real-world companies:

Decreased costs

- Siemens Information Systems Ltd. reduced its cost of quality from over 45 per cent to under 30 per cent over a three-year period.
- TATA Consultancy Services saved $4.6 million across all development centers.
- General Dynamics Advanced Information Systems reduced staff maintenance costs by 64 per cent while doubling the size of the organization.

On-time delivery

- General Motors improved the per cent of milestones met from 50–85 per cent.
- Raytheon North Texas Software Engineering improved schedule performance by 8 per cent with a 50 per cent decrease in variation.
- JP Morgan Chase reduced average slippage of project delivery dates by 70–80 per cent.
- Tufts Associated Health Plans achieved 100 per cent on-time delivery of major IT projects in one, full year.

Enhanced productivity

- IBM Australia Application Management Services improved account productivity over 20 per cent.
- SAIC System and Network Solutions Group doubled its productivity.
- Warner Robins reduced effort to deliver test programs sets by 25 per cent.

Better quality

- Siemens Information Systems Ltd. reduced defect density an average of 71 per cent in three technical areas.
- IBM Australia Application Management Services closed 95 per cent of problems within the customer-specified time frame.
- Tufts Associated Health Plans decreased software defects identified in testing by 25 per cent.

Improved customer satisfaction

- Lockheed Martin Management and Data Systems increased their award fees by 55 per cent.
- Siemens Information Systems Ltd. increased their customer satisfaction index at an average of 42 per cent in three technical areas.
- Northrop Grumman IT, Defense Enterprise Solutions received more than 98 per cent of possible customer award fees.

Impressive return on investment

- Accenture experienced 5–1 ROI for quality activities.
- Siemens Information Systems Ltd. experienced 2–1 ROI over 3 years.
- Reuters experienced over 3–1 ROI from reducing post-release defects.

CMMI (Dev)—Capability Maturity Model Integration (Dev) Version 1.3

CMMI for Development is a reference model that covers activities for developing both products and services. Organizations from many industries including aerospace, banking, computer hardware, software, defence, automobile manufacturing, and telecommunications, use CMMI for Development. This model contains practices that cover project management, process management, systems engineering, hardware engineering, software engineering, and other supporting processes used in development and maintenance. CMMI-DEV commands the largest market share, followed by CMMI-SVC, and then CMMI-ACQ.

CMMI for Development has twenty-two process areas, and CMMI for Services has twenty-four. CMMI can be used in either the "staged" or "continuous" representation. The staged representation, which groups process areas into five "maturity levels," is the most common choice, but an organization can also pick and choose the process areas that make the most sense for them to work on by using the "continuous representation."

There is no difference in content between these two representations. When choosing "Staged", an organization follows a pre-defined pattern of process areas that are organised by "Maturity Level." When choosing "Continuous", they pick process areas based on their interest in improving only specific areas. In the continuous representation, process areas are organised by "Category." (Figures 14.2 and 14.3)

Within the process areas in the CMMI, there are multiple "Specific Goals (SGs)" and "Specific Practices (SPs)." These practices define the expected behaviours of projects and organizations. There are twelve "Generic Practices (GPs)" that provide guidance for organizational excellence including behaviors such as setting expectations, training, measuring quality, monitoring process performance, and evaluating compliance. CMMI and SCAMPI are registered service marks by Carnegie Mellon University.

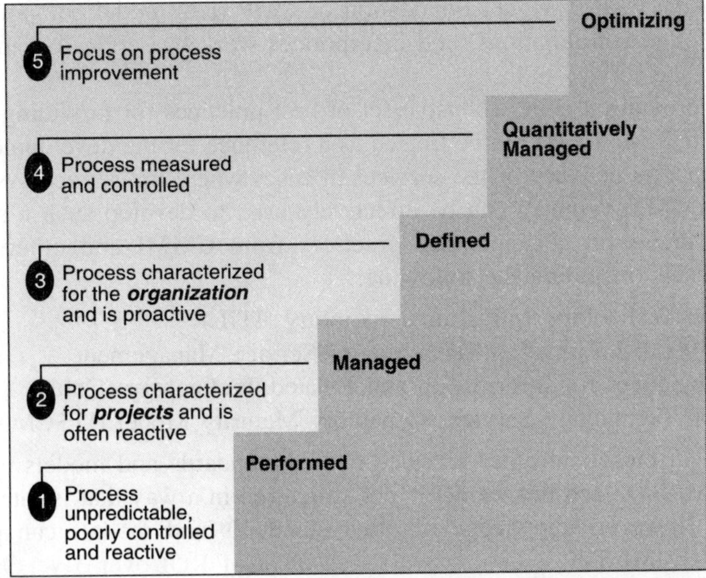

Figure 14.2 Maturity levels of CMMI.

Level	Focus	Process Area	
5 Optimizing	Continuous process improvement	• Organizational performance management	• Causal analysis and resolution
4 Quantitatively Managed	Quantitative management	• Organizational process performance	• Quantitative project management
3 Defined	Process standardization	• Requirements development • Technical solutions • Product integration • Verification • Validation • Organizational process focus	• Organizational process definition • Organizational training • Integrated project management risk management • Decision analysis and resolution
2 Managed	Basic project management	• Requirements management • Project planning • Project monitoring and control • Supplier agreement management	• Measurement and analysis • Process and product quality assurance • Configuration management
1 Initial			

Figure 14.3 Process areas in CMMI.

CMMI (SVC)—Capability Maturity Model Integration (Services) Version 1.3

The CMMI-SVC model provides guidance for applying CMMI practices in a service provider organization. These practices in the model focus on activities for providing quality services to customers and end users. CMMI-SVC integrates bodies of knowledge that are essential for a service provider.

The CMMI-SVC, V1.3 model is a collection of best service practices from government and industry that is generated from the CMMI V1.3 Architecture and Framework.1 CMMI-SVC is based on the CMMI Model Foundation or CMF (i.e., model components common to all CMMI models and constellations) and incorporates work by service organizations to adapt CMMI for use in the service industry.

CMMI-SVC provides a comprehensive set of best practices for providing services. CMMI for Development (CMMI-DEV) can be treated as a reference for the development of the service system, which supports delivery of the service. In cases where the service system is large and complex, the CMMI-DEV model can be effectively used to develop such a system.

CMMI-SVC draws on concepts and practices from CMMI and other service focused standards and models, including the following:

- Information Technology Infrastructure Library (ITIL)
- ISO/IEC 20000: Information Technology—Service Management
- Control Objectives for Information and Related Technology (CobT)
- Information Technology Services Capability Maturity Model (ITSCMM)

Familiarity with these and other service-oriented standards and models is not required to comprehend CMMI-SVC and this model is not structured in a way that is intended to conform to any of them. However, knowledge of other standards and models can provide a richer understanding of CMMI-SVC.

The CMMI-SVC model covers the activities required to establish, deliver and manage services. As defined in the CMMI context, a service is an intangible, non-storable product. The CMMI-SVC model has been developed to be compatible with this broad definition.

CMMI-SVC goals and practices are therefore, potentially relevant to any organization concerned with the delivery of services including enterprises in sectors such as defence, information technology (IT), health care, finance and transportation. Early users of CMMI-SVC include organizations that deliver services as varied as training, logistics, maintenance, refugee services, lawn care, book shelving, research, consulting, auditing, independent verification and validation, human resources, financial management, health care and IT services.

The CMMI-SVC model contains practices that cover work management, process management, service establishment, service delivery and support, and supporting processes. The CMMI-SVC model shares a great deal of material with CMMI models in other constellations. Therefore, those who are familiar with another CMMI constellation will find much of the CMMI-SVC content familiar.

When using this model, one has to use professional judgement and common sense to interpret it for an organization. That is, although the process areas described in this model depict behaviours considered as the best practices for most service providers, all process areas and practices should be interpreted using an in-depth knowledge of CMMI-SVC, organizational constraints, and the business environment. (Figures 14.4 and 14.5)

Organizations interested in evaluating and improving their processes to develop systems for delivering services can use the CMMI-DEV model. This approach is especially recommended for organizations that are already using CMMI-DEV or that must develop and maintain complex systems for delivering services. However, the CMMI-SVC model provides an alternative, streamlined approach to evaluating and improving the development of service systems that can be more appropriate in certain contexts.

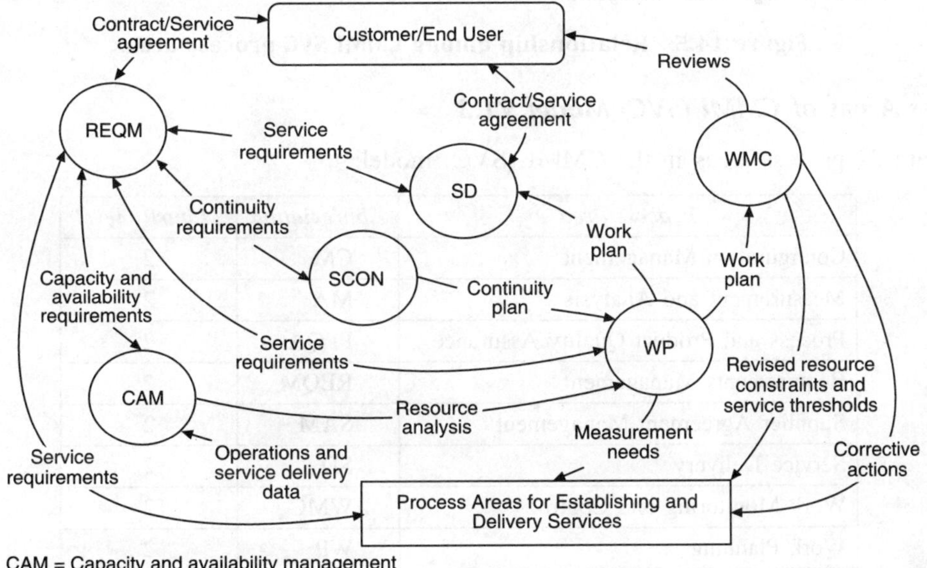

Figure 14.4 Relationship among CMMI SVC process areas.

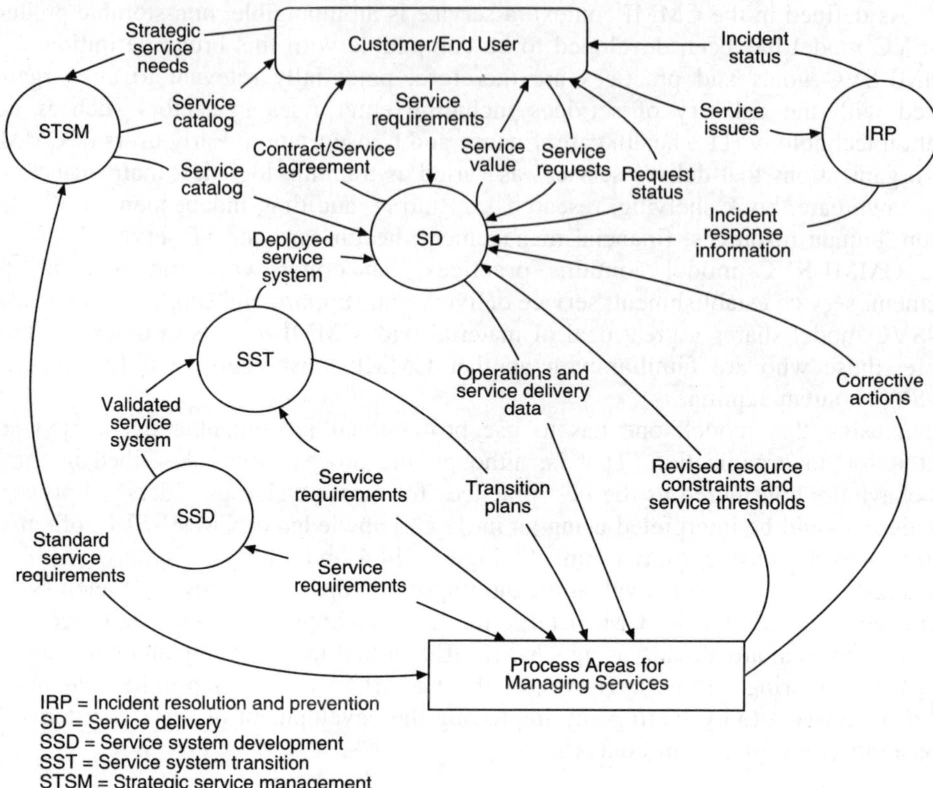

Figure 14.5 Relationship among CMMI SVC process areas.

Process Areas of CMMI (SVC) Model V1.3

There are 24 process areas in the CMMI (SVC) model:

Process area	*Abbreviation*	*Maturity level*
Configuration Management	CM	2
Measurement and Analysis	MA	2
Process and Product Quality Assurance	PPQA	2
Requirements Management	REQM	2
Supplier Agreement Management	SAM	2
Service Delivery	SD	2
Work Monitoring and Control	WMC	2
Work Planning	WP	2
Capacity and Availability Management	CAM	3
Decision Analysis and Resolution	DAR	3
Incident Resolution and Prevention	IRP	3

Process area	*Abbreviation*	*Maturity level*
Integrated Work Management	IWM	3
Organizational Process Definition	OPD	3
Organizational Process Focus	OPF	3
Organizational Training	OT	3
Risk Management	RSKM	3
Service Continuity	SCON	3
Service System Development	SSD	3
Service System Transition	SST	3
Strategic Service Management	STSM	3
Organizational Process Performance	OPP	4
Quantitative Work Management	QWM	4
Causal Analysis and Resolution	CAR	5
Organizational Performance Management	OPM	5

Relationship among CMMI-SVC Process Areas

ISO 9000 Principles of Quality Management

The ISO 9000:2015 and ISO 9001:2015 standards are based on seven quality management principles that senior management can apply for organizational improvement:

1. Customer Focus
   - Understand the needs of existing and future customers
   - Align organizational objectives with customer needs and expectations
   - Meet customer requirements
   - Measure customer satisfaction
   - Manage customer relationships
   - Aim to exceed customer expectations.
2. Leadership
   - Establish a vision and direction for the organization
   - Set challenging goals
   - Model organizational values
   - Establish trust
   - Equip and empower employees
   - Recognize employee contributions.
3. Engagement of People
   - Ensure that people's abilities are used and valued
   - Make people accountable
   - Enable participation in continual improvement
   - Evaluate individual performance

- Enable learning and knowledge sharing
- Enable open discussion of problems and constraints.

4. Process Approach
   - Manage activities as processes
   - Measure the capability of activities
   - Identify linkages between activities
   - Prioritize improvement opportunities
   - Deploy resources effectively.
5. Improvement
   - Improve organizational performance and capabilities
   - Align improvement activities
   - Empower people to make improvements
   - Measure improvement consistently
   - Appreciate improvements.
6. Evidence-based Decision Making
   - Ensure the accessibility of accurate and reliable data
   - Use appropriate methods to analyze data
   - Make decisions based on analysis
   - Balance data analysis with practical experience.
7. Relationship Management
   - Identify and select suppliers to manage costs, optimize resources, and create value
   - Establish relationships considering both the short and long term
   - Share expertise, resources, information, and plans with partners
   - Collaborate on improvement and development activities
   - Recognize supplier successes.

SUMMARY

1. Quality is the need of industries. ISO has attempted to have a uniform set of standards all over the globe.
2. Several organizations have obtained ISO 9000 series certification.
3. The ISO series consists several standards.
4. The European Community has laid emphasis on ISO 9000 in international trade.
5. ISO 9000 quality management systems.

REVIEW QUESTIONS

1. Discuss the concept, need and benefits of ISO 9000 certification.
2. What are the elements of ISO 9001 quality systems?
3. Explain the outstanding features of the ISO 9000 series.
4. What are the seven quality management principles of ISO 9001:2015 series?

CASE STUDIES

1. The Dabbawallas

Mumbai, the commercial capital of India, is a crowded city with a unique geography. Thousands commute from their homes uptown in the suburbs to offices and schools downtown. They leave homes early because of the long commute averaging 70–80 kilometres, lasting up to 2–3 hours. The *dabbawalla*, translated as tiffin carrier, provides a unique service here. At their clients' homes, the mothers, wives, or personal chefs prepare fresh home meal. Dabbawallas collect the tiffin boxes from homes, and using an efficient relay system, pass them down a network of hands, sorting, and delivering them to the offices, factories and schools across the city. The empty tiffin boxes are returned the same day to homes and in some cases, caterers, ready to be cleaned before the client returns home in the late evening.

THE SERVICE PROPORTION

The clients get several benefits: (a) freshly same-day prepared home-cooked meals, with its properties of being healthy, nutritious and personal touch; (b) food of own choice, including special dietary needs and preferences, based on health, regional or religious factors; (c) food of assured taste which they are accustomed to, such as rice, curry, bread, yogurt, garnishes, salads, and vegetables; (d) do not need to carry weight and volume of the tiffin while commuting in crowded trains; and (e) guaranteed delivery on time, with near-zero error rates, and a delivered cost less than the cost of eating out.

THE DELIVERY MODEL

The dabbawallas work like a post office with hub and spoke operations, and an efficient relay system. After travelling up to four hours from outlying villages, a dabbawalla starts work at 9 am. The dabbawalla network is divided into cooperative units of about 15 to 40 men, with two units assigned to each of the local station. One unit of dabbawalla collects the tiffins from the homes and takes them to the nearest railway station on bikes. There, the different tiffins are sorted out for specific central sorting/destination stations, and loaded on to large, rectangular wooden trays. These trays, carrying up to 40 tiffins and up to 100 kilograms, then travel in the local trains down to various stations. At each station, another unit of dabbawallas exchange the tiffins meant to be distributed in that area with tiffins destined for other stations. Some routes involve chains of up to five dabbawallas at set sorting points, who sort tiffins according to the station they have to be carried to for the next leg of their journey. At the destination, the tiffins on the trays are re-sorted for localities and offices. The trays are then carried on heads, hand-wagons, and cycles, delivered to the clients by 12:30 pm, picked up by 2:30 pm, and returned where they came from. The process is reversed, ending at 5:00 pm.

THE SPEED

A Mumbai local halts a station for about 20 seconds or less, thus, the dabbawallas work with clock-like precision and speed. They battle crowds in stations, heavy monsoon rains, and nasty taxi drives, to carry their heavy trays. Still, the lunch boxes reach offices between 11:45 am and 12:30 pm. As noted by a housewife: 'For these dabbawallas, 10 o'clock... they don't stand around for two minutes'. A dabbawalla elaborated, 'Once you have the boxes with you, you can't even stop to go to the toilet because if you are late by even five or 10 minutes, the chain gets disrupted'. Their corporate code of conduct, 'No customer should go without food'. A satisfied client affirmed: "What's amazing is in the past three years, they've never missed a single day... My lunch has never arrived late in all these days".

THE KNOWLEDGE

A majority of the dabbawallas running the system are illiterate, and may not be able to read the addresses. The dabbawallas therefore 'use colours and code markings to ensure faultless delivery'. Each tiffin has, painted on its top, a number of symbols which identify where it was picked up, the originating and destination stations, and the building and the floor to which it is to be delivered. Though there are no addresses, mistake never occurs. For example, a IMII code means that dabbawalla I to deliver the tiffin to the 11th floor of the Maker Towers (a well-known building in downtown Mumbai). The system uses the cognitive and memory structure of the dabbawallas. During the sorting process, each dabbawalla will locate the tiffins that he is responsible for, usually 10–20 at a time.

THE QUALITY

The dabbawallas deliver up to 200,000 tiffins every working day, or 4 million per month. Each delivery involves an average of 20 partner transactions, a total of 800 million transactions per month. As dabbawallas note, "We make a mistake perhaps once in two months, our livelihood depends on delivering efficiently." Thus, the system error rate is 1 per 1.6 million transactions. In contrast, the best in the world practices allow an error rate of up to 3.4 defects per million—or what is termed 6-sigma.

THE ECONOMICS

The dabbawalla system works on the power of human creativity and sincerity, with low capital, without any technology. The 5,000 dabbawallas deliver between 175,000 to 200,000 lunch boxes every working day, for about ₹200 per month for each lunchbox. This amounts to monthly revenues of about ₹35 million ($ 0.75 million). An average dabbawalla earns about ₹7000 per month (or $ 1800 annually), spending less than 5% on association dues, crate, railway pass, and bike maintenance.

THE ORGANIZATION

The Dabbawalla system—dating back to 1890—is run by a cooperative body, the Nutan Trust, with about 5,000 members. The Nutan Trust has a flat structure with only three tiers: the governing council, the *mukadams* (mentors) and the dabbawallas. They operate in cooperative units of 15 to 40 dabbawallas each, supervised by four mukadams. The mukadam is responsible for sorting tiffins, and also for settling disputes, maintaining records of payments, getting new clients, initiating new dabbawallas, helping with substitutes when a dabbawalla needs leave, and ensuring that no dabbawalla undercuts another. Each group pools in the collections, distributes and equally shares the month revenues. The governing council meets with all the members on the 15th of each month, to discuss issues facing the dabbawallas. Besides legal issues, customer service is given the top priority. The rules state, 'If 25 customers complain, the group (of dabbawalla) is thrown out of the organization.' The council uses the membership fee to run pilgrim rest houses, offers grants to meet contingencies such as child education and healthcare, give credit, and offer subsidized facilities for marriage and other occasions. Each dabbawalla is an independent entrepreneur and a shareholder in the Nutan Trust. Everyone feels that they are equal participants in the food service business, not merely an employee. They work six days a week, taking only five days off during March for their annual village festival, the 'Bhairavnath Maharaj Utsav'. They are a tight knit community, hailing from the same region—Pune district, and sharing similar customs. They all wear a distinctive regional uniform, long white shirt, white *dhoti*, and white oval cap.

THE FUTURE

The rise in double income families, with women also working out, trend in many offices to offer free cafeteria meals, a change in customer preferences towards local and global food chains, has limited the growth of dabbawallas over the last one decade. In fact, a recent McDonald's advertisement called upon the local people to 'revolt against the dabbawallas'! However, customer satisfaction rates and loyalty for the dabbawalla service are high. 'Because of pollution, various diseases, and concerns about figure and weight gain, clients prefer home-made food'. In the meantime, the corporates and educational institutions around India are lining up to invite the dabbawallas for lectures and tips on supply chain management and planning. The dabbawallas are also looking to replicate the supply chain in Delhi and Bangalore, as well as in smaller cities such as Nashik. Indian marketers have already begun employing them to deliver free samples and circulars along with meals. An advertiser observed, "It's an excellent rout to get your message across… You could advertise any product using this service".

Questions for Discussion

1. What control systems allow dabbawallas to have such high quality levels?
2. What can the corporations learn from the control systems of dabbawallas?
3. What challenges one might expect while transferring dabbawalla system in other cities?

2. Mohammad Din Tanners and Exporters

In early 1985, Mr. S.M. Pervez, Partner and Director of S. Mohammad Din, was worried about the quality of raw skins purchased for tanning. The output of high quality leather had dropped during the past decade from 70 per cent to a low of 8 per cent of the total available skins. Mr. Pervez was concerned about the increasing proportion of low and medium quality tanned leather. S. Mohammad Din was established in Karachi, Pakistan, in 1965. By 1985, it had developed into a leading exporter of tanned leather from Pakistan. It was owned and managed by partners from the family, and Mr. Pervez was both a partner and a director of the firm. The production capacity of the firm was 2.2 million square feet of tanned leather per month. Exports registered a record value of ₹140 million in 1984 and were expected to rise up to ₹200 million in 1985. Having negligible home trade, their main foreign market was the Federal Republic of Germany. They also had customers in Japan, the Republic of Korea, Romania, the USSR, Spain, Italy and France.

From ancient usage as a writing material, leather had been put to various uses in different periods. It had been used to provide protection from cold weather and as head or body wear. Footware is still preferred in leather as compared to substitute materials. High-fashion ladies' coats and gentlemen's jackets were made of the best quality leather. Italy and the Federal Republic of Germany had specialized in colour dyeing of leather and designing prestige products from high quality leather. These products, such as garments, briefcases, suitcases, shoes, handbags, wallets and saddles, to name a few, required high skill in workmanship and excellence in finish to sell in foreign markets. Italy and the Federal Republic of Germany were the leading producers of these goods, and, as such, the main buyers of tanned leather. The firm purchased sheep, lamb, cow and buffalo skins as raw material through established auction houses on the basis of the highest bid for an offered lot of skins. The auction was open and there was no secrecy about the bids.

Tanned leather was graded in eight qualities. Quality numbers 1 to 7 were exportable, while number 8 was considered rubbish. Ten years earlier, the tanning process resulted in 70 per cent of high quality skins; but over the years, the proportion had fallen, and by the end of 1984 was only 8 per cent. This drastic fall resulted in a very high proportion of low quality and medium quality tanned leather.

The cattle farming profession was not standardized in Pakistan. Scientific approaches to livestock breeding and cattle farming were quite unfamiliar. This resulted in unhealthy and uncared-for animals having defective and low quality skins. Nevertheless, the auction houses did not classify or grade the lots of skins presented for auction. Consequently, tanneries buying skins had to accept lots which included large proportions of lower quality materials. Their problem: What to do with the low quality tanned leather? Poor quality of leather was never acceptable to foreign buyers. Thus, to use this surplus of low quality tanned leather, the firm began manufacturing industrial gloves. The buyers of these gloves did not care about the quality of leather, because they were disposed of after use. They were, however, very cautious about the stitching and finishing standards.

Mr. Pervez wondered what to do with the increasing volume of low and medium quality tanned leather.

Questions for Discussion

1. What alternatives are available to Mohammad Din Tanners?
2. What other uses are there for the lowest quality leather?
3. To what extent would the manufacture of industrial gloves and other products change the character of the company?
4. What are the risks of a tannery expanding into the production of leather goods?

FURTHER READING

Business Today, Quality Revolution, 1995.

www.iso.org

Bureau of Indian Standards, The National Standards Body of India, New Delhi, www.bis.org.in

Sheik Shajahan (2016), Quality Management in Information Technology Industry: A Study with reference to Selected IT Organizations in India, unpublished PhD Thesis, Andhra University, Visakhapatnam.

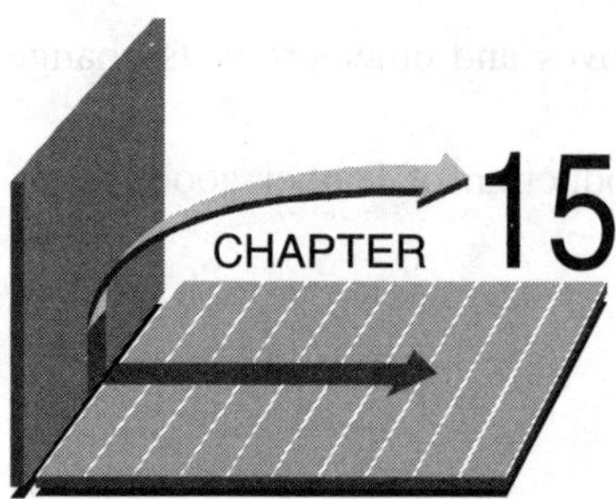

Six Sigma

CONTENTS

INTRODUCTION

Organizations look for ways to improve their production and management processes in order to remain competitive in the market. This calls for ways to reduce production cost, enhance productivity and improve product quality. Therefore, organizations must utilize all the available resources efficiently and effectively to cater to their customers with high quality products at a low price. For these reasons, researchers all over the world proposed several improvement strategies and tools to satisfy organizations' needs. Such initiatives include Total Quality Management, Quality Awards, Total Preventive Maintenance (TPM), Lean and Six Sigma.

The Lean concept, which was initially referred to as the *Toyota Production System*, concentrates on the flow of all the processes rather than on the optimization of individual operations (Lee, 2004). Womack (2002) specified the main components of Lean management system as follows:

- Identify process value from the customer's perspective
- Identify the value stream for each product and eliminate all types of waste currently embedded within the production process
- Try to develop a continuous production process
- Develop the pull management technique within the production lines
- Manage towards perfection.

Six Sigma, on the other hand, is a data-driven methodology used to identify root causes for variations in a production process in order to achieve organizational excellence. Six Sigma is a successful quality improvement technique. Unlike conventional quality improvement programmes like TQM, Six Sigma is known for its ability to produce organization wide results in a short period of time.

GENESIS OF SIX SIGMA

Six Sigma is an old technique and it started with the birth of the concept in mathematics called *normal curve*. In early 1920's, Six Sigma was adopted in the production industry for product variation measurement standard. It was initiated as Three Sigma and was very effectively used in process correction during that time.

In the late 1970's, Dr. Mikel Harry, a senior staff engineer at Motorola's Government Electronics Group (GEG), experimented with problem-solving through statistical analysis. Using this approach, GEG's products were being designed and produced at a faster rate and at a lower cost. With advancement in the manufacturing and production norms, new standards like CPK, Zero Defects and many more came for the measurement and improvement. In the late 1980s, Motorola wanted to improve quality in the products and services offered. Therefore, Bill Smith of Motorola initiated this concept of Six Sigma. Bill Smith, an engineer, and Dr. Mikel Harry together devised a 6-step methodology with the focus on defect reduction and improvement in yield through statistics. Bill Smith is credited as the "Father of Six Sigma". It has been observed that the traditional quality levels like measuring defects in thousands of opportunities, did not provide enough granularities in the process. Measurement of defects per million opportunities has been introduced in the industry and the company took the initiative to create a culture and environment to support the Six Sigma concept. It has been observed that Six Sigma helped Motorola to identify the bottom lines in the business process and instead, the company saved billions as an outcome of the Six Sigma initiatives. Subsequently, Allied Signal began implementing Six Sigma under the leadership of Larry Bossidy. In 1995, General Electric, under the leadership of Jack Welch, began the most widespread implementation of Six Sigma. After that, thousands of companies around the world have adopted Six Sigma for enhancing their business performance which improved them significantly. Six Sigma initiatives have started in almost all sectors of industry ranging from production, process, manufacturing and service, and the results obtained are significant in terms of quality and quantity. The Six

Sigma concept adaptation helped companies to save revenue and to generate business value in the market.

General Electric
"It is not a secret society, a slogan or a cliché. Six Sigma is a highly disciplined process that helps focus on developing and delivering near-perfect products and services. Six Sigma has changed our DNA—it is now the way we work."
Honeywell
"Six Sigma refers to our overall strategy to improve growth and productivity as well as a quality measure. As a strategy, Six Sigma is a way for us to achieve performance breakthroughs. It applies to every function in our company and not just to the factory floor."

Since its inception, Six Sigma has been defined in a number of ways and has many popular definitions. Some of the classical ones which are very relevant in today's context are:

Six Sigma is a highly technical method used by engineers and statisticians to fine tune products and processes.

Six Sigma is a sweeping cultural change effort, to position a company for greater customer satisfaction and competitiveness.

Six Sigma is a comprehensive and flexible system for achieving, sustaining and maximizing business success. It is uniquely driven close understanding of customer needs, disciplined use of facts, data, statistical analysis and diligent attention to managing, improving and reinventing business processes.

Six Sigma is a vehicle for strategic change... an organizational approach to performance excellence. Six Sigma is important for business operations because it can be used both to increase top-line growth and also reduce bottom line costs. Six Sigma can be used to enable:

(i) Transformational change by applying it across the board for large-scale fundamental changes throughout the organization, to change processes, cultures and achieve breakthrough results.

(ii) Transactional change by applying tools and methodologies to reduce variation and defects and dramatically improve business results.

When people refer to Six Sigma, they refer to several things:

- It is a philosophy.
- It is based on facts and data.
- It is a statistical approach to problem-solving.
- It is a structured approach to solve problems or reduce variation.
- It refers to 3.4 Defects Per Million Opportunities.
- It is a relentless focus on customer satisfaction.
- Strong tie-in with bottom line benefits.

The tools used in Six Sigma are not new. It is based on tools that have been around for centuries. For example, Six Sigma relies a lot on the normal curve which was introduced by Abraham de Moivre in 1736 and later popularized by Carl Friedrich Gauss in 1818.

Six Sigma Definitions

Six Sigma is a scientific, systematic and statistical approach to business process improvement and is considered to be an important business strategy.

The name *Six Sigma* refers to the capability of the process to deliver units within the set limits. The Greek letter 'σ' or 'sigma', corresponding to 'S', is a notation of variation in the sense of standard deviation. For a stable process, the distance from the process mean to the nearest tolerance limit should, according to the Six Sigma approach, be at least six times the standard deviation σ of the process output. However, the process mean is also allowed to vary somewhat over time. If the process mean varies at most 1.5 σ from the target value, then on an average at most 3.4 Defectives per Million Opportunities (DPMO) will occur if the output is normally distributed (Table 15.1). 6σ-process corresponds in a sense to a value of 2.0 of the capability index (C_p) or 1.5 for C_{pk} when allowing for a 1.5 σ drift in process mean. According to Bergman and Klefsjo (2003), following is the defectives and opportunities.

Table 15.1 Defectives Per Million Opportunities

Process σ	$(T_U - T_L)/\sigma$	*Value of* C_p	*DPMO when perfectly centred*	*DPMO with a 1.5*σ*-shift that is, when* $C_{pk} = 1.5$
2	4	0.67	46.000	308.537
3	6	1.00	2.700	66.807
4	8	1.33	60	6.210
5	10	1.67	0.6	233
6	12	2.00	0.002	3.4

Source: Bergman and Klefsjö (2003)

The correspondence between 'sigma', capability index $C_p = (T_U - T_L)/\sigma$, the number of defective units with process average on the target value, and the number of defective units when allowing a variation of the process, average upto +/– 1.5 σ from the target value (Figure 15.1).

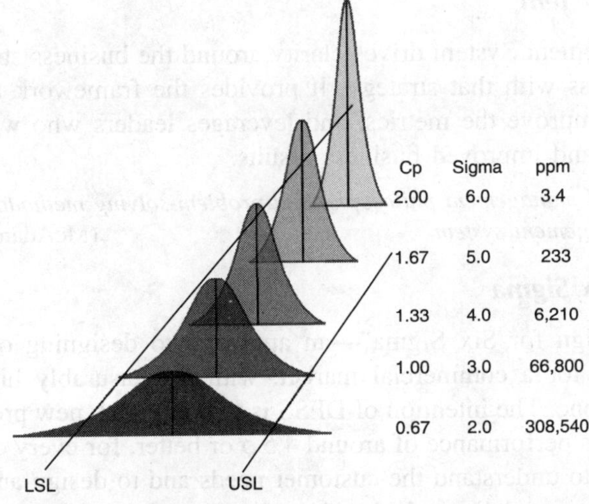

Figure 15.1 Defectives per million opportunities.

In layman terms, Six Sigma is a metric, representing a process that is performing virtually free of all defects. Some scholars and practitioners have attempted to describe Six Sigma in one or two definitions. However, many have concluded that there are at least three definitions—Six Sigma can be viewed as a metric, a mindset, and a management system.

As a Metric

The term "Sigma" is often used as a scale for levels of 'goodness' or quality. Using this scale, 'Six Sigma' equates to 3.4 Defects Per Million Opportunities (DPMO). Therefore, Six Sigma started as a defect reduction effort in manufacturing and was then applied to other business processes for the same purpose."

As a Mindset

Six Sigma is a business improvement approach that seeks to find and eliminate causes of mistakes or defects in business processes by focusing on process outputs that are of critical importance to customers. (Snee, 2004)

Six Sigma is a highly disciplined process that helps us focus on developing and delivering near-perfect products and services. The central idea behind Six Sigma is that you can measure how many defects you have in a process, you can systematically figure out how to eliminate them and get as close to 'zero defects' as possible. Six Sigma has changed the DNA of GE—it is the way we work—in everything we do, in every product we design. (General Electric at www.ge.com)

"Six Sigma is considered an organizational mindset that emphasizes customer focus and creative process improvement. The philosophy of Six Sigma recognizes that there is a direct correlation between the number of product defects, wasted operating costs and the level of customer satisfaction. With this mindset, individuals are prepared to work in teams in order to achieve Six Sigma and its ultimate goal of reducing process variation to no more than 3.4 Defects Per Million Opportunities. Six Sigma's 3.4 parts per million is close to perfection, and that makes it a more attainable and realistic goal to achieve."

As a Management System

The Six Sigma Management System drives clarity around the business strategy and the metrics that most reflect success with that strategy. It provides the framework to prioritize resources for projects that will improve the metrics, and leverages leaders who will manage the efforts for rapid, sustainable, and improved business results.

Six Sigma is a useful management philosophy and problem-solving methodology but it is not a comprehensive management system. (McAdam and Evans, 2004)

DFSS—Design for Six Sigma

DFSS stands for "Design for Six Sigma"—an approach to designing or re-designing a new product and/or service for a commercial market, with a measurably high process-sigma for performance from day one. The intention of DFSS is to bring such new products and/or services to market with a process performance of around 4.5 σ or better, for every customer requirement. This implies an ability to understand the customer needs and to design and implement the new offering with a reliability of delivery before launch rather than after.

DFSS can be used anywhere a new product or service is to be introduced or re-introduced. For many manufacturing organizations, the design and development of new products is very much a part of everyday company life, and a soundly adopted DFSS methodology can make a considerable improvement to the process of 'design and implement'.

The intent of Design for Six Sigma (DFSS) is to:

- Minimize future problems
- Minimize variability
- Maximize satisfaction
- Deliver what is desired in a timely fashion
- Include suppliers in the design process

Within DFSS, there are two approaches to plan change and reduce variation—DMAIC (Define, Measure, Analyze, Improve, Control) to improve existing situations or processes (advocated by GE); and DMADV (Define, Measure, Analyze, Design, Verify) to design a new service, product, or process (proposed by Motorola).

DMAIC Overview

The most important methodology in Six Sigma management is perhaps the formalized improvement methodology characterized by DMAIC (Define-Measure-Analyze-Improve-Control) process (Figures 15.2 and 15.3). This DMAIC process works well as a breakthrough strategy. Six Sigma companies everywhere apply this methodology as it enables real improvements and real results. The methodology works equally well on variation, cycle time, yield, design, etc. It is divided into five phases:

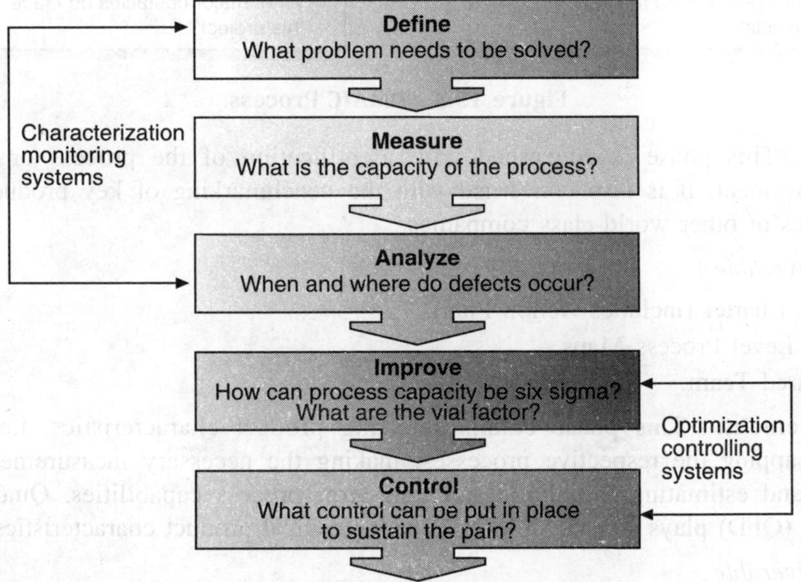

Figure 15.2 DMAIC process.

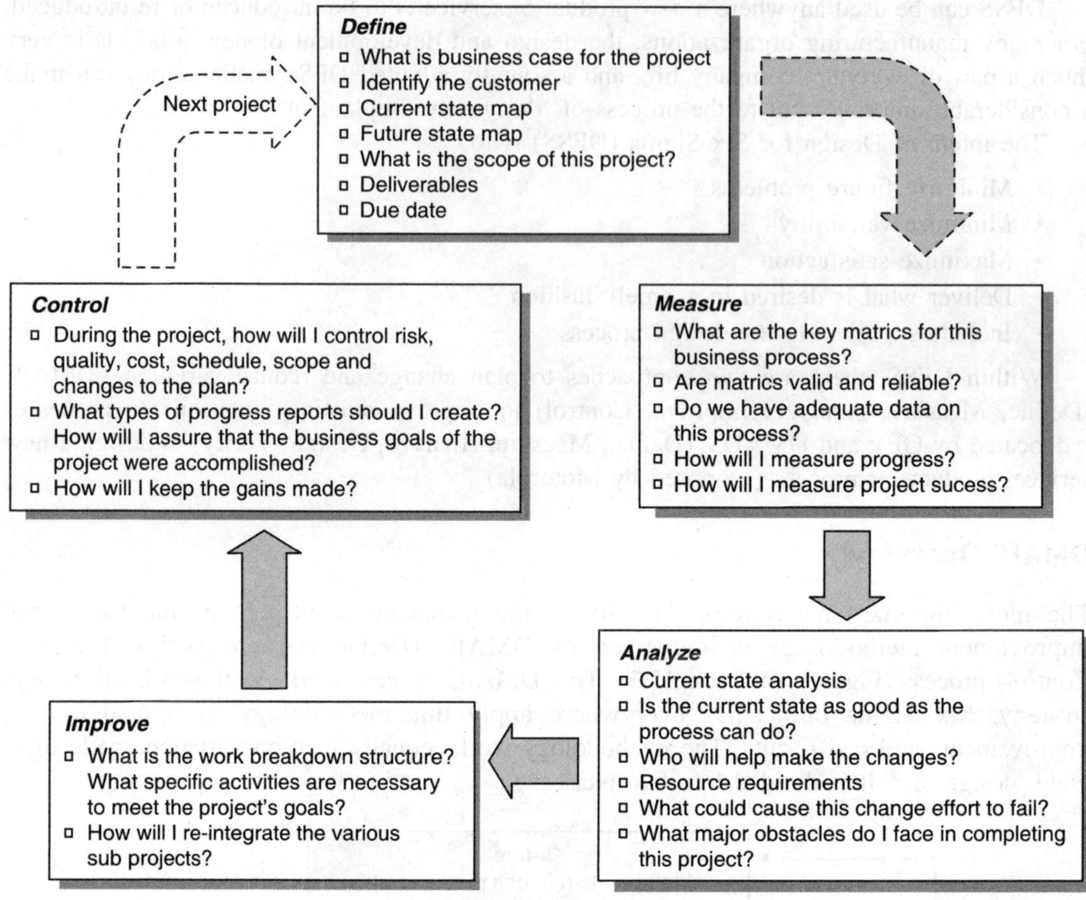

Figure 15.3 DMAIC Process.

Define: This phase is concerned with identification of the process or product that needs improvement. It is also concerned with the benchmarking of key product or process characteristics of other world-class companies.

Key deliverable

- Team Charter (includes Action Plan).
- High Level Process Maps.
- Prepared Team.

Measurement: This phase entails selecting product characteristics, i.e., dependent variables, mapping the respective processes, making the necessary measurement, recording the results and estimating the short- and long-term process capabilities. Quality Function Deployment (QFD) plays a major role in selecting critical product characteristics.

Key deliverable

- Reliable assessment of current performance.

Analysis: This phase is concerned with analyzing and benchmarking the key product/ process performance metrics. Following this, a gap analysis is often undertaken to identify the common factors of successful performance, i.e., what factors explain best-in-class performance. In some cases, it is necessary to redefine the performance goal. In analyzing the product/process performance, various statistical and basic QC tools are used.

Key deliverable

• Validated Root Causes.

Improvement: This phase is related to selecting those product performance characteristics which must be improved to achieve the goal. Once this is done, the characteristics are diagnosed to reveal the major sources of variation. Next, the key process variables are identified usually by way of statistically designed experiments including Taguchi methods and Design of Experiments (DOE). The improved conditions of key process variables are verified.

Key deliverable

• Solutions.
• Process Maps and Documentation.

Control: This last phase is initiated by ensuring that the new process conditions are documented and monitored via Statistical Process Control (SPC) methods. After the "settling-in" period, the process capability is reassessed. Depending upon the outcome of such a follow-on analysis, it may become necessary to revisit one or more of the preceding phases.

Key deliverable

• Process Control Plan

DMADV Overview

DMADV approach was designed to develop a service, product, or process that will successfully address identified issues and maintain it through normal operations (Figure 15.4). A top level

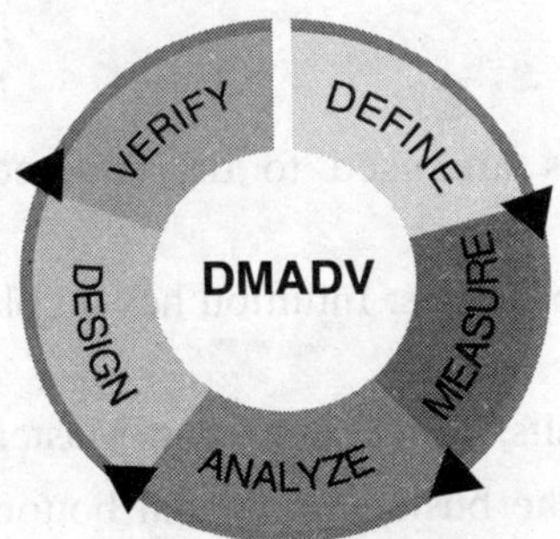

Figure 15.4 DMADV approach.

decision is needed to drive and support the DMADV project, and this can be one basis for its link to strategy implementation. From another perspective, implementing strategies identified in a long-range or strategic plan often involves introducing new services, products, or processes and procedures. Because of its focus on success through thorough analysis, DMADV may be a useful approach to strategy implementation.

There are five major steps to DMADV approach, and component steps to each of those. A key component of the DMADV approach is an active 'toll gate' check sheet review of the outcomes of each of the five steps before proceeding onto the next one.

Define: Identify purpose; identify and set measurable goals from the perspective of both the organization and the stakeholder; develop schedule and guidelines for review; and identify and assess risks.

Measure: Define requirements; define market segments; identify critical parameters for design; design scorecards to evaluate design components that are Critical To Quality (CTQ); reassess risks; and assess production process capability and product capability.

Analyze: Develop design alternatives; identify the best combination of requirements to provide value within constraints; develop conceptual designs; evaluate; select the best components; and develop the best available design.

Design: Develop a high level design; develop exact specifications; develop detailed component designs; develop related processes; optimize design.

Verify: Validate that the design is acceptable to all stakeholders; complete the pilot test; confirm expectations; expand deployment; and document the lessons learned.

In order for DMADV to be successful, the company needs to understand the customer's needs and decide which needs are being met and which needs should be improved upon. Complete evaluations of the existing processes need to be made in order to determine how to satisfy the customers while saving money.

Considering the above two groups of phases, it becomes apparent that the Six Sigma methodology is driven by brilliant, knowledgeable statisticians. Professionals in the project management field may find valuable opportunities to contribute to enhancing these methodologies by incorporating promising practices used in maximum projects most of the time, while keeping in mind the planned short duration of Six Sigma projects.

DMAIC versus DMADV

Similarities

- Six Sigma methodologies are used to drive defects to less than 3.4 per million opportunities.
- Data intensive solution approaches. Intuition has no place in Six Sigma—only cold, hard facts.
- Implemented by Green Belts, Black Belts and Master Black Belts.
- Ways to help in meeting the business/financial bottom line numbers.
- Implemented with the support of a champion and process owner.

Differences

DMAIC and DMADV sound very similar as the acronyms share the first three letters. But that is about where the similarities stop.

There are some differences in the two methodologies. DMADV helps clarify client needs as it relates to services or products. It also assists in matching the requests of the client by creating business models. On the other side, DMAIC is utilized to clarify the work processes and how they fit into the organizational goals. In addition, it creates work process enhancement to lessen or completely eliminate defects.

The contrast shows that DMADV generally comes into the picture when the product is in the beginning stages and it requires a maturing process in order to develop into what the customer is requesting. If there is a service or commodity already established but not rising to customer demands, DMAIC is useful.

THE SEVEN QUALITY CONTROL TOOLS

The Seven Quality Control tools (7QC tools) are graphical and statistical tools which are most often used in QC for continuous improvement. Since they are so widely utilized by almost every level of the company, they have been nicknamed as 'Magnificent Seven'. They are applicable to improvements in all dimensions of the process performance triangle—variation of quality, cycle time and yield of productivity. Each one of the 7QC tools had been used separately before 1960. However, in the early 1960s, they were gathered together by a small group of Japanese scientists lead by Kaoru Ishikawa, aiming to provide the QC Circles with effective and easy-to-use tools. They are—Cause-and-effect diagram, Check sheet, Control chart, Histogram, Pareto chart, Scatter diagram and Stratification.

Cause-and-effect Diagram

An effective tool as part of a problem-solving process is the cause-and-effect diagram, also known as the *Ishikawa diagram* (named after its originator) or *Fishbone diagram*. This technique is useful to trigger ideas and promote a balanced approach in group brainstorming sessions where individuals list the perceived sources (causes) with respect to outcomes (effect). As shown in Figure 15.5, the effect is written in a rectangle on the right-hand side and the causes are listed on the left-hand side. They are connected with arrows to show the cause-and-effect relationship.

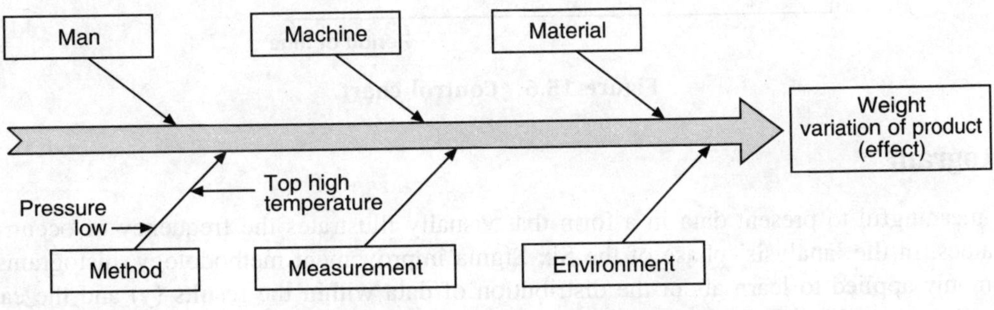

Figure 15.5 Fishbone diagram.

Check Sheet

The check sheet is used for specific data collection of any desired characteristics of a process or product that is to be improved. It is frequently used in the 'measure' phase of the Six Sigma improvement methodology, DMAIC. For practical purposes, the check sheet is commonly formatted as a table. It is important that the check sheet is kept simple and that its design is aligned to the characteristics that are measured.

Control Chart

Control chart is a very important tool in the 'analyze, improve and control' phases of the Six Sigma improvement methodology. In the 'analyze' phase, control charts are applied to judge if the process is predictable; in the 'improve' phase, to identify evidence of special causes of variation so that they can be acted on; in the 'control' phase, to verify that the performance of the process is under control.

The original concept of the control chart was proposed by Walter A. Shewhart in 1924 and the tool has been used extensively in industry since the Second World War, especially in Japan and the USA, after the year 1980. Control charts offer the study of variation and its source. They can give process monitoring and control, and can also give direction for improvements. Control charts can separate special from common cause issues of a process and can give early identification of special causes so that there can be timely resolution before many poor quality products are produced.

Shewhart control charts track processes by plotting data over time as shown in Figure 15.6. This chart can track either variables or attribute process parameters.

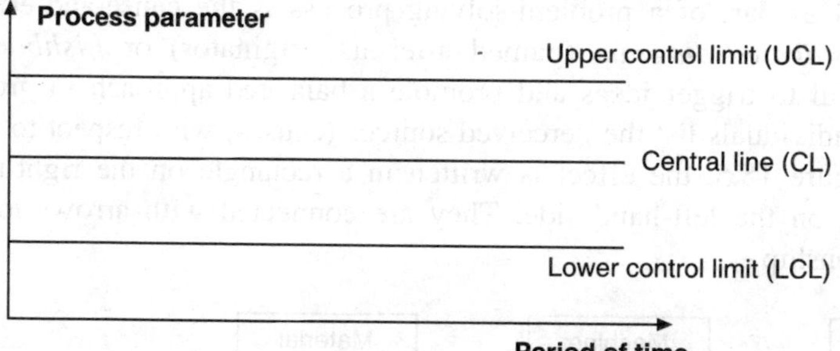

Figure 15.6 Control chart.

Histogram

It is meaningful to present data in a form that visually illustrates the frequency of occurrence of values. In the 'analysis' phase of the Six Sigma improvement methodology, histograms are commonly applied to learn about the distribution of data within the results (y) and the causes (x) collected in 'measure' phase and they are also used to obtain an understanding of the potential for improvements (Figure 15.7).

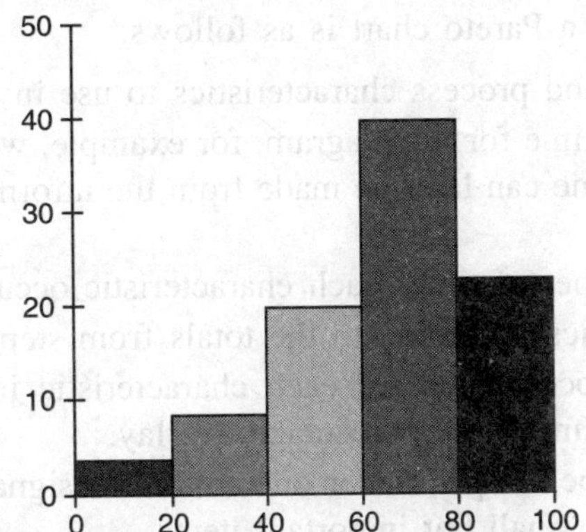

Figure 15.7 Representation of a graph.

Pareto Chart

The Pareto chart was introduced in the 1940s by Joseph M. Juran, who named it after the Italian economist and statistician Vilfredo Pareto, 1848–1923. It is applied to distinguish the "vital few from the trivial many" as Juran formulated the purpose of the Pareto chart. It is closely related to the so-called 80/20 rule—"80 per cent of the problems stem from 20 per cent of the causes," or in Six Sigma terms "80 per cent of the poor values in *y* stem from 20 per cent of the *x*." In the Six Sigma improvement methodology, the Pareto chart has two primary applications. One is for selecting appropriate improvement projects in the 'define' phase.

Pareto charts are extremely beneficial because they can be used to identify those factors that have the greatest cumulative effect on the system, and thus screen out the less significant factors in an analysis. Ideally, this allows the user to focus attention on a few important factors in a process. Here, it offers a very objective basis for selection based on, for example, frequency of occurrence, cost saving and improvement potential in process performance. The other primary application is in the 'analyze' phase for identifying the vital few causes (*x*) that will constitute the greatest improvement in *y* if appropriate measures are taken (Figure 15.8).

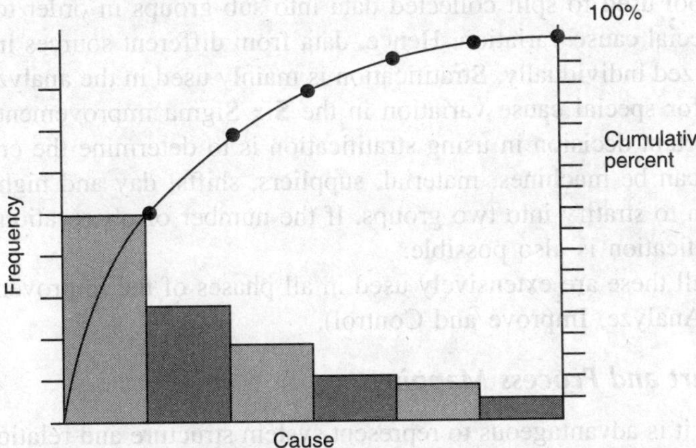

Figure 15.8 Pareto chart.

A procedure to construct a Pareto chart is as follows:

1. Define the problem and process characteristics to use in the diagram.
2. Define the period of time for the diagram, for example, weekly, daily, or shift. Quality improvements overtime can later be made from the information determined within this step.
3. Obtain the total number of times each characteristic occurred.
4. Rank the characteristics according to the totals from step 3.
5. Plot the number of occurrences of each characteristic in descending order in a bar graph along with a cumulative percentage overlay.
6. Trivial columns can be lumped under one column designation, however, care must be exercised not to omit small but important items.

Scatter Diagram

A scatter diagram is a tool for analyzing relationships between two variables. One variable is plotted on the horizontal axis and the other is plotted on the vertical axis. The pattern of their intersecting points can graphically show relationship patterns. Often, a scatter diagram is used to prove or disprove cause-and-effect relationships. While the diagram shows relationships, it does not, by itself, prove that one variable causes the other. In addition to showing possible cause-and-effect relationships, a scatter diagram can show that two variables are from a common cause that is unknown, or that one variable can be used as a surrogate for the other.

In the 'improve' phase of the Six Sigma improvement methodology, one often searches the collected data for x that has a special influence on y. Knowing the existence of such relationships, it is possible to identify input variables that cause special variation of the result variable. It can then be determined how to set the input variables, if they are controllable, so that the process is improved.

Stratification

Stratification is a tool used to split collected data into sub-groups in order to determine if any of them contain special cause variation. Hence, data from different sources in a process can be separated and analyzed individually. Stratification is mainly used in the analyze phase to stratify data in the search for special cause variation in the Six Sigma improvement methodology.

The most important decision in using stratification is to determine the criteria by which to stratify. Examples can be machines, material, suppliers, shifts, day and night, age groups and so on. It is common to stratify into two groups. If the number of observations is large enough, more detailed stratification is also possible.

In Six Sigma, all these are extensively used in all phases of the improvement methodology (Define, Measure, Analyze, Improve and Control).

Process Flow Chart and Process Mapping

For quality systems it is advantageous to represent system structure and relationships using flow charts. A flow chart provides a picture of the steps that are needed to understand a process.

The process flow chart provides a visual representation of the steps in a process. Flow charts are also referred to as *Process Mapping* or *Flow Diagrams.* Constructing a flow chart is often one of the first activities of a process improvement effort, because of the following benefits:

- Gives everyone a clear understanding of the process
- Helps to identify non-value-added operations
- Facilitates teamwork and communication
- Keeps everyone on the same page.

In every Six Sigma improvement project, understanding the process is essential. The flow chart is therefore, often used in the 'measure' phase. It is also used in the 'analyze' phase for identifying improvement potential compared to similar processes and in the control phase to institutionalize the changes made to the process.

There are many symbols used to construct a flow chart; the more common symbols are shown in Figure 15.9.

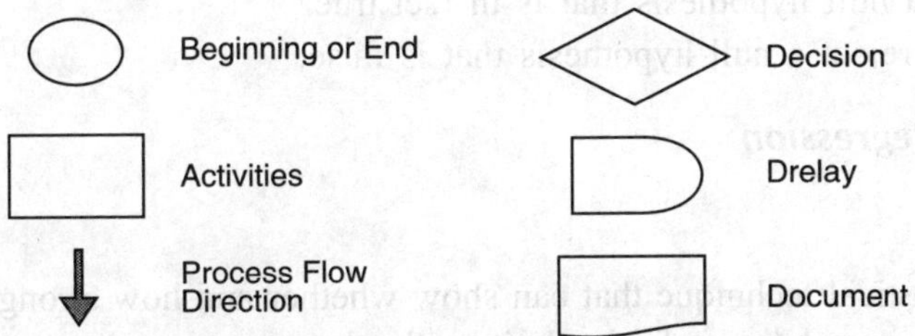

Figure 15.9 Symbols used in a flow chart.

Process Mapping

An alternative (or supplement) to a detailed process flow chart is a high-level process map that shows only a few major process steps as activity symbols. For each of these symbols Key Process Input Variables (KPIVs) to the activity are listed on one side of the symbol, while Key Process Output Variables (KPOVs) to the activity are listed on the other side of the symbol. Note that a KPIV can be a CTQx, and a KPOV can be a CTQy.

Hypothesis Testing

Hypothesis testing begins with the drawing of a sample and calculating its characteristics/ "statistics". A statistical test (a specific form of a hypothesis test) is an inferential process, based on probability, and is used to draw conclusions about the population parameters. In industrial situations, management frequently needs to decide whether the parameters of a distribution have particular values or relationships. That is, the management may wish to test a hypothesis, that the mean or standard deviation of a distribution has a certain value or that the difference between two means is zero. A statistical hypothesis is usually done by the following process.

- Set up a null hypothesis (H_0) that describes the value or relationship being tested
- Set up an alternative hypothesis (H_1)
- Determine a test statistic, or rule, used to decide whether to reject the null hypothesis

- A specified probability value, denoted as σ, that defines the maximum allowable probability that the null hypothesis will be rejected when it is true
- Collect a sample of observations to be used for testing the hypothesis, and then find the value of the test statistic
- Find the critical value of the test statistic using σ and a proper probability distribution table
- Comparing the critical value and the value of the test statistic, decide whether the null hypothesis is rejected or not.

The result of the hypothesis test is a decision to either reject or not reject the null hypothesis, i.e., the hypothesis is either Six Sigma for Quality and Productivity Promotion rejected or reserve judgement on it. In practice, the management may act as though the null hypothesis is accepted, if it is not rejected. Since they do not know the truth, they can make one of the following possible errors when running a hypothesis test:

1. Can reject a null hypothesis that is in fact true.
2. Can fail to reject a null hypothesis that is false.

Correlation and Regression

Correlation

Correlation is a statistical technique that can show whether and how strongly pairs of variables are related. Although correlation is fairly obvious, the data may contain unsuspected correlations. We need to suspect there are correlations, but do not know which are the strongest. An intelligent correlation analysis can lead to a greater understanding of the data.

The scatter diagram, discussed earlier, describes the relationship between two variables, say x and y. It gives a simple illustration of how variable x can influence variable y. A statistic that can describe the strength of a linear relationship between two variables is the sample correlation coefficient (r). A correlation coefficient can take values between –1 and +1. A value of –1 indicates perfect negative correlation, while +1 indicates perfect positive correlation. A zero indicates no correlation.

The equation for the sample correlation coefficient of two variables is:

$$r = \frac{\sum (x_i - \bar{x})(y_i - \bar{y})}{\sqrt{\sum (x_i - \bar{x})^2 \sum (y_i - \bar{y})^2}}$$

where, (x_i, y_i) $i = 1, 2... n$, are the coordinate pair of evaluated values.

Regression

Regression analysis is a statistical tool for the investigation of relationships between variables. More specifically, regression analysis helps one understand how the typical value of the dependent variable changes when any one of the independent variables is varied, while the other independent variable is held fixed. Most commonly, regression analysis estimates the conditional expectation of the dependent variable, given the independent variables—that is, the average value of the dependent variable when the independent variables are fixed. Less commonly, the focus is on a quartile, or other location parameter of the conditional distribution of the dependent variable given the independent variables. Regression analysis is widely used for prediction and forecasting, where its use has substantial overlap with the field of machine learning. Regression analysis is also used to understand which among the independent variables are related to the dependent variable, and to explore the forms of these relationships.

DESIGN OF EXPERIMENTS (DOE)

DOE is a systematic approach to investigate a system or process. A series of structured tests are designed in which planned changes are made to the input variables of a process or system. The effects of these changes on a pre-defined output are then assessed.

DOE is important as a formal way of maximizing information gain while resources required. It has more to offer than 'one change at a time' experimental methods, because it allows a judgement on the significance to the output of input variables acting alone, as well as input variables acting in combination with one another. The statistical approach to experimental design is necessary if we wish to draw meaningful conclusions from the data. Thus, there are two aspects to any experimental design—the design of experiment and the statistical analysis of the collected data. They are closely related, since the method of statistical analysis depends on the design employed.

The Design of Experiments plays a major role in many engineering activities. For instance, DOE is used for:

1. Improving the performance of a manufacturing process. The optimal values of process variables can be economically determined by application of DOE.
2. The development of new processes. The application of DOE methods early in process development can result in reduced development time, reduced variability of target requirements and enhanced process yields.
3. Screening important factors.
4. Engineering design activities such as evaluation of material alternations, comparison of basic design configurations, and selection of design parameters so that the product is robust to a wide variety of field conditions.
5. Empirical model building to determine the functional relationship between x and y.

Classification of Design of Experiments

There are many different types of DOE. According to the allocation of factor combinations and the degree of randomization of experiments, they may be classified as follows:

- ***Factorial design:*** This is a design for investigating all possible treatment combinations which are formed from the factors under consideration. The order in which possible treatment combinations are selected is completely random. Single- factor, two-factor and three-factor factorial designs belong to this class, as do $2k$ (k factors at two levels) and $3k$ (k factors at three levels) factorial designs.
- ***Fractional factorial design:*** This is a design for investigating a fraction of all possible treatment combinations which are formed from the factors under investigation. Designs

using tables of orthogonal arrays, Plackett–Burman designs and Latin square designs are fractional factorial designs. This type of design is used when the cost of the experiment is high and the experiment is time-consuming.

- ***Randomized complete block design, split-plot design and nested design:*** All possible treatment combinations are tested in these designs, but some form of restriction is imposed on randomization. For instance, a design in which each block contains all possible treatments, and the only randomization of treatments is within the blocks, is called the *randomized complete block design.*
- ***Incomplete block design:*** If every treatment is not present in every block in a randomized complete block design, it is an *incomplete block design.* This design is used when we may not be able to run all the treatments in each block because of a shortage of experimental apparatus or inadequate facilities.
- ***Response surface design and mixture design:*** This is a design where the objective is to explore a regression model to find a functional relationship between the response variable and the factors involved, and to find the optimal conditions of the factors. Central composite designs rot table designs, simplex designs, mixture designs and evolutionary operation (EVOP) designs belong to this class. Mixture designs are used for experiments in which the various components are mixed in proportions constrained to sum to unity.
- ***Robust design*:** Taguchi (1986) developed the foundations of robust design, which are often called *parameter design* and *tolerance design.* The concept of robust design is used to find a set of conditions for design variables which are robust to noise, and to achieve the smallest variation in a product's function about a desired target value. Tables of orthogonal arrays are extensively used for robust design.

In Six Sigma training, DOE is sometimes positioned in the 'improve' phase because it can be used to optimize a process.

ANALYSIS OF VARIANCE (ANOVA)

The ANOVA procedure is one of the most powerful statistical techniques. ANOVA is a general technique that can be used to test the hypothesis that the means among two or more groups are equal, under the assumption that the sampled populations are normally distributed.

FAILURE MODES AND EFFECTS ANALYSIS (FMEA)

Failure Modes and Effects Analysis (FMEA) is a set of guidelines, a process, and a form of identifying and prioritizing potential failures and problems, in order to facilitate process improvement. By basing their activities on FMEA, a manager, improvement team, or process owner can focus the energy and resources of prevention, monitoring, and response plans where they are most likely to pay-off. The FMEA method has many applications in a Six Sigma environment in terms of looking for problems not only in work processes and improvements but also in data collection activities, Voice of the Customer efforts and procedures.

There are two types of FMEA—one is design FMEA and the other is process FMEA. Design FMEA applications mainly include component, sub-system, and main system. Process FMEA applications include assembly machines, work stations, gauges, procurement, training of operators, and tests.

Benefits of a properly executed FMEA include the following:

- Prevention of possible failures and reduced warranty costs
- Improved product functionality and robustness
- Reduced level of day-to-day manufacturing problems
- Improved safety of products and implementation processes
- Reduced business process problems.

Within a design FMEA, manufacturing and/or process engineering input is important to ensure that the process will produce design specifications. A team should consider including knowledgeable representation from design, test, reliability, materials, service, and manufacturing/process organizations.

BALANCED SCORECARD (BSC)

The concept of a Balanced Scorecard became popular following research studies published in the *Harvard Business Review* articles of Kaplan and Norton (1992, 1993), and ultimately led to the 1996 publication of the standard business book on the subject, titled "*The Balanced Scorecard*" (Kaplan and Norton, 1996). The authors define Balanced Scorecard (BSC) as "*organized around four distinct performance perspectives—Financial, Customer, Internal, and Innovation and learning. The name reflects the balance provided between short- and long-term objectives, between financial and non-financial measures, between lagging and leading indicators, and between external and internal performance perspectives.*" As data are collected at various points throughout the organization, the need to summarize many measures—so that top level leadership can gain an effective idea of what is happening in the company—becomes critical. One of the most popular and useful tools used to reach that high-level view is the BSC. It is a flexible tool for selecting and displaying "key indicator" measures about the business in an easy-to-read format. Many organizations not involved in Six Sigma, including many government agencies, are using BSC to establish common performance measures and keep a closer eye on the business.

A number of organizations that have embraced Six Sigma methodology as a key strategic element in their business planning have also adopted BSC, or something akin to it, for tracking their rate of performance improvement. One of those companies is General Electric (GE). In today's business climate, the term "balanced scorecard" can refer strictly to the categories originally defined by Kaplan and Norton (1996), or it can refer to the more general "family of measures" approach involving other categories.

COST OF POOR QUALITY

The Cost of Poor Quality (COPQ) is the total cost incurred by high quality costs and poor management. Organizations, both public and private, that can virtually eliminate the COPQ can become leaders of the future. Conway (1992) claims that in most organizations 40 per cent of the total effort, both human and mechanical, is wasted. If that waste can be eliminated or significantly reduced, the per-unit price that must be charged for goods and services to yield a good return on investment is also reduced and often ends up being a price that is competitive on a global basis. One of the great advantages of Six Sigma is to reduce the COPQ, and hence, to improve profitability and customer satisfaction (Figure 15.10).

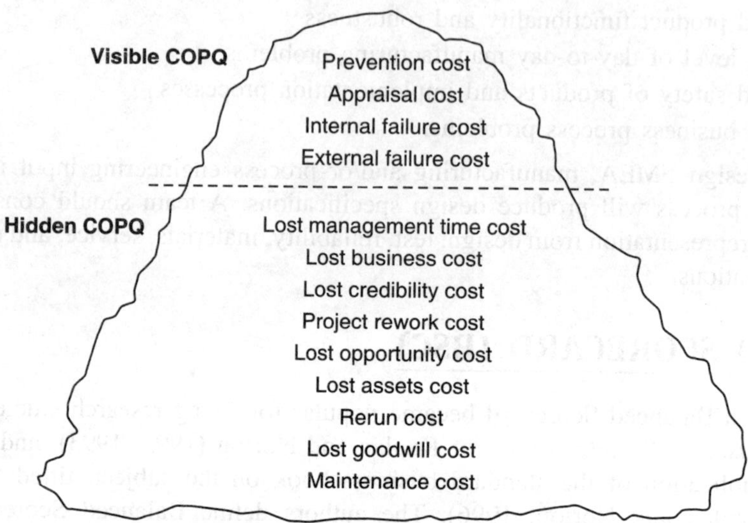

Figure 15.10 Cost of poor quality.

BINOMIAL DISTRIBUTION

In this distribution, the random variable only takes two values—such as a coin toss (heads or tails). For example, if we are working with defectives in a process, we can have parts that are defective or not defective—hence, only two possible values. If we have a series of coin tosses, for instance, we have n coin tosses and the probability of occurrence of head is p, then the random variable x is said to have a binomial distribution with parameters n and p. The random variable can take on values 0, 1, 2, ..., n and counts the number of successes (where getting a head can be termed as success).

The following conditions have to be met for using a Binomial Distribution:

- The number of trials is fixed
- Each trial is independent
- Each trial has one of two outcomes—event or non-event
- The probability of an event is the same for each trial.

POISSON DISTRIBUTION

This describes the number of times an event occurs in a finite observation space. For example, a Poisson distribution can describe the number of defects in the mechanical system of an airplane or the number of calls to a call centre. It is often used in quality control, reliability/ survival studies, and insurance. It is defined by one parameter—lambda, which equals the mean and variance. As lambda increases, the Poisson distribution approaches a normal distribution. Whenever, we are working with defects or when the exact probability of an event is not known (only the average is known), then we use the Poisson distribution.

NORMAL DISTRIBUTION

Normal distribution is the most widely known and used of all distributions. Since the normal distribution approximates many natural phenomena well, it has developed into a standard of reference for many probability problems. A bell-shaped curve is symmetric about its mean (Figure 15.11). The normal distribution is the most common statistical distribution because approximate normality arises naturally in many physical, biological, and social measurement situations. Many statistical analyses require the data to come from normally distributed populations. Mean (μ) and standard deviation (σ) are the two parameters that define normal distribution where mean is the peak or centre of the bell-shaped curve and standard deviation determines the spread in the data. Approximately, 68 per cent of observations are within +/– 1 standard deviation of the mean; 95 per cent are within +/– 2 standards deviations of the mean; and 99 per cent are within +/– 3 standard deviations of the mean.

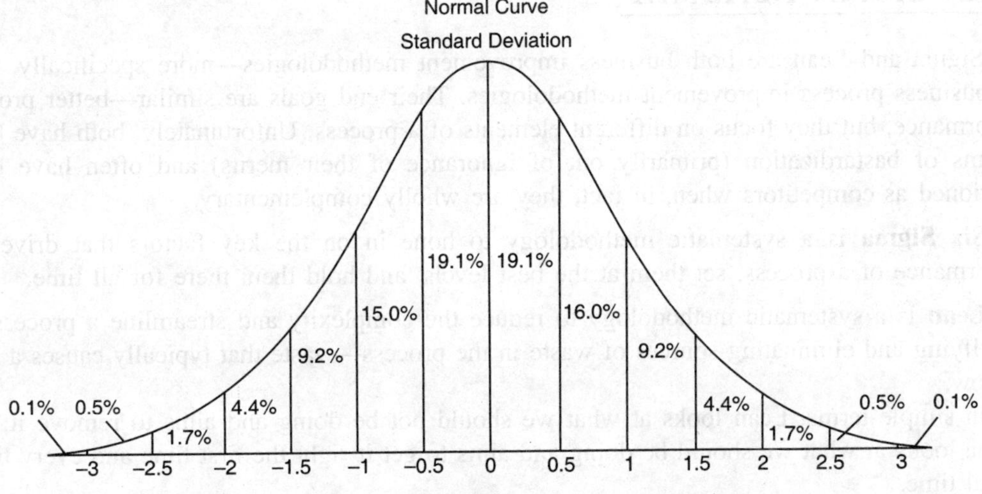

Figure 15.11 Bell-shaped curve.

Seven Steps for Six Sigma Introduction

When a company intends to introduce Six Sigma for its new management strategy, following are the seven seven-step procedures:

1. Top-level management commitment for Six Sigma is first and foremost. The CEO of the corporation or business unit should genuinely accept Six Sigma as the management strategy. Then, organize a Six Sigma team and set up the long-term Six Sigma vision for the company.

2. Start Six Sigma education for Champions first. Then start the education for WBs, GBs, BBs and MBBs in sequence. Every employee of the company should take the WB education first; then some of the WBs receive the GB education; and finally some of the GBs receive the BB education. However, usually MBB education is practiced in professional organizations.
3. Choose the area in which Six Sigma will be first introduced.
4. Deploy CTQs for all processes concerned. The most important is the company's deployment of big CTQs from the standpoint of customer satisfaction. Appoint BBs as full-time project leaders and ask them to solve some important CTQ problems.
5. Strengthen the infrastructure for Six Sigma, including measurement systems, Statistical Process Control (SPC), Knowledge Management (KM), and Database Management System (DBMS) and so on.
6. Designate a Six Sigma day each month and have the progress of Six Sigma reviewed by top-level management.
7. Evaluate the company's Six Sigma performance from the customers' viewpoint, benchmark the best company in the world, and revise the Six Sigma roadmap if necessary.

LEAN SIGMA ROADMAP

Six Sigma and Lean are both business improvement methodologies—more specifically, they are business process improvement methodologies. Their end goals are similar—better process performance, but they focus on different elements of a process. Unfortunately, both have been victims of bastardization (primarily out of ignorance of their merits) and often have been positioned as competitors when, in fact, they are wholly complementary.

Six Sigma is a systematic methodology to hone in on the key factors that drive the performance of a process, set them at the best levels, and hold them there for all time.

Lean is a systematic methodology to reduce the complexity and streamline a process by identifying and eliminating sources of waste in the process—waste that typically causes a lack of flow.

In simple terms, Lean looks at what we should not be doing and aims to remove it; Six Sigma looks at what we should be doing and aims to get it right the first time and every time, for all time.

Lean Sigma is all about linkage of tools and not using tools individually. In fact, none of the tools are new—the strength of approach is in the sequence of tools. The ability to understand the theory of tools is important. There are many versions of the Six Sigma Roadmap, but not so many that fully incorporate Lean in a truly integrated Lean Sigma. The roadmap follows the basic tried and tested DMAIC (Define, Measure, Analyze, Improve, and Control) approach from Six Sigma, but with Lean flow tools as well as Six Sigma statistical tools are threaded seamlessly together throughout. For example, despite being considered most at home in manufacturing, the best Pull Systems were used for controlling replenishment in office supplies. Similarly, Workstation Design applies equally to a triage nurse as it does to an assembly worker. The roadmap is a long way, removed from its Six Sigma predecessors and is structured into three layers:

- Major phases
- Minor phases
- Tools and deliverables (how and what)

Benchmarking for Six Sigma

Benchmarking is a standard by which something can be measured or judged. This term was first used by surveyors. They set a benchmark by marking a point of known vertical elevation. Therefore, benchmark becomes a point of reference for a measurement. We benchmark every day. We compare our performance, lifestyle, or a game of golf with friends and peers.

Benchmarking helps us to:

- Identify areas for breakthrough improvements,
- Establish higher targets, and new priorities.

Note that benchmarking is not a simple comparison and a subsequent blind copy of what seems to be the best. We must carefully analyze the outcome of benchmarking and focus on what adds maximum value in our business context. There are three types of benchmarking:

Internal Benchmarking

It compares critical-to-business processes or products across the organization on key critical-to-quality parameters such as turn-around-time or cost.

Functional Benchmarking

It compares similar functions or processes with industry leaders in that area.

Competitive Benchmarking

It focuses on direct competitors in terms of their products, services, processes, and customers. The following flowchart summarizes the benchmarking process.

Six Sigma in Different Organizations

Motorola: The Cradle of Six Sigma

The first organization to embrace the new quality movement in the form of Six Sigma was Motorola, established by Paul V. Galvin in 1929. Starting with car radios, the company thrived after the Second World War and moved its product range *via* television to high technology electronics, including mobile communications systems, semiconductors, electronic engine controls and computer systems. Today, it is a leading international company with more than $30 billion in sales and around 130,000 employees. Galvin succeeded his father as President in 1956, and as CEO and Chairman in 1964.

Until the 1970s, quality assurance and quality control groups functioned as policemen—they just inspected the product for defects when completed. Motorola realized that in order to compete with Japanese companies in quality and other far-east companies in cost, they would have to rethink the function of quality control. In 1981, Galvin decided to make total customer satisfaction as the fundamental objective of his company and set a goal of a ten-fold improvement in process performance over the next five years.

During 1981–1986, seminar series were set up and about 3,500 people were trained. At the end of 1986, Motorola had invested $220,000, whereas cost savings topped $6.4 million. The intangible benefits included real improvements in performance and customer satisfaction, alongside genuine interest from top-level management in statistical improvement methodologies and enthusiastic employees. Motorola needed well-trained experienced personnel who would be more than the policemen and these personnel would, through their expertise, assist production to optimize processes, eliminate or minimize defects and continuously improve customer satisfaction.

Despite such incredible success, Motorola was still facing a tough challenge from Japan. The Communication Sector, Motorola's main manufacturing division, presented their ideas for an improvement programme to Mr. Galvin in a document titled "*Six Sigma Mechanical Design Tolerancing*". At that time, Motorola possessed data indicating that they were performing at 4 Sigma, or 6,800 DPMO. By improving process performance to 6 Sigma, i.e., 3.4 DPMO in the following five years, the Communication Sector estimated that the gap between them and the Japanese would diminish.

In 1987, when Bob Galvin was the Chairman, Six Sigma was started as a methodology in Motorola. To ensure that the organization could accomplish the milestones of the Six Sigma programme, an aggressive education campaign was launched to teach people about process variation and the necessary tools to reduce it. Spending upwards of $50 million annually, employees at all levels of the organization were trained. Motorola University, the training centre of Motorola, played an active role in this extensive Six Sigma training scheme.

Motorola focused on top-level management commitment to reinforce the drive for Six Sigma, convincing people that Six Sigma was to be taken seriously. The general quality policy at that time also reflected the company's Six Sigma initiative. For example, the quality policy for the Semiconductor Products Sector explicitly states the quality policy as follows: "*It is the policy of the Motorola Semiconductor Products Sector to produce products and provide services according to customer expectations, specifications and delivery schedule. Our system is a Six Sigma level of error-free performance. These results come from the participative efforts of each employee in conjunction with supportive participation from all levels of management.*"

Savings estimates for 1988 from the Six Sigma programme totalled $480 million from $9.2 billion in sales. The company soon received external recognition for its Six Sigma drive. It was one of the first companies to capture the prestigious Malcolm Baldrige National Quality Award (MBNQA) in 1988. The following year, Motorola was awarded the Nikkei Award for Manufacturing from Japan. Motorola adopted "Six Steps to Six Sigma" for guiding the spread of process improvement. Process was greatly improved throughout the company, both in manufacturing and non-manufacturing areas of operation.

General Electric (GE)

General Electric (GE) has the unique distinction of being at the top of the Fortune 500 companies in terms of market capitalization. Market capitalization means that if someone multiplies GE's outstanding shares of stock by its current market price per share, GE is the highest-valued company listed on all US stock exchanges. The monetary value exceeds the gross domestic product of many nations around the world. Even though Motorola is the founder of Six Sigma, GE is the company which has proven that Six Sigma is an exciting management strategy.

GE began moving towards a focus on quality in the late 1980s. Work-Out®, the start of its journey, opened its culture to ideas from everyone, everywhere, decimated the bureaucracy and made boundary-less behaviour a reflexive, natural part of its culture, thereby creating a learning environment that led to Six Sigma. Now, Six Sigma, in turn, has been embedding quality thinking—process thinking—across every level and in every operation of GE around the globe.

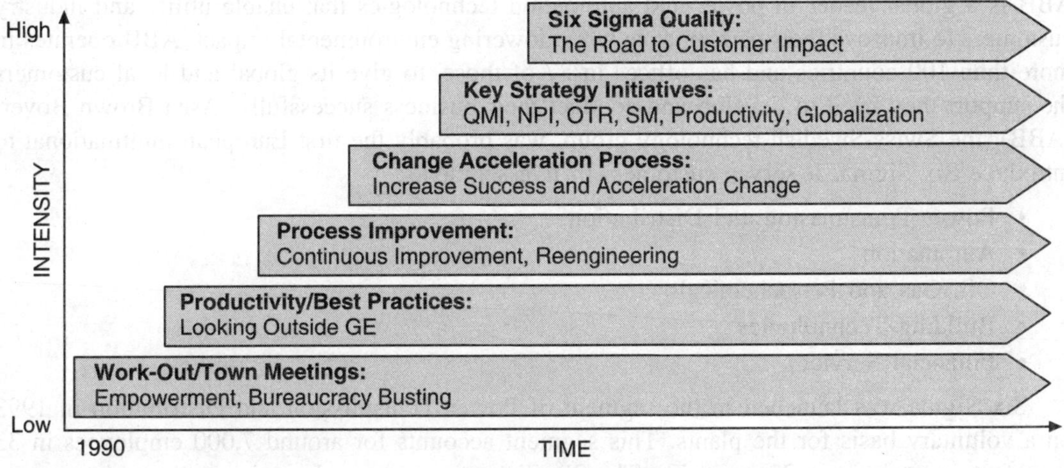

Figure 15.12 GE's evolution towards quality.

GE is indeed the missionary of Six Sigma. It began its Six Sigma programme in 1995 and has achieved remarkable results since then. An annual report of GE states that Six Sigma delivered more than $300 million to its operating income. In 1998, this number increased to $750 million. At the GE 1996 Annual Meeting, CEO Jack Welch described Six Sigma as, "*Six Sigma will be an exciting journey and the most difficult and invigorating stretch goal we have ever undertaken. ... GE today is a quality company. It has always been a quality company. ... This Six Sigma will change the paradigm from fixing products so that they are perfect to fixing processes so that they produce nothing but perfection, or close to it.*" This speech is regarded as a milestone in Six Sigma history.

GE listed many examples as typical Six Sigma benefits (General Electric, 1997). A few of them are as follows:

- GE Medical Systems described how Six Sigma designs have produced a 10-fold increase in the life of CT scanner X-ray tubes—increasing the "up-time" of these machines, the profitability, and the level of patient care given by hospitals and other health care providers.
- Super-Abrasives described how Six Sigma quadrupled its return on investment and, by improving yields, is giving it a full decade's worth of capacity despite growing volumes—without spending a penny on plant and equipment capacity.

- The plastic business, through rigorous Six Sigma process work, added 300 million pounds of new capacity (equivalent to a free plant), saved $400 million in investment, and was to save another $400 million by 2000.

Six Sigma training has permeated GE, and experience with Six Sigma implementation is now a prerequisite for promotion to all professional and managerial positions. Executive compensation is determined to a large degree by one's proven Six Sigma commitment and success.

Asea Brown Boveri Limited (ABB)

ABB is a global leader in power and automation technologies that enable utility and industry customers to improve their performance while lowering environmental impact. ABB operates in more than 100 countries and has offices in 87 of those, to give its global and local customers the support they need to develop and conduct their business successfully. Asea Brown Boveri (ABB), the Swiss-Swedish technology group, was probably the first European multinational to introduce Six Sigma. It serves customers in five segments:

- Power Transmission and Distribution
- Automation
- Oil, Gas and Petrochemicals
- Building Technologies
- Financial Services

Six Sigma was launched in the segment of Power Transmission and Distribution in 1993 on a voluntary basis for the plants. This segment accounts for around 7,000 employees in 33 manufacturing plants in 22 countries. The Six Sigma programme has remained consistent over the years, the drive has matured and commitment has been generated by successful results. Six Sigma has been implemented by all transformer plants and has spread into other ABB businesses, suppliers and customers because of its own merits. The overall objective of ABB at the beginning of Six Sigma was customer focus, in addition to cost reduction, cycle time reduction and self-assessment programmes. Since 1993, several initiatives have been attempted with the objective of finding a pragmatic approach.

In late 1993, ABB asked Michael J. Harry, a Six Sigma architect at Motorola, to join as Vice President of ABB, and asked him to be responsible for Six Sigma implementation. During his two years with ABB, he devoted much of his time to the business area for power transformers. His emphasis was on cost-saving results, performance measurements, training courses and a formalized improvement methodology. It was his consistent philosophy that Six Sigma should be carried out based on voluntary participation and active involvement. His message was clear—introduction in each plant was a decision to be made by the local plant management. It was not forced on any plant by the business area headquarters. Plants interested in Six Sigma sent employees to BB courses at the headquarters and substantial cost savings were achieved immediately by project team activities led by trained BBs. The first BB course was held in 1994. Since then, more than 500 BBs have graduated from the business area's Six Sigma training courses. The BB course has been in much demand over the years and at an early stage, significant cost savings were required in the mandatory homework projects.

In the early days of Six Sigma at ABB, plants started to identify key process and product characteristics to be assessed, and created measurement cards to be used for data collection in workshops. They developed a database for data storage and reported DPMO values to the headquarters. It became clear that a specific process in one plant could be compared to similar processes of other plants. "*This is really benchmarking*" and "*DPMO values disclose problems*" were obvious conclusions. The characteristics were readily available, both in terms of a single process and a combination of processes. This was also true for the improvement rate. Efforts were highly successful in developing a standard set of characteristics to be measured in the production of transformers across plants. Six Sigma has become ingrained in the operation. Over the years, success has bred further success. More than half of all plants apply Six Sigma actively with excellent results, whereas the remaining plants have focused more on training and measurements than on project improvement work. Plants Six Sigma Experiences and Leadership were not forced to introduce Six Sigma, but the reporting and measurement of process performance, by means of DPMO, were made mandatory.

Plants have been very much pleased with their Six Sigma programmes. A quality manager in Scotland, states that "*Six Sigma is the strongest improvement approach that has been around for a long time.*" The Six Sigma initiative at ABB has generated a great deal of positive feedback from customers and suppliers, both to the headquarters and to the individual plants. It has achieved remarkable results through the application of Six Sigma. The results include reduction of process variation leading to products with fewer defects, increased yields, improved delivery precision and responsiveness, as well as design improvements. Most projects have been centred on manufacturing processes, but also a good number of projects in non-manufacturing processes have been completed. They include front end clearance, invoicing, reducing ambiguity in order processing, and improving production schedules.

Some of the key critical reasons for the success of Six Sigma at ABB are complex and interrelated. However, 10 secrets of success which stand out and are specific to ABB are shared below:

Endurance: Endurance from key people involved in the initiative is essential—CEO, Champion and BBs. The CEO as the number one believer, the Champion as the number one driver, and the BBs as the number one improvement experts.

Early cost reductions: For all plants launching Six Sigma, the early improvement projects have brought confidence and determination.

Top-level management commitment: The top-level management has dedicated the time, attention and resources needed to achieve the goals set—commitment is put into practice.

Voluntary basis: Voluntary basis has enabled Six Sigma to grow on its own merits and not as a forced compliance.

Demanding BB course: The BB course held at the headquarters has been thorough and demanding. It has been a vehicle for deployment and brings the Six Sigma framework and the improvement methodology into the company.

Full-time BBs: ABB has utilized full-time BBs which are preferable to part-time BBs. One major reason is that a full-time BB has enough time to dedicate to carrying out and following up improvement projects. After completing a few projects, a BB moves back into operations and become a part-time BB.

Active involvement of middle managers: Active involvement of middle managers who are usually BBs or GBs is essential. They are, in fact, the backbone of improvement efforts.

Measurement and database building: Measurements and measurement systems are the important basis of Six Sigma. In addition to these, database building and information utilization are also a key factor of Six Sigma success. ABB has done excellent jobs on these.

One metric and one number: One metric on process performance presents one consolidated number for performance, such as sigma level or DPMO. Such simplicity effectively reduces complacency, which is the arch enemy of all improvement work.

Design of experiments: Simple design of experiments such as factorial designs are successfully used at ABB. Factorial experiments are well utilized today, either as a stand-alone approach or combined with the seven QC tools.

Samsung SDI: A Leader of Six Sigma in Korea

The first National Quality Prize of Six Sigma was given to two companies. One is Samsung SDI and the other is LG Electronics, which are virtually the leaders of Six Sigma in Korea. Samsung SDI was founded in 1970 as a producer of the black/white Braun tube. It began to produce the colour Braun tube from 1980 and has now become the number one company for Braun tubes in the world. The market share of Braun tubes is 22 per cent. The major products are CDT (color display tube), CPT (colour picture tube), LCD (liquid crystal display), VFD (vacuum fluorescent display), C/F (colour filter), Li-ion battery and PDP (plasma display panel). The total sales volume is about $4.4 billion and the total number of employees is about 18,000, including 8,000 domestic employees. It has six overseas subsidiaries in Mexico, China, Germany, Malaysia and Brazil.

The CEO of Samsung SDI, Son Wook, declared the slogan, "*True leader in digital world*" as the Six Sigma vision, at the end of 1996. The definition of Six Sigma in the company is:

> Six Sigma is the management philosophy, strategy and tool which achieves innovative process quality and development of world number one products, and which cultivates global professional manpower, and a way of thinking and working from the viewpoint of customer satisfaction.

Six Sigma is basically a top-down management tool. For implementation of Six Sigma, executive officers (i.e., Champions) should be the leaders of Six Sigma. In Samsung SDI, the following points have been implemented for Champion leadership:

- *Champion education:* All Champions take the Champion education course of four days, and they obtain the GB certification.
- *Champion planning:* Each Champion is supposed to plan a "Six Sigma roadmap" for his or her division, twice a year. The Champion selects the themes of projects and he/she supervises the Six Sigma plan for his/her division.
- *Champion day:* One day each month is designated as the Champion Day. On this day, the Champions wear Six Sigma uniform, and discuss all kinds of subjects related to Six Sigma. Examples of Champion planning, best practice of Champion leadership, and best practice of BB projects are presented on this day.

The development system of Samsung SDI is based on ECIM (Engineering Computer Integrated Manufacturing). ECIM is a tool for maximizing the company's competitiveness from the viewpoint of customer demand through efficient development process, technology standardization, PDM (Product Data Management) and DR (Design Review). The DFSS process of Samsung SDI follows the IDOV (Identify, Design, Optimize, Verify) process, and after each step, DR helps to validate the process. There are four different types of design review (DR). Each one reviews and validates the previous immediate step. For instance, DR1 reviews the product planning and decides whether DFSS process can flow to the next step or not. As Samsung SDI launched their DFSS programme, they went through a rigorous process of matching the broad set of DFSS tools with their existing Product Development Process (PDP).

Samsung SDI has deployed Six Sigma across all areas of management, one of which was their product development organization, with numerous DFSS projects focused on improving design as well as on completely new innovations. SDI led Samsung Electronics to become the largest producers of televisions and flat panel display monitors in the world. Their flat panel displays for TVs and computer monitors were rated the number one value independently by two large electronic chains in the United States. Samsung SDI and Samsung Electronics, both as world leading companies, have maintained a mutually supportive relationship. The two launched an amazing string of technologies and products that are setting them up to become a powerhouse multinational company in their own right.

Within six months of launching DFSS, SDI had a well-designed system of scorecards and tool application check lists to manage risk and cycle-time from the voice of the customer to the launch of products that meet customer and business process demands. The culture of SDI embraced this disciplined approach and they have realized tangible benefits in a very short period of time. SDI is literally putting DFSS developed products on store shelves today using product development methods they initiated just two years ago. One of them is OLED, which is recently emerging as a new type of display. As a result of a successful DFSS project, Samsung SDI became the first company in the world to produce the 15.1" XGA AMOLED display.

"*Victory or defeat in corporate competition hinges on how efficiently a company operates and how successfully it differentiates itself from its competitors. Samsung SDI has been devoted to Six Sigma with great results since its introduction back in 1996. We will double our efforts for Six Sigma and deliver zero-defect products and services in all business areas. This is, we believe, a sure way to attain our goal of customer satisfaction,*" said by Soontaek Kim Samsung, CEO, Samsung SDI, (January, 2002).

Transformation HSBC's US Futures Business with Six Sigma

In a business environment where many questioned the applicability of Six Sigma, the Quality team at HSBC transformed an under-performing unit in HSBC's Investment Banking unit with a single DMAIC project, using Six Sigma tools such as Process Mapping, Activity Based Costing and Data Partitioning. The result—a 274 per cent improvement in net income and a business 100 per cent focused on continuous improvement.

Situation analysis: A business undergoing massive change

The story starts with Karl Fruecht, Managing Director and Head of US Futures at HSBC Securities (USA) Inc. Karl was responsible for a business that generated over $30 million revenue in 2002, yet was only marginally profitable. The Futures business was a most unlikely candidate for a Six Sigma project given the trading floor culture and the shortage of success stories regarding Six Sigma at Investment Banks, however, Karl was not afraid to look at his business differently and wondered whether Six Sigma could be used to help the Futures business achieve its goals. The business was going through an unprecedented change. Most Futures markets around the world had already shut down their "open outcry" trading floors in favour of electronic trading platforms. However, the US Futures exchanges were resisting these changes. This presented the difficult problem of having to sustain two platforms—a support infrastructure to execute trades *via* the open outcry trading floors of the Chicago Mercantile Exchange and the Chicago Board of Trade; and the need to prepare to compete in a world dominated by electronic exchanges. Costs were rising to support two platforms as revenues per contract were falling due to the inevitable pricing pressure created by more efficient electronic trading systems.

For professionals in the US Futures industry, these were difficult times as many faced the reality that they may one day need to reinvent their careers when the proverbial "lights go out" at the Chicago exchange floors. The challenge Karl faced was considerable—how do you motivate and mobilize a team to fix problems when the future looks so bleak? Realizing that Six Sigma's team-based approach to problem-solving could help him fix some problems while improving morale, Karl called the Six Sigma Quality team for help.

Focus on improving the cost/income ratio

While the potential of the Six Sigma approach was apparent, the problem to be attacked was not. The HSBC Quality Team, led by Dan Stusnick, a certified Black-Belt, interviewed and surveyed staff in New York and Chicago to identify problems that could be the focal point of improvement projects. The surveying process identified numerous issues worth exploring, but none seemed to have the potential to dramatically impact bottom line performance. In a bold move, Karl decided to focus on a single project goal—to significantly improve the bottom line performance of the US Futures Business.

By chartering a project focused on a cost/income metric, Karl committed his business to a broad Quality Initiative with a mandate to look at all the factors contributing to bottom line performance. Karl opened the door to a full assessment of the business during the define, 'measure and analyze' phases of the project that would broadly explore opportunities to reduce costs while improving revenue.

During the early stages of the project, now titled "*The Futures Quality Initiative*", Dan Stusnick led the core team on an assessment of core processes using SIPOC and process mapping to understand the activities that went into servicing a customer and ultimately executing and clearing a Futures transaction. While mapping the core process helped identify non-value added activities, process mapping alone was not enough—the team needed to understand the cost drivers of the services, and how the services were consumed by customers in order to understand the nature of the profitability problem.

Improve phase

The 'analyze' phase has provided a list of issues that influenced capacity to varying degrees, not the least of which was the need to refocus Sales efforts on the right types of customers. Other problems that had a significant impact on net income were also identified, including:

- Market losses on trading errors (usually miscommunicated orders) amounted to $765,000 in 2002, or about 40 per cent of net income
- Past due accounts receivable were growing, and consuming a growing amount of back office time to resolve

- Research services, including a live "Squawk Box" narrative from the floor of the CBOT cost over $1 million, yet it was unclear if they were receiving adequate revenues from the customers who required the service
- Electronic order corrections: over $400,000 in effort wasted to correct orders each year
- Other issues were identified as productivity issues, such as the need to optimizing shift
- Coverage of the 24-hour desk and the need to reduce time spent on administrative activities.

Outcome

Ultimately, projects must show results, and the Futures Quality Initiative is no exception. When the project started, net income stood at $1.9 million, and had been more or less unchanged for several years. Furthermore, the business was in jeopardy due to the changing dynamics of the markets as electronic trading became a factor. As a result of the project:

- Net income climbed to an all time high of $3.1 million during 2003 as many of the improvements were being implemented.
- In 2004, Futures net income climbed $7.1 million, a 274% increase since the project began.
- Project results were achieved with a 10% reduction in headcount and in a declining commission environment.
- While not measured, the improvement in morale was noticeable. After the execution of the 'improve' phase projects, the transformation of the Futures business was apparent. The entire business had been mobilized to address problems that had a direct impact on net income, and each of the core team have gone an extra step for achieving Green Belt Certification.

The Futures Quality Initiative was innovative for several reasons:

- With the help of a committed Champion, it proved that the Six Sigma tool kit is relevant in an Investment Banking and Capital Markets Trading environment.
- It showed how DMAIC could be applied broadly as a business assessment tool and a vehicle to implement rapid changes that directly impact bottom line income.
- It showed how ABC analysis can help a business focus efforts on developing the right customers. Where capacity is limited, it must be channelled to the right types of customers—not all business was good business.
- It involved everyone in efforts to optimize capacity and significantly improved morale.

Six Sigma as a powerful business strategy has been well recognised as an imperative for achieving and sustaining operational and service excellence. While the original focus of Six Sigma was on manufacturing, today it has been widely accepted in both service and transactional processes. Although the total package may change as a part of the evolutionary process, the core principles of Six Sigma will continue to grow in the future. Six Sigma has made a huge impact on industry and yet the academic community lags behind in its understanding of this powerful strategy. Six Sigma is a company-wide management strategy for the improvement of process performance with the objective of improving quality and productivity to satisfy customer demands and reduce costs. It is regarded as a new paradigm of management innovation for company survival in the 21st century.

SUMMARY

1. Six Sigma concept was initially referred as Toyota Production System.
2. Six Sigma refers to the overall strategy to improve growth and productivity as well as a quality measure.
3. Six Sigma is important for business operations because it can be used to increase top line growth and also to reduce bottom line costs.
4. It refers to 3.4 Defectives Per Million Opportunities (DPMO) if the output is normally distributed.
5. The most important methodology in Six Sigma management is perhaps the formalized improvement methodology characterized by DMAIC (define-measure-analyze-improve control) process.
6. The five major steps are DMADV (Define; Measure; Analyze; Design and Verify)
7. The Seven Quality Control tools (7QC tools) are graphical and statistical tools which are often used in QC for continuous improvement. They are—Cause-and-effect diagram, Check sheet, Control chart, Histogram, Pareto chart, Scatter diagram and Stratification.

REVIEW QUESTIONS

1. Explain the concept of Six Sigma.
2. Explain major steps of DMADV process.
3. Distinguish between DMAIC and DMADV process.
4. Explain Quality Control Tools.

CASE STUDY

Wipro Technologies: Thrust on Quality

Wipro Limited was established in 1945 and commenced its operations in 1946 as a vegetable oil company. In the early 1980s, Wipro diversified into the Information Technology sector with Liberalization hitting India in the 1980s. This has been a fascinating transformation from a vegetable oil company into a global IT services giant. Today, Wipro Technologies has become a world service provider, delivering technology-driven business solutions that meet the strategic objectives of clients. Wipro has 40 plus 'Centres of Excellence' that create solutions related to specific needs of industries. Wipro can boast of delivering unmatched business value to customers through a combination of process excellence quality frameworks and service delivery innovation.

A strong emphasis upon building a professional work environment, leaders from within, and having a global outlook for business and growth, have led to innovation of people processes on a continued basis. Over the years, Wipro has significantly strengthened its competency-based people processes and demonstrated innovative practices in talent acquisition, deployment, and development, based on strategic needs. A leading provider of communication networks in the US required improvement in the product performance of a telecom application using Six Sigma methodologies.

Integrating Six Sigma concepts was also intended to bring rigor in effective upstream processes of the software development life cycle. Implementation of Six Sigma methodologies brought in quantitative understanding, cost savings, and performance improvement towards product quality. Some of the key challenges involved were:

- Reduce the data transfer time
- Reduce the risk
- Avoid interruption due to LAN/WAN downtime
- Parallel availability of the switch for other administrative tasks during the same period.

Evolution of Six Sigma

Wipro is the first Indian company to adopt Six Sigma. Today, Wipro has one of the most mature Six Sigma programmes in the industry ensuring that 91 per cent of the projects are completed on schedule, much above the industry average of 55 per cent. As the pioneer of Six Sigma in India, Wipro has already put around ten years into process improvement through Six Sigma. Along the way, it has scaled Six Sigma ladder, while helping to roll out over 1000 projects. The Six Sigma programme spreads right across verticals and impacts multiple areas such as project management, market development and resource utilization.

Six Sigma at Wipro simply means a measure of quality that strives for near perfection. It is an umbrella initiative, covering all business units and divisions so that it could transform itself in a world class organization. At Wipro, it means to:

- Have products and services meet global benchmarks
- Ensure robust processes within the organization
- Consistently meet and exceed customer expectations
- Make quality a culture within.

Implementation of Six Sigma

Wipro has adopted the project approach for Six Sigma, where projects are identified on the basis of the problem areas under each of the critical Business Processes that adversely impacts the business significantly.

Wipro has evolved following Six Sigma methodologies:

For Developing New Processes

- *DSSS (Developing Six Sigma Software) + Methodology:* Wipro employs DSSS methodology for software development. The methodology uses rigorous in-process metrics and cause analysis throughout the software development life cycle for defect-free deliveries and lower customer cost of application development.
- *DSSP (Designing Six Sigma Process and Product) Methodology:* Used for designing new processes and products.
- *DCSM (Design for Customer Satisfaction and Manufacturability) Methodology:* Used for designing for customer satisfaction and manufacturability.

For Improving Existing Processes

- *TQSS (Transactional Quality using Six Sigma) Methodology:* Used for defect reduction in transactional processes.
- *DMAIC Methodology:* Used for process improvement in non-transactional processes.

For Reengineering

- *CFPM (Cross Functional Process Mapping) Methodology:* Used for cross functional process mapping.

The financial gain that Wipro has achieved by using Six Sigma has been one of the high points. As the Six Sigma initiative started maturing, Wipro identified two major phenomenons—the biggest projects had all been completed, and the Yellow-belt culture had cured little problems before they became big ones.

At this point, the project-oriented Six Sigma culture began to give way to the sustaining culture. The Six Sigma process resulted in an achievement of close to 250 per cent, Six minutes for 1 MB transfer and 18 minutes for average data transfer. The set target was 200 per cent.

Since quality is customer-driven, the objective of Six Sigma Implementation at Wipro has continuously been on integrating and implementing approaches through a simultaneous focus on defect reduction, timeliness, and productivity. This has translated to lower maintenance costs, schedule-overrun costs, and development costs for customers. Measurements and progress indicators have been oriented towards what the customer finds important and what the customer pays for. Towards this, Six Sigma concepts have played an important role in:

- Improving performance through a precise quantitative understanding of the customer's requirements, thereby bringing in customer focus
- Improving the effectiveness in upstream processes of the software development life cycle by defect reduction (software defects reduced by 50 per cent) and cycle time reduction (rework in software down from 12 per cent per cent to 5 per cent)
- Waste elimination and increase productivity upto 35 per cent
- Cost of failure avoidance (installation failures down from 4.5 per cent to 1 per cent in hardware business)
- Tangible cost savings due to lower application development cost for customer.

Analysts remarked that Six Sigma was an indisputable success at Wipro, whether in terms of customer satisfaction, improvement in internal performance, or in the improvement of share-owner value. The results of achieving Six Sigma are rapid and overwhelming at Wipro. Its unique methodology provides Six Sigma knowledge and skills to the client, enabling the client to create ownership, generate results and sustain success.

Questions for Discussion

1. Explain WIPRO's initiation in implementing Six Sigma.
2. What are the changes it has to make?
3. Explain the role of Quality Manager in implementing Six Sigma.

FURTHER READING

DMADV: An Approach for Developing New Initiatives, *Innovation Insights* #20, The Pennsylvania State University, USA, 2008.

Garrison and Noreen, *Managerial Accounting and the Business Environment*, 11th ed., The McGraw-Hill Companies, Inc., USA, 2010.

Satya S. Chakravorty, Six Sigma Implementation, *International Journal of Production Economics*, Vol. 119(1), pp. 1–16, 2009.

Sowdamini, T., *Six Sigma Practices: A Study of LG Polymers*, unpublished PhD Thesis, Andhra University, Visakhapatnam, 2014.

www.designsixsigma.com.

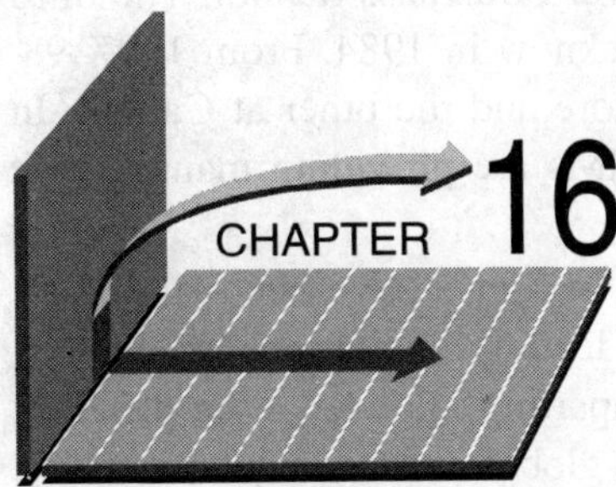

Management Education

CONTENTS

INTRODUCTION

Management education has become part of the learning process of all human beings. For a peaceful, prosperous, happy and healthy career, one has to understand the philosophy and principles of management. Several management institutions, professional associations in India, global B-school formula and agenda for future B-schools have been imparting knowledge on management education.

This chapter focuses on brief profiles of management institutions, information for study abroad, and the role of professional organizations in India for the cause of management development.

MANAGEMENT EDUCATION

Management education in India is a post-Independence development. The first management school was started at Andhra University, over five decades ago, in 1957. Later, management education spread to other universities. The Government of India established two Indian Institutes of Management, at Calcutta and at Ahmedabad, in 1961. The IIM Calcutta was started with technical assistance from the Sloan School of Management of the Massachusetts Institute of Technology, and IIM Ahmedabad with the collaboration of Harvard Business School. The third IIM was established in 1972 at Bangalore, and the fourth at Lucknow in 1984. From 1997–98, the Government of India has started two more IIMs, one at Indore and the other at Calicut. In 2008 one more IIM was established at Shillong. Thus, seven IIMs are providing management education alongwith several universities and other institutions.

In addition, several national and international management institutes have been started by industrialists, philanthropists and national leaders. Some of the leading institutions are located at the metropolitan centres, cities and other towns which are imparting knowledge on different disciplines of management. Some institutes are focussing on global management, some on functional areas, some on rural management, construction management, etc. Almost all the universities are also offering both degree and diploma courses. In India, universities offer only MBA courses, and the institutes issue Post-Graduate Diploma in Management (PGDM) certificates, which are considered to be equivalent to MBA Degrees. At present, over 1200 management institutes and universities are offering management programmes in India.

There is a shortage of 20,000 MBAs in the country in the wake of globalization, strategic alliances, resourcing, re-engineering, benchmarking, downsizing and growth of competition in the world market. Presently, the IIMs and other recognized Management Institutions (MIs) can provide 3,000 MBAs to industry. Hence, there is a requirement for training graduates through management education, and also in practical handling to prepare them to meet global challenges by inculcating leadership qualities and long-term perspectives for network management in a broad socio-economic context. India already has about 500 MIs recognized by the All India Council of Technical Education (AICTE), besides the commerce and business management departments of Indian universities.

Where then is the need for encouraging MBAs from foreign universities (through Distance Learning Programmes) like the Association of Professional Engineers, Scientists and Managers, Australia (APESMA); Wigan and Leigh College UK; Deakin University of Australia; American College of London; Monetary Institute of International Studies, Monterrey; Hottem Street London (HSL); Templeton, Oxford University; Solvay Business School, Belgium; Warwick Business School, England; Schiller International University, London; Newport University, California; Amsterdam Institute of Finance, the Netherlands; Pacific Western University, Honolulu; University of Canterbury, New Zealand and so on? AICTE also intends to check the credibility and authenticity of some foreign MIs/universities coming to India. "Any Institute which enters India should sign a memorandum of understanding (MoU) with AICTE of the Government of India", emphasizes Prof. Rame Gowda, Chairman of AICTE.

In India, there is a sea change in management education during the last five decades. In 1958, there were only nine B-schools in India. Gradually, the number of B-schools has been increased to 58 in 1978, 87 in 1988, 697 in 1998, and 1149 in 2007. The growth was from five per cent in 1968 to 452 per cent by 2007 (Table 16.1).

Table 16.1 Growth of management education in India

Year	*Number of business schools*	*Growth percentage*
1958	09	–
1968	14	05
1978	58	44
1988	87	29
1998	697	610
2007*	1149	452

*as on 31-08-2007

Source: AICTE: Hand Book, 2007–08.

When we observe the B-schools in various regions of India—the central region, eastern region, northern region, north-west region, southern region, south-west region and western region—there was tremendous increase in the number of students pursuing management education (Table 16.2).

Table 16.2 State-wise positions of management institutions in India as on 31-08-2007

Region	*State/UT*	*No. of B-schools*	*Intake*	*Average intake per institute*
Central	Madhya Pradesh	56 (4.87%)	6275 (5.15%)	112
	Chhattisgarh	05 (0.43%)	490 (0.40%)	98
	Gujarat	33 (2.87%)	3503 (2.87%)	106
Eastern	Mizoram	–	–	–
	Sikkim	–	–	
	Orissa	44 (3.43%)	3928 (3.22%)	89
	West Bengal	27 (2.34%)	2565 (2.10%)	95
	Tripura	01 (0.09%)	60 (0.05%)	60
	Meghalaya	–	–	–
	Arunachal Pradesh	–	–	–
	Andaman & Nicobar Islands	–	–	–
	Assam	06 (0.52%)	352 (0.29%)	59
	Manipur	01 (0.09%)	30 (0.02%)	30
	Nagaland	01 (0.09%)	60 (0.05%)	60
	Jharkhand	07 (0.53%)	975 (0.80%)	139
Northern	Bihar	10 (0.87%)	1050 (0.86%)	105
	Uttar Pradesh	135 (11.75%)	174445 (14.31%)	55
	Uttarakhand	16 (1.39%)	1320 (1.08%)	83
North-West	Chandigarh	–	–	–
	Haryana	36 (3.13%)	4445 (3.65%)	123
	Jammu & Kashmir	09 (0.78%)	560 (0.46%	62

Region	State/UT	No. of B-schools	Intake	Average intake per institute
	New Delhi	33 (2.87%)	5180 (4.25%)	157
	Punjab	36 (3.13%)	4000 (3.28%)	111
	Rajasthan	52 (4.52%)	5775 (4.74%)	111
	Himachal Pradesh	05 (0.53%)	300 (0.25%)	60
Southern	Andhra Pradesh	195 (16.97%)	21660 (17.75%)	111
	Pondicherry	01 (0.09%)	60 (0.05%)	60
	Tamil Nadu	142 (12.35%)	11285 (9.26%)	79
South-West	Karanataka	104 (9.05%)	8315 (6.82%)	79
	Kerala	37 (3.22%)	2545 (2.09%)	69
Western	Maharashtra	155 (13.49%)	19449 (15.96%)	125
	Goa	02 (0.17%)	240 (0.20%)	120
	Daman & Diu	–	–	–
All India		**1149 (100%)**	**121867 (100%)**	**106**

Source: AICTE: Hand Book, 2007–08.

The number of B-schools in various regions was: 94 in central region (Madhya Pradesh, Chhattisgarh, Gujarat); 67 in eastern region (Mizoram, Sikkim, Orissa, West Bengal, Tripura, Meghalaya, Arunachal Pradesh, A&N Islands, Assam, Manipur, Nagaland, Jharkhand); 161 in northern region (Bihar, Uttar Pradesh, Uttarakhand); 171 in north-west region (Chandigarh, Haryana, Jammu & Kashmir, New Delhi, Punjab, Rajasthan, Himachal Pradesh); 338 in southern region (Andhra Pradesh, Pondicherry, Tamil Nadu); 141 in south-west region (Karnakata, Kerala); 157 in western region (Maharashtra, Goa, Daman & Diu). In all 1149 B-schools, the intake was 1,21,867 students in 2007 with an average intake of 106 in each B-school.

By 2008, there are about 1200 B-schools in India offering management programmes. Management education has become an important factor for the career development of an employee in the global organizations. Millions of employees are showing their interest to pursue management education.

The Government of India and different states have been encouraging and establishing many B-schools. The B-schools have grown in terms of quantity and quality. There are certain factors to be considered for meeting the challenges of business. Some B-schools in India have been globally accredited and considered to be world class. Some are on the way to become world class, and some others are in the initial stage.

The challenges of Indian B-schools are the following:

- Focus from national to global
- International accreditation
- AICTE approval
- NAAC rated
- NBA rated
- ISO 9001: 2000 certification

- Internationally accredited curriculum and teaching
- Global alliances
- World class environment.

One of the studies reveals that top ten best B-schools in 2006 were:

- IIM—Ahmedabad
- IIM—Bangalore
- IIM—Calcutta
- ISB—Hyderabad
- XLRI—Jamshedpur
- IIM—Lucknow
- MDI—Gurgoan
- SP Jain—Mumbai
- ICFAI—Hyderabad
- IMT—Ghaziabad.

Information for Studying Abroad

Many Indian students wish to study for a management degree or diploma or Ph.D. abroad, preferably in the USA, UK or Australia. But they do not get proper information to apply for admission. Students are advised to go through the section giving information on GMAT. Colleges and universities in the United States receive thousands of applications every year for admission from students abroad. A large number of these applicants are from India. The selection process for the admission is long and difficult.

An applicant for admission to a graduate school offering Masters and Ph.D. degree programmes should have successfully completed 16 years of education in India. This requirement is met by a student who has successfully completed 12 years of high school and four years of college. American admission officers argue that irrespective of what an Indian university may label its degrees, the one granted after 16 years of successful education should be counted as equivalent to an American B.A. So it is advised that students complete four years of college after the higher secondary certificate.

The degree of the applicant who requires admission is then evaluated on the basis of his academic record at school and college. The record should be excellent, not just above average. They consider the score of GMAT. There are several reasons for the advice that only the excellent student should try to go abroad for his/her advanced degree. But several students attempt to study abroad and successfully complete their studies and get good placements.

PROFESSIONAL ASSOCIATIONS

There are several professional associations actively associated with management education and development in India. Any management association is a group of persons joined together for furthering a few common objectives decided on the mutual understanding of these individuals. It helps the members to have an identity; an opportunity to interact with each other; learn from the experience of other organizations; an opportunity to explore contemporary issues; an opportunity to get better jobs; an opportunity to develop more competence and strengthen the profession.

The associations have regular meetings, conferences, workshops, seminars and training programmes on different areas of management. Usually, they conduct annual conferences in which several members attend from all over India and abroad and discuss the changes in and challenges to the profession. It helps the members to share their experience. Sometimes, they also hold exhibitions on their activities. They conduct training programmes, both in-house and outside the organization. All the functional areas of management have different professional associations with varied objectives and mission.

These professional organizations are striving hard to spread management philosophy all over India and in other countries. The aims, objectives and activities of these professional associations in India are discussed briefly here:

- All India Management Association (AIMA)
- Association of Indian Management Schools (AIMS)
- National Institute of Personnel Management (NIPM)
- Indian Society for Training and Development (ISTD)
- National HRD Network (NHRD Network)
- Indian Institute of Materials Management (IIMM)
- International Industrial Relations Association (IIRA)
- Indian Society for Applied Behavioural Science (ISABS)
- Federation of Indian Chambers of Commerce & Industry (FICCI).

AIMA

In 1957, the All India Management Association was created as an apex body with active support from the government. AIMA was intended as a cause group—a body to pool management thought in the country, a forum to develop a national managerial ethos, an organization to facilitate furtherance of the profession and its contribution to society. Today, after more than three decades, AIMA is recognized for its national stature, upheld by a broad base of 53 local management associations, over 12,000 professionals as individual members, and over 400 corporate organizations as institutional members.

AIMA is represented on a number of committees of the Government of India, the IIMs and professional bodies, besides being an active member of AAMO (the Asian Association of Management Organizations), which is the regional body of the World Management Council. The Association maintains close links with a number of overseas professional bodies like the American Management Association, British Institute of Management and others.

AIMA also conducts a national competition for management students, national management games, the National Competition for Young Managers, the National Management Convention and other national events in the field of management. The membership of AIMA is open to institutions, corporate bodies and individuals who have distinguished themselves in the propagation of professional management. Individuals are conferred designatory qualifications and experience.

The Centre for Management Education is a new venture of AIMA to give focus to management education activities and to become a national centre for competency testing for managerial professionals. Pioneers in distance education, it conducts the Post-Graduate Diploma in Management which was started in 1976 and is now conducted nationally and in 12 other countries. Currently, more than 5,000 working managers are enrolled in the various distance/open learning programmes of AIMA-CME in India and 12 neighbouring countries. The Centre has a wide reach in conducting examinations for its courses in over 50 cities in India and 20 overseas locations.

CME has embarked on a major programme called Management Education through Technological Advancement (META), which envisages using multimedia computer and TV-based technologies to create world class management education programmes. In view of changing needs, the curriculum is upgraded. The "FOCUS 2000" curriculum is modern, both in content and pedagogy. The telescopic course pack is designed to boost the revamped programme and contains, besides books and study guides, case books, video and audio cassettes and computer software (wherever applicable).

The distance/open learning programmes were founded in the realization that the flexibility of distance/open learning would be particularly suitable for busy managers, for whom full-time study or even the regular commitment of a part-time course was not practical. The continuous growth and attraction for managers for this mode of learning is based on the following precepts practised by AIMA-CME.

The flexibility and openness of the system allows self-paced learning without taking a break from work. The telescopic multimedia course pack is a specially designed course with texts, readings, study guides, audiotapes, videotapes and computer software. Therefore, a busy executive can optimize time by choosing a medium appropriate at a particular time in his or her schedule. The teaching philosophy, which coerces managers to make constant links between the course and their work experience, leads to improved job performance and a more lasting learning experience.

AIMS

The Association of Indian Management Schools (AIMS) was established as the professional body of Indian Management Schools in Bangalore on 27 August 1988. The formation of this association meets a long-felt need in the field of management education.

Mission: To function as a professional association of management education concerned with the quality of management, manpower training and development, management research, curriculum development and take all such steps on its own or in collaboration with other agencies for the promotion of management education in India.

Major activities: In pursuit of the above mission, the association had embarked on a number of projects and activities. Some of the key ones are:

- annual management education conventions, which bring together management schools, its silent system and HRD specialists;
- developed a set of criteria for the recognition of management schools and submitted the same to AICTE and the Ministry of HRD;
- based on extensive consultations, developed a Standard Management Education curriculum for the benefit of Indian management schools;

- organized a national Colloquium on Management Education in May 1989 to look at the kind of likely developments in the country and outside, and map new directions for management education;
- organized a number of case workshops for the benefit of management teachers; and
- established professional links with a number of regional and international Management Schools Network.

Membership: More than 90 management schools in the country are members of the Association. More are in the process of becoming members. Today, AIMS is the second-largest management schools network in the world. Institutional membership is available to all management educational institutions in India imparting long-duration management education programmes of quality.

The Canadian collaboration: To pursue its goal of contributing to quality upgradation of the Indian management education system and to further open it up to the development in the West, a collaborative project was developed with the Canadian Consortium of Management Schools (CCMS) with funding from CIDA. The project's central focus is to enhance the quality of degree-level management education, networking of these institutions, exchanging experience with other national and regional bodies, and effective interaction and collaboration with the collectivity of Canadian management schools through CCMS. This Canadian $500,000 project has the approval of the Government of India and is now operational.

NIPM

The National Institute of Personnel Management is the premier all-India institute of professionals engaged in personnel management, industrial relations, labour welfare and human resource development. The mission of the association is concern for human excellence.

NIPM is a professional, non-profit society registered under the Societies Registration Act, 1960. It has a nation-wide membership of over 7,500 individual members and over 250 institutional members spread over 41 branches.

NIPM was established in 1980, with the amalgamation of the erstwhile IIPM (founded in 1948 at Calcutta) and NILM (established in 1950 at Bombay). Its national office is located at Calcutta, with branches in most capital cities and major industrial towns in the country. New branches are added every year, depending upon the congregation of members in major industrial locations.

Objectives: NIPM firmly believes in the dignity of human beings at work and their relationship within the enterprises. Keeping this in mind, NIPM is striving to:

- spread the message of professional management in human resource management and development;
- promote an awareness of professional personnel management at all levels in different organizations;
- organize activities and programmes at both the national and branch levels with a view to upgrade the skills and professional standards of its members.

The main objectives of the institute, as enshrined in its constitution, are to:

- spread the knowledge on the approaches, principles, practices, techniques and methods regarding personnel management, industrial relations, labour and social welfare and industrial jurisprudence in all their bearings;
- serve as a forum for exchange of ideas and experiences and collection and dissemination of information on management in general and personnel management, industrial relations, human resource development and labour and social welfare, in particular;
- sponsor, promote, encourage, conduct and contribute to study and research and to impart instruction in any subject touching any or all aspects of personnel management, industrial relations, labour and social welfare, industrial legislation and industrial jurisprudence, including their social, sociological, political and economic background and context;
- promote and safeguard the status and the interests of personnel management, industrial relations and labour welfare work and the interest of those engaged therein; and
- represent the institute and its interests before local, state and central authorities and other organizations, commissions, boards, enquiry bodies, etc. in India and abroad.

Administration: NIPM's policies and programmes are charted out by the Central Executive Council, which conducts all the affairs of the Institute. It is headed by a president and supported by a vice-president and five regional vice-presidents, besides other office bearers and members, elected nationally once in two years. The branches are governed by branch executive committees headed by a chairman and supported by two vice-chairmen and other office bearers and committee members, elected once in two years. The National Office Secretariat is managed by a full-time executive director with adequate support staff at Calcutta.

Membership: The membership of NIPM is open to individuals who are professionally qualified in the field of personnel management and are actively engaged in the practice of personnel management for a number of years. Corporate enterprises are also admitted as members. All membership should be proposed and seconded by corporate members. The different categories of membership are: corporate; associate; student; life; and institutional. Educational institutions and government labour departments are given concessional subscription rates. The fee structure for all categories except for the institutional category is fixed by the AGM periodically. The CEC decides the institutional membership fee.

Conferences: NIPM organizes a national conference every year in different locations in the country, besides several symposia and seminars. Over 600 delegates attend these conferences, which serve as a vital forum for exchange of experience, understanding new trends and establishing and renewing professional contacts. The conferences dwell at length on a topical theme, chosen after detailed discussion and analysis.

Seminars and training programmes: NIPM has been in the forefront of conducting many national seminars and training programmes, attracting the attention of several top executives and trade union leaders, as well as non-personnel executives, besides personnel professionals themselves.

Research: NIPM gives priority to research in the human resources management area; research projects are undertaken periodically, on topical themes. Mention should be made of Pre-Employment Background of Successful Personnel Officers', which was financed by the Planning Commission.

Code of ethics: The institute has adopted a code of ethics for its members from March 1983. Every new member gets a copy of the code, to which wide publicity is given through journals and branch newsletters.

Publications: The institute publishes a quarterly journal, *Personnel Today*. It serves as a medium of communication for the latest events, new trends and live case studies for its members.

Books and monographs: NIPM has published several books, some of which are:

- *Personnel Management in India*
- *Readings in Personnel Management*
- *HRM Response to New Corporate Initiatives.*

These books are prescribed as textbooks by many universities and management institutions. NIPM has also published over 20 monographs and research papers. In addition, several branches have also brought out many monographs, besides their own regular newsletters as well as other local publications.

NIPM news: The institute brings out a bi-monthly newsletter: *NIPM News*, covering various activities of the national office as well as the branches, and apprising the members of the latest national and international news in the personnel field. It also publishes *Personnel Update*, providing members with the latest national/international developments, on a chosen subject connected with human resources management.

Fellowship: NIPM confers fellowship on senior professional members who make outstanding contributions in the field of human resources management and to the cause of the institute.

Representation: NIPM is represented in several government bodies, such as the Bureau of Public Enterprises, Tripartite Industrial Relations Committee, Central Board for Workers' Education, etc.

PG diploma: In order to suitably equip the future entrants to the profession, NIPM conducts a Post-Graduate Diploma Examination in Personnel Management. Its curriculum was evolved by the institute at a national seminar at Mumbai in 1971. First started in 1978, the examination is held twice a year—in June and December, at over 20 centres in the country. The diploma is recognized by the Government of India and several state governments, including Andhra Pradesh, Goa, Karnataka, Kerala, Bihar, Rajasthan and West Bengal. Several cash awards, medals and other citations for meritorious scholars are awarded by different industrial charitable and other organizations.

The institute also awards silver medals to the students of other institutions offering post-graduate courses in personnel management who secure the highest marks in the personnel management or industrial relations papers in their final examination. The NIPM-PGDPM is managed and administered by a separate NIPM-DPM Trust.

NIPM is a member of the International Industrial Relations Association, Geneva (IIRA) and the Asia-Pacific Federation for Personnel Management (APFPM), which in turn is affiliated to the World Federation of Personnel Management Associations (WFPMA). NIPM also regularly interacts with IPM, UK and the Society for Human Resources Management, USA. NIPM maintains close contact with the International Labour Organization, Geneva, and its area office at New Delhi.

ISTD

The Indian Society for Training and Development (ISTD), a premier institution in the field of Human Resources Development (HRD) in the country, was established in 1970 as a non-profit society aimed at spearheading the HRD movement in India. Since then, ISTD has been endeavouring to professionalize and continuously upgrade the training and development function in India, with its headquarters at New Delhi.

The society is affiliated to the International Federation of Training and Development Organizations (IFTDO) and is a founder member of Asian Regional Training and Development Organizations (ARTDO).

Managed by a national council with a president at the apex level, ISTD operates through various chapters. At the moment, 34 chapters are operating in the country. The society, with its all-India network, has more than 3,000 professionals from the government, industry, education, science and technology sectors as its members.

Objectives: ISTD seeks to bring together individuals and institutions from the above sectors to evolve and develop HRD practices in India. Apart from upgrading the professional skills of its members, ISTD also aims at:

- promoting continuing education in training;
- designing and organizing need-based training programmes;
- helping to establish professional institutions, libraries and laboratories in HRD;
- Publishing training literature; and
- Research in and Development of HRD activity.

Activities: ISTD organizes a national convention every year, attended by delegates from India and abroad, to discuss future perspectives for HRD. This gives members a national platform to update their professional knowledge and also share views with decision makers.

In addition, both at the national and chapter levels, a large number of seminars, workshops, lectures and symposia are organized every month. This provides an opportunity for the HRD practitioner to build a professional profile at the national as well as international level. Every convention of the society provides a welcome opportunity to gather in pursuit of the professional and institutional objectives.

National HRD Network

National HRD Network is an association of professionals committed to promoting the HRD movement in the country. It is a non-profit organization registered under the Society's Act, 1860 and the Bombay Public Trust Act, 1950. It is dedicated to developing human resources through education, training, research and experience sharing. The Centre for HRD XLRI has played a significant role in the HRD movement in India and the growth of National HRD Network. IIM Ahmedabad has provided institutional building support.

The philosophy of the network is that every human being has the potential to do remarkable things. The National HRD Network functions through local networks at the regional and area levels through its executive board and its office at Ahmedabad at apex level.

Vision: A network to perpetuate, sustain intellectual brilliance, build human potential and stimulate organizations to create, contribute and perform at a national and international standard, to make the human being a primary resource in developing any production capability or changing anything with anticipation and creating the future.

Mission: It endeavours to build a strong foundation of theory, research and practice in the area of human resources management for application in business, academic, government, consulting, social and service organizations, all towards the realization of the human potential. The mission is to promote HRD movement in the country through making organizations, institutions and all other human activity healthy, collaborative and worthwhile, and strive to make the human potential understood, recognized and directed to do remarkable things.

Purpose: To make human beings discover their inner potential, acquire capabilities, empower themselves and others towards delivering the highest quality of results through collaboration, simultaneously contributing to the health and well-being of their togetherness.

The key tasks performed by HRD Network are to:

- communicate HRD ethos through various training forums;
- update client organizations on the state-of-the-art developments in the field of human resources management;
- desist from parochializing human resources development for HRD professionals only, and to involve line managers actively;
- act as a consultative body enabling and developing practical solutions for real-life organizational problems and giving them a strategic direction;
- act as a network for the diffusion of ideas and sharing of mutual experience, such that any advancements in the field of related fields, both at home and abroad, percolates down to all levels of organizations; and
- give impetus to the rapidly growing number of professionals in the field through scholarships, research grants and other non-financial incentives.

Under the aegis and technical guidance of the network, the vast physical and intangible resources or organizations will be synergistically coupled with the knowledge resource of the academicians—thus giving a tremendous boost to theoretical research and practical applications in the field of human resources management.

IIMM

The Indian Institute of Materials Management is the only all-India body of professionals dealing with materials management and logistics. The members are drawn from public and private sectors as well as government bodies including railways and defence. It is a charter member of the International Federation of Purchasing and Materials Management (IFPMM), which represents 40 countries from all the six continents, and has a membership of over 100,000.

One of the important objectives of the institute is to elevate the professional status and expertise of its members. It has been conducting post-graduate and graduate diploma courses which are approved by the Government of India. The institute, on behalf of the National Association of Purchasing Management (NAPM), USA, organizes the prestigious International Purchasing Managers (IPM) in India.

The institute, through its membership and regional branches all over the country, represents a wide spectrum of professionals engaged in various facets of materials management and responsible for the planning, acquisition, control and distribution of materials and services. Presently, the need to introduce and implement modern tools and techniques of materials management is beginning to be widely recognized in public, private, joint and cooperative sectors.

The following are the objectives of IIMM:

- To secure a wider recognition and promote the importance of efficient materials management in commercial and industrial undertakings.
- To safeguard and elevate the professional status of individuals engaged in the materials management faculty.
- To constantly impart advanced professional knowledge and thus improve the skill of the person engaged in materials management functions.
- To propagate and promote among the members the strict IIMM Code of Conduct and Ethics.

Activities: Today, IIMM has 32 branches and 19 chapters all over India with a membership of over 6,000 individual and institutional members, drawn from the public, private, joint and cooperative sector industries.

The graduate diploma course has been formally recognized by the Ministry of HRD, Government of India in 1981 for the purposes of appointment to superior posts in the government and in government undertakings. The PG diploma is approved by the All India Council for Technical Education (AICTE), New Delhi. The above courses are controlled at the national level by a board of studies consisting of directors (personalities from the academic and professional fields). The faculty is drawn from experts in industry and educational/professional institutions, from all over the country. The director general of IFPMM, in a recent communication to the BOS chairman, informed the good news of accreditation of the GDMM course by the international body of IFPMM.

The institute distributes to members, free of cost, *The Materials Manager,* a bi-monthly publication covering various aspects of materials management, its modern trends and research activities. Most of the branches have their own newsletters to serve as a medium of communication between the organization and its members.

IIRA

The International Industrial Relations Association was established in response to a growing need to develop and exchange knowledge on industrial relations at the international level, providing the academic and the practitioner with a forum for discussion and research.

The aims of the IIRA are of a purely scientific character, without regard to political or philosophical considerations. The association does not endorse opinions on policy questions. IIRA promotes the study of industrial relations throughout the world in several relevant academic disciplines, by such means as:

- encouraging the establishment and development of national associations of industrial relations specialists;

- facilitating the spread of information development of national associations of industrial relations specialists;
- organizing worldwide and other congresses and publishing their proceedings; and
- promoting internationally planned research, by such means as organizing study groups on particular topics.

The IIRA has 33 national industrial relations associations and 44 institutional associate members in 21 countries. It has some 1,500 individual associate members in nearly 90 countries and territories. Major IIRA activities include the IIRA world congress, regional conferences, study groups and publications. Indian Industrial Relations Association (IIRA) is an active professional body in India and conducting several programmes to meet the requirements of the field.

IIRA seeks to promote the study of industrial relations throughout India in several relevant academic disciplines through research, conferences, publications, etc. Its membership is open to individuals, trade unions/employer organizations or other bodies concerned with industrial relations, students, teachers and others associated with universities, colleges and other academic institutions interested in human resources/industrial relations. Registered under the Indian Societies Registration Act, the association is affiliated as a full member and as the national chapter of the International Industrial Relations Association. The headquarters of the IIRA is the International Management Institute, New Delhi.

ISABS

The Indian Society for Applied Behavioural Science (ISABS) is a national, non-profit, voluntary, professional organization funded by a group of behavioural scientists engaged in applying their knowledge and skills for the well-being of persons and organizations. Its members work as independent consultants, trainers, counsellors, academicians, training managers, personnel and human resource development managers in industrial and non-industrial organizations, and as community change agents.

ISABS was registered in January 1972 as a professional body under the Societies Registration Act of 1860. Over the past 24 years, ISABS membership has grown considerably. Most of its growth has been brought about through its professional development and internship programmes.

ISABS programmes/labs focus on human processes and aim at helping people to unblock themselves and discover creative ways of relating and working. The programmes/labs are designed with a view to:

- enabling participants to gain insights into their own behaviour and its impact on others,
- providing the participants an opportunity to identify and work on issues critical to their own growth and effectiveness,
- enabling them to channelize their energies in meaningful directions, and
- developing professionals capable of facilitating experience-based learning.

ISABS utilizes experience-based learning (L-Group/T-Group/sensitivity training groups/encounter groups and such self-analytical groups) processes as its main training method.

Experiencing, reflecting, hypothesizing/conceptualizing and experimenting are the chief ingredients of the process of learning in a laboratory setting.

FICCI (Federation of Indian Chambers of Commerce and Industry)

FICCI is an employers' association with its headquarters at New Delhi. It has been serving in several areas of commerce and management to promote trade, commerce and industry in India.

The management and HRD committee of FICCI plays a catalytic role in initiating and supporting activities aimed at improving and updating managerial skills through appropriate human resource development programmes. A brainstorming session was organized to identify priority areas and strategies with respect to entrepreneurial and executive development programmes to be pursued by FICCI under the auspices of the management and HRD committee. Adequate attention was also focused on creating and reinforcing interfaces between industry and management development agencies in the country.

The following activities are undertaken by the committee.

1. Training programmes.
2. Special lectures by prominent experts from within and outside the country.
3. Institution of awards for outstanding persons in different fields of business management.
4. Publication of books, brochures: *Business Alert*, *Quality Quest*, etc.
5. Brainstorming sessions/meetings among members of the M&HRD committee and invitees.
6. Conducting workshops/seminars on management aspects.

GLOBAL B-SCHOOL FORMULA

The B-schools are to be globalized. Global B-school Formula contains the following parameters:

- Accreditation by any leading global player (AACSB, EQUIS, AMBA)
- GMAT for admissions
- Experience for 2–6 years
- Strong executive MBA based MBA/PGDBA
- Board of Governors from industry/academics
- Large student capacity
- Faculty–student ratio 1:5
- Faculty with strong industry experience
- Faculty representation on corporate boards
- Consultancy and training experience
- Strong book publishing record
- Publications in global journals
- Research record
- Case research and publishing record

- Strong student and faculty exchange programmes
- Case teaching record
- Strong pedagogy
- Updated curriculum matching with industry needs
- Placements with good companies
- A world class infrastructure
- 100 per cent hostel accommodation
- A strong digital library with global databases.

AGENDA FOR FUTURE B-SCHOOLS

- Single test for admissions
- Global accreditation
- Diverse faculty resources of high quality
- Conferences, seminars, workshops
- Consultancy, research and training
- Global networking
- Focused research through centres of excellence
- Proactive student participation
- Strong industry campus interface
- High degree of intellectual capital.

SUMMARY

1. Several management institutions offer management programmes in India.
2. Any management association works for a common understanding of individuals on managerial issues.
3. The professional associations strive hard to spread the message of management philosophy.
4. Some professional associations in India are: AIMA, AIMS, NIPM, ISTD, NHRD Network, IIMM, IIRA, ISABS, FICCI.
5. All the management associations are conducting several programmes, conferences/ seminars, consultancy, etc.

REVIEW QUESTIONS

1. Explain briefly the growth of management institutions in India.
2. What are the main objectives of different management associations?
3. Discuss the functions of management/professional associations in India.
4. What are the roles and responsibilities of professional associations?

CASE STUDY

Administrative Staff College of India

Ever since it was established in 1956, the Administrative Staff College of India (ASCI), Hyderabad, pioneered post-graduate management training in India. ASCI's synergistic blend of management development, consultancy, and research have set the pace for professionalizing Indian management. Every year, over 150 management development programmes stimulate strategic thinking, reformist leadership, and state-of-the-art managerial skills among practising managers occupying decision-making positions at functional and policy levels in the government, industry, and service sectors in India and abroad. Close to 50,000 Indian and overseas participants have benefited from the ASCI experience. Several administrators, management professionals and entrepreneurs have benefited substantially by attending training programmes in the college. Recently, the Chief Minister of Andhra Pradesh and the ministers attended the programme conducted by the college.

Over 500 national and international organizations who consulted ASCI have learnt new, creative and strategic approaches to understand and confront problems, enhance performance, and achieve competitive dominance in consonance with the college's recommendations. Hundreds of books and research papers published by its faculty, cycled back in training, have helped its participants enrich understanding, and discover solutions to cope with environmental uncertainties. The college library, one of the finest in the country, has an impressive collection of over 60,000 books and 550 journals, monographs, periodicals, consultancy reports, research studies and documents, constantly updated to stay in tune with ever-changing times. The library provides bibliographical information services. A state-of-the-art computer centre with Pentium-based computers is in place. A campus-wide computer network connects all academic and administrative departments.

Housed at Bella Vista, the palace of the erstwhile prince of Barer, the college campus, architecturally aesthetic with verdant surroundings spread over 10 acres, provides a perfect setting for participants to study, discuss, reflect, and introspect. Bella Vista offers participants a home away from home—comfortable single-occupancy air-conditioned accommodation, excellent dining facilities, and indoor and outdoor recreational facilities. ASCI offers short duration, non-residential training programmes at its New Delhi centre. Construction work for the Centre for Management Education at College Park located in picturesque Banjara Hills, less than five kilometres away from Bella Vista, is in progress. The proposed centre will offer intensive long-term skill development programmes in technology management, infrastructure management and hospital management.

Research on management issues in Indian organizations has been one of the major activities of ASCI. The main objective of research is to incorporate new learning in training and to introduce research-based training and policy workshops. After the integration of the academic activities in 1984, research has been one of the major pillars of ASCI. During the last 10 years ASCI has published about 40 books and 15 research papers in professional journals. Research sponsored by external agencies is one of the major thrusts. In 1995–96, the research budget of the college was ₹70 lakhs. The faculty of ASCI has wide exposure and experience on different aspects of management, with excellent skills. At any point of time, the faculty has 20 major research projects. During the last three/four years, several national and international agencies have sponsored research at ASCI.

The college is not offering any regular management programme for budding managers. It offers consultancy services for different organizations. Some of the areas in which consulting assistance has been provided by ASCI include strategic planning, organizational restructuring, human resources management and development, organization culture building, project management, financial restructuring, organization management, forest management, energy management and business process re-engineering. Over 570 assignments have been carried out since 1965.

ASCI provides consultancy for improving management practices in organizations, leading to improved economic performance and long-term effectiveness. The ASCI Consultancy Team comprises faculty members representing different functional and sectoral areas of management and uses a multi-disciplinary approach to problem solving.

Questions for Discussion

1. What are the strengths of ASCI?
2. Suggest new programmes to be offered by ASCI.

FURTHER READING

AICTE Publications, New Delhi, 2007–2008.

ASCI, News Letters.

Griffin, *Management*, AITBS Publishers, New Delhi, 1998.

Satya Raju, R., *HRM Response to New Corporate Initiatives*, NIPM, Kolkata, 1996.

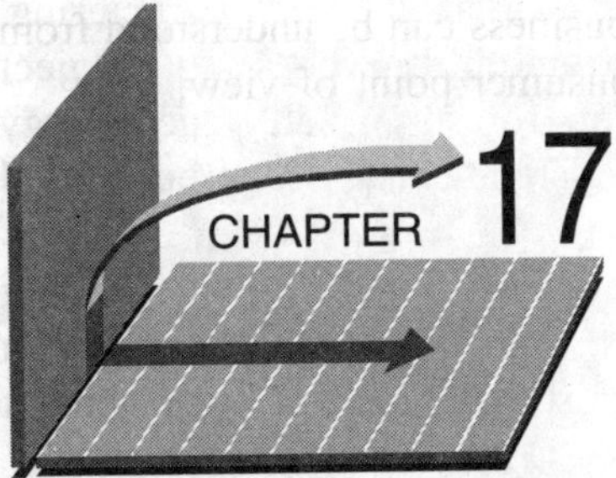

International Management

CONTENTS

INTRODUCTION

The study of international management is concerned with managerial issues related to the flow of people, goods, and money, with the ultimate aim of managing effectively in global business. The environmental factors that affect domestic firms are usually more critical for international corporations. Managers have to interact with employees who have different educational and cultural backgrounds and value systems; they must also cope with different legal, political, and economic factors.

Though business has been conducted on a global scale for many years, international business has gained greater importance in recent years.. A company is considered to be a foreign company if it has specified the place of business. There must be some storehouse, godown or premises providing connection between the locality and the business. Foreign companies operating in India are bound by the provisions of Section 592 to Section 602 of the Indian Companies Act, 1956.

CAUSES OF INTERNATIONAL BUSINESS

In the globalized era, international business is highly needed. It means any commercial transaction taking place across boundary lines of a sovereign entity either between two companies or countries. The important causes for entering into international business can be understood from the Government point of view, company point of view and consumer point of view.

Government Point of View

- Increasing earning from foreign exchange
- Diplomatic relations
- To have competitive advantage
- Interdependency for mutual benefit of nations
- Core competency of nations
- National image
- To meet foreign trade targets
- Infrastructure development
- WTO and international agencies support.

Company Point of View

- Expansion of business
- Corporate vision
- Incentives and business impact
- To utilize human talent
- New business ventures
- Managing sustained business
- Technology advantage
- Building corporate image
- Human resource advantage

Consumer Point of View

- Availability of various products/services
- Choice of location
- Time saving
- Nearness to global company.
- Cost reduction
- Qualitative products/services
- Consumer rights protection

Mode of Entry

There are different modes of entry in international business. Some of them are:

- Exports
- Contract manufacturing
- Management contracts
- Collaboration
- Mergers and acquisitions
- Turnkey projects
- Counter trade [pure barter, buyback and counter purchase].
- International licensing
- Contract marketing
- Joint venture
- Foreign direct investment
- Takeovers

Influencing Factors

- Economic environment of home country, host country and at global level
- Social environment relating to national taste, language, values and beliefs, demography, literacy rate, female workforce, double income families and impulse buying (customers buy after seeing the product, i.e. instance buying)
- Political environment of home country, host country and global levels
- Cultural environment relating to food habits, social class, family system, community units, etc.
- Technology environment at domestic and international levels
- Legal environment at home country, host country and international levels.

DOMESTIC AND INTERNATIONAL ENTERPRISES

The characteristics of domestic and international enterprises are illustrated in Table 17.1.

Table 17.1 Characteristics and practices of domestic and international enterprises

Environment	*Domestic enterprise*	*International enterprise*
Educational environment		
Language (spoken, written, official)	One	Multiple
Education system (quality, level, extent)	No or little constraint	Great constraint
Socio-cultural environment		
Values, attitudes (toward achievement, risk taking, scientific method, work)	Homogeneous	Heterogeneous
Social organization (authority, status, roles, institutions, mobility, social systems)	Similar	Different
Political-legal environment		
Political orientation (power, ideologies)	Country-centred	Transnational
Legal environment (laws, codes, regulations)	Fairly uniform	Different
National sovereignties	One	Many
Government policies, regulations	Same	Different
Economic environment development (underdeveloped, industrialized)	At similar stages	At different stages
Economic system (capitalistic, mixed, Marxist)	Similar	Different
Planning:		
Scanning the environment for threats and opportunities	National markets	Worldwide markets
Organizing:		
• Organization structure	Structure for domestic operations	Global structure

Environment	*Domestic enterprise*	*International enterprise*
• View of authority	Similar	Different
Staffing:		
• Sources of managerial talent	National labour pool	Worldwide labour pool
• Manager orientation	Often ethnocentric	Geocentric
Leading:		
• Leadership and motivation	Influenced by similar culture	Influenced by many different cultures
• Communication lines	Relatively short	Network with long distances
Controlling:		
Reporting system	Similar requirement	Many different requirements

Forms of International Business

The forms of international business are:

1. Exportation
2. Licencing agreement
3. Management contracts
4. Joint ventures
5. Subsidiaries

The Environment for International Business

The environment for international business is influenced by several factors. External and internal factors including political, cultural, social, economic, technological, legal and financial factors influence considerably the establishment and management of the business. The international relations between the domestic and foreign countries, international bodies like the United Nations, European Community and the Organization of Petroleum Exporting Countries also influence international business.

The business environment in India is favourable to several multinational companies. As a result, the number of foreign companies operating in India has been growing steadily over the years. The number of foreign companies has increased from 565 in 1993–94 to 903 in 1998–99.

JAPANESE VERSUS US MANAGEMENT APPROACHES

There is a distinction between Japanese and US management approaches in managing the business enterprises. Table 17.2 explains the basic issues relating to such managerial approaches in managing the business enterprises.

Table 17.2 Managerial approaches

Japanese management	***US management***
Planning	
Long-term orientation	Primarily short-term orientation
Collective decision making (ring) with consensus	Individual decision making
Involvement of many people in preparing and making the decision	Involvement of a few people in making and "selling" the decision to person with divergent values
Decision flow from bottom to top and back	Decisions initiated at the top flowing down
Slow decision making; fast implementation of the decision	Fast decision making, slow implementation requiring compromise, often resulting in sub-optimal decisions
Organizing	
Collective responsibility and accountability	Individual responsibility and accountability
Ambiguity of decision, responsibility	Clear and specific decision responsibility
Informal organization structure	Formal, bureaucratic organization structure
Well-known common organization culture and philosophy; competitive spirit toward other enterprises	Lack of common organization culture, identification with profession rather than with company
Staffing	
Young people hired out of school; hardly any mobility of people among companies	People hired out of schools and from other companies; frequent company changes
Slow promotion through the ranks	Rapid advancement desired and demanded
Loyalty to the company	Loyalty to the profession
Very infrequent performance evaluation for new (young) employees	Frequent performance evaluation for new employees
Appraisal of long-term performance	Appraisal of short-term results
Promotions based on multiple criteria	Promotions based primarily on individual performance
Training and development considered a long-term investment.	Training and development undertaken with hesitation (for fear of turnover)
Lifetime employment common in large companies	Job insecurity prevailing
Leading	
Leader acting as a social facilitator and group member	Leader acting as decision maker and head of the group
Paternalistic style	Directive style (strong, firm, determined)
Common values facilitating cooperation	Often divergent values; individualism, sometimes hindering cooperation

Japanese management	*US management*
Avoidance of confrontation, sometimes leading to ambiguities; emphasis on harmony	Face-to-face confrontation; emphasis on clarity
Bottom-up communication	Communication primarily top-down
Controlling	
Control by peers	Control by superior
Control focus on group performance	Control focus on individual performance
Saving face	Fixing blame
Extensive use of quality control circles	Limited use of quality control circles
Japanese organizations	**American organizations**
Lifetime employment	Short-term employment
Slow evaluation and promotion	Rapid evaluation and promotion
Non-specialized career paths	Specialized career paths
Implicit control mechanisms	Explicit control mechanisms
Collective decision making	Individual decision making
Collective responsibility	Individual responsibility
Holistic concern	Segmented concern

JAPANESE MANAGEMENT PRACTICES

The Japanese government coordinates business activities in terms of planning and implementing a long-term industrial and economic policy. Within the Japanese government there are six "economic bureaucracies", of which MITI (The Ministry of International Trade and Industry) and the Ministry of Finance are the most important.

The following culture is discernible in most Japanese organizations:

- A common light grey uniform for workers and management alike
- A spacious common canteen
- Arrival at the work place fifteen minutes earlier than the scheduled time
- Morning limbering-up exercises
- Common toilets
- Stress on tidiness, orderliness and cleanliness
- Open offices without cabins and partitions
- Daily shop-floor meetings
- Stress on punctuality and attendance
- Emphasis on interaction and sharing of information leading to consultative decision making
- Small group activity, particularly quality circles

- Encouragement to those offering suggestions for organizational excellence
- Team work
- Organizational and individual discipline
- Adherence to physical and financial targets
- Achievement of higher levels of productivity
- Sense of responsibility and commitment to the organization
- Quality consciousness; emphasis on training
- Customer orientation
- Cost effectiveness both in products and services
- Greater accent on human resources
- Lifetime employment

THE ROLE OF GLOBAL MANAGERS

In recent years, several companies are globalizing with one or some of the objectives of opening new markets, obtaining more profits, acquiring products for the home market or other foreign markets, satisfying managements' desire for expansion, protecting domestic or foreign markets, acquiring technology, achieving geographic diversification, or to guarantee supply of raw materials. According to Howard Perlmutter, the managers of international companies have three primary attitudes: ethnocentric, polycentric and geocentric. When foreign countries and their people are considered to be inferior to the home country, the attitude is called *ethnocentric*. In the *polycentric* attitude, managers feel that the environment differs from one country to another and the decision making is based on the foreign environment. Managers in the *geocentric* attitude recognize both similarities and differences among nations and try to procure effective and efficient processes, people and materials from all over the world.

When economies are globalizing all over the world, the need of the hour is to have global leaders to manage multifaceted industrial organizations. The scope of a manager is extended from local or regional to global or cross-national.

Management education is also globalizing with vast expansion, and networks among different institutions have become a common phenomenon to improve the quality of education all over the world. Several strengths are there in Indian business education, besides some constraints. Some common features of business education in India are: a functional approach to the study of management; manufacturing orientation in the curriculum; use of half-baked Indian case material or old American case material; limited contact with Indian industry; shortage of professional faculty; a superficial coverage of the Indian business and economic environment; inadequate coverage of international management; lack of skill development; inadequate research orientation; lack of information about global locations, networks and developments; inadequate computer accessibility, etc.

According to Stephen Rhinesmith, the following competencies are essential to become a global manager.

Managing competitiveness: Managers should constantly scan their environment for changes in market, competitive and suppliers conditions, as well as socio-economic and political trends that may affect their organizations.

Managing complexity: Skills to manage trade-offs of many competing interests as well as inherent contradictions and conflicts that exist in all global organizations.

Managing adaptability: Entails developing a global corporate culture with the values, belief systems and norms of behaviour.

Managing teams: A multicultural environment which requires cultural sensitivity and managerial skills to lead, understand, manage and supervise people from a wide range of cultures in a broad range of situations.

Managing uncertainty: While providing structure and taking advantage of opportunities that arise from the lack of structure, managing learning which requires managers to not only learn about themselves on a continuing basis, but also to train and develop others and facilitate constant organizational learning so that it can be responsive and adaptive to global change and challenge.

In addition, the following qualities are required for managing businesses for results: innovation; quality of life; knowledge; socio-economic development; high ethical standards; sacrifice; forgiveness; truthfulness; respecting elders; focus on significant issues; and identifying opportunities.

Seven spiritual values required for managers are: National service through industry; fairness; harmony and cooperation; struggle for betterment; courtesy and humility; adjustment and assimilation; and gratitude. In Japan, the top managements emphasize quality of the product/service. For the international competitive edge, commitment to quality is required for the competitive advantage of a firm or nation. The issues relating to change in the organizational structures are: multiple layers to be rejected, moving towards horizontal management; developing customer-led strategies, not product-led; loving our people; initiating a cultural change; improving quality of work life; developing partnerships; learning to work with customers and suppliers; providing leadership; spending as much as one can on training. These are adopted by several countries for successful management.

The traits of successful leaders in India are: professionalism; innovative thinking; high knowledge; quality consciousness (Lakshmanbhai R. Gandhi and Ramachandrabhai R. Gandhi of Vadilal Ice Cream); affordable price, smart pricing strategy; developing mass market (Karsanbhai K. Patel of Nirma Chemical Works); fair price, strong marketing strategies (Aspi R. Balsara of Balsara Hygiene Products); pursuit of excellence; grow or perish policy; internationalism (K.M. Mukherjee and Ashok Aikat of Sonodyne Electronics); honesty, dedication, Japanese culture, innovations (Jyothi Mukherjee of Bharat Biscuits); commitment, technology and vision (Chandramohan of Punjab Tractors); satisfying the customer, employing women (Satya Prakash Mathur of Sumeet); service to society through industry, sacrificing nature (K.V.K. Raju of Nagarjuna Steels); innovation, loyalty to customers, commitment to quality (Ramabai B. Patel and Indravadan A. Modi of Cadila Laboratories); employee cooperation, customer support (P. Rangachar of Yeken India).

A recent study in India revealed that the qualities considered essential for choosing the best chief executives are: leadership ability, profit orientation, ability to attract and retain talent, having the best industrial relations policies, honesty, and the ability to establish an international presence. The study further stated that the best chief executives were: Ratan Tata (Tata Sons); K.L. Chugh (ITC); R. Bajaj (Bajaj Auto); Ambani (Reliance Industries); S.M. Datta (Hindustan

Lever); A. Birla (Indian Rayon); D. Setha (Tata Chemicals); A.B. Godrej (Godrej); J.J. Irani (Tata Steel); L.M. Thapar (Crompton Greaves); H.V. Goenka (RPG Enterprises); Nusli Wadia (Bombay Dyeing); Vijay Mallya (UB Group); M.R. Chhabria (Shaw Wallace).

Many managers are thinking and acting like this: thinking globally, acting locally; acting globally with local resources; globalizing the business; training global managers, etc. Let us hope that the mission of our nation would certainly be fulfilled soon, when the present generation of students and other people understand their roles and responsibilities by understanding the attitudes of managers and also other experience of successful Indian managers.

SUMMARY

1. Under the liberalization era, international management is playing an important role in managing business enterprises.
2. There is a distinction between domestic and international enterprises.
3. There are different forms of international business.
4. Japanese and US management practices and the distinction of the various practices should be understood to create the right environment and corporate culture.
5. The role of global managers is very important in a liberalized economy like India.

REVIEW QUESTIONS

1. Explain the characteristics of domestic and international business.
2. What are the various forms of international business?
3. Discuss the Japanese vs US management approaches.
4. What are the various Japanese practices in organizations?
5. Examine the role of global managers.

CASE STUDY

Indian School of Business (ISB)

Some of the corporate giants and visionary leaders thought of having a novel management school in India. They proposed to start an Indian business school in India to offer a high quality management education programme. It is expected to be the number one in the country and also a highly recognized business school in the world. The leaders who deliberated on the subject were Ratan Tata, Anil Ambani, Kumarmangalam Birla, Keki Dadiseth, Adi Godrej, K.V. Kamath, Anand Mahindra, Rajat Gupta, Jairam Ramesh, Purnendu Chatterjee and Anupam Puri, and others, the chiefs of the leading organizations in India.

In several meetings spread over the last two years (1996–98), some of corporate India's most high-profile personalities have been working together on what is arguably the first ever joint venture of its kind, a management university, a business management institution on the lines of the world's best business schools. In the last few weeks of August 1998, this unique venture reached its final stage. After visiting several places in India, they decided to establish the school in Hyderabad, which is the capital city of the state of Andhra Pradesh.

The business school, which will have a collaboration with one of the three top business schools in USA—Wharton, Harvard Business School or the North Western University (Kellogg School)—will be located at Hyderabad. It will have a capital cost of ₹200 crores, of which ₹80 crores has already been committed by the industrial groups represented by the who's who of India's corporate sector.

The land and other facilities will be provided by the Government of Andhra Pradesh. The management university will offer both—an MBA programme as well as a Ph.D. programme. At a later stage, the school will offer a bachelor's programme in business management (BBA) on the lines of US business schools. In fact, the school's programmes will be of the same format as those at US business schools. It will conduct executive development programmes in various fields of management.

The proposed school will have the same contact/teaching hours and similar faculties and courses as US business schools. The idea for setting up a global management school in India was initiated in 1996 by the global leader in management consulting, McKinsey & Co. Its worldwide managing partner, Rajat Gupta, and the chief of its Indian operations, Anupam Puri, then set the ball rolling by roping in the high-fliers of India's corporate sector. McKinsey is one of the world's largest recruiters of top talent from business school campuses across the world, and it recognizes that the focal point of business activity is fast shifting to the Asia-Pacific region.

About 150 students are expected to enrol in the first year for the MBA programme. The school will open its doors to candidates from around the globe. Already, more than 150 faculty members of Indian origin at the top 20 US business schools have been tapped for the proposed institution. Today, many are enthusiastic about signing on at the new Indian schools. In fact, the first Dean of the school could well be an Indian who has the reputation of being among the world's best-known management gurus. In addition to the funds that leading Indian companies—including MNCs operating there—will work out, at least three major global corporations have offered to sponsor various departments, library and research facilities at the school. The school will also have a high-powered international advisory board, which will include the top chief executives of some of the better known Fortune 500 companies.

Questions for Discussion

1. What will be the impact of the proposed Indian School of Business on management institutions in India?
2. What are the strengths and weaknesses of the business school?
3. What should be the role of the Indian School of Business?

FURTHER READING

Chatterjee, Bhaskar, *Japanese Management—Maruti and the Indian Experience*, Sterling Publishers, New Delhi.

Economic Times, Hyderabad, July 7, 1999.

Iacocca with Novak, William, *An Autobiography*, Bantam Books.

Pascale, R.T. and Anthos, A.G., *The Art of Japanese Management—Application for American Executives*, Warner Books, New York, 1982.

Peter, Thomas, J. and Waterman, R.H., Jr., *In Search of Excellence—Lessons from America's* best run companies,

Ravi, N. (Ed.), *The Hindu* Speaks on Management, Kasturi & Sons Ltd., Madras, 1996.

Stoner, James, A.F., *Management*, Pearson/Prentice Hall, New Delhi, 2005.

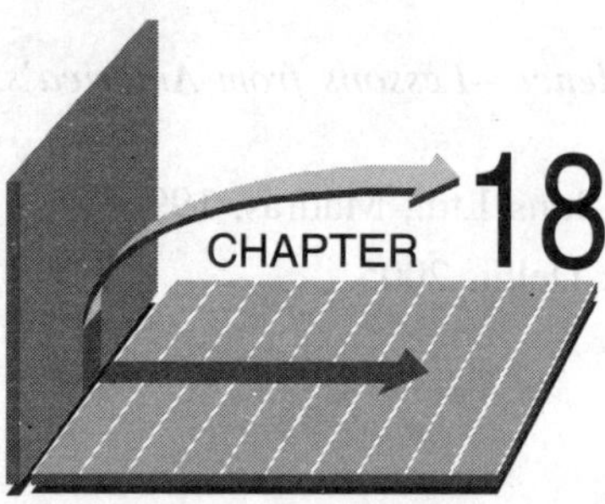

Productivity Management

CONTENTS

INTRODUCTION

Productivity is a universal concept which reflects the relationship between output and input. Productivity is a ratio between output and input. The formula for it is productivity = output/input. It is doing the right things, and also doing things right. It is a form of efficiency, an effective utilization of resources, a ratio, a measure of the rate of return. Productivity bargaining is an ongoing process which seeks improvement, in the way products and services are designed, manufactured, sold, used and maintained. Productivity is finding better ways to do the most with the resources the organization has. It is the process of creating conditions in which every employee—chief executive to peon—contributes towards improvements. It becomes a way of life. An employee becomes a source of improvement rather than a mere resource for management. It emphasizes organizational productivity, long-term gains and synergy. In a liberalized economy, several productivity bargaining agreements were concluded in Indian organizations. In India, the industrial relations scenario has shown a steady improvement in the recent years after introducing economic reforms. The man-days lost due to strikes and lockouts declined significantly from 34.57 million in 1991–92 to 19.20 million in 1994–95 (*Economic survey 1995–96*).

COMPETITIVE ENVIRONMENT

Porter states: "The principal goal of a nation is to produce a higher and rising standard of living for its citizens." The ability to do so depends upon the productivity with which a nation's labour and capital are employed. The productivity of human resources determines employee wages; the productivity with which capital is employed determines the return it earns for its holders. A nation's standard of living depends on the capacity of its companies to achieve higher levels of productivity—and to increase productivity over time.

The essence of formulating a competitive strategy is relating to a company and its environment. The five competitive forces—bargaining power of buyers, bargaining power of suppliers, and rivalry among current competitors—the threat of new entrants and substitutes reflect the fact that competition in an industry goes well beyond the established players (Porter, 1980). In coping with these competitive forces, there are three potentially successful generic strategic approaches to outperforming other firms in an industry: overall cost; leadership; differentiation and focus. The ILO understanding of the role of productivity matters in a socio-economic development is: first, productivity growth is essential for socio-economic development; second, productivity growth is a leading factor in raising the standard of living of workers; third, productivity growth must generate additional resources for additional employment opportunities; and fourth, productivity growth is a common concern of government, employees and trade unions. As companies design strategies to meet the new realities of global competition, unions need to jettison their traditional passivity and start contributing to productivity, quality and flexibility. The four factors to be considered are training, work redesign, employee ownership, and the new workforce.

WORLD CLASS MANUFACTURING

Improving high performance is the present trend for world class manufacturing. The following are the attributes for world class manufacturing:

- Products with high quality
- Products at competitive price
- Products with several enhanced features
- Products in a wider variety
- Products delivered with shorter lead times
- Products delivered on time
- Flexibility in fulfilling products demand.

Every organization has to design the product as per the consumer innovation. For this, continuous innovation of product design is needed. Innovation is a process of converting an invention into some useful product, which can satisfy human wants either directly or indirectly. The steps for new product development are:

- New product strategy development
- Idea generation
- Screening and evaluation
- Business analysis
- Development
- Testing
- Commercialization.

The practice of world class manufacturing are: (a) providing a flexible response to the customers, needs; (b) transparent information flow; (c) people respect humanity; (d) the owners provide leadership; (e) employees are given cross-functional inputs; (f) operators have a sense of ownership of equipment they use; (g) suppliers' manufacturing facility is simply viewed as a remote work centre.

The goal of world class manufacturing is continual and rapid improvement. Continual improvement in quality, cost, lead time, customer service, flexibility is required. Gunn says, "World class manufacturing rests on three pillars: computer integrated manufacturing (CIM), total quality control (TQC) and just-in-time (JIT) production methods."

Maskell included the following aspects:

- A new approach to product quality
- Just-in-time (JIT) production technique
- Managing change in the way of workforce
- A flexible approach to customer requirements

In the USA, three core strategies of world class manufacturing are: customer focus, quality and agility (ability to quickly, efficiently and effectively response to change).

VALUE ENGINEERING

One of the major techniques of cost reduction and cost prevention is value engineering. In this approach, all functions are carried out at minimum cost without compromising quality. According to the Society of American Value Engineers (SAVE), "Value analysis is the systematic application of recognized techniques, which identify the function of a product or service, establish a monetary value for the function and provide the necessary function reliably at the lowest overall cost." It is an organized approach to reduce cost at various stages of production without compromising quality of product.

Value engineering is to be applied under the following conditions:

- Company's products show decline in sales.
- Company's prices are higher than those of competitors.
- Raw materials cost has become higher.
- When a new product is developed.
- When manufacturing cost is rising disproportionate to the production volume.
- When rate of return on investment is reduced.
- When the organization is unable to meet delivery commitments.

PRODUCTIVITY AGREEMENTS IN INDIAN ORGANIZATIONS

Various long-term settlements were concluded with the inclusion of the productivity bargaining concept in different organizations in India. Some recent bargaining issues relating to some Indian industries are briefly detailed below.

BHPV Ltd.

Both the parties recognized that the engineering industry should grow at a rate in order to meet the nation's economic and strategic needs, and also to generate the required resources to meet the urgent needs to modernize the industry and that BHPV being essentially a jobbing industry, had requirements peculiar to it which necessitated special attention. This would necessitate further intensification of all efforts by both parties to achieve viability of the industry. To this end, the parties committed themselves to work together to attain higher levels of production, productivity and profitability. Joint efforts would be made continuously in the following areas: minimizing material handling cost and avoiding material wastages; improvements in yields; reducing operating cost; reducing energy consumption; improving quality in all operations; improvement in housekeeping; continuously adopt better work practices; training of workers in multi-trades; reducing unauthorized absenteeism; improving customer service; attaining full capacity utilization; and effective strengthening of the participative forums.

It was also realized that: retraining, redeployment and readjustment of manpower were essential for the organization, and hence there was a need to keep the manpower at the optimum level and achieve the best utilization of human resources; achieve better overall productivity; increase the profitability and growth of the organization; and continue to have a reasonable share in the highly competitive market in which the company had to operate.

HPCL–VR

In the context of ongoing environmental changes in the petroleum sector in India and their effect on the day-to-day activities of the corporation, an urgent need was felt by the management and the unions to take such actions as were considered necessary and feasible to improve the performance of the corporation, and to meet the future challenges jointly.

Accordingly, through discussions the unions and the management arrived at a consensus to take concrete actions for enhancing productivity through better role play by the unions. The role of the unions, as jointly identified and listed is to:

- bring sustained improvement in the performance of the corporation in physical and financial terms, including quality improvement;
- continuously upgrade "value addition" and achieve a quantum jump in productivity and profitability;
- reduce operating costs including establishment cost and revenue expenses to the utmost minimum level;
- improve effective utilization of all resources, including human resources, through organizational restructuring;

- continuously improve quality in operations, services and products so as to ensure better customer service to achieve excellence in customer satisfaction;
- constantly adopt better working practices;
- create and sustain a climate and systems for enhancing merits/performance; and
- continuously support in achieving ISO 9000 accredition and bringing about Total Quality Management (TQM).

Due to introduction of new technology or upgradation of existing technology, if any surplus manpower is generated, the same will be discussed with the union and will be reassigned/ redeployed in any other process/section as per the requirements. They will be given necessary training as may be required.

In the case of additional facilities in a unit block/off-site facilities within battery limits, the existing manpower will handle the job without any additional manpower. However, if the need was felt, an IE study will be conducted within a reasonable period of time for assessing the actual manpower requirement, and the same will be implemented. It was agreed that all shift personnel of the instrumentation, electrical, general fitter, welder and field machinist sections would attend the jobs arising during the starting and shutting down of the plant except T&I and other planned shutdowns in all existing units. It was also agreed that the usual emergency jobs and running repairs will be carried out by the shift personnel. And also depending on the job requirements, the personnel will be asked to continue the job in the succeeding shift. It was further agreed that the general shift workmen will also undertake all the maintenance jobs in all the existing units.

In shifts, as and when there was manpower available more than the normal requirement (due to leave relief), such manpower will be reassigned wherever the requirement of manpower was needed for running the plants/units. At the time of shutdown, the shift complement will be decided at the discretion of the management.

The onus of deciding the number of workmen required during shutdowns/exigencies of work to be carried out, would be solely at the discretion of the management.

In promotion to higher grade within the non-management cadre, the present system of selection by DPC will continue. The union will cooperate in redesigning the performance appraisal format within three months from the date of signing of the settlement.

HSL

HS Labour Union and HS Staff Association agreed to the full implementation of identified good work practices as finalized and mutually agreed with effect from 1 February 1992. HS Labour Union and HS Staff Association further agreed that restrictive practices coming in the way of production and productivity would be completely eliminated.

In order to achieve progressive reduction in man-days per unit during the next four years, the management, HS Labour Union and HS Staff Association agreed to the following norms.

It is hereby agreed to achieve the target of 200 man-hours per Gross Equivalent Tonne in the Steel Complex, progressively by 1992–93 by elimination of restrictive practices and implementation of good work practices.

It is also agreed that overall productivity levels including the outfit wing of the yard should reach 3,000 man-days per unit of production by improving man-day utilization through implementation of good work practices.

HS Labour Union and HS Staff Association agreed with the management to step up production commensurate with the increased wage levels. It was also agreed to formulate a productivity linked incentive scheme for achieving a higher level of production and productivity norms over those stipulated above.

Industrial peace and harmony will be maintained and every effort will be made to increase productivity.

The practice of discussing production targets with workers at shopfloor level will be introduced and the workers' representatives assured that they will give all cooperation to ensure fulfilment of targets. It was recognized by both the parties that discipline at all levels is essential for the smooth functioning of the company. They, therefore, assured full cooperation for maintaining discipline and optimizing production and productivity.

NTPC

The National Thermal Power Corporation (NTPC), while making an unequivocal commitment to maintenance of industrial peace and improvement of generation and construction efficiency, the unions agreed to:

- extend to the management full support and cooperation in improving productivity and discipline in the project/division/offices,
- cooperate and work out ways and means to identify and eliminate all wasteful practices,
- introduce the system including revision thereof relating to time keeping, attendance procedure and gate control for ensuring attendance, punctuality, etc.,
- work out a system of redeployment and rotation of employees as may be required, and
- identify and eliminate non-uniform practices at different places.

ONGC

The unions agreed that discipline at all levels was of utmost importance for the smooth functioning of the organization and for improving productivity of the employees. They, therefore, assured full cooperation to the management in maintaining discipline, and in their efforts to improve productivity of employees. Indiscipline of any kind will not be compromised at any cost.

The commission and the unions also agreed to have cooperation in:

- minimizing overtime,
- creating a healthy climate for industrial relations, promoting efficiency all around, and making every effort to increase productivity, and
- ensuring a high level of performance, consistent with safety, health, environment, inputs and sustained efforts to achieve not only the targets of production, but also improve upon them.

Pyrites, Phosphates and Chemicals Ltd.

It was agreed to mechanize various mining and related activities and introduce innovative ideas to economize on the cost of production and to achieve higher productivity. It was further agreed that the management will establish norms based on improved performance with mechanization and the union will give full support in implementing it. The union agreed to increase productivity by 15 per cent and to cooperate wholeheartedly to make all the schemes successful.

BEML

It was agreed to continue to adhere to the existing industrial climate of coordination, understanding and sense of cooperation. They continued the existing spirit of resolving disputes and differences peacefully through negotiations and constitutional means, and thereby contribute to industrial peace, productivity and overall efficiency of the company.

The parties agreed to achieve the highest efficiency, performance and productivity consistent with safety, health and other measures, viz. effective handling of resources, reducing wastages, improving quality and diminishing cost.

To achieve optimum utilization of human, machine and material resources by promoting productivity-oriented practices, the personnel will be redeployed and redistributed wherever required. The management ensured training consistent with skill, dignity and the earnings of employees, keeping in view modernization and sophistication. They also agreed to make effective contribution to achieve excellence by adhering to the following objectives:

- Harmony and cooperation
- Striving for betterment
- Effective strengthening of participative forums
- Reduction of absenteeism
- Efforts will be made to improve the quality of work life, job satisfaction and job enrichment.
- Necessary facilities will be provided to improve the skill of employees
- Cooperate and maintain discipline at all levels
- Further improve housekeeping
- Further improve safety consciousness among employees at all levels
- Further improve customers service and delivery.

Bharat Electronics Ltd., Ghaziabad

The agreement began with the following general statement: “In the context of increasing competition, fast changing technological environment and the need to retain the leadership role of the company in the chosen fields of electronics, both the unions and the management commit themselves to work together (i) to achieve higher levels of production, productivity and profitability; and (ii) to attain the optimum utilization of manpower through retraining, redeployment, increased availability of the employees at the workspot, avoidance of overtime and redefining of work assignment consistent with the changing product mix and technological processes."

TELCO

The union agreed to support the management to optimize the utilization of manpower through flexibility of movement, redeployment of excess manpower and also by advising the workmen/ employees to carry out the normal work during periods of high absenteeism with the available manpower.

Due to fluctuation in production schedules, if any workman/employee was rendered idle for a period of time, the workman/employee would be required to work on any other job in any section or department on loan-in and loan-out basis so as to earn their efficiency bonus as well as to optimize the utilization of manpower.

Bhilai Steel Plant, Bhilai

The resolution states: Efforts are made for more effective and better utilization of the available manpower through the following, wherever possible:

- By reorganizing, restructuring/rationalizing the work
- By job enrichment
- Elimination of non-productive working habits/practices
- Elimination of the forced idleness, wherever existing
- By selective optional re-deployment with protection of wages
- Reducing unauthorized absenteeism
- By productive bargaining
- Improvement in the skill of the employees through technical education and re-orientation.

Thermax Pvt. Ltd., Pune

The agreement states: "With the increasing felt need of diversification and the introduction of new products and designs, it is necessary that the workmen adopt the multi-skills concept by suitable retraining and upgradation of their skills.

In order to implement the one-man crew concept effectively, it is felt necessary to train some of the workmen in skills supplementary to their own skills as per the requirements of the jobs such as fitters being trained to do gas cutting and tack welding or welders trained to do minor machining jobs, etc.

The training programme pertaining to multi-skills will be implemented in the shop floor in consultation with the union representatives. The representatives of the workmen have been informed that there will not be any extra benefits accruing out of this concept since it has been agreed in the Productivity Linked Earning Scheme that no workmen will be retrenched due to the implementation of the scheme.

By introducing the multi-skills concept effectively the crew size in a work centre will be automatically reduced and members of the work centre will be equally loaded and utilized to the fullest extent which will result in higher work centre and Plant Performance Index and all the workmen will thus benefit in terms of higher work centre and Plant Productivity Linked earnings."

Damodar Valley Corporation

The union's statement was: "The DVC Karmachari Sangh extends whole-hearted cooperation to the corporation for the following:

- To ensure that Plant Load Factor of DVC does not fall below 50 per cent,
- To maintain productivity in all other spheres, and
- To conform to all-India norms to reduce overtime to the maximum extent, subject to proper manning."

Bajaj Auto Ltd., Pune

The agreement provided for a minimum hike in wages of Rs. 695 per month per worker (as opposed to the union's initial demand for a minimum hike of Rs. 2,800 per month) subject to two main conditions: productivity of the workers would have to go up by 20 per cent over and above the prevalent standards, and a worker would attend to two machines running simultaneously when asked to do so. Workers are liable to disciplinary action if they flouted productivity norms.

Indian Aluminium Company Ltd., Ranchi

The agreement says: "The union and the management agree that rationalization of work standards and work methods which may also include mechanization of operation and handling and rationalization of crew strength are to be undertaken to achieve higher productivity. The workmen will extend full co-operation to management in this regard. To improve productivity and work efficiency, changes in work practices were agreed upon. It is also agreed that there shall not be any retrenchment or loss of earnings of existing workmen as a result of rationalization, mechanization or method of changes."

Hindustan Copper Ltd.

The agreement states that: "Both the management and representatives of unions agree that HCL should grow at a faster rate and aim to meet the nation's requirement, improve the quality of worklife, work culture and industrial peace. In order to achieve these, both the parties agreed to work together by:

Jointly pursuing in promoting industrial peace and harmony; achieving highest efficiency by way of excellence in performance and productivity consistent with safety, health and other measures; improving utilization of installed capacity of the plants; maintaining discipline at all levels; improving housekeeping and working conditions; resolving all disputes by mutual dialogues.

Both management and unions are committed to create a healthy and safe working environment for all employees in the copper industry and jointly promote effective functioning of bipartite forums and statutory committees.

SUGGESTED FRAMEWORK

It would have been observed that several measures were taken for union–management cooperation for increasing productivity. No doubt, industry would flourish when there is a positive attitude to achieve the mission of the enterprises.

The important areas on which the managements and unions can work together for better results are: employee welfare; grievances management; matching of skills; job ability and education with remuneration; participation in decision making; encouragement of a positive culture; introduction of safety measures at work; and social security, training and development.

Productivity agreements are needed in the areas of efficient handling of raw materials; reducing costs; controlling operating costs; procurement of materials at economic prices; improving quality; reducing energy consumption; better housekeeping and work practices, reducing unauthorized absenteeism; better capacity utilization; redeployment of people with skill and abilities; identification of wasteful practices; improving customer satisfaction, etc.

Meaningful productivity bargaining is possible when the following conditions are satisfied:

- The general environment must be favourable for launching an effort for productivity improvement.
- The workers and their unions must not only be taken into confidence but must support the productivity movement.
- The management must have a clear idea about the prevailing practices and levels of production, otherwise, fixation of norms will be difficult.
- Infrastructural facilities should be provided by the management.
- Management must be professionalized.
- Negotiation skills should be improved and
- The productivity agreement must be drafted with great care and confidence.

According to a study by the ILO, direct means of raising productivity are better management by reducing work content of the product; process research; process planning; operator training; reducing the ineffective time of a plant, etc.

The insights gained during the two-year White Collar Productivity Improvement Research Project led the American Productivity Center to the following general observations:

- White collar productivity improvement is found on basic issues of vision, orientation and management practices.
- Attention to operational issues will enable productivity improvements to take place.
- Training and coaching are required to deliver services effectively.
- Organizational systems and processes offer a major opportunity for productivity improvement.
- Management of white collar work is both possible and desirable.

- Justification of technology is best linked to critical features of service development and delivery.
- Service reliance is a key to ongoing productivity improvements.
- It is dependent on some critical success factors, such as innovations, risk taking, emphasis on service, a flexible methodology, technology and inputs.

Productivity would increase when the companies adopt the 5S model and also follow a four-phased approach: assessment phase, foundation phase, basic productivity improvement phase, and advanced productivity improvement phase. In order to improve productivity, all organizations have to follow the under-mentioned basic elements (Monga, 1992).

- Commitment of top management and trade unions.
- Creation of productivity culture and environment.
- Employee empowerment to do Kaizens.
- Creating a mechanism to involve all employees from a peon to the managing director.
- Technology modernization.
- HR development.
- Sharing gains of productivity.
- Audit and evaluation of productivity.
- Integration of productivity with corporate plans, budgets, performance appraisals and long-term strategies.

Productivity ratio must be at least 1 for any organization for survival. If it is more than 1, the organization is in a comfortable position. Therefore, the managements of the organization have to follow some strategies for improving productivity. Some of them are:

- Increased output for the same input.
- Decreased input for the same output.
- Proportionate increase in the output is more than the proportionate increase in the input.
- Proportionate decrease in the input is more than the proportionate decrease in the output.
- Simultaneous increase in the output and decrease in the input.

For a high performing organization, the features required are: management commitment; organizational awareness; management responsibilities; productivity goals; reward system; visible productivity measures; quality improvement; employee involvement; integration of productivity with budgeting, planning and financial reporting systems.

In Modi Xerox, first the company followed an employee involvement strategy in 1979. Later, it implemented quality of work life in 1980; participative work practices in 1985; and high-performing organization practices in the 1990s with the objective of productivity through people. For a successful productivity improvement programme, the guidelines to be adopted for overall corporate strategy are: creating awareness; productivity measurement; productivity evaluation; productivity planning; productivity improvement and productivity reporting.

SUMMARY

1. Productivity is doing the right things, and also doing things right.
2. World class manufacturing is required now.

3. Value engineering helps a lot in reducing costs.
4. Several companies have productivity agreements between unions and managements.
5. Productivity growth is essential for socio-economic development.
6. Public sector and private sector unions and managements have concluded agreements for improving productivity.

REVIEW QUESTIONS

1. What is productivity? What is the role of productivity?
2. Discuss the attributes for world class manufacturing.
3. Why value engineering is essential?
4. What are the productivity agreements in Indian organizations?
5. Explain the measures for increasing productivity.

CASE STUDIES

1. Hi-Class Woollen & Textile Mills

On 1 December 1985, Mr Zaman, the Marketing Manager of Hi-Class Woollen & Textile Mills, Lahore, was called by his boss, Mr Zubair, the Marketing Executive Director, and was told that the Board of Directors was going to meet on 10 December 1985 in order to discuss and find a solution to the company's current problem of falling profits. Mr Zaman, being the direct link between the company and the market, was asked to make a comprehensive presentation in the meeting on how the company might control its falling profits through a better marketing system. Established in 1954, Hi-Class Woollen & Textile Mills utilized Pakistan's wool crop for the production of yarn for the indigenous hand-tufting carpet industry. It also made blankets for the armed forces, and woollen overcoating and tweed for the general market. However, it imported wool tops from the UK to produce worsted fabrics.

In 1960, the present group of industries acquired control of Hi-Class. The event marked a significant change of direction for the Mills. The group brought versatile skills in industrial management and a wide range of experience. Within a short period of time, the worsted spinning capacity was increased by 85 per cent and that of powerlooms by 238 per cent. The group was managing a wide range of other industries, including rayon, nylon, chemicals, cellophane, general and life insurance, mining and two other textile mills. In all these areas of activity, it practised a consistent policy of ensuring high dividends for thousands of shareholders.

Over the years, Hi-Class had evolved into the largest worsted and woollen textile mills in the country. Its production services, including top-making, dyeing, spinning, weaving and finishing, were located within a single complex. The quality of all raw materials used at the mills met the highest international standards. The finest wool was imported from Australia, polyester fibre from Europe and Japan, the chemicals from the Federal Republic of Germany, Switzerland and the UK.

Hi-Class had a general product line-up including worsted and woollen fabrics, shawls, yarn as well as blankets. Its other branded products included varieties to save the demand of different segments of the market, i.e. men, women, summer and winter, old and young groups, casual and formal. Hi-Class had its own R&D department, and with its special expertise, it had developed the ability to use all five principal fibres, viz. nylon, acrylic, polyester, wool and cotton, in their pure and blended forms. It had achieved the capability of making fabrics ranging from 6 oz (170.1 gm per linear yard) to 24 oz (680.4 gm per linear yard). The product development and design department was creating 1,500 designs every year.

Of the production of Hi-Class, 90 per cent was absorbed by the domestic market. The remaining 10 per cent was exported to a few casual importers from the Middle-East countries. The company did not have an independent export office. Production was carried out to the orders of the whole sales on receipt of a negotiable amount of security money at the time of their confirmation. The minimum order quantity was 1,000 metres, and at least three months delivery time was necessary to execute the order. Goods were sold on a cash basis only.

There were only six to seven comparatively smaller domestic woollen textile units which could compete with Hi-Class on the basis of an integrated production system. However, lately many small weavers had cropped up in the market. They had imported smaller capacity weaving looms and were posing a major threat to the company. These small weavers imported yarn and paid tariff duties much less than what Hi-Class paid for its raw materials. It was feasible for these small units to price their products below those of Hi-Class because of their low overhead costs. They enjoyed the benefits of being small organizations and could meet the orders of small retailers, departmental stores and garment manufacturers directly. They required less delivery time, and needed just a token down-payment as security at the time of confirmation of their orders. As a cumulative result of the above factors, a considerable share of the Hi-Class market was being taken away by these small weavers. Hi-Class Woollen & Textile Mills was not only experiencing a downward sloping sales curve, but was also facing the problem of a considerable increase in the costs of production because of the trend of increasing raw material prices in world markets.

The company was afraid of adopting the policy of increasing the prices of its products for the following reasons:

- Newly emerged small weavers were producing and marketing similar quality at prices lower than those of Hi-Class.
- Strict product differentiation could not be maintained in the market because the costly designs of Hi-Class were quickly copied by the competitors, who did not hire designers.
- The demand for such products was extremely sensitive to price.

Mr Zaman realized that he must have some more and detailed information regarding the company and the market before he could decide what to do. He wondered what specific steps he should take so that he could successfully make his presentation on 10 December 1985 to the board of directors.

Questions for Discussion

1. Discuss the use of branding, and whether a branding strategy might be helpful in Hi-Class.

2. What strategic recommendations might Mr. Zaman make to his management to address the company's current problems?
3. In other industries, how do large companies with high overhead costs manage to compete against smaller, lower-overhead-cost producers?

2. Maruti Suzuki India Ltd.

MSIL, one of the best managed multinational company had a strife in the Manesar Plant on 18 July 2012 between the management and workers. It resulted in a lockout for about a week. It is not known that some incidents were experienced earlier.

The violence at Maruti Suzuki on 18 July 2012 started when a supervisor, Samsher Singh, used a casteist abuse against Dalit worker, Jiyalal, after which Jiyalal allegedly slapped the supervisor. The management had suspended Jiyalal after receiving a complaint. There was no action against the supervisor. Workers went to meet the management at around 3.00 p.m. when the shift ended demanding that Jiyalal should be reinstated. They came out of the meeting at around 7.00 p.m. without succeeding. According to the management, hundreds of workers then went on rampage, beating the management and setting fire to the factory. According to the workers, they were goons hired by the company who went on rampage, beating workers and setting fire to the factory.

When the fire was brought under control, the charred body of Avnish Kumar Dev, the GM of HR, was found in the office. The company accused that the workers' had killed him. The police have issued hundreds of arrest warrants against workers, including some who were not even in the factory at that time. But how could workers 'plan' that Samsher Singh would abuse Jiyalal? How could they plan the invasion by the bouncers? If it is true that someone planned the violence, it could only have been the management. Even Dev's wife had asked, why were the police not called in sooner, given that a posse of them was waiting outside the factory? All these questions need to be answered. Instead, the company declared a lockout and refused to pay wages for the month of July; hundreds of workers were facing charges of murder and thousands of dismissal. 116 workers had been arrested. Committee members were being severely tortured in police custody and the police had been sitting in workers' homes the entire night threatening and intimidating the family members to give up their sons or risk having other male members of the family be arrested instead.

The Maruti plant at Manesar was opened in 2007 and workers there had many serious grievances, including the inhuman pace of work—the only time they got to go to the toilet was during two 7-minute tea breaks and the 30-minute lunch-break. On an average, the workers produce one car in 43 seconds. In a day, upto 1750 cars are produced. The balance sheet of the company indicates that only 2.02 per cent of their total revenue was spent on the wage bill of the entire workforce employed. More than two-thirds of the workforce consisted of contract and non-permanent workers. Wages increased by only 5.5 per cent between 2007 and 2011, while the consumer price index increased by 50 per cent—a huge cut in real wages. Contract workers received ₹6000–7,000—less than half the pay of permanent workers—for the same work. Meanwhile, profits of the company went up by 2,200 per cent over the last ten years. The workers wanted to negotiate better conditions and pay, especially for the contract workers, and formed the Maruti Suzuki Employees' Union (MSEU) in 2011, because the management-sponsored Maruti Udyog Kamgar Union (MUKU) was not taking up their demands. But, the management refused to recognise MSEU and got its registration rejected by the Haryana government. A series of strikes followed as workers tried to get their union recognised and victimised union leaders to be reinstated. Finally, with no solution in sight, the suspended union leaders accepted VRS in October 2011. However, the workers did not give up their efforts to form a union. This time, the management in collusion with the government allowed the Maruti Suzuki Workers' Union to be registered, in the hope of controlling it in the same way that they controlled MUKU. But workers insisted that the new union take up their demands, including the demand that contract workers should be on same pay-scales as permanent workers doing the same work. Negotiations were deadlocked when violence occurred.

It is very clear that the real issue in this struggle is the right of workers to form and belong to a union of their choice. The right to freedom of association and to unionise and bargain collectively is among the ILO Core Conventions. And those were fundamental rights enshrined in the Indian Constitution. These rights should be guaranteed to all workers. Yet, they found both state governments and the central government colluding with employers to violate these fundamental rights.

The demands of workers:

- Lift the lockout in the Maruti Suzuki Manesar factory.
- Release all the arrested workers.
- Conduct an impartial enquiry into the incident of 18th July 2012 at the Plant.
- Reinstate all dismissed workers. Pay the workers wages for July 2012.
- Respect the right to Freedom and Association and to unionize and bargain collectively.
- Pay equal wages to contract workers and punish companies violating the Contract Labour Act.

Another major issue is the contract labour system, which allows companies to employ workers for years-on-end on miserable wages and in terrible conditions without ever making them permanent. This is also linked to their resistance to unions: contract, casual and temporary workers can be easily dismissed if they join a union. Managements say this is to give them some degree of flexibility, but flexibility is not the reason. If they want flexibility, they can employ temporary workers when demand is high and in low demand, the management can even layoff permanent workers government does not refuse them permission to do this. But why employ contract workers for years-on-end to do perennial jobs of the company, as in the case of Maruti Suzuki? Of course, the main reason is to save on wages and to keep this workforce held to ransom with the threat of dismissal over their heads all the time. Governments act in complete collusion with all these anti-worker operations of these companies. Employing contract workers in permanent jobs has become the norm, in keeping with policies of globalization. There is no relief for workers even from the courts which are increasingly allowing this practice on the plea that they cannot interfere with the policy matters of governments. It is clear the workers have to fight this on their own. With the cost of living spiraling upwards endlessly, the restlessness of 'workers will only increase against the greed of capitalism which treats them inhumanly like beasts of burden. "We create all the wealth in the world. We will stand together. We will have justice," one of the workers lettered.

Questions for Discussion

1. What are the main issues in the case?
2. How do you maintain industrial harmony in the company?

FURTHER READING

Ahluwalia, I.J., *Productivity Trends in Indian Industry: Concerns for the Nineties*, *Productivity*, **31**, 1, April–June, 1990.

Belcher, J.G., Jr., *Productivity Plus*, Universal Book Stall, New Delhi.

Hoerr, J., What should unions do now? *SPAN*, February, pp. 11–17, 1992.

Monga, R.C., *Dynamics of Productivity Management*, *Productivity*, **33**, 1, April–June, 1992.

Panneerselvam, *Production and Operations Management*, PHI Learning, New Delhi, 2003.

Sahay, B.S. et al., *World Class Manufacturing: A Strategic Perspective*, Macmillan, New Delhi, 2000.

Venkata Ratnam, C.S., *Unusual Collective Agreements*, Global Press, New Delhi, 1993.

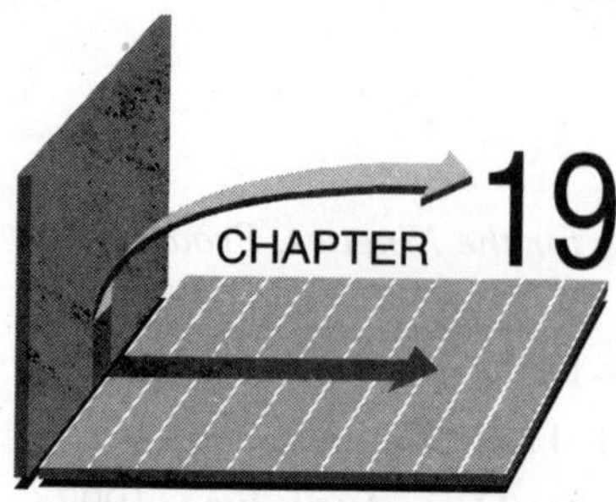

Executive Education

CONTENTS

INTRODUCTION

At present, the world is considered to be a global village with a flat structure. The business has become globalized. Educational institutions, companies and organizations have been expanding their operations globally. Therefore, executive education has become a prime concern for the CEOs, top management professionals and managers all over the world. Executive education, or management development has become a part of the professional career of any corporate CEO or manager at different levels. As a result of several changes in the global labour markets, the role and responsibilities of the executives have been expanded from local to global. The global managers require knowledge on various new areas of management. They should acquire new knowledge and skills to manage the organizations for competitive advantage. The need of the hour is to prepare global leaders to face the new challenges.

According to the latest available estimate by *Business Week*, the international B-school watchdog, executive education in the US is $800 million per annum business. And the largest share of it is provided by business schools. At the same time, schools stand to gain from the associations formed with corporate movers and shakers through this route in terms of placements. For corporates, these programmes aim at training selected managers/high performers in specific skills to take on more responsibility within an organization. A couple of years ago, as per the EMBA survey by *Business Week*, 163 companies sent 21,000 employees to such courses in 2005.

KINDS OF PROGRAMMES

In India, business schools, by and large, used to offer only standardized two-year courses focused on training fresh graduates. However, over the past four years, many B-schools have started paying more attention to this very different breed of students—working executives. And they are creating special courses tailored to the needs of working executives.

There is a whole host of institutes, of all grades, queuing up to woo this very lucrative and under-served segment of MBA aspirants—candidates who are three years into a job or five, or even 10 and more. Short-term executive training programmes or workshops have been on the rise year after year. Another popular format of learning is longer duration courses—spanning a year or more on a part-time basis. The latest addition, however, is 11–18 months full-time residential courses. There is a vast scope for executive education in India because about 5,000 corporates are creating wealth in the country. Each would have an average of at least 30 managers.

There are two kinds of executive education programmes: Management Development Programmes (MDPs) and Executive MBAs (EMBAs). MDPs are short duration programmes along the lines of a management workshop. There are two kinds of MDPs: *customized* and *open enrolment*. These last between a day and a fortnight. The fastest growing segment of the market internationally is customized programmes tailored to the requirements of a single company. Open enrolment programmes are different in that they are open to all. So, the school picks a topic like marketing, innovation, strategy or change management which it thinks will attract participation, and any company may send its employees to attend the programme. In India, these programmes last anything between 1–7 days.

EMBAs, on the other hand, are courses of longer duration for working executives. They require consistent effort over a period of time on the participant's part. Most of these programmes fall within the 6–36 months range. The delivery is a mix of on-campus and off-campus teaching via project work or VSAT.

EXECUTIVE EDUCATION ABROAD

The global top twenty B-schools in 1993 were:

1. University of Michigan
2. University of Virginia (Darden)
3. Northwestern University (Kellogg)
4. Duke University (Fuqua)

5. Stanford University
6. Harvard University
7. University of Pennsylvania (Wharton)
8. Columbia University
9. Institute European d'Administration des Affiares (INSEAD)
10. University of North Carolina (Kenan-Flagler)
11. Pennsylvania State University (Smeal)
12. Massachusetts Institute of Technology (Sloan)
13. University of Tennessee
14. University of California at Los Angeles (Anderson)
15. Carnegie Mellon University
16. Dartmouth College (Amos Tuck)
17. Cornell University (Johnson)
18. Babson College
19. Southern Methodist University (Cox)
20. Indiana University.

There was a vast change during the last 15 years. As per the latest study, the global top twenty B-schools in 2007 were:

1. Duke Corporate Education (USA/UK/India)
2. IMD (Switzerland)
3. Harvard Business School (USA)
4. IESE Business School (Spain)
5. Babson Executive Education (USA)
6. University of Chicago GSB (USA/UK/Singapore)
7. Columbia Business School (USA)
8. Thunderbird School of Global Management (USA/Russia)
9. MIT: Sloan (USA)
10. Ashridge (UK)
11. HEC (Paris/France)
12. UNC: Kenan-Flagler (USA)
13. Emory University: Goizueta (USA)
14. Ipade (Mexico)
15. Center for Creative Leadership (USA/Belgium/Singapore)
16. IAE Management and Business School (Argentina)
17. INSEAD (France/Singapore)
18. Stockholm School of Economics (Sweden/Russia)
19. University of Pennsylvania: Wharton (USA)
20. Boston University (USA).

There is a sea change in the executive education in the liberalized environment. Several B-schools have been focusing their attention on this aspect.

The factors considered for ranking were: course director's credentials; participants' feedback; preparation; course design; teaching materials; faculty; new skills and learning; follow-up; aims achieved; facilities; value for money; future use; international clients; international participants; overseas programmes; partner schools; and faculty diversity and commitment.

The global top B-schools have been offering several programmes to the executives of different companies. Some are long term up to three years, and some are short term, either customized or open enrolment programmes. Selective programmes of various B-schools are briefly given in the following section.

Selective Executive Programmes in B-schools

University of Michigan

- General management programme
- Advanced HR executive programme
- HR executive programme
- Management of managers
- Global leadership programme
- Activity-based costing programme
- Business acumen for high-potential leaders
- The big picture—integrating marketing strategy and execution
- Family business: generational challenges and growth
- Healthcare management series—physicians/clinicians/administrators
- Positive leadership: building extraordinary personal leadership capabilities
- Positive leadership: creating spectacular organizational success

University of Virginia

- General management programme
- Managing critical resources
- Young managers programme
- Sales management and marketing strategy
- FM for non-finance managers
- Transformational leadership
- Creating high performance workplace

Northwestern University

- Advanced executive programme
- Executive development programme
- Business to business marketing strategy
- Creating worldclass quality

Duke University

- Advanced management programme
- Manager development programme
- Strategic marketing programme
- Competitive strategies to the telecom industry
- Executive programme for corporate counsel

Stanford University

- Stanford executive programme
- Organizational change programme for executives
- Financial management programme
- Executive programme for smaller companies
- Strategic marketing management programme

Harvard University

- Advanced management programme
- International senior management programme
- Programme for management development
- Owner/presidents manager programme
- Achieving breakthrough service
- Managing information services resource

University of Pennsylvania

- Executive MBA programme for 2 years (weekend classes, Friday and Saturday, and international seminar)
- Advanced management programme
- The international forum for chief executives
- Executive development programme
- Finance and accounting for non-financial managers
- Advanced industrial marketing strategy

Columbia University

- Executive programme in business management
- Executive programme in international business
- Marketing management programme
- Creating the customer oriented firm
- Managing strategic innovation and change
- Achieving sustainable turnaround
- Managing cultural diversity

INSEAD (Institute European d'Adminsitration des Affaires)

- Advanced management programme
- International executive programme
- Young managers programme
- European marketing programme
- Management of people
- Managing the multinational enterprises

University of North Carolina

- The executive programme
- Young executives programme
- Programme for technical managers
- Global executive programme

Massachusetts Institute of Technology

- Programme for senior executives
- Executive programme in corporate strategy
- Current issues in managing information technology
- Management of technology programme
- International management programme
- Product design, development and management
- Leading change in complex organization
- Corporate strategy

University of Tennessee

- Executive development programme
- Cost management programme
- Marketing and customer value programme
- Executive development programme for distribution managers
- One year MBA programme
- Sixteen months, weekend—executive MBA, physician executive MBA, professional MBA

University of California at Los Angeles

- The executive programme
- Advanced executive programme
- Medical marketing programme
- Purchasing executive programme
- Managing the information resource programme

Carnegie Mellon University

- Programme for executives
- Programme in engineering design

Dartmouth College

- The executive programme on strategic management
- Tuck executive programme
- Minority business executive programme
- Effective management of production programme
- Strategic cost management programme
- MBA update programme
- Business essentials for the information security professional
- Directors consortium
- Finance essentials for strategy execution
- Gateway to business management
- Online bridge programme
- Leadership and strategic impact

Cornell University

- Executive development programme
- Managing the next generation of manufacturing technology
- Manufacturing executive programme
- Purchasing executive programme
- The effective executive programme
- Financial management
- Food, beverage and restaurant management
- General and strategic management
- Human resource management
- Marketing
- Operations management
- Property-asset management and real estate

The Babson College

- The consortium for executive development
- Strategic planning and managing in retailing
- Developing managerial effectiveness
- Technology managers programme
- Leadership and influence programme
- Programmes for individuals and teams
- Strategic management
- Software functional design for IT professionals
- Innovation summit

Southern Methodist University

- Management of managers
- Financial planning and control for oil and gas company managers
- Financial techniques for improved operating effectiveness
- Leading high performance sales organization
- SMU mid-management programme
- Custom executive education programmes

Indiana University

- Indiana partnership for management development
- The professional manager
- Managing business strategies
- Indiana business seminars

Emory University

- Educative development programme
- FM for non-financial manager
- Marketing strategies for competitive advantage
- Investor relations

University of California

- The executive programme
- Managing in the global economy
- Strategic management for innovation programme
- Management development—a comprehensive approach
- Competitive strategies for high tech products

University of Hawaii

- Advanced management programme
- Hawaii management programme
- Self-managing work teams
- Innovative compensation packages

University of Illinois of Urbana Champaign

- Programme for international managers
- Specialized programme for international managers
- PEATA—Illinois business programme

International Institute for Management Development

- Programme for executive development
- Managing corporate resources

- Seminar for senior executives
- International programme for senior executives
- Mobilizing people

London Business School

- Senior executive programme
- Accelerated development programme
- Competing globally: the view from Japan
- Interpersonal skills for senior managers

University of Pittsburg

- Management programme for executives
- Executive programme for expanding business
- Benchmarking
- Improving negotiation skills
- Target marketing

University of Southern California

- Executive programme
- Certificate in management effectiveness
- Advanced management programme
- Asia/Pacific business outlook conference
- The service driven organization

University of Texas of Austin

- Management for engineers, computer and science professionals
- Customer service: the real competitive advantage
- Managing strategy for a changing environment
- Quality excellence programme
- Quality self-assessment workshop

University of Wisconsin—Madison

- The executive programme
- Leadership audit and high performance leadership
- Business to business marketing strategy
- Programme for professional sales skills

Some innovative programmes are as follows:

- Managing cultural diversity (Columbia University)
- Productivity through quality (Tennessee University)
- Managing critical resources (Virginia University)

- Leadership development (Boston University)
- Global leadership programme (Michigan University)
- Minority business executive programme (Dartmouth College)
- The international forum (Pennsylvania University).

EXECUTIVE EDUCATION IN INDIA

Several B-schools have been offering programmes on executive education. Some are long duration for one year or two years, and some are for two days to one week. Sometimes, certification programmes for about two to six months are also being offered.

There are two sub-categories in EMBAs residential and non-residential courses. The former is a recent development. The participants stay and learn on campus much like in a postgraduate 2-year management programme. Only few institutes at this moment are offering full-time residential courses of around a year's duration. These are: Indian School of Business, Hyderabad; Indian Institute of Management Ahmedabad: one year postgraduate programme in management for executives; Indian Institute of Management Kolkata: one year postgraduate programme for executives; Indian Institute of Management Bangalore; Indian Institute of Management Lucknow; Indian Institute of Management Indore; Indian Institute of Management Kozhikode; IMI, New Delhi: 11-month postgraduate programme in international management; XLRI, Jamshedpur: one year general management programme for working executives; IMT, Ghaziabad: 15-month postgraduate diploma in business management (Executive); ICFAI Business School: one year executive postgraduate programme.

Several universities and B-schools are offering executive education programmes in India. Some of them are: Andhra University, Department of Commerce and Management Studies, Visakhapatnam; Alliance Business Academy, Bangalore; Bharathidasan Institute of Management, Trichy; Department of Management Studies, IIT-Delhi; Faculty of Management Studies, Delhi University, Delhi; Goa Institute of Management, Goa; Great Lakes Institute of Management, Chennai; ICFAI Business Schools, Hyderabad (multiple campuses); Indian Institute of Forest Management, Bhopal; Indian Institute of Foreign Trade, New Delhi; Institute of Management Technology, Ghaziabad; Institute of Rural Management, Anand; KJ Somaiya Institute of Management Studies & Research, Mumbai; Lal Bahadur Shastri Institute of Management, New Delhi; Management Development Institute, Gurgaon; Narsee Monjee Institute of Management Studies, Mumbai; National Institute of Industrial Engineering, Mumbai; Nirma Institute of Management, Ahmedabad; SP Jain Institute of Management & Research, Mumbai; Shailesh J. Mehta School of Management, IIT-Bombay; Symbiosis Centre for Management and Human Resource Development, Pune; Symbiosis Institute of Business Management, Pune; T.A. Pai Management Institute, Manipal; Vinod Gupta School of Management, IIT-Kharagpur; Welingkar Institute of Management Development & Research, Mumbai; Xavier Institute of Management, Bhubaneswar.

SPECIFIC PROGRAMMES

The customized and open enrolment programmes are offered by several B-schools in India. Some of them are briefly presented here.

Some Universities and B Schools

- Programmes on general management
- Functional areas of management
- Change management
- Leadership development
- Soft skills
- Communication skills
- Entrepreneurship
- Family business
- Women managers
- Business ethics.

Department of Commerce & Management Studies, Andhra University

- General management programmes
- Management programmes for executives
- HR for non-HR professionals
- FM for non-FM professionals
- Retail management
- Negotiation skills
- Research methods for executives
- Value-based management
- Creativity and innovations
- Employee discipline.

Indian School of Business

- One year executive programme
- Leadership development programme
- Negotiation skills
- Creativity
- Worldclass manufacturing
- Family business management
- General management
- Strategy
- Leadership and change management
- Sales and marketing
- Finance
- IT / operations
- Strategic retail management
- Real estate management
- Mergers and acquisition strategy
- Scenario planning

ASCI (Administrative Staff College of India)

- General management programme
  - GMP for senior executives
  - MDP for women executives
  - Advanced management programme (study tour to France, Switzerland, Netherlands and Belgium)
  - Programme for young managers
  - Strategic management
- Economics programmes
  - New tax regime
  - VAT and works contract tax
- Energy, environment, technology programmes
  - Leadership for industrial environmental management
  - Environmental management
  - Management for environmental professionals
- Financial management programmes
  - Mergers and acquisitions
  - Management audit
  - Managing costs
  - Corporate finance for decision makers
  - Capital markets
  - Strategic financial management
  - Tax reduction at source & e-filing of returns
- Human resource management programmes
  - HR audit
  - Communication skills for managers
  - Leadership through NLP
  - Developing emotional intelligent leadership
  - Strategic HRM
  - Leadership and organization development
  - Negotiation skills
  - Managing creativity
  - Mentoring and career mapping
  - Management of change
  - Effective HR training & development
  - Managing HR in organizations
  - Managing performance
  - Personality development
  - Competency management

- HRM for line managers
- Transactional analysis for interpersonal effectiveness
- Improving work culture
- Effective trade union management

- IT, innovation & technology programmes
  - Enterprise IT security
  - e-procurement
  - Software project management
  - Business intelligence
  - Data mining
  - IT enabled knowledge management
- Marketing management programmes
  - Sales management
  - Strategic marketing
  - Brand management
- Operations management programmes
  - Inventory management
  - Procurement procedure for World Bank aided projects
  - Project and contract management
  - Urban transport management
- Health studies programmes
  - Medical audit
  - Improving quality in health care
  - Core management skills for health professionals
  - Marketing for hospital administrators
- Urban governance programmes
  - Change management for achieving continuous water supply in urban areas
  - Certificate programme in urban management in india
  - Strengthening urban management in India
  - International programme on continuous water supply in cities

Management Development Institute

- Strategic management programmes
- General management programmes
- Finance & economics programmes
- HRM programmes
- Information technology programmes
- Operations management programmes
- Business communication programmes
- Human behaviour and organization development

Indian Institutes of Management [A, B, C, I, K, L]

- Executive education open programme
- Executive PG programme in management
- Management development programme
- Advanced management programme
- Effective communication for managers
- IT for non-IT professionals
- Strategic thinking for business management
- New business environment
- Production strategies
- Marketing strategies
- Financial strategies
- HR strategies
- Technology management
- Management of taxation
- Manufacturing excellence
- Leadership skills
- Finance for non-finance executives
- HR for non-HR executives
- Managing for high performance
- E-leadership
- Managerial motivation and team building
- Logistics and supply chain management
- Six sigma
- Retail strategies
- Business ethics
- Corporate social responsibilities
- Going global: strategies for international business
- Developing positive work culture
- Building strong brands

International Management Institute [IMI]

- Several programmes on functional areas
- HR directors programme
- Globalization and management
- Trade unions
- Negotiation skills

Xavier Labour Relations Institute [XLRI]

- Emerging trends in personnel selection
- Building excellence with human capital
- Several programmes on all functional areas

IMPACT OF GLOBALIZATION

In recent years, a few Indian companies also have started their own leadership development centres at different places with the collaboration of some B-schools to impart knowledge continuously for their executives. They are: Infosys, Satyam, Wipro, SAIL, Hindustan Petroleum, banks, and some financial institutions.

Some B-schools have started their programmes in different countries. Kennedy School of the USA had an MoU with IIMA for offering a collaborative programme in Ahmedabad and launched in 2007. Some private B-schools of India have started their programmes abroad. Harvard Business School launched its first Indian executive education programme "Building a Global Enterprise in India" in February 2008 at Hyderabad International Convention Centre, with a course fee of Rs. 1.8 lakhs for five days. Some B-schools in India had MoUs to launch their joint programmes in India and abroad. Pearl School of Business had entered into some MoUs with Babson, Nottingham and Asian Institute of Technology.

During January 2007, the Kennedy School's newest executive education programme was launched in India. "Governance Challenges for India: A mid-career programme for IAS Officers—Phase V," a four-week programme designed and developed by the Kennedy School in collaboration with the Indian Institute of Management Ahmedabad (IIMA) is taking place on the IIMA campus. Kennedy School's Academic Dean Mary Jo Bane and IIMA Director Bakul Dholakia inaugurated the programme. Renowned economist, Y.K. Alagh, delivered the keynote address, calling it "a significant day in India's quest for powering itself into the twenty-first century".

The four-week long programme will train approximately 100 Indian Administrative Service (IAS) officers who have between 26–28 years experience. "Looking forward, this first day of 2007 brings us together to embark on a month-long journey of learning from each other and jointly enhancing our understanding of the governance challenges for India," said Akash Deep, Assistant Professor of Public Policy of Kennedy School and faculty co-chair of the programme. He further said, "At the dawn of the year 2007, that marks the 60th year of India's independence, the Kennedy School was thrilled to be a part of the process of transition and to do so with those who were best placed to lead that transition." According to Professor Sebastian Morris, IIMA faculty co-chair, "the objective of the course is to think together about how to make good governance happen. Good governance is achieved through good policies which, besides having laudable objectives, must also be incentive compatible so they will not require continual administrative energies and support. Through the programme, the participants will attempt to examine this idea using their experience."

A three-year agreement to design, develop and deliver the programme was signed by the Kennedy School and the Government of India, Department of Personnel and Training (DoPT) through which approximately 360 IAS officers will be trained during the period. Faculty from the Kennedy School and IIMA collaborated to design an integrated curriculum which is being delivered jointly by 12 Kennedy School and 14 IIMA faculty members over the course of the month-long programme. Sessions focusing on governance, political economy, and policy analysis will be taught through cases as well as through lectures and specially designed exercises in which participants will work in small and large groups to develop ideas and solutions. In addition, guest lectures will be delivered on a wide range of public policy topics by experts from other research institutions and public sector organizations in India.

The Kennedy School's degree programmes and executive education programmes have drawn senior officials from around the world for several decades. On an average, the school's student population is 43 per cent international, with students and participants representing more than 80 countries.

SUMMARY

1. Executive education is highly required by the corporate world.
2. Executive education has become an income generating source to B-schools and creating additional value among corporate executives.
3. As executive education is a mutually beneficial activity, several companies are approaching B-schools for offering various programmes.
4. Top B-schools abroad and in India had network with several global companies and local organizations offering short duration and long duration programmes.
5. As per their requirement, even MBA programme has been reduced from two years to one year.
6. B-schools are functioning now without any boundaries.

REVIEW QUESTIONS

1. What are the types of executive education programmes?
2. Discuss executive education abroad.
3. Explain executive education in India.
4. What is the impact of globalization on executive education?

CASE STUDY

The Hard Work of Failure Analysis

It hardly needs to be said that organizations cannot learn from failures if people do not discuss and analyze them. Yet, this remains an important insight. The learning that is potentially available may not be realized unless a thoughtful analysis and discussion of failure is done. For example, for Kaiser [Permanente's] Dr. [Kim] Adcock, it is not enough just to know that a particular physician is making more than the acceptable number of errors (in misread x-rays). Unless a deeper analysis of the nature of the radiologist's errors is conducted, it is difficult to learn what needs to be corrected. On a larger scale, the US Army is known for conducting "after action reviews" that enable the participants to analyze, discuss, and learn from both the successes and failures of a variety of military initiatives. Similarly, hospitals use Morbidity and Mortality (M&M) conferences (in which physicians convene to discuss significant mistakes or unexpected deaths) as a forum for identifying, discussing, and learning from failures. This analysis can only be effective if people speak up openly about what they know and if others listen, enabling a new understanding of what happened to emerge in the assembled group. Many of these vehicles for analysis only address substantial failures, however, rather than identifying and learning from smaller ones.

An example of effective analysis of failure is found in the meticulous and painstaking analysis that goes into understanding the crash of an airliner. Hundreds of hours may go into gathering and analyzing the data to sort out exactly what happened and what can be learned. Compare this kind of analysis to what takes place in most organizations after a failure.

As noted above, social systems tend to discourage this kind of analysis. First, individuals experience negative emotions when examining their own failures, and this can chip away at self-confidence and self-esteem. Most people prefer to put the past mistakes behind them rather than revisit and unpack them for greater understanding.

Second, conducting an analysis of a failure requires a spirit of inquiry and openness, patience, and a tolerance for ambiguity. However, most managers admire and are rewarded for decisiveness, efficiency, and action rather than for deep reflection and painstaking analysis.

Third, psychologists have spent decades documenting heuristics and psychological biases and errors that reduce the accuracy of human perception, sense making, estimation, and attribution. These can hinder the human ability to analyze failure effectively.

People tend to be more comfortable attending to the evidence that enables them to believe what they want to believe, denying responsibility for failures, and attributing the problem to others or to "the system." We would prefer to move on to something more pleasant. A rigorous analysis of failure requires that people, at least temporarily, put aside these tendencies to explore unpleasant truths and take personal responsibility. Evidence of this problem is provided by a study of a large European telecom company, which revealed that very little learning occurred from a set of large and small failures over a period of twenty years. Instead of a realistic and thorough analysis, managers tended to offer ready rationalizations for the failures. Specifically, managers attributed large failures to uncontrollable events outside the organization (e.g. the economy) and to the intervention of outsiders. Small failures were interpreted as flukes, the natural outcomes of experimentation, or as illustrations of the folly of not adhering strictly to the company's core beliefs.

Similarly, we have observed failed consulting relationships in our field research in which the consultants simply blamed the failure on the client, concluding that the client was not really committed to change, or that the client was defensive or difficult. By contrast, a few highly learning-oriented consultants were able to engage in discussion and analysis that involved raising questions about how they themselves contributed to the problem. In these analytic sessions, the consultants raised questions such as *"Are there things I said or did that contributed to the defensiveness of the client?", "Was my presentation of ideas and arguments clear and persuasive?"*, or *"Did my analysis fall short in some way that led the client to have legitimate doubts?"* Raising such questions increases the chances of the consultants learning something useful from the failed relationship, but requires profound personal curiosity to learn what the answers might be. Blaming the client is much more simple, comfortable, and common.

Recent research in the hospital setting by [A.L.] Tucker and Edmondson shows that health care organizations typically fail to analyze or make changes even when people are well aware of failures. Whether medical errors or simply problems in the work process, few hospital organizations dig deep enough to understand and capture the potential learning from failures. Processes, resources, and incentives to bring multiple perspectives and multiple minds together to carefully analyze what went wrong and how to prevent the occurrence of similar failures in the future are lacking in most organizations.

Conducting an analysis of a failure requires a spirit of inquiry and openness, patience, and a tolerance for ambiguity.

Thus, formal processes or forums for discussing, analyzing, and applying the lessons of failure elsewhere in the organization are needed to ensure that effective analysis and learning from failure occurs. Such groups are most effective when people have technical skills, expertise in analysis, and diverse views, allowing them to brainstorm and explore different interpretations of the causes and consequences of a failure. Because this usually involves the potential for conflict that can escalate, people skilled in interpersonal or group process, or expert outside facilitators, can help keep the process productive.

Next, skills for managing a group process of analyzing a failure with a spirit of inquiry and sufficient understanding of the scientific method are essential inputs to learning from failure as an organization. Without a structure of rigorous analysis and deep probing, individuals tend to leap prematurely to unfounded conclusions and misunderstand complicated problems. Some understanding of system dynamics, the ability to see patterns, statistical process controls, and group dynamics can be very helpful. To illustrate how this works in real organizations, we review a few case study examples below.

EXAMPLES OF SYSTEMATICALLY ANALYZING FAILURE

Edmondson et al. report how Julie Morath, the Chief Operating Officer at the Minneapolis Children's Hospital, implemented processes and forums for the effective analysis of failures, both large and small. She bolstered her own technical knowledge of how to probe more deeply into the causes of failure in hospitals by attending the Executive Sessions on Medical Errors and Patient Safety at Harvard University, which emphasized that, rather than being the fault of a single individual, medical errors tend to have multiple, systemic causes. In addition, she made structural changes within the organization to create a context in which a failure could be identified, analyzed, and learned from.

To create a forum for learning from failure, Morath developed a Patient Safety Steering Committee (PSSC). Not only was the PSSC proactive in seeking to identify failures, it ensured that all failures were subject to analysis so that learning could take place. For example, the PSSC determined that Focused Event Studies would be conducted not only after serious medical accidents but even after much smaller scale errors or "near misses." These formal studies were forums designed explicitly for the purpose of learning from mistakes by probing deeply into their causes. In addition, cross-functional teams, known as *Safety Action Teams*, were formed in certain clinical areas to understand better how failures occurred, thereby proactively improving medical safety. One clinical group developed something they called a *good catch log* to record information that might be useful in better understanding and reducing medical errors. Other teams in the hospital quickly followed their example, finding the idea compelling and practical.

In the pharmaceutical industry, about 90 per cent of newly developed drugs fail in the experimental stage, and thus drug companies have plenty of opportunities to analyze the failure. Firms that are creative in analyzing failure benefit in two ways. First, analyzing a failed drug sometimes reveals that the drug may have a viable alternate use. For example,

Pfizer's Viagra was originally designed to be a treatment for angina, a painful heart condition. Similarly, Eli Lilly discovered that a failed contraceptive drug could treat osteoporosis and thus developed their one-billion-dollar-a-year drug, Evista, while Strattera, a failed antidepressant, was discovered to be an effective treatment for hyperactivity/attention deficit disorder.

Second, a deep probing analysis can sometimes save an apparently failed drug for its original purposes, as is seen in the case of Eli Lilly's Alimta. After this experimental chemotherapy drug failed clinical trials, the company was ready to give up. The doctor conducting the failed Alimta trials, however, decided to dig more deeply into the failure—utilizing a mathematician whose job at Lilly was explicitly to investigate failures. Together, they discovered that the patients who suffered negative effects from Alimta typically had a deficiency in folic acid. Further investigation demonstrated that simply giving patients folic acid along with Alimta solved the problem, thereby rescuing a drug that the organization was ready to discard.

Failure analysis can reach beyond the company walls to include customers. A systematic analysis of small failures in the form of customer breakdowns was instituted at Xerox using a network-based system called *Eureka*. By capturing and sharing 30,000 repair tips, Xerox saves an estimated $100 million a year through service operations efficiencies. The Eureka analysis also provides important information for new product design.

ANALYZING EMPLOYEE AND CUSTOMER DEFECTIONS TO CAPTURE THE LESSONS

To help build an organization's ability to analyze its own failures, outside sources of technical assistance in analyzing failures can be engaged. For example, Frederick Reichheld at Bain and Company has demonstrated the value of a deep and probing analysis of failure in the areas of customer and employee defections. In one instance, the fact that most customers who defected from a particular bank gave "interest rates" as the reason for switching banks seemed to suggest that their original bank's interest rates were not competitive. However, his additional investigation demonstrated that there were no significant differences in interest rates across the banks. Careful probing through interviews indicated that many customers defected because they were irritated by the fact that they had been aggressively solicited for a bank-provided credit card, and then had their applications turned down. A superficial analysis of customer defection would have led to the conclusion that the bank's interest rates were not competitive. A deeper analysis led to an alternate conclusion: The bank's marketing department needed to do a better job of screening in advance the customers to whom it promoted such cards. *Failure analysis can reach beyond the company walls to include customers.*

The importance of analysis related to employee turnover at another company, where managers became concerned when they observed high turnover among sales people and conducted an investigation. Many of the employees gave "working too many hours" as the reason for their defection. Initially, it appeared that the turnover may not have been such a bad thing—after all who needs employees who are not committed to working hard? However, further data collection revealed that many of the employees who quit were among their most successful salespeople, and had subsequently found jobs that required, on an average, 20 per cent fewer hours. Once again, deeper probing and analysis yielded a truer understanding of the situation.

BENEFITS OF ANALYZING FAILURE

In addition to the technical aspects of systematic analysis, discussing failures has important social and organizational benefits. First, discussion provides an opportunity for others who may not have been directly involved in the failure to learn from it. Second, others may bring new perspectives and insights that deepen the analysis and help to counteract self-serving biases that may colour the perceptions of those most directly involved in the failure. After experiencing failure, people typically attribute too much blame to other people and to forces beyond their control. If this tendency goes unchecked, it reduces an organization's ability to mine the key learning that could come from the experience.

Lastly, the value of the learning that might result from analyzing and discussing simple mistakes is often overlooked. Many scientific discoveries have resulted from those who were attentive to simple mistakes in the lab. For example, researchers in one of the early German polymer labs occasionally made the mistake of leaving a Bunsen burner lit over the weekend. Upon discovering this mistake on Monday mornings, the chemists simply discarded the overcooked results and went on with their day. Ten years later, a chemist in a polymer lab at DuPont made the same mistake. However, rather than simply discarding the mistake, the Dupont chemist gave the result some analysis and discovered that the fibers had congealed. This discovery was the first step towards the invention of nylon. With similar attention to the minor failure in the German lab, they might have had a decade head start in nylon, potentially dominating the market for years.

These first two sections have dealt with inadvertent failures. If a firm can identify and analyze such failures, and then learn from them, it may be able to retrieve some value from what has otherwise been a negative "result." But failure need not always be considered from a "defensive" viewpoint. Our third section describes an "offensive" approach to learning from failure—deliberate experimentation. The three activities presented earlier identifying failure, analyzing failure, and deliberate experimentation—are not intended to be viewed as a sequential three-step process, but rather as (reasonably) independent competencies for learning from failure. They can be sensibly examined alongside each other, since each is easily inhibited by social and technical factors.

Questions for Discussion

1. What are the main issues of the above case?
2. What is the lesson you can learn from the case?

FURTHER READING

Byrne, John A. and Greene, Cynthia, *Business Week's Guide to the Best Executive Education Programmes*, McGraw Hill Inc., New York, 1993.

Satya Raju, R., *Globalisation and Executive Education*, Andhra University, Visakhapatnam (Mimeo), 2008.

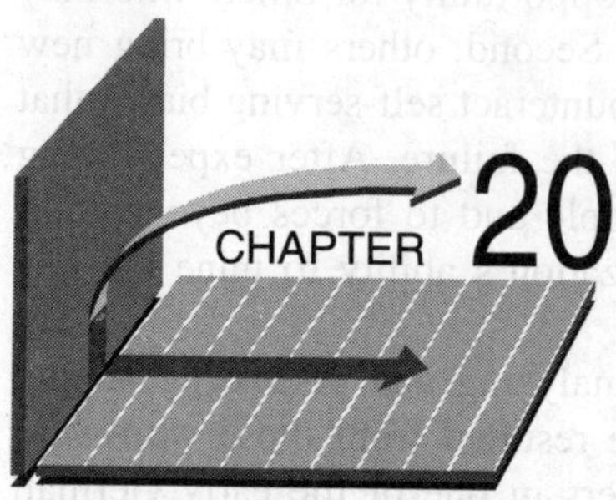

Knowledge Management

CONTENTS

INTRODUCTION

In recent years, several changes have been observed in the global economy. Some global changes are: the world has become flat; closer interaction between nations and people; significant increase in exports volume; drastic increase in foreign direct investment; hike in turnover in foreign exchange markets; rapid increase in the time spent on international telephone calls; increasing demand for internet and e-business and more involvement of people with international associations. These changes led to the importance of knowledge management in the global organizations. At present, several universities, colleges, large business houses have been thinking of this concept and trying to introduce knowledge management techniques for competitive advantage.

THE CONCEPT

Knowledge Management (KM) is defined as creation of some system in the organization, where the entire knowledge base of the people who work for a company or organization is accessible to each of them. In knowledge managed organizations, the knowledge resource should not be locked inside the heads of their people. The basic aim of creating a knowledge management system in any organization is to collect, store and disseminate knowledge among its employees to improve the bottom-line performance. It provides the knowledge worker with the tools he needs and maximizes his capabilities within the organization. Through knowledge management, corporates look for information sharing and resource optimization. The main aim of knowledge management is to capture the knowledge residing in the employees of an organization and to share it across the organization.

Peter Senge in his book *The Fifth Discipline: The Art and Practice of Learning Organization,* used the concept "learning organization". It led to the popularity of the concept of Knowledge Management (KM). According to him, people continually expand their capacity to create results they truly desire; where new patterns of thinking are nurtured; where collective aspiration is set free and where people are continually learning how to learn.

Peter Senge says a learning organization may possess the following features:

- It continuously expands its capacity to create its future.
- It believes in its people to acquire competitive edge over others.
- It encourages its people to learn continuously the ways and means that produce the desired results.
- It provides scope for collective learning by motivating total employee involvement, and nurturing their creative and innovative ideas.
- It develops structure and designs, best suited to its employees so as to enhance organizational capabilities.

As per some studies, in the modules of any Knowledge Management System (KMS), three major functional areas are observed: building and maintaining the knowledge store (creation of a knowledge bank); utilizing the knowledge stores (facilitating the use of knowledge), and creating a knowledge culture.

As per the studies conducted, the advantages of KM companies are: productivity increase (50 per cent); process improvement (19 per cent); transparency of structures and processes (18 per cent); increased focus on customers and improved customer satisfaction (18 per cent); improvement in facilities forecasting and decision making (17 per cent); greater exchange of information (13 per cent); success in market leadership (8 per cent), and improvement in staff qualification and staff satisfaction (7 per cent).

PROCESS

The process of knowledge management contains the issues relating to the concept of knowledge and trivia for the company; identifying the parts of the organization where such knowledge is generated; value addition to data and information for converting it into knowledge; drawing it out from people, organizing the contents of the depository and ensuring its accessibility to everyone; and making the knowledge base intelligent and capable of renewing itself continuously.

The basis of knowledge management rests in the communication, where vast amount of data, information and knowledge are processed daily at high speed and with accuracy. The most codified system in the world for gathering, sorting and disseminating information exists in the Associated Press System (APS). Not only does the APS offer a model for information management at the micro level, it is also a global system which provides a model for companies attempting to link officers, suppliers or customers electronically on a worldwide basis. The information flow through the AP system is examined below. A plane crashed in Wisconsin. AP reporters gather information on the crash and instantly transmit it to the state bureau in Milwaukee, which then relays the story to the central office in New York for final editing and dissemination. Dissemination takes place on a regional or global basis, depending on the interest levels of the information generated. All information generated globally moves through APS's New York office. There are AP centres in London and Tokyo, where information from various hemispheres is processed. London and Tokyo centres inform daily to the New York international desk, which chooses how and where to disseminate the news.

New operations are organized hierarchically for the speedy transmission of knowledge and information; employees are trained in writing and editing. They also learn to judge what information is useful and what is not; all writing takes place in a prescribed style for easy comprehension and quick editing; a common lexicon speeds up oral communication and creates a team atmosphere; accuracy checks are built into the work flow; an information hierarchy is established so that information flow is disseminated on a priority basis. Information is also coded so that it reaches its destination in a timely fashion. Archival data, information, and knowledge are stored for easy access.

Next, the company must realize that Electronic Date Interface cannot handle all communication needs. A human communication system must be developed. Some of the steps that can be taken are: conduct a communication flow study to determine how information is moving between operation before technology is implemented; create a customized communication flow and workflow system based on these findings; train employees in the written skills required to operate on an electronic basis; create a common lexicon among suppliers that build team consciousness; establish common operating procedures; build human and electronic accuracy checks.

The World Bank launched a knowledge management system to serve as a learning house for knowledge about development. The Bank's sectoral networks are leading the effort through the following activities: building communities of practice, developing an on-line knowledge base, establishing help desks and advisory services, building a directory of expertise making key statistics available, providing a space for professional conversation, providing access to transaction information and establishing external access and outreach to clients, partners and stakeholders. Knowledge management is expected to change the way the World Bank internally and transform its relationship with all those it deals with the outsiders.

PARAMETERS

Studies revealed that the most admired knowledge enterprises had the following eight key knowledge performance attributes:

1. Overall quality of knowledge management programmes (Xerox, Ernst and Young, Monsanto)

2. Top management support for knowledge management (Buckman, Hewlett-Packard, British Petroleum)
3. Contribution of knowledge to innovation (Lucent Technologies, 3M, Nokia)
4. Maximizing intellectual assets (Intel, Lucent Technologies, Monsanto)
5. Effectiveness of knowledge sharing (Ernst and Young, Xerox and Intel)
6. Culture of continuous learning and knowledge creation (Lucent Technologies, 3M and Nokia)
7. Creating customer value and loyalty through knowledge management (Lucent Technologies, Arthur Anderson, Ernst and Young)
8. Contribution to shareholder value (Microsoft, Intel, Lucent Technologies).

Intellectual, rich companies provide an insight into how successful knowledge management and knowledge leverage strategies work in different industries. The companies that have managed to leverage their knowledge based assets and intellectual assets are the ones that top the list in terms of market value. The following are the top 10 recipients of US patents in 1998: IBM (2,682 patents); Canon (1,934 patents); NEC (1,632 patents); Motorola (1,428 patents); Sony (1,321 patents); Samsung Electronics (1,306 patents); Fujitsu (1,205 patents); Toshiba (1,194 patents); Eastman Kodak (1,125 patents); Mitsubishi (1,120 patents).

In the past, the top fifteen US companies with the higher market valuation were: Microsoft ($ 375 billion); General Electric ($ 335 billion); Intel ($ 200 billion); Merch ($ 195 billion); Wal Mart ($ 194 billion); Pfizer ($ 172 billion); Exxon ($ 161 billions); IBM ($ 159 billions); Coca Cola ($ 158 billions); Cisco Systems ($ 155 billion); MCI World Com ($ 152 billions); AT&T ($ 149 billions); American International Group ($ 141 billions); Lucent Technologies ($ 149 billion); Citi group ($ 133 billions).

CORPORATE EXPERIENCE

One of the largest knowledge corporations in the world is Anderson Consulting. The very basis of a business organization is knowledge management. Over the past two decades, Anderson Consulting has created a formal structure for the flow of knowledge within the organization. Its knowledge exchange seeks to capture, store and spread the learning generated internally and externally by its 33,000 consultants across 47 countries. The basis of Anderson's knowledge exchange programme is Lotus Notes, which replicated knowledge seamlessly and continuously across the globe.

McKinsey launched a knowledge management project as far back as 1987 to document the core knowledge of their experts and to build a database of their practices. This is supported by a number of interesting initiatives. Ernst & Young has been focusing on knowledge of their experts and to build a database of their practices and has been focusing on knowledge management as a key business process since 1993. Through its Centre for Business Knowledge, it has created 70 company-wide communications of interest or networks, where people with common interest and expertise trade ideas supported by their own database of information. A knowledge officer attends all project meetings, picking up spoken aloud thoughts, ideas generated and discarded in the course of discussion and intellectual by-products. The purpose is to capture all knowledge which may be useful in future.

At Wipro Infotech Software and Service Group, knowledge management enables rapid development of high-quality solutions, expediting the recognition, capture and distribution of innovation through the enterprise. At Sun Pharmaceuticals, the emphasis is on retrieving information process of knowledge management. At Dr. Reddy's Labs, the emphasis has shifted from training to encouraging and shared learning. The focus of responsibility has shifted from being taught to wanting to share. Dr. Reddy's Labs, along with its group companies, Cheminor Drugs, has set up a learning centre, Ankur—equipped with learning resources like CD-ROMs, videos, audio tapes, and books—where cross-functional teams pass on their experience on specific projects to others.

The California-based software solutions provider, Informix, is using the Internet as the central nervous system for its brain with the aim of making the jobs easier at Amtrex Applications. Customer and supplier feedback is a critical source of knowledge. Its knowledge system, Prodash—proactive, professional, productive databased management with synchronization and harmony—aims at collating all correct knowledge on customers and influences, refining and storing this information for proactive databased management and management of key corporate accounts. Forbes Marshal employs a concept named *technology keeping*, where 25 people track the knowledge generation throughout the world in 25 specific fields, store it, structure it and make it available to the right individuals in the organization.

Someone pointed out that Microsoft is like "Godzilla—it screws up but keeps coming!" A good example of a failure to replace America Online Services Division is Microsoft Network, which failed to replace either America Online or the Internet. The company has $ 10 billion in cash, with approximately $ 6 billion invested in research and development. In 1999, Microsoft was an exemplary case of a company that is learning to leverage the biggest competitive advantage of all knowledge.

Airfreight, a courier company, has created a new knowledge centre. At this centre, people work on converting the intimate understanding of trucking routes that a few employees have information into, that everyone else can access and use to plan their own work. The RPG Group has created a Knowledge Integration Programme (KIP) so that all kinds of innovation within the group—from best practices in supply-chain management to time saving solutions for the Y2K problem—are immediately made part of common pool of knowledge for everybody to access.

The concept of KM was being practised by Infosys much before the term got currency. They started off with the body of knowledge—a set of documents that captured in a structured format the experiences and insights of the people as they worked on different projects. Today, the body of knowledge covers not only software development and tool issues, but also like travel trips, loans, etc. Today, the Infosys knowledge base is an in-house development system, which is available across all the units of the company on the Intranet. It started leadership development centre about a couple of years ago to develop people from different perspectives.

The digital dashboard is a knowledge management solution from Microsoft. It is an interface that resides in Outlook 2000 and integrates information from various backend resources. The information could come from any Microsoft application like SQL server, Exchange or Office 2000.

In the telecom sector, one of the hottest researches in this area is being tackled by companies set up by Indians. People like Gururaj Deshpande of Sycamore, Mukesh Chatter, Jagdeep Singh, Hemant Kanakai, Kiran Mazumdar Shaw and Paradeep Sindhu are developing cutting-edge products that will reshape the telecom world. In software, the Indian software industry is the fastest growing industry world-wide. Out of the 59 companies that achieved CMM level, 5 – 9 are Indian. In pharmaceutical industry, research is focusing on genetics. Genetics work is basically software, and India excels in software. Plus, over 14 per cent of the researchers in American research laboratories are of Indian origin. Entertainment is becoming increasingly digitalized. India has one of the largest English speaking, digitally educated pool of workers, making it an ideal base for outsourcing animation work.

In 1996, at the Daves World Economic Forum, McKinsey & Co's first Indian chief, Rajat Gupta told a skeptical world that by 2000, airlines would stress more on their ideas and service strategies than on their aircraft. The world heard for the first time about high definition TV from Arun Netravali, an Indian. He stepped into Noble Laureate Arne Enzia's shoes as the president of Bell Labs, after he had served as its first chief scientist. The pride of the University of Michigan, C.K. Prahlad, has offered the first management solution for developing economies—the theory of the strategic stretch. Viswanathan Anand is the world's number one chess player. He specializes in beating computers and is the undisputed world champion in the fast-evolving game of speed chess, which requires knowledge and speed of thought. In the field of economics, Amartya Sen provided the world its first every-mathematical index to measure welfare, and the first interface between the high ground of moral philosophy and practical economies. A fourteen-year-old Indian boy, Govind Jajoo told the chief of Microsoft (Indian) that he wanted to take up a course to become a certified systems engineer.

In the present competitive era, knowledge management plays a key role for the success of any organization. A proper knowledge management solution requires a well-defined plan. The idea of planning is to decide each and every aspect of knowledge management—the components that would be available to each employee, how it would be available, various information capturing mechanisms, etc. Essentially, the delivery should be a knowledge base and useful across the organization. In every organization, the top management needs to be involved in the planning process. The vision and values of top management and other professional managers help a lot to manage the knowledge workers at workplace. The knowledge worker is to be trained and retrained in the areas in which he requires knowledge continuously, and strategies are to be adopted to retain the knowledge workers. The professional manager of an organization has to play the role of evangelizing (developing awareness about the importance of knowledge), supporting (identify, run and back projects that find, nourish and distribute knowledge) and disseminating (present the knowledge based practices in intelligible and useful forms). Professional managers have to function to know how to tap the knowledge of the workers, when to utilize the resource, and how to retain the knowledge workers for a long time or life time. Long time relationships are to be established by involving them in the process of ownership and management. The success of an organization in achieving the mission and attaining the values is based on the best knowledge management practices in the present century. Therefore, the professional managers of the corporate world should develop the required skills to manage knowledge workers and knowledge organizations.

INDUSTRIAL ERA vs KNOWLEDGE ERA

The following changes are observed from industrial era to knowledge era.

Industrial era	*Knowledge era*
• Tangible	• Intangible
• Finance focus	• Balanced set
• Event driven	• Process driven
• Cost	• Value
• Periodic reporting	• Instant access
• Past orientation	• Future orientation
• Value in things	• Value in flows
• Production statistics	• Innovation statistics
• Metrics for reporting	• Metrics for managing
• Standards	• Customized

SUMMARY

1. The globalization process created knowledge society, which requires knowledge management in the corporate world.
2. Knowledge management is creation of some system in the organization towards accessibility of the entire knowledge base.
3. There are several advantages of knowledge management.
4. The process includes generation of knowledge, value addition to the data, converting information into knowledge, organizing for accessibility to all in the organization.
5. Several companies are following knowledge management.
6. There is a vast change in the knowledge era.

REVIEW QUESTIONS

1. Define knowledge management. What are its advantages?
2. Explain the process of knowledge management.
3. What are the knowledge parameters followed by different companies?
4. Discuss the knowledge management initiatives of some companies.
5. What are the changes from industrial era to knowledge era in managing business?

CASE STUDY

Bharat Petroleum Corporation Limited

During his annual inspection visit to one of the refineries during the mid-2001, Mr. S. Behuria, the Chairman of Bharat Petroleum Corporation Limited (BPCL), wondered if the corporation would survive the impending privatization or if its ownership would change. How could he motivate employees to be ready for upcoming competition in 2002 when state-owned enterprises in India would be privatized? Would workers deal with the momentum of the proposed organizational redesign process or would everything crumble with full deregulation of the petroleum industry?

HISTORY OF THE COMPANY

Bharat Petroleum Corporation Limited (BPCL), a government owned company incorporated under the Companies Act, 1956, is in the business of refining, storing, marketing and distributing of petroleum products. The paid-up capital of BPCL is ₹300 million, of which the Government of India (GOI) holds 66.2%. The balance (33.8%) of the equity is held by foreign institutional investors, financial institutions, employees and other investors.

The history of BPCL dates back to 1975 when the GOI, pursuant to an agreement, acquired Burmah–Shell Refineries Limited (BSR). The Burmah–Shell Oil Storage and Distributing Companies of India Ltd. (BSM), a foreign company established in 1928, was in the business of distribution and marketing of petroleum products in India. Burmah–Shell Refineries Limited was renamed Bharat Refineries Limited (BRL) in 1976 and to BPCL in 1977. Burmah–Shell Refineries Limited was incorporated in 1952 as a company under the Companies Act. Between 1991 and 1994, the GOI had disinvested part of its holdings to financial institutions and BPCL employees. As a result, the equity holding of the GOI was reduced to 66.2%. The GOI planned to fully divest its shares by the end of 2002.

CRISIS

Bharat Petroleum Corporation Limited operates in the retail, lubricant, liquefied petroleum gas (LPG) and aviation fuel sectors. With the ongoing liberalization process in India, sectors like LPG and lubricants have been deregulated. Bharat Petroleum Corporation Limited owns one refinery in Mumbai, which has a capacity of 7–8 million tons, and it sells about 16–18 million tons of crude per year. As the market is controlled in the retail business, there is national pool of oil, controlled by the Oil Coordination Cell (OCC), which distributes crude to the three main oil retailers in India. There is one private firm in the industry, Reliance Petroleum, which cannot openly compete in the market, but which has its own refinery. The output generated from its refinery is bought and distributed by one or more of the three state-owned enterprises (SOEs), i.e. BPCL, Hindustan Petroleum Corporation Limited (HPCL), and Indian Oil Limited (IOL), all three of which had enjoyed a monopoly under the administered pricing mechanism (APM) of the GOI. With full deregulation of the industry proposed in 2002, the market structure will change and there will be open competition in the industry. One of BPCL's service managers reflected, "In the lubricants sector, BPCL had a market share of 12–16%. In 1999, when the market share came down to 4%, there was worry about what will entail when the entire sector is deregulated."

Retention of market share would be a serious threat, with the entry of new local (private) and global players in this sector, in the country. Bharat Petroleum Corporation Limited ought to redesign itself and shift from a mindset operating under a regulated market to a lean, agile, competitive, and customer-oriented player to compete for market share.

INDUSTRY ENVIRONMENT AND MARKET STRUCTURE

The business environment saw many changes after the initial phase of deregulation. India's petroleum retail sector is currently dominated by SOEs, and private domestic firms such as Reliance and Essar Oil have been barred from tapping the market directly. This market structure faces impending change. With new private investment, both BPCL and HPCL will be well positioned to attract investment and increase their market share at the expense of IOC, the leader. Naturally, the concern remains that the strategic sale of HPCL will simply be palmed off to SOEs as in the case of Burmah Petroleum.

India's demand for petroleum products is expected to increase after liberalization, and is therefore attracting the attention of multinational oil companies and other private Indian players. Domestic private firms are trying to complete the construction of their refineries to exploit future prospects. This is bound to increase competition in this lucrative sector. This will mean a significant loss in the market share of the SOEs. Deregulation would also bring other changes, such as the determination of product prices by import parity prices. Margins set by competitive pressures will be more volatile and highly uncertain. Dealers and distributors may shift their allegiance and consequently, the existing firms may lose retail sites and LPG warehouses. Firms may react by offering minimal facilities in their highway segment of retail outlets to keep costs low and reduce lead times.

Trained and experienced manpower in the industry will be lured away by the entrants. Non-fuel offerings such as convenience stores and ATMs are likely to be threshold activities, especially in metros and urban markets. One of BPCL's managers summed up, "The increasing demand for hydrocarbons in India is a tremendous opportunity. The major concern is the possible and inevitable loss of market share due to an increase in the number of players in the market place. The greatest challenge will be to retain our customers and remain profitable."

REDESIGN STRATEGY

A BPCL manager reflected on strategy, "Our broad strategy is to win the deregulated environment, focus on customer service, and improve our profitability. In order to beat the competition, a very strong customer focus is needed in the whole organization. It is necessary to understand and respond quickly to customers' need and expectations. The speed at which the staff responds in the market will determine the success of the corporation. The major focuses in the competitive scenario will be customer loyalty. The whole organization has to align itself to meet customer requirements and to acquire new competencies and skills."

In the refinery sector, which is still regulated, BPCL has a capacity of 7–8 million tons, whereas it sells about 16–18 million tons of crude per year. To address this gap, BPCL acquired Kochi Refineries, which has a capacity of about 8 million tons and is looking to expand opportunities in the refinery business. Following the international model, opportunities in related and unrelated diverse fields in the non-fuel sector are experimented.

Bharat Petroleum Corporation Limited hired the internationally renowned consultancy firm McKinsey to formulate a strategy for retailing effectively and the opening convenience and grocery stores. The deregulation of the industry forced top management to realize that BPCL had to focus on its customers and make decisions faster. That would be possible only by de-layering the hierarchical organization and by empowering its staff. Two senior managers of BPCL pointed out, "Most employees do not understand the nature of the business, what we are doing. Our core competence is not refining crude oil but selling products. This is where the market will be after deregulation. The aim of redesign was to be ready for change. This meant changing ourselves to be tuned to the external changes. Our national competitors are Reliance and MRPL (a joint venture by the Birla Group of Companies) and foreign competitors will be Castrol, TotalEI (Fina, BP, and ExxonMobil), as was witnessed with the deregulation of the lubricants sector."

Organizational redesign started in 1998 with the help of consultancy firm Arthur D Little and its group of consultants. They formed a project group with over 30 people drawn from different functions and regions with a general manager as their leader. It was called Project CUSECS, meaning customer service and customer satisfaction. Their main thrust areas were better customer service, profitability, creation of strategic business units (SBUs), and division of the organization into regional units.

The redesign of BPCL saw the change of the organization structure from a functional to a divisional enterprise, with six SBUs spread over four geographical regions (north, south, east and west). Before the redesign at the corporate level, the structure was functionally oriented, consisting of the functions of sales and distribution, information systems (IS), marketing and HRM. In this structure, although depots reported to the divisional manager, there was very little coordination at the field level among the sales officers and the operational officers. One of the senior managers summed it up, "The functional structure made it difficult for senior managers to focus on developing and implementing strategies for particular business such as lubricants and LPG. It created a bottleneck between the process of strategy formulation and its implementations." The redesigned structure had six SBUs: (a) refinery; (b) retail; (c) industrial/commercial; (d) lubricants; (e) LPG; and (f) aviation. The HRM functions (both human resources service and human resource development) played a critical role in the redesign process. As one of the members of the board of directors pointed out, "BPCL has undergone a very interesting HRD powered transformation process… it was orchestrated by Mr. Arun Maira and his team from Arthur D Little. Instead of providing BPCL with a package of vision, strategy, structure, process … he asked the management to carry through a very broad visioning exercise. Some 2500 managers participated. It resulted not only in a clear corporate vision, identification of shareholders, and statement of core values, but visions were collectively evolved by each function, department, branch and section. This envisioning and agenda setting was facilitated by trained individuals, many of them volunteers from functions other than HRM."

The main theme of the vision is "Business partner first, business partner last". The themes vary for each SBU. For the lubricants SBU, it is "survive today, to be there in the future". For the retail SBU, it is "people above oil. We care for you, we exist because of you".

The necessity and the competencies required for the redesign were summed up by a senior manager of BPCL, "Competition is with both national and multinational companies. The key to compete is to deliver quality products at a cheaper price, cut costs and keep costs in control. There should be a concern for financials by all stakeholders with a profit building motive and sustaining the bottom line. The required functional competency is in selling and distributing products. Customers, both internal and external, should be satisfied. The challenge is to mine this situation with effective leadership at all levels."

The redesigned organization has four elements: (a) corporate centre; (b) SBUs; (c) support services; and (d) lateral thinking mechanisms. The corporate centre has four directors (marketing, financial, refineries and personnel). The marketing director and his team of eight members are responsible for leading and coordinating the brand building and brand management functions of SBUs. The finance director and his team of six members are responsible for leading and coordinating the strategy development effort at the corporate level. The directors facilitate the SBUs in developing and integrating their respective strategies across the businesses. They also assist top management in optimally allocating resources while managing the business portfolio.

The support services are HRM, finance, IS and engineering and projects (marketing). Executives in each embedded unit report to the head of that SBU. For example, the embedded HRM function in the LPG SBU reports to the head of the LPG SBU. Dedicated teams called *shared services* perform the support tasks that have enterpriseswide or regionwide implications and that are not business specific. This is done to bring down the operating costs of these services by pooling some of the activities outside the business.

Before the redesign, the organization was 'totally hierarchical', according to some executives. Today, it is mostly participatory and team based with absolute delegation of authority. An example of this is the new performance management system, it is open. Most personnel understand the role they have to play. One of the managers pointed out, "The attitude shift has taken place in a span of three years only." BPCL recruited generalists and trained them to be specialists. Most senior managers at BPCL are generalists; only a few are specialists. One of the managers pointed out, "Due to the historical recruitment structure, the personnel are generalists while we need bright specialists like MBA graduates. If we cannot look into this, there would be a wide gap as 70% of our recruits are not as good as our competitors, they are average. The profile, experience and expertise for the job are not there."

One of the vehicles used for facilitating the change process has been communication. Plenty of communication workshops have been conducted, in which staff from various locations, irrespective of their positions in the organization, have participated. This had brought about much better understanding and commitment to the change process.

HUMAN RESOURCE MANAGEMENT AT BPCL ("It is a great place to work".)

The HRM function has been classified along with the other support services like finance and information systems. The support services are organized into three types of structures: (a) embedded support services; (b) shared support services; and (c) corporate services. Before the redesign, the regional HR manager was responsible for all the functions in the region, and all the personnel in the region reported to the regional manager. The regional manager had a very formal relationship with the corporate HRM department. Now, each SBU has HRM personnel between as 'Embedded HRM' who assist the SBU in HRM issues like transfers, organizational learning, performance appraisal and discipline. The embedded HRM departments:

- administer the performance management system;
- plan the workforce;
- design functional training programmes and deliver them;
- anchor organizational learning;
- transfer workers within business units; and
- manage discipline.

The shared services entail support task that have enterprisewide and regionwide implications. They are not confined to being business specific and are transactional in nature. All SBUs and entities share teams performing these tasks. Pooling some of the activities together outside the businesses leads to economies of scale. The HRM services team in each region is headed by the head of regional services, who is supported by the HR manager (employee relations), responsible for recruitment of non-management staff.

The role of HRM function is to provide support to the main business. The HRM function should provide information and support proactively. It should know the business the company is in. It should not concentrate only on HRM practices, but also implement those practices in helping the business.

RECRUITMENT PROCESS

Recruitment at BPCL takes place mostly at the entry level. The company believes in building its human potential rather than having it from the market. Until now, it was seen as a lifetime job, and people worked their way up to management. The redesign entailed strengthening the field force to boost marketing and customer focus. The consultants advised a 50% increase in the sales force and frontline staff, but without any additional recruitment. The sales force was increased by redeploying management staff from the back office and retraining them. After the initiation of the redesign process, there has been a hiring freeze. Recruitment is done only for specialized and new jobs. Competency mapping will be introduced.

Selection within the organization is done by matching the job profile and appraisal. The scope for promotion is limited at BPCL. The average age at BPCL is 35–40. A promotion can be expected only after three years. There is a system of job rotation. To occupy a responsible position, an executive needs to have work experience in at least three departments. One of the managers reflected: "There is no clear-cut policy on promotion."

RETRAINING AND REDEPLOYMENT

Retraining and redeployment play a very important role after the redesign process. It is a part of the business strategy to redeploy and transfer personnel. The excess workforce is trained and redeployed. But the decision to redeploy is not taken ad hoc. Retraining and redeployment are discussed first with the personnel and then carried out. This is a big challenge, as employees do not want to be redeployed. One of the senior managers pointed out: "After the implementation of an ERP system in the areas of dispatch, logistics, project and HRM, there is a surplus in the workforce. We were trying to find new opportunities and to train the excess workforce to absorb them where they can build new competencies."

PERFORMANCE MANAGEMENT SYSTEM

The extensive team-based structures proposed by Arthur D Little were pilot-tested with six retail projects. Visionary leadership and planning (VLP) workshops were held to clarify shared-visions, document the current situation, and devise concrete plans for bridging the gap between vision and reality. During the redesign process, the consultants understood that the new organization needed new competencies and a new mindset to make the redesign successful. The functional perspective needed to be changed into a team-based, collaborative, cross-functional mindset. It was a difficult task. Employees were invited to participate in learning experiences throught the foundations of learning (FOL) programme, which was designed to develop their abilities to work in high performing cross-functional teams. One example of the many observations is: "In one of the questions before the new performance management system (PMS), there were four options in the performance appraisal system on the question of the dependability of the subordinate: (a) generally dependable; (b) dependable; (c) mostly dependable; and (d) trustworthy. Supervisors who did not know the difference between these terms could hamper the career of a bright subordinate as the terms are ambiguous and can be represented in different ways." One of the managers reflected, "One of the critical elements in the success of a redesign of an organization is to reward process. The only reward for good performance we have today is promotion. As the number of vacancies is always limited, all eligible staff in a job group cannot be promoted. Rewarding good performers/teams is a solution to achieve performance. A task force is looking into a reward structure that has a combination of monetary and non-monetary reward."

RIGHTSIZING/RETAINING

BPCL is a public enterprise; there is no scope of rightsizing. Hence, efforts are made to retrain and redeploy personnel from departments that have a surplus of workforce. A current example is in the refinery after the implementation of ERP. One of the managers pointed out, "Voluntary retirement schemes (VRS) should come in immediately. We should have a policy like that of

Indian Oil Company, where employees have a choice to opt for VRS. Interviews are held of the employees who opt for VRS scheme. These interviews form the basis for deciding whether VRS should be given or not. IOC does not give VRS to an employee if he wants to quit, and just let him quit. This will bring some scope for new recruitment of professionals within the company."

CHANGES IN PERFORMANCE

Bharat Petroleum Corporation Limited decided to measure performance in both financial and customer satisfaction terms. Financial performance was measured by return on capital employed (ROCE), return on investment (ROI), and internal rate of return (IRR). Customer satisfaction was measured by market share and customer loyalty index. The index was constructed on the basis of periodic customer surveys. The capabilities of key business (corporeity and business strategies, IS plan, brand strategy, and HRM strategy) were gauged by the quality of their outputs. For example, the retail SBU measures its performance by assessing return on capital employed, customer loyalty index, cycle time of retail engineering projects, security of sties, and morale of the staff.

A series of activities were taken by consultants to implement the redesign mechanism and link it to performance. The performance of retail outlets was monitored closely. Dramatic improvements were seen in the resolution and prevention of customer complaints, as well as in the reduction of open items (accounts receivable). Productivity and operating efficiency increased; the increase was felt throughout the units. Both managerial and non-managerial personnel understood the need of the hour after going through an intense communication process and felt the need to do their best to save their company from imminent competition.

The redesign process, the reinforcement of HRM strategies, and the communication exercise together reduced absenteeism, improved morale, and heightened employees' co-operation with management. Employees felt that they had to put in their best to fight the challenge. This saw the beginning of innovations in product, process, systems, and management at all levels.

CONSTRAINTS

Some nationalistic and protectionist ministers have opposed the planned sell-off because the government will be relinquishing much of its influence over the pricing of fuels, a particularly sensitive issue that has precipitated unrest and caused criticism of past governments, and because they feel that the companies will not be sold at a fair price. The process of privatization has so far raised only ₹50 billion (US$1 billion), against a governmental target of ₹120 billion (US$2.4 billion).

FUTURE OUTLOOK AND IMPLICATIONS

Along with Reliance and Essar Oil, foreign operators such as Shell, BP, ExxonMobil and Petronas are expected to bid for controlling stakes. Private investment will then enable investment in marketing and retail infrastructure, which should lead to improved service levels, if not lower prices. The surge in the companies' share prices reflects the investor's confidence that the biggest hurdles have now been navigated and should help the Indian government to get its privatization agenda back on track after several months of uncertainty.

Questions for Discussion

1. What changes have taken place in the business environment after liberalization and after the deregulation of the LPG and lubricant sectors?
2. What were the major challenges confronted by BPCL after liberalization?
3. Given the future outlook of the petroleum sector, what role can be played by BPCL to continues to remain competitive?

FURTHER READING

Charles Despres and Danielle Chauvel, *Knowledge Horizons,* Butterworth Heinemann, Boston, 2001.

Morey, Daryl et al., *Knowledge Management*, University Press, Hyderabad, 2001.

Rao, Madan Mohan, *Leading the Knowledge*, Tata McGraw-Hill, New Delhi, 2003.

Senge, P.M., *The Fifth Discipline: The Art and Practice of a Learning Organization*, Toronto, Currency Double Day, 1994.

Tiwna, Amrit, *Knowledge Management: Toolkit*, Pearson Education Asia Singapore, 2000.

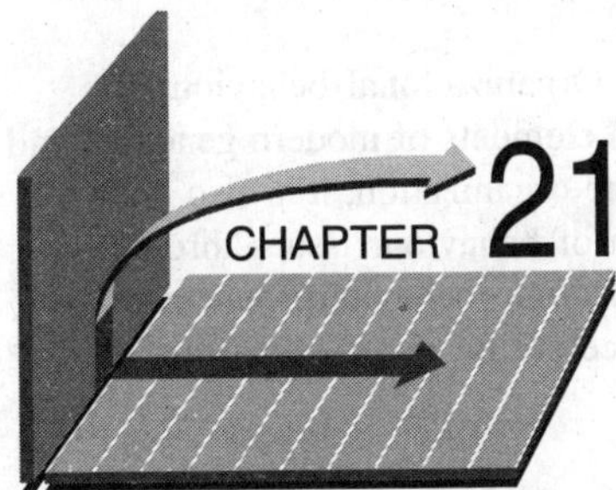

Introduction to Organizational Behaviour

CONTENTS

- Introduction
- Definitions
- Influencing Factors
- Models or Theories
- Individual Behaviour
- Group Dynamics
- Interpersonal Relations

INTRODUCTION

Organizational behaviour is interdisciplinary. It is linked to different behavioural sciences, such as psychology, sociology, social psychology, anthropology and political science. We can understand the behaviour of people at workplace when we study this subject.

DEFINITIONS

ROBBINS and SANGHI: Organizational behaviour is concerned with the study of what people do in an organization and how that behaviour affects the performance of the organization. It emphasizes behaviour as related to concerns such as jobs, work, absenteeism, employment turnover, productivity, human performance and management. The behaviour of people working in an organization should be known to any management in order to manager them effectively. It is related to psychology of people, sociology, social psychology, anthropology, political sciences and other related areas.

FINANCIAL TIMES MASTERING MANAGEMENT SERIES: Organizational behaviour is one of the most complex and perhaps the least understood academic elements of modern general management, but since it concerns the behaviour of people within the organization, it is also one of the most critical...its concern with individual and group pattern of behaviour issues thrown up in the modern business world. As it is based on individual and group behaviour, managers have to consider both individuals and groups to manage them successfully.

INFLUENCING FACTORS

The factors that influence behaviour in organizations are: the individual, the group, the organization, and the environment.

Individual: Organizations represent some individuals. The individual is an important person or central figure of an organization. Individual background, expectations, aptitude and organizational environment are very important to satisfy every individual.

Group: In every organization, groups are common. Their performance is very important. Group behaviour and their work related aspects decide their satisfaction in the organization. People in the group require cohesiveness. Some persons influence the entire group and change the work environment.

Organization: In any formal organization, people representing some individual and groups have great influence on various aspects. The organizational image is based on the behaviour and satisfaction of the people in the organization.

Environment: Organizations are also influenced by environmental factors, such as technology, climate, and social, political and economic factors. In addition, internal and external environmental factors also play a major role.

MODELS OR THEORIES

The following are the models of organizational behaviour:

- Autocratic model
- Custodial model
- Supportive model
- Collegial model

In the autocratic model, the manager or leaders expect the employees to work as per the direction given. There is no two-way participation. The power of the leader plays a major role. The employees have to follow the directions of the management.

The custodial model focuses on employee security, welfare and well-being. Employees feel happy because of their work environment. The management acts as the custodian of people.

The supportive model includes employee participation and involvement. The management maintains cordial human relations. Organizational climate supports the expectations of employees. Managers support employees to reach their goals in the organization.

The collegial model is based on team work of employees and managers. The principle of mutual contribution by the employer and the employee plays a prominent role in this model.

These models are observed in different organizations. Employee behaviour is to be based on managers' behaviour. Sometimes, managers are introverts or extroverts. Employees have to understand managers' behaviour and work in teams for maximum contribution to the organization.

INDIVIDUAL BEHAVIOUR

Individual employees and the group of employees play a significant role in organizational effectiveness. The individual's behaviour is to be understood by managers. The factors influencing the individual behaviour are: traits, gender, abilities, values, physique, development aspects, motivation, attitudes, perception, social and cultural aspects.

Personality

Personality is a pattern of stable and characteristics of a person that influences the behaviour towards goal achievement. The personality of an individual is based on several factors. There are several theories of personality development. Erikson viewed that personality development is continued throughout the life of a person, and we have to understand how individuals resolve their conflicts for personality development. The influencing factors of personality are: biological factors (heredity, physical features), cultural factors, family and social factors, and situational factors.

According to Erikson there are eight stages of personality development: *trust, atonomy, initiative, industry, identity, intimacy, generativity,* and *integrity*. Cattell says the personality factors which influence the individual decision for high score or low score are:

- Outgoing or reserved (more intelligent or less intelligent)
- Higher or low ego strength (emotional stability)
- Dominant or submissive
- Surgency (optimistic) or desurgency (pessimistic)
- Parmia (adventurous) or Threctia (timid)
- Autla (imaginative) or prakernia (practical)
- Shrewdness or artlessness
- Radicalism or conservatism
- Self-sufficiency or group dependence
- High self or low self concept control
- High or low agric tension.

According to Carl Jung, people strive for self-actualization, have a darker self, have both masculine and feminine qualities, and have a personal role. Jung also described three levels of personality: (a) a conscious level (daily reality); (b) an unconscious level (contains our own unique complexes); and (c) a collective conscious level (store of universal and evolutional experiences).

Cognitive Theory

Kelly's cognitive theory considered the whole person in terms of their perceptions, attitudes and goals. This is also called *personal construct theory*. Individuals construct and experiment their personality in their world of work. The decisions taken by the management are based on the perceptions, attitudes and goals of individual employees. Based on various experiences, the British Psychological Society has prepared some guidelines and codes of practice on psychometric tests.

As it was difficult to take data from one individual person (ideography), Kelly developed the *repertory grid* to measure an individual's construct of the world. It helps to measure the person's own constructions of the world. Based on this, it can be understood how the employee behaves and feels about his job in the organization. The important parameters are:

- Interesting
- Skilled
- Physically demanding
- Job satisfaction
- Safe working conditions
- Clean working conditions
- A job in which the employee is respected
- A job in which the employee reaps gains
- A job in which the employee feels to move about.

Based on the individual personality, managers have to produce a good team of people. It is the strength of any organization. Individual differences can be combated with some measures, such as creating organizational ambience for the development of talented employee, systematic appraisal of employees, creating thought leaders, and encouraging talent and employee partnership in business.

Perception

Perception is the basic cognitive or psychological process. It is a process by which individuals organize and interpret their sensory impressions in order to give meaning to their work environment.

There are three factors that influence perception:

1. Situation:
   (a) Time
   (b) Work setting
   (c) Social setting.

2. Perceiver:
   (a) Attitude
   (b) Motive
   (c) Interest
   (d) Experience
   (e) Expectation.
3. Target:
   (a) Novelty
   (b) Motion
   (c) Sound
   (d) Size
   (e) Background
   (f) Proximity
   (g) Similarity.

Internal and external factors also influence perception. Internal factors are individual needs and desires, individual personality, and individual experience. External factors are size, intensity, frequency, and status.

Based on the perception, rational decision making process of individuals has the following steps:

- Define the problem.
- Identify the decision criteria.
- Allocate weights to the criteria.
- Develop alternatives.
- Evaluate alternatives.
- Select the best alternative.

GROUP DYNAMICS

The concept of group dynamics was popularized by Kurt Lewin during 1930. A group is a collection of individuals in which there is interaction among people, sharing of certain norms and values, perceptions and interdependence.

Groups are common in any organization. A group means two or more individuals interacting and interdependent to achieve objectives or any task of an organization. Groups may be formal or informal. Formal group behaviour is different from that of informal groups of an organization. Formal groups are employee unions, any group of employees to perform some task. Informal groups are based on several factors, such as department, region, religion, and social status. Formal groups have organizationally recognized formal structure, roles and responsibilities. Informal groups are neither formally recognized nor have formal structure. Both the groups are usually found in organizations to perform certain functions for organizational and individual development.

Types of Groups

The following are the different types of groups:

- Formal groups (as per the structure of the organization)
- Informal groups (non-structural)
- Command groups (determined by organizational chart)
- Task groups (organizational chart determines on job basis)
- Friendship groups (social alliances).

Reasons for Groups

The following are the important reasons for joining groups:

- Status
- Security
- Self-esteem
- Affiliation
- Power
- Goal achievement
- Protection
- Satisfaction.

Theories

There are many theories of group development. Some of them are explained here briefly.

1. ***Propinquity theory:*** In this theory, individuals associate with others because of their spatial or geographical clones. Employees of a particular department form a group because of their closeness.

2. ***Activities, interactions and sentiments (AIS) theory:*** This theory is based on the employees and their activities and interactions. For instance: employees working on a project of a software organization have a group based on their work.

3. ***Balance theory:*** People are associated because of their attitudes, aptitudes and similar thinking. Similar attitudes of individuals are life style, work, culture, education, politics, etc.

4. ***Five-stage model:*** The following are the five stages in group development: (a) forming, (b) storming, (c) norming, (d) performing, and (e) adjourning.

The first stage is forming group development. In this stage, the group is in a dilemma for structure, leadership objectives, and activities. In the storming stage, they have mixed feelings and experiences. Possibility of conflicts is there. Then, the group has to manage the conflict. In the norming stage, group cohesiveness can be observed. The group shows willingness to share and work together. In the next performing stage, the group members accept to perform any role individually to achieve the goals. In the last stage, the group is adjourned. The members stop their individual work and wind up that activity.

Group Decision Making Techniques

There are three group decision making techniques: (a) interacting groups, (b) brainstorming, and (c) nominal group. In the interacting groups, members interact with each other face to face to take decisions. In brainstorming, the group generates some ideas, discusses various alternatives, and takes decision. Whereas, in the nominal group technique, individual members meet face to face to pool their judgement. Whatever may be the technique, decisions are to be taken at the right time for organizational effectiveness.

INTERPERSONAL RELATIONS

Interpersonal relations are highly essential in any organization. It means relationship between two or more persons. Interpersonal competence refers to the degree to which you are accurately aware of your impact on others, and of the impact of others on you. Your role in any organization is related to superiors, subordinates and colleagues.

Interpersonally competent managers should be able to engage in any mutually helpful relationship, achieve personal goals, aware of their impact on others and others' impact on them, and allow subordinates to challenge their views.

Interpersonal relationship is highly essential in any organisation. Increasing interpersonal awareness is developed by Joseph Luft and Harry Ingham. It is a schematic model that shows how people expose themselves to others and receive feedback from others. This is nicely explained by Joseph and Harry as Johari Window, which has the following four parts:

1. Arena—known to the self and others
2. Blindspot—known to others but not to self
3. Closed—known to self but not to others
4. Dark—neither known to self nor others.

The following factors help a lot in resolving interpersonal problems:

- Importance of relationship
- Ability of confront
- Use of empathy
- Use of one language
- Focusing on behaviour
- Use of descriptive statements
- Exploring alternative behaviour
- Selection of time
- Importance of privacy
- Use of non-verbal behaviour.

For developing interpersonal relationship, forming first impression, developing mutual expectations, honouring psychological contracts, developing trust and influence are essential.

Organizational Development

Organizational development is a long-term effort led and supported by top management to improve an organisation's visioning, empowerment, learning and problem solving processes. It consists of the following components:

- Organisational culture
- Organisational conflict
- Employee commitment
- Management of change
- Management developments
- Organisational effectiveness.

The ultimate objective of organizational behaviour study is to develop organizations through effective management by following several models and practices.

SUMMARY

1. Organizational behaviour is concerned with the study of people working in organizations.
2. It is interdisciplinary.
3. Individuals, groups, organization and environment influence organizational behaviour.
4. Every employee's personality and perception are essential to understand organizational behaviour.
5. Groups in an organization play an important role in taking decisions.
6. Interpersonal relations are to be developed in any organization for effectiveness.
7. Organizational development is highly essential.

REVIEW QUESTIONS

1. Define organizational behaviour and explain its models.
2. Define perception.
3. Discuss the factors influencing individual behaviour.
4. What are the factors influencing group behaviour?
5. Discuss the factors influencing personality.
6. Explain interpersonal relations.
7. Define organizational development and list out its components.

CASE STUDY

Head Hunting

Sunrise Steel Works (SSW) is a rerolling mill, situated near Jamshedpur. By melting iron, it converts into blooms, rods and wires. Since the construction industry in the country is booming, there is good demand for usable and products. SSW, with it rerolling technique, is able to compete well with major steel plants like SAIL and TELCO.

SSW has decided to expand the plant at Jamshedpur and for this, has acquired necessary plant and equipment. It was looking for an experienced metallurgical engineer with blast furnace experience in major steel plant to head its operations.

SSW has requisitioned the services of a Head Hunter Firm (HHF) to focus on Vizag Steel Plant to poach a couple of its experienced metallurgical engineers. SSW gave an indication that it would pay a minimum of fifty per cent more than what the candidate was presently drawing, which could go up to one hundred per cent for a deserving candidate.

Normally, Indians are homesick and would like to have a job nearer to their homes or at least in the same state they come from. Cashing in on this attitude, SSW wanted candidates belonging to Bihar or West Bengal who could get attracted to a job nearer home. HHF demanded that SSW should pay one month's salary as service charges if a candidate is selected and joined. SSW should also meet HHF's administrative expenses on actual cost.

HHF started its hunting and finally located six engineers of Vizag Steel Plant who approximated SSW's requirements. HHF sent brief resumes of these six candidates to SSW whose CMD shortlisted three 'targets' and asked HHF to focus on them. HHF contacted those three candidates over phone and stated that an attractive job as Head of Operations was waiting and if they are interested, they should come for preliminary briefing at a designated local star hotel. Each candidate met the head hunter separately and obtained full briefing about the job description and organization profile. One candidate, after studying the profile of the company, did not show any interest. Another candidate, Mukharjee, was interested only if the job was offered at its 24-Paraganas plant. After verifying with the principles, the candidate was promised posting in West Bengal after one year's service at Jamshedpur plant. But this did not satisfy the candidate and he, too, dropped out.

The third candidate, M.K. Dubey, was interested and started bargaining for better terms. After two rounds of discussions, the head hunter arranged a meeting between the Deputy Managing Director of SSW and Dubey at a star hotel in Vizag. After protracted negotiations, a high salary was fixed. Perks like furnished housing, company car and medical facilities were offered. Interest-free vehicle loan was promised for purchase of a car after one year of service. The job was on a 3-year contract, which could be extended. Dubey was satisfied with the terms but said that he would like to visit the Jamshedpur plant and that he would require three month's time to give notice to his present employer. SSW arranged return rail ticket to visit the plant and offered to reimburse three months' notice pay if the candidate decided to join service early in Jamshedpur.

Dubey visited the plant but was silent for over a fortnight. SSW was eager to know when Dubey would join service. Dubey finally broke the news; he was not interested in the offer, which was conveyed to SSW. The reasons for turning down the lucrative offer were surprising. Dubey reasons that (a) though he was from Bihar, the law and order situation was not good in the State and he had a peaceful life at Vizag; (b) the SSW factory was located some 35 km from Jamshedpur; (c) there was no housing facility at the plant site; (d) above all, there was no surety of job security; and (e) he was happy at Vizag Steel Plant where he has been provided with accommodation, school was very near, good playgrounds, recreation centre, good medical facilities, there was no parochialism or favouritism in the organization, and merit had a premium. The cost of living was comparatively cheap. On the whole, the quality of life was good at Vizag Steel. This would amply offset the lucrative salary increase.

Questions for Discussion

1. Was it ethical for SSW to poach another organization through head hunters just to get its required human resource?
2. Was the apprehension of job insecurity of Dubey right? What steps should SSW take to attract deserving candidates?
3. If Dubey goes along with SSW's inflated salary figures and he is hired, what possible problems could he face?

FURTHER READING

Davis, Keith, *Human Behaviour at Work*, Tata McGraw-Hill, New Delhi, 1975.

Fred Luthans, *Organizational Behaviour*, McGraw-Hill Kogakusha Ltd., Tokyo, 1977.

Laurie J. Mullins, *Management and Organizational Behaviour, Financial Times*, Pitman Publishing, London, 2000.

Richard Seel, Culture and Complexity, New Insights into Organizational Change, *Organisations and People*, No. 2, 2000.

Robbins, Stephen P. and Sanghi, Seema, *Organizational Behaviour*, Pearson, New Delhi, 2008.

Robbins, Stephen P., *Organizational Behaviour*, Prentice-Hall of India, New Delhi, 1991.

Schein, E.H., Organizational Culture, *American Psychologist*, **45**, No. 2, pp. 109–119, 1990.

Organizational Culture and Effectiveness

CONTENTS

- Concept
- Importance
- Characteristics
- Functions
- Competitive Advantage/Disadvantage of Culture
- Cross-cultural Dimensions
- Organizational Effectiveness
- Managing Conflicts

CONCEPT

According to New Storm and Keith Davis, organizational culture is a cognitive framework consisting of assumptions, beliefs, values and norms that are shared by an organization's members. This culture might have been consciously created by its key members, or it may have simply evolved in course of time. It represents a key element of the work environment in which employees perform their jobs. This idea of organizational culture is somewhat intangible, for we cannot see it or touch it, but it is present and pervasive. Richard Seel defines organizational culture as the emergent result of the continuing negotiations about values, meanings and properties between the members of the organization and with its environment. It is the result of all daily conversations and negotiations between the members of an organisation.

Organizational culture can be understood as a product of all the organization's features, its people, its successes and failures. It reflects the past and shapes the future. According to Toyohiro Kono, the concept of organization culture is composed of three basic elements such as shared values, decision making patterns and overt behavioural patterns of organizational members.

There are at least six popular meanings which are ascribed to organizational culture. They are as follows:

- Observed behavioural regularities in the interactions, languages and rituals of the organizational members.
- The norms which evolve over a period of time in working groups.
- The dominant values which are exposed by the organization (or by the dominant members of the organization).
- The philosophy which guides the decision and policies of an organization.
- The rules of the game (The Ropes) one must learn in order to survive and be accepted in the organization.
- The feeling and climate that pervades and gets conveyed in the day-to-day sanctioning of the organization.

Thus, organizational culture can be understood as a cognitive factor and totality of assumptions, beliefs, norms, values, work culture learnt, shared and exhibited among the organizational members. It represents a key element of the work environment in which the employees perform their jobs. It surrounds and affects everything that happens in an organization.

IMPORTANCE

Organizational culture is as the old as organization itself. It is a binding force for the smooth voyage of the organization. People in the organization may come and go, but organizational culture remains. Organizational culture is the foundation on which the organization stands firmly. The productivity, employees' commitment to work and organization, morale, employee performance, and satisfaction depend, to a large extent, on the culture of the organization; even retention of talented work forces, to a considerable extent, is also influenced by the culture of the organization. Organizational culture is important to a firm's success for several reasons. Culture gives an identity to the employees (a defining vision of what the organization represents). It is also an important source of stability and continuity to the organization, which provides a sense of security to its members. At the same time, the knowledge of organizational culture helps newer employees to interpret what goes inside the organization, by providing an important context for events that would otherwise seem confusing.

Culture can be seen as a glue that holds an organization together—a means by which members communicate and coordinate their efforts. At the same time, its responsibility is to accommodate flexibility. In other words, avoidance of uncertainty and maintaining stability is important in the short run, while retaining the character of flexibility is important in the long run. In this manner, culture plays a third duel role, in that it enables stability to behaviour and organizational change in the long run. Rohit Deshpande and Parasuraman stated that firms run into trouble when they fail to explicitly take into account their corporate cultures, or when they make major changes in strategy or enter different phases of their life cycles.

CHARACTERISTICS

The following are the characteristics of culture:

- Innovation and risk taking
- Attention to detail
- Outcome orientation
- People's orientation
- Team orientation
- Aggressiveness
- Stability
- Culture is learnt
- Culture is historically based
- Culture as commonly held beliefs, attitudes and values.

Influencing Factors

Cultural differences affect the organizational work behaviour within countries and cultures, organizational behaviour across countries and cultures. Most significantly, the knowledge of organizational behaviour across different cultures helps in understanding the beliefs, attitudes, interpersonal relationship among workers, executives, clients, suppliers, and alliance patterns from various countries. Employees' behaviour is influenced by their values, beliefs and attitudes which reinforces the behaviour of the organisation.

Culture influences organizational behaviour in two ways. Employees bring their societal culture to work with them in the form of customs and language. Organizational culture, a by-product of societal culture, in turn affects the individual values/ethics, attitudes, assumptions and expectations. The term *societal culture* is used here instead of national culture because the boundaries of many modern nation-states were not drawn along cultural lines. The former Soviet Union, for example, included 15 republics and more than 100 ethnic nationalities, many with their own distinct language. Meanwhile, English speaking Canadians are culturally closer to Americans. Societal culture is shaped by various environmental factors shown in the left-hand side of Figure 22.1.

Once inside the organization's sphere of influence, the individual is further affected by the organization's culture. Mixing of societal and organizational cultures can produce interesting dynamics in multinational companies. For example, with French and American employees working side by side at General Electric's medical imaging production factory in Waukesha, Wisconsin, the unit head, Claude Béchamel has witnessed some culture shocks.

In North American and Northern European cultures, time seems to be a simple matter. It is linear, relentlessly marching forward, never backward, in standardized chunks. To the

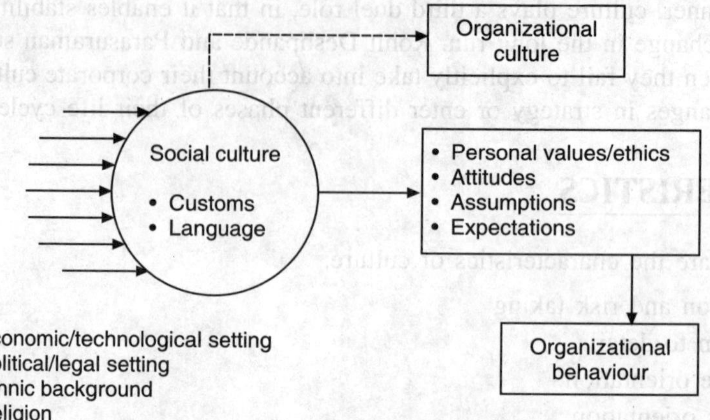

Figure 22.1 Cultural influences.

Americans, time is like money: it is spent, saved or wasted. Americans are taught to show up 10 minutes early for appointments. When working across cultures, however, time becomes a very complex matter. Imagine a New Yorker's chagrin when left in a waiting room for 45 minutes, only to find a Latin American Government official dealing with three other people at once. The North American resents the North American's impatience and apparent self-centredness. This vicious cycle of resentment can be explained by the distribution between monochromic and polychromic time. The former is revealed in the ordered, precise, schedule driven use of public time that typifies and even caricatures efficient Northern Europeans and North Americans. The latter is seen in the multiple and cyclical activities and concurrent involvement with different people in the Mediterranean, Latin Americans and especially Arab culture.

Monochromic and polychromic are relative rather than absolute concepts. Generally, the more things a person tends to do at once, the more polychromic he is. Monochromic people prefer to do one thing at a time.

Low context cultures, such as that of the United States, tend to run on monochromic time while high context cultures, such as that of Mexico, tend to run on polychromic time. People in polychromic view time as flexible, fluid and multidimensional. During the Islamic holy months of Ramadan in Middle Eastern nations, for example, the faithful fast during daylight hours, the general pace of things markedly slows down. Managers need to reset their mental clocks when doing business across cultures.

FUNCTIONS

The functions of organizational culture are as follows:

- Culture creates boundary.
- Culture communicates a sense of quality to organizational members.
- Culture promotes the generation of commitment to do something for the sake of organization to a larger extent than one's individual self-interest.

- Culture improves social system consistantly. It is the adhesive, helps the organization and the employees what they commit to do in the organization.
- Culture can promote sense-making and control mechanism which, in turn, shapes the attitudes and behaviour of the employees.

The business world is rapidly changing, bringing about immense changes in the way organizations are strategizing to survive, sustain and grow in order to remain functional. The opening up of the economies the world over is making it imperative for most organizations to look inward to take stock of their business goals, strategies and future growth. It is due to tremendous competition, and obsolescence in products and services being offered by them. To counter such phenomenon, the only cutting edge strategy available to organizations today is to become learning organizations capable of acquiring, incubating and disseminating knowledge throughout the organization.

When organizations begin to embrace knowledge, they are left with little choice but to become global in their vision and are required to internationalize themselves in terms of their operations. While changes in technology are inevitable, the resultant adjustments that are needed to be made both externally and internally are more crucial. The workflow, structures, processes (both technical and human) need to be aligned differently to suit the new needs to facilitate the smooth functioning of the organization.

Culture identifies the principal goals, work methods and behaviours, how individuals interact/address each other, how friendships and personal relationships are conducted. It guides organizational memberships, how the boundaries are maintained, who is an insider and who is an outsider, etc. Culture reduces ambiguity, facilitates organizational commitment, makes consistency in the behaviour of the employees, and provides information on how things are done and what is important.

Recruitment and selection related areas of management development, have an impact on the organization's culture. According to Van Mannen and Schain, "organizational socialization is an important process by which an individual is taught and learns what behaviour and perspectives are customary and desirable within the work setting as well as what once are not." Leadership also plays an important role in developing organizational culture. According to Schain, Culture and leadership... are two sides of a coin. In fact, there is possibility under emphasizing in leadership research which is the only thing of a real importance that leaders do is to create and manage culture."

COMPETITIVE ADVANTAGE / DISADVANTAGE OF CULTURE

Culture can provide a source of competitive advantage. Michael Porter has argued that nations derive competitive advantage from a set of country level factors, such as the availability of resources, the size and sophistication of the market, the nature of government intervention, and the type of strategic linkages or networks. Many argue that the effective institutional arrangements, such as the methods of financing and nature of ownership, the structure of union, and the role of government are responsible for the success of "Japanese management". Culture is deeply embedded in the institutional arrangements. Thus, culture and institutional configurations work interactively to create potential competitive advantage or disadvantage.

France's many industrial innovations can be attributed to the nature of the education system, which places high value on engineering and administrations, and the close relationship between state and industry. These features are considered responsible for technological success. In Denmark, it was raised by the daily newspaper, *Morgenavisen*. It warned that the competitiveness of Danish companies entering the common market could be constrained by the cultural influence of introvert. In Norway, there is a sign above the SAS check-in counter for business class which reads: "Euroclass–Full Price". It has been designed to make the class distinction more culturally acceptable.

Thus, each country has its unique institutional and cultural characteristics, which can provide sources of competitive advantage. However, that may have provided a source of competitive advantage in the past, but can become Achilles heel in the future. Managers, therefore, need to evaluate the extent to which national culture can interface with their company's efforts to respond to strategic requirements, now and in future.

CROSS-CULTURAL DIMENSIONS

G. Hofstede, based on a cross-national study of a large sample (more than 100,000), suggested a comprehensive framework of four dimensions to study cultural differences: *power distance*, *uncertainty avoidance*, *individualism* vs *collectivism* and *masculinity* vs *feminity*. He has also prepared an instrument to measure these aspects both in societies and in organizations. Martin proposed that culture operates at three levels: *integrated* (common characteristics); *differentiated* (different characteristics in different sub-groups), and *fragmented* (containing contradiction and confusion in the complexity of the dynamics). He proposed that the culture of an organization can be, studied from all the three perspectives. This may provide a deeper understanding of the organizational culture.

While the other frameworks discussed have used instruments, in this framework, qualitative anthropology study is more relevant. Panda and Gupta stucked the culture of one organization and found that while employee welfare reflected different perspectives (region/branch/department-wise differences), customer care, employee care and ethics show both integrated and fragmented perspectives (showing an integrated organizational culture with weak sub-cultures).

Panda and Gupta also identified three roles for a leader from a symbolic interpretative perspective: the leader as a symbol, the leader as a hero in the organizational stories, and the leader as a manager of rituals.

Dutch researcher G. Hofstede, in order to find the common dimensions of culture across the countries, gathered data from surveys with 116,000 respondents working in IBM from more than 70 countries around the world. The underlying concept of dimensions is described here.

1. **Power distance:** This dimension measures social equality, i.e. to what extent a society accepts unequal distribution of power in families, institutions and organizations. Inequality of power in an organization is generally manifested in hierarchical superior-subordinate relationships.
2. **Uncertainty avoidance:** This is a representation of a society's tolerance for uncertain situations. It measures to what extent a society manages those situations by providing specific and conventional rules, regulations and norms, by rejecting aberrant ideas on behaviours, by accepting the possibility of absolute truths and the accomplishments of

expertise. Countries which score high in uncertainty avoidance discourage risk-taking behaviour and innovation.

3. **Individualism vs collectivism:** Individualism gauges to what extent individuals in a country consider themselves as distinct entities rather than as members of cohesive groups. Collectivism, on the other hand, emphasizes on social ties or bonds between individuals. Individualistic society considers self-interest as more important than group goal.
4. **Masculinity vs feminity:** This dimension refers to what extent dominant values in a society emphasize masculine social values like a work ethic expressed in terms of money, achievement and recognition as opposed to feminine social role, which shows more concern for people and quality of life.

ORGANIZATIONAL EFFECTIVENESS

Organizational effectiveness is an organization's ability to achieve its objectives and meet the needs of its various stakeholders, notably employees, owners, customers, etc. It is the degree to which an organization attains its short- (ends) and long-term (means) goals. It is the maximization of profit or return in the organization by all means. Likert viewed that it is an interrelationship among three variables, viz. *independent variables*, such as leadership styles, organizational structure, and technology, *intervening variables*, such as perceptions, attitudes, values, and motivational forces, and *dependent variables*, such as production, sales, and employee turnover.

The influencing factors of organizational effectiveness are:

- Productivity
- Efficiency
- Quality
- Absenteeism
- Control
- Flexibility
- Planning and goal setting
- Managerial skills
- Training and development
- Job satisfaction.
- Motivation
- Profits
- Growth
- Turnover
- Conflict/Cohesion
- Goal consensus
- Interpersonal skills
- Value of human resources
- Morale

MANAGING CONFLICTS

Organizational conflicts are sometimes common. In a small family, we can observe some conflicts. When the organization is functioning with several people with diverse background, conflicts will certainly arise. Conflict means competitive or opposing action of incompatibles; antagonistic state or action; struggle resulting from incompatible needs, drives, wishes, demands; hostile encounter.

Effects and Types

Conflicts create both positive and negative effects. The potential positive effects of conflict are: increased motivation, enhanced problems, group cohesiveness, reality adjustment, increased knowledge, enhanced creativity, contribution to goal attainment and incentive for growth. The potential negative effects are: decrease in productivity, erosion of trust, coalition formation with polarized positions, secrecy and reduced information flow and problem of morale.

Different types of conflicts can be observed. Those are: internal conflicts, interpersonal conflicts, and group dynamic conflicts.

Internal conflicts are disturbance within oneself. These conflicts involve emotional dissonance for individuals due to a gap between their thoughts and happenings. Sometimes, these conflicts hamper their daily life and immobilize some individuals.

Interpersonal conflicts are between one person and another.

Group conflicts might be intragroup or intergroup. Intragroup conflicts are among members of the same group, and intergroup conflicts are among different groups.

Conflict Matrix

Conflicts arise because of high concern for self and low concern for others. Figure 21.2 clearly explains the five positions.

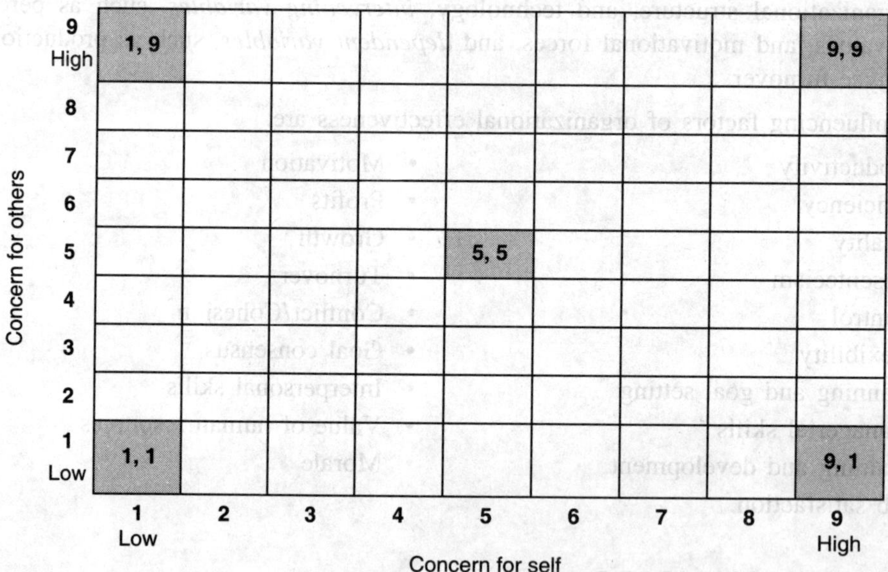

- Avoiding [1, 1]—Low concern for others, high concern for self
- Obliging [1, 9]—High concern for others, low concern for self
- Compromising [5, 5]—Equal concern for both self and others
- Dominating [9, 1]—High concern for self, low concern for others
- Collaborating [9, 9]—High concern for self, high concern for others

Figure 22.2 Conflict matrix.

Employees have to compromise for some changes. Collaborative attitude of employees always leads to better performance and results.

Stages of Conflicts

There are three stages of conflicts. Stage one conflicts are related to day-to-day irritations and activities. The behaviour of employees may not be tolerable. Such conflicts can be minimized with understanding employees and taking positive measures. Stage two conflicts are due to the win-lose attitude of employees. Employees feel that they are losing and are insecure. In such a case, management can manage the situation by providing proper environment for security and safety. Stage three conflicts are related to win. Employees feel that they have to win in the process of dispute settlement. Such conflicts can be resolved through negotiations, mediation, arbitration, etc.

SUMMARY

1. Organisational culture is relating to human actions values and behaviour.
2. It has greater impact on organizational effectiveness.
3. It has several characteristics such as innovation, people's orientation, aggressiveness, stability, beliefs, attitudes and values.
4. Cross-cultural aspects of the organization should be considered for managing the business.
5. The functions of culture are to be studied for effective management of an organization.
6. There are cultural dimensions across the countries resulting in power distance, uncertainty avoidance, individualism and collectivism.
7. Organizational effectiveness is influenced by several factors.

REVIEW QUESTIONS

1. Define culture and elaborate various characteristics of organization culture.
2. Explain the influence of culture on organizational behaviour.
3. What are the different functions of culture in an organization?
4. Explain the importance of culture.
5. How does culture across countries affect the organization?
6. What are the factors that influence organizational effectiveness?

CASE STUDY

Asian Windman

Tulsi Tanti, Chairman of Suzlon Energy Ltd., is today one of India's ten richest men. But this man certainly was not born with a silver spoon in his mouth. A first generation entrepreneur, Tanti has made it big on his own, of course with a little help from his siblings. He was a small textile businessman in Gujarat. It was in 1994 when his firm was passing through troubled times that an idea breezed into his head and life changed for India's wind power man forever. Today, Tanti's Suzlon Energy deals in wind energy—an uncharted sector where he saw potential, ventured into it, and made it big.

A commerce graduate and a diploma holder in mechanical engineering, Tanti originally hails form Gujarat and is presently in Pune. This man around 50 started his career as a textile businessman in Gujarat. But he found the prospects were stunted due to infrastructural problems. The biggest of them all was the cost and unavailability of power, which formed a high percentage of operating expenses of textile industry.

In 1990, Tanti invested in two windmills and realized its huge potential. In 1995, he formed Suzlon and gradually quit textiles. Today, in 2007, Suzlon Energy is the sixth largest wind energy company in the world and the largest in Asia. It is presently building perhaps one of the world's largest wind parks at 1,000 MW capacity.

And yes, like most other CEOs from India, Tanti's Suzlon is currently concentrating on a global expansion drive. It has acquired Hansen Transmissions, a Belgian maker of wind-turbine gearboxes. Tanti is also building a rotor-blade factory in Minnesota and has invested $ 60 million in a factory in Tianjin, China. In short, this young at heart Indian is all set to make India a wind power export hub.

Suzlon went public in 2005 through a 100 per cent book built issue, carrying a price band of Rs. 425 to Rs. 510 a share. The issue was oversubscribed 51 times, and Suzlon was listed in October 2005 at Rs. 692. On the day of listing, Tanti's 69.78 per cent holding in Suzlon was valued at Rs. 13,901 crores. At current prices of over Rs. 750 a share, the market value was over Rs. 15,000 crores.

In the beginning, life was not so sweet for Tanti. Confronted in 1994 with escalating power costs, Tanti's young textile business was in dire straits. With survival at stake, he suddenly saw a solution that was literally blow in the wind. Commissioning two windmills to supply electricity for the family's factories in Gujarat, he realized that he had stumbled into a promising business opportunity. In a power starved nation, renewable energy had a favoured future.

"Our country needs power for its economic growth, and clean, green power is the best option," sad Tanti in an interview to a news website recently. Acting on this belief, he radically shifted his enterprise. In 2006–07, Suzlon reported annual revenues of $ 850 million. This was twice as much as the previous year.

In fact, 1994 was a watershed year for Tanti. Since then, he has been Asia's top wind man and one among India's growing crop of new billionaires. The 70 per cent stake that Tanti and his three brothers owned in their Bombay Stock Exchange listed company is worth $ 4.3 billion. The stock had risen 60 per cent since Suzlon's first daily close, giving Tanti an entry into the billionaire club.

Now situated in Pune, a city famous for its engineering skills, Suzlon is a prime example of India's emerging story in manufacturing, less told than the technology services tale. The company already ranked as one of the world's largest producers of wind energy in terms of installed capacity. Tanti is aiming high and wants to close the gap with Suzlon's biggest European competitors, Denmark's Vesta Wind Systems, Germany's Enercon and Spain's Gamesa.

At home, where it still makes 90 per cent of its sales, Suzlon had 35 per cent of the market. The country is among the top five wind power users, which collectively accounted for 70 per cent of the global capacity. With its mission to provide "Power for all by 2012", the Government of India has introduced legislation making it compulsory for electricity distributors to get a specified quantum from renewable energy sources. No wonder, Tanti's stars seem on the rise at present.

Questions for Discussion

1. What are the key issues in the case?
2. Discuss how Tanti has to prepare to face new challenges.

FURTHER READING

Davis, Keith, *Human Behaviour at Work*, Tata McGraw Hill Book Company, New Delhi, 1975.

Fincham, Robin and Rhodes, Peter, *Principles of Organisational Behaviour*, Oxford University Press, New Delhi.

Harigopal, K., *Management of Change*, Leveraging Transformation, Response Books, New Delhi, 2001.

Luthans, Fred, *Organisational Behaviour*, McGraw-Hill, Kogakusha, Tokyo.

Laurie J. Mullins, Management and Organisational Behaviour, *Financial Times*, Pitman Publishing, London, 2000.

Pareekh, Udai, *Understanding Organisational Behaviour*, Oxford University Press, New Delhi.

Robbins, Stephen P. and Sanghi, Seema, Organisational Behaviour, Pearson Publishers, New Delhi.

Robbins, Stephen P., *Organizational Behaviour*, Prentice-Hall of India, New Delhi, 1991.

Seel, Ricahrd, Culture and Complexity, New Insights into Organisational Change, *Organisations and People*, Vol. 7, No. 2, 2000.

Schein, E.H., Organizational Culture, *American Psychologist*, Vol. 45, No. 2, pp. 109–119, 1990.

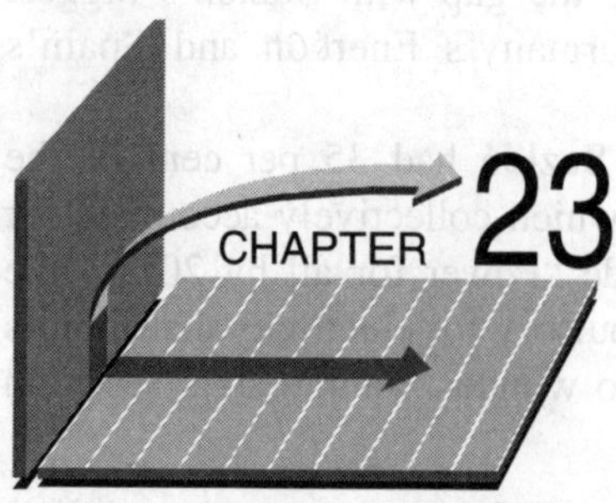

Organizational Change

CONTENTS

INTRODUCTION

Change is certain. One should prepare oneself for change. Any change taking place in the social, political and economic environments is creating a marked impact on organizations as well as for individuals. The pace of change has varied from place to place. Most of all, the developments have occurred over the span of a hundred years—and these developments are likely to be accelerated in the new millennium. Change is constant and permanent. In the competitive environment, change is the need of business. Therefore, managers are expected to learn how to manage change. Human resources play a major role in the change process of any organization. Change is defined as "to make or become different, give or begin to have a different form". A simple definition could be, organizational change is one which ultimately affects the pattern of work and/or relationship within an organization.

CONCEPTUAL ISSUES

Social sciences are not as exact as natural sciences. It is a lucky state of affairs that only during the last few centuries a few straightforward properties of nature could be discovered in every branch of natural sciences and those revolutionized the search of knowledge in these fields. Darwin's theory of evolution, Mundelein's periodic table, Mendel's law of inheritance, Copernicus, Galileo and Newton's contribution to Physics are some instances. Such a breakthrough in social sciences has not yet been possible. Even two centuries ago, chemists searched for the elixir of human immortality or the process to make gold. Neither the elixir nor gold has been discovered, but the search was not in vain. Science has progressed. Almost in a similar fashion, theories are built to understand, explain and guide organizational phenomena. There is no grand theory. But attempts are being continuously made to systemize the experiences and learning about organizational phenomena and organizational change. Theories are being developed in the context of present realities and the store of knowledge. Managing organizational change would mean anticipating needs for such changes, deciding upon the required changes, initiating and implementing the changes ensuring that the changes are stable and enduring.

Change is continuous and intrinsic to an organization: The changes that occur are minute in nature to be observed, but take place continuously. The stability that is seen is apparent. An organization is conceived to be in a state of flux (like the universe)—the elements of its systems and sub-systems always undergoing subtle changes. Each time an employee acts on a task or system, he might not be acting on what is consistently the same. There occur minute changes, though all elements are apparently configured as earlier. Such configuration is well understood, taking an example from human physiology, in terms of the brain structure where a number of cells are destroyed and created every day.

Organizations are conceived as normatively stable structures and change perceived as disruptive, forcing the organization to modify, restructure and reconfigure. Changes occur slowly and can be anticipated. Others occur so quickly that they do not permit sufficient time for individuals/organizations to cope with them, as in the case of natural calamities, such as typhoons, earthquakes (for example, the recent Tsunami disaster in Asia). Some others may result in unpredictable shifts, causing a metamorphic change. Apparently, organizations, like individuals, have a tolerance level for impinging forces at which level they successfully adopt or adjust to and may even be exerting control over the forces. When the impacting forces are extremely forceful, beyond an organization's tolerance level, it could be at the mercy of these forces. Even then, some organizations could be creative or make drastic shifts in their strategy and direction to emerge out of this turbulence, whereas others may get lost in it.

One view of change is that it is an intentional pattern that is regular and stable with identifiable cause–effect relationships and that it signifies a more from a state of quasi-equilibrium to one of equilibrium. Such an assumption is influenced by physical sciences, with well-defined laws governing the relationships among the physical and chemical matters. However, change in social and organizational systems is more dynamic and complex, and often functions as a non-linear feedback system with no clearly identifiable and predictable cause and effect relationship. One can neither intend the future of change with certainty, nor control it in defined ways as it evolves by an interplay of various forces that are complex and unpredictable. Social systems always exist in a state of quasi-equilibrium, and interventions may or may not facilitate its course that determines it.

Change by its nature tends to be bipolar. It is continuous and discontinuous, it is characterized by stability and instability, it is predictable and unpredictable, it is intrinsic as well as extrinsic to the organization. Managing change, therefore, does not entail choosing either pole but reconciling these opposites in productive ways.

Changes may be said to take place at three levels:

1. *Micro changes*—that people face in their personal lives.
2. *Organizational changes*—those changes in any institution that influence people's lives.
3. *Macro changes*—that significantly affect people universally, such as the collapse of the Berlin Wall and communism in Eastern Europe.

TYPES OF CHANGE

To change is to move from the present to the future, from a known state to a relatively unknown state. To be able to adopt or deal with the impact of change forces, organizations may plan for, experience or undergo change. The possible types of changes are classified here.

Happened change: This change is unpredictable. It takes place naturally due to external factors. It is profound or traumatic, for it is out of direct control and produces a future state that is largely unknown. This type of change occurs when an organization reaches a plateau in its life cycle.

Reactive change: Changes that are clearly in response to an event or a series of events are called *reactive*. Most of the companies are engaged in reactive, often incremental change. These changes are attempted when the demand for a company's product/service registers an increase or decrease, or a problem/crisis occurs or develops.

Anticipatory change: Changes carried out in expectation of an event or a series of events are called *anticipatory changes*. Failing to anticipate future events can have destructive consequences for organizations. Their anticipation of change, may tune in or reorient themselves to future demands. Tuning in would involve making incremental changes (dealing with a sub-system as a part of the sub-system) in anticipation of a changing environment. It involves changing the organization from the existing state towards a designed future state, and managing the transition process.

Planned change: Planned change (developmental change) is undertaken to improve upon the current way(s) of operating. It is a calculated change, initiated to achieve a certain desirable output/performance and to make the organization more responsive to internal and external demand. This type of change, where the future state is being consciously chosen, is not as threatening. However, it does require system/subsystems level (techno-social) support to survive.

Incremental change: Changes directed at the micro-level and focused on units/sub-units/components within an organization are called *incremental changes*. Changes are brought in gradually and are usually adaptive in nature. It is assumed that these small changes help set in the larger change process and lead the system slowly in a healthier direction.

Operational change: This is required when an organization needs to improve the quality of its products or services due to external competition, customers changing requirements and demands or internal organizational dynamics. Operational changes are bringing in new technology, re-engineering the work processes, quality management, better distribution and delivery of products and enhancing interdepartmental coordination, etc.

Strategic change: Change that is addressed to the organization as a whole or to most of the organization's components is called *strategic change.*

Directional change: A change in direction may become imperative for an organization due to the severe competition or regulatory shifts in government policy and control (for example, on pricing, import, export restrictions). Directional change is critical when the organization is developing a new strategy.

Fundamental change: It entails a redefinition of the current purpose or mission of the organization. It may be necessitated by drastic changes in the business environment, the failure of the current corporate leadership, problems with employees' morale or a low turnover, or union's attitude.

Total change: The organization is constrained to develop a new vision, and a strong link between its strategy, employees and business performance. The organization has to make a turnaround or perish. Total change is necessary to extricate the organization from the rot that has set in due to long-term failure of business, employee-organization, value incongruence, estrangement of operations from the reality of the business environment, and power concentrated in the hands of few people who could be furthering their own personal interest at the cost of the organization. A new vision and drastic surgery could be the only way out for the organization.

Transformational change: Such a change involves the entire or a greater part of the organization. It could be a change in the shape (size and complexity), structure (systems, ownership and the like), and nature (basic assumptions, culture, technology, etc.) of the organization.

Revolutionary change: Abrupt changes in organizational strategy and design represent revolutionary change. Such change comprises the 3Es.

- Envisioning, which is to articulate a clear and credible vision and a new strategy to realize the vision.
- Energizing, which is mobilizing of employees, and individuals, for change.
- Enabling, which is to provide the necessary resources, support structures and processes, for example, the appropriate information systems, suitable changes in administration policy and procedures, a fitting compensation/reward system and a task force.

PROCESS OF CHANGE

Individual change is determined by individual characteristics, such as knowledge, attitudes, beliefs, needs, and expectations. A total change in an organization can be carried out by changing the behaviour of all the individuals through some practical participative strategy. Bringing about total behavioural change in all the groups and members in an organization usually entails the most difficult long-range effort. It is a slow, painful process to use in a total cultural change in an organization.

An organization can be compared with any other open system organization, it can be described in terms of its birth, growth, maturity, sensibility, decline, entropy or death. Any organization, like other organizations, passes through these stages and, in the process, changes itself from one form to another. In order to meet the critical concerns of each stage, organizations go through some rapid, visible, shake-ups of their structure, policies, procedures, techniques, personnel, etc. These changes may be viewed as revolutionary changes. Evolutionary periods are characterized by the dominant management styles used to achieve growth, while revolutionary periods are characterized by the dominant problems that must be solved before growth continues.

Reflexive behaviour and reactive changes share the characteristics of responding to immediate symptoms, while purposive behaviour and proactive changes respond to underlying forces producing the symptoms. However, the management may decide to go in for planned change to cope with complex problems of modern society and the growth of behavioural sciences. Resistance to change could be overcome on an enduring basis by systematically planning and implementing the process of change. Kurt Lewin identified the following phases in the process of planned change (Figure 23.1).

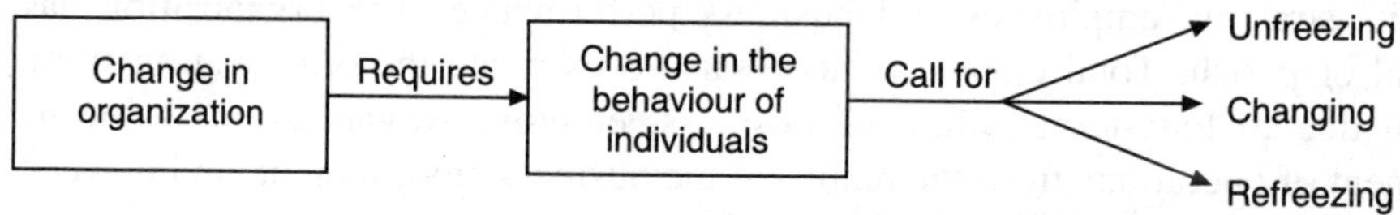

Figure 23.1 The change process.

1. *Unfreezing:* The focus of this stage is to create the motivation to change. Managers can begin the unfreezing process by disconfirming the usefulness or appropriateness of the employee's present behaviour or attitudes.
2. *Changing:* Change involves learning. The purpose is to help employees learn new concepts or points of view. Role models, mentors, experts, benchmarking the company against world-class organizations, and training are useful mechanisms to facilitate change.
3. *Refreezing:* Change is stabilized during refreezing by helping employees integrate the changed behaviour or attitude into their normal way of doing things. This is accomplished by first giving employees the chance to exhibit the new behaviour or attitudes. Once exhibited, positive reinforce is used to reinforce the desired change. Additional coaching and modelling are also used to this point to reinforce the stability of the change.

MODELS OF CHANGE

The following models are explained briefly for understanding change in the organizations:

1. Force field analysis
2. Expanded process model

3. Action research
4. Resistance to change
5. Planned change model
6. Systems model of change.

Force Field Analysis

Kurt Lewin introduced the force field analysis for implementing change. It identifies the driving and restraining forces of change. According to the force field theory, the present situation in which change is to be attempted is a quasi-static equilibrium of driving forces and restraining forces. Organizational stability, quasi-stationary equilibrium, occurs when these driving and restraining forces balance each other in such a way as to maintain a constant level of functioning for a whole.

The present equilibrium can be changed by strengthening the driving forces or by awakening the restraining forces.

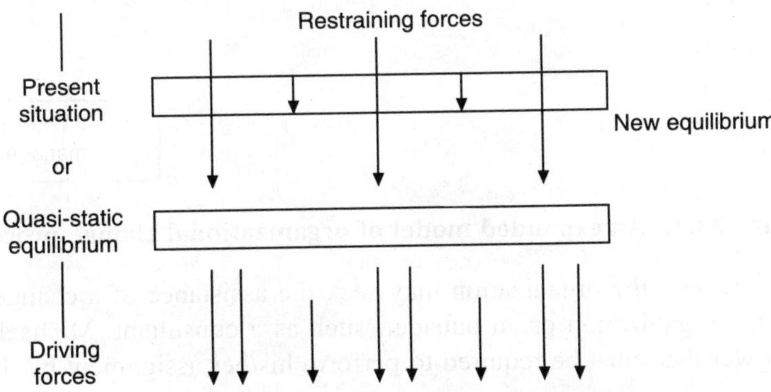

Figure 23.2 Lewin's change model.

The driving forces are: dissatisfaction with the present equilibrium, conflicts in the organization, changes in organizational goals, difference in personal and organizational goals, desire for innovation, low productivity, and rising costs, etc.

Restràining forces may be personal or organizational. Individuals may resist change in general for various reasons of which they may or may not be aware. It arises when an individual perceives a change as a threat to the security of personal advantages associated with the status quo, and also from the result of anticipated disadvantages that accompany change.

Expanded Process Model

The expanded process model looks at planned change from the perspective of top management. The mode incorporates Lewin's concept as a part of the implementation phase. In this approach, top management of the organization perceives that certain forces or trends call for change, and the issue is subjected to the organization's usual problem solving and decision making process. Alternatives for change are generated and evaluated, and an acceptable one is selected.

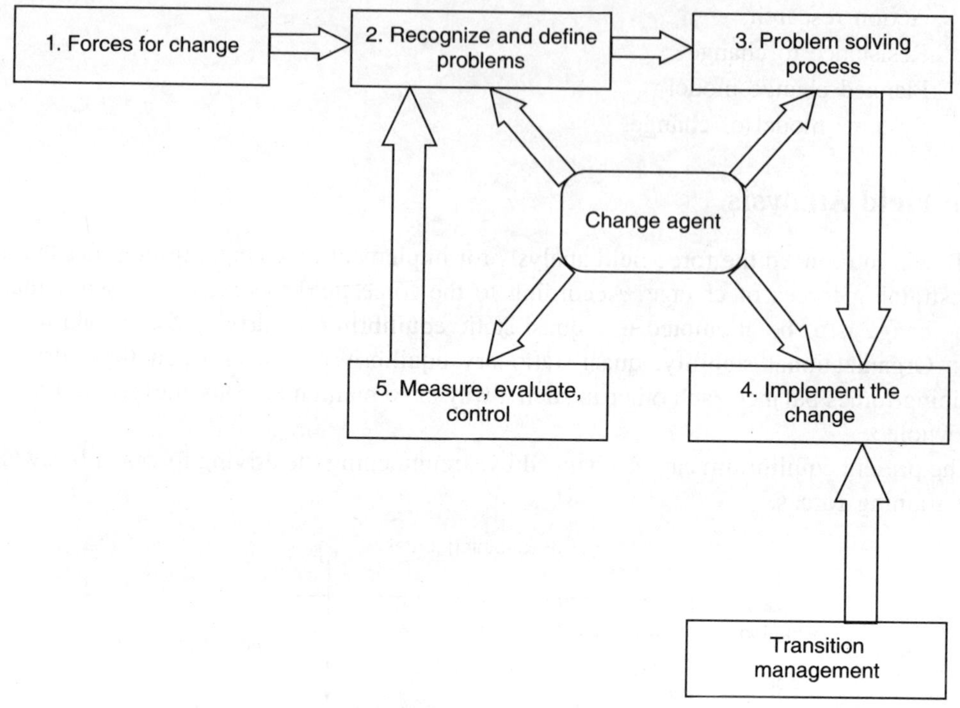

Figure 23.3 An expanded model of organizational change process.

Early in the process, the organization may seek the assistance of a change agent. He may be a member of the organization or an outsider, such as a consultant. Michael Beer described five sources of power that must be required to perform his/her assignment by the change agent:

- High status given by members of the client organization
- Trust in the change agent based on maintaining his role in the organization
- Expertise in the practice of organizational change
- Established credibility based on experience
- Dissatisfied constituencies inside the organization.

Under the direction and management of the change agent, the organization implements the change, through Lewin's unfreeze, change and refreeze process. The final step is evaluation and control. However, the change agent brings in new ideas and viewpoints that help members look at old problems in new ways. Change often comes from the conflict that results when the change agent challenges the organization's assumptions and generally accepted patterns of operation.

Action Research

Another view of the organization change process is action research, which is based on a research model. The research, or change agent is usually an outside person, who is involved in the total change process: From diagnosis to evolution, the research process is usually composed of in-depth searching, asking questions, interviewing employees and evaluating records, all of which lead to an analysis and synthesis of information. The research questions of employees and searching lead to the development of suggestive actions for the organization. The researcher uses the initial data gathered in the early stages as points of comparison for data gathered during and after any subsequent change that may be made in the organization. The researcher can evaluate the effects of the changes in the organization. This can provide valuable information to both the organization and the researcher.

Resistance to Change

Change is common. However, when change is introduced in an organization, employees resist it. The reasons are the following:

Individual resistance

- *Perception:* Employee and unions feel change leads to some negative implications.
- *Loss of freedom:* Employees feel that they may lose freedom in the organization.
- *Lack of security:* When changes are introduced, employees resist them because they are afraid of losing their jobs later.
- *Fear of the unknown:* Employees do not express any particular problem but they are fearful.
- *Economic factor:* Employees feel that their income will be reduced.

Organizational resistance

- *Maintenance of stability:* When change is there, the stability of organizational structure, design is difficult.
- *Organizational culture:* Culture change may not be possible immediately when change is introduced.
- *Past agreements:* As organizations enter into some agreements earlier, sometimes change is difficult.
- *Resources for investment:* Additional resources for investments may be difficult when change is introduced.
- *Threat to power:* Change creates threat to some group's power in the organization.

Managing change

- The behaviour of employees is to be understood before introducing change.
- The management has to follow participants style in the change process.
- Employees are to be given freedom, and security of job even after change.
- Training and development for human resources help a lot before introducing change.

Planned Change Model

Another model that has occupied a place of prominence in bringing about planned change in organizations is the planning model. Developed by Lippit et al., it was later modified and refined by Kolb and Frohman.

The planned change model is based on the principle that information must be freely and openly shared between the organization and the change agent and that this information must be able to be translated into action.

- *Scooting:* This is the phase where the change agent and the organization jointly explore the need for and areas requiring change.
- *Entry:* Refers to the development of mutual contract and mutual expectations.
- *Diagnosis:* Refers to the stage where specific improvement goals are identified.
- *Planning:* This is the stage where actual and possible reasons for resistance to change are identified, in addition to planning for specific improvement goals.
- *Action:* This indicates the implementation of the steps identified in the planning stage.
- *Stabilization and evaluation:* This is the phase where evaluation is undertaken to determine the extent of success of the planned stage and the need for further action or termination.
- *Termination:* Refers to the phase where a decision is made to leave the system or to end and begin another.

Though the above phases have been described sequentially, the change agent and the manager can modify the strategies and approaches, depending on the diagnosis and re-diagnosis of the problem as indicated by the feedback arrows shown in Figure 23.4.

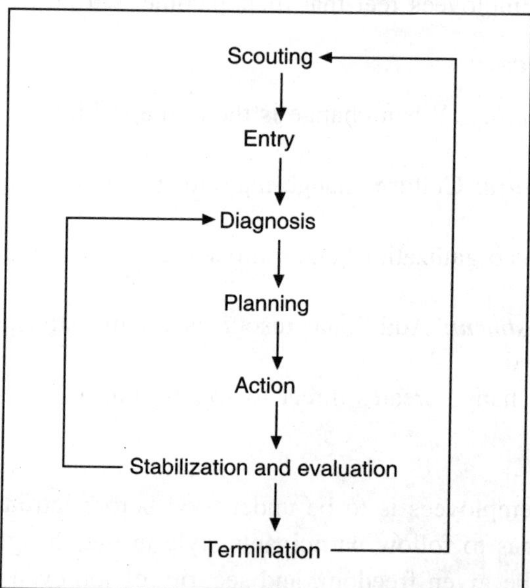

Figure 23.4 Seven-step process in change.

Transition management

Organizational change will not happen overnight or over a weekend. It takes time for employees to absorb even simple changes. Much more time and effort may be required for employees to adopt to complex changes. Such changes need to be managed, not merely implemented.

Transition management is the process of systematically planning, organizing and implementing change, from the disassembly of the current state to the realization of a fully functional future state within an organization. An interim management structure or interim positions may be created to ensure creativity and control of the business during the transition. Communication of the changes to all involved, from employees to customers and suppliers, plays a key role in transitional management.

Systems Model of Change

The systems approach takes a 'big picture' perspective of organizational change. It is based on the notion that any change, no matter how large or small, has a cascading impact throughout an organization. A systems model of change offers managers a framework to understand the broad complexities of organizational change. The three main components of a systems model are *inputs*, *target elements of change*, and *output*.

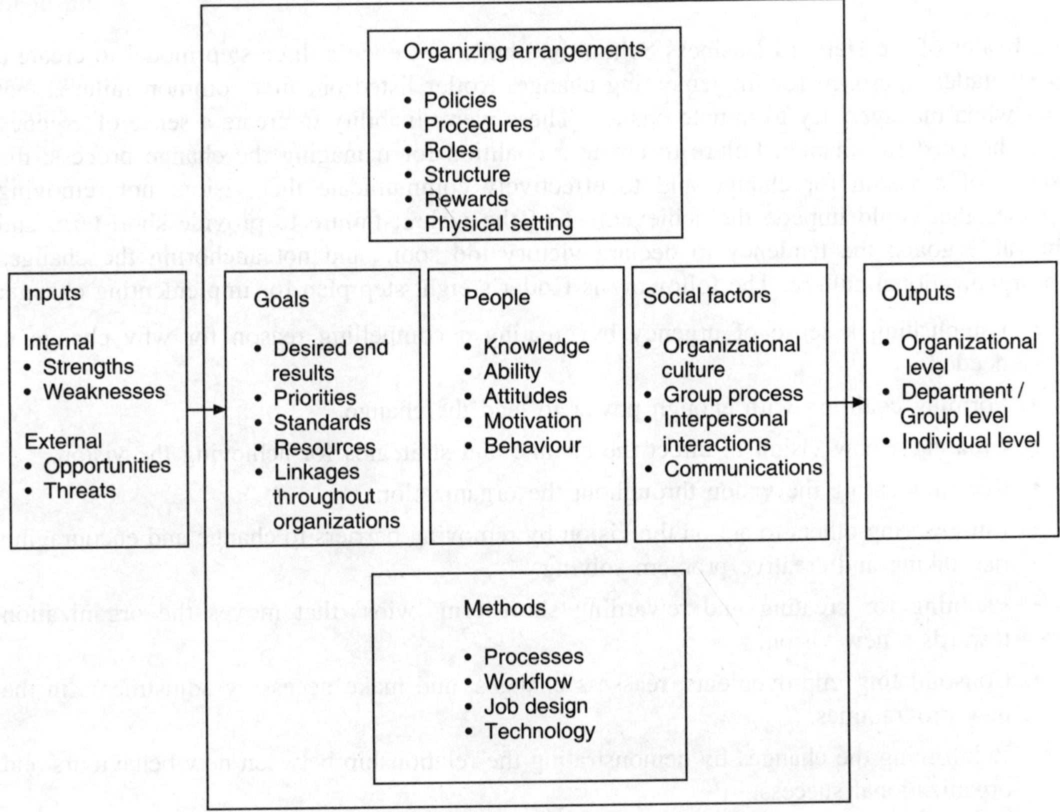

Figure 23.5 A systems model of change.

All organizational changes should be consistent with an organization's strategic mission and the resulting strategic plan. A strategic mission statement describes an organization's ultimate purpose. A strategic plan outlines an organization's long-term direction and actions necessary to achieve planned results. Organizations tend to commit resources to counterproductive or conflicting activities when organizational changes are not consistent with their strategic plan.

The target elements of change represent the components of an organization that may be changed. Change can be directed at realigning organizing arrangements, social factors, methods, goals and people. The choice is based on the strategy being pursued or the organizational problem at hand.

Specifically, a change in organizing management leads to additional changes in social factors, methods, goals and people. People are the hub of all changes. Change will not succeed unless individuals embrace it in one way or another.

The output represents the desired end results of a change. Once again, these end results should be consistent with an organization's strategic plan. Change may be directed at organizational level, department/group level or individual level.

IMPLEMENTING CHANGE

John Kotler of the Harvard Business School had built on Lewin's three-step model to create a more detailed approach for implementing change. Kotler listed out first common failures that occur when managers try to initiate change. These were: inability to create a sense of urgency about the need for change; failure to create a coalition for managing the change process; the absence of a vision for change and to effectively communicate that vision; not removing obstacles that could impede the achievement of the vision; failure to provide short-term and achievable goals; the tendency to declare victory too soon; and not anchoring the changes into organizational culture. The following is Kotler's eight-step plan for implementing change:

- Establishing a sense of urgency by creating a compelling reason for why change is needed.
- Forming coalition with enough power to lead the change.
- Creating a new vision to direct the change and strategies for achieving the vision.
- Communicating the vision throughout the organization.
- Empowering others to act on the vision by removing barriers to change and encouraging risk taking and creative problem solving.
- Planning for creating and rewarding short-term 'wins' that moves the organization towards a new vision.
- Consolidating improvements, reassess changes, and make necessary adjustments in the new programmes.
- Reinforcing the changes by demonstrating the relationship between new behaviours and organizational success.

The first four steps essentially extrapolate on the 'unfreezing' stage. Steps 5 through 7 represent 'movement', and the final step works on 'refreezing'. So, Kotler's contribution lies in providing managers and change agents with a more detailed guide for successfully implementing change.

SUMMARY

1. Organizational change is affecting the process of work and relationship within an organization.
2. As it has a greater impact on the organizational success, the corporate world should prepare for meeting the challenges of change.
3. There are different types of changes.
4. Some of them are happened change, reactive change, anticipatory change, planned change, incremental change, operational change, strategic change, etc. The process of change helps a lot in changing the behaviour of people.
5. There are different models of change. Some of them are Lewin's change model, expanded process model, planned change model. For implementing change, usually Kotler's eight-step plan is adopted.

REVIEW QUESTIONS

1. Explain the process of change.
2. Explain Lewin's change model.
3. What is the systems model of change?
4. Explain the expanded model of organizational change.
5. What are the different forces influencing organizational process change?
6. Why people resist change?
7. How do we implement change?

CASE STUDIES

1. Vimta Labs*

Dr. S.P. Vasireddi walked into the room when it was two minutes to nine in the morning for an appointment with the case writer at nine. He had already finished a meeting with his key personnel to review the previous day's operations and the plans for the day. He told the case writer that he had started his career as a lecturer after doing M.Sc. in Chemistry from Nagpur University in 1972. Later, he completed his Ph.D. in less than 2 years. Since he was not happy with the work he had done on rare earth's complexes, he wanted to join industry and do more in it. In 1976, he joined Mineral Exploration Limited (MEL) in Nagpur itself, when public sector jobs were very attractive. He soon realized that he was underutilized in his job: he took it as an opportunity to understand other related areas and spent time in other research departments. In 1979, he was transferred to Hyderabad, a homecoming for him which made him happy for the next 2 years. There also, he felt restless, as the job did not provide him with sufficient challenges and freedom to explore and work in other interesting areas. He resigned his job

* The case was prepared by K. Ramachandran, Associate Dean, ISB, Hyderabad.

on 1st July 1984 without having any clear idea as to what entrepreneurial activity he would pursue. He visited officials in various industrial development agencies and interacted with the industry people and by the end of July, he decided to set up a testing laboratory in Hyderabad.

INDUSTRY SCENE

The analytical laboratories industry has always been overcrowded, especially with the presence of a large number of small firms undertaking a variety of tests. Sri Ram Institute for Industrial Research in New Delhi was the only significant player in the private sector involved in providing analytical laboratory services in a significant way when Vasireddi contemplated entering this business. There were quite a few large government-run laboratories also set up in different parts of the country to offer often specialized services. They strictly followed government regulations. There were general complaints that the quality of service of these labs was not satisfactory, as they did not always have very small sized to provide general analytical services in their neighbourhood. Quality consciousness was not very high. Besides, those who wanted to set up labs with multiple specialties would have to obtain multi-departmental and multi-point clearances. Customers did not have much choice, and had to pay for the services instantly. Laboratories constantly monitored the fee collected by competitors, and often undercut each other.

The major inputs of the laboratories consisted of chemicals bought from large companies in India and abroad. Imports required upfront payment while Indian companies gave 30 days credit to reliable parties. They also gave 5–6 per cent cash discount for payment on delivery. Major materials suppliers were Sigma Aldrich, E-Merck and Glaxo, who fixed their own terms. Vimta built up good relationship with their input suppliers over the years. Though the company did not receive long periods of credit, they never faced shortage of inputs. Vasireddi added that they always bought the best quality inputs for their use. Smaller laboratories bought in small quantities. Government laboratories followed standard purchase procedures, which were not very attractive to some of the best suppliers. Some of the laboratories ran out of chemicals sometimes, affecting their services.

In the area of environmental studies (especially Environmental Impact Assessment), large organizations, such as Kirloskar Consultants, National Environmental Engineering Research Institute of India and Tata Consultancy Services, had entered the scene. Engineers India also had some presence in the market for a while. In any case, this was not a major business for any of them at any time.

INVESTMENTS

Vasireddi and his brother-in-law pooled all their savings and started Vimta Labs with an investment of ₹0.4 million to test geological samples and water. The Department of Industries in the government refused to register it as an industrial enterprise as it was doing only laboratory testing; it was only after several meetings and persuasion that they agreed to register Vimta as an industrial enterprise. His initial clients included National Aluminium Company and his erstwhile employers, MEL. Vimta did not reject any work so long as their costs were covered;

however, they ensured that their services were excellent. They imported essential equipment in 1984 for geological land water testing and the next year for physical testing. He got a further loan of ₹0.9 million in November 1985 to import equipment for geological and water testing, and material testing. During this period, he visited several well-known laboratories and institutions and some industrial firms to understand their activities.

Vasireddi borrowed a further ₹1 million in 1986 to procure more equipment. Next year, the Department of Environment of the Government of India recognized Vimta Labs as a laboratory equipped to certify hazardous materials. The other 11 laboratories equipped to do the same were all government-run. At that time, the annual business with Coal India alone came to ₹0.80 to 0.90 million. In 1988, he sold most of his personal properties and invested the same in the business. It was the fourth organization in the country to have a Plasma Emission Spectrometer. After persistent efforts, the health authorities in the government approved Vimta Labs capabilities in undertaking testing for drugs and pharmaceuticals industry.

They moved into a new factory in Cheralapalli on the outskirts of Hyderabad in 1990 after making the firm a limited company. To finance further investment, they borrowed ₹62 million from the Industrial Development Bank of India consisting of ₹43 million as term loan, ₹5 million as equity, and the balance as foreign currency loan in 1991. Rupee devaluation and further delays (some equipment were stuck for custom clearance for 15–20 months) forced them to revise the project cost upwards, which left a gap of ₹13 million. ICICI Venture, a venture capital company, and some of Vasireddi's friends together filled this gap. They went public in September 1993 and raised ₹27 million to finance growth. By April 1994, Vimta Labs moved into a much larger new building specially made for their requirements.

The balance sheet and profit and loss account for 1992 to 1999 and details of acquisition of plant and machinery are given in the appendix.

MARKET

The customers ranged from individuals to large private and public sector organizations who wanted services in product development, testing and/or export certification. The demand for environment impact assessment and related tests went up especially since the early 90s. According to Vasireddi, the company's reputation as one of the best 20 laboratories in the world has led to an aggregate client strength of 6,000 in 1991. The number has been subsequently pruned to 1,500 by eliminating very small clients. In later years, Vimta specialized in performance testing, trouble shooting and export certification. Some clients said, "Vimta Labs normally takes only one month as against six months taken by others for the same tests." Once one of the public sector laboratories located in Hyderabad city asked Vimta to conduct a test for them essentially because Vimta could do it quicker than them.

Vimta continues to be rated as the best laboratory to undertake environmental studies in 1999, had many a major company as its client. This list included Larsen & Toubro, Gujarat Ambuja Cement, ACC, Aditya Aluminium, Hindalco, ITC, CMPDI of Coal India, Cairan-energy, Hardy Exploration, Cochin Refineries, National Mineral Development Corporation and National Thermal Power Corporation. In addition, Vimta undertook subcontracting assignment from international firms, such as ERM, Tetra-tech-USA and Gibb Env., UK. About half the income of the company came from this division. The value of each assignment varied from ₹0.4 to 4.50 million in 1999. Vasireddi expected the 1999–2000 revenues from environment related assignments to be ₹24 million. However, he felt that long-term growth prospects in the environmental area were limited.

Nearly 30 per cent of Vimta's revenue in 1999 came from analytical testing, which included testing of food, chemicals, drugs and pharmaceuticals, minerals, metals, petroleum products, and engineering and building materials. Most of the food testing was for export certification. They did chemicals testing for the Bureau of Indian Standards and contraceptives testing for the Ministry of Health and Family Welfare. Customers for lubricants testing were users of power generators from core sector and transport corporations. Organizations involved in infrastructure projects, especially in the public sector, constituted the customers for engineering and building materials. They did minerals and metals testing for a number of major firms in the metallurgical industry. These assignments varied widely in terms of fee, ranging from ₹2,000 to 200,000. While this business promised good growth possibilities, they faced shortage of equipment to work with. Besides, Vasireddi felt the need to update them as the equipment were more than a decade old. He said that he always believed in the use of latest equipment. He planned to further modernize in a couple of years, but knew that technology obsolescence was fairly fast in this area.

Clinical research was an area where Vimta had had hardly any domestic competitor. Here, its capabilities were rated on par with international clinical research organizations of Europe and North America. Vimta tested/researched new pharmaceutical formulations before they were accepted by regulatory authorities. Their clients included pharmaceutical companies, such as Ranbaxy, Cipla, Dr. Reddy's, Pfizer, Sun and IPCA. Some of their international clients were Lagap Pharmaceuticals (UK), Ethypharm (France) and Zenith Goldline (USA).

Since July 1998, Vimta has a joint venture with Gosstandart of Russia in the name of Vimta Rostest (P) Ltd., primarily to certify food and agricultural products exported to Russia. In 1999, this business generated one million rupees business per month.

Vimta's Toxicology division was shut down in 1997–98 when the prospects for it fell. The laboratory and equipment were still retained.

Pricing was based on a combination of factors including expenses, client attitudes, urgency and prevailing market price. On an average, they had 75 per cent gross profit on sales. He, however, priced flexibly for new clients; according to Vasireddi, he used to give some credit in payment for bulk work. Most of the other's sundry work was on cash down basis. The industrial slowdown in the late 90s showed that Vimta faltered in collections. In 1997–98, he stopped giving credit altogether and decided that they would not proceed with work unless paid for in advance. For instance, if a client paid only part of the money, they would do work only for that. He said, "no money, no service" was his new motto. However, there were occasions when the clients took a little longer to settle the bills when the assignments had different phases, and paid for in installments. Even government departments started paying fast to get timely and efficient service from Vimta Labs. They did not advertise their services anywhere.

Vasireedi organized one day seminars for different industries, such as Aquaculture, metallurgy, industrial toxicology and pharmaceuticals in association with specialist government supported bodies. These seminars covered technology inputs and often financial and marketing aspects as well, with some of the key faculty drawn from within. Most of the participants came from Andhra Pradesh and nearby places. These seminars were held in the company auditorium, which could accommodate 150 people. Besides, Vasireddi often permitted student researchers to make use of their facilities free of charges.

As part of such programmes, participants were taken around in groups to show the laboratory and its facilities. Vasireddi took personal interest in selecting faculty; Vimta offered local hospitality to the participants. Each programme had a mailing list of about 300 to 400 people. These programmes were self-sustaining. While some seminars were paid for by industry participants, several others were sponsored by government departments or national laboratories. He also said that their seminar room was often used as a classroom to develop capabilities in their own people. By 1999, this was not a significant activity, though they had one or two such programmers held in Vimta in a year. He was the Vice President of the Drugs and Pharmaceuticals Association of Andhra Pradesh for some time. He organized a one-week programme as part of the association's activities, a day of which was underwritten by Vimta Labs, which included a visit to their works.

HUMAN RESOURCES

The company had employed a total of 164 people in 1995, of whom 75 were scientists and engineers. They had 17 people with Ph.D. on their rolls. There were 47 technicians and 42 administrative and supporting staff too. Vasireddi said that he rarely advertised for personnel. He added that hardly anybody left him except for personal reasons. He paid competitive salaries much higher than those paid in government laboratories and other research institutions. Vasireddi told the case writer that he believed that Vimta Labs was not just a laboratory; it was a scientific community dedicated to ensure quality service to mankind. About 60 per cent of the scientists and engineers were rotated from one division to another, depending on work requirements.

In 1982, he formed a 14-member team of qualified marketing professionals for developing business. This team was disbanded in 1995 when he realized that they were able to generate mainly government orders, which anyway was not very large. Also, they tended to commit business on credit, which often became bad debt later. Since then, scientists themselves took care of marketing; Vasireddi found them to be very effective in this role too.

Dr. Rao (Director, Laboratory) joined Vimta in 1990 from a National Engineering and Environmental Laboratory. Similarly, Dr. Thomas (Additional Director, Laboratory) joined Vimta in January 1994 after spending about 32 years in various industrial research organizations. Vasireddi knew Dr. Rao from his Nagpur days and had met Dr. Thomas at some conference. Besides, Vimta had a panel of experts also in various fields to seek advice when necessary.

The case writer spoke to Dr. Thomas about his team. He said it was a young and dynamic team that worked as a family. He added that some of them were highly acclaimed in their respective areas of specialization and held independent views. He felt that Vasireddi treated his colleagues very well and respected their worth.

ORGANIZATION AND SYSTEMS

Vasireddi as the Chairman and Managing Director headed the organization. The other two key promoters, namely Harriman and Prasad, operated as Director (Technical) and Executive Director, respectively. While Harriman had technology background, Prasad had training in commerce. The organization chart of Vimta had six divisions, namely Quality Assurance and Training, Drugs and Pharmaceuticals, Chemicals, Biosciences, Environment, and Material Testing till 1998 when he restructured the organization to have just three divisions, viz. Environmental, Analytical and Clinical.

They have developed a Laboratory Information Management Services and have obtained ISO 9002, ISO Guide-25 and EN 450001 certifications of quality. In April 1998, Vasireddi was nominated to the Research Council (Governing Board) of the National Physical Laboratory.

His wife, who was the head of the MIS department, perepared a three-page report every morning giving details of the previous day's financial transactions, situation in the operations, and the market. The systems were revised as the organization expanded, and in 1999, the three-page report was prepared once a week. This was the basis for their weekly reviews. Vimta made yearly plans for operations and expansion.

Vimta used to be visited by a variety of people including clients, potential clients and scientists. The case writer noted that four overseas experts in different fields had visited Vasireddi the same day he was there. They were entrusted with four different people to be taken care of, and he could have his meeting with Vasireddi as scheduled.

NEW CHALLENGES

Vasireddi realized that he had reached a stage where some major decisions needed to be taken. He was somewhat concerned about new competition, modernization and staff reduction, among others.

By the mid-90s, SGS India Ltd. had established operations in several parts of the country. It was a subsidiary of a large Swiss MNC, specializing in analytical testing and inspection business. SGS India has branches in all major cities in the country, but were small in size just to meet the exports inspection requirements of customers. By 1998, SGS had successfully entered the analytical segment, especially with respect to government business. However, Vasireddi said that SGS was not able to make much headway in the environmental segment. He admitted that SGS was a big company and he had to find some way to fight them. He expected the newly formed Vimta Rostest to capture significant market share in cities, such as Kochi, Coimbatore, Kakinada and Khandla in inspection activities.

As part of efforts to expand market, Vimta was doing trial orders for some other international clients too. It was working three shifts in 1999 for want of enough number of equipment to execute order. While the fee for domestic assignments ranged from ₹0.6 to 1.0 million, that for international was ₹1.2–2.5 million. Vasireddi hoped that the trial orders would lead to regular business.

Finance was yet another area of concern to Vasirddi. Vimta had very little in terms of working capital borrowings in 1999. He was negotiating a one-time settlement of ₹41 million for an outstanding of ₹105 million they owed to the Industrial Development Bank of India in terms of principal and penal interest. This would involve quarterly payments of ₹8.20 million till the amount was totally repaid.

As part of a restructuring exercise, he wanted to reduce the manpower almost by half and have the following mix:

Scientists and engineers	:	32, including 10 scientist managers and 7 Ph.D.
Technical assistants	:	12
Trainee scientists and technicians	:	15
Administration and supporting staff	:	23

He hoped that reduction in number of employees would be seen as a positive measure by the staff. He wanted to provide them with more training and empowerment to achieve increase in productivity.

Questions for Discussion

1. What was the nature of opportunity that Dr Vasireddi identified?
2. How did he build his business?
3. What do you think of Vimta's performance?
4. What should it do?

Appendix–I

Balance Sheet as on 31 March

(Figures in million)

Particulars			*1999*	*1998*	*1997*	*1996*	*1995*	*1994*	*1993*	*1992*
Sources of funds										
1.	Shareholder's funds									
	(i)	Share capital	36.07	36.07	36.07	36.07	36.07	35.20	16.95	11.40
	(ii)	Share application money	0.00	0.00	0.00	0.00	0.00	0.00	1.70	0.40
	(iii)	Reserves and surplus	9.56	9.56	15.08	24.30	21.73	16.27	5.00	1.40
2.	Loan funds									
	(i)	Secured loans	107.54	90.96	78.74	67.30	58.81	44.89	44.76	19.80
	(ii)	Unsecured loans	0.12	0.12	0.11	0.35	1.03	0.00	4.10	–
		Total	153.29	136.71	130.00	128.02	117.64	96.36	72.51	33.00
Application of funds										
1.	Fixed assets									
	(i)	Gross block	99.90	99.00	96.70	94.43	91.82	87.60	48.50	18.10
	(ii)	Less depreciation	23.66	19.51	15.53	11.77	7.90	4.00	1.70	0.60
	(iii)	Net block	76.24	79.49	81.17	82.67	83.92	83.60	46.80	17.50
	(iv)	Capital W/P (incl. capital advances and pre-operative expenses)	0.00	0.00	2.33	2.40	1.68	0.00	22.00	14.60
		Subtotal	76.24	79.49	83.50	85.07	85.60	84.20	68.80	32.10
2.	Current assets, loans and advances									
	(i)	Inventories	10.03	15.20	14.40	15.50	12.03	5.10	1.96	1.20
	(ii)	Sundry debtors	17.35	17.50	22.19	18.87	13.55	5.56	4.50	2.80
	(iii)	Cash and bank balances	0.28	1.10	0.75	0.75	0.43	1.00	0.12	0.30
	(iv)	Other current assets	1.20	0.86	0.91	0.60	0.31	0.10	0.14	0.30
	(v)	Loans and advances	2992	3.22	2.44	3.83	2.76	1.50	0.94	1.00
	(vi)	Investment	0.48	0.00	0.00	0.00	0.00	0.00	0.00	0.00
		Subtotal	32.26	37.88	40.69	39.56	29.08	13.26	7.66	5.60
3.	Less: current liabilities and provisions									
	(i)	Current liabilities	5.44	0.91	4.78	4.70	4.26	5.20	4.20	4.70
		Net current assets	26.82	1.97	35.91	34.87	24.82	8.06	3.46	0.90
4.	Miscellaneous expenditure (to the extent not written off or adjusted)									
	(i)	Profit and loss account	7.35	8.79	10.59	8.09	7.22	4.10	0.25	–
		Total	51.29	36.71	130.00	128.03	117.64	96.36	72.51	33.00

Profit and Loss Account for the Year

(Figures in million)

Particulars		*1998–99*	*1997–98*	*1996–97*	*1995–96*	*1994–95*	*1993–94*	*1992–93*	*1991–92*
Income									
(i)	Income from operations	29.41	23.37	33.57	37.14	34.03	19.36	15.93	8.80
(ii)	Increase/decrease in W/P	(4.95)	1.39	(1.51)	2.90	5.88	2.76	0.85	1.00
(iii)	Other income	0.77	0.25	0.33	0.08	0.10	0.11	0.22	0.10
	Total	25.23	25.01	32.39	40.12	40.01	22.23	17.00	9.90
Expenditure									
(i)	Chemicals and consumables consumed and testing expenditure	8.59	7.50	6.02	4.91	4.86	3.27	2.60	2.00
(ii)	Payment and benefits to employees	6.93	6.10	5.32	6.50	5.12	2.82	2.80	1.90
(iii)	Administrative, selling and general expenses	10.88	10.59	10.40	9.27	9.20	3.08	2.60	2.20
(iv)	Finance charges	19.64	16.77	14.32	12.15	11.40	8.06	4.30	2.30
(v)	Depreciation	1.23	4.18	4.13	3.98	4.03	2.35	1.10	0.50
	Total	50.27	45.14	40.19	36.81	34.61	19.58	13.40	8.90
	Profit before amortization and prior period adjustments	(25.04)	(20.13)	(7.80)	3.32	5.40	2.65	3.57	1.00
	Less: Amortization of preliminary expenses	1.32	1.35	1.20	0.75	0.44	0.44	0.01	–
	Profit/Loss before tax	(26.36)	(21.48)	(9.00)	2.57	4.96	2.21	3.56	1.00

Details of Plant and Machinery Acquisition

(Figures in million)

Year	*Amount*
1992–1993	19.22
1993–1994	27.65
1994–1995	2.95
1995–1996	3.07
1996–1997	2.04
1997–1998	0.74
1998–1999	0.51

Weekly MIS Report—VIMTA LABS LTD.

From 01-04-1999 to 30-10-1999

Amount ₹

Particulars	*Environment*	*Analytical*	*Clinical research*	*Total*
Order booked	1,02,66,700	84,88,187	52,46,000	2,40,00,887
Sales—Cash	–	34,57,709	–	34,57,709
Credit	1,17,60,138	55,24,466	40,56,750	2,47,99,063
Receipts				
1998–1999 (Actual)	20,33,578	9,89,220	8,93,124	39,15,922
1999–2000 (Estimated)	92,78,469	70,42,251	34,31,975	2,36,68,617

For a Typical Work

Particulars	*Environment*	*Analytical*	*Clinical research*	*Total*
Order booked	–	1,95,175	–	1,95,175
Sales—Cash	–	1,01,994		1,01,994
Credit	3,76,900	4,33,543	–	9,12,437
Receipts				
1998–1999 (Actual)	12,996	–	–	12,996
1999–2000 (Estimated)	4,05,650	2,93,655	–	7,12,301

Provisional Profit and Loss Account as on 30-09-1999

[1999–2000—(6 months)]

(I)	**Income**		
	Testing charges		20.89
	Increase/decrease in work-in-progress		0.00
			20.89
(II)	**Expenditure**		
	Chemicals and consumables	1.50	
	Other testing expenses	3.01	4.51
	Payments and benefits to employees		3.16
	Administrative, selling and general overheads		4.51
			12.18
(III)	**Profit before interest, depreciation and amortization**	8.70	
	Interest #		1.09
	Depreciation		2.12
	Miscellaneous expenses		0.66
			3.87
(IV)	**Profits before tax**	4.84	
	Less: (i) Provision for bad and doubtful debts		0.00
	(ii) Provision for tax		0.00
(V)	**Profit after tax**		**4.84**
	Add: Interest waived by IDBI		0.00
	Add: Surplus/(Deficit) b/f from previous year		(–) 42.88
(VI)	Surplus/(Deficit) carried over to balance sheet		(–) 38.05

Interest payable to IDBI on account of one time settlement

2. ICECD*

The International Centre for Entrepreneurship and Career Development (ICECD) was sponsored by Mrs. Hina Shah in early 1986. Mrs. Hina obtained a postgraduate degree in Science, and after marriage, joined with her husband Ashok in his business in 1973. Mr. Ashok and a friend of him were jointly running two small-scale units in Surendranagar at that time and were finding it difficult to manage both the businesses between them. When Mrs. Hina joined them, they thought she would take care of the management of one of the factories, while either Ashok or his friend would concentrate completely on marketing. Hina, however, evinced a lot of interest in marketing and liked travelling, and gradually took over the marketing functions of both the units. She identified new products and with the help of Mr. Ashok established a new small-scale unit to manufacture one of those new products. The Shahs and their friend started a fourth unit soon afterwards and, at the end of 1977, opened a full time marketing office in Ahmedabad. Mrs. Hina and Ashok shifted to Ahmedabad and took charge of this office.

It was around this time that the Centre for Entrepreneurship Development started looking for a woman to run their Entrepreneurship Development Programmes (EDPs) exclusively for women. They were looking for a person who had some industrial experience, managerial exposure, and above all, drive and initiative, and were happy to recruit Hina as an EDP trainer. She organized EDPs for women in different parts of Gujarat. In 1983, when the Entrepreneurship Development Institute of India (EDII) was formed, she was recruited there along with four other coordinations and CEO's Director. Although she was supposed to organize EDPs for women, gradually she had to get involved in other organizational work. This was mainly because there was a spurt in efforts to organize EDPs all over the country, but individuals and institutions who could impart were in short supply. EDII was the leading institution which could help various state level agencies to organize EDPs, and such assignments took Hina to different parts of the country and put her in touch with several people. By 1984, she was well known in the area of EDP so much as that organizers of training programmes help specifically. She was somewhat frustrated there, partly for lack of time to organize women specific activities. She quit the job at the end of 1985.

Towards the end of 1979, Government and Development Institutions had started recognizing the possibilities of developing entrepreneurship through training. Activities on these lines picked up soon after and industrial development institutions started looking for people and organizations who could organize EDPs. They allocated huge sums of money for this purpose. The early 1980s saw an increasing appreciation for organizing EDPs exclusively for women. Although several state level institutions and commercial banks started offering EDPs, very few of them had the expertise to understand and offer training to meet the special requirements of women in becoming entrepreneurs.

In 1984–85, Mrs. Hina travelled to countries such as UK, Switzerland, Austria, Sri Lanka and Pakistan. She visited international development agencies located in these countries. She spent hours together visiting and talking to people at UNIDO, ILO and Common Wealth Secretariat. These visits enabled her to learn a lot about the way the international aid and

* The case was Prepared by K. Ramachandran, Associate Dean, ISB, Hyderabad.

consulting agencies worked. She maintained records of these people whom she met, especially of those people who were associated with women's industrial development agencies. Nobody apparently thought that ICECD would be a success when Mrs. Hina went ahead with sponsoring the institute in early 1986. Her family members and friends thought it would be a part time activity for Hina who had already a comfortable income form her industrial activities. Mr. Ashok, however, noted that she had great faith in the potential and possibilities of EDPs for women which many others (who were also offering similar training) did not have. She worked hard and was sincere to the core. She analyzed and understood the requirements of women as entrepreneurs, and in fact the ICECD training programmes underwent refinement over a period of time. There was more emphasis on motivational aspects than on management training. ICECD wanted to be a leading institution to undertake entrepreneurship development activities for women. They were willing to open up, monitor and offer all their resources for development of women entrepreneurs all over the world.

ICECD had support from various individuals at senior levels in academic and development agencies. Its governing body consisted of eminent people in entrepreneurship. It kept record of the travel plans of these and other people who were closely associated with it. The Centre had 17 people, including Mrs. Hina making the top management. There are five trainers who coordinated EDPs, two research associates and seven supporting staff. A Niesbud publication listing the names of organizations conducting EDPs helped ICECD to identify potential customers. Since Mrs. Hina was fairly known to many of them, it was not difficult for the Centre to mobilize business. Moreover, ICECD's charges for services rendered to organize women EDPs were on cost basis and very reasonable comparatively.

One of the initial activities ICECD undertook was to organize an EDP for women in Ahmedabad and Baroda at the initiative of a local industries association. Mrs. Hina did not have much contact there and so started talking to known people to find out whether they could suggest any useful contacts there. They suggested some names whom she contacted and with the help of the sponsoring agency, she built up a list of useful persons in Baroda. She visited most of them whom she thought would be able to help ICECD either in the short run or in the long run or both. She believed that it was important for a person to know whom to contract, how to contact and when to contact. These addresses in Baroda came handy when they were asked to organize a programme in Baroda which was not far from Baroda and where they did not know many people. They also held meetings with officials of various development agencies to explain the objectives of the EDPs and the nature of assistance sought. There were also other contacts who were remotely connected with the programme, such as some business contacts.

Coordinators stayed in hotels in major cities, but in small places like Baroda, they preferred to stay in the government circuit house or similar places. Often, there were problems in such places when VIPs arrived there and the coordinator had to vacate. Once a coordinator had to vacate her room in the circuit house at a short notice and did not know where to go, as there were no hotels there. She contacted a dealer of Mr. Ashok's products who came forward to help her. Coordinators were given complete freedom when they were in the field. They submitted a report at the end of each programme. ICECD fixed no limits on the individual expenses, except that it explained to the person (before going into the field) the details of budget and funds available. It was left to the individual to use discretion. Coordinators in general felt happy working with ICECD. Mrs. Hina kept in touch with a large number of people all over the world. She wrote a letter every two months to about 400 people who were directly involved in women EDPs. These letters carried information of interest to the addresses regarding ICECD activities. For the purpose of sending such letters, she prepared something like a newsletter and asked her secretarial staff to insert specific portions from that indifferent letters. Over a period of time, the system was built up. Later on, Mrs. Hina did not spend much time on that as she delegated the work to her subordinates. She also sent personal notes of greetings to several people on days of importance, such as birthdays and wedding anniversaries.

Initially, in 1986–1987, she attended several international conferences at her own cost, where she met many people of importance from different parts of the world. She prepared a list of the institutions which worked for international development agencies and tried to know more about their activities and got associated with them. As a matter of policy, ICECD kept a file for each place under which two sets of addresses were kept. One, of people who could provide general support and two, who could be involved in the training programme. They expanded this list as and when specific projects came up for a particular place and prepared a list of addresses for faculty, organization and infrastructure. When the case writer reached Mrs. Hina's office, there was a huge parcel lying on her table ready for dispatch. It carried the address of a lady in Pakistan who, Mrs. Hina said, had asked for six bottles of a special oil. Mrs. Hina was requested to carry it when she travelled to Pakistan the next week. Although the oil costs very little, it was important for the person in Pakistan and she decided to carry it without any hesitation.

The ICECD has by now conducted seven trainers training programmes related to the development of women. The centre maintained contacts with the trainers of even the first programme, who were sent a small questionnaire seeking information of their activities bimonthly. Based on their feedback, the centre collected further information. In case of necessity, they contacted the individual or the programme sponsors for detailed information. Wherever some of these trainers changed their positions, they tried to contact the new incumbent and kept the chain alive. These contacts were found useful when they undertook a major research project to evaluate the performance of women entrepreneurs in India on behalf of the Industrial Development Bank of India. So far, they have organized seven trainers programmes, five for Indian trainers, one for international participants held in India and one in Africa. In the five programmes for Indian trainers, they had trained 101 people, of which 83 were women. Altogether, they were formally associated with 45 EDPs for women, of which 15 were completely under the control of ICECD. In instances where they helped others to implement EDPs, only the expenses were collected from them.

Questions for Discussion

1. Why Hina Shah started her own organization?
2. What are the strengths of Hina Shah?

FURTHER READING

Fincham, Robin and Rhodes, Peter, *Principles of Organizational Behaviour*, Oxford University Press, New Delhi.

Harigopal, K. *Management of Change, Leveraging Transformation*, 2nd ed., Response Books, New Delhi.

Luthans, Fred, *Organizational Behaviour*, McGraw-Hill, Kogakusha, Tokyo.

Pareekh, Udai, *Understanding Organizational Behaviour*, Oxford University Press, New Delhi.

Robbins, Stephen P., *Organizational Behaviour*, Prentice-Hall of India, New Delhi, 2000.

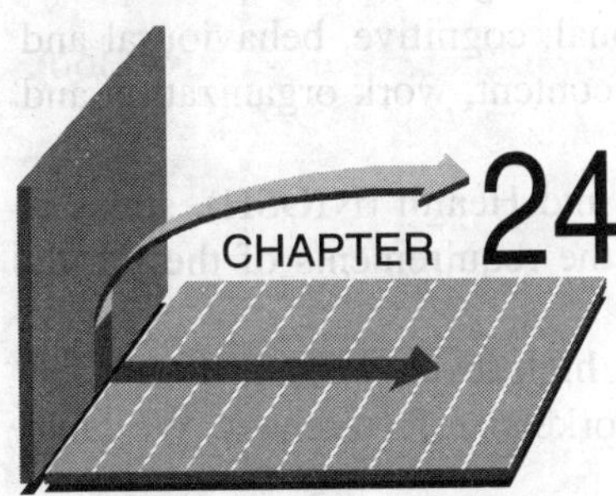

Managing Stress and Burnout

CONTENTS

INTRODUCTION

Stress means hardship or strain or adversity. In recent years, stress has become a common problem. Despite some research done in the area of stress, troublesome areas still remain. There is a lot of work being done on employee stress, reflecting perhaps the fact that job stress directly influences the performance of the employee and productivity.

CONCEPT OF STRESS AND BURNOUT

Stress is a feeling that is created when we react to a particular event. It is the body's way of rising to a challenge and preparing to meet a tough situation with focus, strength, stamina, and heightened alertness. Stress is a non-specific response of the body to any demand, according to Hans Selye.

Keith Davis defines stress as a condition of strain on one's emotions, thought processes and physical condition.

According to Fred Luthans, stress is an adaptive response to an external situation that results in physical, psychological, and/or behavioural deviations for organizational participants. The European Commission defined stress as a pattern of emotional, cognitive, behavioural and psychological reactions to adverse and noxious aspects of work content, work organization and work environment.

According to the National Institute of Occupational Safety and Health (NIOSH), stress is the harmful physical and emotional responses that occur when the requirements of the job do not match the capabilities, resources or needs of the worker.

Burnout is above the degree of stress. When the stress is at high level, we call it burnout. It is a syndrome of exhaustion and fatigue that decreases the workers' effectiveness. We have to take some measures to manage it.

CAUSES OF STRESS

There are several causes of stress. Some of them are:

1. **Work environment:**
   (a) Overload of work
   (b) Fear
   (c) Insecurity
   (d) Risk of losing job
   (e) Behaviour of colleagues
   (f) Role ambiguity.
2. **Physical stressors:**
   (a) Noise
   (b) Chemical hazards
   (c) Temperature extremes
   (d) Physical trauma
   (e) Radiation
   (f) Poor posture
   (g) Vibration
   (h) Handling of heavy goods
   (i) Monotonous tasks
   (j) Night shifts
   (k) Overtime.
3. **Emotional stressors:**
   (a) Anger
   (b) Challenges
   (c) Shock
   (d) Competition

(e) Conflicts
(f) Contradictory instructions
(g) Negative thoughts
(h) Time pressures
(i) Structural changes
(j) Monotonous tasks.

4. **Others:**
(a) Lack of job security
(b) No participation in decision making
(c) Unreasonable demands
(d) Lack of effective communication
(e) Long hours of work
(f) Excessive time spent away from home and family
(g) Office politics
(h) Conflicts among workers
(i) Inadequate wages.

CONSEQUENCES OF STRESS

The following are the consequences of stress:

1. *Violence has become an increasingly serious problem:* According to two studies, United States of America has the distinction of having the highest violent crime rate of any industrialized nation. On an average, 20 workers are murdered each week in the US, making homicide the second highest cause of workplace deaths. As per the recent study, India ranks first.

2. *Absenteeism:* According to a survey, the number of employees claiming themselves sick because of stress tripled from 1996 to 2000. The European Agency for Safety and Health at work reports that over half of 550 million working-days are lost annually in the US from absenteeism due to stress.

3. *Quitting jobs:* A government study in the USA reported that more jobs had been lost due to job insecurity. This is not only the problem of the USA. but of the entire world. To retain the employee in the organization means promising a healthy work life, and if organizations fulfil this, then they can have potential candidates working for the good of the organization.

4. *Others:*

- Unnecessary interpersonal conflicts
- Attachments to the current days of doing things and therefore resistance to change
- Prevarications that cloud issues and confuse priorities
- Procrastination in decision making and implementation
- Dullness in terms of creative problem solving
- Chaotic activity and disorganization
- Absenteeism

- Days off for genuine sickness
- High staff turnover
- Lethargy and slow working
- Resentments
- Disloyalty
- Secrecy
- Hidden agendas
- Hostility or resentfulness in the organization
- Negativity or cynicism towards planning outcomes and management
- Poor judgment with respect to both working relationship
- Clumsiness and accidents
- Loss of focus and absentmindedness
- High level of mistakes.

STRESS SCALE

The Holmes–Rahe Social Adjustment Scale reveals the impact of stress on different issues as follows:

Event	Score
• Death of spouse	100
• Divorce	73
• Marital separation	65
• Jail term	63
• Death of close member of family	63
• Personal injury or illness	53
• Marriage	50
• Dismissal from job	47
• Marital reconciliation	45
• Retirement	45
• Change in health of family member	44
• Pregnancy	40
• Sex difficulties	39
• Gain of new family member	39
• Business readjustment	39
• Change in financial state	38
• Death of close friend	37
• Change to different line of work	36
• Change in number of arguments with spouse	35
• Major mortgage	31
• Foreclosure of mortgage or loan	30
• Change of responsibilities at work	29

- Son or daughter leaving home 29
- Trouble with in-laws 29
- Partner begins or stops work 29
- Outstanding personal achievement 28
- Beginning or ending school 26
- Revision of personal habits 24
- Trouble with boss 23
- Change in hours or conditions of work 20
- Change in residence 20
- Change in schools 20
- Change in recreation 19
- Change in social activities 18
- Small mortgage or loan 17
- Change in sleeping habits 16
- Change in number of family get-togethers 15
- Change in eating habits 15
- Vacation 13
- Christmas 12
- Minor violations of the law 11

BURNOUT

Burnout is unmanageable stress. When stress is not managed, it creates more stress, which leads to burnout. It is common to some people. According to Rogers, about 18 per cent of business owners, managers, professionals and technical personnels in the USA suffers from organizational burnout. It is found among several service providers, like doctors, counsellors, police officers, nurses, teachers, executives and employees. In corporate world, executives have more problems because of high targets, increasing competition, high employee expectations, continued pressure of work and long hours of work. One study reported that information overload causes ill-health among 62 per cent of managers in Australia compared to 52 per cent worldwide.

The symptoms of burnout are related to the personality of industrials. It creates alienation, powerlessness, low self-esteem, poor teamwork, nastiness, dependency behaviour, individual breakdown, etc. The behavioural symptoms of burnout among employees are: absenteeism, hopelessness, sabotage, malpractices, non-compliance, falling short of deadlines, sensitiveness, interpersonal and group conflict, low productivity, goal confusion, back stabbing, lack of teamwork, etc.

Models of Burnout

There are three dimensions of burnout. They are as follows:

1. *Depersonalization:* An employee alienates or distances himself from others.

2. *Lack of personal accomplishment:* This scale envisages that excessively low level of personal involvement and low achievements are the main indicators of emotional burnout.
3. *Emotional exhaustion:* It is related to chronic fatigue, frustration and powerlessness experienced by employees due to high stress, exceeding tolerable limits.

MANAGING STRESS AND BURNOUT

Several strategies are to be followed to reduce stress at workplace and in daily life. Some of them are:

- No single method is uniformly successful; a combination of approaches is generally most effective.
- What works for one person does not necessarily work for someone else.
- Stress can be positive as well as negative. Appropriate and controllable stress provides interest and excitement and motivates the individual to greater achievement, while a lack of stress may lead to boredom and depression.
- Stress may play a part in making people vulnerable to illness. A physician or psychologist should be consulted if there are any indications of accompanying medical or psychological conditions, such as cardiac symptoms, significant pain, anxiety or depression.
- Organizational interventions can be of many types, ranging from structural (e.g. staffing levels, work schedules, physical environment) to psychological (e.g. social support, control over work, participation).
- Individual approaches are required. Training is required for reducing stress.
- Training helps prevent stress.
- Becoming aware of the signs of stress.
- Balancing work life.
- Changing personal and work attitudes and behaviour.
- Small physical exercises.
- Making use of the available courses.
- Having healthy diet.
- Offering the employee frequent short intervals.

ORGANIZATIONAL ACTIVITIES

One of the first things an organization can do is to recognize the role management plays in the stress–work equation. This process can include the following steps:

- Senior managers and employees should meet to acknowledge the importance of the issue and agree to a corporate policy on work areas.
- The policy should be jointly 'owned' by the organisation and those it protects.
- The policy should begin with a statement of goals that are linked to local health and safety legislation.
- Management outlines areas that the organization can take responsibility for implementing.

- Employees outline areas that they can take responsibility for implementing.
- Management determines the need for carrying out risk assessments.
- Specific steps should be delineated to eliminate work-related stress injuries.
- The organization must ensure there is support for confidential health monitoring.
- All stakeholders agree on a process for publicizing the policy.

STRESS AND BURNOUT REDUCTION STRATEGIES

Job conditions: With some jobs, the nature of the work can lead to stress. Management should ensure that workload is not too heavy, build in rests or breaks, and avoid overly long work hours. With routine tasks or overly hectic jobs, the organization should emphasize how meaningful the work is by putting it in the context of organizational goals and performance. People should have access to the big picture of what they are trying to accomplish. Also, allow them as much of a sense of control over their work as possible. Controlling the timing of breaks, the set-up of the workplace and various other issues can give the employees a great sense of ownership and pride in the work.

Management styles: A great deal of stress at work can be a result of a manager's style in dealing with employees. Managers should have appropriate training or skills in dealing with others. Employees should be part of a decision-making team with their manager. Managers should be more like coaches or mentors, and should be good communicators and sensitive to family issues of employees.

Interpersonal relationships: Employees who are isolated from others should have opportunities to connect with co-workers. The social environment at work is important. While little work will get done if the workplace is excessively social, there should be some ability for people at work to bond with others.

Work roles: People's job responsibilities should be clear. Conflicting or uncertain expectations should be avoided. Often, people have too many hats to wear or too many competing tasks to complete. An effort should be made to rationalize the job and work expectations.

Career concerns: It is important for people to have some sort of career plan. Whenever there is job uncertainty or lack of opportunity for growth, some employees will experience stress. Also, changes to the workplace can be worrying to many people. Whenever there is restructuring or reorganizing, ensure the plan includes timely and individual feedback to everyone affected.

Environmental conditions: The workplace should be as pleasant as possible. Avoid crowding, too much noise, noxious odours, or ergonomic problems.

MANAGING WORK-LIFE BALANCE

- Reviewing workloads to ensure that people are not taking on more than is reasonable. If people are being given more work than is realistic for the time allotted, then nobody wins. The organization will not meet its deadlines and performance will suffer.
- Setting predictable workloads. Try to prepare for unexpected shifts in workload, schedules, and responsibilities for at least the next three months.

- Exploring the possibility of flextime with staff that may be eligible.
- Asking what steps the organization has taken to show it recognizes family and personal obligations of employees by exploring the circumstances of the programmes or actions.
- Many organizations have work-life balance programmes that assist employees in taking care of personal issues that often decrease their efficiency and productivity at work. Generally, these programmes improve employee satisfaction and loyalty. Explore the possibility of offering programmes that focus on improving employees' physical and mental wellness. Programmes may include weight training or cardiovascular activities, stretching and relaxation sessions (e.g. yoga, visualization) and artistic focussed (e.g. photography classes, dance classes). These programmes can be implemented in-house or with outside resources, such as exercise clubs or art studios.

SUMMARY

1. Success is strain of a person at workplace.
2. Stress has become a common problem.
3. It is harmful to the society.
4. Causes of stress are related to work environment, physical stressors, emotional and other stressors.
5. Stress has several consequences.
6. Some of them are: violence, absenteeism, quitting jobs, conflicts and unhappiness.
7. Stress can be managed by following some strategic and yoga exercises.

REVIEW QUESTIONS

1. Define stress. Discuss the sources of stress.
2. Explain the concept of burnout.
3. What are the consequences of stress and burnout?
4. Explain the strategies for managing stress.

CASE STUDIES

1. Man or Machine?

To

The Chairman
Teffer India, Mumbai

Dear Mr. Chibber,

Thank you very much for the wonderful farewell you gave us last evening. We have been given many farewells in the past, as we moved from one city to another, from one division to another. But this one will have lasting impact, probably because we are leaving the country this time. I will certainly miss the lovely people at Teffer, people who will stay with you for many years. These people, like Shuklaji, give every moment of their lives to further the cause of Teffer. I despair about them as I will be leaving them when India is going through some testing times, professionally. And it is with these people in mind that I want to leave with you some thoughts to ponder over. We have known each other for long and that gives me the courage to voice some concerns, which, I hope, you will think about. As you often say, Teffer puts its people first, then its products and processes.

I was amazed how many people had such wonderful things to say about my husband. I know people usually say the right things at farewells, but I knew what I heard yesterday was not feigned. I am happy that my husband means so much to all of you and that he is such a critical part of the organization. I am also happy to see how much he is loved. I do believe that it is the sum total of all the love one gets that goes on to become a blessing.

As a wife, I do get to meet a number of your managers from time to time, but they have been simple social encounters. Yesterday brought to the fore Shuklaji's professional profile very sharply. For me, he has been just a husband, not a senior vice-president. Maybe what Mr. Bhalla said is true: "Wives need to be told how good their husbands are because they won't believe it otherwise." He evoked a lot of laughter, but there was some truth in that statement. In all my 17 years with Shuklaji, not once have I or my children judged him on his performance, his upward mobility at Teffer or what he brings home. To a large extent, I think Shuklaji himself has contributed to that ethos because he rarely discusses his company at home. I'd read about the brand wars, about high court judgements, about your mergers in the papers, but I learnt nothing from Shuklaji. Because that's how he is. He does not like to bring the workplace home.

My interaction with other managers has been merely at a social level and chat confined to my children's lives, my music and the counselling centre I run at home. But last evening when everybody said such wonderful things about Shuklaji, I realized how little of his life we got to share! In the 15 waking hours in a day, Shuklaji spends 10 hours at office, one hour commuting. Of the remaining four hours which he spends at home, close to two hours are spent on the telephone, which leaves us just two hours (which these days is taken up by interviews to the press). Isn't that amazing? It must be worse in your case! No wonder then that people whom he worked with are affected by his attention and care, and more people benefit form his time.

This brings to mind what another wife once confided. Apparently, her husband's secretary once told her in jest: "Please send him to work in a good mood, or he gets irritable the whole day with all of us." She was taken aback. "Whom do I call and tell? "Please keep the stresses and pressures low at work or else he comes home and growls at all of us," she asked tearfully. I wonder if life was like this earlier. I hardly expect Shuklaji to help in the kitchen; he always looks tired and worn out. So much so that when the kids hear his car, they whisper, "Dad's back", not "Yay! Dad's back!" My responses have also altered with the changing times. Today when Shuklaji comes home, I don't ask him, "Did you have a nice day?" That sounds far fetched. Instead, I ask him, "Was the merger signed?"

Mr. Chibber, there is far too much stress building up at work, which infects an otherwise peaceful family life. Have you noticed that? Fortunately, Shuklaji is not a short-tempered person. When he is stressed, he remains silent. But my friend's husband, who heads a beverage company, has become very irritable. So much so that when his daughter hears his car in the driveway, the little girl rushes about putting her toys away, switching off the television, all the 'extra' lights and fans, walks, waits on tiptoe behind the curtains, gauging her father's mood when he enters the house. No, isn't that was? What is happening to us? Mr. Chibber, what happened to the days when fathers and children rushed into each other's arms? Last month, and this one is very telling, a seven-year-old boy was brought to me by his mother. The boy had started that by picking up my telephone and yelling: "Get the … crates moving if you want to save your …" Clearly, the boy's father does most of his dynamic sales reviews over dinner. The point is, that man was never known to ever talk like that. "It's happened to him over the past few years," his wife says.

Shuklaji also says: "How tough these times are." When he has a chance, he tells the boys: "Your life ahead is going to be very tough. Nothing is going to come to you on a platter. It's for you to grab the opportunity and run, keep your nose to the grindstone and slog like a horse." I am frightened when I hear this. Should we scare our children with our own myopic vision of life? I know he means well, when he says, "Kanta, I see the bloodshed every day, what you learnt yesterday is useless tomorrow. You have to be on your guard, awake, alert and watchful."

The last time I heard those kind words was when my grandmother recounted to us her memories of Partition. For mangers like Shuklaji, life has become one long guerrilla war. They are always watchful, cautious. My brother, who is 50, is going to Wharton for a two-month refresher course this month, just when his youngest son is taking the Class X board exams. "Can't it wait Dad?" he pleaded, but my brother, who was trying to lighten the moment, said, "Darling, if I wait, there will be no college for you to go to," Exaggerated it may have been, but it struck me that our preoccupation with success is reaching diabolic proportions.

Success is nice, who doesn't want it? But what I fear is, will there be any bonding left based on love? Someone told my son yesterday: "Because a great man like your father." What if my son does not become as great as his father? Will we all still love him?

How time flies! Seventeen years! And it seems like yesterday when I got married to Shuklaji. He was then just confirmed after his three-year training and you were his new division's head! Today, you are the chairman and Shuklaji is being posted to the Asia-Pacific office as the group head for market operations. These are successful events in your lives and I am sure both of you worked very hard for it. Yesterday, in your farewell speech you said: "Behind every successful man there is a woman…" Please do not misunderstand what I am about to say, but that sentence jars.

I can't see how I could have contributed to his success. He is on a whirlwind rush between one goal and the next. All I do is sit and watch the panoramic view, like surfing channels on television. The staccato changes of goals, the sudden highs and lows—I don't understand his world anymore. During the past four years, even though we are all together, we are not in reality together. I manage the house, the boys' education, I fix light bulbs, leaking faucets, fight with MTNL, negotiated the sale of our land in Delhi, drive my boys to cooperage for their cricket coaching and maths tuitions, scour the city for size 10 shoes, wait up at night praying that the older one returns safely after a Bon Jovi concert, sit chin up at a meeting with my younger one's headmaster who tells me: "Mrs. Shukla, your son spends Hindi class launching paper missiles, stuck to chewing gum!" Shuklaji has been very busy, I could hardly meet him to discuss my problems.

But all that is fine, I suppose. Most mothers are doing all that and much more these days. But still, we are grass widows. I have barely any time to handle the variety of problems at home, where am I going to find the time to enable Shuklaji's success? I don't even know what he is chasing.

He has succeeded single handedly. Alone, just as his sons are working at their success alone. Mr. Chibber, I am not complaining, I am only worried, deeply worked about what is happening to men like Shuklaji. Fortunately, he is with Teffer, which is a caring organization. You have invested tremendously in his growth and development. In the last seven years alone, Shuklaji has been to 15 management development programmes. He knows so much about his work and he is always at it. But I wonder if he knows enough about his sons.

Two months ago, my younger boy won the Bournvita Quiz Contest. I was on TV but Shuklaji was in Thailand. We taped it for him, but he hasn't had the chance to see it. It's been one thing after another. First, it was the orientation for this new position for which he had to fly back to Bangkok. The day he came back, there was the annual review, so he went to the office straight from the airport to work on his presentation. The next morning he was leaving for Sri Lanka for a new launch conference. When he retuned after four days, the directors from New Jersey were here and all of you went off to Goa for a week.

It's been like that for as long as I can remember. The corporate train never stops. But you know it wasn't like this even as recently as four years ago? We did spend some evenings together. We attended family weddings together, we even celebrated our wedding anniversary. During the past two years, we haven't been together even on his birthday. I wonder about the quality of life that people like Shuklaji are leading. What do they get out of life? One rung up every year? Does that make up for missing out the compassion and presence of one's own family? In November last year, his sister's daughter was getting married. Shuklaji had sworn he would take the day off. But as luck would have it, the proviso days, the sale of 'Amigo' to Delaware went into court, Shuklaji returned after 36 hours, well after the doli had left!

Shuklaji's parents feel very bad about him. He works so hard to be able to give us a good life, they say TRUE. But what about him? He has severe acidity and is down to fruit for breakfast and bland food at other times. But how can a diet help if your lifestyle is wrong to start with? Take December last year. The purchase of Megalo was being negotiated. For three weeks he came home in the middle of the night. Then some legal issues stalled the acquisition. And when my older son explained the details to me, I was surprised. How could Teffer have problems, I thought. Then there was bad press and he was caught up with that. One thing or the other kept him high till February end when the deal fell through. Just as I thought, at last some peace, the deal was hot again. Again, he went through the rush and tumble of courts, registrars and God knows what else. He came home with huge reams of paper, and worked on his laptop every night. Suddenly, he was off to France to discuss the deal. He came back after a week only to enter the whirl of annual appraisals. And right in the midst of that came that horrible incident of the Foods Directorate's accusation on quality. For six weeks, the battle went on from newspapers to court to damage control.

Doesn't that sound like some non-stop thriller? If just watching him was so exhausting, I wonder what he must feel when he is assailed by so many emotions and mood swings! We never see him; during the last three years, we have seen more of him in the press. Every other day there is some newspaper correspondent intruding on our dinner. The interviews are longer than the quotes. Last week one correspondent stayed on till 11.30 pm. Now that is really too much?! Later, I learnt he used the opportunity to also research some articles he was doing on brand value. Shuklaji felt he had to help the lad. "After all, Teffer has grown some terrific brands; the experience must be passed on," he said. Ever since the Megalo takeover, he has come to be known as a takeover artiste. A new tag. So there are now TV channels interviewing him, chat shows, breakfast shows… And if it is not these, he has seminars to attend, syndicates to facilitate, all kinds where he is called to deliver lectures…all that means four days a week of media interaction.

Yesterday, I asked Dhiren Bakshi, your HR director, whether all this was simply a function of Shuklaji's seniority. What he said gives food for thought. He said: "Naturally, the media will approach the senior, the successful, but there is also a growing need among professionals to market themselves as products."

What is happening is that the individual has lost complete sense of his personal identity and related roles and become a corporate product. His time is completely devoted to preparing the 'product', shining it, polishing it, and presenting it to the world and being preoccupied with how he comes across to his audience—be it the board, his team, trade bodies or the general public.

In the process, the professional ends up being more of an enigma than a person and is unwittingly continuously 'working' on the image. Like Rajiv Mittal who had to drag himself away last night to attend some bureaucrat's daughter's wedding. Why? Because as he said: "The chaps from Dennet, Tylo, Argie will all be there. Teffer will stand out if I don't go."

I could see Ranji's dilemma—he is so caught up in this whole image circuit. Competitive warfare has found new battlegrounds. Why, even we have been victims of this imaginary. Our social life has become so hectic that I have to maintain a diary! We are constantly being invited for something or the other. Some of them are difficult to refuse, because we have to maintain an image. I'm sure you know how stressful it is.

Can you feel the heightened pitch of competition? What I see and hear today is a different mosaic of feelings, far different from the simple tapestry of the past. And frankly, I don't think this has anything to do with Shuklaji's career progression, but the general environment. There seems to be a mad rush; everyone is rushing to get somewhere, destination unknown. Even the reasons are different. Around 10–15 years ago, people worked hard to become successful, to be seen as good, for increments and that odd promotion. Today, every year could take you up two rungs. Managers work harder to remain successful, salient and relevant. Even companies are working harder to grow bigger and bigger, there were new markets, new channels, new partners, more acquisitions, more mergers, new ventures—the preoccupation is with 'getting there before the competition does'.

So, today, managers like Shuklaji are working to keep the company highly successful. The company's success is their success. Training programmes are being devised to make every trainee a better packaged product, smarter, cleverer… but only professionally. Meanwhile, the individuals have lost their way: they climb mountains, some reach the top and realize they had climbed the wrong mountain, others scale newer heights, onward and upward, leaving behind their individuality. People, hereafter, are going to be harder hit when they retire because their feeling of self-worth will drop from a higher plane.

Two months ago, a lady who works with me was heading for a breakdown. On probing, I learnt the family was unable to cope with the imminent relocations of the father to another city. "I am not sure if we should live separately. I can't displace my kids at this stage in their schooling and my husband agrees," she wept. But did Mr. Sharma agree in his heart? What he told me was very painful, "I know it is very hard on the kids to be displaced like this. I have thought about it and am willing to chase my career alone. Yes, I will miss them, but, at least, they will have continuity... I wonder if I am doing the right things, I will miss out on so much of their growth..."

I asked him: "Will you lose your job if you decline the transfer?" "No, I won't lose my job. But I will get stuck. My growth will be stunted. These days, youngsters coming out of campus are pitching for the managing director's post! It's like being on a treadmill that is running at 80 kmph. If you stop, you crash. If you try and match the pace, your heart is going to pack up. I don't know if I am emotionally ready for the sacrifice. I could get bitter. Then again, for how long will my firm agree to my terms? If everyone says no to a transfer, what will happen to the company we built? You can't blame the company—business has to grow. It either helps me grow or helps itself grow. The choice is clear. But, is giving it all up a solution? Then what happens to my family? Okay, for three or four years, I will coast along with a halo around my head as the man who could look opportunity in the eye and say: Thanks, but, no thanks. Then what happens to my future?" he asked.

I could see this dilemma. More than that, I say his pain. The pain of a father who, in today's times, must be ready to be separated from his family. Shuklaji comes home at every night, but he comes home. He is there on call. But what about men who relocate alone? I can read Sharma's mind. He probably says: "It's not my company's fault. It's not even my family's fault that they find this transfer inconvenient. It's my fault that I want to run this race..." Sharma and his family know that what he earns is valuable. He has provided is certainly helping the family. And sustaining that comfort has now come to mean distancing the breadwinner from the beneficiaries. Careers must go on. Bread and even jam must be earned. But the need to keep up the charade is killing people. Like a long running soap opera that refuses to end, with new angels and twists in the plot to keep the serial on air. And that is the stress I am referring to. Of course, many families have made optimal arrangements. Like a friend who runs a successful cosmetics company lives alone while his family is in a different city. But isn't such an arrangement born out of a desire to appear agile and successful in a world that recognizes only the runners and not the others?

What is happening is mangers today are losing touch with themselves and their true nature. The preoccupation with the trappings of life have dulled their senses. That is not to say that companies must not grow or men must not seek growth. But I ask, doesn't all this hurt you? Would you be happy with a manager who takes in the volumes but sits alone at night missing his family?

I am not talking of loneliness, I am talking of the missed paragraphs in life. The point is, many of them do not even realize it. They keep up hoping things will change. Meanwhile, I ask you, is there something you can do to make it all bearable? If you can manoeuvre the cleverest of takeovers, surely you can take care of the human emotion through the organization. You need to stay in touch with the manager's feelings, find solutions so that the human quality in a manager is not destroyed. I really don't know how or what you will do. But this is what I want to leave with you, to think about. Can we save our managers? If Teffer has been successful all these years, they say it was because the managers never lost their human quality. I fear that quality is being slowly eroded. In some distant period in future, they will unearth the ruins of our civilization and conclude, "Man in the 21st century had lost the ability to use his amygdala, the seat of human emotions…".

With best wishes,
Mrs. Kanta Shukla

Questions for Discussion

1. Explain the feelings of Mrs. Kanta Shukla.
2. How do you tackle this type of situation?

2. Swagat Engineering Corporation

On 15 June 1985, the workers of Swagat Engineering Corporation were shouting at the main gate of Visakha Steel Plant (VSP) with some slogans. The CMD of the VSP called the general manager (personnel) and the personnel officer (contract labour) and directed them to settle the issue immediately.

Swagat Engineering Corporation (SEC) was started by three entrepreneurs—Balan, Raman and Rajan—as a small enterprise in 1980 in Visakhapatnam. Raman and Rajan were engineering graduates from IIT Kharagpur, and Balan was a union leader with plus-two qualification. Balan had three years' experience in a similar engineering corporation earlier. After identifying vast scope and potential for engineering contracts, they took up contract jobs by contributing ₹5 lakhs each towards the initial investment. The number of workers in the concern was increased from 20 to 60 by 1984. All the workers were members of the Steel Contract Labour Association (SCLA) affiliated to INTUC.

The firm made substantial profits since its inception. Labour-management relations were also harmonious. The workers were paid above the statutory wages and were provided other facilities, like medical and clothing allowances. Some engineering contractors enhanced the wages keeping in mind the increasing cost of living.

Visakhapatnam is a jewel on the east coast of India, with a natural harbour and a beautiful landscape. It was a sleepy seaside fishing village in the seventeenth century and has now become a beehive of industrial activity due to the tremendous growth of large, medium and small-scale industries and subsequent growth of the informal sector in the city. Visakha Port Trust is the sole catalyst in transforming the seaside village into the "City of Destiny" and the "City of Steel". The port was built in 1933. A decade later, Hindustan Shipyard was started after which there was a lull in the industrial activity for about a decade. After the 1950s, the city witnessed the setting up of many large, medium and small enterprises. About 35 large and medium enterprises started functioning giving employment to about 40,000 persons. Over a lakh were absorbed in the informal sector. All the expansion programmes and some emerging units were expected to employ another 10,000. Visakha Steel Project (VSP), which is an integrated steel plant with a massive investment of about ₹8,500 crores, has been under construction with a direct employment potential of 15,000 small enterprises, and employment potential of another 60,000 people. Several entrepreneurs are eager to start their ventures in Visakhapatnam.

The Visakha labour market consists of both the organized and unorganized sectors, but the share of unorganized labour is quite significant, representing over 60 per cent. Rapid industrialization has attracted a large number of migrants from various places. Most of the workers are members of labour unions affiliated to central unions like INTUC, HMS, CITU. Regional parties like the Telugu Desam also have their labour fronts.

There is also the problem of about 12,000 displaced persons from the area taken over by VSP, whose major demand has been that they should be provided employment by VSP. Around 2,000 displaced persons have been absorbed, while the rest have been working with the contractors of VSP, having about 30,000 contract workers under about 300 contractors.

On 2 January 1985, the workers of SEC approached the management and demanded that wages should be enhanced by 20 per cent; bonus enhanced by 10 per cent for the year 1984, and weekly holidays be given for the watch and ward staff. The SEC management refused to entertain their demands. The management, in the meanwhile, was busy in preparing work order proposals and was also trying hard to obtain fresh orders. The workers sought the assistance of SCLA regarding their demands. The SCLA, in turn, submitted a charter of demands to the management for redressal. The union leaders were invited by the management for discussions on 15 March, but they could not arrive at any amicable settlement. In spite of repeated requests, the management did not pay attention to the emerging situation. Ultimately, on 1 May, the union submitted a strike notice stating that the workers would go on strike from 15 June onwards if their demands were not met. They sent a copy each to the personnel officer (contract labour), VSP, and the Assistant Commissioner of Labour (ACL), for their information and necessary intervention.

On 29 May 1985, the ACL arranged a meeting between the workers and managers. He tried to convince them to follow the wage policy of similar enterprises executing contract works in VSP, but in vain. After two days, on 1 June, the ACL invited Mr Balan and his two partners to his office and had the following discussion.

ACL: Mr. Balan, as your firm is doing well, why don't you consider the union's demands which are quite reasonable?

Balan: Sir, it is a characteristic feature of labour in our country to demand more wages and better working conditions without improving productivity. If we secure profits, it is due to our own efforts but not out of their sweat.

ACL: Please do not forget, when you were working as an employee in Swastik Engineering Corporation, you came to me with similar problems.
As a union leader, you fought for workers' rights. I supported your arguments and helped you in reaching amicable settlements.

Balan: You did your duty as a conciliation officer. It was neither a favour to me nor to my union members.

ACL: Ok, I did my duty. Even now, I have to do it sincerely to maintain industrial harmony in this organization, and also to ensure that there would not be any losses due to delays.

Balan: You do whatever you can. I do not agree with your views.

ACL: I once again advise you to settle the issue at the earliest. If all the contract labours go on strike, you cannot do anything. I will also take some action on my part.

Balan: Today, I am leaving for Delhi for finalizing a long-pending contract. I do not know when I will come back. You may exercise your power.

Questions for Discussion

1. What are the main issues in the above case?
2. How do you tackle the above situation?
3. What is the role of the management and the union for maintaining industrial harmony?

FURTHER READING

Cary, L. Cooper and Roy Payne, *Stress at Work*, John Wiley and Sons, Chichester, 1978.

Davis, Keith, *Human Behaviour at Work*, Tata McGraw Hill, New Delhi, 1981.

French, J.R.P. and Caplan, R.D., *Stress at Work*, John Wiley and Sons, New York, 1978.

Hammonds, K.H., Work: More Complex than we thought, *Business Week*, September, 1993.

Jackson, Paul and Reima Soumi, *Workplace Design and Organisational Effectiveness*, 2006.

Kaila, H.L., Pai., S., Ravishankar, S., and Dhar, U., *Stress Management* (Western and Indian Techniques) Himalaya Publishing House India, 2001.

Subbulaxmi, Santha, Productivity and Stress, *Management*, Vol. 11, No. 3, July–September, 2002.

Sharma, Radha R., Executive Burnout—Contribution of Role Related Factors, *Indian Journal of Industrial Relations*, Vol. 38, No. 1, July, 2002.

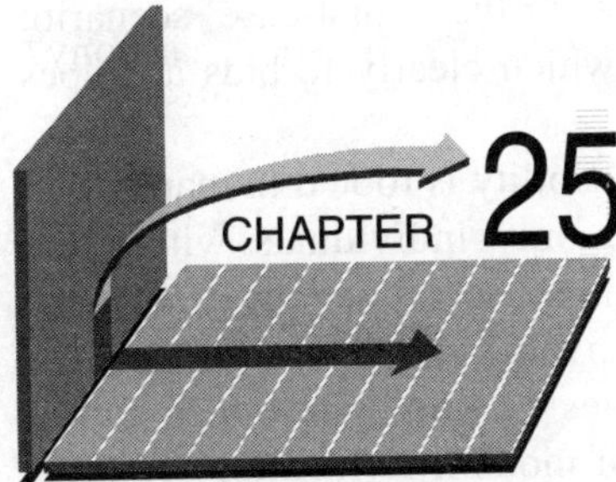

Managing Business Values

CONTENTS

- Conceptual Issues
- Ethical Dilemmas
- Corporate Experiences
- Role of Executives

CONCEPTUAL ISSUES

Business ethics and values are the desired norms of behaviour, exclusively dealing with commercial transactions. According to Sekhar R.C., one can convert values into rules of behaviour that can then be described as ethics. It means values plus knowledge equals ethics, which in business includes values governing commercial transactions not only among persons and among organizations, but also among persons within organizations and political processes that regulated such transactions. It follows from a comprehension of the concept that ethics stand for an individual's personal attitudes and beliefs concerning what is right or wrong, good or bad. Ethics differ from organization to organization, person to person, country to country, and culture to culture because they are not absolute, but relative.

A famous consultancy firm, called, Karve suggested CATWOE model, which is adopted from systems management for resolving ethical questions. CATWOE is an acronym for ethical decision-making representing customers (C); actors who carry out the decision (A); transformation process or the decision maker (T); worldwide predominantly held (W); owners

(O); and environment (E). The model suggests that it is in the long-term interests of stockholders involved in the decision that the area manager should: (a) decline to pay the bribe; (b) appraise the top management of the decision; (c) try to resolve the issue in the proper manner, with the help of top management intervention at higher levels and threat of counter exposure, if necessary; (d) take customers into confidence to cater for the 'worst-case' scenario; and (e) ask the top management to propagate a code of ethics which clearly forbids all types of bribes and illegal payments.

The application of the concept of organizational social responsibility is rooted in managerial ethics. This is because organizations cannot make decisions; only individuals within the organizations can do that. As decisions relating to any organization's social actions project the values of corporate managers, the organization's social responsiveness is determined on the basis of executives' value culture. It is in this context the studies on corporate ethics gain a currency of literature. Further, business ethics are the backbone of modern civilization. Today's corporate business is complicated, comprehensive, and competitive. Technological advances have enabled to specialize and globalize. In the present socio-economic environment, it is a vital issue, to achieve individual as well as social goals. Finally, it is said that there exists a certain synergy between corporate governance and business ethics which is expected to exist in the corporate world. The bedrock of good corporate governance is the quality of leadership and core values.

ETHICAL DILEMMAS

Management of corporate ethics is considered under two general categories: ethical dilemmas and ethical lapses. An ethical dilemma is an ethical issue which has two conflicting and valid views. A classic example is whether tobacco companies or liquor marketers should be allowed to advertise or not. Allowing them to do so would be encouraging unhealthy behaviour, but not allowing them to advertise would violate their freedom of speech and hamper their ability to do business. An ethical lapse, on the other hand, occurs when managers make unethical decisions. Thus, any managerial action which does not have the sanctity of business ethics is an ethical lapse. The alleged nexus between Tata Tea and ULFA in Assam, which hit the headlines for some period, is an interesting point.

Several philosophers and management experts have developed a number of models and systems to help people resolve ethical dilemmas. There are three fundamental ethical approaches or business for business managers: the *utilitarian*, the *moral rights*, and the *social justice* approaches. The utilitarian approach judges the effects of a particular action on a particular group in terms of what provides the greatest good for the greatest number of people. This approach focuses on 'actions' rather than on the motives behind the actions. The moral rights approach judges whether actions are in accordance with the accepted principles of moral and legal rights. Also known as *deontology*, it stresses on the rights of human beings to life and safety, a standard of truthfulness, privacy, and so on. The social justice approach judges actions in terms of whether they are consistent with the maintenance of fairness, equity and impartiality in the distribution of rewards and costs among individuals and groups. In other words, this approach implies that individuals as members of organizations should agree to confirm to the shared values and goals of their respective enterprises.

Steven Brenner and Earl Molander conducted a survey among the practising executives to identify the factors that influence ethical standards. According to them, public disclosure by publicity and media coverage is the most important determinant of ethical standards, and the other factors being public awareness, government regulations, professionalism in business managers, new social expectations, and top management emphasis on ethical action, in that order.

Brenner and Molander also stated that most often managers find themselves involved in conflict of interest situations with their superiors, customers, subordinates, competitors, regulators and suppliers. They added that the most common conflicts of interest related to: honesty of communication; gifts, entertainments and kickbacks; fairness and discrimination; breaking of laws; honesty in contracts; firings and lay-offs; and pricing practices. To assist the managers who are frequently confronted with these dilemmas, many firms are establishing written codes of ethics. Amanda Bennett studied corporate codes of ethics and confirmed the earlier findings relating to conflict of interest situations. The issues centre round bribes and kickbacks, political contributions, authenticity of books, misappropriation of corporate assets, and confidentiality of corporate information, etc. Pradip N. Khandwala's study on 30 senior and top level executives from India's leading public enterprises revealed that whether there were any core values that the management strongly emphasised to the staff. S.K. Chakraborthy of IIM-C had presented nicely the issues relating to the values for managers, value system in the East and West, managing self and society, etc.

High product quality, high productivity, improved work ethic and culture, team-work and cooperation were most commonly stressed values. Whereas integrity, sense of belongingness, employee orientation, cost control, customer orientation, and safety at work were somewhat less frequently stressed values. Further, meeting social obligations was least commonly emphasized core value. Vikram Karve considered an ethical dilemma faced by a newly appointed area manager of an IT company. A state-of-the-art product was to be launched on a certain date that had been widely announced and there were heavy customer bookings. Three days before the launching date, however, the manager's deputy told him the trucks transporting the product had been detained at the octroi post for want of some documents, and the octroi inspector was demanding bribe for the immediate clearance of the consignment. "Should we pay the bribe?" the deputy manager asked him.

The indian corporate sector scenario is not what it was prior to 1991. The package of economic reforms implemented over the last one decade has intensified the competition by opening the market for MNCs, with a reduced role for direct public investment and a concerted drive to woo foreign investment through numerous concessions. Now, in the liberalized business environment, Indian companies are compelled to replace old ethos and give priority to enhancing shareholders' values, maximum scope to professional management, participative decision-making and transparency in dealings, besides providing competitive service to customers. This is a period of transition from a controlled economy to a market-driven economy, characterized by basic and fundamental philosophical changes.

Georgetown University, Washington D.C., concluded a seminar with the following issues:

- Ethical behaviour cannot be assured simply by writing and distributing an ethical code of conduct.

- Since ethics is a constant, living interpersonal process, we need always to be working at it. If it is not improving, it is deteriorating.
- The process of ethical behaviour can no longer be assured by an authoritarian fiat or a command from the top. People today prize their freedom and individuality too highly for mere commands to be effective. Individuals must freely agree with, and commit themselves to, the principles and values that the corporation stands for.
- Agreement is an exercise of intelligence. Therefore, values which are proposed must be reasonable. Commitment is a matter of free choice and, therefore, values which are proposed must be desirable.
- It is within the climate of a corporation that certain values are recognized by the membership to be reasonable and desirable. The climate grounds and supports values.
- The creation of an ethical climate is the indispensable means, therefore, ethical behaviour is to be promoted in a modern corporation.

According to R.W. Austin, a sound code has the following principles:

- A member of the profession should have acceptable standard of excellence within a recognized body of knowledge.
- A code of conduct of the profession (not imposed) should be followed.
- Each member of the profession will place the interest of society before his personal interest.

According to Barry Posner and Warren Schmidt, the values and ethics of the executives are as follows:

- To make the organization effective
- Profit maximization and stockholders interest should not be the goals of the organization
- Attending to customers is very important
- Integrity and priority for the company's interest
- Maintaining organizational standards and revealing true picture of the organization
- Spouses are important in helping their mates grapple with ethical dilemmas
- Managers should seek others' advice in handling ethical dilemmas.

Corporate ethics implies the conduct of business operations in such a way that management always respects the rights of all parties concerned. The level of business morals remains unmeasured. Periodically, there are business scandals. All executives agree on the need of ethical conduct of business, and the top management has to take lead in following and implementing. The executives have to get feedback from their subordinates in informal meetings/get-togethers in order to correct themselves, which is in the practice of some organizations, like Indian Navy, Indian Army and Air Force. Arranging *Rampunch* and *Radakhana* would be useful to get such feedback.

The factors which help a lot in increasing ethical standards are: provide clear guidelines for ethical behaviour; teach ethical guidelines and their importance; set up controls that check on illegal or unethical deeds; conduct frequent and unpredictable audits; and punish trespassers in a meaningful way.

CORPORATE EXPERIENCES

Some corporate values of different companies are quite interesting. The values have been actualized in the companies. Some of them are:

- *Tata Steel:* Providing services at a reasonable price; increasing productivity; increasing quality of products; improving public utilities; creating good and healthy relationship; contributing to the well-being of the community; providing adequate welfare and recreational measures.
- *Infosys:* Creation of wealth through ethical and legal means; fairness and social concern.
- *Grindwell Norton:* Care, concern and respect of human beings; uncompromising ethical behaviour; freedom; sense of ownership; willingness to accept responsibility; continuous improvement and high achievement orientation.
- *Reliance Industries:* Honesty; integrity; respect; fairness; citizenship and caring.
- *Marico:* People; products and profits.
- *Indian Oil:* Integrity; interaction; value based training; team spirit; anger prevention at work; social welfare.
- *NTPCL:* Business ethics; customer focus; organizational pride; mutual respect and trust; innovation and speed; total quality for excellence.
- *Ford:* People; products; profits; and honesty; and integrity.
- *3M:* Innovation; integrity; individual growth; product quality, and reliability; problem solving.
- *IBM:* Dedication; innovation; trust; and personal responsibility.
- *Core values of Japanese companies:* Group orientation; diligence; aesthetics and performance customer and innovation; respect for people; competition silence; perception of time.

ROLE OF EXECUTIVES

Executives should avoid the following unethical practices: gifts, gratuities, bribes and call girls; price discrimination, unfair pricing; dishonest advertising; unfair competitive practices, cheating customers; unfair credit practices, over-selling; price collusion by competitors; dishonesty; unfairness to employees; other factors. Usually, the influencing factors to take unethical decisions are: superiors and top management; ethical climate in industry; behaviour of equals in the organization; lack of company policy for values; personal financial needs.

If business management is to be a profession, it must meet the basic requirements of the profession. One of these requirements is an internally developed code of conduct that can profess as the code by which the members of the profession will live. The code has to call on the executives to assume the duty of: placing the interests of his company before his private interests; placing the interest of society before his own and company's interest, and revealing the truth in all cases of involvement.

It is well known that managerial ethics are highly required to manage any organization successfully. Though the code of ethics is known to all the executives, sometimes they are in a dilemma to implement/follow the code. The twenty first century executives require strict adherence to the code, principles and also other practices, to have competitive advantage.

SUMMARY

1. Business ethics are desired norms of behaviour dealing with common transactions.
2. Ethics are highly essential for competitive advantage.
3. Several studies reveal ethical aspects at various places and companies.
4. There are different approaches to ethics.
5. Corporate experiences reveal various ethical aspects.
6. The role of executives is very significant in creating ethical culture.

REVIEW QUESTIONS

1. Define business ethics and values. Why values are essential?
2. Explain ethical dilemmas.
3. Discuss corporate experiences of values.
4. What is the role of executives in maintaining business values?

CASE STUDY

The Ethical Company

Bharat Gears Limited, a medium sized unit manufacturing gears for two-wheelers, is located at Palampur near Rajkot. Its headquarters is in Mumbai and has been a family-owned enterprise of the Maheshwaris. The company was making moderate profits, and there was job satisfaction amongst the employees. The recent Gallop Survey showed employee satisfaction levels at 67 per cent. The average tenure of employees was five years, which was a matter of surprise to other companies in Palampur. It was common for employees in that area to search for greener pastures, once they had a little experience. Bharat Gears Limited has won the Best Ethical Performance Award by the State government for the last three consecutive years.

Balaji was a very satisfied worker at Bharat Gears. He was the first employee to join his unit and has completed twelve years of his service. An efficient worker, he had also been felicitated with the 'Best Employee Award' twice. Balaji was nearing 50 and his experience and enthusiasm kept other supervisors on their toes. Due to his performance, he had become a cherished and valued employee for the management and his peers alike. Aditya, Human Resource Manager, often took some important decisions after consulting Balaji.

One day, Balaji was working on the Gear Cutting Machine. It was a new machine, imported from Pfaff, Germany. Balaji did not have complete knowledge of the machine's functions. While working, a small slip near the meshed wires found his legs trapped inside the machine. The next moment, all he knew was a terrible pain. He was in a pool of blood. His fellow workers rushed to get him out. To the dismay of all, both his legs had to be amputated. Balaji's physical disability made him discontinue the job. He surrendedered to his fate, and accepted that the mishap had happened due to his negligence. As per the rules in HR Handbook, within a week's time, the company gave him full compensation and paid towards all the medical expenditure. As a good gesture from the top management, he was allowed to stay in the staff quarters. Aditya Singh spoke to Balaji and assured him of a suitable job for his son Sameer, who was Balaji's only hope. Sameer was a young engineer working with Tanushree Cables at Vadodara. The company was humane in its attitude towards Balaji, one of its trusted and valued employees.

Paresh, one workshop engineer in Bharat Gears, was looking for a change to another company. This fact was known to Aditya. Paresh, being close to the HR manager, had intimated him of his success at the final interview at Container Corporation of India, a public sector undertaking, which, he hoped, would give him greater stability. Aditya had promised the job to Balaji based on this premise.

After a month, Sameer presented himself before Aditya. The HR manager welcomed him and made him go through the selection process of Bharat Gears. He was satisfied with Sameer as an able and prospective candidate, who could easily fit into Paresh's shoes. He asked Sameer to contact him in a couple of days.

Meanwhile, he called Paresh and enquired as to when he was joining Container Corporation. Paresh's reply made him heavy on heart. Paresh quoted of a last minute rejection at Container Corporation due to medical grounds (though not important for the job, but PSUs had to comply). Aditya was now in a dilemma. He did not know what to answer to Paresh. He discussed this problem with a friend over the coffee table and ruminated late at night. When Sameer reported to the HR office, Aditya apologized about his inability to induct Sameer at present. Though he did not disclose the details to Sameer, he could make out that Aditya was in a fix. He was surprised because Aditya was the one for whom his father had high regard and trust. Aditya promised Sameer to give him first preference in Bharat Gears whenever next vacancy arose. For the time being, he requested Sameer to continue at Vadodara.

Sameer replied that he had resigned from Tanushree Cables after Aditya's assurance. Not only the job at Bharat Gears suited his profile better, it also made possible for him to stay with his handicapped father.

He reminded Aditya of the commitment he had given to his father. Due to his commitment, Balaji had asked Sameer to quit his job and report at Bharat Gears. Aditya was in a big trouble. His efforts at securing a job for Sameer in adjacent factories at Palampur did not yield any results. He felt guilty for not keeping his word. Aditya needed a solution so that he could do some justice with the old lieutenant of Bharat Gears—a motivated, cherished and valued worker who had met with an accident. Not finding a job for his son Sameer, who had left a good job due to his assurance, pricked Aditya's conscience.

Questions for Discussion

1. What are the main issues in the above case?
2. What are the lessons that we can learn from the case?

FURTHER READING

Andrews, K.R., Ethics in Business, *Harvard Business Review*, September–October, 1989.

Chakraborthy, S.K., *Ethics in Management*, Oxford University Press, Bombay, 1995.

Drucker, Peter F., *The Frontiers of Management*, Heinemann Publishers, London, 1986.

Satya Raju, R., Fragrance of Values and Ethics at Work Place for Fruits in Twenty First Century, *IIRA World Congress*, Vol., given May 27–June 2, Tokyo, 2000.

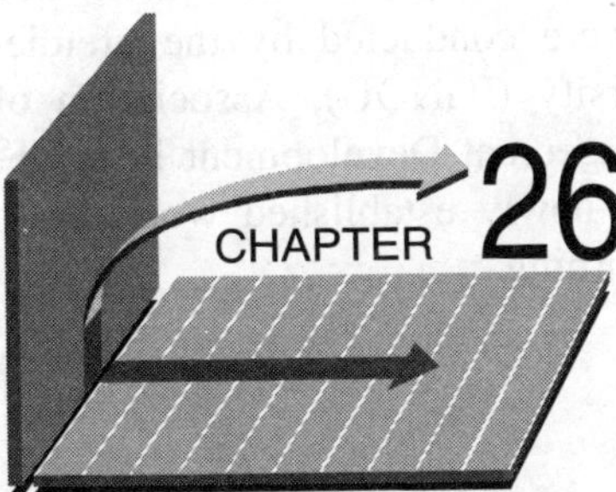

Case Method of Learning

CONTENTS

INTRODUCTION

The Case Method of Learning was first introduced in 1871 by Christopher Langdell in the Harvard Law School. When the Harvard Business School was opened in 1908, there were no cases on hand. The first dean of the school, Edwin F. Gay, had stated that they used to have oral presentations by business executives. Cases were first used in 1911–12 when A.W. Shaw started the course in business policy. A Case Book on Marketing was developed during 1919–20 for the first time, and later it gradually gained momentum. Since 1922, some books on the case method were recommended for several business schools.

The Asian Institute of Management, Manila, has also introduced the case method of teaching in its management programme. In India, the Indian Institute of Management, Ahmedabad adopted the case study method in the early 1960s in collaboration with Harvard Business School. Gradually, several management schools and other IIMs also implemented this method of teaching. In the 1980s and 1990s, several programmes were conducted by the premier management institutes, Indira Gandhi National Open University (IGNOU), Association of Indian Management Schools (AIMS), and Association of Management Development Institutes in South Asia (AMDISA), etc. Indian School of Business, a newly established world class institution, has also been focusing more on case method of learning.

THE CONCEPT OF THE CASE METHOD

Sharplin says that a case is a written description of an organization covering a certain period of time. A good case places students in a realistic situation where they can practise making decisions without the accountability for making mistakes which the real world imposes.

The case method is an approach to learning by doing. This method should expose the students to as many aspects of business activity as possible. The student's role is the collection and analysis of facts thus developing decision-making skills.

A case is a written description of an enterprise, usually containing information about numerous facets of the enterprise, its history, external environment and internal operations. The terms *case, case study, case history, case record, case problem, case report*, are used interchangeably. Maloun of the Harvard Business School of Management suggested some distinction between *case* and *case problem* in 1931. According to him, a *case* is used to denote a case where the decision is *stated,* while *case problem* is used to denote a case which *ends with a question* rather than a statement of the company's decision. In actual practice, all these concepts are used as synonymous terms.

The nature of several students and managers is to delay making decisions until they are satisfied with the quality and quantity of the information available. However, a good student and a good manager is one who makes the best decisions possible under the circumstances. Sometimes, one has to make certain decisions with assumptions before making decisions. A major benefit of using cases is derived from the process of evaluation, not necessarily from finding the one right answer (Henry Rath).

CASE REPORT AND CASE STUDY

The distinction between a case report and a case study is as follows (Jain, Sagar and others):

1. A case report is produced primarily for teaching and training purposes, not intended to generate new theories, principles or formulations. Instead, it is to serve any one or more of the following purposes:
   - To illustrate an abstract argument.
   - To help students develop a general insight into a real-life situation.
   - To develop operational skills and mental faculties.

A case study may be used as a teaching tool, but this is not its central purpose. The main purpose is to facilitate new insights into current knowledge and theory in the field.

2. Cases are either typical or problematic; often a case will have both characteristics. Events in the near past are preferred; a case may be fictitious although life cases are preferred. There is no emphasis on typical and problematic cases. Generally, the selection of a case is dictated by the intended purpose of the case study.
3. In a case report, the emphasis is on obtaining the "whole story". Useful guidelines for locating appropriate cases, for securing the cooperation of people concerned and for reporting have been developed. In a case study, the methodology is a crucial consideration. It is as good as its methodology of research.
4. In a case report, it is described to the end, and information is provided on the event, its background, its conclusion and the author's analysis and conclusion are not included. In a case study, it is described in full. The author's conclusions also are included.
5. In a case report, length is an important consideration. A very lengthy case is cumbersome and often unmanageable for class use. A case may run to 50 pages. In a case study, length is not an important consideration. The important thing is to get all the data, analysis and discussion.
6. In a case report, it is not important to identify the persons, places, organizations and products by their real names. In fact, fictitious names are preferred to real names for two reasons: (a) to protect all concerned from any harm which might be caused to them if their real identities were made known, and (b) to permit a more objective and dispassionate discussion of the case study. Names may be omitted only when it is justified on the grounds of research strategy of ethics.
7. In a case report, the identity of the author is not important, whereas in a case study, the author's identity is very important: the findings are often evaluated in the context of the author's standing.

CASE STUDY AND ROLE PLAY

The distinction between a case study and role play is as follows:

1. A case study presents a problem for discussion, whereas, role play places a problem in a life-like setting.
2. The problem in a case study is derived from previous events and the problem in role play involves ongoing processes.
3. The problem in a case study involves others. But the problem in role play involves the participants themselves.
4. A case study emphasizes the *facts,* but role play emphasizes the *feelings*.
5. A case study is an intellectual exercise, whereas role play is emotional involvement.
6. A case study defines action or solution and traits in the exercise of judgement, whereas, role play provides for execution of action or solution and traits in emotional control.

OBJECTIVES OF THE CASE METHOD

E.R. Schoen and P.A. Sprague stated the following four objectives of the case method:

- Helping students to acquire the skills of putting textbook knowledge about management into practice.
- Getting students out of the habit of being a receiver of facts, concepts and techniques into the habit of diagnosing problems, analyzing and evaluating alternatives and formulating workable plans of action.
- Training students to work out answers and solutions for themselves, as opposed to relying upon the authoritative crutch of a professor or a textbook.
- Providing students with exposure to a range of firms and managerial situations, thus offering them a basis for comparison when they begin their own management career.

Some other authors have stated the following objectives of the case method:

- To recognize the existence of a problem, identify the policy issues involved, and apply the appropriate policies in the analysis of the problem situation.
- To develop skills in situational analysis and decision making in simulated-to-life situations.
- To afford practice in the give and take of problem analysis, defend one's own views and pinpoint the weaknesses in other's analysis of the same problem.
- To learn to solve a problem in the minimum time with minimal outlay of energy and effort, even when the problem posseses new and vital elements that are totally unfamiliar.
- To develop skill in the transfer of training, this implies the upgrading of an ability to think one's way creatively through new situations, transferring knowledge and problem-solving techniques from prior situations to new situations.

CATEGORIES OF CASES

There are several thoughts on categorization of cases. The simplest method is by length and use. Some are long and some are short cases. Harvard cases are long and contain about 50 pages. Short cases are with limited objectives providing a focal point for a brief analysis of a specific problem. Cases can also be categorized as "individual problem", "isolated incident," "organizational problem", or a combination of these. Case problems might be either real or designed or even fictitious.

Another classification reveals that cases are of two types:

- Vignette case, involving two, three or more issues. More often there is only one issue and it contains minimum of facts, but still requires a decision to be made from the organizational point of view.
- Long cases which contain the full description of the organization and the functional areas of the management.

Advantages

Charles Gragg in his classic article—"Because wisdom can't be told" brings out the merits of the case method very well, as follows:

1. It distributes knowledge and facts.
2. It improves participants' skills in problem analysis, communication and decision making.
3. It affects attitude formation, and particularly brings home to the participants that nothing is absolutely "right" or "wrong" in the field of human behaviour.

Disadvantages

The case method of study has the following disadvantages:

1. A student may "sit through" a discussion and take no part at all, or at best, merely make some comments based upon what he has heard, rather than on a true study of the case.
2. It is time-consuming and requires several hours of private work.
3. It is a dangerous belief that answers to case problems can be applied directly to the problems of the students in their employment
4. A case cannot hope to impart the knowledge of a company's background and the real situation.
5. Sometimes, the case method of teaching may give exposure to a critical approach by ignoring a positive attitude.
6. The faculty cannot hope to cover all the material in the course by using case studies alone.
7. The case leader needs more *skill* than *knowledge*.
8. Often, information is irrelevant, ambiguous and contradictory, and cases have no unique answer.
9. The instructor does not solve the problem, and the teaching is ineffective in several cases.

THE PROCESS OF CASE PREPARATION

The following process of case preparation is usually followed by the students of business schools:

- Read the case.
- Read the case again.
- Prepare a list of major opportunities and problems.
- Analyze the alternatives in terms of opportunities and problems.
- Understand how the organization can implement the suggested strategy.
- Re-evaluate the proposal in terms of the qualitative criteria.
- Prepare notes for an oral presentation and also for a final written report.

ACTION SKILLS REINFORCED BY CASES

- Think clearly in complex, ambiguous situations.
- Devise reasonable, consistent, creative action plans.
- Apply quantitative tools.
- Recognize the significance of information.
- Determine vital missing information.
- Communicate orally in groups.
- Write clear, forceful, convincing reports.
- Guide students' career.
- Apply personal values to organizational decisions.

GUIDELINES FOR PREPARING A CASE

- The students should know the facts.
- The students should consider the organizational mission.
- The case analysis should be developed around some accepted model or models.
- Case analysis should be built up around certain strategic issues of questions which are important to the organization.

Some authors suggested the following methods:

- First of all, understand the threats and opportunities of the organization through environmental audit.
- Next, analyze the strengths and weaknesses through organizational audit.
- Then identify the strategic issues and the problem.
- Describe the past and present strategies and also the internal and external environment.
- Evaluate the past and present strategies and also the strategic alternatives and choices.
- Last, explain how your strategies improve organizational mission accomplishment, evaluation and implementation of the strategies.

ANALYTICAL TOOLS

There are several tools which have been stated to be effective in strategic decision making. Some important tools are:

- SWOT analysis
- Financial ratio analysis
- Quantitative risk analysis
- Breakeven analysis
- NPV method.

Usually, the first two are used in several situations.

THE ROLE OF A CASE LEADER/TEACHER

The teacher needs an open mind and tolerance; he should have the depth of knowledge. She/ he should have a picture of what managers do every day with an understanding of the management profession.

The teacher has to create a classroom environment. If he refrains from the pedagogical sins (sarcasm, personal cross-examination, discourtesy, self-approval, self-consciousness and talkativeness), he can hope for the best without worrying about the technique whereby it can be achieved as expanded by Kenneth R. Andrews. The following role is to be played by the case leader/teacher:

- Guide
- Moderator
- Tension reliever
- Inquisitor
- Role player
- Prompter
- Clarifier
- Answer-giver
- Pattern discerner
- Summarizer
- Integrator
- Full participator with the students.

The teacher has to prepare teaching notes. The case writer's note may be used as an aid. The following items are usually used as guidelines:

- The course for which the note is prepared; the purpose of the course and positioning of the case
- The objectives of the case
- Student preparation
- Teaching strategies to be used
- Analysis of the major issues
- Past experience
- Possible assignments to the students.

CASE WRITING

Case teaching and case writing are two different functions of a case teaching faculty. Some can be experts on case teaching but do not write cases. Those who write cases can teach the cases very effectively. The case writer has to follow certain norms for writing cases for the benefit of management students. The phases for writing the cases are: selection of some incident, collecting data, preparing structure, releasing and presentation.

The case starts with a case lead. It is an indication that something is important form the case writer view point. A topic which can be discussed from different perspectives is required from learners' point of view.

Data collection might be based on some factual data from the various sources or observations. Sometimes, interviews will be arranged with the person concerned. A detailed analysis of the case is to be structured. The narration of the case should be preferably in the past tense. The case should disguise certain issues and obtain permission to release. Then, the case is to be presented for discussion in the class.

Do's and Don'ts for Case Writing

Do's

- Right reasons for writing the case
- Teaching value
- Organizing material and preparing outline of the case
- Scheduling time
- Writing in a simple language
- Gap between drafting and editing stages
- Writing in appropriate style.

Don'ts

- Injecting values of teacher
- Praising the case teacher
- Providing solutions.

Guidelines for Case Writing

- Developing thinking
- Dividing the case into paragraphs
- Use the past tense and the active voice
- Simplicity
- Revise/rewrite
- Proper documentation
- Using simple words
- Using effective language
- Making positive checks for accuracy
- Based on facts or fiction.

CASE ANALYSIS AND PREPARATION

According to Fred R. David, the following are the guidelines for case analysis and preparations.

- View your case analysis and presentation as a product that must have some competitive factor to differentiate it favourably from the case analysis of other students.

- Prepare your case analysis in advance of the due date to allow time for reflection.
- Develop a mindset or 'why', continually questioning assumptions and assertions (your own as well as others).
- The best ideas are lost if not communicated to the reader, so as ideas develop, think of their most appropriate presentation.
- Maintain a positive attitude about the class, working with problems rather than against them.
- Keep in tune with your professor and understand his or her values and expectations.
- Since business policy is a capstone course, seek the help of professors in other specialty areas as needed.
- Other students will have strengths in functional areas that will complement your weaknesses, so develop a cooperative spirit that moderates competitiveness in group work.
- Read your case frequently as work progresses, so do not overlook details.
- When preparing a case analysis as a group, divide into separate teams to work on the external analysis and internal analysis. Each team should write its section as if it were to go into the paper; then give each group member a copy.
- At the end of each group session, assign each member of the group a task to be completed for the next meeting.
- Have a good sense of humour.
- Capitalize on the strengths of each member of the group; volunteer your services in your areas of strength.
- Set goals for yourself and your team; budget your time to attain them.
- Become friends with the library.
- Foster attitudes that encourage group participation and interaction. Do not be too hasty to judge group members.
- Be creative and innovative throughout the case analysis process.
- Be prepared to work. There will be times when you will have to do more than your 'share'. Accept it, and do what you have to do to move the team forward.
- Think of your case analysis as if it were really happening; do not reduce case analysis to a mechanical process.
- To uncover flaws in your analysis and to prepare the group for questions during an oral presentation, assign one person in the group to actively play the 'devil's advocate'.
- Do not schedule excessively long group meetings; two-hour sessions are about right.
- A goal of case analysis is to improve your ability to think clearly in ambiguous and confusing situations, do not get frustrated that there is no 'single best answer'.
- Push your ideas hard enough to get them listened, listen to others and try to follow lines of thinking; follow the flow of group discussion, recognizing when you need to get back on track; do not repeat yourself or others unless clarity or progress demands repetition.
- Do not confuse symptoms with causes; do not develop conclusions and solutions prematurely; recognize that information may be misleading, conflicting or wrong.

- Work hard to develop the ability to formulate reasonable, consistent, and creative plans; put yourself in the strategist's position.
- Develop confidence in using quantitative tools for analysis, they are not inherently difficult; it is just practice and familiarity you need.
- Develop a case-writing style that is direct, assertive and convincing; be concise, precise, fluent and correct.
- Have fun when at all possible. It is frustrating at times, but enjoy it while you can; it may be several years before you are playing CEO again.
- Acquire a professional typist and proofreader. Do not perform either task alone.
- Strive for excellence in writing and technical preparation of your case. Prepare nice charts, tables, diagrams and graphs. Use colour and unique pictures. No messy exhibits!
- In group cases, do not allow personality differences to interfere. When they occur, they must be understood for what they are and put aside.
- Do not forget that the objective is to learn; explore areas with which you are not familiar.
- Pay attention to detail.
- Think through alternative implications fully and realistically. The consequences of decisions are not always apparent. They often affect many different aspects of a firm's operations.
- Get things written down (drafts) as soon as possible.
- Read everything that other group members write and comment on them in writing. This allows group input into all aspects of case preparation.
- Provide answers to such fundamental questions as what, when, where, why and how.
- Adaptation and flexibility are keys to success; be creative and innovative.
- Do not merely recite ratios or present figures. Rather, develop ideas and conclusions concerning the possible trends. Show the importance of these figures to the corporation.
- Support reasoning and judgment with factual data whenever possible.
- Neatness is a real plus; your case analysis should look professional.
- Your analysis should be detailed and specific as far as possible.
- A picture speaks a thousand words, and a creative picture gets you an "A" in many classes.
- Let someone else read and critique your paper several days before finalization.
- Emphasize the 'strategy selection' and 'strategy implementation' sections. A common mistake is to spend too much time on the external and internal analysis parts of your paper. Always remember that the 'meat' of the paper or presentations, the strategy selection and implementation sections.
- Make special efforts to get to know your group members. This leads to more openness in the group and allows for more interchange of ideas. Put in the time and effort necessary to develop these relationships.
- Be constructively critical of your group members work. Do not dominate group discussions. Be a good listener and contributor.
- Learn from past mistakes and deficiencies. Improve upon weak aspects of other case presentations.

- Learn from the positive approaches and accomplishments of other classmates.
- Be considerate, dependable, reliable and trustworthy.

EVALUATION OF A CASE

Whether a case is good or not is evaluated as per the following questions:

- Is the case born out of a real situation?
- Does the case describe a typical situation?
- Is the practice and theory nexus clear?
- Is the case focused on decision making?
- Does the case lend itself to the purpose?
- Does the decision making require not only analysis but also judgement?
- Does the case stand by itself?
- Is the length of the case right enough for the intended learning?

Evaluation

Cases can be written for different purposes. The evaluation of a case depends largely on the purpose for which it was intended. Cases are not always prepared exclusively for a single purpose. In evaluating cases, the following classification of purposes is helpful:

- A case may be the report of a researcher's observations of reality as part of the process of collecting data to construct and/or test a hypothesis, to fulfill a thesis or to design a course.
- It may be a story about an incident or how a manager, businessman or entrepreneur handled a situation. It is used as a teaching note.
- A case describing a situation in which certain techniques are supposed to be useful may be used for the specific purpose of making the student practice and get exercise in performing the techniques.
- A case may be used as a substitute for reality so learners can practice, exercise and develop their skills.
- Having made the distinction among the four purposes, it is important to recognize interrelationships among them. Sometimes a research case may be used as a teaching-learning case, with or without modifications.
- At times, when the case collection process does not unearth the kind of problem a professor is seeking, he may be tempted to write a case which is the composite of several different real situations. This is called an armchair note.

The effectiveness of the management programme of a school/institute depends upon the effective implementation of the case study method of learning. It has already been accepted that the case study method is well accepted by students of management and also the faculty, all over the world. Therefore, management colleges/institutes should concentrate more on writing and teaching cases on different areas of management, focusing on regional, national and international problems. Training programmes in Indian organizations should cover the case method of learning for right and effective decision making by executives and officials.

SUMMARY

1. The case method of learning was first used in the nineteenth century in Harvard Law School.
2. The case method is an approach to learning by doing.
3. Several premier management schools gradually introduced the case method of learning.
4. There is a clear distinction between a case report and a case study and a case study and role play.
5. The main objective of this method is to help the student in acquiring practical knowledge to solve problems and also to take the right decisions.
6. The student has to prepare well in discussing a case by following the guidelines.
7. The case leader also has a role to play in case discussion as a guide or moderator or clarifier.
8. The evaluation of a case depends upon the purpose for which it was intended.

REVIEW QUESTIONS

1. What is a case? Distinguish between
   (a) a case report and case study,
   (b) a case study and role play.
2. What are the categories of cases?
3. Discuss the advantages and disadvantages of the case method of learning.
4. Explain the role of a student in case preparation.
5. Discuss the role of a case leader/teacher.
6. How does one evaluate a good case?

FURTHER READING

Broom, H.N., *Business Policy and Strategic Action*, Prentice Hall, Inc., Englewood Cliffs, New Jersey, 1969.

Cullition, J.W., *Handbook on Case Writing*, Asian Institute of Management, Philippines, 1973.

Gragg, C., "Because Wisdom can't be Told", *Harvard Alumni Bulletin*, October 19, 1940.

Harvard Business Review, HBR Case Method Series 1–3, Boston, Harvard Business School, 1960–65.

Jauch, L.R. and Glueck, W.F., *Business Policy and Strategic Management*, McGraw-Hill, New York, 1988.

McNair, M.P., *The Case Method at HBS*, McGraw-Hill, New York, 1954.

Sharplin, A., Strategic *Management*, McGraw-Hill, New York, 1985.

Glossary

Accountability: It is the obligation to carry out responsibility and exercise authority in terms of performance standards established.

Action research: The method through which organizational development and change agents learn what improvements are needed and how the organization can best be aided in making improvement.

Affiliate: A company owned or controlled by another corporation through ownership of 10 per cent or more of outstanding voting stock.

Auditing: The process of verifying the validity of an organization's financial statements and records by outsiders or by members of the organization.

Balance sheet: A statement showing a company's assets, liabilities and net worth at a given time.

BCG matrix: A corporate portfolio management approach that examines the rate of market growth and market share of each of a corporation's business units to help top management develop a balance between those business units that absorb cash and those that provide it.

Behaviour modification: An approach to motivation based on the law of effect that behaviour which leads to rewarding consequences tends to be repeated, and behaviour with negative consequences tends not to be repeated.

Benchmarking: Comparing a company's practices and processes with the world's best standards for the purpose of closing the gap with them.

Board of Directors (BOD): An apex body for decision making; the members of the board exercise their authority and responsibility collectively.

Boston Consulting Group (BCG): A two-by-two product portfolio analysis using market growth rate with relative market share. (It defines its segments as dogs, cats, stars and question marks. These different businesses are categorized in terms of cash flow.)

Break-even analysis: A mathematical procedure for studying the relationships between cost, sales volume and profit.

Budgets: Formal quantitative statement of the resources allocated to specific programmes or projects for a given period.

Bureaucratic control: A method of control that employs strict rules and regulations to help ensure desired behaviour by organizational units often used by multinational enterprises to control subsidiaries.

Business unit strategy: The level of strategy that concerns a portion of a company which is large and distinct enough to be considered a separate business.

Capacity planning: The determination of the amount of products of services that an operations system should be capable of producing.

Case method: It is a method of training through which case studies provide learning experiences that help the learner to develop habits and skills of analysis, reasoning, imagination and judgement.

Centralization: It is concentration of authority at certain central points within an organization.

Chain of command: The hierarchy of authority, encompassing all organization members, which extends from the top to the bottom of the organization.

Challenge of change: The strategy implementation process involves a change, either minor or major, if it affects a large number of people cutting into deeper issues like beliefs, values, etc., it is a major change.

Change agent: The individual leading or guiding the process of a change in an organizational situation.

Channel: The medium of communication between a sender and a receiver.

Chaos management style: When both the Board of Directors and top management have little or no involvement in the decision-making process of the company, their style is described as the *chaos management style*.

Charismatic leaders: Those leaders, who, through their personal vision and energy, inspire followers and have a major impact on their organization; also called *transformational leaders*.

Client system: The individual group or organization which is the target of a planned change.

Closed system: A system that does not interact with its environment.

Coercive power: The negative side of reward power, based on the influencer's ability to punish and seek conformance from subordinates.

Collaborative bargaining: The process of negotiating and administering agreements between labour and management concerning wages, working conditions and other aspects of the work environment.

Command group: A group composed of a manager and his or her subordinates, who interact with each other towards a common objective.

Commission Groups: Groups whose members are usually appointed by government officials, charged with administrative, regulatory, or legislative tasks.

Committee: A formal organizational group, usually relatively long-lived, created to carry out specific organizational tasks.

Communication network: A set of channels within an organization or group through which communication travels.

Competition: The situation in which two or more parties strive towards mutually incompatible goals and cannot interfere with each other.

Competitive advantage (or edge): The position achieved by a business enterprise over its competitors by intensifying functional differentiation of its products, exploiting competitors' weaknesses, taking aggressive initiatives through search for improvements/innovations and by superior competitive performance.

Computer-Aided Design (CAD): The process of designing products interactively with computers.

Computer-Based Information System (CBIS): A formal system for providing various levels of management with information through the use of computers.

Conceptual skill: The mental ability to guide and coordinate an organization's activities by understanding the organization as a whole, as well as an understanding of the interdependence of its parts.

Contingency approach: The view that the management techniques that best contribute to the attainment of organizational goals might vary in different types of situations or circumstances.

Continuous improvement: Constant, ceaseless attempts to fulfil the customer's expectations.

Continuous-process production: A production technology that yields long flows of homogeneous materials, such as oil refining.

Continuous reinforcement: A reinforcement schedule in behaviour modification, in which individuals are immediately rewarded/punished for their good/bad behaviour.

Controllable variable: A part of a problem situation that can be manipulated to achieve a solution.

Controlling: The process of monitoring actual organizational activities to see that they conform to planned activities, and correcting flaws or deviations.

Cooperation: The process of working together to attain mutual objectives.

Coordination: The integration of the activities of the separate parts of an organization to accomplish organizational goals.

Corporate social responsibility: The concept that corporations have an obligation to act for the good of society.

Corporate values: Beliefs held by managers of an organization concerning what is desirable or good. The broad objectives pursued by a business enterprise and the priority attached to these objectives give some idea about its corporate values.

Critical Path Method (CPM): A network analysis technique used to schedule and control work on projects for which the time required to complete the task is specified/limited.

Cultural control: A method of control that emphasizes implicit and informal leading based on a broad company culture, associated with many large Japanese companies.

Data: Raw, unanalyzed facts, figures and events.

Decentralization: The delegation of power and authority from higher to lower levels of an organization, often accomplished by the creation of small, self-contained organizational units.

Decision making: The process of identifying and selecting a course of action to solve specific problems.

Decision Support System (DSS): An easily accessible microcomputer-based information system that aids individual managers in planning and decision making.

Decoding: The interpretation and translation of a message into meaningful information.

Delegation: It is the entrustment of responsibility and authority to a subordinate and the creation of accountability for the successful accomplishment of the task.

Delphi method: A survey of expert opinion that includes each expert's review of the other's ideas; the expert's identity is not disclosed to the others in order to ensure that the decision is not through consensus.

Departmentalization: The grouping into departments of work activities that are similar and logically connected.

Diversification: This results when a firm adds new products or enters into new markets which may be related or unrelated to the existing business.

Divestment strategy: *Divestment* implies stripping or getting rid of loss-making operations or units.

Division of work: The breakdown of a complex task into components so that individuals are responsible for a limited set of activities, instead of the task as a whole.

Dysfunctional conflict: Any conflict that results in decreased efficiency and greater factionalism within an organization.

Effectiveness: The ability to determine appropriate objectives doing the right things.

Efficiency: The ability to minimize the use of resources in achieving organizational objectives; in common parlance, *smart work.*

Electronic Data Processing (EDP): Storage and analysis of data using computers.

Electronic mail (E-mail): Data and text circulated through interlinked computers.

Empowerment: Giving people the power to solve problems and ensure quality.

Encoding: The translation of information into a series of symbols for communication.

Entrepreneur: The originator of a new business venture; a person who starts a business activity and ventures to take risk.

Environmental factors: These are both global and national factors which influence business the important factors being economic, technological, socio-cultural, political, legal, and international.

Equity theory: A theory of job motivation emphasizing the role played by an individual's belief in the equity or fairness of rewards and punishment in determining his or her performance and satisfaction.

Expectancy approach: A method of motivation specifying that effort to achieve high performance is a function of the perceived likelihood that high performance can be achieved and will be rewarded if achieved, and that the reward will be worth the effort expended.

Expert power: Power based on the belief or understanding that the influencer has specific knowledge or relevant expertise which the influencer does not have.

Expert System (ES): An advanced computer program that emulates the problem-solving abilities of human experts through the use of artificial intelligence.

Export Processing Zone (EPZ): A physically fenced-in industrial estate developed by host country governments to facilitate manufacture by foreign as well as domestic investors, primarily for exports.

External audit: The check of a firm's financial statements and records for validity, accuracy and completeness by accounting personnel from outside the organization.

External environment: The environment outside the organization (government, political, social, economic, cultural factors, etc.).

Fail-safe: Technical or procedural solutions incorporated within the product's design to minimize error.

Fear of failure: The fear of not reaching organizational/personal goals and of potential public embarrassment if such failures are recognized.

Fear of success: Fear of the burden and stress that may accompany success and the envy and dislike it generates in others.

Financial budget: Budgets that detail how the organization intends to spend money during the financial year, and where that money will come from.

First-line managers: Managers who are responsible for the work of operating employees only, and who do not supervise *other* managers. They are the first or the lowest level of managers in an organizational hierarchy.

Fishbone diagram: A method designed by quality guru Kaoru Ishikawa to trace the causes and effects of problems.

Forecasting: The attempt, using specific techniques, to predict outcomes and project future trends.

Foreign Direct Investment (FDI): The primary measure of cross-border investment of TNCs. FDI involves giving managerial controlling power to the foreign investor.

Formal authority: Power rooted in the general understanding that specific individuals or groups have the right to exert influence within certain limits by virtue of their position within an organization.

Franchise: A business arrangement in which a person gets the right to manufacture, market or distribute the products or services of a company and use the company's name to do business.

Functional conflict: Any conflict that has positive, constructive and non-divisive results.

Functional layout: The organizing of physical production arrangements to foster a specific purpose such as storage or sales.

Functional-level strategy: The level of strategy that establishes a framework for the management of organizational functions, such as marketing or production, so that they conform to the business unit-level strategy.

Functional organization: A form of departmentalization in which employees are divided according to the functions they perform: production, marketing, finance, etc.

Game theory: A method of analyzing and predicting the rational behaviour of people in competitive and conflict situations.

General Manager: The individual responsible for all activities such as production, marketing and finance, for an organization.

Geocentric: The attitude that accepts both similarities and differences among countries and takes a balanced view towards the management of operations in every nation.

Global village: In a liberalized economy, the boundaries between cultures and nations are blurred and people think of the world as a "global village".

Goal: The basic purpose for which an organization has been brought into existence.

Grapevine: The various paths through which informal communication is passed through an organization, including the single-strand "gossip", "probability" and "cluster" chains.

Group cohesiveness: The degree of solidarity and positive feeling held by individuals towards their group.

Group Decision Support System (GDSS): The use of a computerized information system in a group meeting to make more efficient use of information for group decisions.

Hawthorne effect: The possibility that workers who receive special attention will perform better simply because they receive that attention; one interpretation of Elton Mayo and his colleagues' studies.

Holding company: A company having control over one or more firms through ownership of the latter's stocks.

Human resource audit: The analysis and appraisal of an organization's current human resources.

Human Resources Information System (HRIS): A system, frequently computerized, for collecting, storing, maintaining, retrieving, and validating data concerning an organization's personnel.

Human resources planning: Planning for the future personnel needs of an organization, taking into account both internal activities and factors in the external environment.

Human skill: The ability to work with, communicate with, and motivate individuals to work in groups.

Inspection: A system of comparing products and services with specified requirements to ensure conformity.

Induction and orientation: Activities intended to ease an individual's entrance into an organization through introducing the individual to the organization and providing information on it.

Influence: Any action or example of behaviour that causes a change in the attitude or behaviour of another person or group.

Informal communication: The grapevine or any communication within an organization that is not officially sanctioned.

Informal groups: Unofficial groups created by members of an organization without the express encouragement of managers.

Informal organization: The undocumented and officially unrecognized relationship between members of an organization, which inevitably emerge out of the personal and group needs of employees.

Information ownership: The possession by certain individuals of unique information and knowledge concerning their work.

Inputs: Resources from the environment that enter any system, such as an organization.

Installation: The part of a management science effort in which a mathematical model is developed and used with actual data.

Integration: The degree to which employees of various departments work together in a unified way.

Internal audit: The monitoring within an organization of the validity, accuracy and completeness of its financial statement and records.

Internalization: The third dimension of a management science effort in which the concepts and methodology of management science become part of the thinking of managers, allowing them to recognize appropriate times to use these techniques.

Job enlargement: The combining of various operations at a similar level into one job to provide more variety for workers, and thus increase motivation and satisfaction.

Job enrichment: The combining of several activities from a vertical cross-section of the organization into one job to provide the worker with more authority and responsibility.

Job-shop production: The production of small batches of custom-made products.

Job specialization: The division of work into standardized, simplified tasks.

Just-In-Time (JIT): A production system that eliminates inactive production inventory through delivery to the production line of parts and suppliers exactly when they are needed.

Kaizen: A Japanese term implying continuous improvement, involving every employee in every company function at all levels of an organization.

Large batch/mass production: The production of large quantities of similar items, often on an assembly line.

Lateral communication: Communication between departments of an organization that generally follows the work flow, thus providing a direct channel for coordination and problem solving.

Leader-member relations: The quality of interaction between a leader and his or her subordinate; according to Fred Fielder, it is the most important influence on the manager's power.

Leadership: The process of directing and inspiring workers to perform the task-related activities of the group.

Leadership functions: The group maintenance and task-related activities that must be performed by the leader, or someone else, for a group to perform effectively.

Leadership styles: The various patterns of behaviour favoured by leaders during the process of directing and influencing workers.

Leading: The process of directing and influencing task-related activities of organization members.

Linear Programming (LP) model: A mathematical model used to determine the optimum allocation of limited resources to attain a goal.

Local Area Network (LAN): An intra-organizational, user-oriented computer network that allows users to communicate with each other and to share facilities for data storage.

Management: The process of planning, organizing, staffing, directing and controlling the work of organization members and of using all available organizational resources to reach stated organizational goals.

Management audit: A systematic, comprehensive examination of the quality of management in an organization in order to bring about improvement.

Management by crisis: A management style which focuses on problems as they arise.

Management by Objectives (MBO): A formal set of procedures that establishes and reviews progress towards common goals for managers and subordinates.

Management game or Business game: An educational or training activity in which a trainee is required to take decisions as if in real-life management problem and is then presented with the results of each decision.

Management Information System (MIS): A formal, usually computerized, structure for providing management with complete and up-to-date information.

Management performance: The measure of how efficient and effective a manager is, or how well he or she determines and achieves appropriate objectives.

Management Science (MS): Mathematical techniques for modelling, analysis and solution of management problems.

Managers: Individuals who plan, organize, lead and control other individuals in the process of pursuing organizational goals.

Market niche strategy: A marketing strategy which aims to focus on small gaps or niches in the market, and then introduces suitable products at competitive prices to capture those small markets.

Matrix organization: An organizational structure which is a combination of the functional and product types of organizations.

Mentors: Individuals who pass on the benefits of their knowledge to other individuals who are usually younger and less experienced.

Message: The encoded information sent by a sender to a receiver.

Middle managers: Managers in the mid-range of the organizational hierarchy, who are responsible for other managers and sometimes for some operating employees.

Mission: The unique reason for an organization's existence that makes it different from all others.

Mission statement: Formal description of what a quality improvement project intends to accomplish.

Motivation: Is the technique adopted by managers to create willingness on the part of subordinates to give their best to the organization.

Network analysis: A technique used for scheduling complex projects that contain interrelationships between activities or events.

Networking: The linking of groups of computers, either intraorganizationally or interorganizationally, so that they can communicate with each other and share common data bases and resources.

Niche strategy: In marketing management, *niche* means focusing around a product or a market; it is a strategy involving a very low degree of risk and represents the typical behaviour of small companies.

Noise: Anything that confuses, disturbs, diminishes or interferes with smooth communication.

Objectives: The targeted goals of an organization towards which resources and efforts are channelled.

One-way communication: Any communication from the sender without feedback from the receiver.

Open system: A system that interacts with its environment.

Operational plans: Plans that detail the implementation of strategic plans.

Operations: The production activities of an organization.

Operations management: The planning, organizing, directing and controlling of an organization's production/operations system.

Operations system: The organizational system or subsystem whose function is to transform inputs into desired outputs.

Organizational conflicts: Disagreement between individuals or groups within the organization stemming from the needs to share scarce resources or engaged in interdependent work activities, or from differing statuses, goals, or cultures.

Organizational culture: The set of important understandings, such as norms, values, attitudes, and beliefs, shared by organizational members.

Organizational design: The determination of the organizational structure that is most appropriate for the strategy, people, technology, and task of the organization.

Organizational Development (OD): At the heart of organizational development is the concern for the vitalizing, energizing, actualizing, activating and renewing of organizations through technical and human resources.

Organizational goals: The purpose, mission and objectives that are the reason for an organization's existence and that form the basis of its strategy.

Organizational life cycle: The pattern of developmental changes that typically occurs in an organization.

Organization and Method (O&M): The body of knowledge concerned with the examination of the method of an organization covering any or all aspects of organization from classical procedures to management structure. O&M is often an application of methods of study and sometimes work measurement techniques to office procedures.

Organizing: The process of arranging an organization's structure and coordinating its managerial practices and use of resources to achieve its goals.

Outputs: Transformed inputs that are returned to the external environment as products or services.

Out of control: Situation during which the critical parameters of a process exceed pre-defined limits.

Overload: The condition of being unable to meet all the various performance expectations held by oneself and others.

Pareto analysis: A technique used to identify the most important cause of a problem using the Pareto principle.

Partial reinforcement: In behaviour modification, a schedule of reinforcement in which rewards are given intermittently.

PDCA cycle: A four-step process of Plan-Do-Check-Act, devised by Japanese firms on Ed Deming's principles.

Performance appraisal: The process of evaluating an individual's performance by comparing it to existing standards or objectives.

Planning: The process of establishing objectives and suitable courses of action before taking action.

Poka-yoke: Shigeo Shingo's principle of eliminating errors by eliminating the possibility of making mistakes.

Policy: A standing plan which is a guideline to decision making, where a manager has certain discretion or it is solutions to recurring problems.

Polycentric: The attitude that all countries are different and difficult to understand; therefore, foreign offices must be relied upon to know what works best in their own countries.

Positive reinforcement: In behaviour modification, any consequence that results in the repetition of a given behaviour.

Post-action control: A control method that uses the results of a completed action to guide changes in future activities.

Power: The ability to exert influence; that is, the ability to change the attitudes or behaviour of individuals or groups.

Pre-action controls: A control method that budgets for all necessary material, financial, and human resources before an action is begun.

Production: The transformation of organizational resources into finished goods and services.

Productivity: A measure of the performance of a worker or an operations system relative to resources utilization; or output divided by input.

Program Evaluation and Review Technique (PERT): A network analysis technique, using estimates of time required to complete tasks, which is used to schedule and control projects for which task completion times cannot be predicted fairly precisely.

Programme: A single use that covers a relatively large set of organizational activities and specifies major steps, their order and timing, and the unit responsible for each step.

Programmed decisions: Solutions to routine problems determined by rule, procedure, or habit.

Purpose: The primary role of an organization in society or the aim of producing a good or service.

Qualitative forecasting: A judgement-based forecasting technique used when hard data are scarce or difficult to use.

Quality assurance: Activity that confirms whether or not a product or service meets the specifications promised by the supplier or expected by the customer.

Quality circle: Periodic meeting of labour and management personnel to solve quality control and productivity problems.

Quality control: The process of ensuring that goods and services meet predetermined standards.

Quantitative overloading: The situation that occurs when an individual is given more tasks than he or she can accomplish at a given time.

Ratio analysis: The process of stating key figures from an organization's financial statement as fractions or percentages of one another, to assist in the assessment of its financial performance or condition.

Realistic Job Preview (RJP): A description provided by an organization's financial statement as fractions or percentage of one another, to assist in the assessment of its financial performance or condition.

Reality shock syndrome: An individual's reaction to the difference between high job expectations and the frustrating day-to-day realities of the workplace.

Recruitment: The development of a pool of candidates in accordance with a human resources plan for applying a job.

Refreezing: Transforming a new behaviour pattern into a norm through reinforcement and supporting mechanisms.

Responsibility centre: Any organizational unit that is headed by a manager responsible for the unit's activities; major types include revenue, expense, profit and investment centres.

Reward system: A system of performance motivation through wage increases, bonuses, promotions, and so on.

Risk: 1. Probability of loss or failure in a business venture or related to a particular decision or course of action.

2. Hazard (e.g. fire, accident, etc.) covered by a contract of insurance.

Risk management: Function associated with reducing the risk or loss to a firm, particularly loss due to fire, accidents, etc.

Role conflict: A situation in which an individual is confronted by two or more incompatible demands.

Role perception: The individual's understanding of the behaviour needed to accomplish a task or perform a job.

Satisfiers: Positive motivating factors in the work environment, including achievement, responsibility, recognition, and advancement.

Scalar principle: The concept that a clear line of authority through an organization must exist if delegation is to work successfully.

Scenario construction: The building of a logical, hypothetical description of sequences of events so as to examine the dynamics of alternative sets of conditions.

Scientific management: A management approach, formulated by Frederick Taylor and others between 1890 and 1930, that sought to scientifically determine the best method for performing any task and for selecting, training and motivating workers.

Sensitivity training: An early personal growth technique at one time fairly widespread in organizational development efforts, that emphasizes increased sensitivity in interpersonal relationships.

Seven 'S': Strategy, structure, system, staff, style, skills and superordinate goals of an organization.

Simulation models: Models (usually computerized) of situations that are too complex for standard mathematical equations to describe effectively.

Situational leadership theory: An approach to leadership developed by Paul Hersey and Kenneth H. Blanchard that described how the leaders should adjust their leadership style in response to their subordinate, expressing desire for achievement, experience, ability and willingness to accept responsibility.

Span of management: The number of subordinates who can be effectively managed by a supervisor or manager.

Staff: The individuals or groups who provide line managers with advice and services.

Staffing: The process of recruiting, placing, training, and developing personnel.

Stakeholders: Those groups or individuals who are directly or indirectly affected by an organization's pursuit of its goal.

Standing committees: Permanent committees that exist to respond to a continuing organizational need.

Statistical Process Control (SPC): Use of statistical methods to analyze a production process to prevent undesirable variations.

Statistical quality control: Use of statistical techniques to ensure that the product conforms to specifications.

Steering controls: Controls designed to detect any deviation from a predetermined standard, and to allow corrections to be made prior to the completion of a specific sequence of actions. Also known as feed forward controls.

Stockholders: Owners of corporate stocks, also called shareholders.

Strategic business unit (SBU): A term developed by General Electric Co., USA to identify distinctive business or product divisions, each responsible for growth and profitability, and each of which may be planned independent of the other businesses.

Strategic control: The process of checking strategy implementation progress against the strategic plan at periodic or critical intervals to determine if the corporation is moving towards its strategic objectives.

Strategic decisions: These decisions encompass the definition of the business, products and markets to be served, functions to be performed and major policies needed for an organization to execute these decisions to achieve objectives.

Strategic management: It is a stream of decisions and actions which leads to the development of an effective strategy or strategies to help achieve corporate objectives.

Strategic planning: The active formulation by top management of an organization's objectives, and definition of the strategies for achieving them.

Strategic plans: Comprehensive plans designed to define and achieve the long-term objectives of the organization.

Strategy: The broad programme for defining and achieving an organization's response to its environment over time.

Stress: The tension and pressure that result when an individual views a situation. It is the wear and tear caused by life.

Structure: The arrangement and interrelationship of the components of an organization—or it is the "Manner in which a building or organization or other complete whole is constructed..." (Oxford dictionary)

Subsystems: Those parts comprising the whole system.

Superordinate goals: Higher-level goals that encompass lower-level goals; also, the significant meaning or guiding concept that an organization imbibes in its members.

Synergy: A situation in which the whole is greater than its parts. In organizational terms, the fact that departments that interact cooperatively can be more productive than if they operate in isolation, for example, 2 + 2 = 5.

Taguchi methods: Techniques developed by Genichi Taguchi to cut variables and, therefore, costs, to a minimum in design and production.

Task force: A temporary group formed to address a specific problem.

Task structure: A work situation variable that, according to Fred Fiedler, helps determine a manager's power. In structured tasks, the manager's power is diminished.

Team building: A method of improving organizational effectiveness at the team level by diagnosing barriers to team performance, and improving inter-team relationships and tasks accomplishment.

Telecommuting: The use of computers to enable individuals to work at home, sending only the work (via telephone or data network) to the work place.

Theory X: The assumption that the average employee dislikes work, is lazy, has little ambition and must be directed, coerced, or threatened with punishment to perform adequately.

Theory Y: The assumption that the average person can enjoy work, be committed to objectives and seek responsibility.

Theory Z: According to William Ouchi, the management believes that the key to productivity and quality is the development and participation of all employees.

The Peter Principle: In a hierarchy, every employee tends to rise to his level of incompetence.

Total Quality Management (TQM): It is an approach to improving the effectiveness, of flexibility, of a business as a whole. It is essentially a way of organizing and involving the whole organization, every department, every activity, every single person at every level.

Transactional analysis: An approach to improving interpersonal effectiveness, sometimes used in organizational development efforts, which concentrates on the styles and content of communication.

Uncontrollable variable: A part of a problem situation that cannot be manipulated in the short run, and thus constrains the set of feasible solutions.

Unfreezing: Making the need for change so obvious that the individual, group, or organization can readily see and accept that change must occur.

Unit production: The production of individual goods or services that are tailored to a customer's specifications.

Valence: The value or motivating strength of a reward to the individual.

Vertical communication: Any communication that moves up or down the chain of command.

Vertical information system: Means through which data are transmitted up and down the managerial hierarchy.

Video conferencing: Meeting held via telecommunications, usually by satellite television transmission, rather than by face-to-face contact.

Waiting-Line Model (queuing): A management science technique for determining the most appropriate number of servicing units in situations with waiting lines.

Wholly owned subsidiary: A company completely controlled by a parent or holding company. The parent or holding company owns the entire voting stock of the subsidiary company.

Zero-Base Budgeting (ZBB): A budgeting approach in which all of the organization's activities, the existing ones and the proposed new ones, are considered on an equal footing in resource allocation decisions, rather than using the previous years' budget as a starting point.

Zero-defect: A defect-free product or service used as a target by companies in quality practices.

Bibliography

Ahluwalia, I.J., Productivity Trends in Indian Industry: Concerns for the nineties, *Productivity,* **31**, 1, April–June, 1990.

AICTE Publications, New Delhi, 2007–2008.

Allen, Louis, A., *Management and Organisation*, McGraw-Hill, New York, 1980.

Andrews, K.R., Ethics in Business, *Harvard Business Review*, September–October, 1989.

Anthony, R.N., Dearden, J. and Bedford, N.M., *Management Control Systems,* Richard D. Irwin, Home Wood (Illinois), 1984.

Baig, E.C., America's Most Admired Corporations, *Fortune*, January 1987.

Bank, John, *The Essence of Total Quality Management*, Prentice-Hall of India, New Delhi, 1995.

Barnard, C.I., *The Functions of the Executive*, Harvard University Press, Cambridge, 1937.

Belcher, J.G., Jr., *Productivity Plus*, Universal Book Stall, New Delhi, 1991.

Broom, H.N., *Business Policy and Strategic Action*, Prentice Hall, Inc., Englewood Cliffs, New Jersey, 1969.

Business India, December, 2007.

Business India, April, 2008.

Business Today, March, 2008.

Business Today, April, 2008.

Business Today, Quality Revolution, 1995.

Business World, January, 2008.

Byrne, John A., and Greene, Cynthia, *Business Week*'s Guide to the Best Executive Education Programmes, McGraw Hill Inc., New York, 1993.

Chakraborthy, S.K., *Ethics in Management*, Oxford University Press, Bombay, 1995.

Chatterjee, Bhaskar, *Japanese Management—Maruti and the Indian Experience*, Sterling Publishers, New Delhi.

Chester, Barnard, *The Functions of an Executive*, Harvard University Press, Cambridge, 1938.

Cooper, Cary L. and Roy Payne, *Stress at Work*, John Wiley & Sons, Chichester, 1978.

Cullition, J.W., *Handbook on Case Writing*, Asian Institute of Management, Philippines, 1973.

Davis, Keith, *Human Behaviour at Work*, Tata McGraw-Hill, New Delhi, 1975, 1981.

Drucker, Peter, F., *The Frontiers of Management*, Heinemann Professional Publishing Co., London, 1986, 1987.

Drucker, Peter, F., *Management—Tasks, Responsibilities*, Practice, Allied Publishers, Bombay, 1980.

Economic Times, Hyderabad, July 7, 1999.

Fielder, F.E., A Theory of Leadership Effectiveness, McGraw-Hill, New York, 1967.

Fincham, Robin and Rhodes, Peter, *Principles of Organisational Behaviour*, Oxford University Press, New Delhi.

Flippo, E.B., *Personnel Management*, McGraw-Hill, New York, 1984.

Fortune, **157**, No. 5, p. 40, 2008.

Fred, Luthans, *Organisational Behaviour*, McGraw-Hill, Kogakusha, Tokyo. 1996.

French, J.R.P. and Caplan, R.D., *Stress at Work*, John Wiley & Sons, New York, 1978.

Friedman, Thomas L., *The World is Flat,* Penguin Books, London, 2005.

Government of India, Bureau of Indian Standards, New Delhi, 2000.

Gragg, C., Because Wisdom can't be Told, *Harvard Alumni Bulletin*, October 19, 1940.

Griffin, *Management*, AITBS Publishers, New Delhi, 1998.

Harigopal, K., Management of Change, *Leveraging Transformation*, Response Books, New Delhi, 2001.

Hammonds, K.H., Work: More Complex than we Thought, *Business Week*, September, 1993.

Harvard Business Review, HBR Case Method Series 1–3, Boston, Harvard Business School, 1960–65.

Herzberg, F. et al., *The Motivation to Work*, John Wiley & Sons, New York, 1959.

Hoerr, J., What should unions do now? *SPAN*, February, pp. 11–17, 1992.

Iacocca with Novak, William, *An Autobiography*, Bantam Books.

Indian Management, June, 2008.

Jackson, Paul and Reima Soumi, *Workplace Design and Organisational Effectiveness*, 2006.

Jauch, L.R. and Glueck, W.F., *Business Policy and Strategic Management*, McGraw-Hill, New York, 1988.

Juran, J.M., *Leadership for Quality: An Executive Handbook*, New York, The Free Press, 1989.

Kaila, H.L, Pai, S., Ravishankar, S., and Dhar, U., *Stress Management* (Western and Indian Techniques); Himalaya Publishing House, India, 2001.

Kanji, G.K. and Asher, M., *100 Methods for Total Quality Management*, Response Books, New Delhi, 1996.

Koontz, H. and Weihrich, Heinz, *Essentials of Management*, McGraw-Hill, New York, 1990.

Koontz, Harold and O'Donnell, C., *Principles of Management*, McGraw-Hill, New York, 1972.

Laurie, J.M., Management and Organizational Behaviour, *Financial Times*, Pitman Publishing, London, 1999.

Laurie, J. Mullins, *Management and Organisational Behaviour, Financial Times*, Pitman Publishing, 1999.

Maslow, Abraham, H., *Motivation and Personality*, Harper & Row, New York, 1954.

McClelland, David C., *The Achievement Motive*, Appleton-Century-Crofts, New York, 1953.

McNair, M.P., *The Case Method at HBS*, McGraw-Hill, New York, 1954.

Monga, R.C., Dynamics of Productivity Management, *Productivity*, **33**, Vol. 33, No. 1 April–June, 1992.

Oakland, J.S., *Total Quality Management*, Butter Worth-Heinemann, Oxford, 1989.

Pareekh, Udai, *Understanding Organisational Behaviour*, Oxford University Press, New Delhi, year.

Panneerselvam, R., *Production and Operations Management*, 3rd ed.. PHI Learning, Delhi, 2003.

Pascale, R.T. and Anthos, A.G., *The Art of Japanese Management—Application for American Executives*, Warner Books, New York, 1982.

Peter, Thomas J. and Waterman, R.H., Jr., *In Search of Excellence—Lessons from America's Best Run Companies*, Harper & Row, New York, 1982.

Prasad, L.M., *Principles and Practice of Management*, Sultan Chand & Sons, New Delhi, 1990.

Rangnekar, S., *In the World of Corporate Managers*, Vikas Publishing House, New Delhi, 1996.

Ravi, N. (Ed.), Speaks on Management, *The Hindu,* Kasturi & Sons Ltd., Madras, 1996.

Robbins, Stephen P. and Sanghi, Seema, *Organisational Behaviour*, Pearson Education, New Delhi, 2006.

Sahay B.S., et al., *World Class Manufacturing: A strategic perspective*, Macmillan, New Delhi, 2000.

Satya Raju, R., Fragrance of Values and Ethics at Work Place for Fruits in Twenty First Century, *IIRA World Congress*, May 27–June 2, Tokyo, 2000.

Satya Raju, R., A Perspective on Executive Education, *University News*, September 2008.

Satya Raju, R., Rising India: Changing Global Labour Market, Seminar Volume, Andhra University, Visakhapatnam, 2008.

Satya Raju, R., *Globalisation and Executive Education*, Andhra University, Visakhapatnam (Mimeo), 2008.

Satya Raju, R., *HRM Response to New Corporate Initiatives*, NIPM, Kolkata, 1996.

Satya Raju, R., *ISO 9000 Certification in Indian Industries—The role of professionals* (Mimeo), Andhra University, Visakhapatnam, 1997.

Sayles, L.R., *Managerial Behaviour*, McGraw-Hill, New York, 1997.

Schein, E.H., Organisational Culture, *American Psychologist*, **45**, No. 2, pp. 109–119.

Senge, P.M., The Fifth Discipline: *The Art and Practice of a Learning Organization*, Toronto, Currency Double Day, 1994.

Seel, Richard, Culture and Complexity, New Insights into Organisational Change, *Organisations and People*, **7**, No. 2, 2000.

Sharma, Radha R., Executive Burnout—Contribution of Role Related Factors, *Indian Journal of Industrial Relations*, **38**, No. 1, July, 2002.

Sharplin, A., *Strategic Management*, McGraw-Hill, New York, 1985.

Steiner, G.A., *Business and Society*, Random House, New York, 1971.

Stoner, James, A.F., Freeman Edward, R. and Gilbert, Daniel, R. Jr., *Management*, 6th ed., Prentice-Hall of India, New Delhi, 1995.

Stoner, James, A.F. and Wankel, Charles, *Management*, Prentice Hall, Englewood Cliffs, New Jersey, 1987.

Subbulaxmi Santha, Productivity and Stress, *Management*, **11**, No. 3, July–September, 2002.

Toffler, A., Future Shock, *The Adaptive Corporation*, Toronto, 1988.

Venkataratnam, C.S., *Unusual Collective Agreements*, Global Press, New Delhi, 1993.

Venkataratnam, C.S. and Srivastava, B.K., *Personnel/Human Resource Management*, Tata McGraw-Hill, New Delhi, 1994.

Vroom, V.H., *Work and Motivation*, John Wiley & Sons, New York, 1954.

Wofford, J.C. et al., *Organisational Communication*, McGraw-Hill, Kogakusha, Tokyo, 1977.

www.bsl.org.uk

www.iso.ch

Author Index

Organization Index

Subject Index